1988

ON LANGUAGE

ROBERT P. STOCKWELL

ON LANGUAGE

Rhetorica
Phonologica
Syntactica

a Festschrift for
Robert **P.S**tockwell
from his Friends
and Colleagues

Edited by
Caroline Duncan-Rose
Theo Vennemann

ROUTLEDGE
London and New York

First published in 1988 by
Routledge
11 New Fetter Lane, London EC4P 4EE

Published in the USA by
Routledge
in association with Routledge, Chapman and Hall, Inc.
29 West 35th Street, New York, NY 10001

© 1988 Collection and pages ix and xx-xxiv
C. Duncan-Rose and T. Vennemann

Typeset in 10pt Times Roman by Leaper & Gard Ltd,
Bristol, England

Printed and bound in Great Britain by Mackays of Chatham PLC, Kent

All rights reserved. No part of this book may be
reprinted or reproduced or utilized in any form or
by any electronic, mechanical, or other means, now
known or hereafter invented, including photocopying
and recording, or in any information storage or
retrieval system, without permission in writing from
the publishers.

British Library Cataloguing in Publication Data

On language: rhetorica, phonologica,
   syntactica: a festschrift for Robert P.
Stockwell from his friends and colleagues.
1. Linguistics
I. Stockwell, Robert P. II. Duncan-Rose C.
III. Vennemann, T.
410   P121

ISBN 0-415-00312-1

Library of Congress Cataloging in Publication Data

Data applied for

Contents

Preface	ix
Robert Stockwell: The Student and Teacher ARCHIBALD A. HILL	xi
Robert Stockwell: The Scholar as Teacher ROBERT OCHSNER	xii

Robert Stockwell and the Building of the
    UCLA Linguistics Department
    PAUL SCHACHTER
	xv

Curriculum Vitae of Robert P. Stockwell	xx
Bibliography of Robert P. Stockwell	xxi

Part I: RHETORICA   1

1. Correctness and Norms of Language   3
   RENATE BARTSCH

2. Written and Spoken Language in South Asia   22
   WILLIAM BRIGHT

3. Chaucer, Livy, and Bersuire: The Roman Materials in *The Physician's Tale*   39
   WILLIAM H. BROWN, JR

4. How Relevant is 'External Evidence' for a Theory of Grammar?   52
   VICTORIA A. FROMKIN

5. Chaucer and the Pun-Hunters: Some Points of Caution   66
   ARCHIBALD A. HILL

6. Two Cheers for Prescriptivism   79
   MICHAEL B. KAC

7. Middle English *enst*, Not *evest*   86
   SHERMAN M. KUHN

8. Creoles, Triggers, and Universal Grammar   97
   DAVID LIGHTFOOT

9. The Rise and Fall of the Vernacular   106
   RONALD K.S. MACAULAY

CONTENTS

10.	Hypercorrection and the Creole Continuum: -s and -d in Liberian English JOHN VICTOR SINGLER	116
11.	Is Internal Semantic-Pragmatic Reconstruction Possible? ELIZABETH CLOSS TRAUGOTT	128
12.	Notes on Black and Red American English WOLFGANG VIERECK	145

Part II: PHONOLOGICA   159

13.	Old English Ablaut Again: The Essentially Concrete Character of Dependency Phonology JOHN M. ANDERSON	161
14.	The Late Old English Type *leinten* 'Lent' KLAUS DIETZ	183
15.	Prothetic Alif and Canonical Form in Egyptian CARLETON T. HODGE	195
16.	Proto-Burmese as a Test of Reconstruction ROBERT B. JONES	203
17.	Redefining the Scope of Phonology PETER LADEFOGED	212
18.	The 'Akzentumsprung' of Old English *ēo* ROGER LASS	221
19.	From Latin to Romance: The Vowel Systems CARLOS P. OTERO	233
20.	The Rule Dependence of Syllable Structure THEO VENNEMANN	257

Part III: SYNTACTICA   285

21.	Objects (Direct and Not-So-Direct) in English and Elsewhere STEPHEN R. ANDERSON	287
22.	A Note on the Definition and Description of True Anacolutha NILS ERIK ENKVIST	315
23.	On the Principle of 'Weight' in English PETER ERDMANN	325
24.	Tale of Two Passives: Internal Reconstruction in Ute TALMY GIVÓN	340

25.	The Unity of English/German Contrasts: Inferring a Typological Parameter JOHN A. HAWKINS	361
26.	The Group Genitive and Type 24 Languages FRED W. HOUSEHOLDER	381
27.	Transitivity: Intransitivization vs. Causativization: Some Typological Considerations Concerning Verbs of Action YOSHIHIKO IKEGAMI	389
28.	Minor Movement Rules FREDERICK J. NEWMEYER	402
29.	On the Basicness of Certain Types of Passives: Some Evidence from Child Acquisition SUZANNE ROMAINE	413
30.	Non-Restrictive Relative Clauses JAMES PETER THORNE	424
31.	On the Subject of Bare Imperatives in English ARNOLD M. ZWICKY	437

Addresses of Authors and Editors   451

Preface

Robert P. Stockwell thinks of himself as a grammarian — not as an Anglist, not as a dialectologist, not as a phonologist or syntactician or historical linguist; indeed, the remarkable catholicity of his achievements in linguistics seems to make that term the only appropriate one.

This *Festschrift* in his honor, as both the title and the range of topics suggest, reflects that catholicity — but only in part. Some of Professor Stockwell's contributions to our discipline, extending far beyond the impact of his research, are mentioned in the prefatory essays which follow: one by Archibald Hill on Robert Stockwell the student, one by Robert Ochsner on the scholar as teacher, and one by Paul Schachter on the builder of one of the world's most prestigious departments of linguistics.

The thirty-one articles are arranged according to the three categories suggested by the subtitle. **Rhetorica** — with this venerable term to be understood in its broad medieval sense — comprise studies ranging from considerations of stylistic variation to the analysis of linguistic norms, from the etymological identification of a single rare lexical item in Middle English texts to the methodology of theory construction. **Phonologica** and **Syntactica** comprise those papers in which problems of one of these two subdisciplines of linguistic theory predominate, even though more general considerations of linguistic theory may also be encompassed.

It was with deepest sorrow that we learned of the death, shortly before this *Festschrift* appeared in print, of one of our contributing authors. Professor James Peter Thorne (Department of English Language, University of Edinburgh), had been a close friend of Robert P. Stockwell for many years.

We wish to express here our immense gratitude to Professor Jacek Fisiak (Institute of English, Adam Mickiewicz University, Poznań, Poland) for his invaluable assistance and encouragement during the initial stages of conceptualizing and compiling the *Festschrift.*

We are proud to have played a part in bringing together the tributes of so many distinguished colleagues, who join with us in presenting this volume to Professor Stockwell and to the academic community.

Caroline Duncan-Rose
Theo Vennemann

Robert Stockwell: The Student and Teacher

ARCHIBALD A. HILL

Robert Stockwell has certainly been, for very many of his students, a leader and an inspiration. Such a relation to his students is a principal characteristic of a good and successful teacher, but Professor Stockwell, to give him the formal title I seldom use in addressing Bob, is more, because he has been, over the years, a leader and an inspiration to his teachers as well.

My relation with Bob began forty years ago, when I returned to the University of Virginia from military service and found that I was quite thoroughly out of touch with the development of the kind of scholarship which meant most to me, linguistics. Furthermore, I wanted to demonstrate that knowledge of the structure and signal system of language was relevant to scholarship and understanding in literature. I remember with gratitude the years when Bob was studying such subjects and I, in turn, was studying them with him. It is, therefore, fitting that I should contribute to this *Festschrift* an article on a subject that is one of the fields that we both were interested in, the contribution of linguistic analysis to the understanding of one of our greatest poets, Chaucer.

I can only say that it is for me a matter of great regret that time makes it difficult for me to follow Bob's footsteps as he goes ever farther forward in scholarship and the dissemination of knowledge and understanding. As I think of the happy days when we were together in study and learning, I cannot keep the words of Horace out of my mind:

> Eheu fugaces, Postume, Postume,
> labuntur anni ...

Robert Stockwell: The Scholar as Teacher

ROBERT OCHSNER

There is a game that assistant professors play a bit like the taunting word play of children. It begins as one baby assistant professor tells another about the intellectual giant he studied under, and then the other responds with a more gigantic tale of his mentor's high octane IQ and superhuman achievements in teaching or scholarship. It's the young academics' version of my daddy's bigger than yours is.

For Robert Stockwell I want to avoid the verbal puffery of this gamesmanship, yet I find it impossible to describe him in simple terms. He really is exceptional. Anyone who meets him for the first time immediately recognizes what makes him a remarkable teacher and scholar: it is the quality of his intellect, combining brilliance with a quickness of perception which can, sometimes, overwhelm students or render colleagues in a state of speechless agreement.

I've seen this happen several times in committee meetings where I participated as a student representative. Professor Stockwell gets to the point and resolves an issue, it almost seems, before the rest have begun working. In anyone else, this ability to intellectually dominate a group of his peers would be the mark of an academic bully. But Professor Stockwell is the most spontaneously kind person I have ever met. He's not a saint exactly, not with the scholarly equivalent of a knockout punch for flimflam research or dishonest teaching. Yet this intolerance for false learning is balanced against his genuine concern for students' success in his classes.

The first time I took a class from Professor Stockwell he warned us not to misinterpret his sudden bursts of excitement as imaginary acts of violence. Even forewarned, it took a while to become accustomed to his lectures and to recognize, as he muscled into topics, that he was leaving a clear path for us to follow behind. Or, if we took the initiative, that he would enthusiastically step aside. The result was first-rate instruction.

What I remember best is how he responded to questions, proceeding in rapid-fire sequence from point to point. Like most students, I was a little intimidated at first, then thoroughly impressed as the range of his scholarship became evident. Indeed, our class responded so well that we began asking questions as a way to gauge the extent of Professor Stockwell's knowledge of linguistics. Contests of this sort must test the patience of any instructor, but Professor Stockwell never became annoyed; rather, I was the one who became annoyed, especially since I figured to have a special advantage; yet, as it turned out, I would inevitably lose. With my background in TESL and English literature, I was certain to find something he would not be familiar with. Not so. It may be that other students have exposed a few arcane bits of linguistic knowledge that are not part of Professor Stockwell's scholarly universe. If so, it hardly matters; such missing details would only make the knowledge he possesses seem even more impressive.

After measuring my own ignorance in this way, I stopped looking for comparisons and, instead, learned to appreciate the qualitative strengths of his comprehensive mind. A fortunate decision, for rarely does a student have the opportunity to learn from someone who takes risks, who assimilates ideas in grand fashion in order to produce a definitive work in contrastive linguistics (e.g., *The Grammatical Structures of English and Spanish*, with J.D. Bowen and J.W. Martin, 1965) or to undertake a description of English syntax amid the swirl of changing linguistic theory (*Major Syntactic Structures of English*, with Paul Schachter and Barbara Partee, 1973; and *Foundations of Syntactic Theory*, 1977). Like that of all great and memorable scholars, his work encompasses more than fashionable topics and trends, providing instead a record of an individual mind that links past with present, as occurs in Professor Stockwell's historical studies of language. His numerous articles on English philology and reviews of this scholarship extend across three decades, at a time when research in this area was never popular.

The scholarship that underlies a Stockwell course explains his remarkable ability to reduce seemingly complex ideas to their basic components. Students leave his class, as I did, understanding material that had initially seemed impossible to grasp. And considering the complexity of much of the subject matter he teaches, the success of his courses underscores an extraordinary talent as a teacher, a talent wonderfully augmented by his kindness and generosity.

On one occasion — I could cite many others — Professor Stockwell offered his home as the meeting place for an informal seminar on applied linguistics. This offer was itself a generous thing to do, especially with twenty or so graduate students and about ten faculty members to receive as host. As he briefly showed us his home, one student noticed the orchids in his backyard, so he invited her outside to have a closer look. While she was admiring them, he went to another part of the garden, pulled out his pocketknife, and snipped off two of the prize-winning cymbidium orchids for her to take home. This spontaneous generosity complements his many other virtues as a teacher and scholar.

Robert Stockwell deserves more than the clumsy praise of a former student. If I had the ability, I would write a philosophical essay on the quality of his teaching and research, something akin to Whitehead's *Aims of Education,* or attempt to describe in literary form his special gifts as a thoughtful, insightful, and fully likable person. But perhaps the best way to honor him is to say that I try to model my career on his, while recognizing that I can never do as much, with as much grace and intellectual force, as he has done.

Robert Stockwell and the Building of the UCLA Linguistics Department

PAUL SCHACHTER

In 1956, when Robert Stockwell joined its faculty, the University of California, Los Angeles had no department of linguistics. In 1973, however, when Stockwell completed his inaugural term as Chairman, the UCLA Linguistics Department had for some time been recognized as among the best in the United States.[1] Of course the period in question was one of considerable **general** growth for the field of linguistics in this country. Thus it is quite probable that UCLA would have had a department of linguistics by 1973 even if Stockwell had chosen to go to some other university in 1956. But under these circumstances it is also quite probable that it would be this **other** university whose linguistics department would have enjoyed the reputation enjoyed by UCLA's in 1973 — and, indeed, ever since.[2] As one who has good reason to be glad that Stockwell made the choice he did, I am very pleased indeed to have been asked by the editors of this volume to chronicle the role played by my colleague and former teacher Robert Stockwell in the building of the UCLA Linguistics Department.

Stockwell was invited to join the faculty of UCLA's Department of English in 1956 on the recommendation of William Matthews, an eminent English philologist who had been at UCLA since the late 1930s. Matthews had heard Stockwell present a paper at the Winter 1955 meeting of the Modern Language Association of America and the two had spoken at some length after the presentation. The resultant invitation came at a time when Stockwell had already decided that he wanted to return to academia — he had been teaching Spanish and Portuguese in the US State Department's Foreign Service Institute since earning his doctorate from the University of Virginia — and he forthwith accepted it.

Together with Matthews, Stockwell quickly redesigned the graduate program in English language, and he himself assumed sole responsibility for all courses and seminars on Modern English — which, in his hands, were courses and seminars in general linguistics as well. He also established collegial relations with the other linguists on campus. These included Harry Hoijer of the Anthropology Department, a distinguished student of Edward Sapir's who, like Matthews, had come to UCLA in the 1930s, and, subsequently, two younger linguists who joined the UCLA faculty in the late 1950s: William Bright, also then in the Anthropology Department, and

Jaan Puhvel of the Classics Department.

In addition, Stockwell took an active part in the UCLA–Philippines Project, initiated in 1958 under a grant from the Rockefeller Foundation, and directed by Clifford Prator of the English Department. This large research, teacher-training, and materials-development project involved work on both Philippine languages and the teaching of English in the Philippines, and contributed in various ways to an expanded interest in linguistics at UCLA. So did the passage in 1958 of the National Defense Education Act, which provided (and continues to provide) support for the study of less-commonly-taught languages.

By 1960 Stockwell and the other UCLA linguists, who had taken to meeting on a more or less regular basis to present their research or to hear visiting speakers, felt that there was enough academic and administrative support for linguistics at UCLA to warrant the introduction of an interdepartmental MA degree program in general linguistics. The proposal for such a program that Stockwell drafted in that year was approved, and the interdepartmental program was initiated in 1961 under the direction of a committee consisting of Hoijer, Bright, Puhvel, and Stockwell, with Hoijer as Chairman. It was soon obvious that the interest of the students and the quality of the by-then-available faculty was sufficient to justify an interdepartmental PhD program in general linguistics, and the proposal for such a program, again drafted by Stockwell, was approved in 1962. Two years later the interdepartmental BA program that Stockwell drafted was also approved.

The Committee on the Linguistics Program was chaired by Hoijer for two years and by Bright for one. Stockwell became its Chairman in 1964. By this time the UCLA administration had also established a nonteaching Center for Research in Language and Linguistics, chaired by Puhvel. This Center provided the Linguistics Program with administrative support and started the book collection that was soon to be inherited by the Linguistics Department. The proposal for such a department was drafted by Stockwell in 1965, and the department came into official existence on 1 July 1966, with Stockwell as Chairman, a position he held until 1973. (The Center had been dissolved in 1967.)

The faculty of the new department included, in addition to Stockwell and Bright (Hoijer chose to remain in Anthropology and Puhvel in Classics), four people for whose presence at UCLA Stockwell was to a greater or lesser degree responsible. In chronological order of Stockwell's involvement in their careers, these people were myself, William Welmers, Peter Ladefoged, and Barbara (Hall) Partee.

I had been Stockwell's student in his first Modern English class in 1957, and I was also his first doctoral student. He was largely responsible for my joining the staff of the UCLA–Philippines Project in 1961 and for my subsequent faculty appointment. Welmers had been recommended by

Stockwell to Wolf Leslau, Chairman of the Near Eastern Languages Department (subsequently the Near Eastern **and African** Languages Department) for a senior appointment in African languages that the UCLA administration made available in 1960. As for Ladefoged, Stockwell had successfully urged the English Department to make a place for him in 1962. The department, at Stockwell's request, had purchased a sound spectrograph, and both David Abercrombie (Ladefoged's teacher) and Martin Joos had recommended Ladefoged to Stockwell as a promising young phonetician who would make good use of the new equipment.

The appointment of Barbara Partee to a position in the English Department (but earmarked for transfer to the Linguistics Department) in 1965 was a reflection of Stockwell's early recognition of the significance of the Chomskyan revolution in linguistics. In 1958 Stockwell had attended the Third Texas Conference on Problems of Linguistic Analysis, where, hearing Noam Chomsky for the first time, he had immediately been persuaded of the superiority of Chomsky's approach over the structuralist approach in which Stockwell himself had been trained. (My own most vivid experience as a student was in a seminar taught by Stockwell in 1958, when, immediately after his return from the Third Texas Conference, he told us, essentially, to drop everything we had been doing and join him in learning as much as possible, and as quickly as possible, about transformational generative grammar!) When Stockwell went on sabbatical leave for the 1963-4 academic year, he went to MIT to study with Chomsky, and there he met the first group of MIT PhD candidates in Linguistics, among them Partee, for whose subsequent invitation to UCLA he was responsible.

As Chairman of the new Linguistics Department, Stockwell of course played an important role in all the faculty appointments and recruitments that took place during his term of office. These included Victoria Fromkin, who received, in 1965, one of the first UCLA Linguistics PhDs and who, after two years in the UCLA Speech Department, joined the Linguistics Department in 1967. Others appointed or recruited by Stockwell during this period include four who are still members of the department — George Bedell, Raimo Anttila (who had originally been a member of the Indo-European Studies subdepartment of Classics), Thomas Hinnebusch, and Edward Keenan (hired to replace Partee, who left in 1972) — as well as several prominent linguists who have since moved elsewhere, among them Theo Vennemann, Talmy Givón, Joseph Emonds, and Sandra Thompson.

In addition to the central role that he played in the building of a strong faculty, Stockwell also played a key role in a number of other events that helped to enhance the prestige of the new department. One of these was the 1966 appointment of Bright as Editor of *Language*, the journal of the Linguistic Society of America. Stockwell was a member of the LSA Executive Committee in 1965 and thus took part in the Winter meeting of the Committee, at which the chief item of business was to find a replacement for the recently-deceased editor, Bernard Bloch. Bright's name was not on the original list of candidates, and it was Stockwell who was responsible for having it added. He was also responsible for getting the UCLA administration to promise space and financial support for the journal if Bright should get the appointment. It was, of course, Bright's own merits that ultimately won him the editorship that he held for twenty-two years, but if it had not been for Stockwell, Bright would presumably never even have been considered for the position.

The 1966 LSA Institute at UCLA is still remembered as one of the most successful ever. No doubt this was due in large measure to Puhvel's efforts as Director of the Institute, but Stockwell also played an important part in the Institute's success. Not only had he joined Puhvel in the negotiations with the Society to hold the Institute at UCLA, but he was also responsible for persuading Noam Chomsky to accept that year's LSA Professorship, entailing the teaching of two courses at the Institute, which remains the one LSA Institute at which this most influential of American linguists has taught.

It was at this LSA Institute that Stockwell persuaded Bruce Fraser — a linguist who was then employed by the US Air Force in a position where he could influence funding for linguistic research — of the potential interest of a project aimed at producing a comprehensive generative grammar of English. The proposed UCLA Syntax Project was forthwith funded, with Stockwell, Partee, and myself as Principal Investigators, and with a number of graduate-student research assistants who have since become prominent in one or another area of linguistics. The book that ultimately resulted from this project[3] helped to establish UCLA as a center for significant syntactic research.

Naturally the graduates of any department are among the most important bases for evaluating the department, and the UCLA Linguistics Department was fortunate in having many extremely gifted graduates during Stockwell's inaugural term as Chairman — students in whose selection and training Stockwell himself typically played a significant role. It would be invidious to list some arbitrarily-chosen subset of these graduates here, but I should at least mention some of those who subsequently themselves became members of the Department. This list includes (in addition to Fromkin, who was actually graduated before departmental status was achieved) Givón, Hinnebusch, and Russell Schuh.

I should also mention in this connection a piece of very clear evidence of the contribution that Stockwell's teaching made — and continues to make — to the quality of the UCLA Linguistics Department's graduates: namely, Stockwell's being awarded one of the UCLA Alumni Association's Distinguished Teaching Awards in 1968. Competition for these awards is university-wide, and only five awards are given each year. An important part of the case for an award is always letters from present and former students. Letters of the 's/he changed my life' variety are generally not very common, but in Stockwell's case there were in fact many such.

Thus it is clear that Stockwell made crucial contributions of a number of different kinds to the growing distinction of the UCLA Linguistics Department — a distinction that was well established by the end of his inaugural term as Chairman in 1973. Also well established by then was the **distinctiveness** of the department: the characteristics that have given it its special place in the American linguistic scene. Among these characteristics were — and are — strength in the analysis of a wide range of languages (European, African, Asian, American, Pacific), strength in a truly **linguistic** phonetics, and strength in theoretical approaches that constitute a kind of 'loyal opposition' (and sometimes one not so loyal) to the dominant paradigm. Clearly the linguistic scene in the United States would have been very different today — and, I think it is fair to say it would have been considerably impoverished — had the UCLA Linguistics Department never existed. And equally clearly, without Robert Stockwell, though a UCLA Linguistics Department would presumably have existed today, **the** UCLA Linguistics Department surely would not.

NOTES

1. According to the 1970 Roose-Andersen report (Kenneth D. Roose and Charles J. Andersen, *A Rating of Graduate Programs.* Washington, DC: American Council on Education, 1970), the UCLA Linguistics Department ranked below only MIT's in both the quality of its faculty and the effectiveness of its doctoral program.

2. During Stockwell's second term as Chairman, 1980–4, the UCLA Linguistics Department was again ranked second only to MIT's in a national survey (Lyle V. Jones, Gardner Lindzey, and Porter E. Coggeshall (eds.), *An Assessment of Research-Doctorate Programs in the United States.* Washington, DC: National Academy Press, 1982).

3. Robert P. Stockwell, Paul Schachter, and Barbara Partee, *The Major Syntactic Structures of English.* New York: Holt, Rinehart and Winston, 1973.

Curriculum Vitae of Robert P. Stockwell

1946	BA in English and Greek, University of Virginia.
1949	MA in English, University of Virginia.
1952	PhD in English Philology, University of Virginia. Dissertation: *Middle English Phonology.* Dissertation Director: Archibald Anderson Hill.
1952–6	School of Languages, Foreign Service Institute, Department of State (in charge of Spanish and Portuguese language instruction); co-authored the FSI Spanish text, the main instructional tool at FSI for the next 20 years and the principal model for the MLA *Modern Spanish* and the ALM series of language texts from Harcourt Brace Jovanovich.
1956–66	Professor of English, UCLA. Responsible for graduate and undergraduate courses in history and structure of English language.
1966–	Professor of Linguistics, UCLA. Responsible for graduate and undergraduate courses in historical linguistics, history of English, syntactic theory, historical theory.
1963–6	Chairman, Interdepartmental Program in Linguistics, UCLA.
1966–73	Chairman, Department of Linguistics, UCLA.
1980–4	Chairman, Department of Linguistics, UCLA.

Visiting Professorships (summers): 1955, 1956 Georgetown University; 1960 University of the Philippines; 1961 University of Texas; 1965 University of Michigan; 1979 University of Salzburg.

Fellow of the American Council of Learned Societies, 1963–4.
Distinguished Teaching Award, UCLA Alumni Association, 1968.
Distinguished Teaching Award, UCLA Graduate Student Association, 1968.

Associate Editor, *Language*, 1973–82
Associate Editor, *Hispanic Linguistics*, 1983–
Associate Editor, *Folia Linguistica Historica*, 1976–
Associate Editor, *Studia Anglica Posnaniensia*, 1984–

Bibliography of Robert P. Stockwell

1. 1951. 'Some Old English Graphemic–Phonemic Correspondences: *æ*, *ea*, and *a*', with C.W. Barritt, *Studies in Linguistics, Occasional Papers* 4 (monograph).
2. 1953. 'Concerning Description and Hypothesis', *Studies in Linguistics* 11: 1–2.
3. 1955. 'The Old English Short Digraphs: Some Considerations', with C.W. Barritt, *Language* 31: 372–89.
4. 1955. 'The Phonemic Interpretation of Semivowels in Spanish', with J.D. Bowen, *Language* 31: 236–40. Reprinted in Martin Joos (ed.), *Readings in Linguistics*. New York: American Council of Learned Societies, 1958.
5. 1955. 'The Preparation of the Foreign Service Institute Spanish Materials: A Case History', *Monarch* 8: 33–50.
6. 1956. 'Spanish Juncture and Intonation', with J.D. Bowen and I. Silva-Fuenzalida, *Language* 31: 641–65. Reprinted in Martin Joos (ed.), *Readings in Linguistics*. New York: American Council of Learned Societies, 1958.
7. 1956. 'A Further Note on Spanish Semivowels', with J.D. Bowen, *Language* 32: 290–2. Reprinted in Martin Joos (ed.), *Readings in Linguistics*. New York: American Council of Learned Societies, 1958.
8. 1956. 'On Phonemes and Allophones', *Hispania* 39: 325–6.
9. 1956. 'The Apocopation of Certain Adjectives in Spanish', with J.D. Bowen, *Hispania* 39: 349–51.
10. 1956. Review article on *The Field of Yiddish*, by Uriel Weinreich, *Language* 32: 374–84.
11. 1957. Review of *The National Interest and Foreign Languages*, by W.R. Parker, *Language* 33: 497–502.
12. 1957. 'Orthography and Respelling in Teaching Spanish', with J.D. Bowen, *Hispania* 40: 200–5.
13. 1957. *FSI Spanish: Basic Course* (three volumes), with J.D. Bowen and I. Silva-Fuenzalida. Washington, DC: US Government Printing Office.
14. 1957. Review of *James Douglas on English Pronunciation c. 1740*, by Borje Holmberg, *Language* 33: 246–53.
15. 1957. 'A Rejoinder (on the Respelling Issue)', with J.D. Bowen, *Hispania* 40: 463–4.
16. 1957. Review of *The Pronunciation of English*, by Daniel Jones, *Language* 33: 614–21.
17. 1958. 'The Phonology of Old English: A Structural Sketch', *Studies in Linguistics* 13: 13–24. Reprinted in Charles T. Scott and Jon L. Erickson (eds.), *Readings in the History of the English Language*. Boston: Allyn and Bacon, 1968, 136–45.
18. 1958. Review of *Audio-Visual Aids in Language Teaching*, by Ruth Hirsch, *Studies in Linguistics* 13: 3–4.
19. 1959. 'Structural Dialectology: A Proposal', *American Speech* 35: 258–68.

Reprinted in H.B. Allen and G.N. Underwood (eds.), *Readings in American Dialectology*. New York: Appleton Century Crofts, 1971, 314–24.

20. 1959. 'Further Notes on Old English Phonology', with R. Willard, *Studies in Linguistics* 14: 1–2.
21. 1959. Review of J.R. Firth (ed.), *Studies in Linguistic Analysis*, in *International Journal of American Linguistics* 25: 254–9.
22. 1959. Review of *Spoken English*, by David T. Thomson and Robert P. Lyons, with J.D. Bowen, *The MST English Quarterly* 9: 2–4.
23. 1959. 'A Test of Speech Intelligibility', with A.L. Larr, *The Volta Review* 61: 403–8.
24. 1960. 'The Place of Intonation in a Generative Grammar of English', *Language* 36: 360–7. Reprinted in H.B. Allen (ed.), *Readings in Applied English Linguistics*. New York: Appleton Century Crofts, 1964. Also reprinted in Dwight Bolinger (ed.), *Readings on Intonation*. Harmondsworth: Penguin, 1972.
25. 1960. Review of *English Intonation: Its Form and Function*, by Maria Schubiger, *Language* 36: 544–8.
26. 1960. *Patterns of Spanish Pronunciation*, with J.D. Bowen. Chicago: University of Chicago Press.
27. 1961. 'The Middle English "Long Close" and "Long Open" Mid Vowels', The University of Texas *Studies in Literature and Language* 2: 529–38. Reprinted in Roger Lass (ed.), *Approaches to English Historical Linguistics*. New York: Holt, Rinehart and Winston, 1969, 154–63. Also reprinted in Charles T. Scott and Jon L. Erickson (eds.), *Readings in the History of the English Language*. Boston: Allyn and Bacon, 1968, 196–205.
28. 1961. 'Scribal Practice: Some Assumptions', with C.W. Barritt, *Language* 37: 75–82. Reprinted in Roger Lass (ed.), *Approaches to English Historical Linguistics*. New York: Holt, Rinehart and Winston, 1969, 133–41.
29. 1961. Review of *The Groundwork of English Intonation*, by Roger Kingdon, *International Journal of American Linguistics* 27: 278–83.
30. 1962. 'On the Analysis of English Intonation', *Proceedings of the Second Texas Conference on Problems of Linguistic Analysis in English*. Austin, Texas: University of Texas Press.
31. 1962. Review of *The First Five Minutes*, by R. Pittenger, C.F. Hockett, and J. Danehy, *International Journal of American Linguistics* 28: 293–6.
32. 1962. 'Literature, Language Teaching, Linguistics', *ACLS Newsletter* 12: 1–8.
33. 1962. 'Foreign Language Learning Ability', with P. Pimsleur and A.L. Comrey, *Journal of Educational Psychology* 53: 15–26.
34. 1963. 'The Transformational Model of Generative or Predictive Grammar', in Paul L. Garvin (ed.), *Natural Language and the Computer*. New York: McGraw-Hill, Chapter III, 23–46.
35. 1963. Review of *Generality, Gradience, and the All-or-none*, by Dwight L. Bolinger, *Language* 39: 87–91.
36. 1964. 'Grammar? Today?', *Journal of the Conference on College Composition and Communication* 15: 56–9.
37. 1964. Review of *Modern English Structure*, by Barbara M.H. Strang, *Language* 40: 483–7.
38. 1964. 'On the Utility of an Overall Pattern in Historical English Phonology', *Proceedings of the Ninth International Congress of Linguists*. The Hague: Mouton. Reprinted in Roger Lass (ed.), *Approaches to English Historical Linguistics*. New York: Holt, Rinehart and Winston, 1969, 88–96. Also reprinted in Charles T. Scott and Jon L. Erickson (eds.), *Readings in the*

History of the English Language. Boston: Allyn and Bacon, 1968, 206–12.
39. 1964. 'Transformational Grammar in Perspective', *English Studies Today*, Third Series, 51–67. Edinburgh: Edinburgh University Press.
40. 1965. *The Sounds of English and Spanish*, with J.D. Bowen. Chicago: University of Chicago Press.
41. 1965. *The Grammatical Structures of English and Spanish*, with J.D. Bowen and J.W. Martin. Chicago: University of Chicago Press.
42. 1965. Review of *Internal Structure of Clauses in English and Main Sentence Elements in the Book of Margery Kempe*, by Alfred Reszkiewicz, *Language* 41: 155–66.
43. 1968. 'Contrastive Analysis and Lapsed Time', in James E. Alatis (ed.), *Georgetown Monograph Series on Languages and Linguistics*, No. 21. Washington, DC: Georgetown University Press, 11–26.
44. 1968. *Integration of Transformational Theories of English Syntax*, with Paul Schachter and Barbara Partee. Two vols., pp. xi + 1057. (US Air Force Systems Command, Hanscom Field, Bedford, Mass.). Reviewed in *Language*, Sept. 1972, by Paul Chapin. Reprinted by National Technical Information Service, US Dept. of Commerce, # AD 703300, Washington, DC, 1970. RPS is principal author of chapters entitled 'Case Placement', 'Nominalization', and 'Relativization' (pp. 37–84, 445–526, and 527–624) and coordinator of the project.
45. 1969. 'Mirrors in the History of English Pronunciation', in E. Bagby Atwood and Archibald A. Hill (eds.), *Studies in Language, Literature, and Culture of the Middle Ages and Later.* Austin: University of Texas Press, 20–38. Reprinted in Roger Lass (ed.), *Approaches to English Historical Linguistics.* New York: Holt, Rinehart and Winston, 1969, 228–46.
46. 1972. *Linguistic Change and Generative Theory*, ed. with R.K.S. Macaulay. All original papers. Bloomington, Indiana: Indiana University Press.
47. 1973. *Major Syntactic Structures of English*, with Paul Schachter and Barbara Partee. Full revision of *Integration of Transformational Theories of English Syntax* (1968). New York: Holt, Rinehart and Winston.
48. 1973. 'The Role of Intonation: Reconsiderations and Other Considerations', in Dwight L. Bolinger (ed.), *Readings on Intonation*, Harmondsworth: Penguin, 1972. Also (pre)published in *Working Papers in Phonetics* 21, UCLA, Nov. 1971, 25–49.
49. 1973. 'Problems in the Interpretation of the Great English Vowel Shift', in M. Estellie Smith (ed.), *Studies in Linguistics: Papers in Honor of George L. Trager.* The Hague: Mouton. Reprinted in D.L. Goyvaerts and G.K. Pullum (eds.), *Essays on the Sound Pattern of English.* Ghent: E. Story-Scientia, 1976.
50. 1977. *Foundations of Syntactic Theory.* Englewood Cliffs, NJ: Prentice-Hall.
51. 1977. *Workbook in Syntactic Theory and Analysis*, with Dale E. Elliott and Marian C. Bean. Englewood Cliffs, NJ: Prentice-Hall.
52. 1977. 'Motivations for Exbraciation in Old English', in Charles Li (ed.), *Mechanisms of Syntactic Change.* Austin: University of Texas Press.
53. 1978. 'Perseverance in the English Vowel Shift', in J. Fisiak (ed.), *Recent Developments in Historical Phonology.* The Hague: Mouton.
54. 1980. 'Summation and Assessment of Theories', in Edith Moravcsik and Jessica Wirth (eds.), *Current Approaches to Syntax.* New York: Academic Press.
55. 1984. 'On the History of the Verb Second Rule in English', in J. Fisiak (ed.), *Historical Syntax.* The Hague: Mouton.
56. 1986. 'Assessments of Alternative Explanations of the Middle English

Phenomenon of High Vowel Lowering when Lengthened in the Open Syllable', in *Proceedings of the Fourth International Congress on English Historical Linguistics.* The Hague: Mouton.

57. 1986. 'Grammar as Speaker's Knowledge versus Grammar as Linguists' Characterization of Norms', in Dieter Kastovsky and Aleksander Szwedek (eds.), *Linguistics Across Historical and Geographical Boundaries.* Berlin: Mouton de Gruyter and Co.
58. 1987. 'The English Vowel Shift: Problems of Coherence and Explanation', with D. Minkova, in Dieter Kastovsky, Gero Bauer, and Jacek Fisiak (eds.), *Luick Revisited.* Tübingen: Gunter Narr.
59. 1987. 'A Rejoinder to Lass', with D. Minkova, in Dieter Kastovsky, Gero Bauer, and Jacek Fisiak (eds.), *Luick Revisited.* Tübingen: Gunter Narr.
60. 1988. 'Verb Phrase Conjunction in Old English', with D. Minkova, in Thomas Fraser (ed.), *Papers from the Eighth International Conference on Historical Linguistics.*

Part I
Rhetorica

1

Correctness and Norms of Language

RENATE BARTSCH

CORRECTNESS IN LINGUISTICS

'Linguistic correctness' has always been a basic notion in traditional grammar, which has been concerned with what the correct expressions in a language are (conditions of well-formedness of expressions) and what the correct use of these expressions is (conditions of use of expressions). Lexica and grammar books have provided lists of correct basic expressions (words and idioms) and patterns and examples of correct complex expressions, plus examples and descriptions of their use. These two basic aspects are traditionally called form and function of language. In the last sixty years or so, methods of linguistic description came into focus, and later the focus shifted toward the construction of theories which would provide explanations for various linguistic phenomena, e.g., that language is learned (in certain ways), that language changes (in certain ways), and that linguistic expressions can be interpreted and can serve as a means of orientation about the world and as a constitutive part of actions. In all these later endeavors, from the development of linguistic description to theory formation from certain points of view, the notion of linguistic correctness has played a central role in all kinds of correctness judgments, those of linguists themselves and those elicited by linguists from native speakers. Their intuition about correctness in different respects was the starting point for the reconstruction of linguistic structures and even processes that were supposed to underlie these intuitions as a kind of mechanism.

Itkonen (1974 and 1976) has pointed out that correct expressions and the correct use of these form the data for theoretical linguistics, and that this involves collecting not only utterances, but also judgments about the correctness of these utterances, because only correct utterances should be the basis for construing grammar. He has looked at these judgments of correctness as intuitions about norm-governed behavior and at the activities of the grammarian as conceptual analysis of the normative notions that regulate this behavior. In his view, grammar is the same kind of non-empirical science as is mathematics or logic. According to Itkonen, linguistic rules, as we find them in theoretical linguistics, are different from rules of language, of which speakers can become aware when they try to explicate their intuitions. The first are hypotheses about the most effective and elegant or adequate way in which the second, the rules of language, can be described.

Although I think Itkonen is right in making a distinction between rules of language and rules of theoretical linguistics, the difference is rather complicated; moreover, it is not the same for different types of linguistic theory. Nor can I agree with his claim that theoretical linguistics is a non-empirical science. The main reason is that what the most adequate way of describing linguistic expressions is depends on what assumptions are made initially, and these assumptions can be empirical claims about the organization of human cognitive faculties or even claims about the physiological and biological organization of the brain. Descriptions are then adequate not only insofar as they deliver the correct linguistic expressions, but also insofar as they are formulated on the basis of these assumptions and thus depend on empirical claims. The problem is that these claims cannot be proven in linguistics, and certainly not by pointing out that the description based on them gives the correct linguistic results, because such an argument is simply circular.

Other basic assumptions that involve certain empirical claims and lead to certain ways of constructing a grammar are facts of actual language behavior, different from judgments about correctness and often in conflict with these judgments, or facts of language change, which should be explained by linguistic theory (for both aspects see Labov 1972). These facts require that behavior be interpreted by taking into account both social norms and possible systematizations of the patterns of actual linguistic behavior in the human cognitive faculties. The notion of norm, on the one hand, and the notion of systematization, on the other, make it possible to analyze change, linguistic heterogeneity, and repeated deviance from correctness in terms of conflicts among norms, among systematizations, and between norms and systematizations, and in terms of strategies for solution of these conflicts (see Bartsch 1981).

Further, adequate description depends on whether one wants to make empirical assumptions of this kind at all, because even without such assumptions, adequacy of description, besides providing for the correct expressions of a language, depends on considerations of generality of the rules, simplicity of the application of the rules (for example, preference for intrinsic rule order above extrinsic rule order), the size of the set of basic notions, and the possibility of broad application of whole complexes of rule applications in subroutines. A further basis for determination of adequacy might be possible integration of linguistic theory, especially grammar, into the general theory of truth and information, and into the general theory of action. This point of view leads to grammars that can be part of a theory of interpretation, as we find it in philosophy of language, where formal grammar is based on the notions of truth and, more recently, also on information, such that grammatical rules are compositional and recursive, parallel to the build-up of truth conditions.

From the above considerations, it follows that there is not just one relationship between intuitions of correctness, formulated in correctness judgments, and rules formulated by theoretical linguists, but there are as many relations as there are different goals and assumptions under which grammars are constructed.

Besides the theoretical points of view mentioned, there is, of course, the point of view of language teaching, which does not permit simply taking one of the theoretically oriented grammars as the basis for teaching languages. Traditional functional grammar, aided by some structuralist methodology such as substitution, still dominates language teaching in schools, and not just because of a theoretical deficit among language teachers. It is widely recognized that language teaching requires its own theory, depending on the special goals of teaching a language and the conditions under which it has to take place.

Although, apparently, all scholars and teachers of language start from the basic assumption that a grammar or, more broadly, a linguistic theory should take into account correct expressions and the correct use of these expressions and somehow describe them in a comprehensive manner, the ways and kinds of description differ considerably, depending on different basic assumptions and goals. Especially, the degree of empiricality differs, as does the degree of normativity. Insofar as a linguistic theory claims to describe and produce correct expressions, it is always normative at least to the extent that it reinforces existing judgments of correctness.

Note that description of norms of a language is itself empirical, and is descriptive rather than prescriptive, because it describes which norms hold in a speech community. One can describe these norms without at the same time advocating them. A theory of language norms is a descriptive endeavor; it represents the empirical fact that in community X the norms A hold, and in community Y, the norms B. A special theory of linguistic norms reports an empirical fact, which is a social fact. In being empirical in this way, it is very different from mathematics or from logic. A general theory of norms is partly empirical and partly philosophical, but it is not a normative theory in the sense that it advocates certain norms: it investigates types of norms, their functions, their justification with respect to assumed values, and their systematic properties.

In what follows, I want to elaborate on the foundations of certain notions of correctness associated with linguistic forms and their use and call attention to the kinds of norms that provide the establishment of these notions of correctness. Roughly, we can say that the norms are the social reality of the correctness notions: the correctness concepts exist in a community by being the content of norms.

TYPES OF CORRECTNESS IN LANGUAGE

1. Correctness of the basic means of expression

As far as correctness of the sounds of a language is concerned, there are two questions: which ones are sounds of the language, and what is the range or latitude of pronunciation that delimits a sound such that it is recognizable as that sound, is easily recognizable, or is nearly perfect, such that it can serve as a model for imitation of the sound? Actually, perfectness of a sound as a certain sound is not an inherent quality, but rather a social phenomenon: speakers who are accepted as providing the models by their pronunciation determine what the sound has to be like. A sound is perfect, or nearly perfect, if it is like the sounds of the kind produced by the people who give the models.

Phonology, traditionally, answers the question of which sounds are in a language. The question is answered in two parts: first, what are the basic sounds, and second, what are the combinations? The sounds are classified into those which form functional oppositions, especially in that they distinguish meanings, and those which do not form such oppositions with each other and thus can be identified within a system in which equivalence makes no difference with respect to meaning. As to the possible combinations, there are language-specific rules. For example, stops in final position are [−voice] in German; that this rule is called 'final devoicing of stops in German' suggests that a process is involved, in which a voiced stop gets devoiced. Such a rule, interpreted as a process, is not a norm, because a norm only says that every stop in final position **is** without voice; a speaker does not have to imagine a voiced stop in this position and then devoice it when pronouncing it. Linguistic norms that define correctness of forms never say how these forms have to be made. For the function expressions have in society, it does not matter how they are produced; only the final result of production matters. The norms regulate only the product, not the production.

People exhibit strong normative attitudes and behavior with respect to phonological correctness. Sounds of their language are selected by their perception apparatus from all sounds received. What is perceived, out of what is received, is that which makes a difference from the relevant points of view — here, for conveying information. People welcome and reward sounds of their language produced by babbling infants, thus reinforcing the production of these sounds; they disregard and discourage the production of other sounds.

Auditory correctness of an actual sound means that it lies within accepted boundaries for the realization of a sound-concept; these boundaries are relative to the context in which the actual sound occurs. The accepted range of quality of a sound X is thus a complex of sound-realization types $(X_1, X_2, ..., X_n)$ for the n typical contexts in which it occurs in the language under consideration. An example of such a complex would be the set of types of contexts in which voiced dental stops can occur, where each type of context affects the quality of the stop in a different way. But sound-concepts can also be organized with respect to additional, morphological-semantic points of view. We can construct a complex including the context types and the qualities of voiced dental stops in these context types, which additionally include the context types in which the voiced stop is realized not in a voiced but in an unvoiced manner; then one X_i of the complex would be [dental stop, −voice] in context type ___#. In German, the concepts of voiced stops would thus contain the fact that they are unvoiced in final position. From a morphophonemic point of view, these are adequate concepts of voiced stops in German. The corresponding concepts in English will be different, since they do not include devoicing in final position. Each X_i itself is a range of realizations of the sound with small qualitative differences. These realizations are recognized as typical for the linguistic community that speaks the language in question as its mother tongue.

Another group of notions of auditory correctness defines acceptable boundaries for loudness and for pitch or tone. The norms that govern these aspects are often different for different social strata: talking in a loud voice when this is not required because of intervening noise may, for example, be a sign of lower class. For natural reasons, women speak with higher pitch than men; in England, however, where pitch is higher generally than in continental Europe, social convention requires middle-class women to speak in an even higher voice in order to maintain normal pitch-distance between male and female. Prime Minister Thatcher had to unlearn talking in very high women's pitch: as in public speaking generally, this dominant marker of femaleness was likely to destroy the effectiveness of the Prime Minister's political message, distracting from the content of what she had to say because whatever she said would be very strongly marked by high pitch as 'women's talk' — even more so in foreign countries than in England.

The norms that keep intact the notions of auditory correctness are never presented to people by description, but by models. There are models for correct pronunciation and tone who have had speech education at teacher academies or theater schools. Most speakers on television and radio in Germany have received speech education at theater schools or television academies. The norm of High German pronunciation (*Bühnen-Aussprache*), fixed 86 years ago by Siebs (1898/1961 and 1969), has been used by teachers of speech up to the present.

Another medium for the realization of language, besides speech, is writing. This second medium can be related directly to the semantic content and to syntactic functions of the language, or it can be related to the primary medium, sound, and via this detour related to semantic content and syntactic functions. With the direct relationship, we get a script consisting of characters or pictures. With the other, we get a letter-based script which in more or less detail is a mapping of sounds; in the extreme case of a phonetic alphabet, it is a one-to-one mapping. In any event, the script had to be fixed by explicit conventions. These conventions are subject to deliberate change now and then in the history of a language, and they are subject to negotiations and regulations in case there are competing systems of writing and spelling. In the Netherlands, there have been several committees in the last century which revised the spelling, lately mainly from the point of view of congruency with phonetic distinctions and equivalences. This point of view has been taken to even greater extremes in the system of spelling for Afrikaans (Berits 1983).

Differing points of view lead to contradictory results in devising spelling: historical considerations about roots and the derivation of words, morphological considerations such as the representation of identical meaning in an identical fashion in different contexts of appearance, and phonological, as well as phonetic, considerations. The results are often a compromise between points of view and are thus inconsistent from any one point of view. The whole discussion about Dutch spelling reforms is an excellent example of the conflicts involved (cf. Booij *et al.* 1979 and Schaap 1980). The results reached by the officially appointed committee on spelling are codified and become obligatory. There are two different codes of spelling in the Netherlands right now: one more conservative with regard to morphological history, and one that follows to a greater degree the phonological and even phonetic development of the language. From its main point of view, each code shows inconsistencies due to compromise with the competing point of view. Though both codes are in use, people are required to stick exclusively to one or the other within a text. But to many, including educated writers, this is difficult; on a single page, we often find several spellings of the same word or one code applied to one word, the other code to another. It is the task of secretaries, editors, and proofreaders to create a unified spelling for a text. Here, certainly, two separate codes lead to a great deal of insecurity of writing and additional work in editing.

2. Correctness of lexical items

In every language there are restrictions on word morphology. Possible stems or root words are mainly affected by phonological restrictions.

Possible morphological derivations and compound words are mainly affected by morphological restrictions, which are partly phonologically based because they must conform to the possible sounds and combinations of sounds in a language. Not everything that is morphologically possible in a language is realized. The actual words are a conventionally determined open list, i.e., a list to which new words can be added. The set of actual words consists of a subset of the possible words plus a subset of loans that are not yet adapted to native morphological restrictions; after adaptation the latter are counted as members of the first subset.

Since words are coded separately (organized, that is, in lists rather than in rules), the correctness notion is very simple: what is in the list, i.e., the lexicon, is correct. The lexicon is stored in the 'collective' memory of the speech community. Often it is codified in lexica in the form of books or computer disks. For the individual speaker, on the other hand, basically what is familiar to him, as a word of his language, is correct. He will base his correctness judgments on his own memory in the first place, but accept additionally what is stored in public lexica.

Not all the speakers of a language have the same vocabulary: there is a common stock of everyday words, and people in specialized fields of knowledge know words which most people outside that field may not know. The whole vocabulary of a language is organized in subgroups of items for which certain subgroups of people know and handle the correctness notions with respect to the form of a word and with respect to its use ('division of linguistic labour' — a term coined by Putnam 1975).

The simple correctness standard of being on the list or not cannot be applied to new words or to loans newly introduced into the language. Since these words are not on the list, they are incorrect at first sight, or at least do not belong to the set of correct words. Here, the notion of acceptability plays a role: is the word formed according to the patterns of word formation of the language out of existing roots, stems, and affixes such that the parts are semantically compatible if combined according to the semantic combinations, or at least one of them, that correspond to the type of construct? If it is a new word that is not constructed out of existing morphemes, then the method of introducing it plays an important part: is the context of use sufficient to supply enough information about what its content can be? Or, for a loan word: is it a word of a language with some prestige, or of a language known at least to the leaders of the group which would have to accept it first? Is it a word from a native dialect which is spoken by people who play a role outside their native region, in areas where the standard language or neighboring dialects are used? Is the loan word adjustable to the phonological and morphological restrictions of the language such that its origin is still recognizable and its original meaning can to some extent be ascertained from knowledge about the original language and culture in which it was or still is used? And, important in all these cases, is there a need for the new word, or is there already a word that performs the tasks of the new word well enough and without stigmatization? Acceptability depends on all these points. If the new item is acceptable to a significant subgroup, then it will be adopted first by that group and later in the speech of the community as a whole, to the extent that it is useful there. The moment a word is adopted by a group, i.e., has been put into use, it acquires correctness standards: there are now criteria for its further use and for recognition of its proper form and appearance.

3. Correctness of syntactic form

There is not much of syntax needed as long as language use is restricted to reporting about the immediate speech situation; the hearer can see for himself what is going on, and language is used more to direct attention to certain parts of the situation than to give a precise description. This is true not only with respect to indicatives, but also with respect to questions and to imperatives or requests that can be satisfied directly in the situation of utterance. Here, what is said and what happens occur more or less simultaneously or follow each other immediately. This has been the situation in teaching language to apes and to small children. It is a situation where not much talk is necessary for successful communication, and word order and inflection are not really important in preventing serious problems of ambiguity. Thus, a notion of syntactic correctness is not necessary, since interpretation can fare well without it. Also in early pidgin stages (see Bickerton 1977), there is no notion of syntactic correctness employed, nor does one exist as yet for the pidgin; everything that works is acceptable. Generally, notions of correctness are not employed for their own sake, but are developed and employed only when they are really necessary. This is also the reason why spoken language is much more free in its syntax, up to ignoring syntactic form altogether in utterances of which the interpretation is largely supplied by other than linguistic information — by the situation itself or by previous knowledge of the content of what is said. There are many situations where people do not speak in sentences, but say only one or several words, in an order that is certainly not given by syntax, and where contextual, gestural, and intonational clues suffice for interpetation. These situations hold especially when emotions are being expressed: the content is known to the hearer already, and the speaker knows this. If interpretation of speech is secured anyhow, syntax does not matter. A very regular instance of this is in answering questions. Since the question itself supplies the presupposed information in a syntactically explicit manner, it can be answered by just one word or by pairs of words, such as 'John Mary, and Bill Suzy' in answer to 'Whom do John and Bill love?'. An answer in which the missing syntactic form is supplied by the previous question is just a special case of the general condition for minimal or no syntactic form: that the information necessary for interpretation can be presupposed.

Spoken language is syntactically less restricted in general, besides having also certain syntactic patterns that are not used in written language. In speech, people normally accept this freedom from a strict notion of syntactic correctness, except in situations where it would hinder understanding and in teaching situations. In the latter, even when communication works well with unregulated constructions, parents and teachers usually correct children and language learners so that they can learn the syntax needed for written language and for communication about unknown events, things, and relationships lacking sufficient situational clues for interpretation. Motivation for learning syntax depends on several factors: the prestige of the people providing the models of correct speech, the wish to please them and to avoid neglect and other penalties, and the drive to get to know parts of the world that are next door and farther away. Communication about things and events that are not present or are unknown, with the purpose of gathering knowledge about them, generally requires a set of consistent syntactic signals, such that in the syntactic forms the facts are represented clearly.

Syntax has to get the facts straight, so to speak. In order to learn how this is done, one first has to learn syntax *vis-à-vis* the facts. Thus far, the somewhat naive picture of how sentences represent information about facts is true: there has to be a mapping between facts and texts, but it can be defined in different ways for different languages. In any case, it has to be defined one way or the other. This means that in **just** those situations where syntax is not really necessary for successful communication (that is, where speech does not transmit information that is really new, but only directs attention to it), syntax has to be learned for the sake of communication about other, strange, and faraway situations and their interrelations. Situations of learning syntax are to that extent certainly 'unnatural': they themselves do not provide motivation for learning syntax because in them, syntax is not really needed.

This might be part of the trouble with the efforts to teach syntax to apes. They do pretty well at learning words and combining them up to three items, even forming new compound words, but syntactic restrictions pose a problem for them because these are not needed in the situations in which apes apparently live and communicate; signs are used for directing attention toward something within the situation of communication itself or a direct continuation of it. Children, on the other hand, appear to have, at least, broader cognitive interests and abilities that make it necessary for them to communicate about situations and things out of reach and out of sight and about possible relationships among these. For the representation of such relationships, there have to be available cognitive means, and it is possible that the syntax of a language is to a great extent just a mapping of these, such that it preserves basic cognitive relationships. Different syntaxes are, so to speak, different mappings of these relationships, which preserve cognitive structures to a degree sufficient for orientation about the world by means of language.

On the other hand, the syntax of a language provides a socially controllable intermediate structure between basic cognitive operations, or at least possibilities for specifying such operations, and publicly accessible and controllable states of affairs. Thus syntax, which is learned *vis-à-vis* the facts, provides a socially induced structuring which the facts permit, on the one hand, and which basic cognitive types of operation permit, on the other. We can say that syntax, with respect to situations and events and their interrelations, selects structures in a socially coordinated way. Situations and their relationships represented under this selective view are what we call facts. Thus facts are language-dependent selections of structurings and systematizations which the world permits, by being as it is. In this way, a certain homomorphism between syntax and facts is secured, and what the facts are, though not whether something is a fact, is socially determined insofar as the human possibilities of cognitive operations leave a range of freedom. Facts are situated within the possibilities left open by the basic cognitive restrictions on handling data provided by perception and lexical information, to begin with, and by already available syntactically structured information, in a recursive manner. It is recursiveness of syntax and, likewise, of cognitive operations that makes it possible to build up complex information from parts that are basic relative to the syntactically complex representations of information.

Written language *per se* is largely independent of the situations of writing and reading. It has to make explicit, by description, information which in daily speech can be available in the situation. Besides more lexical items, this requires a large amount of socially controllable syntactic construction. There are also situations in which spoken language requires strong syntactic restrictions. Formal speech is an example, as in lectures about involved matters. Strict syntactic form is also necessary in stories and songs that report history, not only for facilitating recollection, but for keeping the facts straight about events that happened long ago and are not recoverable independently. The same precision is required in formulating predictions or plans about the future: if once distorted by ambiguity in the historical text, history cannot be recovered; if predictions and plans are distorted by ambiguity, one does not know what to expect and what to do. The exactness required in these matters is not possible without proper syntactic form. Those responsible for conveying the history of nonliterate peoples, who had to learn the old stories by heart in exact form and wording, performed for their language a task similar to that performed by written language in literate societies. Syntactic form is stabilized in 'frozen' texts generally, whether oral or written ones; that these frozen texts are reference points or models for the notion of syntactic correctness has led, in the history of languages, to different degrees of standardization and also to tensions between conservative models and new models that are a compromise between the old models and new developments due to change in spoken language, change in conditions of life, and modernization.[1]

The question, now, is whether there are separate notions of syntactic correctness for written and for spoken language or only one, that of written language, to which formal speech, less formal speech, and informal speech are adjusted to greater or lesser degrees. Schoolteachers, up to now, have assumed the latter, as is shown by their correction behavior: in school, spoken language has always been criticized and corrected against the standard of written language. Especially in primary schools, teachers require pupils to answer in syntactically fully explicit sentences, although a one-word answer, a pair-answer, or a chain of these would be perfectly correct, both semantically and pragmatically. Perhaps this is done for the purpose of teaching syntax, but the trouble with such exercises is that they occur in contexts where syntactic explicitness is not only unnecessary, but pragmatically incorrect, because it expresses information that need not be expressed since it is fully available from the context in an unambiguous way. The availability of information from the context is systematically taken into account in the production of texts and is conceptualized in the notions of correctness of texts. We have examples of texts (question-answer dialogues) in which the sentences are perfectly correct but which become less acceptable, not to say incorrect, as texts, by overextending a notion of syntactic correctness such that every statement, whatever the context, has to be expressed as a full-fledged sentence. It is a case of hypercorrection with respect to the use of syntactic form.

In everyday speech, correction activity, oriented toward the written or formal standard, depends on how much one is aware of speaking a language different from written language. In Switzerland, spoken language (*Switzerdüits*) is accepted as an independent language, side by side with the written language (Standard German). This acceptance shows in the use of *Switzerdüits* in semiformal situations in business and school. Written language there has no influence on everyday speech, though it has some normative force with respect to formal oral language use. Likewise in Austria, spoken language is not subject to the norms of written German, but is independent, though less so than *Switzerdüits*, the orientation toward written Standard German being stronger in Austria. The political independence of these two countries certainly contributes to awareness of having their own spoken languages that are not Standard German. In these cases we can certainly speak of different sets of syntactic norms (as well as other linguistic norms) for written and spoken language. In Bavaria, a German state with a strong notion of identity that is also recognized by other Germans, the Bavarian language or dialect is conceived of as having local prestige, though it is considered a dialect of German. Spoken language in Bavaria, depending on region, is influenced mainly by Bavarian but also by Franconian and Swabian dialects in the respective regions; many of the overall south German features are accepted or even promoted in schools, even in written language, certainly as far as lexical items are concerned, and this practice is backed up by Bavarian politics. The notion of correctness for writing is mainly that of Standard German, but some regional notions of correctness are incorporated, at least as alternatives though not replacing standard forms obligatorily. Formal spoken language, of course, contains more regional features than written language.

In other German states, where there is less feeling of tribal or regional identity, correction of spoken language to conform to Standard German is accepted in all school situations and by people of middle and higher social strata; there, except in informal conversations in villages, between local people of local origin and local occupations, the standard of written German is also the measure that is incorporated in the notion of correctness for spoken language.

This acceptance of the correctness notions of written language does not mean that everyday spoken language conforms to them: tolerance for deviance from these standards of correctness is great or small, depending on social position and type of situation. Although dialects are, of course, constituted by their own notions of correctness, as any language necessarily is, the norms that stabilize these notions have a lower normative force because they are superseded by the norms of the standard language in nearly all situations of public life. This is what makes languages (in the linguistic sense of the word) dialects, which are not accepted as separate languages. There are too many situations in which forms that are correct according to the standard of a given dialect are evaluated according to the correctness notions of the standard language and thus considered incorrect. Dialects are not languages in a sociological sense, because their correctness notions are superseded by those of the transregional standard in all official or transregional contexts, and especially in schools. In these contexts, the norms of the standard language clearly are the only valid ones, and this means that there the notions of correctness of the standard language are the only ones: every utterance that does not conform to them is incorrect.

This notion of correct and incorrect speech has very decisive consequences outside school: in Germany, a person who does not use the case markings correctly is considered unfit for any white-collar job. Different word order is more acceptable; order of term-phrases that fill in the places, or valencies, of the verb is relatively free in German anyway, especially in spoken language where certain particles and special referring constructions that are not part of the syntax of written language are used: *Mein Vater, der ging weg* ('My father, he went away'), or even *Er ging weg, mein Vater* ('He went away, my father'), instead of *Mein Vater ging weg* ('My father went away'); and sometimes we hear something like *Mein Vater, der ging weg, ging er*, used systematically by some people in story-telling. These construction types occur systematically in spoken language, but are not part of written language, at least not in German. A more famous example is the use of the definite determiner in front of proper names (*der Hans, die Frieda*). Though this is now a feature of standard spoken language in conversations generally, in all social strata, it is not accepted in written language, except in personal informal letters, and not in formal speech. With regard to these examples, everyday spoken language seems to have its own notions of syntactic correctness. Another case involves patterns of word order that deviate from the position of finite and non-finite verbs in sentences of written German; certain patterns of this kind are also considered incorrect in spoken language. *Hast Du genommen mein Buch?* and *Du hast genommen mein Buch* are incorrect versions of *Hast Du mein Buch genommen?* and *Du hast mein Buch genommen.* The first two will be accepted as occasional infelicitous sentence constructions of a speaker who does not do this systematically, but the systematic use of these constructions by Germans is strongly stigmatized and corrected; they are accepted from non-Germans, however, without correction. They are a marker of being a foreigner, like *Du Buch nehmen* instead of *Willst Du dieses Buch nehmen?* or *Du nimmst dieses Buch* or *nimmst Du dieses Buch?* or *Nimm dieses Buch!* The diference between the first type and the second is that the former is correct in inflectional morphology and unambiguous, whereas the latter, lacking the correct inflectional morphology, is at least four times ambiguous. Although the first is interpretable according to the rules of the language, and the second is interpretable in situations that give sufficient additional information, these constructions are generally unacceptable except when spoken by someone of whom one does not expect better anyway.

We thus have a hierarchy of notions that pertain to acceptability and correctness of syntactic form:

(1) syntactically correct according to the standard of written language
(2) syntactically incorrect according to written standard, but acceptable in everyday spoken language
(3) syntactically incorrect and not acceptable in everyday spoken language of native speakers
(4) otherwise incorrect and unacceptable but can, if at least understandable and interpretable, be acceptable when used by people of whom one does not expect correct speech.

What is not understandable and not interpretable is absolutely unacceptable. If one has higher expectations with regard to the ability of a person to handle the correctness notions of a language, one will find that person's production of incorrect speech more unacceptable; with higher expectations, that is, acceptability of incorrect speech is lower. Note that sometimes perfectly correct speech with respect to the correctness notions treated so far can be unacceptable, as, for example, in situations in which more casual speech is appropriate, or less explicitness is required. Here other correctness notions than the grammatical ones come into play to determine acceptability.

Thus far I have discussed notions of correctness that pertain to linguistic forms; I did not include notions of correctness of texts because a text, in my opinion, is not a linguistic form. To judge a text from the point of view of linguistic form just means to determine whether it is correct from phonemic or graphemic, morphemic, and syntactic points of view. There are standard forms of different kinds of text that make them recognizable as a text of this kind or that: a letter, a story, a poem, a report, etc., but there is no notion of a text-form *per se*. This is because there must be a property of coherence which makes a text a text, distinct from a mere collection of sentences; and this property cannot be captured on the formal level of the text itself. It can only be captured on the basis of interpretation, by considering reference to established referents, presuppositions and other assumed knowledge of speaker and hearer, goals, and motivations of behavior. Therefore, the notion of 'text grammar', which has been widely criticized (for example, by Dascal and Margalit 1974) since it was introduced in the early days of Textlinguistics by Van Dijk (1972), is nothing comparable to a sentence grammar and is, in the linguistic sense, no grammar at all. Formulating correctness conditions for texts is not a matter of finding correctness conditions for linguistic forms. Correctness of texts, in some of its aspects, belongs under the heading of correctness of use of linguistic forms, together with semantic and pragmatic correctness; in other aspects, it belongs under the heading of correctness of actions and series of actions. Two different kinds of correctness are involved in both pragmatic correctness, including aspects of stylistics, and correctness of texts:

(1) correctness of the use of linguistic forms
(2) correctness of communication as a part of rational interaction.

In fact, when judging from the first of these points of view, we always presuppose correctness from the second. This is necessary because, when we judge the adequacy of the use of linguistic forms for performing certain communicative actions or series of these (as in texts and dialogues), we have to be able to find out the intended action before we can judge whether the linguistic expression used in that action is adequate for performing that action. On the other hand, to determine the performed action, we generally have to rely on the correct use of the linguistic forms; indeed, this is presupposed in interpretation. In cases in which one finds semantic or pragmatic contradictions if an utterance is interpreted according to the correct use of its parts and syntactic structure, and no indirect interpretation can be derived by pragmatic principles, one can assume that the linguistic forms are used in a way that is different from established use and thus are used incorrectly. One also presupposes in such cases that the intended actions are, in fact, consistent, but wrongly performed with respect to the use of linguistic forms.

In this paper I shall omit the treatment of the different notions of correctness of the use of linguistic forms and refer the reader to the literature.[2] Instead, I want to make some remarks about the relation between the notions of linguistic correctness and norms of language.

THE RELATION BETWEEN NOTIONS OF CORRECTNESS AND NORMS

Notions of correctness and norms are intimately related. We could embed the conjunction of all correctness notions for utterances into one norm, which then would not need to say more than 'Speak correctly, as specified by the whole set of correctness notions!'. This would be too crude, because different notions of correctness are associated with different normative forces, often conditionally, relative to certain types of situations and groups within the population. Different notions of correctness are the content of different norms. The norms can be organized in subsets, according to certain properties which they have.

How are norms related to the corresponding notions of correctness? The norms are the constellations in social reality that create, delineate, and secure the notions of correctness. These norms consist of relationships between people, in which it is determined what the models or standards which have to be followed are, who has to follow which models, who provides the models, and who enforces, if necessary, following the models. There are central models and less central models: by the same social relationships, it is also determined which people provide the central models, which ones have to follow the central models within acceptable margins of deviation and are then secondary models for other people who then follow the secondary models within acceptable margins of deviation. These, further, may be tertiary models for still other people. Since people have to be acquainted with the models relevant to them, the hierarchy of models roughly corresponds to social hierarchies between groups: availability of contact with models that are more central in the hierarchy diminishes with social distance. The availability of written models to broad groups of the population after cheap printing techniques were developed and the availability, via radio and television, of models trained especially in correct speech have led to a general availability of the central models. But even so, models which are closer to one's own speech and therefore seem more familiar can be followed more easily and provide a more realistic motivation for following them: they are not strange, because they are to a great extent compatible with one's own notions of correctness, which have been built up by means of primary socialization in one's local and familiar surroundings, including linguistic surroundings.

The hierarchy of models is a social fact, which is evident in the different degrees of acceptability of speech that is incorrect when measured against the central models: the farther a person is away from the central models socially, the more acceptable it is when he produces incorrect speech. Generally speech is judged as correct or incorrect relative to the models that are supposed to be the models of the speaker. These are the village teachers for village populations, or local officials and merchants. The teachers are the officially provided models, who for a long time have been local people with better education and teacher training. Now, more and more primary teachers are not local people, and this makes a difference in the role they play as models: bigger steps are required of local people when the model they have to follow is a stranger. On the other hand, radio, television, and newspapers provide so much additional input into the process of acquiring varieties of the standard that this difficulty is less severe.

Despite all the changes in the last seventy years in the patterns and media of communication, there is still a hierarchy in the orientation toward the central models. The educated people follow the central models, provided by (high) literature, handbooks, and personal models. People with less education follow the more educated ones: their teachers and other civil servants; the least educated follow, often enough, not their schoolteachers, if they have any, but those people who are one step higher on the social ladder, or they follow subgroup leaders who have enough prestige to compete with those models who are socially and economically better off. This whole construction, consisting of a center, a graded range around it, vague boundaries, and an area outside of the standard, which is represented by the models with their different degrees of centrality, is an idealized structure of social relationships that exists with regard to the task of securing and reinforcing the notions of correctness of speech.[3] This construction of orientation and order in the social background that carries and supports the standard is modified in reality by additional factors. In a society, an economically and politically strong group can be a stronger model than educated people, but this makes a difference only if such a group is not itself oriented toward educated models. Or people may have reasons to follow local leaders or subgroup leaders with prestige and this, too, makes a difference if these leaders do not orient their speech toward the standard provided by interregional, educated, or otherwise influential speakers.

Generally, the social reality of a norm consists in relationships between norm authorities or subauthorities, norm enforcers, norm codifiers, and norm subjects, any of whom, in the case of linguistic norms, can also fulfill the other roles. These interrelations build up the force of the norm by providing models and correcting speech behavior with respect to them. Acts of correction are aided by rewards or penalties. The other part of the norm, besides normative force and possible conditions restricting application, is the norm content. This consists of a notion of correctness, or a whole set of such notions, which can be spelled out explicitly or exemplified by models. If only examples are provided as models, speakers construct a concept or a complex of concepts, using their normal capacity of concept formation to abstract the relevant features from the exemplifying situations. In this way they construct semantic concepts, concepts of sounds and sound patterns, and concepts of syntactic patterns; the boundaries of these concepts are provided by the relevance of certain features and by acts of correction applied to overgeneralization. By acts of especially authorized correction, the degree of deviance from the models is limited. A second level of concept formation is the systematization of the concepts built on the basis of perception of speech and its use. These systematizations can take place from different points of view and can thus lead to extensions beyond what is learned in primary concept formation. Order and other relationships among the constructed concepts of basic items and patterns are established — for example, the formation of recursive rules on the basis of observed patterns and relationships among them, especially as there is substitution of patterns into other patterns or even in the same ones.

In this way, a whole network of semantic, syntactic, morphological, and phonological relationships is constructed among the respective kinds of concepts formed on the first level of concept formation, and can then, furthermore, be constructed among the constructs of the second level. The concepts of the first level are the content of linguistic norms. The systematizations of these on the second level are of a different kind: insofar as they are real, they can be mapped homomorphically (i.e., preserving structure) on relationships and operations in the heads of speakers. Systematizations of this kind have been formulated by theoretical linguists as linguistic rules, which are ontologically quite different from norms of language, which are social entities. The connection between norms and linguistic rules or systematizations exists via the norm contents which are concepts constructed by individual speakers, the formation of which is restricted by human cognitive abilities, by states, events, and things in reality, and by social control exerted by providing models and correcting deviance outside the accepted margins, which vary with different conditions of language use. The intersubjectivity of these concepts is only secured by these restricting factors. The restrictions on the possibilities of human perception and cognition, and the outside reality of the world, give the objective restrictions, and the social control provides the social or intersubjective restrictions. These objective and intersubjective restrictions together, apparently, are sufficient to secure the formation of concepts and systematizations of concepts by individuals such that they are similar enough to make possible both communication and the coordination of people's knowledge.

In conclusion, we can state that linguistic norms are the social reality of concepts of linguistic correctness; this social reality secures the coordination concerning form and use of linguistic forms in a speech community.

NOTES

This article is in large part identical with pp. 1-17 and 70-72 of my book *Norms of Language*, Longman's Linguistics Library, 1987, and has been printed with the kind permission of Longman: London and New York.

1. For these topics, especially the role of classical languages in standardization of modern languages, see Bartsch (1984b); see also the case studies by Subbayya (Rayjashree) (1980), and Musa (1981, 1984).
2. The notion of correctness of texts is mainly based on the notion of text coherence, on which work has been proceeding in Textlinguistics for more than 15 years; see, for example, Van Dijk (1977). Notions of semantic and pragmatic correctness have been treated in Bartsch (1979a, 1979b, and 1984a). A more formal treatment of certain aspects of pragmatic correctness has been given by Groenendijk and Stokhof (1984).
3. We find further empirical evidence for this construction in Subbayya (Rayjashree) (1980); this study of the standardization of Marathi has been reported extensively in Bartsch (1984b).

REFERENCES

Bartsch, R. 1979a. 'Semantical and Pragmatical Correctness as Basic Notions in the Theory of Meaning', *Journal of Pragmatics* 3: 1-43.
—— 1979b. 'Die Rolle von pragmatischen Korrektheitsbedingungen bei der Interpretation von Außerungen', in G. Grewendorf (ed.), *Sprechakttheorie und Semantik*. Frankfurt: Suhrkamp Verlag, 217-46.
—— 1981. 'The Concepts "Rule" and "Norm" in Linguistics', *Lingua* 58: 51-81.
—— 1984a. 'Concept Formation, Truth, and Norm'. Paper presented at the 1983 Cleves Conference 'Meaning and Lexicon'. Centrale Interfaculteit, Universiteit van Amsterdam, MS.
—— 1984b. 'The Influence on Linguistic Norms by Language Standardization'. Centrale Interfaculteit, Universiteit van Amsterdam, MS.
Berits, J. 1983. 'Proposed Spelling Reform for Dutch', *Language Planning News Letter*, July 1983. Honolulu: East-West Center.
Bickerton, D. 1977. 'Some Problems of Acceptability and Grammaticality in Pidgins and Creoles', in S. Greenbaum (ed.), *Acceptability in Language*. Den Haag: Mouton, 27-37.
Booij, G.E., *et al.* 1979. *Spelling*. (Spektator Cahiers 2) Groningen: Wolters-Noordhoff.
Dascal, M., and A. Margalit. 1974. 'A New Revolution in Linguistics? — "Text Grammars" versus "Sentence Grammars"', *Theoretical Linguistics* 1: 195-213.

Van Dijk, T.A. 1972. *Some Aspects of Text Grammars*. The Hague: Mouton.
—— 1977. *Text and Context. Explorations in the Semantics and Pragmatics of Discourse*. London: Longman.
Groenendijk, J., and M. Stokhof. 1984. *The Semantics of Questions and the Pragmatics of Answers*. University of Amsterdam dissertation.
Itkonen, E. 1974. *Linguistics and Metascience* (Studia Philosophica Turkuensia II) Kohemäki: Societas Philosophica et Phaenomenologica Finlandiae.
—— 1976. 'Was für eine Wissenschaft ist die Linguistik eigentlich?', in D. Wunderlich (ed.), *Wissenschaftstheorie der Linguistik*. Kronberg: Athenäum, 56–76.
Labov, W. 1972. 'The Study of Language in its Social Context', in *Sociolinguistic Patterns*. Philadelphia: University of Pennsylvania Press, 183–259.
Musa, M. 1981. *Language Planning in Sri Lanka*. Dacca: Bhuiyan Muhammad Imram PWD.
—— 1984. *Language Planning for Language Development: The Modernization of Bengali*. Honolulu: Institute of Culture and Communication, East–West Center, MS.
Putnam, H. 1975. 'The Meaning of "Meaning"', *Mind, Language, Reality*. Philosophical Papers, Vol. 2. Cambridge: University Press, 215–71.
Schaap, G.C. 1980 (ed.). *De Spelling van de Nederlandse Taal*. Derde bijgewerkte drik. Publikatie van de Centrale directie Voorlichting van het Ministerie van Onderwijs en Wetenschappen. s'Gravenhage: Staatsuitgeverij.
Siebs, Th. 1898/1961. *Deutsche Hochsprache. Bühnenaussprache*. 18. durchgesehene Auflage. Herausgegeben von Helmut de Boor und Paul Diels. Berlin: de Gruyter, 1961.
—— 1969. *Deutsche Aussprache. Reine und gemäßigte Hochlautung mit Aussprache-Worterbuch*. 19. umgearbeitete Auflage. Herausgegeben von Helmut de Boor, Hugo Moser und Christian Winkler. Berlin: de Gruyter.
Subbayya (Rayjashree K.S.) 1980. *The Standardization of Language. A Case Study of Marathi*. University of Mysore dissertation. Mysore-6: Central Institute of Indian Languages.

2

Written and Spoken Language in South Asia

WILLIAM BRIGHT

Twenty years ago, I had the pleasure of organizing a conference on sociolinguistics at UCLA, the proceedings of which were subsequently published (Bright 1966). For me, and for other participants in the conference who had worked in India, such as John Gumperz and Paul Friedrich, the field of sociolinguistics had taken shape as a very direct result of our experiences in South Asia. We had gone there with backgrounds in post-Bloomfieldian structural linguistics, but we had returned with the realization that new methodologies were needed to cope with such phenomena as diglossia, code-switching, widespread multilingualism, and social dialect. (For a survey of the whole literature which has grown up on these topics in South Asia, see Shapiro and Schiffman 1981.)

Among the phenomena with which we were poorly prepared to deal was the relationship between written and spoken language in South Asia, which has several aspects. One is the multiplicity of writing systems, and the fact that radically different scripts are sometimes used for very similar speech varieties, as in the case of Hindi and Urdu. Another aspect was the diglossic distinction between 'literary' and 'colloquial' language — complicated by the fact that 'literary' language is not simply the written variety, but more accurately that of formal speech. Still another aspect involved some paradoxical attitudes towards written language: on the one hand, high prestige is attached to literacy, but on the other hand, where the most prestigious literary texts of all are involved — the Vedas, and later Sanskrit literature as well — great value is set upon oral transmission and memorization. But in considering the complexity of written language in India, we were at a disadvantage in the 1950s, since few of us were experienced in studying written language as such: the post-Bloomfieldian dogma was that writing was in fact only a secondary reflection of **real** language.

It is in fact only in the last few years that many general linguists have begun to take written language seriously. (Let me refer to just one field which currently seems to be coming into its own with the help of sociolinguistic insights: this is the study of the social functions of written language and of literacy, as related to and compared with the functions of spoken language — cf. Goody 1977, Tannen 1982a, b.) The American 'structuralist' linguists of the 1930s through the 1970s were frequently involved in research on previously unwritten American Indian languages; perhaps in reaction to the 'philological' outlooks of their predecessors, they tended to emphasize speech, and to see writing as a mere derivative — not truly worthy of being called 'language'. By contrast, the school of transformational generative grammarians, who came into prominence from the 1960s onward, were concerned at first mainly with English and other standardized languages; and perhaps in counter-reaction to the structuralists' views, they went in a different direction as regards speech vs. writing. On the one hand, since generative syntax dealt most often with major world languages, presented in standard orthography, it was taken for granted that writing was indeed a form of language; but relationships or differences between what is written and what is spoken were generally ignored. On the other hand, generative phonology, as codified in Chomsky and Halle's *Sound Pattern of English* (1968), offered the startling proposal that English orthography — previously maligned by linguists as seriously out of correspondence with the modern spoken language — could in fact be seen as very close to a psychologically real 'underlying representation' of English pronunciation; but again, the generativists tended to ignore the characteristics which **differentiate** the basic structure of written language from that of speech. Recently, however, a more balanced view, informed by sociolinguistic awareness, seems to be gaining prominence. Many researchers would now say that language has at least three **manifestations**: spoken, written, and signed (as in the sign language used by the deaf). Written language, especially in societies with long traditions of literacy and of highly valued written literature, tends to acquire its own distinctive structures on all levels: phonology, grammar, semantics, and discourse — and its own sociolinguistic functions in terms of class dialect, register, etc. It is within this framework that I wish to examine the history of spoken and written language in South Asia.[1]

1. HISTORICAL ORIGINS OF WRITING IN SOUTH ASIA

One of the world's significant early scripts is, of course, that of the Indus Valley civilization, often called Harappan, after one of the main archaeological sites. The known inscriptions in this writing system, which has not yet been deciphered, date from around the first half of the third millennium BC, at a period when most scholars believe that Sanskrit speakers had not yet entered the Indus Valley. It is widely hypothesized that the language of the Harappan civilization belonged to the Dravidian family, for two reasons. First, although languages of that group are now concentrated in

South India, they are known to have occupied a wider area in the past; and one Dravidian language, Brahui, is still spoken in Baluchistan, just west of the Indus Valley. Second, a significant number of Dravidian borrowings can be identified in the oldest Vedic texts, reflecting the earliest period of contact between Sanskrit speakers and the ancient Harappan population (Emeneau 1954). However, the corpus of Harappan writing is limited primarily to very short texts — typically of five or six characters — found almost exclusively on about 2,500 stone seals, and in clay impressions of those seals. Since some of the impressions are found still attached to bales of trade goods, it is inferred that a major function of the writing was in labeling merchandise. But no bilingual inscriptions have been found; and although two large (and overlapping) concordances of the Harappan inscriptions have been published (Mahadevan 1977, Koskenniemi et al. 1973), all attempts at decipherment still remain speculative — though there are indications that the script was basically logographic, with some development in the direction of phonologically defined signs.[2]

One of the most surprising things about the Harappan script is that it seems to have disappeared from use along with the decline of the Indus Valley civilization — leaving South Asia with no trace of a writing system for some 2,000 years, until, in the third century BC, two scripts, Brāhmī and Kharoṣṭhī, made their appearance in the stone-carved edicts by which the Emperor Aśoka Maurya propagated Buddhist principles throughout the subcontinent. I deliberately say 'no trace of a writing system', because various scholars have found it hard to believe that anything so valuable as a writing system could be simply discarded, and have looked for evidence that the Harappan script may have simply gone 'underground'. On the one hand, they have pointed to the so-called 'graffiti' which are found on potsherds from all over South Asia during the post-Harappan period, and some of which bear geometrical resemblances to Harappan characters. But since these graffiti lack the patterned nature characteristic of writing systems, and since there is in any case no way to match them phonologically or semantically with Harappan characters, most scholars have regarded them as mere potters' marks (Gupta and Ramachandran 1979: xxi). On the other hand, some writers have called attention to graphic similarity between Harappan signs and those used in the later Brāhmī script; but again, in the absence of phonetic correspondences, these similarities cannot be taken seriously as anything but accidental coincidences of universal geometrical patterns. Another argument is that writing must have existed continuously in South Asia, but that it was on perishable materials, such as cloth or bark, which have not survived (cf. Pandey 1957: 16). On this hypothesis, the Aśokan texts are significant for the history of writing only because they were the first of their type to be carved in stone, and therefore to endure. But the Harappans had inscribed their characters not only in stone and clay, but also in other durable materials, such as ivory and copper; so it is difficult to believe that the extensive archaeological research which has been carried out in South Asia would not have turned up **some** examples of pre-Aśokan writing, if any such had indeed existed. Some fragmentary pre-Aśokan inscriptions on coins, plaques, vases etc. have indeed been reported; but all of these turn out to be vulnerable to skepticism as regards date (cf. Goyal 1979: 30–45).

Such considerations have led scholars such as Goyal (1979), Verma (1971, 1979), Dani (1963), and Upasak (1960) to claim that pre-Mauryan India was essentially scriptless, and even that the Kharoṣṭhī and Brāhmī scripts were developed under direct orders from the Emperor Aśoka himself. To the latter hypothesis, Gupta and Ramachandran (1979, 123-4) object that 'We do not have a single reference from the ancient world regarding a king or emperor inventing a totally new script and popularizing it' — but of course the Korean King Sejong (1419–52) is traditionally said to have done precisely that (Jensen 1969: 211).

2. THE AŚOKAN SCRIPTS

The edicts of the Emperor Aśoka, dating from around 253–250 BC, are found over a large part of South Asia, and in several writing systems. On the northwestern frontier, some inscriptions are in Greek and Aramaic — the principal languages of foreign contact in that area. Most other inscriptions are in the Prakrit dialect of Aśoka's capital in Magadha (now part of Bihar state, in eastern India); but they are in two different writing systems. One of these, Kharoṣṭhī, was written from right to left, like Aramaic and other Semitic scripts; it was used only in the northwest, and eventually died out. The other script, Brāhmī, was written mainly from left to right; it was used in the larger part of the subcontinent, and eventually developed into the many different major and minor scripts used down to the present time in India and southeast Asia. Both systems were phonologically based, and they introduced a novel method of transcribing both consonants and vowels in a systematic way. Instead of writing both consonantal and vocalic phonemes as independent letters, as is done in Greek, or writing the vowels only as inconsistent or optional diacritics to consonant symbols, as is done in many Semitic writing systems (e.g. Hebrew, Aramaic, and Arabic), the new Indic scripts adopted the strategy of writing each CV sequence as a unit (called in Sanskrit an *akṣara*), specifically by regarding the short vowel *a* as inherent in all consonant symbols, and by writing all other vowels as **obligatory** diacritics — attached to the top, to the bottom, or to either side of the consonant. Table 2.1 illustrates the system for Kharoṣṭhī, Brāhmī, and two important major scripts of the present day — (Deva)Nāgarī, used for Hindi and other north Indian languages, and the Kannaḍa script of South India. Compare the rightmost

WRITTEN AND SPOKEN LANGUAGE IN SOUTH ASIA

column, which shows how the same syllable would be written in the Urdu adaptation of the Arabic script; note that here the superior line which marks *a*, the inferior line which marks *i*, and the superior curl which marks *u* and *o* are all optional, used mainly in students' primers.[3]

It is of interest to note that there is perhaps only one other writing system in the world which indicates CV combinations by vowel diacritics obligatorily attached to consonants. This is the Ethiopic, which is well known to have been derived from South Semitic sources around AD 350 (cf. Jensen 1969: 343–4). Writing systems such as these have created problems for scholars who have attempted typologies of writing systems. A system which writes consonants and vowels separately and independently, as in most European languages, is called an alphabet; a system with a unitary symbol for each CV combination, like Japanese *kana* or Sequoyah's Cherokee script, is called a syllabary. But we lack a name to distinguish a system like the Semitic, where a single symbol can indicate *k*, *ka*, *ki*, *ku* etc. And we also need a separate term for the systems used in South Asia and in Ethiopia, which differentiate *ka*, *ki*, and *ku* by single yet complex symbols, in which consonantal and vocalic elements are combined (cf. Voegelin and Voegelin 1961). The term 'semi-syllabary' has been suggested, and may prove useful.

Table 2.1: Semitic and Indic consonant symbols

	Kharoṣṭhī	Brāhmī	Nāgarī	Kannaḍa	(Urdu)
ka	ꡔ	+	क	ಕ	کَ
kā		ᚠ	का	ಕಾ	کَا
ki	ꡔ	ᚠ	कि	ಕಿ	کِ
kī		ᚠ	की	ಕೀ	کِی
ku	ꡔ	±	कु	ಕು	کُ
kū		±	कू	ಕೂ	کُ
ke	ꡔ	+	के	ಕೆ	کَے
kē				ಕೇ	
ko	ꡔ	ᚠ	को	ಕೊ	کو
kō				ಕೋ	

These questions are of more than merely terminological importance, as is illustrated in the influential textbook on writing by Gelb (cf. Verma 1971: 2-4). On the one hand, Gelb wishes to establish a general principle that 'writing ... must pass through the stages of logography, syllabography, and alphabetography in this, and no other order'; hence, he says, 'it is absurd to speak of the development of the Ethiopic (or Sanskrit) syllabaries from a Semitic alphabet'. Rather, he wants to say that 'both the Ethiopic and Sanskrit writings are further developments from a Semitic syllabary' (Gelb 1963: 201). Elsewhere, however, Gelb declares that Brāhmī letter forms were 'freely invented' (144). And in still another passage (188), Gelb admits that the terms 'alphabet' and 'syllabary' are inadequate, not only for Indic and Ethiopic scripts, but for those of the modern Semitic languages as well. It appears that a universal evolutionary progression, such as Gelb proposes, will need to be based on a more adequate typology of script types.

As has been noted, some writers have proposed that both Kharoṣṭhī and Brāhmī scripts were new inventions within South Asia, in spite of the fact that we have no evidence concerning the process of their development. Other writers have accepted the likelihood that Kharoṣṭhī was an adaptation from the Aramaic script, considering the facts that they were used in the same northwestern area, that they were both written from right to left, and that a fair number of Kharoṣṭhī symbols show significant similarities in shape and pronunciation to the corresponding Aramaic symbols. However, some of these writers have denied that Brāhmī can have the same Aramaic inspiration; they point to the fact that Brāhmī was written in the opposite direction, and that it is harder to find significant correspondences in shape and sound. In this view, Brāhmī must represent either a survival of the Harappan writing system, or an independent new invention. Finally, still other writers, including most European Indologists (especially Bühler), have believed that Brāhmī **was** derived from Aramaic writing; they mention that a few Brāhmī inscriptions are written from right to left, or else partially in the boustrophedon style of alternating directions, and they point to the undoubted similarities of certain Brāhmī letters to those of similar sound in Aramaic, e.g. g. All scholars, to be sure, recognize the important fact that both Kharoṣṭhī and Brāhmī scripts were systematically expanded, with reference to any known previous model, so as to convey all the phonological contrasts in place of articulation and manner of articulation which are characteristic of Sanskrit, Prakrit, and of South Indian languages generally; it is clear that the Kharoṣṭhī and Brāhmī scripts as we know them were elaborated by ancient pandits who had a high degree of sophistication in phonetics. (For tables showing the symbols of the relevant Semitic and Indic scripts, see Jensen 1969: 302, 316, 365, 367.)

I believe that scholars have not given enough attention to one particular argument in favor of a Semitic origin for the Aśokan scripts. This is their unusual character, described above, whereby vowels are indicated as obligatory diacritics attached to consonant symbols. The only other writing system known to use this principle is the Ethiopic, which is clearly derived from Semitic sources. It seems to me that the Ethiopic and the Indic developments can be accounted for in the same way, as an extension of the Semitic practice of writing vowels as **optional** diacritics; thus even if one is disinclined to see the letter shapes of Kharoṣṭhī and Brāhmī as derived from Semitic sources, it is nevertheless likely that the Indic **principle** of vowel-writing can be explained as an instance of 'stimulus diffusion' from a Semitic model. However, another problem is even more difficult: was Brāhmī script, or some predecessor of it, used during the 2,000 years that preceded Aśoka's reign? Or was Sanskrit literature, from the Vedic through the Classic periods, composed and transmitted in a purely oral medium? This has been a matter of intense controversy.

3. ORALITY VS. LITERACY IN ANCIENT INDIA

The majority view among European Indologists has been that Sanskrit-speaking culture was basically oral; that not only the Vedas, but also the Brāhmaṇas, the Purāṇas, the epics, and classic literature in general were composed and transmitted orally; and that even that epitome of sophistication, the Sanskrit grammar of Pāṇini, was elaborated without the use of writing. But other scholars, especially in India, have insisted that a continuous tradition of literacy must have existed, though the written documents themselves have not survived. The problem is that, even though we find mention of writing in Classical Sanskrit texts, it is hard to determine the exact period from which a text dates, and even harder to rule out the possibility that the references to writing are late interpolations. I will attempt to summarize the major types of evidence which bear on this dispute.

3.1. The Greek evidence

The most easily datable evidence is that from the Greek writers who visited India during and following the time of Alexander the Great (cf. Gopal 1977). This material is in some ways unsatisfactory, since it consists largely of fragments quoted by later Greek and Roman authors; furthermore, there is a tendency in much Greek writing on India to emphasize the spectacular and fabulous. However, a few statements seem straightforward and relevant. First, Nearchos, a general of Alexander's army, was reported by Strabo's *Geography* as stating that 'the Hindus wrote letters (*epistolás*) on linen cloth that is very closely woven' (Jones 1930, vol. 7: 117). However, in an adjacent passage, Strabo also quotes Nearchos as saying, of the ancient Indians, that 'their laws, some public and some private, are unwritten'. It has been supposed that, in speaking of 'laws', Nearchos was referring to *smṛti*, the Sanskrit term literally meaning 'remembered', which is applied to post-Vedic literature known to have been transmitted orally from early times. A possible interpretation for the evidence from Nearchos, then, is that writing was known, and perhaps used for commercial purposes, but not for religious or legal texts.

Second, the Roman writer Quintus Curtius, in his *History of Alexander the Great*, cites an unknown Greek source as stating that 'the tender side of the bark of trees receives written characters like paper'; the reference is evidently to birch bark. These two quotations indicate that writing was known at least in some parts of South Asia around 326 BC.

On the other side of the balance, however, is a much-quoted statement by the Greek envoy Megasthenes, who some 25 years later visited the emperor Candragupta Maurya, known to the Greeks as Sandracottus. Megasthenes commented on the lack of serious crime in ancient India, and his observations were recorded by Strabo as follows (in the translation of Jones 1930, vol. 7: 86–9): 'Megasthenes says that when he was in the camp of Sandracottus, although the number in camp was forty thousand, he on no day saw reports of stolen articles that were worth more than 200 drachmae; and that too among a people who use unwritten laws only. For, he continues, they have no knowledge of written letters, and regulate every single thing from memory...'

This quotation has been cited by many scholars to indicate that, at least in the parts of South Asia visited by Megasthenes, oral transmission was still dominant. However, some of the terminology in the quotation is troubling: if Megasthenes 'on no day saw reports of stolen articles' worth over 200 drachmae, this clearly implies **written** reports. However, examination of the original Greek text suggests a more appropriate translation: *mēdemían hēméran ideīn anēnegména klémmata* is literally 'not-one day to-see brought-back stolen-articles'. That is, the participle *anēnegména*, which Jones translated as 'reported', could equally well refer to stolen articles **recovered**. This fits better with the statement by Megasthenes that no writing system was in use during the reign of Candragupta Maurya — only about 50 years before the time of the Aśokan inscriptions.

It has been suggested that Megasthenes, like Nearchos before him, observed that justice was regulated by the oral *smṛti* tradition, and that he then jumped to a false conclusion that writing was not used at all (cf. Gopal 1977: 51). At any rate, the Greek evidence as a whole can be interpreted in terms of the hypotheses already stated: that, in the early Mauryan period, writing existed in some parts of South Asia, perhaps used for certain limited purposes, but not used for law or administration. (It should be noted, however, that Gopal 1977, after carefully marshalling his evidence, wishes to use it to argue for the creation of the Brāhmī script in the early Mauryan period: I cannot agree that such a conclusion is required.)

3.2. The Buddhist tradition

Since the Brāhmī texts are in fact the Buddhist edicts of the Emperor Aśoka, it is natural to look to other early Buddhist texts for evidence of writing. Such evidence is found in the Pali scriptures, as reported by Rhys Davids (1903: 107-20). The oldest reference is in the *Sīlas*, thought to date from around 400 BC, which contains a list of frivolous activities forbidden to Buddhist monks; one is called *akkharika*, i.e. the tracing of *akṣaras* or written symbols on the skin of a person who is then supposed to guess what was written. In the *vinaya* texts of perhaps a century later, the term *lekha* 'writing' first occurs, as the name of a skill which monks were allowed to learn, and which was used both for official notices and for personal letters. However, as Davids notes (1903: 109), 'it is a long step from the use of writing for such notifications ... to the use ... for the purpose of writing down any books'. And in fact the Pali literature strongly suggests the absence of anything that could be called 'scriptures'. For one thing, the monastic rules give detailed lists of all objects which monks were allowed to own, or not allowed; but there is no reference to books or manuscripts. Again, the *Anguttara Nikāya* refers to the danger that religious texts will be lost if the chain of oral transmission is broken; and a definition of scholarship is given which does not mention reading, but rather 'repeating over to oneself'. If, in a monastic settlement, no member knows the 227 Rules of the Order, it is prescribed that a monk shall be sent to a neighboring group to learn the material by heart; this is to be done even if it violates a rule forbidding monks to travel during the rainy season.

It should be noted that it is difficult to assign dates to the early Buddhist texts, or to rule out the possibility of subsequent changes or additions. However, Buddhist tradition ascribes the oral formulation of the Pali canon to the first century after the Buddha's death, and it was supposedly not written down until the first century BC. Whatever the accuracy of these dates, they strongly point toward the same hypothesis suggested by the Greek data — namely that, in the early Mauryan period, writing was used in India for certain purposes, but that oral transmission was obligatory, to the exclusion of writing, for the extensive and important texts of the sacred Buddhist canon.

3.3. The Hindu tradition

It is well known that oral transmission of the Vedas and other Sanskrit literature has been practiced in India from ancient times to the present. In fact, the earliest record of written Sanskrit dates from only the first century BC (Verma 1979: 106) — much later than the Prakrit inscriptions, at a time when Sanskrit can no longer have been widely spoken. Yet some earlier writings in Sanskrit must have been on perishable material, and so vanished. Scholars differ as to their estimates of the dates when writing is first referred to in Sanskrit literature, and when it was first **used** for literary purposes. However, the general view of European scholars in the twentieth century is typified by the following quotations:

> References to writing occur ... in the Sūtra literature [sixth to second centuries BC], but there is no clear mention of it in the Vedas, Brāhmaṇas or Upaniṣads. This negative evidence, however, is not wholly conclusive, and some form of script may have been used by merchants ... (Basham 1954: 394)
>
> During the period when the Vedic civilisation was being built up, no form of writing was employed in India, and in its absence the technique was evolved of preserving intact the Vedic literature by means of oral tradition. Even when writing was introduced, this oral tradition persisted in the various departments of knowledge, and it continued as a basic feature of Indian education down to modern times ... use of writing was only slowly adopted in the Brahmin schools, and in the early period its function lay primarily in business and administration ... It is unlikely that much literature existed in manuscript form before the second century BC. (Burrow 1955: 64–5)
>
> The first form of the Indian alphabets now used ... could have been introduced to India about 800 BC ... and ... must have been adapted by Sanskrit-speaking specialists, with great finesse, to the Indian phonetic system ... The presence of writing is also shown by the terminology of the oldest legal texts, by the canonical literature of the Buddhists and the Jains, by the Rāmāyana, and by reports of the Greeks. [I comment on these points below.] ... At the beginning, writing served only practical aims. For literary purposes, it entered into usage among the peoples in general only in a secondary and progressive way. But in India, the bearers of literature clung resolutely to the oral tradition for a long time ... Dissemination by recitation was frequent, even for secular or semi-secular works, especially the Epic. Brahmanical teaching, including that of grammar, had been entirely oral at a previous date; Pāṇini attests the existence of writing, but not its use in teaching; his grammar, with its supplements, gives reason to believe in a purely oral tradition. (Renou 1957: 32–4)[4]

It is necessary to comment on the evidence which Renou mentions regarding writing in Classical Sanskrit times. The Buddhist and Greek materials have been mentioned above. Renou's mention of old legal materials presumably refers to supposed mentions of writing by the Vedic sage Bṛhaspati — but these are, of course, known only through quotations by much later writers. The statesman Kauṭilya composed the *Arthaśāstra*, perhaps the world's first treatise on political science, the received text of which contains many references to writing in an administrative context; but again, we cannot be sure about the date of Kauṭilya himself, or about the antiquity of the received text (cf. Goyal 1979: 26–7). Similar qualifications must be applied to mentions of writing in the Jain canon and in the epic.

The testimony related to Pāṇini's Sanskrit grammar, commonly believed to date from the fourth century BC, is discussed further by Agrawala (1963: 25):

> The text of the *sūtras* has been handed down to us almost intact by the method of oral transmission by which Sanskrit learning through the ages has descended from generation to generation through a succession of teachers and pupils ... instead of being conserved in writing ...

Memorization is of course aided in this instance by the extreme brevity of Pāṇini's rules; thus his last sutra is *a a* — which, given appropriate 'metarules' of interpretation, is understood as meaning that the phonemic short /a/ is realized as phonetic shwa [ə]. But elsewhere, Agrawala points out (312–13):

> Writing was known in the time of Pāṇini ... Though teaching was oral in those days, ... Pāṇini hints at the use of the writing in several significant expressions. These are (1) *grantha* ['book'], (2) *lipikara*, a writer, [and] *yavanāni lipi* ['Greek writing'] ...

It is significant to recall that Pāṇini lived in the northwest, where he was most likely to be aware of Greek, Aramaic, or Persian scripts; and indeed, his term *lipi* 'writing' is apparently a loanword into Sanskrit from Old Persian *dipi*.

The evidence of the Pāṇinian tradition and of other early materials thus all point toward the likelihood that writing was known and used in South Asia from a date in pre-Mauryan times which we cannot specify exactly, but that it was probably restricted mainly to commercial and other practical purposes, and only adapted to sacred or secular literature in later times. This in turn suggests that the tradition of oral composition and of verbatim transmission was maintained in India well into the Classic period of Sanskrit literature.

In opposition to the above views, however, some Indian scholars — perhaps from patriotic motives — have not only denied that the Aśokan scripts could have been derived from a foreign source, but have also maintained that writing has existed in India since Vedic times.[5] Thus Wakankar (1983) writes:

> According to Indian tradition it is [the god] Ganesha, the younger son of Shiva Maheshwara, who created the ... logical Phono-graphy [and] incised the Letters after the Mantras delivered by Shiva ... To state that all these [Vedic hymns, in diverse meters] were composed without aid of writing and without aid of counting each letter is unbelievable ... Shiva Maheshwara is the most popular deity of South India; but in the grammatic tradition he is the earliest of the Grammarians ... the first grammarian is identified with Nataraja Shiva; the Sound categories are attributed to Shiva who is fond of going into cosmic dance ... [T]he sages ... went to him for acquiring some device to save the Vedas from being lost. Understanding their worries, Nataraja Shiva Maheshwara gave them 14 aphorisms, called Shivasootras, delivering them by striking his trinklet.

[The Śivasūtras are a listing of the morphophonemic classes into which Pāṇini divides the Sanskrit phonemes; they are traditionally given as a sort of prologue to his grammar. The term 'trinklet' is Wakankar's rather strange translation of Sanskrit *ḍamāru*, a type of hand drum.]

> Shiva Maheshwara's Categories of Sound trickled down to the Grammarian Panini ... Now we come to Ganesha, the First of the School of Vedic scribes ... *Ganesha-Keelaka* says in clear terms that He (Ganesha) incised writing ... inspired by the Mantras of Shiva enunciated earlier ...

I will not attempt to comment in detail on Wakankar's mythological account of the origin of Sanskrit speech and of writing; however, it is striking that he believes the Vedas and their meters **could** not have been elaborated without the use of writing. Yet the metrical structures of the Vedas, like the melodic patterns traditionally associated with the various meters of Classical Sanskrit poetry, can never have been a complication, but rather an aid to the memory; we can always remember the words to a song better than we can those of purely spoken poetry, and those of poetry better than prose. Furthermore, it seems to me a tribute to Hindu culture, rather than an act of derogation, to recognize that a complex literature could be developed and perpetuated by the human mind and memory alone, without the 'artificial' extension of writing systems.

4. OTHER PARTS OF THE WORLD

The roles of literacy and orality in South Asia may profitably be compared with what is known from other regions where oral traditions have been important. The famous studies by Lord (1960) and Parry (1971) on the oral epic in southeastern Europe showed that oral narratives still chanted by peasant bards in Yugoslavia are based not on verbatim repetition, but on a constant overall pattern within which individual performers can use varying recombinations of formulaic expressions — and also showed that a similar process is likely to have given rise to the Homeric epics of preliterate Ancient Greece. Goody (1977: 116-20) reports the same processes in present-day oral literatures of West Africa; so it may well be that Classical Sanskrit literature — and even the Vedas — originated in such structures of 'controlled improvisation'. But India, from a very ancient date, perfected the skills of word-for-word repetition and memorization, and institutionalized them for Hindu, Buddhist, and secular literature. Parallels, with less historical depth, can be found elsewhere in the world. Finnegan (1973, 1977) reports extensive verbatim memorization in West Africa (in cultures different from those studied by Goody), and so does Sherzer (1982: 319-20, n. 2) for the Cuna Indians of Panama. Field workers among North American Indian groups, such as myself among the Karok of northwestern California, have heard how, less than 100 years ago, children were required to repeat each sentence of the myths narrated by their grandparents, so as to ensure accurate transmission. Where musical features of rhythm and melody are involved, the human memory can of course stretch even farther; consider a singer in our own society who has memorized words and music for twenty or thirty full-length operas — or the symphony conductor who works without a score. Again in our own society, we can consider the extensive repertories of numerous musicians, in the folk and jazz traditions, who cannot read a note of written music.

Thus there is reason to believe that the capacities of human memory, though they may have been neglected and downgraded by modern European societies, are in fact — with proper training — capable of the prodigies of retention which have long been customary in Hindu culture. Doubts concerning such capacities, such as those quoted above from Wakankar, are to be sure also expressed by some Western writers, as in the extensive work on literacy and orality by Ong (e.g. 1982: 65-7) — though he concedes the Cuna evidence presented by Sherzer. My own belief is that there is no serious reason to deny that the human mind can perform awesome feats of memory, in situations where a culture has developed a tradition for such practice, and where major prestige is attached to oral transmission. This is where we must think sociolinguistically, in terms of **attitudes** toward speech vs. writing as alternative manifestations of language.

5. CONCLUSION

A traditional Indian view is expressed by Ananda Coomaraswamy as follows (1947: 27):

> From the Indian point of view a man can only be said to *know* what he knows by *heart*; what he must go to a book to be reminded of, he merely knows of ... From the earliest times, Indians have thought of the learned man, not as one who has read much, but as one who has been profoundly taught.

It appears, then, that a society may have knowledge of writing, and yet assign it to restricted functions — the use of merchants, perhaps, as opposed to the purposes of religion or of literary art. A possible parallel comes from Minoan Greece: the Mycenaean civilization used the Linear A and B scripts for bills of lading, cargo manifests, etc.; but so far as we know, they did not use them for literature. Following the collapse of Minoan civilization, Greece apparently did without a writing system for some centuries, until the Phoenician-based alphabet was introduced; during this period, of course, the *Iliad* and the *Odyssey* were in the oral tradition, taking the forms which we now know — just as in India, around the same time, the Hindus were apparently also producing and transmitting literature without the aid of writing.

A parallel from a different branch of culture comes from Native America. It is generally said that the American Indian did not use the wheel. This is true, except that the Aztecs (and their Meso-American neighbors) **did** know about wheels — but they used them only on children's toys. It was not that these people lacked the ability to invent the wheel, but rather that they chose not to ascribe any important function to it (Vaillant 1950: 153).

It is useful to remember that Plato, who lived when the alphabet was a relatively novelty in Greece, warned that it would corrupt human memories, fostering both credulity and mistrust (Jowett 1892: 1.484–8). For centuries afterwards, Latin and Greek were normally read **aloud**, the written text being conceived basically as an aid to spoken performance; not until AD 384 does St Augustine report his astonishment on observing that his teacher, St Ambrose, was capable of reading **silently**. In medieval England, written contracts were at first regarded with suspicion: a man's spoken word was his bond, it was felt, but a piece of paper was just a piece of paper (cf. Clanchy 1979). Since then, of course, European society has succumbed to what Jorge Luis Borges (1960) has called 'the cult of the book'; nowadays it is writing, not speech, which most educated people regard as basic, and indeed as a necessity. Nevertheless, to quote Coomaraswamy once more (1947: 19), 'necessities are not always goods in themselves, out of their context; some, like wooden legs, are advantageous only to men already maimed'.

NOTES

1. For general references on the history of writing, including South Asian systems, see Gelb (1963), Diringer (1968), and Jensen (1969). For more specific discussions of the history of writing in India, see Bühler (1895, 1896), Pandey (1957), Dani (1963), Sircar (1965), Verma (1971), and Gupta and Ramachandran (1979) (with the review by Salomon 1982).
   Versions of this paper have been presented at the University of Washington and the University of Ottawa. I am indebted for encouragement and advice to A.L. Becker, M.V. Deshpande, M.B. Emeneau, Roy Andrew Miller, P.B. Patel, Shana Poplack, Richard Salomon, and Deborah Tannen.
2. For general accounts of this script, and of attempts at its decipherment, see Dani (1963: 12–22), Jensen (1969: 353–6), Zide and Zvelebil (1970), Bright (1982, 1983). For a recent major effort to decipher the Harappan language in terms of Sanskrit, see Rao (1982).
3. Becker (1984: 143–4) has commented that the typical shape of the Indic *akṣara*, as now used even for non-Indic languages such as Burmese, Javanese, and Balinese — consisting of a consonantal center with vocalic marks above, below, before, and after it — has come to be a metaphor in terms of which all other phenomena can be organized. From Zurbuchen (1981: vi) he quotes part of the prologue to a Balinese shadow play, in which the graphemic unit is invoked:

> There is a god unsupported by the divine mother earth,
> Unsheltered by the sky,
> Unilluminated by the sun, moon, stars, or constellations.
> Yes, Lord, you dwell in the void, and are situated thus:
> You reside in a golden jewel,
> Regaled on a golden palanquin,
> Umbrellaed by a floating lotus.
> There approached in audience by all the gods of the cardinal directions ...

4. For a more recent statement, see Kiparsky (1976: 99–103).
5. For convenient synopses of such views, see Naik (1971: 1.7, 49–51, 77–92, 95–9, 2.611–36).

REFERENCES

Agrawala, V.S. 1963. *India as Known to Pāṇini*, 2nd edn. Varanasi: Prithvi Kumar.
Basham, A.L. 1954. *The Wonder that was India.* New York: Macmillan.
Becker, A.L. 1984. 'Biography of a Sentence: A Burmese Proverb', in Stuart Plattner (ed.), *Text, Play, and Story: The Construction and Reconstruction of Self and Society.* Washington, DC: American Ethnological Society, 135–55.
Borges, Jorge L. 1960. *Otras inquisiciones.* Buenos Aires: Emecé.
Bright, William. (ed.). 1966. *Sociolinguistics.* The Hague: Mouton.
——— 1982. Review of *Studies in the Indus Valley Inscriptions*, by J.E. Mitchiner.

Journal of the American Oriental Society, 102: 233-6.
—— 1983. 'Archaeology, Linguistics, and Ancient Dravidian', in Bh. Krishnamurti *et al.* (eds.), *South Asian Languages*. Delhi: Motilal Banarsidass, 108-12.
Bühler, Georg. 1895. *On the Origin of the Indian Brāhma Alphabet*. (*Indian Studies*, 3.) Wien: Tempsky. Reprinted, Varanasi: Chowkhamba Sanskrit Series, 1963.
—— 1896. *Indische Palaeographie von circa 350 a. Chr. — circa 1300 p. Chr.* (*Grundriss der Indo-arischen Philologie und Altertumskunde*, ed. by G. Bühler, 1: 11.) Strassburg: Trübner. Translated as 'Indian Palaeography', *Indian Antiquary*, vol. 33, Appendix, 1904. Reprinted, Calcutta: Sambunath Pandit, 1959.
Burrow, Thomas. 1955. *The Sanskrit Language*. London: Faber and Faber.
Chomsky, Noam, and Morris Halle. 1968. *The Sound Pattern of English*. New York: Harper and Row.
Clanchy, M.T. 1979. *From Memory to Written Record: England 1066-1307*. London: Arnold.
Coomaraswamy, Ananda K. 1947. 'The Bugbear of Literacy', in his *Am I My Brother's Keeper?* New York: Day, 19-35.
Dani, Ahmad Hasan. 1963. *Indian Palaeography*. Oxford: Clarendon.
Davids, T.W. Rhys. 1903. *Buddhist India*. New York: Putnam's. Reprinted, Delhi: Motilal Banarsidass, 1971.
Diringer, David. 1968. *The Alphabet*, 3rd edn. London: Hutchinson.
Emeneau, M.B. 1954. 'Linguistic Prehistory of India'. *Proceedings of the American Philosophical Society* 98: 282-92. Reprinted in his *Language and Linguistic Area*. Stanford: University Press, 1980, 85-104.
Finnegan, Ruth. 1973. 'Literacy vs. Non-Literacy: the Great Divide?' in Robin Horton and R. Finnegan (eds.), *Modes of Thought*. London: Faber and Faber, 112-44.
—— 1977. *Oral Poetry*. Cambridge: University Press.
Gelb, Ignace J. 1963. *A Study of Writing*, 2nd edn. Chicago: University of Chicago Press.
Goody, Jack. 1977. *The Domestication of the Savage Mind*. Cambridge: Cambridge University Press.
Gopal, Lallanji. 1977. 'Early Greek Writers on Writing in India', in L. Gopal (ed.), *In Commemoration of D.D. Kosambi*. Varanasi: Banaras Hindu University, 41-54.
Goyal, S.R. 1979. 'Brahmi — an Invention of the Early Mauryan Period'. In Gupta and Ramachandran, 1-53.
Gupta, S.P., and K.S. Ramachandran (eds.). 1979. *The Origin of Brahmi Script*. Delhi: D.K. Publications.
Jensen, Hans. 1969. *Sign, Symbol, and Script*, 3rd edn. New York: Putnam.
Jones, Horace L. (trans.). 1930. *The Geography of Strabo*, 8 vols. Cambridge, Mass: Harvard University Press, 1930.
Jowett, Benjamin (trans.). 1892. *The Dialogues of Plato*, 3rd edn. Oxford: Oxford University Press.
Kiparsky, Paul. 1976. 'Oral Poetry: some Linguistic and Typological Considerations', in Benjamin A. Stolz and R.S. Shannon (eds.), *Oral Literature and the Formula*. Ann Arbor: Center for the Coordination of Ancient and Modern Studies, University of Michigan, 73-106.
Koskenniemi, Seppo, *et al.* 1973. *Materials for the Study of the Indus Script*, I: *A Concordance to the Indus Inscriptions*. Helsinki: Suomalainen Tiedeakatemia.

Lord, A.B. 1960. *The Singer of Tales.* Cambridge, Mass: Harvard University Press.

Mahadevan, Iravatham. 1977. *The Indus Script: Texts, Concordance and Tables.* New Delhi: Archaeological Survey of India.

Naik, Bapurao S. 1971. *Typography of Devanagari,* 3 vols. Bombay: Directorate of Languages, Government of Maharashtra.

Ong, Walter J., SJ. 1982. *Orality and Literacy.* London: Methuen.

Pandey, Raj Bali. 1957. *Indian Palaeography,* 2nd edn. Varanasi: Motilal Barnarsidass.

Parry, Milman. 1971. *The Making of Homeric Verse.* Oxford: Clarendon Press.

Rao, Shikarpur Ranganath. 1982. *The Decipherment of the Indus Script.* Bombay: Asia Publishing House.

Renou, Louis. 1957. 'Introduction générale', in *Altindische Grammatik,* by Jakob Wackernagel, vol. I, 2nd edn. Göttingen: Vandenhoeck and Ruprecht, 1–125.

Salomon, Richard. 1982. Review of Gupta and Ramachandran 1979. *JAOS,* 102: 553–5.

Shapiro, Michael C., and Harold Schiffman (eds.). 1981. *Language and Society in South Asia.* Delhi: Motilal Banarsidass.

Sherzer, Joel. 1982. 'The Interplay of Structure and Function in Kuna Narrative', in Tannen 1982a: 306–22.

Sircar, D.C. 1965. *Indian Epigraphy.* Delhi: Motilal Banarsidass.

Tannen, Deborah (ed.). 1982a. *Analyzing Discourse: Text and Talk.* (*Georgetown University Round Table on Languages and Linguistics,* 1981.) Washington, DC: Georgetown University Press.

—— (ed.). 1982b. *Spoken and Written Language: Exploring Orality and Literacy.* Norwood, NJ: Ablex.

Upasak, C.S. 1960. *The History and Palaeography of Mauryan Brahmi Script.* Nalanda.

Vaillant, G.C. 1950. *The Aztecs of Mexico.* Harmondsworth: Penguin Books.

Verma, Thakur Prasad. 1971. *The Palaeography of Brahmi Script in North India, from c. 236 BC to c. 200 AD.* Varanasi: Siddharth Prakashan.

—— 1979. 'Comment', in Gupta and Ramachandran: 98–110.

Voegelin, C.F., and F.M. Voegelin. 1961. 'Typological Classification of Systems with Included, Excluded, and Self-Sufficient Alphabets'. *Anthropological Linguistics* 3: 1.55–96.

Wakankar, L.S. 1983. 'Writing in India — Ignorance and Reality'. *CALTIS 83* (Souvenir from seminar on Calligraphy, Lettering, and Typography of Indic Scripts.) Pune: Institute of Typographical Research [unpaginated].

Zide, Arlene, and Kamil Zvelebil. 1970. Review of Knorozov *et al. Language* 46: 952–68.

Zurbuchen, Mary S. 1981. *The Shadow Theater of Bali: Explorations in Language and Text.* Ann Arbor: University of Michigan dissertation.

3

Chaucer, Livy, and Bersuire: The Roman Materials in *The Physician's Tale*

WILLIAM H. BROWN, JR

I.

Greek as well as Latin historians tell the story of Virginia. In the middle of the first century BC, about twenty years before any of the extant versions, Cicero (*De Republica* II.63) comments that it is a familiar story, recorded by many of the great works of literature: 'Nota scilicet illa res et celebrata monumentis plurimis litterarum' (Mueller 1910). Diodorus Siculus' Βιβλιοθηκη (XII.24) gives a synopsis that names Appius but neither Virginia nor her father. Dionysius of Halicarnassus, whose Ρωμαϊκη Ἀρχαιολογια began to appear in 7 BC, recounts it in detail (XI.28 ff.). A century later, Tacitus alludes to Virginia's death in both the *Annals* and the *Histories*. But the Latin Middle Ages apparently knew the story through the brief notice Valerius Maximus gives in the *Facta et Dicta Memorabilia* (VI), done about AD 30, and through Livy's extended account in book III of the *Ab Urbe Condita*, from which all the medieval versions seem ultimately to derive.

Livy reports how the decemvir Appius is captivated by the plebeian maiden Virginia but unable to seduce her with gifts and promises. Appius orders his hireling Claudius to claim her as a slave. When the people protest that wrong, Appius allows her father Virginius, a centurion, to be summoned from camp. Appius then awards Virginia to Claudius despite the appeals by her father, her betrothed Icilius, and the people. Refusing to give the girl over to Appius' lust, Virginius promptly stabs her. The plebs establish their freedom, deposing the decemvirs and restoring their own tribunician authority. Appius kills himself in prison. Virginius has the condemned Claudius spared and sent into exile.

Livy, Dante avers, is the historian 'che non erra'. When Chaucer redacts the story in *The Physician's Tale*, he understandably begins with Livy — 'Ther was, as telleth Titus Livius' (Robinson 1957: VI.1) — even though he takes most of his materials from Jean de Meun's version in the *Roman de la Rose*. Is Chaucer's citation at first hand? Does he supplement Jean de

Meun with Livy, or merely call upon an authority he knows by reputation alone (normally the case when a medieval writer names Homer or Plato, for instance)?

Shannon (1941: 401-7) presents the standard case for Chaucer's using Livy in *The Physician's Tale*. The only evidence Shannon offers, however, is verbal parallels. These argue best when they show Chaucer's reproducing details found in Livy but not in Jean de Meun:

> The juge answerde, 'Of this in his absence,
> I may nat yeve diffynytf sentence.
> Lat do hym calle, and I wol gladly heere;' (VI.171-3)

Jean has no mention of Virginius' being away when Claudius claimed Virginia, or of Appius' summoning Virginius.[1] Presumably Chaucer also takes from the *Ab Urbe Condita* his notice that Virginia was an only child (VI.6), as well as his references both to Virginia's mother (VI.119) and to the many friends Virginius and his daughter each had (VI.4, 135), details not appearing in the *Roman de la Rose*. Shannon cites a number of less convincing parallels between Chaucer and Livy, to which only one addition need be made. 'For certes, by no force ne by no meede' (VI.134) suggests Livy at least as much as it does Jean de Meun. Appius, Livy records, tried to entice Virginia with reward and promise, 'pretio ac spe perlicere adortus' (Conway and Walters 1964: III.44.4), while Jean writes that Appius was not able to frighten the girl, who cared for neither him nor his lechery, 'por ce qu'il ne poait donter / la pucele, qui n'avoit cure / ne de lui ne de sa luxure' (11.5566-8).

Although never directly challenged, Shannon's evidence has not persuaded everybody that Chaucer in fact draws from Livy. Waller (1976: 293, n. 3) points to the dissimilarities between *The Physician's Tale* and the original, at the same time questioning Chaucer's access to Livy. 'A close comparison of the Physician's Tale with *Ab Urbe Condita* 3.44-58', Waller asserts, 'indicates that Livy, concerned with the overthrow of the decemvirs rather than the death of Virginia — and rarely available in fourteenth-century England — was apparently known to Chaucer only by name.' Her demurral about the scarcity of Livy's work is readily met. Manitius (1935: 74) identifies just two manuscripts of the *Ab Urbe Condita* that would have been available to Chaucer; but Waller herself, in a different context, rightly notes how inconsistency and accident prove medieval catalogues unreliable (294, n. 5). Gower certainly seems to use a copy of Livy. Furthermore, even a work of no established availability can have significant influence. Some half dozen of Chaucer's poems attest he had a copy of Boccaccio's *Teseida*, or ready access to one, although no reference to the *Teseida* appears in any medieval or Renaissance collection (Coleman 1982: 92).

The Physician's Tale seemingly preserves little of Livy's emphasis; this causes a major problem for anyone wishing to argue Chaucer's debt to the original.[2] Attempts to explore the tale within the context of the *Ab Urbe Condita* have not been totally successful. Middleton (1973) and Brown (1981) share a reluctance to claim Chaucer knew Livy: Middleton finds 'no convincing evidence' for Chaucer's using any source other than Jean de Meun (11), while Brown notes that Chaucer 'may have consulted Livy' (131). Yet both introduce the *Ab Urbe Condita* into their analyses — on ill-defined grounds. Middleton sets it up as a touchstone for Chaucer's account (10, 13). Discussing Harry Bailly's remarks on the tale, she throws great burden on the sole mention Chaucer has of Livy's name: 'Chaucer prompts us to weigh the Roman civic virtue of Virginius against other classical and Christian virtues which Harry's comment helps to define' (16). Any concern Chaucer has with Roman civic virtue he effectively denies by avoiding reference to Rome or to the Romans; he leaves the story's locale as indefinite as he found it in Jean de Meun.[3] Brown similarly uses the *Ab Urbe Condita* for a touchstone, at one point making the novel and implausible assumption that Livy was readily available in Chaucer's England: 'One might even argue that by mentioning Livy Chaucer encourages us to compare the Physician's version with the facts as recorded by the respected Roman historian.' He then gives a summary of Livy's story 'as it would have been known to Chaucer and his audience' (132). Since Brown is unsure about Chaucer's knowledge of Livy, he should be downright skeptical about any knowledge the audience might have.

Ramsey (1972) and Delany (1981) deal with aspects of the original Chaucer either alters or 'significantly omits'. Ramsey maintains that whereas Livy stresses the abuse of specific Roman liberties, Chaucer emphasizes worldly injustice. Like Delany, Ramsey underestimates Virginia's role in the *Ab Urbe Condita*, asserting she 'gets almost no attention from [Livy] and remains a shadow figure throughout' (190). Delany offers a Marxist/Derridean reading. In her view the original intention of the Virginia story was to glorify popular rebellion, and her discussion of the *Ab Urbe Condita* underscores the plebs' role in overthrowing the decemvirate. Therefore she faults *The Physician's Tale* because Chaucer abandons the social consciousness she imputes to Livy as well as to Jean de Meun, Boccaccio, and Gower. Arguing 'the presence of absence', she claims that 'the social struggle in *The Physician's Tale* is cryingly there *because* of its exclusion, especially once we are aware of its role in the other versions' (57).

Although Ramsey and Delany offer no new evidence regarding Chaucer's use of Livy, they do help clarify the story's political meaning in the *Ab Urbe Condita*. Concentrating on the injustices done by Appius and the decemvirate, they show how Livy asserts the need for personal freedoms, particularly the right of appeal. But by neglecting Livy's treatment of the ideal of chastity, they fail to acknowledge a significant parallel between Chaucer and the original. That parallel strengthens the argument Shannon makes for Chaucer's debt to Livy.

His argument must also be examined in context of the versions by Jean de Meun, Boccaccio, and Gower. Furthermore, it is necessary to reconsider Bersuire's Old French translation of the *Ab Urbe Condita*, which Shannon rejects as a source for *The Physician's Tale*.

II.

Livy emphasizes chastity and chastity's violation, and, except for Bersuire's translation, this is reflected only in *The Physician's Tale* among the medieval versions of the story. Livy in fact stresses the personal as well as the civic virtues responsible for Rome's greatness. In his historiography *pudicitia* is an essential part of the Roman character.

Livy understands history as a literary form that, to be valid, must afford moral instruction. Begun shortly before Augustus assumed the *imperium* in 27 BC, the *Ab Urbe Condita* glorifies the traditional virtues like *fides* that had led Rome to eminence and were now part of the Augustan program. One of Livy's strongest episodes describes how in the fourth century BC the old Roman nobles — proudly electing to die rather than retreat before the Gauls — sit silent and immovable in their palaces, each clutching the ivory staff of office in his hand. The marauding Gauls look upon them with nothing less than reverence, Livy says, these Romans who in their majesty of countenance and gravity of expression showed themselves most like gods ('maiestate etiam quam uoltus grauitasque oris prae se ferebat simillimos dis' (V.41.8)).

Apparently the Virginia story is an adaptation of the enormously popular story of Lucretia. In both a woman dies for the cause of *pudicitia*, giving incentive to a popular revolt against tyranny.[4] Appius' abuse of Virginia caused the decemvirs to be expelled, just as Sextus Tarquinius' violation of Lucretia brought down the Tarquins sixty years earlier. This point begins Livy's account of Virginia: 'ut non finis solum idem decemuiris qui regibus sed causa etiam eadem imperii amittendi esset' (III.44.1). Virginia furnishes a lesson in civil liberty. Justifying his daughter's death before a large crowd, Virginius reminds them that they also have daughters, sisters, and wives. In the calamity of another they have been given warning to guard against similar offenses: 'illis quoque filias sorores coniugesque esse ... aliena calamitate documentum datum illis cauendae similis iniuriae' (III.50.7-8). Appius, too, demonstrates the need to preserve personal freedoms, for after being arrested he invokes those institutions he plotted to destroy. The people mutter to themselves that the one who abrogated appeal had now appealed, the one who crushed the rights of the people had now begged the people's protection, the one who had adjudged into slavery the person of a free citizen was now, being hastened away in fetters, himself needful of the law of liberty:

> prouocare qui prouocationem sustulisset, et implorare praesidium populi qui omnia iura populi obtrisset, rapique in uincla egentem iure libertatis qui liberum corpus in seruitutem addixisset (III.56.8)

Livy binds the defense of *libertas* closely to the exhaltation of *pudicitia*. Icilius angrily notifies Appius that, in protecting his betrothed's freedom, he would sooner die than prove disloyal: '"Me uindicantem sponsam in libertatem uita citius deseret quam fides"' (III.45.11). When Claudius moves to seize Virginia, her father shakes his fist at Appius, defying Appius' attempt to subvert morality and freedom. Virginius has betrothed his daughter to Icilius, not to Appius, and has raised her for wedlock, not for defilement. Does Appius want to hasten into the promiscuous gratification of desire, in the manner of cattle and wild animals?

> Verginius intentans in Appium manus, 'Icilio' inquit, 'Appi, non tibi filiam despondi et ad nuptias, non ad stuprum educaui. Placet pecudum ferarumque ritu promisce in concubitus ruere?' (III.47.7)

Finally, as he grabs the knife to kill his daughter, Virginius assures her that only in this way can he protect her freedom: '"Hoc te uno quo possum" ait, "modo, filia, in libertatem uindico"' (III.48.5).

As Chaucer also will do, Livy reiterates a specific quality in a character. Appius becomes the example of *libido*. In the beginning Livy calls Claudius the accomplice of the decemvir's lust ('minister decemuiri libidinis' (III.44.6)). Appius is beside himself with lust ('alienatus ad libidinem animo' (III.48.1)). Virginius cautions his fellow citizens that Appius' lust has not been extinguished with the death of the girl: 'nec cum filia sua libidinem Ap. Claudi exstinctam esse' (III.50.7). Now, he continues, there no longer is any occasion in his house for Appius' lust: 'non esse iam Appi libidini locum in domo sua' (III.50.9). Virginia, of course, Livy identifies with *pudicitia*. Her betrothed Icilius defends her against the unjust decree by denouncing Appius' lechery. Icilius intends to have his bride chaste ('pudicam habiturus' (III.45.7)). He challenges Appius to vent his fury upon the backs and necks of the men, but to let chastity at least be safe ('pudicitia saltem in tuto sit' (III.45.9)). After Virginia's death, the sorrowing matrons ask if the circumstances leading to her death are indeed the rewards of chastity ('ea pudicitiae praemia esse' (III.48.8)). Then Virginius refers twice to his daughter's chastity. Her life would have been dearer to him than his own, had she been able to live free and chaste ('liberae ac pudicae' (III.50.6)). His wife had died naturally, his daughter had died because she could no longer have lived chaste ('quia non ultra pudica uictura fuerit' (III.50.8)).[5]

III.

Chaucer had access to two, probably three, adaptations of Livy besides Jean de Meun's. Boccaccio includes the story in *De Casibus Illustrium Virorum* (III), completed about 1360, and *De Mulieribus Claris* (LVIII), completed a year or so later. Chaucer uses both anthologies for *The Monk's Tale*. Chaucer's sometime friend Gower, in 1390, offers perhaps the story's first Englishing in the *Confessio Amantis* (VII.5131–306). Although *The Physician's Tale* cannot be dated precisely, it may well have been written after the final recension (1393) of Gower's poem.[6] Even if Chaucer draws only from Jean de Meun, these other three help establish the uniqueness of Chaucer's treatment.

No medieval writer reflects Livy's nationalism and his emphasis on the *ius civile*. His story becomes an anecdote with appended *moralitas*, illustrating, first of all, how lechery corrupts power and justice. In the *Roman de la Rose* Reason concludes that judges commit too many outrages, and then appeals to the very wise Lucan, who said no one can ever discover virtue and great power together:

> Briefmant, juges font trop d'outrages.
> Lucans redit, qui fu mout sages,
> c'onques vertuz et grant poair
> ne pot nus ensemble voair. (11.5629–32)

Boccaccio's two versions condemn Appius for licentiousness and abuse of legal process. Nothing, says *De Mulieribus Claris*, is more destructive than an unjust judge. Whenever he follows the commands of his wicked mind, the system of law is inevitably subverted, the laws' power is broken, virtue's labor is weakened, restraints on evil are relaxed, and, in short, all the commonweal is dragged to ruin:

> Nil pernitiosius iniquo iudice. Hic quotiens sceleste mentis imperium sequitur, omnis iuris ordo pervertatur necesse est, legum potestas solvatur, virtutis enervetur opus, sceleri lexentur habene et breviter omne bonum publicum in ruinam trahatur. (Zaccaria 1970: 240)

Gower's Genius casts Appius as a lecherous king rather than a lecherous judge. The example of Appius teaches a good king to avoid vice's pleasure and to follow virtue:

And thus thunchaste was chastised,
Wherof thei myhte ben advised
That scholden afterward governe,
And be this evidence lerne,
Hou it is good a king eschuie
The lust of vice and vertu suie. (Macaulay 1901: VIII.5301–6)

For Chaucer's confreres the story demonstrates more than simply the abuse of power and justice. Jean de Meun's Reason cites the story while arguing Love's superiority to Justice: 'Donc di ge que mieuz vaut Amor / simplement que ne fet Joutice' (11.5532–3). Judges became necessary only after the world ruled by Love had passed.[7] In *De Casibus Illustrium Virorum* the story prompts an invective against the training lawyers and judges receive. Many things resulted from the censuring of Appius. But the great number of vices in present-day lawyers compels an attack against them of a most justified anger:

Erant qvae in vituperium Appii plurima veniebant: Set cumulata vitiis præsentium leguleorum congeries in se iustissimi furoris impetus reuocauit. (Gourmont and Petit 1520: 83)

Gower places the story near the end of his long final section of Book VII, 'Practique'. This section, like the *De Casibus Illustrium Virorum*, assembles exempla for instructing rulers. In an important sense it culminates Gower's argument about common profit.

Chaucer, however, explains the story's significance without noting the lessons of worldly injustice. The comment at the end of the tale (VI.277–86) first recalls the fate of Appius and his collaborators ('Heere may men seen how synne hath his merite' (VI.277)). The rest of this comment expounds the certainty of divine justice. It builds up to a homiletic commonplace — 'Forsaketh synne er synne yow forsake' (VI.286) — that expands the focus from the story's malefactors to the whole of fallen mankind. Chaucer stresses the seductiveness of evil. Appius, who flouted due process and family integrity before all Rome, is *parum ad rem* to the 'worm of conscience' and the secret sin known only to God (VI.279–84).

Chaucer's Appius is merely the threat to chastity that the plot requires. The tale examines the suffering his abuses cause, and lauds the precepts that his victims uphold. In the beginning, Chaucer describes Virginia with an array of hagiographical clichés (VI.41–71) — beauty, precociousness, abstinence, to name a few. Then in the story itself (VI.118–276) he emphasizes the goodness of Virginia and her father, along with the wickedness of Appius and Claudius, in a way suggesting some influence from Livy.

Chaucer piles up adjectives that demand unequivocal responses from the audience, reminiscent of Livy's contrasting *libido* with *pudicitia*. On the one side they demand not only approval but sympathy, on the other swift condemnation. In the hundred and fifty-eight lines he devotes to the story proper, nearly half the instances of adjective and noun have either *deere*, *fals*, *cursed*, or *pitous*, and the related words *falsly*, *cursednesse*, and *pitee* reinforce them. Four times *deere* applies to Virginia — 'deere doghter' — then one time each to her father and to her mother. Conversely, Appius is 'this false judge' three times, while his hireling Claudius is 'This false cherl' and Appius' plot 'the false iniquitee'. As predicate adjective *fals* applies to Claudius' testimony, and *falsly* is the way Appius passes judgment on Virginia. Appius' instructions to Claudius are 'this cursed reed', Claudius' complaint against Virginius 'this cursed bille', Appius himself is 'This cursed juge'. All subsequently are hanged who were 'consentant of this cursednesse'. And it is with 'pitous hand' that Virginius will slay his daughter. He announces her fate 'With fadres pitee stikynge thurgh his herte'. After Appius sentences Virginius himself to die, the crowd 'for pitee' saves him; then Virginius, 'of his pitee', saves Claudius from hanging with the rest.[8]

IV.

Do Shannon's verbal parallels, strengthened with these reiterations and by the emphasis on chastity, in fact establish Chaucer's debt to the *Ab Urbe Condita*? Or could Gower and Bersuire have supplied Chaucer with those details Shannon claims came from Livy?

Shannon assumes that Chaucer did not use Gower, and yet the reasons for dating Chaucer's version earlier than Gower's are flimsy.[9] Gower does offer the important details Chaucer supposedly takes from Livy. He mentions Virginia's mother (VII.5137), noting in his Latin summary opposite that Virginia was an only daughter ('vnicam filiam'). He reports Virginius' absence when Appius summoned Virginia to appear:

Whil that hir fader was absent
Sche was somouned and assent
To come in presence of the king (VII.5181–3)

And Virginia's friends have a prominent part in Gower. By appealing to common profit, they win from Appius a two days' delay in the trial that enables Virginius (who knew of Appius' designs) to return from camp.[10]

Despite those details, however, *The Physician's Tale* probably owes nothing directly to Gower. Gower does not share Chaucer's concern with chastity, nor does he offer a model for Chaucer's use of reiteration, two points that link Chaucer to Livy.[11] On the other hand, Bersuire's translation of the *Ab Urbe Condita* afforded Chaucer everything he would have taken from the original itself.[12]

Shannon (1941: 399) too readily dismisses Bersuire as a source for *The Physician's Tale*. He notes that Bersuire does not follow Livy in calling Virginia an only daughter: for Livy's 'unica filia' (III.45.9) Bersuire (1514: III.22) has simply 'ceste pucelle'. Why Shannon considers that omission significant remains unclear. Chaucer makes Virginia not an only daughter but an only child ('No children hadde he mo in al his lyf' (VI.6)). No other version has Virginia an only child.[13]

Bersuire translates Livy accurately but not slavishly.[14] His translation, Shannon affirms, 'offers no evidence in word or phrase that Chaucer made any use of it' (399). Yet Chaucer's 'in his absence' (VI.171) could correspond either to Livy's 'quod pater puellae abesset' (III.44.5) or to Bersuire's 'le pere de la fille estoit en la bataille' (III.22) (cp. 'sed Verginio absenti' (III.46.3) and 'Virginius son pere qui est absent' (III.22)), and Chaucer's 'Lat do hym calle' to either 'placere itaque patrem arcessiri' (III.45.3) or to 'Et pource dist il ie iuge que son pere sera attendu' (III.22). Chaucer could just as easily owe his mention of Virginia's mother to Bersuire as to Livy. Like Livy, Bersuire says that Virginia's mother (and siblings) shared the principles of Virginius ('Perinde uxor instituta fuerat liberique instituebantur' (III.44.3) in Livy, 'et aussi sa fēme et ses enfans estoient bien morigines a lexemple de luy' (III.22) in Bersuire).

Bersuire keeps all of Livy's emphasis on the friends of Virginius and Virginia. For example, when Livy records that Claudius was driven back by the crowd of women and supporters surrounding Virginia, 'a globo mulierum circumstantiumque aduocatorum' (III.47.8), Bersuire writes 'par les femmes q' estoient entour luy et par les aduocas de la pucelle' (III.24).

And Bersuire accounts for other influences Shannon (402, n. 3 and 4) attributes to Livy. Chaucer's two constructions, 'excellent beautee' (VI.7) and 'excellent was hire beautee' (VI.39), suggest Bersuire's 'souueraine beaulte' (III.22) as much as they do Livy's 'forma excellentem' (III.44.4). (The construction 'excellent beautee' occurs at only one other place in Chaucer, *The Shipman's Tale* VII.1193.) Further, Chaucer's 'This mayde of age twelve yeer was and tweye' (VI.30) would owe no more to Livy's 'Hanc uirginem adultam' (III.44.4) than to Bersuire's 'ceste fille qui ia estoit grande' (III.22).

Bersuire carefully preserves Livy's concern with *pudicitia*.[15] Icilius' plea to let chastity at least be safe, 'pudicitia saltem in tuto sit' (III.45.9), Bersuire renders 'mais q' la chastete de nos femmes soit gardee' (III.22). Virginius' sad observation that his daughter died because she could no longer have lived chaste, 'quia non ultra pudica uictura fuerit' (III.50.8), becomes in Bersuire 'poure q'lle ne pouoit plus viure chaste' (III.27). When Icilius avows he will have a chaste bride, 'pudicam habiturus' (III.45.7), Bersuire reinforces the fact of virginity's absoluteness: 'la prendre vierge non pas violee ne corrumpue' (III.22).[16]

A major difficulty in deciding whether Chaucer used Livy or Bersuire's translation is that he took little directly from the *Ab Urbe Condita*. Chaucer gives less than half *The Physician's Tale* to the traditional story. Shannon provides valuable evidence for Chaucer's using Livy. But it has been accepted uncritically. The materials from Bersuire show how slight an argument his verbal parallels offer, even when supplemented with the reiterations and emphasis on chastity Chaucer shares with the *Ab Urbe Condita*. Chaucer would more likely turn to Bersuire than to Livy — the many manuscripts of Bersuire's translation testify to its authority; and it is reasonable to assume that Chaucer would choose contemporary French over Golden Latin. All the evidence for Chaucer's using the original can be explained simply and directly by reference to the French translation.

NOTES

1. Virginius, Jean makes clear, was standing ready to answer Claudius' claim and to confound his adversaries: 'ainz que Virginius palast, / qui touz estoit prez de respondre / por ses aversaires confondre' (Lecoy 1976: 11.5588–90).

2. Many recent students, Hoffman (1967: 22), Ussery (1971: 128), Hanson (1972: 134), Mathewson (1973: 35), Gardner (1977: 297), and Arnold (1981: 174), for example, assume Chaucer knew the original, but offer no supporting evidence.

3. Jean says nothing about the story's locale. Chaucer identifies the locale simply as the 'toun' and 'regioun' where Appius governed: 'Now was there thanne a justice in that toun / That govenour was of that regioun' (VI.121–22).

4. Ogilvie (1970: 477) surmises that Virginia's name itself is a hypostatization of *virgo*.

5. Shortly after Livy's death Valerius Maximus had reduced the story to a brief anecdote illustrating chastity (see note 16 below).

6. Chaucer would have known about Gower's poem after 1390. Manly's point (1928: 76) is still good: 'And we do not know that Chaucer even read the *Confessio Amantis* through, though we can be fairly certain that he had heard of it and knew something about its contents.' Chaucer's version has usually been dated earlier than Gower's because it assumedly shows no influence of the *Confessio Amantis*. By that reasoning *The Physician's Tale* would also predate Boccaccio's two accounts. Tatlock (1907: 155–6) dates the tale about 1388. He believes that it alludes (VI.61 ff.) to the notorious liaison in 1386 between Elizabeth, John of Gaunt's daughter, and Richard II's half-brother, John Holland. Even if that allusion is accepted, however, it cannot establish an early date for the tale — why, after all, would Chaucer necessarily have written 'when the incident was fresh in his mind'? Tatlock argues that Chaucer could not have used the *Confessio Amantis* because Chaucer insists on the names 'Apius' and 'Claudius', whereas Gower employs the traditional names 'Apius Claudius' and 'Marchus Claudius' (152). Chaucer, on the other hand, could be working for clarity while trying not to overburden his pentameters with unneeded syllables. Tatlock also claims that had Chaucer known 'a better account' of the story he would have included Icilius (Gower's Ilicius) to heighten the pathos (152, n. 1). But by omitting Icilius, Chaucer intensifies the inviolability of Virginia's chastity.

Rumbaur (1890: 12–15) does show that Chaucer and Gower treat the story in different ways; but he fails to demonstrate his assumption that Chaucer has not taken from Gower. Another argument for dating the tale earlier than 1390 is its putative similarity to *The Legend of Good Women*. Yet Virginia, who 'floured in virginitee / With all humylitee and abstinence' (VI.44–5), shares little with the rebellious, usually libidinous, coterie Chaucer assembles in the *Legend*. See Overbeck (1967).

7. Fleming (1969: 131, 141 ff.) excellently discusses this problem of the earthly paradise in the *Roman de la Rose*.

8. At one point Chaucer uses this procedure ironically. He reaffirms the baseness of the antagonists when Claudius calls his trumped up petition against Virginius 'this pitous bille', and addresses the judge as 'sire Apius so deere'.

9. See note 6 above.

10. Shannon (1941: 403, n. 1) rightly points out that 'The strength of the friends of Virginius and Virginia and their influence in the daughter's behalf are a conspicuous feature of Livy's story.' These friends, however, do not have the importance in *The Physician's Tale* Shannon implies (398, 403, n. 1 and 2). Virginius would have called many witnesses to disclaim Claudius' testimony ('And eek by witnessyng of many a wight, / That al was fals that seyde his adversarie' (VI.194–5)). Virginius and his daughter both are 'strong of freendes'. Nonetheless, he is forced to tell her, in a scene Chaucer invents, there is no remedy for her except death (VI.235–7). In the end Virginius is saved by 'a thousand peple' (VI.260) who, like Jean de Meun's 'li peuples' (1.5614), are not identified as his friends.

11. The tales of the Clerk, the Man of Law, the Prioress, and the Second Nun also use reiteration or *determinatio* much the same way *The Physician's Tale* does. See Payne (1963: 162–70). Payne concerns himself mainly with *The Prioress' Tale*. Jean de Meun quite likely suggested Chaucer's reiteration of *fals* and *pitee*. Jean employs *faus* or a form of it three times in his first twenty-seven lines. Appius orders Claudius to make through false witnesses a false plaint ('par fauz tesmoignz fausse querele' (1.5561)) against Virginia. After reporting Claudius' testimony, Jean identifies Claudius as the wicked traitor who was the minister of the false judge ('qui du faus juige estoit menistres' (1.5586)). Further, Jean uses *pitie* twice at the end of his account, in instances Chaucer also renders with *pitee*. Virginius is saved from hanging by the citizens who were all moved by pity ('qui fu touz de pitié meuz' (1.5615)); Chaucer reports that the people save Virginius 'for routhe and for pitee' (VI.261). Virginius, in turn, through his pity ('par sa pitié' (1.5624)), saves Claudius from death; Chaucer writes that Virginius, 'of his pitee' (VI.272), saves Claudius.

12. Bersuire completed his Livy about 1355. An earlier, anonymous translation of Livy into Old French has not survived. It was the basis for an Italian version of Livy's first ten books done by Filippo de Santa Croce in 1323; see Samaran and Monfrin (1962: 105–6). Samaran and Monfrin provide a thorough discussion of Bersuire's Livy (100–56) along with a list of its many manuscripts (189–92).

13. Pointing out that Livy's Virginius has other children, Shannon (404, n. 1) claims 'Chaucer intensifies the tragedy by making the only daughter the only child the devoted father had ever had.' But why must she have been in Chaucer's source an only daughter among other children, rather than simply a daughter among other children?

14. Bersuire's prose does become lame when he renders direct discourse. In Livy, for example, Icilius opens his attack on Appius by saying 'You must use iron to drive me away from here, Appius, so that you may do in silence what you wish to be hidden.' The first part ('"Ferro hinc tibi submouendus sum, Appi"' (III.45.6)) Bersuire handles well enough: 'Se tu veulx que ie departe de ce lieu il fauldra que tu

men faces tirer auecques glaiues' (III.22). But with the second part ('"ut tacitum feras quod celari uis"') he loses Livy's subtlety: 'toy Appius veulx tu que pour ta parolle ceste vierge soit corrumpue et violee'.

15. He preserves part of Livy's emphasis on *libido*. He leaves 'minister decemuiri libidinis' (III.44.6) and 'alienatus ad libidinem animo' (III.48.1) untranslated. But he does translate 'libidinem Ap. Claudi' (III.50.7) — 'la paillardise de appius' (III.27) — and 'Appi libidini' (III.50.9) — 'sa paillardise' (III.27).

16. Already in his headnote to the Virginia story (III.22) Bersuire had stressed the theme of chastity by citing book six of Valerius Maximus' *Facta et Dicta Memorabilia*. That sixth book includes the example of Virginia in its first chapter, 'De Pudicitia'. If Chaucer used Bersuire, he would have recognized the reference to Valerius' sixth book, which he apparently consults for the stories of Metellius, Gallus Sulpicius, and Sempronius Sophus in *The Wife of Bath's Prologue*.

REFERENCES

Arnold, Richard A. 1981. 'Chaucer's Physician. The Teller and the Tale', *Revue de l'Université d'Ottawa* 51: 172–9.
Bersuire, Pierre. 1514. *Le Premier volume des grans decades de tit' livius*. Paris: Eustace.
Brown, Emerson, Jr. 1981. 'What is Chaucer Doing with the Physician and His Tale?', *Philological Quarterly* 60: 129–49.
Coleman, William E. 1982. 'Chaucer, the *Teseida* and the Visconti Library at Pavia: a Hypothesis'. *Medium Ævum* 51: 92–101.
Conway, R.S., and C.F. Walters (eds.). 1964. *Titi Livi Ab Vrbe Condita*. Vol. 1. Oxford: Clarendon.
Delany, Sheila. 1981. 'Politics and the Paralysis of Poetic Imagination in *The Physician's Tale*'. *Studies in the Age of Chaucer* 3: 47–60. Norman, Okla.: New Chaucer Society.
Fleming, John V. 1969. *The 'Roman de la Rose'*. Princeton: Princeton University Press.
Gardner, John. 1977. *The Poetry of Chaucer*. Carbondale, Ill.: Southern Illinois University Press.
Gourmont, Jean, and Jean Petit (eds.). 1520. *De casibus virorum illustrium*. Reprint. Gainesville, Fla.: Scholars' Facsimiles, 1962.
Hanson, Thomas B. 1972. 'Chaucer's Physician as Storyteller and Moralizer', *Chaucer Review* 7: 132–9.
Hoffman, Richard L. 1967. 'Jephthah's Daughter and Chaucer's Virginia', *Chaucer Review* 2: 20–31.
Lecoy, Félix (ed.). 1976. *Le Roman de la Rose*. Vol. I. Paris: Champion.
Macaulay, G.C. (ed.). 1901. *The English Works of John Gower*. Vol. II. EETS ES 82. London: Oxford University Press.
Manitius, Max. 1935. *Handschriften antiker Autoren in mittelalterlichen Bibliothekskatalogen*. Hrsg. von Karl Manitius. Leipzig: Harrassowitz.
Manly, John M. (ed.). 1928. *Chaucer's Canterbury Tales*. New York: Holt.
Mathewson, Jeanne T. 1973. 'For Love and Not for Hate: The Value of Virginity in Chaucer's *Physician's Tale*', *Annuale Mediaevale* 14: 35–42.
Middleton, Anne. 1973. 'The *Physician's Tale* and Love's Martyrs: "Ensamples Mo Than Ten" as a Method in the *Canterbury Tales*', *Chaucer Review* 8: 9–32.
Mueller, C.F.W. (ed.). 1910. *M. Tullii Ciceronis Scripta Quae Manserunt Omnia*. Vol. II. Leipzig: Teubner.

Ogilvie, R.M. 1970. *A Commentary on Livy: Books 1-5.* 2nd edn. Oxford: Clarendon Press.

Overbeck, Pat Trefzger. 1967. 'Chaucer's Good Woman', *Chaucer Review* 2: 75-94.

Payne, Robert O. 1963. *The Key of Remembrance.* New Haven: Yale University Press.

Ramsey, Lee C. 1972. '"The Sentence of It Sooth Is": Chaucer's *Physician's Tale*', *Chaucer Review* 6: 185-97.

Robinson, F.N. (ed.). 1957. *The Works of Geoffrey Chaucer.* 2nd edn. Boston: Houghton Mifflin.

Rumbaur, O. 1890. *Die Geschichte von Appius und Virginia in der englischen Literatur.* Dissertation, Breslau.

Samaran, Charles, and Jacques Monfrin. 1962. *Pierre Bersuire: Prieur de Saint-Éloi de Paris.* Paris: Imprimerie Nationale.

Shannon, Edgar F. 1941. 'The Physician's Tale', in W.F. Bryan and Germaine Dempster (eds.), *Sources and Analogues of Chaucer's Canterbury Tales.* Chicago: University of Chicago Press, 398-408.

Tatlock, John S.P. 1907. *The Development and Chronology of Chaucer's Works.* London: Oxford University Press.

Ussery, Huling E. 1971. *Chaucer's Physician: Medicine and Literature in Fourteenth-Century England.* New Orleans: Tulane University Department of English.

Waller, Martha. 1976. 'The Physician's Tale: Geoffrey Chaucer and Fray Juan García de Castrojeriz', *Speculum* 51: 292-306.

Zaccaria, Vittorio (ed.). 1970. *De Mulieribus Claris.* 2nd edn. Vol. 10 in *Tutte le Opere de Giovanni Boccaccio.* Verona: Mondadori.

4

How Relevant is 'External Evidence' for a Theory of Grammar?

VICTORIA A. FROMKIN

When the view of language as a cognitive system replaced the philosophy of behaviorism which dominated American linguistics in the preceding era, there arose a growing concern that linguistic theory should delimit the class of possible grammars to those which are psychologically (and even neurologically) real, i.e. which can be acquired, stored, and accessed in speaking and understanding. In the attempt to formulate 'psychologically real models', some linguists differentiate among the kinds of evidence which can be used to show the reality of a grammar, a lexical entry, an abstract segment, a rule.

A major distinction that has been made is between 'external' and 'internal' evidence. 'External' evidence refers to aphasia data, acquisition data, abnormal language of all kinds including the language of Alszheimer patients, autistic children, schizophrenics, Down's Syndrome patients, etc.; borrowing, orthography, speech and spelling errors, orthography, metrics, casual speech, speech 'under the influence of', language games, historical change, results of perception and production experiments, etc. (Zwicky 1975). Such data are often in some tangible form, i.e., acoustic signals, reaction time, muscle actions, overt judgments, etc.

Internal evidence refers to facts drawn from the overall grammar, significant generalizations, simplicity factors, distributional criteria, morphemic alternations, etc.

It has never been demonstrated why a linguist would regard quantitative data or external evidence as more worthy of consideration, or more highly valued, than internal evidence. As Chomsky (1978) has stated:

Suppose that someone were to discover a certain pattern of electrical activity in the brain that correlated in clear cases with the presence of wh-clauses, relative clauses (finite and infinitival) and wh-questions (direct and indirect). Suppose that this pattern of electrical activity is observed when a person speaks or understands (a particular sentence).

Would we now have evidence for the psychological reality of the postulated mental representations?

He continues:

> We would now have a new kind of 'evidence', but I see no merit to the contention that this new evidence bears ... reality whereas the old evidence only relates to hypothetical constructions. The new evidence might or might not be more persuasive than the old; that would depend on its character and reliability, the degree to which the principles dealing with this evidence are tenable, intelligible, compelling, and so on.

A similar view is expressed by the psychologists Mehler, Morton, and Jusczyk (1984), who ask: 'What relevance do neurophysiological findings have for psychological models?' They distinguish 'the use of data from brain-damaged patients and ... the activity of mapping psychological functions into the brain' and conclude that while the latter activity may be a legitimate one, it is the first aspect which is of interest to psycholinguists. They add that 'with respect to descriptions of the processes of mental activities, there is no special status conferred on biological data'.

Their question may be restated for linguistics: What relevance does external evidence such as aphasia data or speech errors have for our understanding of the nature and structure of human language? And we may conclude in similar fashion that there is no special status for any kind of data which serves as evidence to support some hypothesis in science. It is up to the investigator to show how any data can count as evidence.

If there is no one-to-one mapping between linguistic performance and the stored, internalized grammar which is accessed when we speak or comprehend — and there is no evidence to date that there is such a mapping, although there is strong evidence that such a grammar is utilized during speech in a highly complex fashion — then performance data must be evaluated carefully to see what, if anything, it tells us about the mental grammar, if that is what we are trying to understand. Such data are of course crucial in the construction of linguistic processing models, in determining the interaction of the linguistic grammar with other cognitive and perceptual systems, with knowledge of the world, and with pragmatic knowledge.

However, neither response latencies in phoneme monitoring tasks nor data from jargon aphasics can solve the problem of whether phonological theory should permit highly abstract representations of the underlying forms of morphemes or words, nor can semantic priming experiments nor word substitutions produced by deep dyslexics tell us whether syntactic constraints are independent of semantic notions and should be so represented in a theory of grammar.

When performance data collected from normals or aphasics coincide with the constructs and concepts required by linguistics, they provide, as already stated, additional evidence to support the theory.

In this regard, it is interesting to note that the kinds of errors which occur in spontaneous speech are only 'explainable' by reference to the grammatical components, rules, and units posited on the basis of linguistic evidence alone (Fromkin 1968, 1971, 1973, 1975, 1980). The reason for this is suggested by Bierwisch (1982):

> The analysis of 'spontaneously incorrect' sentences belongs within the realm of psycholinguistics inasmuch as the errors they contain can give some clues to the particular mechanisms of language production, in which the abnormal case — in accordance with a general methodological principle — can lead to conclusions about the factors involved in normal functioning (30f.).

He further suggests that

> the phenomena ... can [also] be of interest in sorting out questions of the linguistic system proper ... It goes without saying that linguistic and psycholinguistic analyses of spontaneous error, if they are to be meaningful, can only be made against the background of significant hypotheses concerning the structure of the language in questions (31).

Although Bierwisch was referring specifically to normally occurring speech errors, the statements are equally applicable to aphasic language.

In support of his position, for example, it was shown (Fromkin 1971) that without the background of the significant hypothesis which posits that phonological segments in a language are composites of semi-independent distinctive features, we would be hard pressed to understand the source of errors such as the following (the intended utterance occurs on the left of the arrow and the actual utterance with the error on the right):

I.
    (1) metaphor → menaphor
    (2) Cedars of Lebanon → ... Lemadon
    (3) is Pat a girl → is bat a curl
    (4) he's a vile person → he's a file person

Klatt (1979) finds 'little evidence in the speech error corpus to support independently movable distinctive features as psychologically real representational units for utterances'.

While I am not ready to concede to Klatt, despite the statistical argument he presents, let us assume he is correct. What this tells us then, is that in the act of speaking, a phonological segment is mapped onto muscular commands as an integrated bundle. But this does not constitute evidence that features are not part of the linguistic representation of lexical items. Klatt concedes that features do seem to figure in perception. Therefore, they must exist even in a performance model.

Buckingham (1980), Lecours and Lhermitte (1969), Blumstein (1973), Green (1969) and others in their analysis of the kinds of phonological errors produced by aphasics show that, as Blumstein states, 'errors occurred most frequently between phonemes related by one distinctive feature', providing further support for the linguistic concept of phonological features which combine to form phonological segments.

However, even if we had no perceptual or production data from normal errors or from the errors produced by aphasics showing that features are independently movable performance units, we could still not abandon them in a theory of phonology without obscuring true phonological generalizations. Phonological rules pertain to classes of sounds specified by features common to their segmental members; historical sound change makes reference to segments sharing the same features etc. We would be unable to explain universal synchronic and diachronic phenomena without these theoretical constructs. Thus these 'external data' are both relevant and irrelevant for grammatical theory.

Another type of speech error — word substitutions — which occur in the speech of both normals and aphasics, demonstrate that the lexicon we access to convey a message is a highly complex interconnected structure organized on many levels or with a number of subcomponents, as is revealed in the next speech errors.

II. WORD SUBSTITUTIONS, produced by normals
  (1) They put him in a straight jacket → They put him in a stuffed shirt
  (2) Are my tires touching the curb → Are my legs touching the curb?
  (3) 'Jack' is the subject of the sentence → 'Jack' is the president — subject of the sentence.
  (4) I didn't want to be a racist — uh — sexist
  (5) That's a horse of another color → That's a horse of another race, I mean color

III. WORD SUBSTITUTIONS, produced by aphasics
(data from Buckingham 1980)
(1) sister → brother
(2) oranges → apples
(3) Easter → Christmas
(4) cactus → plant
(5) accordian → play
(6) sofa → chair
(7) garter → leg

Such word-substitution errors show the kinds of information which must be part of the lexical representation of words and compounds and also that semantic similarities or classes or subclasses have lexical interconnections which are utilized in speaking and comprehending and must therefore be accounted for in a linguistic processing model. These examples, however, do not settle any crucial debates about the organization of a linguistic grammar; nor do the following errors produced by non-aphasic speakers:

IV. IDIOM BLENDS, produced by normals
(1) In one ear and gone tomorrow.
(2) Give him an inch and he'll hang himself.
(3) I hope you won't do anything behind my back → ... do anything on my face.
(4) Two rights don't make a wrong.

While such data have contributed little to advancing viable grammatical models, they do support many of the hypotheses developed by linguists on the basis of linguistic internal evidence, hypotheses which argue that knowledge of a language is represented by an autonomous formal grammar, finite in size, with infinite generative capacity, and with interactive, independent modules or components. The basic concepts of this generative grammar remain unchallenged by the aphasia data collected from brain-damaged patients, or speech errors, or results of psycholinguistic experiments.

Although there are numerous studies concerned with lexical access, particularly in speech perception, the questions now being debated between, for example, those who support a theory of interpretive morphology (Anderson 1982) in which inflectional morphology is outside the lexicon and those who support a lexical morphology in which inflectional forms are in the lexicon (Lapointe 1979, Lieber 1980, Kiparsky 1982, Jensen and Stong-Jensen 1984) have not been resolved by the results of these psycholinguistic experiments to date.

It may not be crucial to any present argument regarding a theory of grammar as to whether the different kinds of information speakers know about a word in their language — its phonological form, its morphemic structure, its syntactic category, its semantic representation, its sub-categorization constraints, its selectional features, and, for literate speakers, its orthographical shape — are included as part of one entry or whether there are interconnected or inter-addressed sub-lexicons each containing a distinct kind of representation.

Studies of aphasics, however, strongly support the notion that there are interconnected sub-lexicons. Evidence is specifically provided for this model by studies of acquired dyslexia (reading and/or writing disorders by individuals who, prior to brain damage, were fully literate). The relevance of such studies to psycholinguistic models of normals was shown in a seminal paper by Marshall and Newcombe (1966) and has been reinforced by numerous additional studies (cf. e.g. Newcombe and Marshall 1985; Patterson 1982; Saffran and Marin 1977; Shallice and Warrington 1975; Coltheart, Patterson, and Marshall 1980, to name just a few).

Some of the characteristics of three of the categories of acquired dyslexia have particular relevance to the organization of the lexicon in psycholinguistic processing models. (The adjectives used to describe these classes should be viewed simply as technical, identifying terms. All examples are taken from the literature cited above.)

V. CHARACTERISTICS OF DEEP DYSLEXIA
  (1) Can read words but not non-words; can repeat non-words.
  Response to non-words: 'no', 'don't know', 'sorry'.
  If urged to try, may respond with a real word, e.g.:
  a. DAKE → 'lake'
  (2) When reading single words aloud, semantically related words may be substituted, e.g.:
  a. JAIL → 'prison'
  b. SOCCER → 'football'
  c. ILL → 'sick'
  d. LARGE → 'big'
  e. CLOSE → 'shut'
  f. GNOME → 'pixie'
  (3) Semantic class substitutions also occur when reading abbreviations or orthographic symbols, e.g.:
  a. LBS → 'inch'
  b. XII → 'BC'
  c. ETC → 'and sons limited'
  (4) Difficulty with grammatical morphemes; errors result in substituted words in same category, e.g.:
  a. FOR → 'and'
  b. HIS → 'she'
  c. BE → 'small words are the worst'

d. SOME → 'one of them horrid words again'
(5) Derivational and inflectional errors are common, e.g.:
  a. ARRIVE → 'arrival'
  b. TRUTH → 'true'
(6) Reading unaffected by word length or spelling regularity.

In spontaneous speech as well as in reading, errors occur in which pseudosynonyms of semantically related words are substituted for the targetted words.

It is interesting to note that little or no improvement is shown in reading sentences rather than single words, as shown by the following:

(7) a. HE WALKED THROUGH THE SUPERMARKET → 'walking ...'
  b. PUT FIVE SHILLINGS ON A GOOD HORSE → 'five bob — best horse'
  c. GOING DOWN THE RIVER THERE WAS A COAL BARGE → 'row ... Thames ... coal ... ship ...'

For these patients there does not seem to be any access to grapheme-to-phonology rules, which would explain why non-words or nonsense forms can not be read. These rules are either 'erased' or inaccessible. In words read correctly, there appears to be a direct pathway from the visual orthographic signal to an orthographic listing and from there to the word's phonological form which can then be 'translated' into pronunciation rules. Since the meaning of these words is known (as is also true through auditory perception), the semantic representation must be accessed through the orthographic and/or phonological representation. In reading, however, since semantically related words are substituted, the route must lead from the orthographic entry to its related semantic representation before the phonology is accessed. The error occurs in selecting an incorrect (but related) 'address' in the semantic sub-lexicon.

The derivational errors which these patients produce lend some support for Cutler and Fay's (1982) suggestion that morphologically derived forms occur together in the lexicon. (See also Fay and Cutler 1977.)

The difficulty these patients have with reading grammatical morphemes, substituting other grammatical morphemes when they read them at all, provides evidence for a separate sub-lexicon of this lexical class (Zurif 1982).

A second category of acquired dyslexia is characterized as follows:

VI. CHARACTERISTICS OF PHONOLOGICAL OR DIRECT DYSLEXIA
  (1) Like deep dyslexics, words can be read well, but non-words poorly, if at all.
  (2) Especially good at reading lexical content words. Reading per-

formance virtually perfect on single morpheme lexical items.
(3) Semantic substitutions never occur.
(4) Bound morphemes, e.g. -*ed* and -*tion*, may cause problems resulting in derivational errors.
(5) Ability to read does not imply ability to understand meaning of the words pronounced correctly.

Schwartz, Saffran and Marin (1980) report on a 62-year-old woman, with severe impairment of the semantic knowledge of words (or a difficulty to access this knowledge) who had retained the ability to read single words aloud, including such irregular words as TORTOISE, LEOPARD, CLIMB, BOTH, OWN, and FLOOD, without knowing what they meant.

Phonologic dyslexia further supports the view that the lexicon is organized into a number of sub-lexicons with parallel phonological, semantic, and orthographic representations for each word or morpheme. These patients apparently go from the printed word stimulus to the orthographic representation and then directly to the phonological listing, bypassing semantics (at least at those times when they can not state the meaning of the word read). Since they are unable to read non-words, their ability to correctly read words can not be due to the use of orthographic-to-sound rules, but only by reference to a phonological representation. In fact, their inability to read nonsense forms suggests that they have no access to such rules. Their difficulty in reading grammatical morphemes provides further evidence for the existence of a separate lexicon for this lexical category. One could envisage a marking of such items in a single lexicon which in some way would make these words difficult to access, but a simpler solution is the sub-lexicon organization.

The third and final category of acquired dyslexia to be discussed in this paper has been called 'surface dyslexia'.

VII. CHARACTERISTICS OF SURFACE DYSLEXIA
   (1) Fluent and effective spontaneous speech.
   (2) Great sensitivity to regularity of spelling; words with irregular spelling cause difficulty, e.g.:
      a. BROAD → [brod] (cf. 'road')
   (3) Kinds of errors show use of grapheme-to-phoneme rules:
      a. DISEASE → 'decease'
      b. OF → 'off'
      c. GUEST → 'just'
   (4) When, after making an error, the patient is asked to give the meaning of the stimulus word, s/he defines (correctly) her/his own (false) response:
      a. LISTEN → 'Liston' — described as 'the famous boxer'

'EXTERNAL EVIDENCE' FOR A THEORY OF GRAMMAR

    b. BEGIN → 'beggin' — 'collecting money'
(5) When a misreading results in a neologism, there is an awareness of the nonlexical status of the response:
    a. ISLAND → [ɪzlænd] — 'there's no such word'
    b. SUGAR → [suǰər] — 'don't know'
(6) Homophones may be read aloud correctly but misinterpreted as to meaning:
    a. BEE → 'be' — 'to be or not to be, that is the question'
    b. OAR → 'or' — 'that's the ore of metal, the raw materials'
    c. BILLED → 'build' — 'to build up, buildings'
    d. SIGHS → 'size is measurement ... or bit of stuff they use in glue'
    e. PAIR → 'pair/pear' — 'it's either two of a kind or it's one for eating'

This last category of 'surface dyslexics' again shows that the lexicon, at least the one accessed for reading and writing, is modular in its organization. The mispronunciation of irregular words (as if on analogy with regular words) shows that grapheme-to-phoneme correspondence rules are used in reading. The phonological representation of words does not seem to be accessed at all. In addition, semantic interpretation seems to be made only through phonology, which accounts for homophonic and homonymic ambiguities as well as inability to provide meaning for mispronunciations which do not match real words. That is, these dyslexics appear to be using the following routes:

ORTHOGRAPHY → PRONUNCIATION
(via grapheme-to-phonology rules)
PRONUNCIATION → MEANING
(via mapping of phonetic representation of word onto phonological representation to semantic representation)

If the phonological representation of a word is not found, as in the case of a nonsense 'pronunciation', e.g. "izland" for ISLAND, there is no way to 'address' the semantic meaning of the stimulus item.

One case of an almost 'pure' surface dyslexic, referred to here as Kram, the name he uses for himself, was first examined by Freda Newcombe, John Marshall, and subsequently by myself in 1981 and 1983. (The complete medical history and results of various intelligence, psychological and performance tests are given in Newcombe and Marshall 1985, and a more detailed description of his reading/writing impairment in Fromkin 1985.)

Despite fluent, appropriate, and intelligible spontaneous speech, Kram's oral reading, writing, and oral spelling show severe impairment. He reads and writes solely by use of his own (non-standard) grapheme ↔ phonology rules, as shown by the following examples:

VIII. KRAM'S READING PRONUNCIATION AND WRITING TO DICTATION

	STIMULUS	READING PRONUNCIATION	WRITING TO DICTATION
a.	'fame'	[fæmij]	FAM
b.	'cape'	[sepij]	KAP
c.	'fight'	[fɪg-hʌt]	FiT
d.	'goes'	[gɔ-ɛs]	GOZ
e.	'thing'	[təhɪŋ]	FiNG
f.	'with'	[waytəhə]	WiV

Kram, like other surface dyslexics can only access the semantic representation of words through the phonology as shown in IX.

IX. MEANING THROUGH PHONOLOGY

	STIMULUS	PRONUNCIATION	MEANING
a.	sum	[sʌm]	'I've got some money'
b.	can	[sæn]	'I don't know. If it was "m" it would be "Sam"'
c.	son	[sɔn]	'if that were a "u" it would be up in the sky'
d.	fame	[fæmij]	'don't know. Is it a word?'
e.	pig	[pɪg]	'oink oink'

It is obvious that Kram does not use the orthography to access the phonology and pronunciation. One sees some similarities to spelling and reading errors of children first learning to read and write, particularly in the use of letter names. We are fortunate that his father has given us notebooks containing his writing pre-accident, and some, but not all, of the rules which he now uses to read from written text or write to dictation are those he used when he could not remember the learned spelling/orthography of a word when he was in school.

Kram has either lost ('erased') the orthographic representation of words or has no way of accessing the phonological representation through the orthography. His 'constructed' rules reflect his phonological system rather than the phonetics, as shown by the fact that in writing to dictation when the auditory stimulus of the word includes an interdental fricative, a [θ] or a [ð] which do not occur in his English dialect, he writes an F or V, respectively.

These cases of acquired dyslexia provide evidence to support a model of the lexicon in which each lexical item has multi-entries. A model in which one word is listed singly with all the information included in that one listing can accommodate the data reported on but in a most inefficient fashion. To account for Kram's disorder, for example, one would have to assume that the orthographic representation of each lexical entry were erased or 'obscured' leaving the phonological and semantic representations intact. The model proposed by Fromkin (1985) can account for his difficulties more elegantly.

For Kram, the 'access pathway' to the orthographical lexicon is blocked. He can only get to the phonological lexicon via his own grapheme-to-phoneme rules which produce a phonological string which can be 'pronounced' via his phonetic rules, or mapped onto an entry in the phonological lexicon if his phonological representation matches an actual address. That entry then points to a semantic address which gives him the meaning. Since his attempt to read the word 'cape' via his rules produced /sepi/ rather than /kep/, and since /sepi/ is not an entry in the phonological lexicon, he cannot provide a meaning for the word and, in fact, is not sure whether or not it is an English word.

These kinds of data provide quite strong evidence for such a lexical organization in a linguistic processing model. To my knowledge, as stated earlier, no crucial linguistic hypothesis is addressed by these data. It may very well be the case, then, that in respect to the organization of the lexicon, there is a one-to-one mapping between the lexicon of the grammar and the lexicon actually processed in linguistic performance.

The 'external' evidence discussed briefly in this paper does seem to meet Chomsky's (1978) criteria cited above; it is persuasive and reliable, and the principles 'dealing with this evidence are tenable, intelligible, [and] compelling'.

'EXTERNAL EVIDENCE' FOR A THEORY OF GRAMMAR

Figure 4.1: Subcomponent of Linguistic Performance Model (for single words)

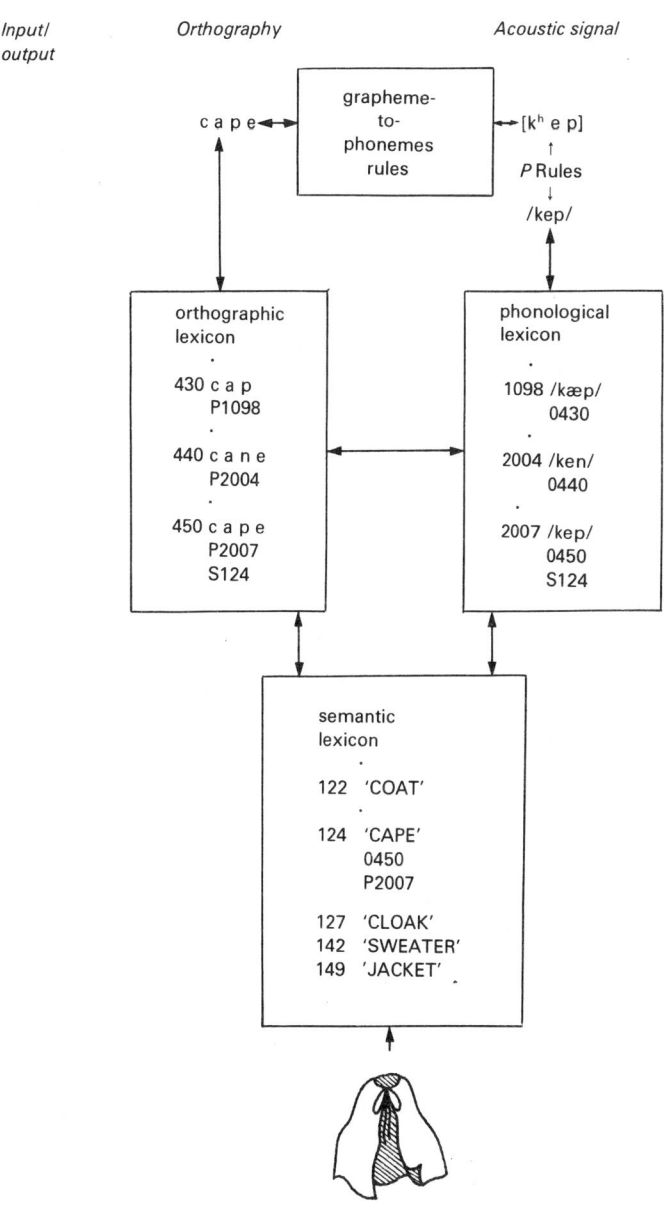

63

REFERENCES

Anderson, S.R. 1977. 'On the Formal Description of Inflection', in W.A. Beach, S.E. Fox, and S. Philosoph (eds.), *Papers from the Thirteenth Regional Meeting of the Chicago Linguistic Society*. Chicago, Ill.: University of Chicago, 111: 15–44.

—— 1982. 'Where's Morphology?', *Linguistic Inquiry* 13: 571–612.

Bierwisch, M. 1982. 'Linguistics and Language Error', in A. Cutler (ed.), *Slips of the Tongue and Language Production*. Amsterdam: Mouton, 29–72.

Blumstein, W.E. 1973. *A Phonological Investigation of Aphasic Speech*. The Hague: Mouton.

Buckingham, H.W. 1980. 'On Correlating Aphasic Errors with Slips-of-the-tongue', *Applied Psycholinguistics* 1: 199–220.

Chomsky, N. 1978. 'On the Biological Basic of Language Capacities', in G.A. Miller and E. Lenneberg (eds.), *Psychology and Biology of Language and Thought: Essays in Honor of Eric Lenneberg*. New York: Academic Press, 208–9.

Coltheart, M., K. Patterson, and J.C. Marshall (eds.). 1980. *Deep Dyslexia*. London: Routledge and Kegan Paul.

Cutler, A., and D.A. Fay. 1982. 'One Mental Lexicon, Phonologically Arranged: Comments on Hurford's Comments', *Linguistic Inquiry* 13: 107–13.

Fay, D.A., and A. Cutler. 1977. 'Malapropisms and the Structure of the Mental Lexicon', *Linguistic Inquiry* 8: 503–20.

Fromkin, V.A. 1968. 'Speculations on Performance Models', *Journal of Linguistics* 4: 47–68.

—— 1971. 'The Non-anomalous Nature of Anomalous Utterances', *Language* 47: 27–52. Reprinted in V.A. Fromkin (ed.), *Speech Errors as Linguistic Evidence*. The Hague: Mouton, 1973.

—— 1973. 'Slips of the Tongue', *Scientific American*, December, 111–17.

—— 1975. 'When Does a Test Test a Hypothesis, or What Counts as Evidence?', in D. Cohen and J.R. Wirth (eds.), *Testing Linguistic Hypotheses*. New York: John Wiley (Hemisphere Publishing Co.), 43–64.

—— 1980. 'The Psychological Reality of Phonological Descriptions', *Proceedings of the Ninth International Congress of Phonetic Sciences*, vol. III, 195–216.

—— 1985. 'Evidence in Linguistics', in R.H. Robins and V.A. Fromkin (eds.), *Linguistics and Linguistic Evidence*. Newcastle-upon-Tyne, England: Grevatt and Grevatt, 18–38.

Green, E. 1969. 'Phonological and Grammatical Aspects of Jargon in an Aphasic Patient: A Case Study', *Language and Speech* 12: 103–18.

Jensen, J.T., and M. Stong-Jensen. 1984. 'Morphology is in the Lexicon!', *Linguistic Inquiry* 15: 474–98.

Kiparsky, P. 1982. 'Lexical Morphology and Phonology', in I.-S. Yang (ed.), *Linguistics in the Morning Calm*. Seoul, Korea: Hanshin, 3–91.

Klatt, D. 1979. 'Lexical Representations for Speech Production'. Paper presented at the International Symposium on the Cognitive Representation of Speech, Edinburgh, 29 July–1 August 1979.

Lapointe, S.G. 1979. 'A Theory of Grammatical Agreement'. University of Massachusetts dissertation.

Lecours, A., and F. Lhermitte. 1969. 'Phonemic Paraphasias: Linguistic Structures and Tentative Hypotheses', *Cortex* 5: 193–228.

Lieber, R. 1980. 'On the Organization of the Lexicon'. Massachusetts Institute of Technology dissertation.

Marshall, J.C., and F. Newcombe. 1966. 'Syntactic and Semantic Errors in

Paralexia', *Neuropsychologia* 4: 169-76.

Newcombe, F., and J.C. Marshall. 1985. 'Reading and Writing by Letter Sounds', in K. Patterson, J.C. Marshall, and M. Coltheart (eds.), *Surface Dyslexia*. London: Routledge and Kegan Paul, 35-52.

Mehler, J., J. Morton, and P.W. Jusczyk. 1984. 'On Reducing Language to Biology', *Cognitive Neuropsychology* 1: 83-116.

Patterson, K.E. 1982. 'The Relation between Reading and Phonological Encoding: Further Neuropsychological Observations', in A.W. Ellis (ed.), *Normality and Pathology in Cognitive Functions*. London: Academic Press, 77-111.

Saffran, E.M., and O.S.M. Marin. 1977. 'Reading without Phonology: Evidence from Aphasia', *Quarterly Journal of Experimental Psychology* 29: 307-18.

Schwartz, M., E. Saffran, and O.S.M. Marin. 1980. 'Fractionating the Reading Process in Dementia: Evidence for Word-specific Print-to-sound Associations', in M. Coltheart, K. Patterson, and J. Marshall (eds.), *Deep Dyslexia*. London: Routledge and Kegan Paul, 259-69.

Shallice, T.D., and E.K. Warrington. 1975. 'Word Recognition in a Phonemic Dyslexic Patient', *Quarterly Journal of Experimental Psychology* 27: 187-99.

Zurif, E.B. 1982. 'Psycholinguistic Interpretations of the Aphasias', in A.R. Lecours, D. Caplan, and A. Smith (eds.), *Biological Perspectives on Language*. Cambridge, Mass.: MIT.

Zwicky, A. 1975. 'The Strategy of Generative Phonology', in W.U. Dressler, and F.V. Mares (eds.), *Phonologica 1972*. Munich: Wilhelm Fink, 151-68.

5

Chaucer and the Pun-Hunters: Some Points of Caution

ARCHIBALD A. HILL

Paull F. Baum remarked more than twenty years ago that 'certain of Chaucer's puns are unmistakably deliberate and have long been recognized; for the rest, no one can be sure'. It is unfortunate that scholars have not followed this warning. What they have followed instead is Baum's listing of puns of which 'no one can be sure'. At this writing, more than two hundred and fifty possible puns have been suggested, and I am sure that more suggestions could be found by further search. The tendency to find puns, often for slight reasons, has grown steadily, and has reached a climax with the books of Thomas Ross and John Gardner.[1]

I should begin, I believe, with a general statement about puns in their relationship to normal lexical usage. It is an axiom that in normal language use, meanings are derived from the contexts in which they occur, and are (again normally) single. A chief contribution of the late Martin Joos was to formulate the principle that meaning is maximally derived from context and only minimally from individual lexical items. Like other entities, individual semantic items are, in Occam's words, not to be needlessly multiplied. Thus the probabilities are weighted against double meanings, and puns are usually to be rejected unless there is evidence supporting them. That is, a meaning is innocent unless proved double.[2]

Any search for a double meaning requires a suggestion or trigger — if there is none, we do not search. One type of trigger is identity of word form, with difference of meaning. A typical example of identity in form and spelling is in such a sentence as 'the *gate* was awkward'. Since in this narrow context, the meaning of *gate* is uncertain, the reader is forced to examine the surrounding contexts, to see what meaning they support, and if they support more than one, the word is a pun.

A second type of trigger for pun-hunting is context. In fact, a double context can be not only the trigger for a hunt for double meaning, but the proof that it is there. For instance, the eleventh edition of the *Encyclopedia Britannica*, in an unsigned article on puns, has the following fully attested contextual pun:

Charles I's Court Jester is said to have made the punning grace 'great praise be to God and little Laud to the devil' for which the archbishop dismissed him from his service.

At this point it can be said, further, that if the pun is contextually supported, absolute identity of the two word forms is not necessary.[3] It is only necessary that the two words be sufficiently similar so that they both reach the consciousness of the hearer or reader. This is what happens with George Kaufman's famous pun, 'One man's Mede is another man's Persian'.

On the other hand, if the trigger for the pun-hunter is verbal rather than contextual, absolute identity of word form is certainly a necessary precondition, though in the absence of contextual support, absolute identity proves merely ambiguity, not double meaning. If the pun-hunter relies on mere similarity rather than identity, not even ambiguity is present. It is nowadays sometimes fashionable for critics to assert that merely similar words 'reverberate' with those of the text, a process which created a tempest over the words said to 'reverberate' with Keats's 'beauty is truth, truth beauty'.[4]

Puns and other word-plays have been with us for a long time, as Bede's story of the English slaves at Rome makes plain — 'non Angli, sed Angeli', as one of a cluster of word-plays from the mouth of the future Pope Gregory. But there is one type of pun which I believe was impossible in mediaeval times. This is the pun in which support comes from spelling alone. Milton in *Lycidas* wrote 'flote upon his watry bear', with three spellings that differ from modern usage. Had he intended (Heaven forbid!) the pun which Oxford students once saw in the line, mere variation in the spelling of *bear* would not have indicated his intention. Only when spelling became fully fixed would writing *beer* have clearly indicated the pun.

To come at last to Chaucer's puns, we can find the type example of a true, double-meaning pun in the description of the Clerk of Oxford:

For hym was levere have at his beddes heed
Twenty bookes, clad in blak or reed,
Of Aristotle and his philosophie,
Than robes riche, or fithele, or gay sautrie,
But al be that he was a philosophre
Yet hadde he but little gold in cofre (*CT* I 293–8).[5]

In this passage, if *philosophre* is read in the light of what precedes, the meaning is 'student of philosophy'. If read in the light of what follows, the meaning is 'alchemist, maker of gold'. This, like other true puns, is the occurrence of a word at the overlapping point of two contexts.

The puns that 'have long been recognized', as Baum said, are all of this sort, and there are not very many of them in the totality of Chaucer's works. I would count thirteen, giving a total nearer to those of the conservative scholars Tatlock, Kökeritz and Robinson, but differing in many of the items.[6] It is not my purpose to discuss the puns I believe to be genuine, but for those who wish to go further with the matter, I list them in a note.

What does interest me is to determine how it has come to be possible for modern Chaucerians to maintain, as does Gardner, that Chaucer's puns 'are easily missed until the fifteenth reading', or that a particular passage is 'loaded with sexual puns'.[7] That is, a belief in Chaucer's fondness for all sorts of word-play has apparently developed to the point where if a given word in a Chaucer line even faintly resembles another word, then the second word is taken to be also present in the meaning. The belief and its results are both in need of skeptical reexamination.

A part of the belief in word-play arises through failure to distinguish true puns from those word-plays which do not involve double meaning. A clear example of the sort of word-play that has often been lumped together with puns is the following.

> Fro Paradys first, If I shal nat lye,
> Was man out chaced for his glotonye
> And chaast was man in Paradys, certeyn (*CT* III 1915–17).

The use of *chaced* has clearly suggested the use of *chaast* in the line following, but has not affected its meaning. The phrase *out chaced* is clearly the modern *chased out*, and the form *chaast* clearly means *chaste*, so that there is no double meaning.[8] It should be added, also, that the quite frequent identical rhymes, thought of as an ornament as long as the meanings of the rhyme-words were different, were a form of this kind of word-play.

Another type of occurrence that has wrongfully been called a pun is no more than a simple uncertainty. A good example is in the description of the dress of the Prioress.

> And thereon heng a brooch of gold ful sheene
> On which ther was first write a crowned A,
> And after *Amor vincit omnia* (*CT* I 160–3).

Baum lists *crowned A* among his possible puns, on the ground that it may have been a letter with a crown-like ornament, or simply a very superior letter.[9] I believe that the first meaning is the more likely; it is unnecessary to think that the letter was both ornamented and superior, as would be required were this a pun.

It is also true that there are occasional double meanings which are not puns, but are innuendoes, involving a suggestion drawn from a whole passage. Such an innuendo is found in the description of the Friar —

He hadde maad ful many a marriage
Of younge wommen at his owene cost (*CT* I 212–13).

Almost all scholars have found this an 'innuendo which Chaucer surely intended', as Robinson's note says. That is, he marries off girls, not out of generosity, but because he had himself seduced them.

Word-plays like that on *chaced/chaast*, uncertainties, and innuendoes are not particularly important except as they contribute to the belief in Chaucer as an inveterate user of rhetorical devices. In any event, these devices do not contribute to multiple meanings over and above the clear meanings present in the text.

I know of no discussion of what constitutes evidence for or against double-meaning puns, and I shall therefore attempt to list the kinds of situations in which a scholar is forced to accept a double meaning, or in which he should avoid doing so.[10] Far and away the most important evidence for the existence of a pun is the presence of two contexts which force reinterpretation. Two meanings for *philosophre* are so fully supported as to be virtually certain. Yet it is well to remember that in questions of interpretation we are always dealing with probabilities, and that the most that we can expect is that some probabilities will be higher than others. If we have measured the probabilities with reasonable accuracy, we have performed our task.

Each of the two meanings of *philosophre* is not merely appropriate to its own context, but is the single most probable meaning for its context. In other instances, the textual meaning is clear, but the proposed secondary meaning is merely possible. An example of such a situation is at line 1313 of *The Book of the Duchess*

... al was doon,
For that tyme, the hert-huntyng.

The dreamer has been describing a royal hunt, so that the obvious meaning is 'hunting of the hart'. A pun on *heart* would fit into the general subject since the poem is an elegy for a dead, and dearly beloved, Duchess. But such a second meaning is not specifically required; it is, as I have just said, merely possible. To find a pun here, then, is a violation of the principle of simplicity.

There is, however, a situation in which a secondary meaning which would otherwise be merely possible, is increased in probability. This occurs when there is something strange in the surface text, and the secondary meaning explains it. An example is the occurrence of *ryche hil* at line 1319 of *The Book of the Duchess*. Hills are not ordinarily described as rich, but Richemont or Richmond is one of the titles of John of Gaunt, and the phrase is then a pun on the name.

One of the most obvious situations making for the improbability of a pun is nonexistence of the punning word. A striking example of such an improbable suggestion is in Gardner's discussion of *Truth*. He says that the word *hord* in the phrase *hord hath hate* has two meanings. One is the Modern English 'hoard', and the other is modern 'horde', meaning a crowd. The second sense that he proposes is not recorded in the *Middle English Dictionary*, and indeed, the word is not recorded in English until 1555, and then only in the sense of a tribe, particularly a Tartar tribe. The transferred sense *crowd* is not recorded until 1613. It is certainly always possible that a word was in existence at a date earlier than its first recording, but absence from the records makes existence at least questionable.[11]

Puns which are dependent on a word or meaning from a foreign language are also improbable. One which was quite properly rejected by Baum is a pun at *Troilus* I 225, where Chaucer ascribes to 'proude Bayard' the thought that he is but a horse, and then says *so ferde it* by Troilus. The suggestion is that *ferde* is a pun on German *Pferd*. What Baum says is that 'This is "unlikely" but would make a bilingual pun if Chaucer knew German.'[12] My own opinion is that it would be unlikely even if Chaucer did indeed know German. In writing in one's native language, foreign words, even if known, are normally at the outer fringes of consciousness, and are therefore unlikely to appear in puns. A case in point is a pun proposed by R.J. Pearcy for the line in the Franklin's Tale.

Withouten coppe he drank al his penaunce (*CT* V 942).

The proposal is that *coppe* is punned with Latin *culpa*.[13] Though as I have said, exact phonological identity is not a necessary condition for puns which are contextually supported, this one is based on the two words alone, so that the difference in pronunciation, spelling (and language!) rules the pun out, conclusively.

It should be said, however, that the kind of bilingual pun which is unlikely is one in which the English word is in the text, and the foreign word is the secondary form. In instances where the foreign word is in the text, and the English word is the secondary form, the pun can be quite likely. Such a pun is that on *Vache* in *Truth*, where it has been shown that a personal name is punned on, the secondary meaning being the English *cow, beast.*[14]

A pun is unlikely if the context which gives the secondary meaning is created by manipulation of the presented text. Baum gives a pun suggestion on the line spoken by the Host to the Monk.

I vowe to God, thou hast a ful fair skyn (*CT* VII 3122).

The proposal is that *ful* (with short vowel) is punned with *foul*, with long vowel. The context for the second meaning is made by dropping out the adjective *fair*, which would then give *foul skin*.[15] Improbability can also be produced by creation of a nontextual context that lacks outside support. Norman Eliason, departing from his usual scholarly caution, creates a nontextual context for lines 118–19 of *The House of Fame*.

> To the corseynt Leonard
> To make lythe of that was hard.

The situation is that the dreamer is weary from a pilgrimage of two miles to the shrine of St Leonard. The usual interpretation of the line is that the dreamer wishes to 'make the bonds of marriage softer'. Eliason interprets it as meaning 'soften the male organ', and says that it is therefore necessary to suppose that there was a brothel beside the shrine.[16]

Puns are improbable if the secondary meaning does not fit the dramatic or emotional tone of the passage. Perhaps the clearest case of a pun that is improbable for this reason is in the apostrophe of Troilus to the empty house of Criseyde. I give the whole of the passage, since I wish to establish the tone.

> Then seide he thus, 'O paleys desolat,
> O hous of houses whilom best ihight,
> O paleys empty and disconsolat,
> O thow lanterne of which queynt is the lyght,
> O paleys, whilom day, that now art nyght,
> Wel oughtestow to falle, and I to dye,
> Syn she is went that wont was us to gye!' (*Tr.* V 540–6).

Of this passage, Robertson has said 'The ironic pun on "queynte" is a bitter comment on what it is that Troilus actually misses'. It seems to me that Eliason is quite right in rejecting this pun as out of keeping 'with the lovely apostrophe of Troilus'.[17] It can be added that the pun would produce a badly mixed metaphor as well.

This is the possible pun discussed at length by William Frost. He says 'In favor of the pun hypothesis is first, Chaucer's inclination toward buried puns, including some of a quite scabrous nature buried not far beneath the linguistic surface.' As examples of buried, scabrous punning he cites the 'stif burdoun' of the Summoner, and the 'queynte fantasye' of the Wife, both of which I discuss below and find uncertain. As for the meaning which I believe is an anatomical metaphor of considerable improbability, Frost brings in support an Italian tray with a picture of Venus in which rays of light stream from the organ in question. For me, what is possible for a goddess is no argument for what is possible for a mortal. It seems to me conclusive, however, that the anatomical meaning for *queynt(e)* in Chaucer is confined to frankly bawdy situations and speech, and is never found in the mouths of elegant speakers. The pun can then be rejected on the grounds that it would greatly and unnecessarily change the total context.[18]

A pun is unlikely if it relies on a narrow context, and in so doing violently changes the larger context in which it is found. An example of such a pun is one suggested by Baum, in the description of the Pardoner (*CT* I 673). The Summoner bore a *stif burdoun* to the Pardoner as they both sang 'Come hider, love, to me!' That is, the Summoner sang a strong bass to the Pardoner's treble, Baum suggests a pun on staff.[19] The best reply to the suggestion is that of Donald R. Howard:

> This possible pun is always dredged up as evidence of a homosexual relation between the two [i.e., Summoner and Pardoner], but the next line, 'Was never trumpe of half so great a soun', enforces the literal meaning (that the Summoner sings a bass accompaniment), and there is not another line that carries out the sexual suggestion.[20]

Howard is clearly following not only the Joos axiom as mentioned above, but is also following an important corollary to it, namely, that in instances where there is a conflict between a narrow context and a wider one, the wider context is to be preferred. As for the conflict, it should be added that the Summoner has been described at length as a heterosexual as 'hot and lecherous as a sparrow'. The proposed pun would give a violent and unnecessary change.

The most extreme form of reliance on a narrow context alone is a pun for which there is no support except similarity of words. One of Gardner's proposed puns is of this sort. Gardner says of the *Parliament of Fowls* 'a parliament of *foules* (fowls or, by a foul pun, fools)'. The words, be it noted, are merely similar, not identical, so that the suggestion of a pun is very unlikely.[21]

There is one possible pun which involves a special problem. This is the pun proposed in Baum's 'Supplementary List', on *farthing/farting* at *CT* III 1967.[22] The problem here is the span of contexts. Line 1967 is 'What is a ferthyng worth parted in twelve?' The line is spoken by the begging friar of the tale, and only 182 lines later is there any mention of farting. Then, finally, in the conclusion of the tale the problem is solved by the use of a twelve-spoked wheel. There can be little doubt that the conclusion of the tale forces the reader to remember and revise his understanding of the meaning of the friar's speech. A pun over such a very long span would scarcely be possible outside of literature, since in everyday speech the intervening material would have driven the original word from memory. In speech, in fact, to establish the pun it would have been necessary to repeat the original statement, as doubtless the friar did when he related the incident at the lord's table.

There are two situations sometimes adduced as evidence of punning which seem to me valueless. One is the piling up of possibilities. In discussing the possible pun on *burdoun* already mentioned, Baum lists not only the meaning 'staff', but also 'young woman', 'joke', and 'hinny', and says that all of these point to an obscene pun.[23] It would seem to me, on the contrary, that if any one of the secondary meanings were punned on, it would decrease the likelihood of punning on the others.

A second situation said to favor the existence of a pun is repetition of a word. An amusing, and certainly startling, example of reliance on this belief is found in a comment on the passage in which Emilye sacrifices to Diana.

Then sodeynly she saugh a sighte queynte
For right anon oon of the fyres queynte,
And quyked agayn, and after that anon
That oother fyr was queynt and al agon;
And as it queynte it made a whistelynge (*CT* I 233–7).

W.F. Bolton comments: 'With four "queynts" and a whistle in five lines, Chaucer leaves no doubt where the fire is.'[24]

Two of the four occurrences are in a Chaucerian identical rhyme, and since the practice was one of the conventional ornaments of Middle English verse, these two occurrences are fully accounted for without punning. The other two are clearly verb forms, so that there is no compelling reason to regard them as punning with the noun. And finally, the whole passage is about the chaste Emilye and the chaste Diana, so that references to the female sexual organs would seem to be out of place dramatically.

The last type of evidence which often turns out to be no evidence at all, is that from cumulative occurrences. Cumulative evidence can be an important support for a conclusion based on individual instances, if the individual instances themselves are genuinely probable. This happens with a series of four name puns at the end of *The Book of the Duchess*. The items are *long castel, walles white, seynt Johan* and *ryche hil* (*BD* 1318–19). The *ryche hil* has already been mentioned as a pun on Richmond; *long castel* is a pun on Lancaster; *Johan* is a pun on John (of Gaunt), and *white* is a pun on Blanche. Each of the puns is highly probable, so that a conclusion that the whole group represents punning on the names of the Duke and Duchess of Lancaster is also highly probable.

Yet if the individual instances are themselves improbable, a conclusion based on them is not strengthened, but greatly weakened. One instance of such cumulative improbability is in the treatment of *queynte* in Ross's study. He devotes more space to these forms than to any other possible puns, and concludes with one which seems to me wildly improbable, in the description of Canacee's magic ring.

> For swich a joye she in hir herte took
> Both of hire queynte ryng and hire mirour,
> That twenty tyme she changed hir colour (*CT* V 368–70).

Of this Ross says

> Does this Oriental heroine change color for shame (embarrassment over the vision she has had in the mirror) or in an allusion to her repeated orgasms, as she takes joy in her 'queynte ryng'? The latter seems preposterous, yet in view of the passages where 'queynte' occurs elsewhere, one can hardly doubt that Chaucer's audience would have raised an eyebrow.[25]

The passage indicates that Ross himself would regard this interpretation as unlikely if it were isolated, but that he relies on other puns on the word for support. In spite of the fact that the word has been called Chaucer's 'favorite obscene pun' my own examination of all the occurrences makes me feel that there are no certain instances of such punning, and only three which seem possible.[26] In consequence, there is no support for a pun in the passage quoted by Ross.

There are two instances, also, of suggestions of puns in clusters in Gardner's books. In both instances the individual puns or double meanings are highly improbable and therefore the conclusions based on them are even more so. The first is in Gardner's discussion of the character of the Host.

> [The Host's] function is undoubtedly allegorical at least in part. The Devil is sometimes pictured as an innkeeper in medieval visual art, and 'Bailey' can suggest imprisoning walls, as in the bailey of a castle; the free supper he promises the best of the storytellers has sometimes been read as parodic of the celestial banquet, that is, the parodic banquet in hell. If we take 'Host' as a pun — and no pun goes past Chaucer unnoticed — he's a parodic Christ.[27]

The second instance of a conclusion based on a cluster of unlikely pun suggestions is in Gardner's interpretation of the character of the Friar as given in the general prologue (*CT* I 208–69). In *Life and Times* Gardner says the Friar is a dreadful man indeed, 'A fornicator, as Chaucer slyly hints through such puns as "a noble post", and perhaps a homosexual as well as a heterosexual, if "famulier" is a double entendre.' He then quotes the Chaucerian passage, giving side glosses. One attacks Franklins as 'the climbing class, just below knights, often accused of prissiness if not homosexuality'. In *Poetry*, Gardner returns to the Friar.

The portrait is loaded with sexual puns. On the innocent level, the Friar pays for the marriage of girls without a dowry 'at his owene cost' (213) because he's generous, but puns suggest that he does so because he himself has gotten them pregnant. As in the seventeenth century, 'cost' may have the sense of (to speak politely) ejaculation; at all events, 'Unto his ordre he was a noble post' (214) — a noble pillar. He is 'well beloved' and 'familiar', both in a double sense, with men as well as women ... When he does go to some widow ... he would 'have a ferthyng, er he wente' (255), but also a 'fair thing', that is, sexual gratification.[28]

Of these double meanings, one is well supported, namely that the Friar (as I have said earlier) is responsible for the condition of the girls he marries off. A pun on 'post' has been discussed briefly and rejected by Eliason.[29] All the rest are Gardner's own proposals. None are forced by double contexts, and if I understand Gardner, he is relying on Latin *mulier* for one. I know of no evidence for his attack on Franklins. His suggestion of a pun on 'cost' relies on a later meaning, and an uncertain one at that, since the obscene sense he suggests belongs to 'spending' and 'expense', not (so far as I know) to 'cost'.

The two hundred and fifty or more proposed puns in Chaucer seem to me highly improbable, and if we should accept any considerable portion of them, I think we would gravely distort our understanding of his work. Yet the many scholars who have pored over Chaucer's poems have been — and are — reasonable men. Why then this growing tendency to hunt for more and more secondary, tertiary, and even quaternary meanings? At least partly because there is an unanswered mystery about how we formulate utterances in either speech or writing. When we make a slip of the tongue, saying perhaps, *eloquent* when the sentence calls for *elegant*, it would seem to indicate that words similar in sound are somehow stored close together in the internal language mechanism. It is therefore tempting to assume that the words on the page bring with them a trailing cloud of similar words, and that the total cloud is a part of the total message. This belief led William Frost to speak of criticism by the *Finnegan's Wake* principle, and led Kenneth Burke to devise the operation which he called 'Joycing'.[30] Perhaps because Chaucer requires the modern student to go over his poems word by word, with dictionary and full apparatus of notes, there is a tendency to place an undue emphasis on individual lexical items, and give insufficient attention to contexts. The result is a collection of conjectural secondary meanings. Chaucer is not, however, the only target of this kind of conjecture. I have seen hidden double meanings ascribed to Keats, Robert Frost, and Hopkins to name only three. Such puns may add to richness of meaning, but only at the expense of validity of interpretation. In that belief I have tried to formulate some principles to curb extravagances of pun-hunting.

NOTES

1. Paull F. Baum, 'Chaucer's Puns', *PMLA* 71 (1956), 225-46. Also 'Chaucer's Puns: A Supplementary List', *PMLA* 73 (1958), 167-70; Thomas W. Ross, *Chaucer's Bawdy* (New York, Dutton, 1972); John Gardner, *The Life and Times of Chaucer* (New York, Knopf, 1977). Also *The Poetry of Chaucer* (Carbondale, Southern Illinois University Press, 1977)

2. The Joos axiom was first given in an unpublished paper before the Linguistic Society of America in 1953, and is fully discussed in Joos's article 'Semantic Axiom Number One', *Language* 48 (1972), 257-65. For an example of my own use of the axiom, see my 'Literary Meanings — Complex or Simple?' in Paul J. Hopper, Harriet Penensick, and Jerome Bunnag (eds.), *Studies in Descriptive and Historical Linguistics, Festschrift for Winfred P. Lehmann* (Amsterdam, John Benjamins, 1977), 109-24. Full bibliography is given there in note 2.

3. It is not possible, I believe, to specify exactly how much similarity must exist in a context-supported pun, but it is clear that there must be several shared sounds, and similarity of stress pattern. The most instructive example I know is a pun from a newspaper column I once saw. A correspondent asked why a woman had gift-wrapped a fish, and the answer was perhaps she did it 'just for the halibut', which puns upon the phrase 'just for the Hell of it'. *halibut — Hell of it* has three pairs of identical consonants, and one pair different in a single distinctive feature. The stress patterns are identical, but in my speech none of the vowels are the same. The pun would have been equally overt with 'just for the smell of it', but not with 'just for the fish of it'.

4. A moderate statement of reaction to Burke's hunting for hidden meanings is that by Merle E. Brown, *Kenneth Burke*, University of Minnesota Pamphlets on American Writers, no. 75, 43. Brown speaks of Burke's 'scatological reductionism', and says that he calls trying to make contextual understanding of Keats's poem 'only a game', while he (Burke) 'must be doing more serious things. Like reducing "Beauty is Truth" to "Poetry is Science", or, as he later does, like transposing some letters and changing others in a Joycean manner, so that the phrase becomes "Body is turd".'

5. All quotations from Chaucer are from F.N. Robinson, *The Works of Geoffrey Chaucer* (Boston, Houghton Mifflin, 1957).

6. J.S.P. Tatlock, 'Puns in Chaucer', *Flugel Memorial* Volume (Stanford University, 1916), 229-32. Helge Kökeritz, 'Rhetorical Word-play in Chaucer', *PMLA* 69 (1954), 937-52. Robinson, *Chaucer,* note to *CT* I 297.
My own list of genuine double-meaning puns is (1) *philosophre, CT* I 297; (2) *cordial, CT* I 443; (3) *pryvetee, CT* I 3164; (4) *lyes, CT* III 302; (5) *eructavit, CT* III 1934; (6) *ars-metrike, CT* III 2222; (7) *taille, CT* VII 416; (8) *blered ys myn ye, CT* VIII 730; (9) *A, Tr.* I. 171; (10) *Vache, Truth* 22; (11) *mede, Truth,* 27. This pun is discussed by James F. Ragan, *Modern Language Notes* 68 (1953), 534-5; (12) *lyght, Purse* 3; (13) *Hevy, Purse* 4. I have not listed those name-puns which, like 'wikked nest' at *CT* VII 2386, or those at the end of *The Book of the Duchess,* consist essentially of translations of names into ordinary language. Since most scholars are agreed on these name puns, they present no problems.

7. Gardner, *Life and Times,* 119, and *Poetry,* 236.

8. This word-play was admired by Tatlock, p. 232. He says of it, 'Chased out, and chaste in, what a beautiful thought! Of course the friar does not know that he is punning, it is merely the way his mind works.'

9. Baum, 'Puns in Chaucer', 235.

10. William Frost, 'A Chaucerian Crux', *Yale Review,* vol. 66, number 4 (June

1977), 551-61, discusses evidence for and against a single pun, that on *queynt* at *Troilus* V 543, but the discussion is inconclusive.

James Brown, 'Eight Types of Puns', *PMLA* 71 (1956), 14-26, discusses types of puns according to whether the two meanings are both literal, both figurative, or one literal one figurative, but does not discuss evidence for and against the reality of puns.

11. Gardner, *Poetry*, 68.
12. Baum, 'Supplementary List', 167, footnote.
13. R.J. Pearcy, *Notes and Queries* 22 (5 May 1975), 198.
14. Edith Rickert, 'Thou Vache', *Modern Philology* 11 (1913), 209-25.
15. Baum, 'Supplementary List', 168.
16. Norman E. Eliason, *The Language of Chaucer's Poetry* (Copenhagen, Rosenkild and Bagger, 1972), 190-1.
17. Durant W. Robertson, Jr., *A Preface to Chaucer* (Princeton, Princeton University Press, 1962), 500. Eliason, *Language of Chaucer*, 109-10.
18. William Frost, 'A Chaucerian Crux', 552-4.
19. Baum, 'Puns in Chaucer', 232.
20. Donald R. Howard, *The Idea of the Canterbury Tales* (Berkeley, University of California Press, 1976), 344.
21. Gardner, *Life and Times*, 218.
22. Baum, 'Supplementary List', 167. The pun was first suggested to Baum by a student, and again, later, by Henry A. Person of the University of Washington. Baum discusses the possibility that the two words *farthing* and *farting* might have been pronounced alike, and cites the parallel pun on *nothing* and *noting* in *Much Ado*. Pretty clearly there is no necessity of identity, and the pun is established (if it is) by contexts, not by special sound-developments.
23. Baum, 'Puns in Chaucer', 232.
24. W.F. Bolton, 'The Topic of the Knight's Tale', *Chaucer Review* I (1966), 224.
25. Ross, *Chaucer's Bawdy*, 178-80.
26. There are a total of 42 occurrences of *queynt* in Chaucer, as listed by the Tatlock and Kennedy *Concordance* (1963 edn., which lumps them all under the single lemma, *quaint*); of these five are fully discussed in the body of the paper. Of the 37 which remain, three clearly refer to the noun and have no secondary meaning.

> And prively he caughte hire by the queynte (*CT* I 3276)
> Ye shul have queynte right ynogh at eve (*CT* III 332)
> Is it for ye wolde have my queynte allone (*CT* III 444)

It is worth pointing out that these are all in the speech of vulgar persons, and that there are no certain uses of the word in the speech of the elegant.

There are three occurrences which seem to me possible puns. They are

> What al this queynte cas was for to seye (*CT* I 3605)
> We wommen han ...
> In this matere a queynte fantasye (*CT* III 515-18)
> O brotil joye! O sweete venym queynte! (*CT* IV 2061)

Without going into a detailed discussion, I can point out that secondary meaning in these lines is supported by general tone, or in some instances by possible covert and partial analogies. None of these force a second meaning, and I believe both general tone and partial analogies are not so powerful as the meaning suggested by the presented text. The remaining forms all clearly refer to the adjective, and a secondary meaning is improbable for all of them. There are eleven from the Canterbury Tales: I 1431, I 3275, I 4051, II 1189, II 1426, III 361 *var.*, V 234, V 239, V 369, V 726, VIII 752.

There are three forms in the *Book of the Duchess*: 531, 784, and 1330.

There are two occurrences, beside the one discussed in the text, in *Troilus*: I 411, and IV 1629.

There are four occurrences in the *House of Fame*: I 126, I 228, I 245, III 1925.

There are two occurrences in the *Legend of Good Women*: F 353, and 2013.

There are nine occurrences in the *Romaunt of the Rose*: 69, 98, 610, 1435, 2038, 2251, 3079, 5199, and 6342.

27. Gardner, *Poetry*, 240.
28. Gardner, *Life and Times*, 131-2, and *Poetry*, 236.
29. Eliason, *Language of Chaucer*, 46, footnote. Eliason ascribes the suggestion of a pun to C.A. Owen, Jr., 'Thy Drasty Rhyming', *Studies in Philology* 53 (1966), 533-64. Eliason says that such a pun would have astonished Chaucer, who 'knew how to manage *double entendres* such as this, taking care to mark them so clearly that no one could miss them, not even the Prioress'.
30. William Frost, 'A Chaucerian Crux'. Kenneth Burke, *A Rhetoric of Motives* (Berkeley and Los Angeles, University of California Press, 1969), 310-11, footnote. He gives there a list of other passages in which he has applied the method.

6

Two Cheers for Prescriptivism

MICHAEL B. KAC

It is incumbent upon academic linguists to have sensible answers to the following two questions:

(1) What ought an educated person to know about language (and what ought an educated English speaker to know about English)?
(2) What is the correct conception of the relationship between the standard and nonstandard varieties of a language?

In the course of thinking over a period of time about these questions, I have come to the conclusion that some cherished dogmas to which most of us at least claim to subscribe must be reevaluated, and that uncritical acceptance of them has done some serious damage which can only be repaired if we subject them to a fresh look. My title specifically mentions prescriptivism, but my concern is actually broader; a reconsideration of prescriptivism is only the wedge by which I hope to open a number of questions.

Antiprescriptivism in linguistics is a result, in large part, of the most basic of the forces responsible for creating modern linguistics as we know it. One of these is the anti-ethnocentrism of modern anthropology, another the powerfully empiricist bias common to the social and behavioral sciences in the beginning half of the present century. The first of these forces had the effect of making linguists' extremely reluctant to accept the idea that one language or variety of language was superior to another, while the second invited linguists to abandon to the fullest possible extent any preconceptions about the nature of language given the ease with which so many of those which had been part and parcel of traditional thinking could be debunked once the database was expanded to include languages other than those of Europe and its close oriental neighbors. Both of these developments occurred for honorable reasons, and in the main they were healthy ones. But even a valid philosophical position can be exaggerated and perverted into something which, in the end, is actually in conflict with the very motives that originally gave rise to it. It is not merely that the road to Hell is paved with good intentions; at every turn is a baby who, cold and shivering after having been thrown out with the bathwater, now waits to exert merciless revenge on all who pass by. This revenge has caused two plagues to be visited upon us, the first being the disastrous decline in verbal skill and concomitant increase in functional illiteracy which is now producing near panic in colleges and universities; the second, in a twist of irony that must be particularly comforting to the worst enemies of our discipline, infects those of us who must teach our subject to increasing numbers of students (many of them juniors and seniors) who do not know what an adjective is. Unfortunately, we are ourselves partly to blame for what has happened, and the time has come to 'fess up and do something about it.

The case for the sort of antiprescriptivism that most of us embrace (or claim to) — I shall call it 'vulgar antiprescriptivism' — looks initially most persuasive. For it is indeed true that grammatical norms change with time, that so-called experts on usage do not always agree (and are, in many cases, quite ignorant of just the subject in which they profess expertise — as is devastatingly documented in Jim Quinn's wonderful *American Tongue and Cheek*), and that too many of the concepts so cherished by Miss Fidditch and her colleagues are but the anachronistic residue of a largely discredited tradition of speculative philosophy. Yes, it is silly to require students to memorize case paradigms for a mostly caseless language, and yes, it is equally silly to view today's vernacular languages the mere detritus of their classical forebears. All of this is true; what I want to question is not its truth but its relevance. For easy (and enjoyable) as it may be to ridicule the adherents of a position for the excesses in which they indulge, the crucial issue remains unaddressed. A philosophy must be considered on its merits, not on what is done in its name.

A second failure of vulgar antiprescriptivism is its inability to distinguish between blind pedantry and an insistence on adherence to standards for which rational justification can be given. Consider, for example, what students beginning logic are taught about the importance of carefully distinguishing between *if, only if* and *if and only if*. We may grant, with H.P. Grice, that commonly observed principles of social cooperation make it possible, and even necessary, to blur some of these distinctions in ordinary parlance; but not all situations are ordinary. Indeed, it is one of the vital functions of education to teach about the world that lies beyond the commonplace and the accessible, thus making it inevitable that the process will be difficult and sometimes even painful. As long as there are circumstances in which language must be used in ways which run counter to the customs and the instincts of the majority (and I think we must admit that there are some), the necessity to prescribe will exist. The real issue, then, is not whether to prescribe, but what, when, how and, most important of all, why. The need for a new, enlightened, prescriptivism will make itself soon felt, I suspect, as a result of the increasing dominance of that most stereotypical of symbols of our age, namely the computer. Natural language capability is one of the professed goals of the drive toward a Fifth Generation of machines, though I must count myself on the side of the skeptics with regard to the question of whether a complete mechanical replication of human linguistic competence is possible. Even assuming, however, that the goal is realizable, it almost certainly lies far enough in the future that we shall have to make do for some time with language specifically tailored to the capability of the machines. Human–machine interaction will, to be sure, grow progressively easier than it is now, but it will be necessary nonetheless to impose certain restrictions on how one is allowed to express one's intentions — restrictions motivated not by cultural prejudice or metaphysical excess, but by the prosaic exigencies of life in a technological world.

An additional element of confusion results from the inability of nearly everyone (prescriptivist and antiprescriptivist alike) to see the difference between favoring a certain kind of language for the purposes that it is best equipped to serve and stigmatizing varieties of language that are not appropriate for these purposes. It is perfectly possible to do the former without doing the latter, i.e. to maintain a standard language and insist on its use in public life[1] without also holding in contempt those who do not command this language natively. The situation to emulate in this regard is the one which obtains in certain parts of Norway, where regional nonstandard speech serves as a positive symbol of local identity but inevitably gives way to the standard in situations calling for it. There is no reason in principle, therefore, why education in a standard language cannot be conducted with an attitude toward other linguistic varieties of sympathy and respect; and the case is very strong for there being a moral obligation to provide such education to those for whom the full range of social opportunities would otherwise be unavailable.

Finally, I find vulgar antiprescriptivism guilty of the Naturalistic Fallacy, of concluding that because certain things **are** so, they ought to be left alone. I suspect that what has happened here is that we have let ourselves confuse the idea that certain things are inevitable (linguistic change, most particularly) with the idea that whatever we see happening around us is the result of forces over which we can exert no control. This is an extremely dangerous trap and occasional excess of zeal is probably preferable to the consequences of falling into it. If, for example, we intend that students be capable of understanding the kind of language employed in philosophy, mathematics, and the sciences, then it is no good to just sit by while the forces of semantic change generalize the sense of *unique* from 'one of a kind' to 'unusual'. A freshman being introduced to set theory whose textbook contains the statement that the null set is unique is ill served by not having been told that in the discourse domain in question, this word is used in an etymologically conservative sense. I do not think that people who use *unique* to mean 'unusual' when engaged in casual conversation ought to be derided as boors; but if I met a university senior majoring in philosophy who did not know the narrower sense, I would be scared. It is not, as a dogmatic prescriptivist would have it, a matter of what *unique* 'really' means, or of defending the sanctity of the language against the depredations of the unwashed; it is simply a matter of there being in our society a kind of weak diglossia corresponding to the division between the academic and secular worlds and thus of the practical necessity of being sure that knowledge of the High variety is adequately transmitted to those in our charge. Should they fail to acquire this knowledge because of our reluctance to traumatize them by drawing them fully into a world that on first exposure seems alien and frightening, then we are not doing our job.

There are, of course, cases where no amount of pragmatic justification of the sort just offered will serve and where we must, inevitably, deal with matters of taste. Let us take as a case in point the growing tendency to treat such words as *media* and *criteria* as grammatically singular mass nouns rather than as plurals. Why this is happening is, of course, due to the fact that Latin and Greek are no longer on the linguistic pedestal. I see no grounds other than personal preference for adhering in these matters to conservative usage (which, by and large, I do), and I think it worthwhile to point out that not even the most rock-ribbed linguistic conservative behaves consistently in regard to loan vocabulary.[2] At the same time, I share with many of my professional colleagues an appreciation for diversity and a dislike of blandness. I do not consider those whose culinary experience is limited to boiled beef and potatoes to be contemptible, but given the opportunity to introduce Peking Duck to someone who has never tasted it, who of us would fail to rise valiantly to the occasion? I am fond of the Latin and Greek plurals for much the same reason. I see nothing wrong, as long as we are honest about what we are doing, in holding our students to some of our own preferences as long as the end result is to add to their store of interesting experiences; nor do I see anything wrong with perpetuating a form of linguistic symbolism which, like the centralized diphthongs on Martha's Vineyard, serves the cause of pride and a sense of distinctive identity. Why should we not allow ourselves the same privilege we so willingly grant to those we study?

I come now to the question of what we ought to teach people about language. This cannot be divorced from the issue of prescriptivism since, if I am right so far, we must somehow succeed in conveying to students the idea that standards of usage are to some extent capricious and arbitrary without at the same time encouraging the mistaken notions against which I have argued above. I think that there is a good model to follow here, and that is the teaching of music. Musicians are taught both theory and performance in a highly integrated way, in the sense that the practice of the best composers provides the models for the former, which in turn makes available a language and a conceptual scheme for talking about the latter. I am quite aware of the evidence that the teaching of grammar by itself does little to improve verbal skill, but I nonetheless think we should at least experiment with a method of instruction which makes it possible for teachers and students alike to speak and think of writing in terms of its technical elements — what, in the old days, used to be called 'mechanics'. I think, moreover, that it is possible to approach the matter of mechanics in a way which lends some real vitality to the subject. I would favor, that is, an instructional program in which the study of grammar is pursued less as a chore and more in the spirit of linguistics itself — to make the study of grammar, in short, a subject of the same sort as chemistry or biology. Study of this subject would begin in earnest in the ninth grade and would be clearly separated from the study of usage,[3] combining some basic linguistics with some basic logic. Students would dissect syllogisms, learn to detect ambiguities, develop a feeling for paraphrase relationships, and acquire at least a bare-bones introduction to the history of the language. I recognize, by the way, that this could not be done either quickly or cheaply; being able to do it at all would require a substantial upgrading in the quality of teachers which could probably not be achieved except by starting from scratch with a much more able pool than the one from which teachers are now drawn. And I would rather not try the experiment at all than have it fail, as did the much vaunted 'New Math', partly because the teachers weren't sufficiently capable. This problem, however, is not unique to the language-skills area.

Let me give some examples of what I have in mind. Imagine that we are dealing with ninth graders in their second semester, and that in the first they have been exposed to something like Fromkin and Rodman's *An Introduction to Language*. Suppose also that these students over the first few weeks of the semester have learned syllogistic logic through the Square of Opposition and that they have been presented with the Principle of Form. The idea is to get them to understand how the form of an argument determines its validity, which means that some attention must be paid to the grammatical structure of the sentences of which an argument consists. The following exercise is now given. Having already learned that arguments in the general form exemplified by (1) are valid,

(1) The trees of New Jersey are green.
    Copper Beeches are trees of New Jersey.
    Therefore, Copper Beeches are green.

students are then given the following invalid argument:[4]

(2) The trees of New Jersey are numerous.
    Copper Beeches are trees of New Jersey.
    Therefore, Copper Beeches are numerous.

The first task would be to actually show that the argument is invalid; next, students would be asked to make suggestions as to why, even though they are of apparently the same form, the arguments (1) and (2) are not both valid. Ultimately, they would be guided to an understanding of the difference between 'distributive' and 'collective' predicates and of the subtleties involved in the notion 'identity of form' illustrated by examples of this kind. A collateral exercise might involve finding other examples of collective predicates and of constructing diagnostic contexts for them.

Consider now a quite different sort of exercise. Students are given the information that the German cognates of the English words *right* and *night* are [rɛxtə] and [naxt] respectively. They are told that German and English are related languages, and then asked to suggest an explanation for the fact that the English words pronounced [rayt] and [nayt] are spelled with the 'silent' digraph *gh*. Once this is established, the next step is to compare the English and German words with the Latin cognates [re:ktus] and [noktem], and from there to proceed to an introduction to Grimm's Law. (Recall that these students have read Fromkin and Rodman — they can be presumed to know some phonetics.) All this might sound quite ambitious for junior high school students, but I doubt it would be any harder than solving quadratic equations by factoring, which is a routine part of ninth grade algebra.

'Ah yes,' says the skeptic, 'but isn't this all very elitist? Who except a bunch of ivory tower academics cares about any of this anyway? How is this going to improve society?'

There is an answer to this question. If you want to create a truly elitist society, one in which a very few (a priesthood, if you will) control everything, the best way to do so is to deny substantive education to the masses. Inevitably, however much we try to keep it from happening, there will be those intelligent enough to learn on their own, ambitious enough to do so, and ruthless enough to use what they know for their own advancement at the expense of the hapless, undereducated majority. Substantive education must include the development of knowledge about language and skill in using it, and there seems no way to do justice to these twin aims without prescriptivism of a sort. The trick is to manage all of this without bringing back Miss Fidditch. It will be interesting to see how well we do.

NOTES

An earlier version of this paper was presented to the Minnesota Center for Advanced Study in Language, Style and Literary Theory. It seemed appropriate for this volume since I owe to Bob Stockwell some of the best examples I know of with which to debunk dogmatic prescriptivism.

1. I use this term in the sense in which it is employed in Richard Rodriguez' *Hunger of Memory* (New York: Godine).

2. For example, I doubt that even Edwin Newman would insist that we say *Spaghetti are good*, or that *et cetera* be pronounced [ɛtkɛtərə]. Abandonment of dogmatic prescriptivism most emphatically does not mean that we can no longer have any fun roasting the pop grammarians.

3. There is one respect in which I would agree with the view, otherwise difficult to defend, that standard English should be taught to the population to whom it is not native as a foreign language, and it is this: there is no automatic presumption in second language instruction that there is something wrong with the student's first language. The reason for dealing with usage separately is thus that the model, second language teaching, is different.

4. I owe this particular example to John Corcoran.

7

Middle English *enst,* Not *evest*

SHERMAN M. KUHN

There are four passages in the *Cursor Mundi* containing a word which the editor transcribed *enst*.[1] The word occurs in two manuscripts of the text, British Library MS. Cotton Vespasian A. 3 (Vsp) and Göttingen University Library MS. Theol. 107 (Göt), as well as in a fragment of the text found in Edinburgh, Library of the College of Physicians (Phys-E). All three are from the Northern area and are regarded as among the best examples of the Northern Dialect of Middle English. Besides these, Richard Morris printed the text of a Northeast Midland copy of the *Cursor,* Oxford, Bodleian Library MS. Fairfax 14 (Frf); a Northwest Midland copy, Trinity College Cambridge MS. R. 3. 8 (Trin-C); and a fragment which is north Midland, rather eastern than western, Oxford, Bodleian MS. Laud 416 (Ld).[2] The poem was originally written early in the fourteenth century, probably before 1325, but the manuscript copies are later: Vsp, Göt, Frf, Trin-C, and Phys-E probably during the last quarter of the century, Ld somewhere about 1460. *Enst* probably occurs also in the poem *Wit and Will* (*Wit & W.*),[3] although the editor transcribed it *eust,* and the letter in the MS is of dubious shape and could certainly have been intended for a *u*. This text, written about 1400, appears on fragments of a manuscript which were used to patch some leaves of a printed copy of the *York Missal* (now in the Cambridge University Library) associated with prominent sixteenth-century Yorkshire families. From his dialect, the copyist was apparently from the Midlands, but occasional Northern forms in his work suggest that he was copying an exemplar in the Northern dialect.[4] The five passages, with manuscript variants, are as follows:

1. Als he þat sibb was to sathan,
   Wit nith and *enst* and iuel witt,
   þe water wissing can he ditt ...
   And spilt þe werk þat iesus wroght. (Vsp 11940-4)
       Wid erd and *enst* and euil witt (Göt 11941)

86

Wiþ erþe & wiþ euel witt (Trin-C 11941)
With erthe and with euyll wyt (Ld 11941)

2. þe princes als his ful faas
   Wit *onst* a night again him ras;
   Als prisun þai him tok for-þi. (Vsp 18551–3)
   Wid *enst* and nith again his ras (Göt 18552)
   Wiþ wraþþe & envye on him roos (Trin-C 18552)
   Wiþ pompe & pride againe him ras (Frf 18552)

3. Bot in pride and in trecheri,
   In nith and *enst* and licheri ...
   þat man right nu his lijf in ledis. (Vsp 23137–41)
   In nith and *enst* and licheri (Göt 23138)
   In niþe and *enest* and licheri (Phys-E 23138)
   In nythe & onde & lecchery (Trin-C 23138)
   & in nyste & in liccherie (Frf 23138)

4. þai þat war fild wit *enst* and hete,
   þat iþenli þair hertes ete,
   þar wormes sal þaim vnder wrote. (Vsp 23279–81)
   þaa þat war fild of *enst* and hete (Göt 23279)
   þat þai war fild of *enist* and hete (Phys-E 23279)
   þo þat euer had wraþþe & nyþe (Trin-C 23279)
   & þa þat ware fulle of enuye & hete (Frf 23279)

5. Alle þis manshedemen, als mani eren in toune,
   þat haues oende and *euste* til þar euen-cristen. (*Wit & W.* G, 8–9)

Enst (or was it *eust*? or *evst*?) was obviously a rare word in late fourteenth-century English. Midland scribes were usually unable to handle it at all and either substituted some other word or simply omitted it. Even the Northern scribe who copied Vsp had trouble with *enst and nith* in example 2. The Northwest Midland scribe of *Wit and Will* must have been trying to copy what he saw before him in his exemplar, but he misspelled *onde* 'malice, hatred' and wavered between *u* and *n* in *euste*. The word is not attested in Old English nor in any Middle English dialect outside the North nor in any Northern or mixed-Northern text except the *Cursor* and *Wit and Will*.

Our dictionaries do not record *enst* as a word. In the *Oxford English Dictionary*, all of Morris's *n*'s are taken to be *u*'s, phonetically [v]'s, and the resulting entry is *Evest*, defined 'envy, malice' and derived from OE *æf*- 'from, away from' (cognate with German *ab*) and OE *ēst* 'grace, favor', etc. The forms listed are *æfest, æfst, æfist, efest*,[5] which appear only in Old English, and *evest, evist, eust, oust,* which are cited only from the *Cursor.* In Stratmann-Bradley also, we find the entry *evest* 'envy, malice', derived from OE *æfest,* and all forms cited from *Cursor.* Both dictionaries suggest comparison with *eft,* a noun which occurs twice in the phrase *eft and nithe* in the *Northern Homilies*[6] and is treated as a possible variant of *evest.* The *Middle English Dictionary* followed the older authorities (wrongly, I now believe), entering *evest* 'envy, or malice', derived from OE *æf-ĕst, æfst,* illustrated by two early quotations, in which the word is spelled *æfest-;*[7] the two *eft* examples from the *Northern Homilies,* which are treated as errors for *efst;*[8] two quotations from *Cursor,* in which the *n*'s are treated as errors for *u;* and the single quotation from *Wit and Will.*

There are serious objections to *æfest* as the Old English etymon of an ME *evest.* In the first place, the expected form of a Northern Middle English reflex of *æfest* would be *avest,* not *evest.* Texts in the Northumbrian dialect of Old English, from which the dialect of Vsp, Göt, and Phys-E is descended, invariably have *æ* (i.e., *æfest, æfist, æfista*), which in an accented syllable[9] would appear as *a* in Northern Middle English. The only dialects of Old English in which the *e* would normally appear are the Mercian and the Kentish, in which the /æ/ from fronting of Germanic /a/ underwent the sound change called 'second fronting' (Karl Luick's *zweite Aufhellung*) to become a sound which, while not so high front as /e/ from Gmc. /e/, was close enough to it to be spelled *e.*[10] As I pointed out in 1939,[11] this change occurred later than the prehistoric sound changes (i.e. in the eighth to early ninth centuries) and could have spread from Mercian into Northumbrian to a very limited extent, if at all. Although *efest does not appear in any of the Mercian or mixed-Mercian texts,[12] the derived adjective *efestig* 'envious' (corresponding to WS *æfestig*) appears in the Mercian gloss to the *Vespasian Psalter,* i.e. *ðes efestgan* (cf. WS *þæs æfestgan*), weak singular, genitive, masculine, glossing *invidi.*[13] The *efestes* in the gloss to the *Benedictine Rule* (see note 5) may be due to Kentish influence, or it may represent mere scribal confusion of *æ* and *e.* It appears in a late West Saxon text, in which *æfest-* would be the expected form.

My dating of the second fronting has been controversial ever since I proposed it in 1939. I shall not repeat or attempt to answer the arguments advanced against the late eighth-century to early ninth-century dating, since Thomas E. Toon has already performed that service for Anglo-Saxonists very effectively.[14] In addition to analyzing the sound changes, as a historical linguist should, and illustrating and explaining orthographic variations in the early OE texts by statistical methods, he has done something that linguists frequently neglect to do: he has consulted the historians. He has shown how the spread of phonetic and phonemic changes are related to the rise and fall of kingdoms, the formation and dissolution of alliances and hegemonies, and the political history of a period in general. I have nothing to add at this time, but I should like to emphasize a few points. Please note that, in Toon's chronology of the early vowel changes (pp. 204–5), his first six changes, ending with *i*-umlaut (or *i*-mutation) were complete, according to most historical linguists, by the close of the sixth century, while the seventh (the raising and rounding of nasalized Gmc. /a/) and the eighth (smoothing) were far advanced toward completion in the seventh century, although they were still in progress in the eighth. It is in these changes that Mercian and Northumbrian most closely resemble each other, and it is no coincidence that the final separation of Mercia from Northumbria occurred in the latter half of the seventh century under the Mercian king, Wulfhere (657–74). If the ninth change, the second fronting, had occurred in the fifth century, as some scholars suppose, it should have been shared by Northumbrian.[15] As Toon points out (p. 152), the second fronting is shared by Mercian and Kentish because, during the eighth and early ninth centuries, Kent was a dependency of Mercia; communication between the two kingdoms was constant, even if not always friendly.

It is true that sporadic examples of *e* for /æ/ from Gmc. /a/ appear in the Northumbrian texts, and some of these may be due to the second fronting. The *Cursor* also contains sporadic examples of *e* where we should expect to find *a*. The instances are rare, however, and most of them are better explained by analogy than by regular phonological development; e.g., *efter* 'after' (probably influenced by *eft* adv.), usually written *after*; *gedir* 'to gather' (cf. *togeder*), usually spelled *gader* or *gadir*. More difficult to explain by analogy are *gedling* for *gad(e)ling* 'vagabond' and *gres* 'grass', from Nhb. *gærs, gers*. It is possible, of course, that a by-form of Nhb. *æfest* with *e* due to second fronting survived until the fourteenth century, but not really probable. It is even more unlikely that the unexpected forms, *euest*, *eust*, etc., would be used exclusively, to the total exclusion of the expected *auest.

A second objection to *evest* arises from the spelling *eust(e)*, which occurs, or is alleged to occur, eight times in the five passages quoted above. This supposedly represents /evst(e)/, with a voiced spirant /v/ followed by the voiceless /st/-cluster. Such a juxtaposition of consonants is not in keeping with what we know of the phonology and spelling practices of either Northumbrian or Northern Middle English. In Old English, only the voiceless allophone of /f/, namely [f], occurred before voiceless consonants. Thus, *æfest* would be pronounced [ævest], with the voiced allophone used between vowels or between a liquid or nasal and a vowel; but *æfste* would represent [æfste]. In the *Cursor* and in *Wit and Will*, the phoneme /v/, spelled *u* and no longer an allophone of /f/, is normally used between vowels or between liquid or nasal and vowel;[16] e.g., *aueril* 'April', *cuunand* 'covenant', *deuls* 'devils', *driue* 'to drive', *selue* 'self', *serue* 'to serve'. The voiceless /f/ is normal before a voiceless consonant. A *u* in that position would represent a vocalic /u/, often but not invariably in a word of Latin or Romance origin. The contrast between /f/ and /u/ may be illustrated by the following pairs: *after* 'after', *auter* 'altar'; *beft* 'struck, beat', *beuté* 'bounty'; *theifs* 'thieves', *theus* 'customs'. When a *u* for /v/ would otherwise appear before a voiceless consonant, a vowel usually intervenes; e.g., *caitiueté* beside *caitifté* 'captivity', *fiuet* beside *fift* 'fifth', *fiueten* beside *fiften* 'fifteen', *giuetes* beside *giftes* 'gifts', *giues* beside *gifs* 'gives', *haues* beside *hafs* 'has'.[17]

There are exceptions to the rules, but they are rare and usually explainable on the basis of obvious analogies, as for example, *caitiuté* 'captivity'. I can think of no such easy analogy in the case of *eust(e)*, the commonest variant of our supposed *evest*.

A third objection has to do with meaning. It is less clear-cut and conclusive than the phonological objections; nevertheless, it seems to me to demand consideration. The commonest meaning of Old English *æfest* is 'envy, jealousy'. The word is used to render Latin *invidia* in translations and glosses, also to render *livor* in the sense 'envy'. It occupies the position of *invidia* in lists of the deadly sins. It occurs fairly often, without any Latin lemma to guide us, in contexts which clearly point to 'envy' or 'jealousy' and rule out such other possibilities as 'anger, hatred', etc. In other instances, the word appears in contexts, by itself or in long lists of sins, where the meaning could be, and very probably is, 'envy' but where something like 'hatred' or 'anger' would make reasonable sense. I have noticed three rare meanings: 'zeal', rendering *zelus*; 'striving, rivalry', rendering *aemulatio*; and, once, 'the Devil', rendering *zabulus*.

OE *æfest* usually appears by itself or in lists of sins, but occasionally it enters into combination with other sin names to form pairs: *æfest & anda* 'enmity', *æfest ne anda*, *æfest & gecid* 'strife', *æfest & oferhygd* 'pride', *anda and æfest*, *elnung* 'zeal' *vel æfista*;[18] or triads: *æfest & geflit* 'contention' *& cyd* 'strife', *biternesse* 'bitternesses' *anda and æfst*, *facen* 'deceit' *& leasunga* 'lies' *& æfeste*, *unrihtwisnesse* 'unrighteousnesses' *& niðas* 'hatreds' *& æfest*. In one of these, the paired items are intended as synonyms, *elnung vel æfista*, a double gloss to *zelus* 'zeal' in the *Lindisfarne Gospels*, John 2. 17. In the other phrases, the components appear to be differents rather than sames, and *æfest* may be assumed to have the common meaning 'envy, jealousy'. None of the phrases occurs with any significant frequency; several occur only once in the entire corpus of OE.

In Middle English, the supposed reflex of OE *æfest* shows a very different semantic pattern. The examples are few, and their uses are restricted. The common Old English meaning 'envy' is hard to find. Of the five examples of the word, only one (the first) occurs in a context that might suggest an interpretation like 'envy' or 'jealousy'. The little boy who destroyed the miniature lakes which the child Jesus had made in the clay could have been motivated by jealousy of another's workmanship. On the other hand, he could have acted out of sudden anger or longstanding hate. Or perhaps he felt anguish or distress at seeing Jesus' skillful work — something akin to *angustia*. The remaining four contexts contain nothing that would suggest envy or jealousy on the part of the malefactors. In each of the five passages, the word with which we are chiefly concerned forms part of something which looks like a set phrase: *enst* (? *eust*) *and nith* (2), *nith and enst* (? *eust*) *and iuel witt* (1), *nith and enst* (? *eust*) *and licheri* (3), *enst* (? *eust*) *and hete* (4), *oende and euste* (? *enste*) (5). The word does not occur independently or in any list longer than a triad. This suggests to me that *enst* (? *eust*) was an old word in the fourteenth century, preserved only in a few rather fixed constructions. Its precise meaning may have been uncertain to the writers, even less certain to the scribes who copied it.

The words substituted for *enst* (? *eust*) in the Midland copies of the *Cursor* may shed a little light on the meaning. In example 2, Trin-C substitutes *wraþþe & envye* for *enst* (? *eust*) *and nith*. Both *nith* and *envie* in Middle English frequently meant 'ill will, enmity, hostility, hatred' and can be taken as roughly synonymous,[19] leaving *enst* (? *eust*) equated with *wraþþe* 'anger, wrath'. In example 4, Trin-C substitutes *wraþþe & nyþe* for *enst* (? *eust*) *and hete*, Since *hete* 'hate' could also be a synonym for *nith*, once more *wraþþe* is left as the equivalent of *enst* (? *eust*). In the same passage, Frf reads *enuye & hete*, and as we have seen, *envie* could mean 'enmity', etc., as well as 'envy'. These substitutions suggest that *enst* (? *eust*) was a stranger to the Midland dialects of the fourteenth century, and that scribes, perhaps influenced by the contexts, felt the word to be either 'anger' or 'hatred', with 'envy' as a remote possibility. Example 3 is more complicated than the others. Here, Trin-C uses the substitute *onde*, which frequently meant 'hatred, malice, enmity', frequently also 'envy', less frequently 'anger, wrath', also, rarely, 'distress, anxiety' (according to the *Middle English Dictionary*), probably the same sense which the *Oxford English Dictionary* defines as 'emotion, perturbation of mind'. This last sense could be translated neatly into German as *Angst*.

The fourth objection is a little matter of minims. Anyone who has had extensive experience with late medieval English manuscripts knows that, in the latter part of the fourteenth century, many scribes began to be careless about the formation of the minim letters: *i, m, n,* and *u*. Instead of beginning the second minim of *n* or the second or third minim of *m* at the top of the preceding minim and making a curved connecting line before starting the down-stroke, a scribe would merely skip from the bottom of one minim to the top of the next, leaving the minims unjoined at the top. Similarly in the case of *u*, instead of joining the two minims with a shallow curved line at the bottom, a scribe would lift his pen at the bottom of the first minim and move directly to the top of the second. Thus, there are many *n*'s and *u*'s that look exactly alike, and *m*'s that could be mistaken for *iii*.[20] The surviving manuscripts of the *Cursor Mundi* were written by scribes who not only were careless about joining minims but also frequently mistook *n* for *u* and *u* for *n*. Sarah Horrall, who has studied the *Cursor* manuscripts much more thoroughly than most of us, reports that *u* and *n* are 'not distinguished' in Vsp (p. 18), that *u* and *n* are 'not always distinguished' in Göt (p. 20), and that *u* and *n* are 'not distinguished' in the portion of Phys-E from which our examples of *enest* (? *euest*) and *enist* (? *euist*) are taken (p. 21).[21]

Cyril Wright's facsimile of a portion of Vsp[22] bears out Horrall's description of that manuscript. In the facsimile, I see 70 *n*'s, of which 42 are completely, or almost completely, closed at the top and look like *n*'s, 27 look like nothing more than two minims and could be mistaken for *u*'s, and one (in *dane* 2.1) is closed at the bottom and looks like a *u*. I see 23 *u*'s, of which two are closed at the bottom like proper *u*'s (in *cum* 1.23 and *Bituix* 2.15), four are closed at the top and look like *n*'s (in *qui* 1.7, *squilk* 1.14, *dun* 2.10, *giue* 2.11), and 17 consist of two separate minims and could be read either way. I do not expect everyone to see precisely as I do, but I believe that anyone who examines the facsimile closely will reach the same general conclusion as I have: *u* and *n* in Vsp cannot be distinguished on the basis of form alone. This partly explains why Morris read all of the controversial letters in the four *Cursor* passages as *n*'s, while the makers of the *Oxford* read them all as *u*'s. I say 'partly' because I suspect that the lexicographers were biased in favor of *u*: reading *u* as [v] provided them with a neat (though false) connection with OE *æfest*.

I may have suffered from a bias in favor of *n* when I first examined my glossy print of *Wit and Will*, fragment G, obtained from the Cambridge University Library. Perhaps I saw *enste* instead of *euste* because I had already perceived the phonetic objections to the latter and because I had seen the possible relationship between *enst* and the German *Angst*. After examining all of the *u*'s (16) and all of the complete *n*'s (26)[23] in the fragment, I am inclined to accept Dickins's reading. The *n*'s are generally closed, or almost closed, at the top, the only dubious one being the first *n* of *manshedemen* (line 8). Five of the *u*'s are closed or nearly closed at the top, so that they resemble *n*'s: *follues* (2), *leute* (5), *louies* (5), *toune* (8), and *euen-* (9). One is closed at both top and bottom, *turned* (10). The rest look like pairs of minims, although the second minim of the *u* in *euste* (9) has a little on-stroke at top left which might suggest that the scribe intended to write an *n*, or merely that he lowered his pen too soon. I accept the form as *euste* but assume that it was copied from a late fourteenth-century manuscript in which the *n*'s and *u*'s were not carefully distinguished.

Of the four arguments against ME *evest*, the first two are conclusive, the third is strongly suggestive, and the last is a warning against one of the pitfalls in late Middle English orthography, into which some lexicographers (including myself) have fallen. The word is certainly not *evest* or any variant like *evst* or *ovst*. If a case can be made for *enst* as an alternative, I believe that we should accept it.

Although no ancestral form of *enst* survives in the Old English texts, there is ample precedent for accepting a derivation from Old English. An examination of any of our historical dictionaries will reveal a considerable number of words which must have existed in Old English although they did not appear in writing until centuries later. The word has cognates in the Germanic languages most closely related to Old English: Old High German *angust*, Middle High German *angest* 'fear, terror, dread; anxiety; anguish, distress'; Middle Low German *angest*, *anxt* 'fear, dread; anxiety; that which causes fear, danger'; Middle Dutch *anxt*, *angest*, *ancst*, and (with loss of *g* or *c* in the consonant cluster) *anst* 'fear, dread; anxiety; awe, respect; shame; danger, peril'; Old Frisian *angost*, (with rounding of [ɑ] before nasal) *ongost* 'fear, dread; anxiety'. All of these, as well as ME *enst*, are descended from the Latin *angustia* 'difficulty, distress', etc., probably pronounced [aŋgustja] in the Vulgar Latin of the Roman merchants and soldiers with whom the Germanic tribes made their earliest contacts with Latin speakers.[24]

After the Angles and Saxons borrowed the Latin word, probably about the same time that it entered Low German and Frisian, certainly while the English were still on the Continent, the word stress was shifted to the first syllable, and the [ɑ] began to round to [ɔ] before the nasal. By *i*-umlaut, [ɔŋgʊstja] became [ɔŋgystja], with the front rounded vowel [y]. The [y], in turn, triggered a type of secondary *i*-umlaut peculiar to Old English, producing something like [öŋgystja].[25] As a result of sound changes in the unstressed syllables, this last became [öŋgɛst(ɪ)], which, if it had been recorded in the eighth century, would probably have taken the written shape *œngest* or *œngist*; cf. *hœngist* 'Hengest' in the early manuscripts of Bede's *Ecclesiastical History*. Later the [ö] was narrowed before the nasal, to produce [ɛŋgɛst], [ɛŋgst], inflected [ɛŋg(ɛ)stɛ], etc. Loss of /g/ in the *ngst*-cluster would then produce the form *enst* [ɛnst] as we see it in Northern Middle English. The forms *enest* and *enist* represent orthographic (perhaps phonetic) variations of the fourteenth century; and the lone example of *onst* is probably due, not to any unumlauted by-form, but to confusion of *o* with one of the varieties of *e* in use around 1400.

All of the sound changes posited are well known and are fully described in the grammars and handbooks of Old English, except perhaps the last, the loss of a palato-velar stop in a consonant cluster. This one is noted, among other reductions of consonant clusters, by Karl Luick,[26] but since Luick offers very few examples, I shall supplement his evidence. The cluster *ngst* appears rarely in Old English but may be seen in *hengest*, *hengst* 'horse, steed', also as a personal name, *Hengest*. In Middle English, *hengest* in its full form is a literary word, perhaps a conscious archaism of the historians and poets. In compounds which were in common use, the *g* was often dropped. In the compound *hengestman*, originally no doubt a servant or an officer in charge of horses, in Middle English 'an attendant, a retainer', etc., in present use 'a henchman', the first element in Middle English appears variously as *hengest-* 1360, *henxt-* 1400, *hengs-* 1345, *hens-* 1393, *heynce-* 1440, *henche-* (fifteenth century). The forms of place names are revealing: Hinksey, Berkshire, appears as *Hengestesige* in a document of *c*959, *Henxteseya* 1389, *Henstesia* 1177, *Hensteseye* 1247–8; Henstridge, Somerset, as *Hengstesrig* 956, *Heynstrugge* 1243; Hinxworth, Hertfordshire, as *Hengstworth* 1196, *Hensteworth* 1199; Hensleigh, Devonshire, as *Hengsteleg* 1228, *Henxtelegh* 1270, (*Suth*)*enstelegh* 1407; Henscott, Devon, as *Engestecota* 1086, *Hengestecoth* 1242, *Heynstecote* 1333.

Other words with clusters containing a nasal followed by a palato-velar stop plus another consonant may be similarly reduced either in Old or in Middle English: OE *lengþ* 'length', ME *length, lenthe, leynth*; OE *lengten, lencten*, also *lenten* 'lent', ME *lencten*, etc., but most frequently *lenten*; OE *strengþ, strencþ, strenþ* 'strength', ME *strengthe, strenth, streinð, strynthe*; OE *drencte*, preterit of *drencan* 'to drown', ME *drencte, drente, dreynte*; OE *gemengeþ* 'mingles, mixes', ME *mengeth, meinth*; OE *swengde*, preterit of *swengan* 'to beat', ME *swende, sweinde*, past participle *sweynt.*

Defining *enst* is difficult because of the paucity of examples and the lack of variety in the contexts. The best I can do at present is: 'Anger, hatred; ? also, anguish, distress'. In any case, I cannot imagine any definition that would call for a semantic jump between *angustia* and *enst* greater than that between the Latin word and some of the meanings recorded for the borrowed forms of it in the Continental West Germanic languages.

NOTES

A portion of this essay was read before the Indo-European Linguistics Session of the Summer Meeting of the Linguistic Society of America, Urbana, 28 July 1978.

1. Richard Morris (ed.), *Cursor Mundi: A Northumbrian Poem of the XIV Century*, EETS, OS, 57, 59, 62, 66, 68 (London, Kegan Paul, 1874–8). Abbreviations used for the manuscripts are those of the *Middle English Dictionary.*

2. I omit fragments printed by Morris which do not contain any of the four passages quoted.

3. Bruce Dickins (ed.), *The Conflict of Wit and Will*, Leeds School of English Language, Texts and Monographs, 4 (Leeds, 1937), Fragment G, p. 19.

4. The text is a mixture of the Northern and Midland dialects, with a few forms, noted by Dickins, which suggest a West Midland connection. 'I should tentatively assign these fragments,' says the editor, 'to the North-West Midland dialect, and to the northern limit of that dialect. Still the possibility of its being a Northern text modified by a West Midland scribe cannot be excluded,' *Op. cit.*, p. 14. I prefer the 'possibility' to the tentative assignment.

5. The form *efest* is listed but not illustrated in the quotations. I have searched the *Microfiche Concordance to Old English*, compiled by Antoinette diPaolo

Healey and Richard L. Venezky, and published by the Dictionary of Old English Project at the University of Toronto, 1980. This invaluable tool for research in Old English contains scores of examples of *æfest* and its variant spellings, *æfist, æfst,* etc.; but the only instance of *efest* that I could find is in H. Logeman (ed.), *The Rule of S. Benet, Latin and Anglo-Saxon Interlinear Version,* EETS, OS, 90 (1888), p. 110, line 8. *Efestes,* sg. gen., is a faulty gloss to *emulationes* but apparently the same word as *æfest.* For Logeman's discussion of the confusion of *e* and *æ* in this text, see pp. xliv–xlv. For his suggestion that the *e* for *æ* may be due to Kentish influence, see p. lxiii.

6. John Small (ed.), *English Metrical Homilies* (Edinburgh, William Paterson, 1862), pp. 35, 130. These homilies are in the MS which contains the fragment of *Cursor Mundi* designated 'Phys-E'.

7. Neither of these examples is a fair representative of a Middle English word. The first is from a transition text, partly ME and partly OE, in A.O. Belfour (ed.), *Twelfth Century Homilies in MS. Bodley 343,* EETS, OS, 137 (London, Kegan Paul, etc., 1909), p. 40, line 28. This homily was copied from an OE exemplar which must have been very close to the third homily in Max Förster (ed.), *Die Vercelli-Homilien,* Bibliothek der angelsächsischen Prosa, 12 (Hamburg, Henri Grand, 1932), pp. 53–71. For *æfest,* see p. 55, line 25. The second example, I regret to say, is simply the wrong word. Somewhere about the year 1200, *ðreo æfesteno* in an OE text was glossed *æfestes;* see S.J. Crawford, 'The Worcester Marks and Glosses', *Anglia* 52 (1928), p. 25. The word *æfesteno* has nothing to do with *æfest* 'envy'; it is the plural of *ǣfesten* (earlier *ǣwfæsten*) 'a legal or public fast'.

8. This *eft* has also been explained as a descendant of OE *eofot* 'crime, guilt'; Eduard Mätzner, *Altenglische Sprachproben,* II, ii (Berlin, Weidmannsche Buchhandlung, 1885).

9. Originally, *af- was a prefix, but in prehistoric OE the word accent was shifted from the root *ēst* to the prefix; the /a/ was then fronted to /æ/, and the /ē/ under weak stress was shortened and sometimes confused with other vowels.

10. For a brief explanation, see my article, 'On the Syllabic Phonemes of Old English', *Language* 37 (1961), 533–4; reprinted in Sherman M. Kuhn, *Studies in the Language and Poetics of Anglo-Saxon England* (Ann Arbor, Karoma Publishers, 1984), pp. 96–7.

11. 'The Dialect of the *Corpus Glossary*', *PMLA* 54 (1939), pp. 14–18; repr. in *Studies,* pp. 14–18.

12. A West Saxon form of the word, *æfeste,* glosses *inuidiam* in Farman's mixed-Mercian gloss to the Rushworth Matthew 27.18.

13. See the 'Mercian Glossary to the *Vespasian Psalter*', in my edition, *The Vespasian Psalter* (Ann Arbor, University of Michigan Press, 1965), pp. 187–273.

14. *The Politics of Early Old English Sound Change* (New York and London, Academic Press, 1983), pp. 202–5.

15. Someone will surely point out that the tenth change, velar umlaut, was shared by Mercian and Northumbrian, but this change was also shared by West Saxon and Kentish; its manifestations, however, were markedly different in the four dialects, indicating that the change began early but was not complete until much later.

16. The voiceless /f/ also occurs in these positions, but that is not relevant to this study.

17. The two examples of *eft* in the *Northern Homilies* are probably not forms of *evest* or *avest.* They have *e* rather than the *a* expected in the Northern dialect; and both must be emended to get the *s.* Perhaps Mätzner was correct in deriving this *eft* from OE *eofot* (see note 8).

18. *Æfest* is usually declined as a strong noun, sometimes masc., sometimes fem.; but this is one of several forms which follow the weak *n*-stem pattern.

19. Although each has other meanings, some of which are not shared by the other. The looseness with which several of these words are used makes semantic comparisons difficult and uncertain.

20. Unless, of course, the scribe has been taught to place a tick above each of his *i*'s — and remembers to do so.

21. Sarah M. Horrall (ed.), *The Southern Version of the Cursor Mundi*, Ottawa Mediaeval Texts and Studies, 1 (University of Ottawa Press, 1978).

22. C.E. Wright, *English Vernacular Hands from the Twelfth to the Fifteenth Centuries*, Oxford Palaeographical Handbooks (Oxford, Clarendon Press, 1960), plate 11. My examples are cited by column and line.

23. The top of the *n* of *-lorne* (line 2) has been cut off. My examples are numbered according to the lines in Dickins's transcription.

24. Angustia is descended from the same Indo-European root as OE *enge* 'narrow, oppressive', etc., OHG, Old Saxon *engi*, Gothic *aggwus*. It has been suggested that OHG *angust* and its cognates are descended directly from the IE root, but such derivation calls for the positing of suffixes and sound changes nowhere else exemplified.

25. Kuhn, 'On the Syllabic Phonemes', pp. 524, 527.

26. *Historische Grammatik der englischen Sprache* (Stuttgart, Tauchnitz, 1964), pp. 894–6.

8

Creoles, Triggers, and Universal Grammar

DAVID LIGHTFOOT

Many research programs make up what we call linguistics, and one of them seeks to find how people attain their mature linguistic capacity under usual childhood circumstances. Derek Bickerton, Hilda Koopman, Claire Lefebvre, Pieter Muysken and others have brought creoles into the empirical range of this program, and this raises some intriguing questions.[1]

An adequate account of language acquisition involves genetic principles which enable children to attain more than they experience, as they all routinely do. It is well known now that there are many principles which hold of people's mature grammars for which there is no direct evidence in their childhood experience; that experience consists of a finite set of utterances made in an appropriate context and does not include lists of 'ungrammatical' sentences, paraphrase relations, etc. In other words, the child's experience is less than the kind of evidence that one finds in *Linguistic Inquiry*, and the child is no 'little linguist'. Explanatory models used in this program say that a grammar emerges in a person after exposure to triggering experience and that this development is guided by principles which are available independently of experience, let us say genetically (cutting some corners — see Lightfoot 1982). In that case, any hypothesis about the genetic principles will affect the kinds of hypotheses which can be made about particular grammars, and vice versa. This applies also to the trigger experience; in fact, any hypothesis about any one of the three entities involved (trigger, mature grammar, genetic principles) will affect hypotheses about the other two entities. This much is simply the logic of the program, but the reality is somewhat different.

Considerable attention has been devoted to properties of particular grammars and to the kind of information which must be available to the child *a priori*, i.e. independently of experience. However, very little serious attention has been paid to the third component in the explanatory model, the trigger experience. Sometimes this has disastrous consequences, as when linguists propose a parametric difference between the grammar of an English speaker and that of an Italian speaker and pay no attention to how the parameter can be set. A useful critical stance for a reader of *Linguistic Inquiry* is to ask how the proposed parameters could be set, i.e. what the trigger experience would have to be; authors almost never specify the trigger and one often finds that the trigger would need to be something which is generally unavailable to children, e.g. information that certain forms do not occur. Ignoring the trigger experience often leads to incoherence.

Let us consider the trigger experience in the normal case. The most obvious point is that not everything that the child hears 'triggers' a device in the emerging grammar. For example, so-called 'performance errors' and slips of the tongue do not entail that the hearer's grammar be amended in such a way as to generate such deviant expressions, presumably because a particular slip of the tongue does not occur frequently enough to have this effect. This suggests that a trigger is something that is robust in a child's experience, occurring frequently. Children are typically exposed to a diverse and heterogeneous linguistic experience, consisting of different styles of speech and dialects, but only those forms which occur frequently for a given child will act as triggers, thus perpetuating themselves and being absorbed into the productive system which is emerging in the child: the grammar. It is clear, then, that triggers, i.e. expressions which set off in the emerging grammar some device which permits them to be generated, are a subset of the child's total experience and consist only of robust elements. The fact that only robust elements are triggers permits the child to steer a course through the flux of experience and not to be 'thrown off course' by exposure to occasional instances of non-normal speech, speech which is not absorbed into the child's productive system. One can ask how small this subset is, and I have argued recently for Depth 0 learnability: that triggers are found only in main clauses, that there is nothing new to be learned from subordinate clauses (Lightfoot 1984).[2] Just how robust an element must be to be a trigger for some parameter may vary from one parameter to the next, and almost certainly does so. So, if we view the acquisition of lexical items as a process of parameter fixing, i.e. fixing feature values, then the work of Susan Carey (1978, etc.) shows that certain features can be established on the basis of just one exposure to the relevant datum; other features require more extensive exposure. In contrast, the work of Carol Chomsky (1969) suggests that fixing the 'subject control' parameter of verbs like *promise* requires quite extensive input and is normally not achieved until a fairly late age. For some discussion of the possible role of maturational factors in determining which parameters can be fixed at which age, see Gleitman (1981). These are interesting research questions, but for now we may agree that not everything a child hears is a trigger.

If that is the normal case, one can easily identify non-normal cases. Sometimes there is no trigger experience, as for Genie (Curtiss 1977) or the wild boy of Aveyron, as portrayed by François Truffaut in 'L'enfant sauvage', or the deaf children raised in non-signing homes studied by

Goldin-Meadow (1979). Sometimes there is a trigger experience which is more diverse and heterogeneous than usual, as for children who are raised in multilingual homes. Or there may be an exceptional amount of degenerate input, as for children raised monolingually by immigrant parents who do not fully command the language in which the children are being raised. All of these non-normal circumstances raise interesting questions about the nature of the trigger experience and the effects of modifying some aspect of a given trigger in some way. We will understand more of these unusual conditions as due attention is paid to the less unusual, more or less regular conditions. Since the trigger experience is a subset of the total experience, little will be gained from those costly experiments in which tape recorders are strapped to the backs of children for months on end, recording what they 'experience'. Much greater insight will come from the study of language change, where one can investigate the causes and effects of certain expressions becoming obsolete, ceasing to be part of childhood experience. In language change one can identify changes in the linguistic environment at some point and, when the record is rich enough, examine the consequences of those changes in the next generation. At least, that is my view of the interest of language change for this research program.

This, then, is one perspective from which work on creole languages can be read. Creoles seem to be languages like any other and they can be investigated on a par with French, Dutch, Chinese, etc., leading to revisions and refinements of theories of Universal Grammar in the usual way. As with French, Dutch, and Chinese, it is possible that a certain creole will manifest unique properties not as yet manifested by speakers of other languages, but very unlikely that it will require postulating special genetic principles which have no detectable effect elsewhere. However, creoles are acquired, at least initially, under highly unusual conditions, where the linguistic experience of a particular generation of children is quite different from that a generation earlier, and, more importantly, where the linguistic input for that generation differs quite dramatically from the capacity the children eventually attain. If we can discover some properties of the grammars which emerge in these people, and if we know something about the kind of childhood experience they had which might have triggered certain aspects of the grammar, we may be able to learn something about triggers in general, and about the limiting cases. The particularly dramatic contrast between the input and the mature capacity of the first creole speakers should make it easier to identify which elements of their experience acted as triggers for the emerging grammars. This is to view the acquisition of creoles as 'first-language learning with restricted input' (Bickerton 1984b).

In what we have called the normal case, then, the **relevant** input for the child, i.e. the trigger experience, is a subset of the total experience, perhaps consisting only of simple clauses, and the total experience involves considerable redundancy in the 'information' available to the child. Under this perspective, the restrictedness of the input to creole-speaking children does not look as dramatic as when one is concerned with the total experience that children have. That is, the difference from the non-creole cases will not be as extensive. The question now arises: to what extent does the creole child lack relevant input for fixing the parameters provided by the linguistic genotype? The answer to this question might be: not at all or not very much. This would explain how children with apparently quite impoverished input nonetheless attain a mature capacity more or less as rich structurally as that of children with a more extensive and more uniform input; it would simply mean that children with apparently impoverished input are not exposed to as much redundant information. Answering the question, of course, will require fairly detailed knowledge of the input to the first creole speakers. This kind of information is sometimes available, and this is one reason why Sankoff's work on Tok Pisin is so important (see Sankoff and Laberge 1973, etc.). Usually, however, the trigger experience of original creole speakers is shrouded in the mists of history, and written records of early stages of creole languages are meagre. This is not to say that no information is available; Bickerton has done interesting detective work on the early context of Saramaccan. See also Singler (1984) for discussion of relevant demographic material for other creole languages, which indicates roughly which languages were available as potential trigger experiences and to what degree.

Under a research program seeking to find how children acquire their mature linguistic capacity, creole languages can be studied profitably in the context of unusual trigger experiences, and one can expect that the sharp contrast between the input and the eventual mature capacity, at least in the early stages of creole languages, will provide a useful probe into the nature of trigger experiences in general. However, one finds claims in the linguistic literature which go far beyond this. Aitchison (1980), for example, asserts that one cannot expect to understand how languages change historically without studying the creolization process, that discussion of historical change 'which contains no mention of pidgins and creoles is somewhat surprising in this day and age'; however, she does not indicate how creoles reveal anything special about the general nature of language change from one generation to the next, i.e. something which is not manifested in the history of non-creole languages, and thus why it is essential for historical linguists to study them. Similarly, Bickerton expects more than insight on the nature of triggers. He expects the study of creoles, or at least plantation creoles, to give 'special evidence' about the nature of the genetic principles, particularly about the value of the unmarked settings of the parameters of Universal Grammar. In general one should be wary of claims that certain areas of data have privileged status and will be the only ones to reveal certain aspects of the mental genotype, although these claims are frequently made. How often have we heard child psychologists say that we **must** study children's speech if we wish to discover something about the linguistic genotype, or aphasiologists say that we **must** study aphasia, creolists say that we **must** study creoles to gain any understanding of how languages change historically? The proof of these claims lies in the interest of the claims made about Universal Grammar by aphasiologists, creolists, *et al.*

The particular form of Bickerton's claim seems to have been changing, which of course is no bad thing. In his articles in *Scientific American* and *Behavioral and Brain Sciences* he was arguing that the grammars of creoles were themselves genetically given; this was his Language Bioprogram Hypothesis.[3] He drew an analogy with Herodotus' story about the king who isolated a child and waited to hear the first word the child produced; the child produced a Phrygian word, which convinced the king that this was the oldest language. The notion was that children who had no real trigger experience would have to rely more or less entirely on their bioprogram, which would thus be manifested directly in the creole grammars. Now there have been many occasions when I was baffled as to how some aspect of English could be attained and I was tempted to say that it was genetically wired in. After all, if the language I am working on is genetically given, the language you are working on is just your problem.

This position, which left unexplained why creole speakers should differ from pathological cases like Genie, seems to have been abandoned in Bickerton's current and forthcoming work, and happily so. Now the basic notion is that every parameter has an unmarked setting, and unless experience instructs the child differently, the unmarked setting will be adopted. And creoles emerge as children select the unmarked setting for every parameter (Bickerton 1984b). (Although this seems to be the position of Bickerton 1984b, his 1984c takes a slightly different position, that parameter settings will either reflect the setting of the superstrate language or the unmarked value.) Four comments on this.

1. Bickerton (1984b: 11) says that apart from creole evidence 'we have no reliable or generally accepted means for determining what are the unmarked settings of any parameters that we may hypothesize and we have no principled, systematic or even explicit means for deciding between alternative parameters'. This is puzzling. The whole point of comparative work is to define correctly the parameters provided in Universal Grammar. Rizzi (1982: ch. 2), to take one of many possible examples, argued that S or S' may be a bounding node for Subjacency, after he considered two other ways of formulating the difference between English and Italian. He further argued that S must represent a less marked setting than S'. The reason was that if the English child had to 'learn' that S was a bounding node, this could be done only on the basis of knowing that certain sentences were ungrammatical; since such information is not available to children, such

101

a property could not be learned and must represent the unmarked case. The Italian child, on the other hand, could 'learn' that S' was a bounding node as a result of hearing certain complex sentences which in fact occur in Italian; those sentences act as a trigger for the marked property.[4] There most certainly is a basis for establishing which settings are marked.

2. As a matter of fact, Bickerton's prime example of a radical creole, Saramaccan, has a marked setting for at least one parameter. Some languages do not allow *wh*-items to be extracted from a subordinate clause. Such languages have been analyzed as having both S and S' as bounding nodes, and this must represent the least marked case. An English child goes to the next level of markedness (where only S is a bounding node) on hearing evidence that the least marked case does not hold, and the Italian child goes to a higher level of markedness (where S' is a bounding node) again on exposure to evidence that requires this. Saramaccan in this respect is like English: Bickerton has informed me that *wh*-items can be extracted from subordinate clauses, as in English.

Responding to an early version of this paper, Bickerton raised the question of how marked settings for parameters could ever arise:

> How did English get data that would cause a more marked setting to be chosen ...? The problem is one of infinite regression. English children set the parameter as they do because the data determine that setting, but the data was produced by an earlier generation which must have had the same setting on the basis of similar data, so you arrive at the conclusion that English must always have had the setting it has now.

This question really amounts to the broader question of why languages change at all. Many careers have been devoted to this matter, but here I will just make two points. First, a marked parameter setting is in some ways like the familiar problem of irregular verbs, and irregular verbs may arise in various ways. So, phonological amd morphological changes may affect a productive class of verbs in such a way that the class eventually has very few members; for a detailed example, consider the account of the English modal verbs in Lightfoot (1979: ch. 2), where it was argued that they became irregular verbs as a result of changes such as the loss of the independent subjunctive mood, some phonological levelling, etc. As a result of their new irregular status, a further reanalysis then took place. Second, Universal Grammar consists of principles and parameters which define the way in which grammars are uniform and the ways in which they may vary. The parameters, including the markedness settings, define the limits to variation, the limits to the kinds of innovations that speakers may make. So, for example, languages have various strategies for asking questions: Chinese has interrogative words in their 'logical' positions, some languages have interrogative words at the front of the clause and a resumptive pronoun in the logical position (*who₁ you saw a woman who met him₁ in New York*), and other languages, like English, have interrogative words at the front of the sentence with a gap in the logical position. Given the existence of, say, the resumptive pronoun strategy in some language, one can imagine speakers introducing as a stylistic variant the gap option, the new generation saying *who you saw?* for the older generation's *who you saw him?* If so, that strategy is necessarily subject to the demands of the Subjacency condition, and S and/or S' may be picked as the bounding node. This is the familiar notion of a fairly rigid genetic program which is open at the edges, as is required to account for the physical development of human beings. Our bodies have many common properties and some degree of variation 'at the edges', and some variation which can be induced by external factors such as excessive carbohydrate intake, etc. It is incontrovertible that languages change from generation to generation. This is due to stylistic innovation and sometimes to borrowing features of other languages; such innovations may in the course of time become 'grammaticized', i.e. they may trigger 'devices' in the grammars of subsequent speakers. Nobody knows why people innovate in this way, but they do, and hence I see no special problem for languages developing marked settings of parameters. Consequently, it seems perfectly legitimate for Bickerton and others to assume that this is a general mechanism of language change; indeed the notion is central to Bickerton's approach. The infinite regress problem does not arise; the mere fact that speakers of one generation utter some forms which occur productively in a later generation does not entail that they have the same parameter setting. We know that this entailment does not go through because we know that grammars may change from generation to generation. (For some discussion of grammar change along these lines, see Lightfoot 1982: ch. 8.)

3. Supposing that we had no evidence along these lines from Saramaccan, I see no reason to expect only unmarked settings in 'radical' creoles. Such an expectation seems to presuppose that marked settings require access to more extensive experience and perhaps to fairly exotic data, and that this is not available to the first speakers of a creole. This presupposition seems to me to be unwarranted. It is not hard to imagine a parameter which could have the marked setting on the basis of readily available data even in the first forms of a creole. For example, suppose that Bickerton is right and that all parameters have an unmarked setting. One parameter seems to be that an NP consists of a Spec and an N', with the order to be fixed depending on the language to which the child is exposed (for this parameter, see Lightfoot 1982: ch. 4). Suppose, with Bickerton, that one of those orders is marked. The marked setting (say, N' Spec) would be established on the basis of data which would be available almost every minute, e.g. expressions like *horse that, trees two*, etc.

103

4. But that raises the question of why one would want to say that either of the two settings for this parameter, Spec N' or N' Spec, should represent a marked value. The same point could be made for the parameter which puts a direct object in front of its verb or behind it, OV or VO; why should one of these values be marked? Why are they not equipotential? It is hard to see that specifying that one value is marked would contribute to solving any poverty of stimulus problem, which is the rationale for all properties of the linguistic genotype, as we saw, for example, with the bounding nodes for Subjacency.

The work which has brought creole languages into the arena of this research program is a welcome development. One always welcomes work on a new language from this perspective and the peculiar circumstances of the way creoles are acquired initially suggests that there may be something to be learned about the limits to triggers, where there are good records revealing the kind of childhood experience that early creole speakers had. I see no reason to expect that creoles will manifest properties of Universal Grammar, relating to the markedness settings of parameters or whatever, which cannot be detected in other languages, and I certainly do not accept this as an empirical conclusion of existing work.

I have tried to suggest here a way of looking at creole languages from the perspective of one research program. At a certain stage of investigation some area of data may provide a useful probe into some aspect of an explanatory model, and I have suggested the kind of probe that creoles might provide at this stage of research in one program: namely, they may be able to cast some initial light on the limits to trigger experiences. In that program, which seeks to find the genetic basis for language acquisition, it is most unlikely that one language or one area of data will manifest particular principles of the linguistic genotype which will not be manifested elsewhere. To make such a claim at this early stage of investigation would certainly be premature. Quite generally, I urge scepticism in the face of all claims to the effect that particular areas of data offer 'special evidence' for the existence of certain principles of the genotype, whether the area of data is creole languages, asphasia, or quantifiers in Kikuyu. Creolists may be able to advance our knowledge about the nature of the trigger experience where early records are rich enough; otherwise creole languages are likely to support claims about Universal Grammar which are qualitatively on a par with the claims supported by the study from this perspective of French and Italian. No more and no less.

NOTES

1. This paper began as a presentation to the Colloquium on Creoles and Universal Grammar at the 1984 Winter meeting of the Linguistic Society of America in

Baltimore. In relating historical change to the concerns of general linguistic theory, it deals with the central issue that has dominated Bob Stockwell's intellectual life. I have spent many hours discussing this issue with him happily and vigorously, and here I seek to broaden the base of our discussions by considering the relevance of creoles for the issue that set off our discussions ten years ago.

2. There are parameters proposed in the literature which seem to require that the child has access to Depth 2: doubly embedded clauses. One example is Rizzi's (1982) S vs. S' parameter as a bounding node: see below. However, I argue that the Italian child has to 'learn' that S is not a bounding node and that this conclusion may be drawn from the possibility of extracting elements from within subject NPs, and thus that the child does not need access to Rizzi's doubly embedded clauses.

3. For discussion of the language bioprogram hypothesis see Bickerton (1984a) and the peer commentary.

4. Rizzi argued that S' must be the bounding node in Italian because of the existence of sentences like *tuo fratello, a cui mi domando che storie abbiano raccontato, era molto preoccupato* 'your brother, to whom I wonder which stories they told, was very troubled,' where *a cui*, he argued, must move directly from its position as the indirect object of *raccontato* to the COMP of the upstairs clause.

REFERENCES

Aitchison, Jean. 1980. Review of Lightfoot 1979. *Linguistics* 18: 137–46.
Bickerton, Derek. 1983. 'Creole Languages', *Scientific American* 249: 116–22.
—— 1984a. 'The Language Bioprogram Hypothesis', *Behavioral and Brain Sciences* 7: 173–203.
—— 1984b. 'Creoles and UG: the Unmarked Case?'. Paper presented at the Winter meeting of the Linguistic Society of America, Baltimore.
—— 1984c. 'Learnability and the Structure of Parameters'. Mimeo, University of Hawaii.
Carey, Susan. 1978. 'The Child as Word Learner', in M. Halle, J.W. Bresnan, and G. Miller (eds.), *Linguistic Theory and Psychological Reality*. Cambridge, Mass.: MIT Press.
Chomsky, Carol. 1969. *The Acquisition of Syntax in Children from 5 to 10*. Cambridge, Mass.: MIT Press.
Curtiss, Susan. 1977. *Genie*. New York: Academic Press.
Gleitman, Lila. 1981. 'Maturational Determinants of Language Growth', *Cognition* 10: 103–14.
Goldin-Meadow, Susan. 1979. 'Structure in a Manual Communication System Developed Without a Conventional Language Model: Language Without a Helping Hand', in H. Whitaker and H.A. Whitaker (eds.), *Studies in Neurolinguistics*, vol. 4. New York: Academic Press.
Lightfoot, David. 1979. *Principles of Diachronic Syntax*. Cambridge: Cambridge University Press.
—— 1982. *The Language Lottery: Toward a Biology of Grammars*. Cambridge, Mass.: MIT Press.
—— 1984. 'The Child's Trigger Experience'. Mimeo, University of Maryland.
Rizzi, Luigi. 1982. *Issues in Italian Syntax*. Dordrecht: Foris.
Sankoff, Gillian, and Susan Laberge. 1973. 'On the Acquisition of Speakers by a Native Language', *Kivung* 6: 32–47.
Singler, John. 1984. Remarks on Bickerton 1984b. Paper presented at the Winter meeting of the Linguistic Society of America, Baltimore.

9

The Rise and Fall of the Vernacular

RONALD K.S. MACAULAY

Unum vernaculum ac domi natum (Varro)

ABSTRACT

In current sociolinguistic work, the term vernacular is being used in such widely differing senses that it may be the source of problems rather than a useful term. The need for well defined terminology to distinguish local varieties, social varieties, age-graded varieties, and speech styles is outlined.

Although, as Saussure pointed out, 'in the matter of language, people have always been satisfied with ill-defined units' (1959: 111), it has been a constant problem for linguistic investigation that it is the basic terms such as LANGUAGE and DIALECT which are hard to define (see Haugen 1966). Some years ago (see Macaulay 1973), I pointed out the risks of confusion when a term such as STANDARD LANGUAGE is used with reference to independent languages and also to dialect differences within a single language. Recently another term with a similar ambiguity, VERNACULAR, has become current in discussions of linguistic heterogeneity. This problem is reflected in the definition in Crystal's *A First Dictionary of Linguistics and Phonetics* (1980: 375):

(1) VERNACULAR A term used in *sociolinguistics* to refer to the indigenous *language* or *dialect* of a *speech* community, e.g. the vernacular of Liverpool, Berkshire, Jamaica, etc.

One problem with this kind of definition is the difficulty in defining a speech community (see Romaine 1980a). Another is that the range of language varieties to be found among the indigenous inhabitants increases exponentially as one moves from communities the size of Liverpool to those as complex as Jamaica. The next in sequence after the *etc.* might be the British Isles or the United States. This is the traditional use of the term 'vernacular' to refer to an independent language. Baugh (1957: 224), for example, cites English 'along with the other vernaculars' in contrast to Latin, and Bloomfield and Newmark (1965: 298) link the establishment of new nations in Europe 'to the rise of the vernaculars'. Fishman (1972) points out that vernacular literacy played an important part in this growth of nationalism. Haugen (1966) uses the term 'vernacular' with reference to an undeveloped language which may later develop into a standard language (his examples are Finnish and Modern Hebrew). Stewart (1962: 19) in his linguistic typology gives as examples of vernaculars 'most tribal languages of Africa and the Americas'. O'Barr (1976), for example, claims that there are about 120 African vernaculars in Tanzania. Common to these examples is the notion of VERNACULAR as a political term rather than a purely linguistic one, though there may be linguistic consequences of the standardization process, when it takes place, through the development of a writing system and the codification of prescriptive norms. Vernacular languages are in an inferior position politically until some social upheaval raises them to the dominant position. There is also a strong association with regionalism; a vernacular is a local language often contrasted with the language of an occupying foreign power. It is, however, difficult to perceive the language spoken in Liverpool or Berkshire in this sense.

In some recent work in sociolinguistics, the term VERNACULAR has been used in a rather different sense. The innovator is Labov who adopted the term BLACK ENGLISH VERNACULAR (BEV) to refer to 'that relatively uniform grammar found in its most consistent form in the speech of Black youth from 8 to 19 years old who participate fully in the street culture of the inner cities' (1972: xiii). There are several interesting aspects to this use of the term 'vernacular' which contrast with the traditional use outlined in the previous paragraph.

In the first place, it is not locally restricted in any narrow sense, since Labov elsewhere refers to 'the great uniformity of the Black English vernacular throughout the major cities of the North and South and even in most rural areas' (1973: 107). Secondly, BEV is explicitly restricted to a particular age-group and Labov (1973: 107–8) insists that there is no evidence that any adults consistently speak BEV, though he does not exclude the possibility. Consequently, BEV as described in Labov 1972 is an adolescent form of speech. Thirdly, ethnicity is a necessary but not sufficient condition for membership in the group. By definition, though not necessarily in practice (see Wolfram 1973), all speakers of BEV are Black but not all Blacks are speakers of BEV. Fourthly, being a speaker of BEV coincides with a number of activities which are known as full participation in the street culture.

Labov's use of the term 'vernacular' in Black English Vernacular is thus well defined and unambiguous. His reasons for choosing the term are clearly stated in Labov 1972. The term he had used previously, NONSTANDARD NEGRO ENGLISH (Labov, Cohen, Robins, and Lewis 1968), was potentially offensive to some people and he was unhappy with the label BLACK ENGLISH which, if used to describe his data, could be taken to imply that all Black Americans speak nonstandard English. The term 'vernacular' has positive connotations without implying conformity with the norms of the standard language, so it was an inspired choice.

Unfortunately, Labov extended his use of the term 'vernacular' to other situations which are less clearly defined. The most dangerous of these is given in Labov 1970 where the vernacular is defined as 'the style in which the minimum attention is given to the monitoring of speech' (46). This is similar to the term CASUAL SPEECH used in Labov 1966: 'By CASUAL SPEECH, in a narrow sense, we mean the everyday speech used in informal situations, where no attention is directed to language' (100). Although there is clear need for a term to describe casual speech in this sense, nothing but confusion can result from the decision to use the same term to describe a manner of speaking and a variety of speech. The ambiguity which can arise is shown in a later statement (Labov 1981: 3):

(2) Each speaker has a vernacular form, in at least one language; this may be the prestige dialect (as in the case of 'RP'), or a nonstandard variety.

'Form' in this quotation could possibly refer to a style of speech (the least monitored), though more likely it is intended to refer to the 'basic' system of an individual's speech, as it were, the basilect of his idiolect. What makes this use of the term 'vernacular' surprising is that, in the earlier article, Labov had been quite explicit that 'the vernacular is the property of the group, not the individual' (1973: 83). The reference to RP in (2) follows on a statement in the earlier article (Labov 1973: 112):

(3) There are communities where the basic vernacular is a prestige dialect which is preserved without radical changes as the adolescent becomes an adult. The class dialect used in British public schools [i.e. private boarding-schools, R.M.] had that well-formed character, and presumably a British linguist raised as a speaker of Received Pronunciation can serve as an accurate informant on it.

One of the surprising points about this is that Received Pronunciation (RP), as its name would suggest, is an accent, not an independent variety of speech. RP speakers are presumed to speak Standard English though not all speakers of Standard English have an RP accent. There is thus the somewhat paradoxical situation that there can be vernacular speakers of the standard language. It seems as if Labov is trying to make the term 'vernacular' do too much work.

A cautionary example of the confusion which this varied use of the term may bring about can be seen in L. Milroy 1980.[1] The word VERNACULAR appears on average on every third page of Milroy's work, so it is important for its meaning to be clear and well defined. It is clear throughout that vernacular is not a term which is socially neutral for Milroy but rather one which refers to a form of speech that is nonstandard and of low prestige (10, 18, 119, 173, 176, 182, 184). In particular, Belfast vernacular 'is an example of a highly focused variety at the lowest stratum' (180). This is appropriate since Milroy is studying the speech of working-class speakers in three districts of Belfast. However, although it had earlier been claimed that 'people use their vernacular most of the time' (12), it turns out that in the sample of working-class speakers Milroy studied 'the base of the vernacular is certainly narrow in terms of the number of speakers at a high level' (193) and women on average 'use the vernacular variably at a much lower level than men' (159). There is something very odd in this situation. The speakers Milroy studied were lower working class and by her own account (see Milroy and Milroy 1977), she had recorded good quality data in group sessions where the participants are well acquainted with each other. What were these people speaking if it was not the vernacular?

It emerges that Milroy is not using the term 'vernacular' to refer to a variety of speech in all its aspects, but rather as an abbreviation for certain marked phonological features which are found only in the most casual speech of some working-class speakers in Belfast. As such, they can be recognized as markers of working-class loyalty in Belfast. Milroy confuses the issue further by frequent reference to VERNACULAR NORMS (8, 61, 106, 119, 131, 132, etc.). One might expect these to be norms of interpretation such as Labov (1966) found in New York City, but Milroy claims that the vernacular norms are 'observable in spontaneous styles' (112) and it turns out that these norms are the same as the phonological features previously mentioned. Thus, when Milroy claims that a speaker approximates to vernacular norms (131-3), what she means is that the speaker uses certain non-standard pronunciations more frequently than other people in the sample. This is very different from Labov's Black English Vernacular which is characterized by a wide range of rules that differentiate it from other varieties of American English.

One is driven to the conclusion that, according to Milroy, there are no speakers of Belfast vernacular, although some people come closer to that ideal than others. The vernacular thus turns out to be as much of an abstraction as Standard English. Milroy's concentration on a chimerical vernacular is all the more disappointing, given the richness of her data (as illustrated in Milroy and Milroy 1977). The careful identification of different spontaneous styles in the earlier paper is largely ignored, and we are left with a few correlations between network connections and certain phonological features.

J. Milroy apparently takes an equally rarified view of the vernacular, judging by his criticism of my Glasgow study (Macaulay 1977). In his review, Milroy complains that '95% of the sociolinguistic complexity remains submerged and out of sight' (1979: 91). With a small judgment sample of 48 respondents, only one-third of them adults, it would have been surprising if the Glasgow study had revealed as much as five per cent of the sociolinguistic complexity of that remarkable city, but even such a modest sounding goal is probably beyond the scope of our present methodology, whatever the size of the sample.

Milroy's conclusion was based on the 'absence of a systematic account of style-shifting' and a 'failure to reach the "vernacular"' (91). What rankled about this criticism was not the reference to the stylistic limitations of the survey, since I had pointed them out myself (though Milroy seems to have been confused by my ironical reference to 'the Queen's English'). What troubled me was that the criticism implied that the samples of speech I recorded in the interviews were somehow not legitimate examples of Glasgow speech. Obviously, no single interview can cover the whole range of a speaker's verbal repertoire, but it does not follow from this limitation that the speech recorded in an interview is not a legitimate part of that repertoire (for a response to Wolfson 1976, see Macaulay 1984). In the Glasgow survey, I was generally satisfied with the quality of speech recorded, given the constraints of the survey situation, and I am familiar enough with the community to trust my own judgment in this respect. (I was born and grew up in a village thirty miles from Glasgow; it was the nearest big city for shopping and entertainment; I have relatives and friends in the city; I worked there for three years; as long as I can remember I have known what Glasgow speakers sound like, from the basilect to the acrolect.) All the respondents I interviewed in the community sample[2] sounded characteristically Glaswegian to me, and I am confident that they would have been recognizable to their friends, though it would also have been obvious that they were not talking to a close acquaintance in intimate circumstances. I believe that they were all speaking the vernacular in Illich's sense of the language used by 'people who mean what they say and say what they mean in the context of everyday life' (1980: 48). I agree that none of them was using the basilect in its most casual style; but, for most of the respondents, the basilect would not be the most casual form of speech.[3] Moreover, a survey that concentrated only on the basilect would not cover much of the sociolinguistic complexity of the city either. As Romaine (1982: 209) has pointed out, Labov's preoccupation with working-class speech may have given a misleading impression of variation in the speech community. Milroy's use of the term 'vernacular' for the most casual style of the basilect makes his criticism appear more general than I believe to be justified.

There is a more general point to be raised about both Labov's and the Milroys' use of the term vernacular that is related to the question of age.

L. Milroy defines an urban vernacular as 'the kind of speech the majority of speakers of a city (usually low status speakers) acquire in their adolescent years' (1980: 24) and claims (though she has not systematically investigated this) that adolescents are 'more consistent vernacular speakers' than adults (191). Labov claims that 'the most consistent vernacular is spoken by those between the ages of 9 and 18' (1973: 83) and defines the vernacular as 'that mode of speech that is acquired in pre-adolescent years' (1981: 3).

In the case of Black English Vernacular, it is reasonable to limit the label to adolescents since that was the age-group Labov studied,[4] but there is no reason why sociolinguistic investigation in general should be focused on this age-group. In fact, there may be a danger in taking adolescent behavior as somehow basic to adult society, when instead such behavior may be an attack on adult values. Hamblett and Deverson (1964) quote a 16-year-old 'mod' from South London as saying 'You'd really hate an adult to understand you. That's the only thing you've got over them — the fact that you can mystify and worry them' (cited by Hebdige 1979: 167) and Hebdige summarizes the attitude of punk rockers: 'The punks wore clothes which were the sartorial equivalent of swear words, and they swore as they dressed — with calculated effect' (114).

It is highly likely that the speech behavior of certain groups of urban working-class adolescents is an example of what Giles (1979: 280) called '"downward divergence" (an accentuation of speech markers by members of subordinate groups)'. In other words, rather than being the basic form of speech underlying the speech behavior of adults, it is a marked form deliberately adopted for group identification and stylistic display, similar in function to the punk rockers' clothes. If this turns out to be an accurate description of the situation, then it would not be surprising that adults are inconsistent users of the 'vernacular' (in this age-marked sense), since their access to the adolescent form of speech would be subject to the same kind of memory limitations as their recollections of childhood rhymes and games.

There are, therefore, a number of separate notions which need to be kept distinct and not lumped together in a single term:

a. LOCAL VARIETY

There is a need for a term to refer to the speech of the natives of a locality. There seems no reason why DIALECT should not be used for this purpose, provided it is clear that dialects are multilayered and not restricted to any stratum of the community. Upper-class speakers are as much dialect speakers as working-class ones if their speech is recognizably 'local'. There is a rather romantic notion, which goes back at least to Wordsworth, that the language of poor, relatively uneducated speakers is somehow more authentic than that of other members of the community, but linguists should not fall into that trap. The only hope of understanding 'the sociolinguistic complexity' (*pace* J. Milroy 1979) of any community is to study the whole range of speech within that community.

b. SOCIAL VARIETY

The kinds of distinctions indicated by the terms STANDARD/ NONSTANDARD, SUPERORDINATE/SUBORDINATE, ACROLECT/ BASILECT, PRESTIGE/STIGMATIZED, as well as all the social class labels, present a confusing picture because sometimes certain terms appear to be used synonymously and at other times to indicate differences. This is probably the trickiest area of the whole sociolinguistic terminology because the terms often carry stereotypical connotations. It may not be possible for linguists to solve this problem without help from sociologists, but at least care can be taken in defining the sense in which terms are being used and avoiding as much as possible the use of synonyms for stylistic purposes.

c. AGE-GRADED VARIETY

There is a pressing need for more accurate information on the continuity of language development. Is it true that the 'basic' form of an individual's idiolect is established in the pre-adolescent years? Are all aspects of language established at the same time or is there a difference between phonological development and syntactic development? To what extent do literacy and education affect an individual's 'basic' form of speech? Is there an age after which no major modification of the individual's 'basic' form of speech can take place? Is all language development essentially cumulative after a certain age? Opinions on these questions can be found in the literature, but there is very little evidence that is relevant to answering the questions. Empirical investigation is needed, but it is probably unrealistic to expect that longitudinal studies will ever be carried out in a form that would provide useful answers.

d. STYLES OF SPEECH

This is another area in which the terminology is badly in need of clarification. Labov (1966) and Trudgill (1974) carefully defined style-shifting in operational terms even though it was based on a perhaps unwarranted assumption about the relationship between speaking and reading aloud. Apart from these two works, there has been little systematic investigation of style-shifting in complex communities. Douglas-Cowie (1978) and

Coupland (1980) are too limited in scope to provide a model and L. Milroy (1980) makes almost no use of the stylistic categories outlined in Milroy and Milroy 1977. In the absence of better-defined categories than CAREFUL/CASUAL, FORMAL/INFORMAL, INTERVIEW/SPONTANEOUS, any strong claims made about style-shifting are likely to be suspect, given the complexity of the factors involved (see Goffman 1964, Hymes 1974).

Perhaps the greatest irony in all of this confusion is that Labov and the Milroys, who have demonstrated the variability of language so effectively, should somehow seem to have faith in a monolithic vernacular. As Rickford has pointed out (personal communication), there is no reason to believe that even the most casual or spontaneous form of speech is monostylistic, since it will be used in a variety of situations, with different participants, and for different ends. The search for a pure vernacular is potentially dangerous, if it leads to an undervaluing of other varieties and a consequent lack of attention to them. The aim of sociolinguistic investigation should be to describe the totality of speech use in the community. Until that is done, it may be safer to use the term 'vernacular' only in contrast to 'classical'.

NOTES

Although I had written most of this paper before the proposal for the *Festschrift* reached me, I feel it is appropriate as a tribute to Bob Stockwell, because of his concern for precision in language. I recently came across a copy of an early draft of my dissertation with his comments on it, including the following: 'I don't see how what follows here supports the first sentence', 'This is a crucial point which your style of presentation has damn near buried. Can't you highlight it more?', 'I'm not convinced' and *passim* 'not clear'. I have tried to follow his exhortation and example in clarity of expression ever since. The present is an attempt to deal with what I perceive to be terminological confusion. I am grateful to Suzanne Romaine, Donald Brenneis, and John Rickford for comments on an earlier version.

1. Romaine (1980b: 267) also remarks on the confused use of the term 'vernacular' by Milroy.

2. I also interviewed samples of teachers and employers, some of whom were not speakers of the local variety of English.

3. All of the respondents, however, probably have a passive knowledge of the basilect which can be exploited for comic or other purposes (see Macaulay 1982).

4. Wright 1975, however, points out that Black ghetto adolescents use many varieties of English in addition to BEV.

REFERENCES

Baugh, A.C. 1957. *A History of the English Language*, 2nd edn. New York: Appleton-Century-Crofts.
Bloomfield, M.W., and L. Newmark. 1965. *A Linguistic Introduction to the History of English*. New York: Knopf.
Coupland, N. 1980. 'Style-shifting in a Cardiff Work Setting', *Language in Society* 9: 1–12.
Crystal, D. 1980. *A First Dictionary of Linguistics and Phonetics*. London: Deutsch.
Douglas-Cowie, E. 1978. 'Linguistic Code-Switching in a Northern Irish Village: Social Interaction and Social Ambition', in P. Trudgill (ed.), *Sociolinguistic Patterns in British English*. London: Arnold, 37–51.
Fishman, J. 1972. *Language and Nationalism*. Rowley, Mass.: Newbury House.
Giles, H. 1979. 'Ethnicity Markers in Speech', in K.R. Scherer and H. Giles (eds.), *Social Markers in Speech*. Cambridge: Cambridge University Press, 251–89.
Goffman, E. 1964. 'The Neglected Situation', *American Anthropologist* 66: 133–6.
Hamblett, C., and J. Deverson. 1964. *Generation X*. London: Tandem.
Haugen, E. 1966. 'Dialect, Language, Nation', *American Anthropologist* 68: 922–35.
Hebdige, D. 1979. *Subculture: the Meaning of Style*. London: Methuen.
Hymes, D. 1974. *Foundations in Sociolinguistics: an Ethnographic Approach*. Philadelphia: University of Pennsylvania Press.
Illich, I. 1980. 'Vernacular Values', *The CoEvolution Quarterly*, Summer, 22–49.
Labov, W. 1966. *The Social Stratification of English in New York City*. Washington, DC: Center for Applied Linguistics.
—— 1970. 'The Study of Language in its Social Context', *Studium Generale* 23: 30–87.
—— 1972. *Language in the Inner City*. Philadelphia: University of Pennsylvania Press.
—— 1973. 'The Linguistic Consequences of Being a Lame', *Language in Society* 2: 81–115.
—— 1981. 'Field Methods of the Project on Linguistic Change and Variation', *Sociolinguistic Working Paper*, No. 81. Austin: Southwest Educational Development Laboratory.
—— P. Cohen, C. Robins, and J. Lewis. 1968. *A Study of the Non-standard English of Negro and Puerto Rican Speakers in New York City*. New York: Columbia University.
Macaulay, R. 1973. 'Double Standards', *American Anthropologist* 75: 1324–37.
—— 1977. *Language, Social Class, and Education*. Edinburgh: Edinburgh University Press.
—— 1982. 'The Sociolinguistic Significance of Scottish Dialect Humor'. Ms.
—— 1984. 'Chattering, Nattering and Blethering: Informal Interviews as Speech Events', in W. Enninger and L. Haynes (eds.), *Studies in Language Ecology*. Wiesbaden: Steiner, 51–64.
Milroy, J. 1979. Review of *Language, Social Class and Education* by R. Macaulay. *Language in Society* 8: 88–96.
—— and L. Milroy. 1977. 'Speech and Context in an Urban Setting', *Belfast Working Papers in Language and Linguistics* 2: 1–85.
Milroy, L. 1980. *Language and Social Networks*. Oxford: Blackwell.
O'Barr, W.M. 1976. 'Language Use and Language Policy in Tanzania: An Over-

view', in W.M. and J.F. O'Barr (eds.), *Language and Politics.* The Hague: Mouton, 35–48.

Romaine, S. 1980a. 'What is a Speech Community?', *Belfast Working Papers in Language and Linguistics* 4: 41–60.

—— 1980b. Review of *Language and Social Networks* by L. Milroy. *English World-Wide* 1: 264–8.

—— 1982. *Socio-Historical Linguistics: Its Status and Methodology.* Cambridge: Cambridge University Press.

de Saussure, F. 1959. *Course in General Linguistics.* New York: McGraw-Hill.

Stewart, W.A. 1962. 'An Outline of Linguistic Typology for Describing Multilingualism', in F.A. Rice (ed.), *Study of the Role of Second Languages in Asia, Africa, and Latin America.* Washington, DC: Center for Applied Linguistics, 15–25.

Trudgill, P. 1974. *The Social Differentiation of English in Norwich.* Cambridge: Cambridge University Press.

Wolfram, W. 1973. *Sociolinguistic Aspects of Assimilation: Puerto Rican English in New York City.* Arlington, Va.: Center for Applied Linguistics.

Wolfson, N. 1976. 'Speech Events and Natural Speech: Some Implications for Sociolinguistic Methodology', *Language in Society* 7: 215–37.

Wright, R. 1975. Review of *English in Black and White* by R. Burling and *Language in the Inner City* by W. Labov. *Language in Society* 2: 185–98.

10

Hypercorrection and the Creole Continuum: -*s* and -*d* in Liberian English

JOHN VICTOR SINGLER

The sight of someone who is obviously American walking down the street of a Liberian city may prompt non-English-speaking Liberian children to break into their imitation of American English: [hərs tərs yərs sərs].[1] While initial consonants may vary, the imitation inevitably contains syllable-final *s*'s (and post-vocalic *r*'s).

An American meeting a pidgin-speaking Liberian for the first time may find that the pidgin speaker's half of the conversation goes something like that found in (1):

(1) hɛlos... gu mɔnẽs... ma nẽs?... ma nẽ josɛs.
    'Hellos... Good mornings... My names?... My name is Josephs.'

It is the final *s*'s found in (1) and final *d*'s like the one in (2) that are the focus of this article. (In (2) and throughout the remainder of the article, the final *d*'s and *s*'s in question are signalled by capitalization.)[2]

(2) The guy wrote a book call *The CryD of My People*.

1. THE CREOLE CONTINUUM

In order to talk about these final *S*'s and *D*'s, it is appropriate to begin by discussing the model of the creole continuum introduced by DeCamp (1971). DeCamp predicts a continuum situation will arise when two conditions can be met:

> First, the dominant official language of the community must be the standard language corresponding to the creole ... Second, the formerly rigid social stratification must have **partially** (not completely) broken down. That is, there must be sufficient social mobility to motivate large numbers of creole speakers to modify their speech in the direction of the

standard, and there must be a sufficient program of education and other acculturative activities to exert effective pressures from the standard language on the creole (351).

DeCamp's description of the creole continuum argues for a chain of varieties from most creolized to most standardized. The gap between the two extremes, i.e. between the basilect and the acrolect, is spanned by a series of intermediate levels (or lects), each of these differing only slightly from the level on either side of it. In the strictest application of the model, each level differs from its immediate neighbor by a single rule. That is, in the diagram in (3), if Y is the stage whose nearest neighbors are X and Z, it possesses one more rule than X and one fewer rule than Z.

(3) Basilect 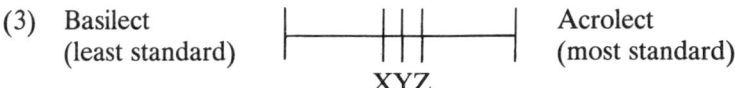 Acrolect
    (least standard)   (most standard)
                        XYZ

Bickerton (1975) refines and instantiates DeCamp's proposal. He shows that the model works best for subsets of the grammar; that is, the aspect system has to be mapped separately from, for example, the pronoun system or the phonology. At the same time, Bickerton's study shows the validity of the rule-chain illustrated in (3).

Various linguists — including Tonkin (1971), Sankoff and Laberge (1973), and Todd (1974) — have noted the strong parallels between the pidgins of West Africa and Papua New Guinea, on the one hand, and creoles, on the other. These pidgins have long histories and display the stability and range of a full language. Indeed, with regard to tense–aspect, Singler (1984) demonstrates the applicability of the creole-continuum model to non-native, i.e. pidginized, Liberian English. An illustration of the chain of rules that expresses non-punctual aspect in the Monrovia variety of Liberian English is given in Table 10.1.

At the basilectal extreme, regardless of the tense of the action and regardless of the nature of the non-punctualness, the AUX *de* is used. The second stage introduces a distinction between continuous actions and habitual/iterative ones: the verb suffix -*ẽ* marks the continuous while *de* marks habitual/iterative. The third step replaces *de* with *kẽ*. Then, the fourth step introduces a past/non-past distinction for continuous actions, the past being marked by the addition of the AUX *wɔ*. Next, in the fifth step, *kẽ* yields to *dɔ*. In the sixth step, the past/non-past distinction appears with habitual/iterative verbs, *dɔ* contrasting with *yustu*. Finally, in the seventh step, *dɔ* is replaced by ∅. The system in Step 7 is essentially the Standard English system though not necessarily with Standard English pronunciation. The chart in Table 10.1 shows seven systems, from the undifferentiated use of *de V* at Lect 1 to a four-way distinction at Lect 7. The

Table 10.1: Non-punctual Marking in Liberian English (Monrovia Region)

STAGE 1 [−PUNCT] → de	1.	−PUNCT de V		
STAGE 2 [−PUNCT] → [−PUNCT][±CONT] [−PUNCT][+CONT] → -ē [−PUNCT][−CONT] → de	2.	+CONT V-ē	−CONT de V	
STAGE 3 de → kɛ̃	3.	V-ē	kɛ̃ V	
STAGE 4 [−PUNCT][+CONT] → [−PUNCT][+CONT][±PAST] [−PUNCT][+CONT][−PAST] → -ē [−PUNCT][+CONT][+PAST] → wɔ -ē	4.	−PAST V-ē	+PAST wɔ V-ē	kɛ̃ V
STAGE 5 kɛ̃ → dɔ	5.	V-ē	wɔ V-ē	dɔ V
STAGE 6 [−PUNCT][−CONT] → [−PUNCT][−CONT][±PAST] [−PUNCT][−CONT][−PAST] → dɔ [−PUNCT][−CONT][+PAST] → yustu	6.	V-ē	wɔ V-ē	−PAST +PAST dɔ V yustu V
STAGE 7 dɔ → ∅	7.	V-ē	wɔ V-ē	V yustu V

model does not require that every speaker fit neatly into a single lect. Rather, speakers command a RANGE along the continuum. Their speech can be expected to span one, two, or even more lects. What the model predicts is that the speaker's range is continuous; that is, one does not expect a speaker to display a mixture of Lect 2 and Lect 5 behavior without also displaying evidence of the intervening Lects, 3 and 4.

The purpose of this discussion of the creole-continuum model has been to demonstrate its orderly and rule-governed character. It must be noted that, in recent years, the continuum model has been both sharply criticized and staunchly defended. Speaking with reference to Guyana, Edwards (1983) rejects the continuum model, while Rickford (1984) argues that it captures generalizations that would otherwise be lost. The study of Liberian English tense–aspect referred to above (Singler 1984), while modifying the continuum model somewhat in language-particular ways, is in agreement with Rickford: the systematicity of the continuum model reflects the fundamentally systematic transition from basilect to acrolect in Liberian English. The quantitative analysis of over fifty speakers in over fifty hours of tape-recorded Liberian speech confirms the effectiveness of the model.

2. HYPERCORRECTION AND RULE OVERGENERALIZATION

As illustrated in the Liberian case, a great part of the value of the creole-continuum model lies in its ability to impose regularity on massive amounts of disparate data. However, some phenomena defy this type of detailed regimentation. Hypercorrection seems to be one such instance. While hypercorrection is identified by DeCamp (1972) and others as the result of overgeneralization, usually its occurrence seems sporadic and unpredictable. As such, it seems an unlikely target for any kind of systematization.

As for the basis for hypercorrection, there is general agreement among linguists that the phenomenon is social in motivation. It is contact with a prestige dialect that triggers the upwardly mobile speaker to correct — or hypercorrect — his or her speech. As such, environments where DeCamp predicts that creole continua will obtain are also environments that are ripe for hypercorrection.

In the Liberian case, examples of hypercorrection are numerous. One example involves the voiceless interdental fricative. Not ordinarily found in the Liberian basilect or mesolect, it shows up in a hypercorrect context in cases like those in (4):

(4) [θɔʔ] 'taught'   [ɛnθayto] 'entitled'

2.1. Intrusive S

The most widespread case of hypercorrection in Liberian English involves word-final S. That it is widespread stems apparently from the fact that the presence or absence of word-final -s is the most salient difference between Standard English and Liberian English, especially the Liberian basilect. As a morpheme, word-final -s has three functions in Standard English: to mark agreement, plurality for regular nouns, and possession.[3] In the Liberian basilect, on the other hand, word-final -s is ordinarily not used in any of these environments. When the verb is non-punctual — as most non-past verbs are — the AUX *de* is used, as in (5).

(5) This time, car *de carry* we now.
     'These days a car takes us there.'

Otherwise, a Ø-form is used. In any event, subject–verb agreement is not marked. As for plurality, Singler (to appear) shows that it is ordinarily not marked. However, in those cases where the head noun is human and definite, *dẽ* is frequently added, as in (6).

119

(6) I use to help my *friend dɛ̃*.
    'I used to help my friends.'

Finally, possession is indicated by word order, as in (7).

(7) Those big-big doll baby what in the store, he go shake the *doll-baby hand*.

With regard to the INTRODUCTION of the Standard English morpheme(s) -*s* along the continuum — that is, the use of -*s* in the Standard non-hypercorrect fashion — this occurs fairly early for plurals (i.e. towards the basilectal end of the continuum) but rather late for agreement and possession.

As to the claim that the presence or absence of word-final -*s* is the most salient difference between Standard English and the Liberian basilect: the Liberian children's imitation of American English referred to above reflects that salience. So do the data in (1). When an upwardly mobile basilectal speaker attempts to speak a variety of English that extends beyond the acrolectal end of that speaker's range, the *S*'s can show up virtually anywhere. They are added to greetings and proper names, as in (1).[4] They are also added to place names, as in (8) and (9):

(8) We went NigeriaS.

(9) That time, from the way MonroviaS, we not find no coaltar, that was so-so rough road.
    'In those days, all the way to Monrovia, there was no paved road, nothing but dirt roads.'

To determiners, as in (10) and (11):

(10) That theS time, my mother came here and he and my father then they born me here in Robertsport.
    'That was when my mother came here, and she and my father had me here in Robertsport.'

(11) But those days ... they have aS time to make their farm.
    'In those days there was a set time for farming.'

To adverbs, as in (12) and (13):

(12) Because actuallyS you alway fear.

(13) First time, we use to ride boat from hereS to Monrovia.
    'Formerly, we would go by boat from here to Monrovia.'

To pronouns, as in (14) and (15):

(14) I won't like for youS to sit down like this.
'I wouldn't want you to be without a job.'

(15) They didn't meet nobodyS there.
'When they got there, there was no one there.'

Indeed, no word is impervious to hypercorrection, not infinitive markers (16), nor negation (17), nor sentence words (18).

(16) When you bring home, Father going toS beat you.
'When you bring [the letter telling of your disrespect] home, your father is going to beat you.'

(17) I am notS in government work.

(18) OhS, we always call it Tabou Waterside.

S even makes its way **inside** words, as in (19) and (20):

(19) He aSttending the same school here.

(20) You all join the people and start making that joySful noise, you see.

The data in (8) through (20) show that S can occur in virtually any syntactic environment. Is there any hope of systematizing the S data? In fact, there is. Moreover, the generalizations that obtain show that the distribution of S can be aligned on a basilect-to-acrolect continuum. The occurrences of S fit into four stages, listed in (21).

(21) STAGES ALONG THE CONTINUUM IN THE USE OF S

	Distribution	Pronunciation
Stage 1:	No restrictions	[s]
Stage 2:	No restrictions	[s]/[z] (phonologically conditioned)
Stage 3:	Restricted to three environments: a. V–S b. $[X\ N\text{–}S\ Y]_{NP}$ c. $[X\ ADJ\text{–}S\ N\ Y]_{NP}$ and $[X\ [N\text{–}S\ N]_N\ Y]_{NP}$	As in Stage 2
Stage 4:	Stage 3c, but not 3a or 3b	As in Stage 2

Of these stages, the first is that illustrated in (8) through (20). In that stage, there are no restrictions on distribution, and *S* is not subject to phonological conditioning. In the Liberian basilect, final consonant clusters are very rare, and final obstruents are devoiced. (Thus, *S* is never immediately preceded by a voiced obstruent.) Somewhat more acrolectally, the second stage occurs. Still there are no restrictions on distribution, and the data in (8) through (20) illustrate this stage, too. The difference between the first and second stages lies in the pronunciation of *S*. At the second stage, devoicing no longer applies to *S*. That is, a speaker at Stage 2 would pronounce *youS* in (14) as [yuz] and *toS* in (16) as [tuz]. For speakers at Stage 2, it is probably the case that *S* is /z/ underlyingly. It should be noted, however, that a speaker at Stage 2 would pronounce *notS* in (17) as [nas]. Thus, it is necessary to posit both a voicing-assimilation rule (22) and a final-cluster simplification rule (23); the assimilation rule must be ordered before the cluster simplification rule.

(22) $/z/ \rightarrow [s] \ / \ \underset{[-\text{VOICE}]}{C} \ \_\_ \ \#$

(23) $C \rightarrow \emptyset \ / \ \_\_ \ \underset{[+\text{CONT}]}{C} \ \#$

(As its structural description indicates, the domain of (23) extends to other environments as well.)[5]

Still more acrolectally, in the third stage, the appearance of hypercorrect forms comes to be restricted to those parts of speech to which the Standard English morpheme -*s* can be attached. That is, while it no longer attaches to adverbs or pronouns or the like, it occurs still with verbs and nouns. Note that the occurrence of *S* with verbs — in the early part of Stage 3, at least — is frequently with verbs whose syntactic position is such that they cannot take -*s* in Standard English. (24) and (25) illustrate this.

(24) That's the heart man we use to callS 'You Too Late'.
     'He's the ritual murderer we used to call "You Too Late."'

(25) He was the only man that they could dependS on.
     'He was the main person that they used to depend on.'

With regard to nouns, *S* is affixed to the head noun of a NP, as in (26) and (27).

(26) You know, my grandfather*S*, he was a strong man.

(27) We scare to advise our childrenS among people.
'We're scared to rebuke our children in front of other people.'

Additionally, it occurs after the adjective in a NP, as in (28), or after the first noun in an N–N compound, as in (29).

(28) Not so much of concreteS house.
'There weren't many concrete houses then.'

(29) I saw some people making cocoaS farm.

At the most acrolectal level of the occurrence of hypercorrect S, that is, in the fourth stage, its distribution becomes quite restricted. It is now limited to sentences like (28) and (29). While these examples are bona fide cases of hypercorrection — concrete and cocoa not being items that lend themselves either to plurality or to being possessors — there are several factors that contribute to the perseverance of S in this environment, i.e. Stage 3c of the schema in (21).

To begin with, in Standard English, as Kiparsky (1982) has noted, irregular plurals can occupy the non-head position of compounds, but regular ones cannot. Thus, *lice-infested* is grammatical, but **rats-infested* is not. This distinction apparently does not hold in Liberian English — at least not for all speakers. Rather, it may be the case that all plurals, whether regular or irregular, may occur in the non-head position of compounds. If this is so, it would then explain forms like those in (30) and (31).[6]

(30) The city mayor say he was going to take a new road for the *logS truck* not to pass in Greenville self.
'The mayor said that he was going to construct a new road so that the logging trucks would not pass through the city of Greenville.'

(31) You got any *peanutS butter*?

It is not possible to determine whether the origin of compounds like those in (30) and (31) lies in hypercorrection or in the fact that — for some speakers — Liberian English permits non-heads, regular as well as irregular, to be marked for plurality. Whatever the cause was originally, once the pronunciation comes generally to be N–*s* N, one cannot describe the situation as one of synchronic hypercorrection. This is the case in (31), where *peanuts butter* has come to be the usual Liberian pronunciation.

Apart from the possibility of marking regular plurality on non-head nouns in compounds, a second explanation for the perseverance of S in this environment involves cases in Standard English where the semantics of possession are subtle. That is, frequently, both noun–noun and noun–'*s*–noun are possible for a given pair of nouns, as in the Standard English sentences in (32).

(32) Standard English
    a. Ms. Harding is the school principal.
    b. Ms. Harding is the school's principal.
    c. He didn't finish his morning work.
    d. He didn't finish his morning's work.

That there seems to be a meaning difference between (32c) and (32d) does not matter. What is crucial is that both sentences can and do occur. Given pairs like those in (32), the question of hypercorrection becomes moot for sentences like those in (33) and (34).

(33) We will now say the schoolS prayer.

(34) We shall be signing off our morningS transmission to carry out our routine maintenance.

A third explanation for the perseverance of *S* in this environment involves adjectives that also function as nouns. Thus, given the two points already raised as contributing to the perseverance of *S*, it is possible that what the Standard English speaker would regard as an ADJ–noun phrase is analyzed by the Liberian English speaker as either a noun–noun compound (where the first noun is plural) or a possessive construction. A reanalysis of the latter sort may explain the presence of *S* in (35).

(35) We study the humanS body.

2.2. Intrusive *D*

In contrast to *S*, the use of *D* is much more restricted, both in terms of the continuum and in frequency of occurrence. Presumably, *D* is modeled on the Standard English past-tense suffix. Liberian English phonotactic constraints make the occurrence of the past-tense suffix reasonably infrequent. The language forbids a word-final cluster that ends with a stop. Thus, for all Liberian speakers, the past tense of *dance* is *dance*. The past-tense *-d* appears only after a vowel, e.g. *agreed,* and then only in fairly acrolectal speech. Moreover, the *-d* is much more likely to occur there if the following word begins with a vowel. Thus, the past-tense *-d* is more likely in *agreed on* than in *agreed with*. Similarly, the syllabic past tense is ordinarily realized as a low front vowel, for example [disaydɛ] as the past tense of *decide*. However, among acroletal speakers, when the following word is vowel-initial, the *d* may be pronounced, e.g. [disaydɛd ɔ̃], *decided on.*

As DeCamp (1972) observes, every instance of hypercorrection is a case of rule generalization, but not every instance of rule generalization is a case of hypercorrection. Certainly for some speakers *D* looks like the educated cousin of *S*. That is, for these speakers, *D* can occur almost anywhere. The data in (36) through (38) come from such a speaker, a disk jockey on a Monrovia radio station.

(36) You can join us tomorrow morning at 10:30 when Aaron Lincoln will be hereD for half-hour summary of activities claiming the attention of the police and that would be of interest to you.

(37) The green boys, the men in armD, they are conducting a massive cleanup campaign today.
'The soldiers are conducting a cleanup campaign today.'

(38) If this is so, would you assureD your brothers and friends that the Defense Ministry will continue to do this in the long run?

For most speakers who insert *D*, however, the environment is strictly limited to cases where *D* breaks up a sequence of vowels across a word boundary. As such, its use represents a generalization based on forms like *agreed on* and *decided on.* Examples of this overgeneralization are given in (39) through (41).

(39) If you goD around the whole world, you will not find the end.

(40) According to the ideaD of this tale, the old lady said it was the red iron make snake to have big tongue.
'The point of the tale, according to the old lady, is that a snake's tongue is forked because it was once burned by a hot iron.'

(41) I don't want any pretty woman, I want one with plentyD of money.

Apparently, the only restriction on *D*-insertion for these speakers is that the *D* must follow a lexical item. (41) is taken from a song by Jones Dopoe, a Liberian singer. A line from the chorus of a different Dopoe song is given in (42a):

(42a) Pretty girl, you eat my money, then you say I am a ugly man.

(42b) is predicted to be not possible: it would require that *D* be tacked on to a function word.

(42b) ?Pretty girl, you eat my money, then you say I aD ugly man.

The question remains as to whether *D*-insertion is a case of hypercorrection or whether it is a case of rule overgeneralization without hypercorrection. For some speakers, like the disk jockey, it seems to be a case of hypercorrection. For most speakers, however, it seems to be phonotactically motivated **non**-hypercorrect generalization. To be sure, the fact that, for the latter set of speakers, *D*-use is limited to a narrowly defined environment is not by itself evidence that this does not represent hypercorrection. Rather, the evidence is social, as it must be when hypercorrection is at issue. An analysis of conversations between Liberians who know each other well and who are of comparable social status reveals no intrusive *S*'s; on the other hand, it does reveal intrusive *D*'s. That is, *D* shows up in sentences like (39) and (40) when the phonological environment is right, even when the social circumstances favoring hypercorrection are absent. The occurrence of *S*, on the other hand, tends to be limited to only those environments where the social circumstances favor hypercorrection.

3. CONCLUSION

It conclusion, while it has been shown elsewhere that the creole-continuum model applies to non-native Liberian English and that the model succeeds there in systematizing and accounting for massive amounts of disparate data, the randomness of instantiations of hypercorrection means that, for such phenomena, the continuum cannot be employed in any strict sense. Thus, no rule-chain is possible for relating levels of hypercorrection one to the other. Nonetheless, an examination of *S*-hypercorrection demonstrates that it is possible to delineate stages in the use of *S* and that the arrangement of these stages parallels the continuum. The stages correspond to their speakers' proximity to Standard English and reflect the degree of distance inasmuch as successive stages represent progressively more accurate approximations of the use and pronunciation of the morpheme -*s* in Standard English.

Finally, while *S* represents a case of both rule overgeneralization and hypercorrection, it seems that — for most speakers at least — *D* illustrates rule overgeneralization without hypercorrection.

NOTES

1. This article is an expanded version of a paper presented at the annual meeting of the International Linguistic Association, held at New York University in March, 1985. I am grateful to those who helped me to gather the data on which this study is

based. In this regard, I am particularly grateful to Boakai Zoludua. Various members of the Liberian speech community have called my attention to examples of hypercorrect *S* over the years; Annie K. Freeman was especially helpful.

2. With regard to the Liberian English sentences used in this study: most examples come from a corpus of fifty hours of Liberian English speech recorded in 1978 and 1980-1. This corpus forms the basis for Singler 1984. The exceptions are the following: (34), (36), (37), and (38), which come from a program broadcast on ELBC, a Monrovia radio station; (41) and (42), which come from the records of Jones Dopoe, a Liberian singer; and (2), (31), and (33).

3. From a phonological point of view, one must add to the list contracted variants of *has* and *is*.

4. The addition of *S* to male Christian names is especially common. There is a model for this: Richards, Williams, and Roberts are common Liberian surnames.

5. In Standard English, *-s* has a third allomorph, [ɨz]. In Liberian speakers who mark the plural use [ɛz]/[ɛ] for sibilant-final stems. Thus, the plural of [bɔs] 'bus' is [bɔsɛz]/[bɔsɛ].

6. I am grateful to John Jesse Rudin for first calling *peanuts butter* to my attention.

REFERENCES

Bickerton, Derek. 1975. *Dynamics of a Creole System*. Cambridge: Cambridge University Press.
DeCamp, David. 1971. 'Toward a Generative Analysis of a Post-creole Speech Community', in Dell Hymes (ed.), *Pidginization and Creolization of Languages*. Cambridge: Cambridge University Press, 349-70.
—— 1972. 'Hypercorrection and Rule Generalization', *Language in Society* 1: 87-90.
Edwards, Walter F. 1983. 'A Community-based Approach to the Provenance of Urban Guyanese Creole'. Paper presented at the York Creole Conference.
Kiparsky, Paul. 1982. 'Lexical Morphology and Phonology', in I.S. Yang (ed.), *Linguistics in the Morning Calm*. Seoul: Hanshin.
Rickford, John R. 1984. 'In Defense of the Creole Continuum'. Address delivered to the Thirteenth NWAVE Meeting, Philadelphia.
Sankoff, Gillian, and Susanne Laberge. 1973. 'On the Acquisition of Native Speakers by a Language', *Kivung* 6: 32-47.
Singler, John Victor. 1984. *Variation in Tense-Aspect-Modality in Liberian English*. UCLA dissertation.
—— to appear. 'Social and Linguistic Constraints on Plural Marking in Liberian English', in Jenny Cheshire (ed.), *English Around the World: Sociolinguistic Perspectives*. Cambridge: Cambridge University Press.
Todd, Loreto. 1974. *Pidgins and Creoles*. London: Routledge and Kegan Paul.
Tonkin, Elizabeth. 1971. *Some Aspects of Language from the Viewpoint of Social Anthropology, with Particular Reference to Multilingual Situations in Nigeria*. Oxford University dissertation.

11

Is Internal Semantic–Pragmatic Reconstruction Possible?

ELIZABETH CLOSS TRAUGOTT

1. INTRODUCTION

Among the time-honored research strategies for reconstructing the linguistic structure of earlier periods has been that of hypothesizing that synchronic irregularity is the residue of earlier regularities that have been disrupted through competing change, analogy, borrowing, or other factors.[1] Extensive work along these lines has been done in the area of internal reconstruction of linguistic structure and change,[2] and most effectively in phonology. There is, for example, the well known work on phonological alternations at morpheme boundaries such as are found in pairs like *house–houses* and *divine–divinity*, and which can be used to infer aspects of the structure of fricatives and vowels in earlier English. Another domain in which the method has been used, but more controversially, has been in reconstruction of word order, largely from the order of synchronically bound forms such as *lion-killer, up-keep* which are controlled by derivational and lexical rules but are hypothesized to represent frozen relics of earlier free forms controlled by syntactic rules (cf. Givón 1971). My purpose in the present paper is to suggest that the semantic range of a form at some given synchronic moment may be used in somewhat similar ways to infer the semantic–pragmatic development of that form. The specific example to be used is *just*, a form which is particularly interesting because its range of meanings is partly dependent on its syntactic status.

No attempt to infer the past from the present can be made without a number of operating assumptions, including the crucial assumption that the more 'likely' ('unmarked', or 'natural') change will have occurred, all other things being equal. Traditional internal reconstruction depends on the assumption that frozen morphological forms point to older, more productive patterns. For example, it is assumed for phonological reconstruction that paradigmatic allomorphy is not original; similarly, Givón's reconstruction of earlier word order from synchronic morphology assumes that syntactic structures become lexicalized, not vice versa. One of the assumptions I am making, for my part, is that there are variation-defining[3] universals of change of the type. If a property Y exists, then property X existed at an earlier time (cf. Greenberg 1978, Givón 1979). Also, grammatical status is significant: there is a cline of grammaticality such that adverbs are more 'grammatical' than adjectives, and the more grammatical a form is, the later it has developed (cf Givón 1979, Lehmann 1982). As in other areas of historical work, assumptions have to be made about 'same' and 'plausibly similar' — these are problematic enough in morphology and syntax (cf. Traugott and Romaine 1985), but even more so in semantics where there is not even a generally recognized formalism for representing lexical and grammatical meanings. However, I am assuming a semantics in which it is possible on the one hand to show relatedness among meanings synchronically, and on the other to decide what are plausible steps along a semantic continuum from one stage to the next. Such a semantics allows for distinctions to be made between the meaning of the form and various invited inferences and implicatures (cf., among others, Geis and Zwicky 1971, Grice 1975, Leech 1983). Furthermore, the meaning itself may best be treated in terms of core and periphery (cf. Coleman and Kay 1981). This claim involves yet another assumption: meanings associated with one form are related unless no connection can be found.[4] It follows that homonymy is to be considered as a last resort. For example, the *might* with which I swing a hammer can be semantically related to the *might* of possibility since physical strength is one of the factors that render possibilities possible, and these two meanings of *might* should therefore be treated as related and not as homonyms. On the other hand, the *can* in which I buy sardines cannot be semantically related by plausible semantic steps to the *can* of ability, and the two forms must be treated as homonyms.

2. THE SYNCHRONIC DATA

We turn now to a sketch of the meanings in Modern English of *just*. No attempt is made here to give an exhaustive account of the possible meanings of this word — such an endeavor would draw us too far afield into theoretical issues about where a difference of meaning can be said to occur. The following glosses form a substantial subset of the meanings most often cited in dictionaries such as the OED, Webster's Third, or the American Heritage Dictionary:

(1) Adj: a. honorable, fair: *just ruler*
b. righteous, legitimate: *just cause*
c. well-founded: *a just appraisal*
d. properly due: *just deserts*

e. fitting: *a just touch of solemnity*
   f. exact, precise: *a just measure*

These adjectival meanings all share the property of legitimacy, fairness, rightness, and being in harmony with some norm. In this they are supported by the meanings of words derived from *just*, such as *justice*, and *justify* (in the sense of both 'demonstrate validity' and 'space properly in printing'). The adverbial meanings may at first seem somewhat different:

(2) Adv: a. precisely, exactly: *just enough salt*
   b. simply: *it's just beautiful*
   c. at the exact moment: *it's just six*
   d. in immediate future or past: *she just arrived; she's just arriving*
   e. merely: *she's just a linguist*
   f. barely: *you just missed the bull's eye*

However, the relation between doing something legitimately or fittingly and doing it exactly, precisely as it should be done, are not really so far apart, especially when the adjectival usage in connection with weights and measures (1f) is taken into account. Both the adjectival and the adverbial meanings bring into play various alternative values: fairness and fittingness bring into play certain types of behavior, while excluding others that are valued less highly or considered excessive; preciseness, too, brings into play and excludes various alternatives that are neither too little nor too much.

Some elaboration on the adverbial meanings is in order here. König (MS) shows that the various adverbial types can be reduced to three, and that these all cohere when considered in terms of scales and boundaries on events, actions, states, and times. He distinguishes:

(3) a. an exclusive scalar particle meaning 'precisely, only, simply' (2a,b)
   b. a temporal adverb (2c,d)
   c. a downtoner like *hardly, merely, barely, scarcely* (2e,f)

He argues that these are separate categories on various grounds, among them the potential ambiguity in pairs like:

(4) a. I just read *Foundations of Syntactic Structure*: 'All (exactly what) I read was *FSS* / In the immediate past I read *FSS*' [ambiguous between (3a) and (3b); cannot mean *'I barely read *FSS*'].
   b. She just got tenure: 'She obtained tenure in the immediate past / She barely obtained tenure' [ambiguous between (3b) and (3c)].

As in the case of many other 'ambiguities', intonation will often disambiguate these.

Like other scalar particles, e.g. *only* and *even*, *just* in its scalar function is the sister to a wide range of focus constituents: S, NP, VP, PP, V, Adj, or Adv (cf. König 1981). Like all scalar particles, it brings into play alternatives to the meaning or value of the focus constituent. As an exclusive scalar particle similar to *only* and *simply*, it excludes the other alternatives brought into play, cf. *I visited just/only Odense* (contrast inclusive scalar particles like *even* which include other alternatives: *I visited even Odense*). Thus *just* can be a constituent of pragmatically negative and positive adjectives: *That is just awful, That is just marvelous*. What makes scalar *just* different from *only, simply* is that it does not evaluate the value of its focus constituent as ranking low.

König suggests that the temporal functions of *just* in (3b) are in complementary distribution as follows. It expresses:

(5) a. identity with the point of reference; this is a time adverb such as *then, this morning*, or time of utterance in constructions involving the present progressive or a momentary copula, cf. *She left just then, She's just having supper, It's just midnight*.
b. immediate precedence in past and present perfect contexts: *Bill just ran, Mary has just left*.
c. immediate future in constructions with futurative progressive, or with a verb having the *aktionsart* of an instantaneous event, such as *leave, arrive*: *She's just going to sing, She's just leaving*.

Although König treats the temporals as one set, it should be noted that those that identify points of reference, (5a), are actually like scalar particles of type (3a) in that they pick out the temporal adverb (*now*), or NP (*midnight*) or the time of utterance and exclude all other times. Types (5b) and (5c), however, do warrant treatment as a separate type, as they do not identify any particular time, nor pastness or futurity in general. Rather, they convey the somewhat fuzzy notion of immediately proximal time, that is, they are deictic to the time of utterance: proximal past and proximal future. However, they are semantically coherent with the scalar particle since they exclude values (in this case points in time) on an ordered scale.

In its downtoning function of 'barely, merely', (2e,f) *just* is syntactically not a scalar particle in that it can itself be preceded by a scalar particle, cf. *only just caught the train*; indeed, a potential scalar or temporal *just* is interpreted as a downtoner in the environment of a scalar particle, cf. *only just six*. Semantically, however, the downtoner shares some properties with the scalar particle *just* in that it too brings alternatives into play. This time, however, the focused element is treated as the uppermost boundary on the bottom (negative) end of the scale, and what is excluded is asymmetric. Whereas scalar *just* excludes both higher and lower values on the scale (if these exist, given cultural assumptions), downtoning *just* excludes everything valued (by cultural standards) as 'above' or 'more than' the focused element.[5] Thus *That is just marvelous* can only under special circumstances be interpreted as meaning 'That is merely marvelous' (what can be excluded above *marvelous*?); similarly, *That is just terrible* can only under special circumstances be interpreted as *That is merely terrible* (what is worse or 'more bad' than *terrible*?).

In sum, the three distinctions between the adverbial meanings of *just* proposed by König and summarized in (3) have been slightly modified as follows:

(6) a. an exclusive scalar particle meaning 'precisely, only, simply' (2a,b,c),
 b. a deictic temporal adverb meaning immediate future or past (2c),
 c. a downtoner (2e,f).

Although the three adverbial meanings are somewhat different, they are synchronically coherent in that they bring to attention alternatives (allowed or disallowed) on an ordered scale. Furthermore, they are coherent with the ordering of states, decisions, actions, etc. along a scale of (culturally determined) fitness, legitimacy, and justness. This means that the adjectival and adverbial meanings should be considered polysemous, not homonymous. The core meaning for the adjective has to do with fairness, and its peripheral meanings have to do with fitness and orderliness; it is the latter meaning which is the core meaning for the adverb.

3. PROJECTION BACK ON THE PAST

Given the synchronic facts outlined here, or some elaboration of them, what can we guess about the paths of change that led to the modern range of meanings? While I have shown that there is no semantic discontinuity between the 'adjectival' and 'adverbial' meanings of *just*, no attempt to account for the semantic–pragmatic changes in the word can ignore the syntactic category differences. It is useful then to start with the syntactic–semantic facts and to see what evidence can be gleaned from considering the process of grammaticalization.

As Lehmann has pointed out, 'It is a fact that most of the adverbs in every language are synchronically derived from nouns, verbs or adjectives' (1982: 87). This suggests that the adverbial meanings are later than the adjectival, and furthermore that they originated in a manner adverb which was directly derived from the adjective meaning 'honorab-ly, fair-ly, exact-ly'. Thus we can infer a period at which it was possible to say something like:

(7) They did it just

in the sense 'They did it justly/fittingly/precisely'.

Given a scale of grammaticalization, a further question is whether there is any difference in degree of grammaticalization among scalar particles, temporal adverbs and downtoners. On purely syntactic grounds, the downtoner would appear to be less grammaticalized than the scalar particle and the temporal because it behaves more like a regular adverb than a particle, in so far as it can itself be preceded by a scalar particle. On the grounds of grammaticalization, then, we can infer:

just: adj > adv manner > downtoner > scalar particle/temporal

Let us now turn to the independent evidence provided by principles of semantic–pragmatic change. We will see that these principles suggest a somewhat different order of development *vis-à-vis* the three 'adverbial' uses of *just*.

One frequently observed semantic change in the histories of languages is the change from more to less concrete or, to put it the other way, from less to more abstract. While recognizing the difficulty of defining such a change, and even suggesting that the terms should be abandond, Kronasser (1952) nevertheless identifies concrete > abstract with generalization in meaning. This generalization, in Kronasser's view, largely involves a shift from a specialized term to a generic term, cf. IE **bhel-* 'shine white' > 'shine'. If we consider the modern meanings of *just*, the adjectival meanings are more concrete in Kronasser's sense since they are largely specialized to moral, legal, and behavioral domains, whereas the adverbial meanings are more abstract as they are less specialized (even in the case of temporal *just*, the temporality itself derives from the focus constituent, not from *just* alone). We may therefore infer on semantic grounds as well as on grounds of grammaticalization that the adjectival meanings precede the adverbial ones.

A second type of semantic change will help provide insight into the possible order of development among the adverbial meanings of *just*. Among well known cases of semantic change are such shifts as were undergone by *boor* ('farmer' > 'coarse-mannered person'), *will* ('want' > (deictic) future), *but* (OE *beutan* 'outside' > connective of contrast), *very* ('true-ly', (cf. *verily*) > intensifier (or 'uptoner')). On the basis of evidence such as this, I have suggested (Traugott 1982) that a shift from less > more personal is common in semantic–pragmatic change. 'More personal' covers a number of different relationships, specifically, more evaluative (cf. *boor*), more subjective (cf. deictic tense *will*), or more intrusive in the utterance (cf. *but*).

In the case of *just*, of course, we start with meanings that are already relatively evaluative since they have to do with norms of behavior (we may, in fact, assume that these meanings themselves developed from less evaluative ones not retained in Modern English). But they are also relatively objective, since 'fair, righteous, fitting' depend largely on socially recognizable canons of law, religion, and appropriate behavior. The adverbial meanings are for the most part more subjective. While the truth value of the exclusion of alternatives brought into play by scalar *just* can be judged by external criteria such as eyeballing or scientific instruments in expressions with numerals and other quantifiers, e.g. *just six letters, just twelve-thirty*, the truth value of the exclusion in most other expressions cannot, e.g. *just the right answer, just what he wanted*. Even in the case of *There are just six letters left, It is just twelve-thirty*, where objective reference to the 'exactness' of *just* is possible, the particle *just* at the same time injects the speaker's point of view into the proposition (contrast *There are six letters left, It is twelve-thirty*, which are semantically the same, but pragmatically quite different). In the case of expressions like *just the right answer* the speaker's viewpoint is intrusive enough to call into question the appropriateness of the common notion that there is no relativity to rightness. The deictic temporal *just* by definition involves the speaker's point of view — how large an interval of time between Dick's leaving and the time of utterance does one allow before one is ready to claim that *Dick just left* is false? Given the criterion of less > more personal, we now have additional evidence that the adjectival meaning preceded that of the scalar particle. Furthermore we may assume that the scalar particle (including the scalar temporal with the immediate present as its focus) preceded the deictic temporal *just* (proximal past and future). The imposition of speaker point of view is particularly clear in the case of downtoning *just* (cf. *just a linguist, just a Laphroig*) where the possibility of external verification by scientific instrument is out of the question, and the speaker is imposing a negative evaluation. We can therefore assume that the downtoner as well as the deictic temporal developed later than the scalar particle.

In summary, we can infer the following changes (where 's', 't', 'd' are short for scalar particle, temporal particle, and downtoner respectively):

CHANGE	PROCESS UNDERGONE
(a) adj > manner adv > s/t/d	grammaticalization
(b) downtoner > s/t	grammaticalization
(c) righteously/fittingly > s/t/d	less > more abstract
	less > more personal
(d) precisely > temporal	less > more personal
(e) precisely > downtoner	less > more personal

It should be noted that (a) and (c) correlate perfectly; however, (b) and (e) predict reverse orders of change. Furthermore, no ordering with respect to the temporal and the downtoner have been inferred on grounds of semantic change. In so far as the downtoner is not restricted to temporals, it seems closer to the scalar particle than to the temporal. In so far as the temporal does not presuppose that alternatives beyond the boundary reached are negative, it seems closer to the scalar particle than the temporal. We can therefore infer only the following order:

$$? > \text{righteous/fitting/precise} > \text{precisely} \begin{array}{l} \nearrow \text{temporal} \\ \searrow \text{downtoner} \end{array}$$

4. THE HISTORICAL EVIDENCE

We turn now to the historical evidence to see how far our hypotheses are borne out by the data; in so far as partially different predictions are made by reference to processes of grammaticalization and processes of semantic change, which is the better predicter?

Just was borrowed into English from French in the later Middle English period (the earliest instances of the adjective cited in the MED are from Chaucer c.1380 and the Wyclif Bible c.1384; those of the adverb date from c.1400). The French forms, which will be discussed below, ultimately derive from the Latin adjective *iust-* and the adverb *iuste*, which pertain to actions and decisions in accordance with ritual, law, and good reason. According to Benveniste (1973: 391), Lat. *iustus* 'just' is related to IE **yous* 'state of regularity, of the normality required by the rules of ritual'. He argues that in Latin the verb *iurare*, the past participle of which gave rise to the adjective, means to engage in 'the act of repeating a certain form of words' (395), and the noun *ius*, which we usually translate as 'law', 'in general, is a *formula* and not an abstract concept' (391). This suggests that the hypothesis put forward in the preceding section is correct: that *just* in the sense of 'righteous, legitimate', etc. originated in a more concrete, less evaluative, meaning.

In Medieval French there were an adjective *juste* and an adverb *justement*. According to Wartburg (1950), the adjective *juste* was also used in earlier Old French in connection with religious norms, i.e. in the sense 'righteous'. According to Wartburg and also Larousse (1975), from the twelfth century on there appear legal and normative meanings ('conforming to that which is legal, legitimate'), and from the end of the thirteenth century also the meaning 'precise, exact' in contexts involving measures and balances (cf. *juste mesure* 'just/exact measure'). The adverb *justement* apparently was used only in the legal sense, not in the sense 'precisely'; this sense did not develop until the sixteenth century.

We may ask how the meaning 'exact, precise' came into being. Righteousness and justness, whether established by religious canons or by law, bring into play alternatives on a scale; in this case the scale, by convention, is implicated to be behavioral — conforming to the regulation of law, Christian doctrine, good manners, or other appropriate form. Extremes of behavior are normally not tolerated in these contexts. We may assume that in thirteenth-century French, as in Modern English, to say that something is just or is justly done is to invite the inference that it is done in precisely the right way, with the appropriate balance. The shift from 'honorable, fair, legitimate' > 'precise' can best be understood as involving the lexicalization of this invited inference. It is hardly surprising that expansion of meaning occurred in the context of measures.

In sum, when *juste* was borrowed into English there was a Medieval French adjective of this form and an adverb marked by *-ment*. The adjective appears in meanings essentially similar to those of MF *juste*: 'righteous, (legally) fair, exact':

(8) c.1384. Wyclif Bible, Luke 5.32: I cam not to clepe iust men but synful men to penaunce 'I came to call not righteous but sinful men to penance' (MED *just(e)* adj 1a)

(9) c.1385. Chaucer *TC* 3.1227: She ... juste cause hadde hym to triste 'She ... had reasonable cause to trust him' (ibid. 3a).

(10) c.1380. Chaucer *HF* 719: Hir paleys ... stant eke in so juste a place / That every soun mot to hyt pacc 'Her (Fame's) palace ... stood in so correct a place that every sound could reach it' (ibid. 4c).

There was also an adverb *justli*. This might appear to be a form part borrowed, part calqued from *justement*. However, it meant not only 'righteously, fairly' as did MF *justement*, but also 'exactly' in contexts of measurement and fit:

(11) c.1391. Chaucer *Astr.* 2.38.32: Yif thou drawe a cross-lyne overthwart the compas justly over the lyne meridional, than hast thou est and west and south 'If you draw a line across the compass exactly over the meridian line, then you have E and W and S' (MED *justli* 2a).

Within a couple of decades a new adverb *juste* appeared in the meaning 'exactly, precisely' of measurement and location:

(12) a. c.1400. *Morte Arth.* 1123: The gyaunt he hyttez Iust to the genitales 'He hits the giant exactly at the genitals' (MED *just(e)* adv a).

b. c.1500. *Altitude Steeple* 27: Let hym ... pitche a staffe the vpper poynte thereof to be *juste* with his yie, he stondyng upp righte therby 'Let him ... pitch a staff, the upper point of which should be exactly in line with his eye when he stands upright by it' (ibid.)

It appears then that adverbial *just* did not arise directly out of an adverbial phrase meaning 'in righteous/fitting manner', but rather out of an adverbial phrase meaning 'in exact degree/location'. Thus the hypothesis made in the previous section was correct that the adverbial meaning had its origins in an adjectival phrase, but was overly broad in allowing 'righteous' and 'fitting' to be possible sources in addition to 'exact/precise'.

We may note that the adverbial use of *just(ly)* in the sense 'exactly, precisely' is an English innovation. Adverbial *juste* appears to have been an incipient scalar particle from the beginning since it is associated with locative prepositional phrases, although it was not restricted to this syntactic category at first; the MED cites two examples without PP, one in the sense 'fittingly' (associated with measurement in a place):

(13) c.1486. *Arms Chivalry* 44: for to make the basinet sitte juste 'to make the basinet (helmet) sit right' (MED *just(e)* adv b)

and one in a temporal sense which will be discussed below.

The manner adverbial *juste* illustrated in (13) did not survive, but the scalar particle was rapidly expanded in the Early Modern English period to its modern range. The scalar particle is clearly syntactically different from the true adverb ('fittingly'), since the scalar particle but not the adverb of manner is sister to another constituent. Also, the adverb conventionally implicates measure but the scalar particle does not. This is a function in part of grammaticalization. In the process, the conventional implicature of measure, location, etc. is lost ('bleached' out); content is now expressed not by *just* but by the focus constituent [*genitales, yie* in (12)].

So far we have considered the relation between the adjective and the scalar particle. Two other meanings need to be considered, the temporal and the downtoner. Both of these develop later than the scalar particle. One adverbial temporal use of *juste* is cited in the MED:

(14) c.1500. *Bevis* (Chet) 89/1728: Graundyneee was the ffirste; He rode oute of tho gatus juste 'G was the first; he rode out of the gates immediately' (ibid. c).

This particular type of construction was not long-lived. What is striking about it is that it does not mean 'precisely then' but rather 'immediately after'. This presumably derives from the inferences invited by the narrative that situations follow each other (in this case, Graundyneee rides out right after hearing a plea for the recapture of Bevis).

By the beginning of the Modern English period, scalar particle constructions with similar deictic properties came into being. What the constructions have in common is that there is no overt time expression. As long as the particle had as its scope the time adverb or the time of utterance it indicated 'precisely at time X', just as in Modern English (5a). But when the scalar particle had as its focus Tense, and an adverb of time was not present, or the reference point was not time of utterance, then some uncertainty could arise concerning what time was being specified.[6] Consider:

(15) 1697. Dryden *Virg. Georg.* IV 430: pleasant Casia just renew'd in prime (OED *just* adv 4).

Because of the ambiguity of *renew'd*, which can be processed as a perfect stative or as a passive participle, this can be interpreted as 'just now in a state of renewedness' (stative) or as 'recently renewed' (passive). Or consider again:

(16) 1719. Defoe *Crusoe* 1.xviii: the captain replied 'Tell his excellence I am just a coming' (ibid.).

This can be interpreted as 'Just now I am starting to come', and indeed this is probably what the captain meant to imply. But hearers know that coming is an action that takes time, and that promises are not always fulfilled on time. *Just*, then, can be interpreted as signalling intention to act in the near future.

The kind of shift postulated here from designating exact time of utterance to deictically proximal time can be found in a number of other expressions; among them is the extension of *right* as in *right now* to *right* in *right away* (immediate future); cf. also the development of *presently* from 'at present' to 'soon', French *tout à l'heure* 'exactly on the hour' to 'in the immediate future, in the immediate past'; there are also similar shifts in the meanings of Gm. *eben* (< 'even, on the same level'), *gleich* (< 'same/similar'). Indeed, it appears that the semantic relation of 'same time' is quite unstable. Potential simultaneity in time between clauses as in *When Jim arrived Jack jumped out of the window* is typically interpreted as sequential time ('After Jim arrived Jack jumped out of the window'). It can even be interpreted as textual contrast in some cases, cf. *While Ron likes wine, Tom likes beer* (cf. *inter alia* Heinämäki 1974, Abraham 1976). I have suggested elsewhere (Traugott 1986) that the tendency to infer temporal asymmetry from simultaneity is related to the linearity of speech and the tendency to view order of clauses as iconic to order of events (cf. Haiman 1984). In the case of *just, toute à l'heure*, etc., clause order is not involved. However, asymmetry, or absence of exact match between the moment of utterance and the present tense of the proposition can readily be inferred, given that many speech acts specify future time, cf. promises, commands, etc. Once it was used to signal immediate future it could then also be extended to the immediate past.

The last development of *just* to be considered here is that of the downtoner. The OED cites the earliest examples toward the end of the seventeenth century, and points out that they are often in the environment of *but* and *only*, e.g.

(17) 1693. Dryden *Juvenal* p.lxxv: Let Horace, who is the Second, and but just the Second, carry off the Quivers (OED *just* adv 5).

It is possible that the downtoner derives metonymically from constructions with *but, only*. But it is also possible, in view of the fact that even from the beginning bare *just* also occurs in downtoning function, that once more an invited inference has become lexicalized. As in the case of *merely* and *only*, *just* excludes 'more' in so far as it means 'precisely'. The negative downtoning meaning may well derive from social inferencing associated with such principles as 'the more the better', and conversely, 'if you can't get more, that's bad'.

We see, then, that the semantic predictions (c)–(e) made in the section on hypothetical semantic reconstruction are correct. The earliest recorded meaning is relatively concrete. The adjectival meanings precede the adverbial, and the scalar meanings precede the temporal and downtoner meanings. Although the downtoner develops later than the temporal, there is no more evidence from the historical data than from the synchronic to assume that it derived out of the temporal rather than directly from the scalar particle.

The independence of the proximal temporal and downtoner meanings of *just* is supported by the development of an adverbial form *juste* in French which has downtoning but not deictic temporal meanings. This form developed in the seventeenth century meaning 'fairly, exactly'. It existed alongside *justement*, which, as mentioned above, itself had acquired the meaning 'exactly' in the sixteenth century. Like English adverbial *just*, French *juste* presumably derived the meaning of exactness and preciseness directly from adjectival *juste* 'exact, precise'. Unlike the English form, however, it did not develop an equivalent scalar particle range, being limited mainly to occurrence with NPs and PPs of location, measure, and time. *Juste* with NP of time can be illustrated by *Il est six heures juste* 'It is just/ exactly six o'clock'. However, there is nothing equivalent to the English deictic immediate future and past construction. Recently a rather restricted downtoning use has developed, usually in the phrase *tout juste*: cf. *Il sait tout juste lire* 'He barely knows how to read' (while Larousse cites a sixteenth-century adjectival use meaning 'hardly sufficient', it claims the adverbial use equivalent to *à peine* is twentieth-century).

5. ON THE RELATION OF *JUST* TO SIMILAR TERMS

Before concluding, a note is in order on the relation of *just* to some other forms with similar meanings, most especially *right*. *Right* has an adjectival meaning associated with justness, and fittingness. As an adverb it can mean 'precisely' as in *right over there, right now*, and, as has been mentioned, it can signal proximal future as in *She will leave right away*. Indeed, at the time when *just* first entered English, derivatives of native *right*, which goes back to Old English and beyond to Germanic, sometimes alternate in manuscripts with *just*.[7] The overlap between the adverbial meanings of *just* and *right* prompted Cohen (1969) to propose that, since there was 'apparently no way to explain the various meanings of "just" from the notion of "righteous"' (1969: 26), it was not unreasonable to assume that they derived by analogy from *right* which had from Old English times the two relevant meanings: 'righteous' and 'precise'. We have seen that in fact the scalar meaning of *just* can be derived without difficulty from 'righteous/fair/legitimate' via the adjectival meaning 'exact, precise', a meaning which had already developed in Medieval French (presumably independently of *right*). Cohen's argument is worth taking up, however, because it highlights two methodological points relevant to the present topic: one concerning the assumption that analogy operates readily in semantic change, the other concerning the possibility that old meanings may continue to put constraints on the path of change, even though they may have lost their status as core meanings.

While it is certainly conceivable that analogy may be a factor in semantic change, it should be hypothesized to occur only in the last resort. The neogrammarians used analogy to explain exceptions to sound laws. At the other extreme, generative linguists have argued that analogy is the basis of grammar simplification; in fact it is **the** basic principle underlying phonological and morphological change (cf. Kiparsky 1968). In both cases analogy is used to account for change in form, and development of formal similarity (diagrammatic iconicity). However, a well recognized principle for semantics is that different form signals different meaning, and vice versa 'semantic sameness is also represented by formal sameness' (Anttila 1972: 89). This is the principle of isomorphic iconicity (Haiman 1980). The question of whether pure lexical synonyms can exist from a pragmatic point of view is still open. In general, linguists assume there are none, or if they exist they are very rare. Analogy, or movement toward same meaning, is therefore methodologically a poor starter for semantic change, except in the weak sense of 'likely process of change'. It is, of course, only in the latter sense that it can be used in the kind of reconstruction from synchronic meanings investigated here, since it requires evidence external to the form itself.

The history of *right* is in fact interesting not so much for its similarities with *just* but for its differences. For one, *right* never developed the range of uses of a scalar particle, being limited mainly to spatial and temporal adverbial constructions (**He right passed his exam, *Right a dozen apples*). More important for our purposes here, however, is its original meaning. *Right* originally had to do with straightness and boundaries. In his discussion of IE institutions, Benveniste points out that Lat. *regio, rex, rectus* derive from a common source related to Gk. *orego* 'stretch (out) in a straight line'. In Lat. a *regio* 'region' is a point reached by a line, a *rex* 'king' is an appointer of lines, boundaries or rules, and *rectus* means 'straight as this line which one draws' (1973: 311f). The metaphoric extension of concrete straightness to abstract morality appears to have had widespread currency in IE. However, the sense of physical straightness was not lost. It is associated with paths and orientation toward some goal. Apparently it is this meaning that in part constrains the uses of adverbial *right* and helps to maintain the differences from *just*, despite neutralization in certain contexts. The original meaning of *right* can be hypothesized to account for the fact that *right* can be an intensifier (meaning 'very'), but not a downtoner, cf. earlier *I am right glad*, now fossilized in expressions like *the right honorable minister.* Whereas *just* excludes more (as well as less), *right* in its linear, directed sense invites the inference that more is possible.

Another lexical item which shares some semantic (but not syntactic) properties with scalar *just* is *very* as in *That's the very spot on which he stood* (cf. *That's just the spot on which he stood*) (Brugman 1984: 34). Here *very*, like *just*, specifies a unique referent among a set of alternatives. In other uses, *very* identifies an extreme on a scale, as in *the very back of the room* (*very* = adj) or intensity, as in *She is very tall* (*very* = adv), but it cannot place a referent on the lowest or negative end of the scale. That is, it cannot be a downtoner, only an uptoner. Again, as in the case of *right*, we can invoke the original meaning: *very* derives from MF *verray* 'true' (cf. Section 2), and, as Brugman points out, still shares many properties with *true/truly*. As such it would hardly be expected to mean 'barely, merely'.

If one holds the view that diachronic facts are totally separate from synchronic ones, it may seem counterintuitive and even theoretically absurd that the original lexical meanings of words like *just, right* or *very* persist in the uses discussed here, and continue to partially constrain their development. However, large numbers of 'desemanticized' and grammaticalized words do in fact show similar evidence of an original core meaning that has controlled and continues to control the path of semantic–pragmatic change they can undergo, and needs to be accounted for in a semantic–pragmatic description of those words. To take one further example, *yet* and *still* both originally signalled continuity and therefore non-perfectivity. *Yet* as the suppletive form of *already* (cf. *He hasn't left yet*) still signals precisely this non-perfectivity. And both *yet* and *still* as concessives continue to show properties of 'durativity: unlike other concessives such as *although, even if,*

141

while, they signal pragmatically that the concessive is an elaboration, continuing the discourse (cf. König and Traugott 1982).

6. CONCLUSION

In conclusion, we have seen that principles of grammaticalization are reliable for internal reconstruction where major category changes are concerned (e.g. adjective > adverb), but relatively unreliable where more delicate distinctions are in question and, as in the case of particle vs. downtoner, there is no fixed morphological structure to go by. This should not be too surprising in light of the fact that Lehmann has found that the parameter of scope (larger scope implies less grammaticalization) frequently does not cohere with other parameters of grammaticalization such as semantic bleaching (1982: 169f).

On the other hand, we have seen that principles of semantic–pragmatic change are very reliable for internal reconstruction of the changes undergone at least by the word *just*. This reliability must of course be tested against numerous further examples. The present micro-study should, however, suggest that we are beginning to know enough about semantic–pragmatic changes to be able to make predictions as well as descriptions of individual changes. Furthermore, it should suggest that the force of the predictions is testable in part through the procedure of inferring the semantic past from the variation of the present; in other words, it has the potential of being as strong as the force of predictions in the area of phonological change.

NOTES

1. This paper, a much revised version of a discussion of *just* and *right* presented at the Modern Language Association's Annual Meeting in December 1982, was completed while I was a Fellow at the Center for Advanced Study in the Behavioral Sciences. I am grateful for support from NSF Grant BNS 76-22943 and the Simon Guggenheim Foundation. Many thanks are due to Christian Lehmann for lively discussion of some of the issues, and to Suzanne Kemmer and Ekkehard König for comments on a draft of this paper. They are, of course, in no way responsible for any errors of fact or interpretation.

2. There is also work on internal reconstruction of paths of transmission; for example, the spread of sound changes across speech communities can be inferred on the basis of closeness to or distance from a focal center (cf. Bailey 1973, Labov and Trudgill in Wang, forthcoming). Such research focuses on inferring the actuation and transition of a change rather than the constraints on it.

3. This term is used by Hawkins, but with reference to synchronic universals that 'have been used to structure certain observed changes in languages and explain their directionality' (1982: 368).

4. There are, of course, 'false friends' that may appear to be related when they are not, e.g. *meal* 'grain, food served at one sitting', but this does not invalidate the general principle.

5. König points out that this may be too restrictive: *I can just reach the ceiling* may be 'close to' rather than 'not comfortably'.

6. John Schneider (personal communication) points out that in South African English *I'll do it just now* means 'I'll do it soon (in about ten to thirty minutes)'. This proximal future sense of *just* with *now* is presumably a projection from the proximal future in contexts without *now*.

7. Cf. entries in MED under *juste* adj 1a.

REFERENCES

Abraham, Werner. 1976. 'Die Rolle von Trugschlüssen in der Diachronie von Satzkonnektoren', in Heinz D. Pohl and Nikolai Salnikow (eds.), *Opuscula Slavica et Linguistica: Festschrift für A. Issatschenko*. Klagenfurt: Heyn.

Anttila, Raimo. 1972. *An Introduction to Historical and Comparative Linguistics*. New York: Macmillan.

Bailey, Charles-James N. 1973. *Variation and Linguistic Theory*. Washington, DC: Center for Applied Linguistics.

Benveniste, Emile. 1973. *Indo-European Language and Society*, trans. by Elizabeth Palmer. Coral Gables, Florida: University of Miami Press.

Brugman, Claudia. 1984. 'The *Very* Idea: A Case Study in Polysemy and Cross-Lexical Generalizations', *Papers from the Parasession on Lexical Semantics of the Chicago Linguistic Society*, 21–38.

Cohen, Gerald. 1969. 'How did the English Word "Just" Acquire its Different Meanings?', *Chicago Linguistic Society* 5: 25–9.

Coleman, Linda, and Paul Kay. 1981. 'Prototype Semantics: The English Verb *Lie*', *Language* 57: 26–44.

Geis, Michael L., and Arnold M. Zwicky. 1971. 'On Invited Inferences', *Linguistic Inquiry* 2: 561–6.

Givón, Talmy. 1971. 'Historical Syntax and Synchronic Morphology: An Archaeologist's Field Trip', *Chicago Linguistic Society* 7: 394–416.

—— 1979. *On Understanding Grammar*. New York: Academic Press.

Greenberg, Joseph H. 1978. 'Diachrony, Synchrony, and Language Universals', in Joseph H. Greenberg, Charles A. Ferguson, and Edith Moravcsik (eds.), *Universals of Human Language I: Method and Theory*. Stanford: Stanford University Press.

Grice, H. Paul. 1975. 'Logic and Conversation', in Peter Cole and Jerry L. Morgan (eds.), *Syntax and Semantics III: Speech Acts*. New York: Academic Press.

Haiman, John. 1980. 'Iconicity', *Language* 56: 515–40.

—— 1984. 'Asymmetry', in John Haiman (ed.), *Iconicity in Syntax*. Amsterdam: Benjamins.

Hawkins, John A. 1982. 'Language Universals and the Logic of Historical Reconstruction', *Linguistics* 20: 367–90.

Heinämäki, Orvokki T. 1974. 'Semantics of English Temporal Connectives'. University of Austin, Texas, dissertation.

Kiparsky, Paul. 1968. 'Linguistic Universals and Linguistic Change', in Emmon Bach and Robert T. Harms (eds.), *Universals in Linguistic Theory*. New York: Holt, Rinehart and Winston.

König, Ekkehard. 1981. 'The Meaning of Scalar Particles in German', in Hans-Jürgen Eikmeyer and Hannes Rieser (eds.), *Words, Worlds, and Contexts: New Approaches in Word Semantics*. Berlin: de Gruyter, 107–32.
—— MS. '"Just": Polysemy or Vagueness'. Chapter of *The Meaning of Focus Particles* (in preparation).
—— and Elizabeth Closs Traugott. 1982. 'Divergence and Apparent Convergence in the Development of *Yet* and *Still*', *Proceedings of the Eighth Meeting of the Berkeley Linguistic Society*, 170–9.
Kronasser, Heinz. 1952. *Handbuch der Semasiologie: Kurze Einführung in die Geschichte, Problematik und Terminologie der Bedeutungslehre*. Heidelberg: Carl Winter.
Larousse. 1975. *Grand Larousse de la langue française*. Paris: Librairie Larousse.
Leech, Geoffrey. 1983. *Principles of Pragmatics*. London: Longman.
Lehmann, Christian. 1982. 'Thoughts on Grammaticalization: A Programmatic Sketch', Vol. I. *AKUP* 48.
MED. 1969–. Sherman M. Kuhn and John Reidy (eds.), *Middle English Dictionary*. Ann Arbor: University of Michigan Press.
Traugott, Elizabeth Closs. 1982. 'From Propositional to Textual and Expressive Meanings: Some Semantic–Pragmatic Aspects of Grammaticalization', in Winfred P. Lehmann and Yakov Malkiel (eds.), *Perspectives on Historical Linguistics*. Amsterdam: Benjamins.
—— 1986. 'On the Origins of "And" and "But" Connectives in English', *Studies in Language* 10: 137–50.
—— and Suzanne Romaine. 1985. 'Some Questions for the Concept of "Style" in Sociohistorical Linguistics. *Folia Linguistica Historica* 6: 7–39.
Wang, William S.-Y. Forthcoming. *Papers from the Symposium on Cultural Transmission*, Center for Advanced Study in the Behavioral Sciences, Stanford, Spring 1984.
Wartburg, Walther von. 1950. *Französisches etymologisches Wörterbuch*. Basel: Helbing und Lichtenhahn.

12

Notes on Black and Red American English

WOLFGANG VIERECK

In the extremely valuable *Bibliography of Pidgin and Creole Languages* (1975) John Reinecke and his associates include chapters on Black American English and American Indian Pidgin English and sum up quite well both the research (especially early research) and the different positions held in these areas.

1.

Taking Black American English first, it must be said that the research descriptions are matter-of-fact even with regard to the 'creolists' (1975: 482).

> Crucial to testing the creolist theory of B[lack] E[nglish] origins is a truly rigorous comparison of black and white speech in Southern communities. ... Also awaiting detailed study are the questions of uniformity versus regional diversity in Southern BE, changes and leveling in the speech of Southern Negroes moving to the North and West, and code-shifting in Southern Negro speech (1975: 483).

More than ever before the second half of the 1970s and the early 1980s (cf. Montgomery's fourth stage referred to below) saw a remarkable advance in the 'rigorous comparison of black and white speech in Southern communities' although, regrettably, quite a few projects did not meet R. McDavid's ambitious requirements, which he outlined as follows for the urban South:

> For each city an investigation should cover pronunciation and grammar and vocabulary of various ethnic, age, and educational groups. The research design should indicate the traditional differences between cultivated, common, and folk speech in the community ...; it must then

indicate the traditional differences between the speech of the community and that of the surrounding countryside; finally, it must assess the differences that have been wrought by the passage of time — whether by mass migration from other areas ... or by the normal centripetal processes of industrialization and urbanization and mass education. ... (1967: 119).

In 'The Study of the Language of Blacks and Whites in the American South' (1981) Michael Montgomery distinguishes between the following four distinct stages in the study of language patterns in this area, considered to be crucial in evaluating the linguistic relationship between the two ethnic groups: the Linguistic Atlas stage, the creolists' stage, the intensive surveys conducted mainly by Labov, Wolfram, and Fasold in the late 1960s and early 1970s both in Northern cities and Southern rural areas (e.g. Wolfram 1974), and finally, since the middle 1970s, the intensive studies conducted in Southern communities using a variety of approaches and providing valuable new data. Some remarks on the second stage are appropriate here. To quote Montgomery:

> The work in this second stage was not based on fieldwork in the conventional sense, but was rather based on personal observations and conclusions of the scholars themselves. Researchers in this second stage did not address the same questions about variation in pronunciation and vocabulary as did earlier Linguistic Atlas studies. Many of them were primarily concerned with making claims about the grammatical system and the grammatical rules of American blacks that it was up to later research to substantiate. They were also interested in showing how the historical record could provide new sources of information on language differences between blacks and whites (1981: 3).

Although no doubt interesting and important, the historical and geographic dimensions the creolists added to the discussion of the speech of American blacks were not really new. Earlier, dialectologists had neither overlooked Africa as a possible source of certain features/words found on the American continent nor ignored the possibility of the influence of the speech of blacks on that of whites (cf. Turner 1949; R. McDavid and V. McDavid 1951). At the time of the 'Black Power' movement of the 1960s, the search for identity of the American black population and, a little later, Alex Haley's much-discussed national bestseller *Roots*, led some creolists to narrow the outlook even in linguistic matters to the Caribbean and Africa and to base their conclusions on questionable evidence, i.e. literary attestations.

In some noteworthy contributions (1967, 1968), William A. Stewart produces 'literary attestations of early Negro and white non-standard dialect' (1968: 18) to show that 'of the Negro slaves who constituted the field labor force on North American plantations up to the mid-nineteenth century, even many who were born in the New World spoke a variety of English which was in fact a true creole language' (1968: 3). To prove this, Stewart produces 'a well-known example of the speech of a fourteen-year-old Negro lad given by Daniel Defoe in *The Family Instructor* (London, 1715)' (1967: 24). Other creolists, however, were more careful with that kind of evidence: 'If Defoe's representation of New World pidgin English were based on accurate information one would expect it to have more in common with other Atlantic pidgins and creoles. ... Defoe's use of pidgin was almost certainly a stylistic device used to lend verisimilitude to his supposedly real-life adventures as well as to supply a touch of the exotic' (Todd 1974: 77). It is not likely that Defoe ever personally encountered African natives. Other, more reliable, evidence that sheds light on the true nature of early Black American English unfortunately remained untouched by Stewart. I mean letters written by blacks (and whites) (cf. Eliason 1956), by overseers both white and black,[1] and the large collection of *Ex-Slave Narratives* (cf. Rawick 1972, 1977, 1979).[2] Such sources must be fully exploited. Hardly anything can be made of another source which Allen Walker Read (1939) used: runaway slave advertizements; they do not contain examples of the English of these slaves but give only impressions of the particular slave's competence in English, as Stewart (1968: 3) rightly noted. It is impossible today to interpret these impressions unequivocally.

Edwards (1974) provides an example of a creolist's narrowed outlook. He notes: 'The *gwine* forms are very widespread in Afro-American dialects. *Gwine* occurs in Jamaica ..., in Gullah ..., and is common in Southern rural Black English, today ... *Gwain* was also common in Southern plantation speech ...' (1974: 16). About its origin Edwards has the following to say: 'The "to go" verbs of the Germanic languages (Eng. *go, going*; Dutch *gaan*) apparently syncretized early with Akan language forms of the word *gwa, gwo, guaá* "to flee"' (1974: 16). Edwards overlooks completely that *gwine* and related forms were still widespread in dialects in the whole southwest of England in the late 1930s (cf. Map 12.1) and that it also occurred in other areas of North America, e.g. in eastern New England (see Map 12.2). Edwards also overlooks the fact that *gwine* is not only common in Southern rural Black English but that it also occurs in Southern White English. Atwood (1953: 41) notes that *gwine* is 'considerably more frequent among Negroes than among [the more rustic of the] white informants. A larger sampling of Negro usage might enable us to classify these and other forms as "characteristically Negro", but the difference would again be one of frequency'. What is needed first and foremost is an honest evaluation of **all** materials and data attainable before a one-sided picture becomes the 'established' point of view. Some of Crawford Feagin's conclusions are examples of the bad consequences of one-sided research. In her sociolinguistic study of the white community of Anniston,

NOTES ON BLACK AND RED AMERICAN ENGLISH

Map 12.1: *Going* and its Variants in Southern English Dialects

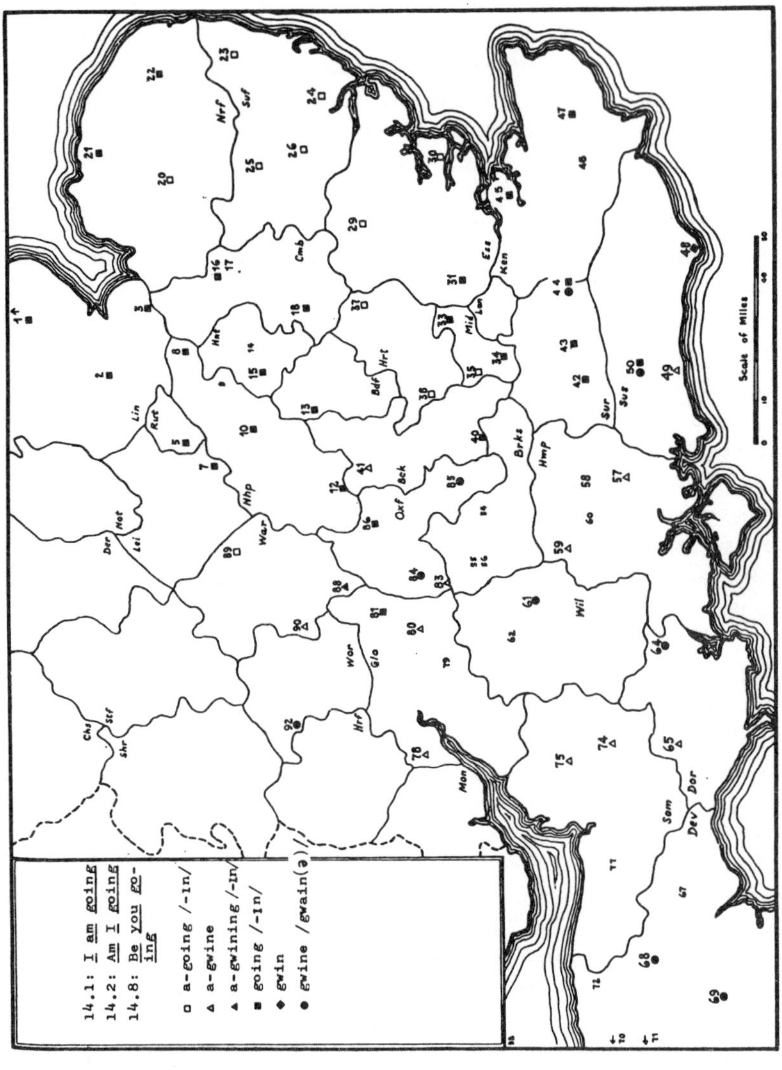

14.1: I am going
14.2: Am I going
14.8: Be you go-
     ing

□ a-going /-in/
△ a-gwine
▲ a-gwining /-in/
■ going /-in/
♦ gwin
● gwine /gwain(ə)

Source: Viereck (1975), vol. II, Map 88.

Map 12.2: The Distribution of *gwain* and *gain* 'Going' in the Eastern United States

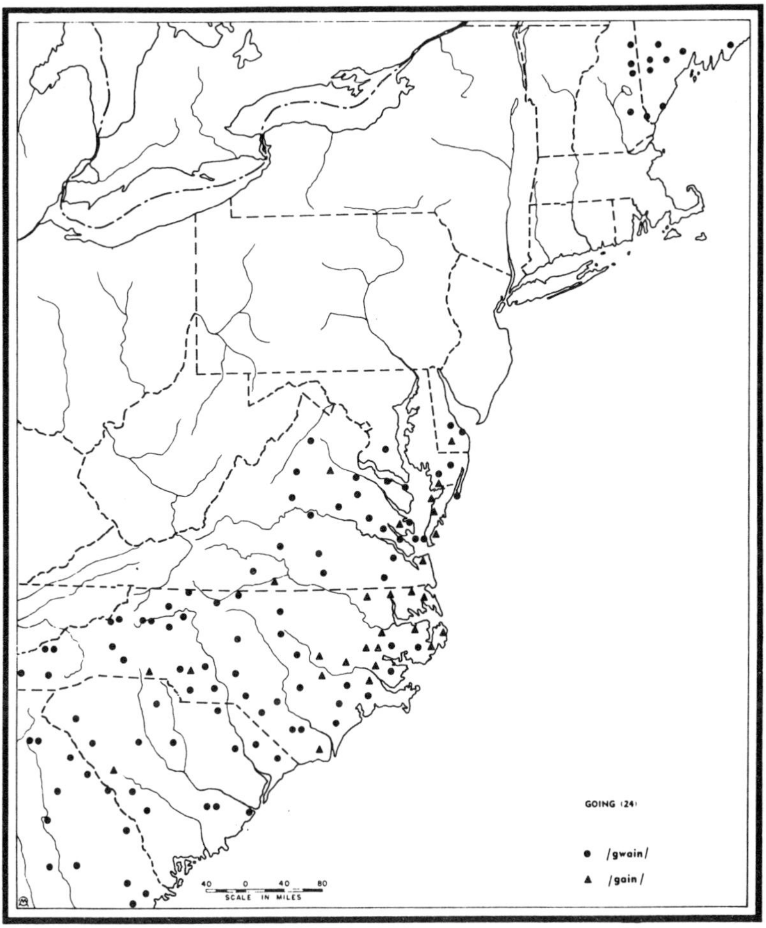

Source: Atwood (1953), Figure 27.

Alabama, she remarks: 'It must be emphasized ... that Black English has certain features which do not occur in Southern White, British dialects, or older stages of English and which are **undoubtedly** grammatical remnants of Creole: (1) remote present perfect *been*; (2) lack of agreement; (3) lack of possessive *-s*; (4) *is* deletion' (1979: 263, my emphasis). With the possible exception of the first-mentioned feature, on which more research is needed, such a statement can be made only when relevant studies pointing out the existence of the features in the English of the mother country are simply ignored.

In his provocative book *Roots of Language*, Derek Bickerton postulates: 'I shall use the word *creole* to refer to languages which ... arose in a population where not more than 20 percent were native speakers of the dominant language and where the remaining 80 percent was composed of diverse language groups' (1981: 4). When we take this to be more than just figures and look at the demographic developments in the South, we realize that this white–black population ratio is hardly ever reached. 'Aside from New England, Virginia and Maryland were the only colonies which developed a very distinctive life during the seventeenth century ... The great majority of the inhabitants [of Virginia] had come at their own expense, receiving fifty acres for each adult member of their families, including a servant or two ... The typical landholding was small, and approximately two thirds of the owners held no slaves, but cultivated their plantations with their own hands' (Hockett 1940: 81ff). Similar was the situation in other parts of the South. Consider two further instances, one from Alabama, the other from Tennessee: 'Those who are not familiar with the South generally think of Alabama as a region of big plantations and a high percentage of Negroes. Such areas certainly existed in Alabama, but the section under discussion was never one of them' (Feagin 1979: 37).

> The population of the Alabama Piedmont has been mainly native-born white southerners ever since the Indians were removed. In what are now the seven northern counties of this section — Calhoun, Cleburne, Talladega, Clay, Randolph, Coosa, and Tallapoosa — the Negro population has remained in the same proportion to whites for 120 years: between 24% and 26% for the area as a whole and between 6% and 48% for individual counties. This contrasts with Dallas County in the Black Belt which has had a Negro population of between 50% and 80% over the same period. In the Piedmont, cotton plantations with slaves were mainly located in the flat bottom land between the Coosa River and the Blue Ridge foothills in Calhoun and Talladega counties. Smaller farms operated by their owners with perhaps one or two slaves were more typical of the rest of the area. In some places, such as Ashland in Clay County, it is known that slaves were never used and that all farming was done by whites ... (Feagin 1979: 42ff).

With regard to certain regions in Tennessee, Lee Pederson points out: 'Black speech in East Tennessee is not easy to evaluate because ... the emergence of blacks as a large and distinctive social group in the region is a phenomenon of the present century' (1983: 142) and 'In 1880 ..., only the rural counties of Hawkins, Jefferson, Hamblen, Blount, McMinn, Loudon, Bledsoe, Bradley, and Marion had black populations in excess of 10 percent of the total population. Nowhere did the figure reach 20 percent in the rural counties, and even Knox County, the most heavily populated unit in East Tennessee, had a black population of less than 16 per cent of its total. Only Hamilton County had a significant black population, scarcely 24 per cent in 1880' (1983: 20). Although one of Bickerton's conditions was met (i.e. the diverse language groups to which the Negroes belonged), the other was not. Consequently, a creole could not develop in such a situation. For the state with the highest Negro population — South Carolina — the following figures are available: in 1790 56.3 percent of the population was white and 43.7 percent black. One hundred years later the black population had increased to 59.8 percent and the white population had decreased, but with 40.1 percent still remained twice as high as Bickerton's figure. The white population in the state as a whole had never been lower than 39.3 percent (in 1880) (Petty 1975: 64). However, this black–white population rate was not the same throughout the state. There were areas near the Atlantic coast, such as Beaufort where the Negro population increased from 76.7 percent to 84.7 percent between 1790 and 1830 (Petty 1975: 73) or All Saints' Parish, Georgetown District, 'once the site of the richest rice plantations in America ... [where] nine blacks to each white ... (lasting throughout the nineteenth century) was the highest ratio of blacks to whites in South Carolina' (Joyner 1981: no page numbering).[3] Thus the two factors favorable for creating a creole are present here — and a creole in areas near the Atlantic coast and on the Sea Islands indeed developed, the well known Gullah or Geechee, legitimately enjoying separate treatment in the *Bibliography of Pidgin and Creole Languages* by Reinecke and his associates (1975).[4] The application of Bickerton's demographic criterion points to the uniqueness of the Gullah area in the United States. In the 'rest' of the country in all probability a creole simply could not develop — with the probable exception of large local plantations where we need further information on the black–white ratio of the people working there.[5]

2.

The section on American Indian Pidgin English in the *Bibliography of Pidgin and Creole Languages* (1975) is understandably quite short. The two opposing views on the English spoken by Indians (or, perhaps, the older and the more recent approach) are succinctly summarized in the introduction, also drawing attention to the fragmentary and not always reliable documentary attestations. Literary attestations, such as those in Defoe's *Robinson Crusoe*, belong to the latter category. As Beverly O. Flanigan (1981: 15) rightly observed:

> The role of literary convention even in the recording of nonfictional documents must not be overlooked, however. Defoe's *Robinson Crusoe*, for example, represents not an actual voyage but a fictional narration in the tradition of what were very probably already highly conventionalized nonfiction commentaries on the speech of aboriginal peoples ... A number of fictional travel accounts of the New World predated *Crusoe*, and such books typically confused African and Indian natives, reflecting the Europeans' confusion about 'exotic' peoples learned of only secondhand.

Furthermore, 'American writers of fiction and drama ... adopted for the first two hundred years the European mode of depicting the Indian as a "noble savage" who spoke an exalted and even poetic British English' (Flanigan 1981: 2). Flanigan also adequately deals with the theory put forward by J.L. Dillard in 1972 and 1975, according to which Indians learned the pidgin, so-called, from blacks with whom they often worked as slaves on the plantations. Whereas a Negro–Indian contact in the Southeast can certainly not be denied,[6] Indians in the Northeast — not to mention those in the West and Southwest — had contact with the British and other Europeans long before they would have seen blacks (cf. also Flanigan 1981: 8ff). Theories, however, should eventually be supported by data, reliable data, that is. More reliable than the literary attestations referred to above are the data collected by George L. Kittredge as early as 1904 on the English or Englishes used by New England Indians in the seventeenth and early eighteenth centuries, which Dillard overlooked. Dillard maintains that 'gradually — almost grudgingly — some attention is beginning to be paid to American Indian Pidgin English' (Dillard 1980: 4) and quotes an article by Ives Goddard from 1976, which in Dillard's bibliography (1980: 463) appears as 1977. Although Dillard tries to play down Goddard's contributions as only providing 'a few more attestations [of American Indian Pidgin English] and a rehash of many already cited' (1980: 406), e.g. by Dillard (1972: 146ff) himself, the evidence presented by Goddard forces Dillard to withdraw his own theory: 'It is quite true that the earliest attestations of A[merican] I[ndian] P[idgin] E[nglish] predate those of W[est] A[frican] P[idgin] E[nglish], and that it therefore cannot be proved that the former represented diffusion from the latter' (Dillard 1980: 407)! Not only are Kittredge's data on the English of Indians in the Northeast, e.g. the letters he produced, unknown to Dillard, this is also true of Hugo

Schuchardt's much earlier short but important piece 'Beiträge zur Kenntniss [sic] des englischen Kreolisch. I.' (1888).[7] Schuchardt gives examples of writings of Indian boys and girls published by the pupils of Indian schools in Pennsylvania around 1880. Among the peculiarities that occur quite frequently in the texts of these 'School News' publications, Schuchardt mentions the following: omission of the *-s* morpheme in the third person singular, present tense, of verbs (*he think*); pronominal apposition or double subject (*my father he took me*); coalescence of personal and possessive pronouns (*he name*); and deletion of the copula (*they working*). All these features are well attested in earlier stages of English and/or present-day varieties of English in the British Isles. Red English is another area that deserves further attention, and this means primarily the collection and analysis of further data.

In this paper I have tried to show that beliefs should not be treated as facts and that all data attainable, linguistic and extra-linguistic, should first be evaluated critically, honestly, and patiently before conclusions are drawn; otherwise these are likely to have to be revised again.

NOTES

1. See Eliason (1956) and Starobin (1974). To avoid misinterpretation of the materials due to normalizations introduced by the editor in view of a broader readership, only originals should be analyzed. Space does not permit me to deal with the many problems of White American English and its development. In this field, too, much work remains to be done. Promising sources have remained almost untapped. To name just one: British private libraries. Since many plantation owners lived in the mother country, a considerable amount of correspondence between them and their overseers on the various plantations must exist in private libraries. In a 1981 paper J. Williamson devoted her attention to the overseers' speech. Since the conference proceedings have not yet been published at the time of this writing, I do not know whether she used original material or relied mainly on those letters already investigated by Eliason (1956) and in the MA theses mentioned by him. Williamson notes:

> Few, if any, have looked at the speech of those Englishmen who became settlers, those Englishmen who bought slaves and from whom the slaves must have learned at least some English. They had no other source from which to learn it. An examination of the features which were a part of the settlers' speech is revealing. Not all of the settlers spoke grammar book standard English' (1981: no page numbering).

Her conclusion is anything but surprising. On other sources relevant for the study of American English, see Viereck (1982). In that paper as well as in my review (Viereck 1983) of J.L. Dillard's 1980 revision of Albert H. Marckwardt's *American English*, I hope to have convincingly shown that Dillard ignores valuable contributions while taking questionable evidence, such as travel reports, seriously. In short, the picture he draws of the development of American English must be revised.

2. That this last-mentioned source is well worth examining is shown by Edgar W. Schneider (1981). His results are also revealing with regard to 'the questions of uniformity versus regional diversity in Southern Black English', the study of which was ranked highly by Reinecke *et al.* (1975: 483).

3. By making use of a very important source of information for the South Carolina lowlands, namely the correspondence from Anglican ministers representing the Society for the Propagation of the Gospel in Foreign Parts, Peter H. Wood noted for St George's Parish that by 1726 'there were more than 13 slaves for every white person' (1975: 159).

4. According to Wood the Sea Island region was the area with 'the most highly concentrated group of Afro-Americans during the Colonial era' (1975: 171, n. 8).

5. Wood (1975) makes a beginning here, if only for South Carolina and only for a moderate-sized farm, by listing the age of the 39 slaves working on the estate of John Cawood in 1726. More revealing in this connection is the following diagram taken from Fogel and Engerman (1974: 195) showing that the larger the farm, the larger was the percentage of persons who were slaves:

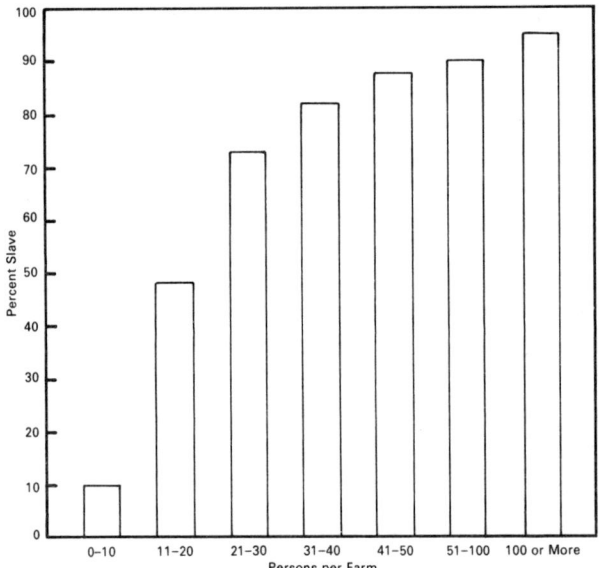

The Percentage of Farm Residents Who Were Slaves, by Size of Farm

'On farms of ten or fewer persons, about 11 percent of the residents were slaves, on average. But on farms of fifty to one hundred persons, 90 percent were slaves. On farms of one hundred or more persons 94 percent were slaves' (Fogel and Engerman 1974: 194). This black–white ratio is quite similar to that found in the Caribbean. Wells (1975) shows that the composition of the population of most of the Island Colonies was completely different from that of the northern continental colonies and states (with the exception of the Gullah territory and the large plantations). Consider a few examples: in 1774 the black–white population ratio was 93.9 percent to 6.1 percent in Jamaica, 88.6 percent to 11.4 percent on the Leeward

Negroes as a Percentage of the Total Population in Four Regions

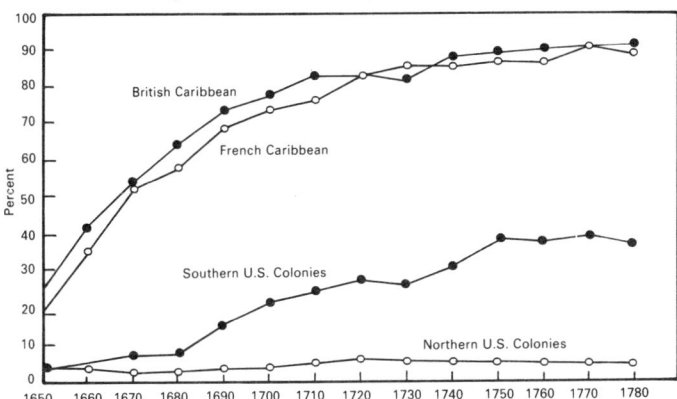

Islands (in 1756) and 95.7 percent to 4.3 percent on Tobago (in 1775). Consider also the following diagram taken from Fogel and Engerman (1974: 21). The linguistic consequences in these regions must have been different, too.

6. Peter H. Wood (1975: 144) provides absolute figures on that contact. According to a report by the governor and council, 17 September 1708, the South Carolina population comprised 4,080 whites, 4,100 Negro slaves, and 1,400 Indian slaves.

7. This article also escaped the attention of the compilers of the *Bibliography of Pidgin and Creole Languages* (1975).

REFERENCES

Atwood, E. Bagby. 1953. *A Survey of Verb Forms in the Eastern United States.* Ann Arbor: University of Michigan Press.

Bickerton, Derek. 1981. *Roots of Language.* Ann Arbor: Karoma.

Dillard, Joey Lee. 1972. *Black English. Its History and Usage in the United States.* New York: Random House.

—— 1975. *All-American English. A History of the English Language in America.* New York: Random House.

—— (ed.). 1980. *Perspectives on American English.* (Contributions to the Sociology of Language. 29.) The Hague, Paris, New York: Mouton.

Edwards, Jay. 1974. 'African Influences on the English of San Andrés Island, Colombia', in David DeCamp and Ian F. Hancock (eds.), *Pidgins and Creoles: Current Trends and Prospects.* Washington, DC: Georgetown University Press, 1–26.

Eliason, Norman E. 1956. *Tarheel Talk: An Historical Study of the English Language in North Carolina to 1860.* Chapel Hill, NC: The University of North Carolina Press.

Feagin, Crawford. 1979. *Variation and Change in Alabama English. A Sociolinguistic Study of the White Community.* Washington, DC: Georgetown University Press.

Flanigan, Beverly Olson. 1981. 'American Indian English in History and Literature:

The Evolution of a Pidgin from Reality to Stereotype'. Indiana University dissertation. (University Microfilms International 1982.)
Fogel, Robert William, and Stanley L. Engerman. 1974. *Time on the Cross.* Vol. I: *The Economics of American Negro Slavery.* London: Wildwood House; Vol. II: *Evidence and Methods.* London: Wildwood House.
Goddard, Ives. 1977. 'Some Early Examples of American Indian Pidgin English from New England', *International Journal of American Linguistics* 43: 37–41.
Haley, Alex. 1974. *Roots. The Saga of an American Family.* New York: Reader's Digest.
Hockett, Homer Carey. 1940 (3rd edn.). *Political and Social Growth of the American People 1492–1865.* New York: Macmillan.
Joyner, Charles. 1981. 'Patterns in Afro-American Creole Language on the Eve of the Civil War: Evidence from the South Carolina Low Country'. Abstracts of Papers on Language Variety in the South: Perspectives in Black and White. A Research Conference on the English Language in the Southern United States. 1–3 October 1981. Columbia, South Carolina.
Kittredge, George Lyman. 1904 (second impr. 1920, third impr. 1921). 'Indian Talk; More Indian Talk'. *The Old Farmer and His Almanack, Being Some Observations on Life and Manners in New England a Hundred Years Ago ...* Cambridge: Harvard University Press, 333–66; 367–78.
McDavid, Raven I., Jr. 1967. 'Needed Research in Southern Dialects', in Edgar T. Thompson (ed.), *Perspectives on the South: Agenda for Research.* Durham, NC: Duke University Press, 113–24.
—— and Virginia G. McDavid. 1951. 'The Relationship of the Speech of American Negroes to the Speech of Whites'. *American Speech* 26: 3–17.
Montgomery, Michael. 1981. 'The Study of the Language of Blacks and Whites in the American South'. Paper presented at the biennial American Studies Association meeting in Memphis, Tennessee, on 1 November 1981.
Pederson, Lee. 1983. *East Tennessee Folk Speech: a Synopsis.* (Bamberger Beiträge zur englischen Sprachwissenschaft, 12.) Frankfurt, Bern: Peter Lang.
Petty, Julian J. 1943 (repr. 1975). *The Growth and Distribution of Population in South Carolina.* Spartanburg, SC: The Reprint Co.
Rawick, George P. (ed.). 1972. *The American Slave. A Composite Autobiography.* 19 vols. Westport, Conn.: Greenwood; 1977, 1979. Supplement Series 1–2.
Read, Allen Walker. 1939. 'The Speech of Negroes in Colonial America', *Journal of Negro History* 24: 247–58.
Reinecke, John E., in collaboration with David DeCamp, Ian F. Hancock, Stanley M. Tsuzaki, and Richard E. Wood. 1975. *A Bibliography of Pidgin and Creole Languages.* (Oceanic Linguistics Special Publication No. 14.) Honolulu: The University Press of Hawaii.
Schneider, Edgar W. 1981. *Morphologische und syntaktische Variablen im amerikanischen Early Black English.* (Bamberger Beiträge zur englischen Sprachwissenschaft. 10.) Frankfurt, Bern: Peter Lang.
Schuchardt, Hugo. 1888 (repr. 1965). 'Beiträge zur Kenntniss [*sic*] des englischen Kreolisch', I, *Englische Studien* 12: 470–4; translated into English by Glenn G. Gilbert (1980) as 'Notes on the English of American Indians: Cheyenne, Kiowa, Pawnee, Pueblo, Sioux, and Wyandot', in Glenn G. Gilbert (ed.), *Pidgin and Creole Languages. Selected Essays by Hugo Schuchardt.* Cambridge: Cambridge University Press, 30–7.
Starobin, Robert S. (ed.). 1974. *Blacks in Bondage. Letters of American Slaves.* New York: New Viewpoints.
Stewart, William A. 1967. 'Sociolinguistic Factors in the History of American Negro

Dialects', *The Florida FL Reporter* 5(2): 11, 22, 24, 26, 30.
—— 1968. 'Continuity and Change in American Negro Dialects', *The Florida FL Reporter* 6(1): 3-4, 14-16, 18.
Todd, Loreto. 1974. *Pidgins and Creoles.* (Language and Society 1.) London and Boston: Routledge and Kegan Paul.
Turner, Lorenzo D. 1949. *Africanisms in the Gullah Dialect.* Chicago: University of Chicago Press.
Viereck, Wolfgang. 1975. *Lexikalische und grammatische Ergebnisse des Lowman-Survey von Mittel- und Südengland.* 2 vols. München: Wilhelm Fink.
—— 1982. 'Das amerikanische Englisch in Forschung und Lehre', *Zeitschrift für Dialektologie und Linguistik* 40: 351-65.
—— 1983. Review of Albert H. Marckwardt, *American English.* Revised by Joey Lee Dillard. 1980. New York, Oxford: Oxford University Press. *Arbeiten aus Anglistik und Amerikanistik* 8: 220-1.
Wells, Robert V. 1975. *The Population of the British Colonies in America Before 1776. A Survey of Census Data.* Princeton, NJ: Princeton University Press.
Williamson, Juanita. 1981. 'The Overseers' Speech'. Abstracts of Papers on Language Variety in the South: Perspectives in Black and White. A Research Conference on the English Language in the Southern United States. 1-3 October 1981. Columbia, South Carolina.
Wolfram, Walter A. 1974. 'The Relationship of White Southern Speech to Vernacular Black English', *Language* 50: 498-527.
Wood, Peter H. 1975. *Black Majority. Negroes in Colonial South Carolina from 1670 through the Stono Rebellion.* New York: W.W. Norton.

Part II

Phonologica

13

Old English Ablaut Again: The Essentially Concrete Character of Dependency Phonology

JOHN M. ANDERSON

In his review of Lass and Anderson (1975), Richard Hogg describes the first chapter, entitled '"Ablaut" in the Old English strong verb', as 'a *tour de force* of abstract generative phonology' (1976: 188). Such a description is clearly double-edged, as is confirmed by Hogg's subsequent discussion (and, indeed, that offered in Chapter 6 of the work under review). Without wanting to seem ungracious, I nevertheless feel constrained to say that I am not sure that the positive 'edge' is fully warranted (for some doubts in this direction see e.g. Dresher 1978: particularly section 3.1). But I am entirely sympathetic to the implication associated with the negative 'edge', that the '*tour*' offered by that part of the book is perhaps rather of the variety offered by Messrs. Cook as far as a synchronic phonological description of Old English (OE) is concerned. That is, specifically, that the kind of 'abstractness' embodied in the analysis is unnecessary, and indeed undesirable.

There are two aspects to this 'abstractness' that I find objectionable. One involves a failure to recognise explicitly the morphological and lexical restrictedness of the rules proposed — despite the use of such 'cover-symbols' as PRES (for all the forms of the present paradigm, including the infinitive) and SV (for strong verb): no distinction is made between the morphophonological and the phonological. The second, related 'abstractness' concerns the deployment of rules which can change, often, quite radically, the feature values for segments. Among them are indeed rules whose application results in derivational 'absolute neutralisation' (Kiparsky 1973a).

I take it that 'absolute neutralisation' is undesirable, and should be represented as (at least) phonologically complex. And I also adopt here the (in a certain respect) even stronger position that synchronic phonological rules, specifically word- (as opposed to utterance-) based rules (Anderson, to appear a, b), preferably do not modify the feature composition of segments except to add further specification. Word-based phonological rules which obey this requirement are to be preferred to alternative formulations which do not: 'structure-building' is to be preferred to 'structure-changing'. Totally excluded are structure-changing rules without SURFACE VISIBILITY, i.e. where the trigger for the change is not apparent on the surface. Derivations which conform to this restriction are WEAKLY CONCRETE. (For related discussion see e.g. Vennemann 1972; Hooper 1976.)

It will be clear that I do not reject another aspect of 'abstractness' criticised by Hogg (1976: 190), viz. the postulation of underlying segments that are not 'fully specified', archi-segments. The notation of DEPENDENCY PHONOLOGY is not amenable to the kind of criticism initiated by Stanley (1967); and, indeed, is naturally adapted to such analyses, whereby derived representations specify subsets of the underlying set of properties associated with a segment. And they allow characterisations which obviate appeal to (other kinds of) 'abstractness', while permitting formulation of the generalisations that 'abstract' characterisations are intended to capture. The notation favours derivations which are weakly concrete.[1]

I want here to reconsider, in this context, the 'ablaut' variations associated with the strong verb in Old English. The rules with which we are concerned are word-based and lexical: the class of verbs affected is characterised precisely by their eligibility for these particular rules.[2] The rules are, moreover, morphologically determined; they affect specific paradigmatic sub-classes. What I am going to suggest is that they do not merely conform to the weak concreteness requirement; they obey a stricter requirement, in that they do not involve feature-changes at all: the derivations at STRONGLY CONCRETE. As we shall see, they provide for progressive 'de-neutralisation' of the segments involved. Such derivations are favoured by the notation.

I am also assuming that phonological rules are not extrinsically ordered; rather, order of application reflects the (inter-)action of universal principles such as the mutual exclusiveness associated with an 'otherwise' or 'elsewhere' condition (Kiparsky 1973b). Thus, specifically, the morphophonological rules which specify the form of the stem in Old English strong verbs are unordered and non-feature-changing. This conjunction of properties defines STRONG DERIVATIONAL CONCRETENESS.

1.

Table 13.1 displays some typical Old English strong verb paradigms from classes I–V, given in their most common (West Saxon) form (though with the addition of the usual editorial macron to indicate representation of an etymological long vowel). At the head of each column is one of the 'cover-symbols' utilised by Lass and Anderson. Each abbreviates a set of morphological specifications: PRES(ENT), as indicated above, includes the present tense paradigm (indicative and subjunctive) plus the infinitive, whose

Table 13.1: Old English strong verb paradigms

Class	PRES	PRET₁	PRET₂	PP	
I	bīdan	bād	bidon	-biden	'(a)wait'
II	bēodan	bēad	budon	-boden	'command'
IIIa	weorpan	wearp	wurpon	-worpen	'throw'
b	breġdan	bræġd	brugdon	-brogden	'drag'
c	bindan	band	bundon	-bunden	'bind'
IVa	beran	bær	bǣron	-boren	'bear'
b	niman	nam	nōmon	-numen	'take'
V	metan	mæt	mǣton	-meten	'measure'

manifestations are represented in Table 13.1 by the infinitive (suffix -*an*); PRET₁ includes the first and third person singular of the preterite indicative, which are both realised as in Table 13.1; PRET₂ includes the preterite subjunctive and the plural and second person singular preterite indicative, the manifestation in the table being that for the preterite plural (suffix -*on*); and PP is the past participle, whose form is as given. The traditional division into classes is based on the reconstructed phonology of the rhyme of the stem syllable; each class displays a different set of alternations in the stem dependent on this. I shall propose (following Lass and Anderson) that the reflexes of these rhyme differences still determine (together with the morphological information) the realisation of the stem vowel in Old English. Hence the class labels have no systematic status in themselves but are used here simply for ease of reference.

In Table 13.2 I offer characterisations, in terms of the notation of dependency phonology,[3] of (the surface manifestations of) the stem vowel in each of the forms in Table 13.1. The segmental representation consists of two sub-segments or GESTURES, each enclosed within a brace, the upper being the CATEGORIAL ('major class'), the lower the ARTICULATORY ('place'). They are joined by a (broken) line of ASSOCIATION, unmarkedly one-to-one but not so, e.g. in the case of diphthongs (one categorial gesture, two articulatory) or affricates (two categorial, one articulatory). Each alphabetic symbol in Table 13.2 is a COMPONENT ('feature') of the gesture concerned. A component may or may not be present (the 'features' are 'unary'); and it may appear necessarily alone, indicated by enclosing verticals, as in '{|i|}', or in combination with (an)other component(s). In the latter case, the components may be hierarchised with respect to each other; one depends on the other, as represented in '{i;a}', [e], where component a depends on component i. Or the components may simply co-occur, as in '{|V,V|}', long (tense) vowel. (Again, the verticals ensure that only the two V components are present in the categorial gesture; there are other segment-classes which involve the co-presence of one or two V components and a C.)

The categorial gesture includes (the potential presence in various combinations of at least) the two components C ('consonantality', tending to

OLD ENGLISH ABLAUT AGAIN

Table 13.2: Old English strong verb stem nuclei

Class	PRES	PRET₁	PRET₂	PP
I	|V,V| | |i|	|V,V| | |a|	|V| | |i|	|V| | |i|
II	|V,V| i;a u;a	|V,V| a;i a;u	|V| |u|	|V| u;a
IIIa	|V| i;a u;a	|V| a;i a;u	|V| |u|	|V| u;a
b	|V| i;a	|V| a;i	|V| |u|	|V| u;a
c	|V| |i|	|V| |a|	|V| |u|	|V| |u|
IVa	|V| i;a	|V| a;i	|V,V| a;i	|V| u;a
b	|V| |i|	|V| |a|	|V,V| u;a	|V| |u|
V	|V| i;a	|V| a;i	|V,V| a;i	|V| i;a

energy reduction) and V ('vocalicness', tending to harmonicity). Presence of V alone is associated with vowels; two Vs represent a tense ('long') vowel. If such a categorial representation is associated with a single articulatory gesture, as in class I PRES and PRET₁, we have a long monophthong; if there are two associated articulatory gestures, we have a long diphthong, as in PRES and PRET₁ of class II. The rules which build word trees on the basis of (among other things) segmental representations (Anderson, to appear a, b) associate with the specification {|V,V|} subconfigurations of the character of (1):

(1)a.   b.

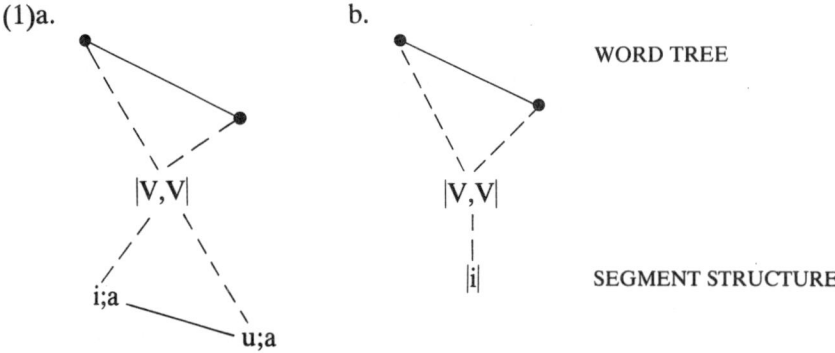

WORD TREE

SEGMENT STRUCTURE

((b) for a long monophthong, (a) for a diphthong): i.e. complex nuclei in which the second segment depends on, or is ADJOINED to, the first. Lax ('short') vowels are associated with a single node in the word tree, but short diphthongs, as in IIIa PRES and PRET$_1$, are assigned a segment internal adjunction of the articulatory gestures only, though the syllable nucleus of course remains simplex (see particularly Anderson, to appear b: section 6; Anderson and Ewen, to appear: Chapters 3 and 7), as represented in (2a):

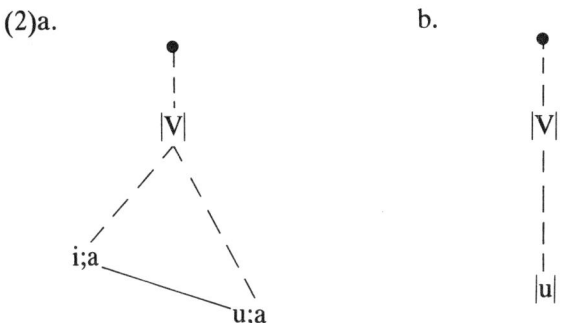

Compare the short monophthong in (2b), as manifested in PRET$_2$ of class II. I am assuming that all these diphthongs are falling and that the dependency relations in (1) and (2) are thus appropriate.

The articulatory gesture with vowels involves combinations of the components a ('lowness', 'sonority'), u ('peripherality', 'gravity') and i ('frontness', 'palatality'). So that we can characterise qualitative differences within the Old English vowel system as in (3):

(3) ⟨i⟩ [i]   i   ⟨u⟩   [u]   u
     ⟨e⟩ [e]   i;a   ⟨o⟩   [o]   u;a
     ⟨æ⟩ [ɛ]   a;i   ⟨a/o⟩ [ɔ]   a;u
                ⟨a⟩ [a]   a

which also records the typical spelling for each vowel. A contrastive status for short [ɛ] (⟨æ⟩) is marginal at best (Colman 1983) and for [ɔ] dialectally and temporally very restricted (Kuhn 1961, Hogg 1982); but the existence of such segment types is confirmed by consistent spelling and/or their distinctive participation in phonological processes (e.g. Breaking in the case of [ɛ]) and/or subsequent history. The long vowel system is identical except for the lack of a long congener to [ɔ] (which develops only later and initially only in the south of the country). On the other hand, despite the fact that in West Saxon [ɔ] can be said with some assurance to have occurred only before nasals, its phonetic distinctness from other short vowels represented by ⟨o⟩ or ⟨a⟩ is suggested by the limitation of this particular spelling fluctuation to putative instances of [ɔ], as well as by the distinctive developments [ɔ] undergoes both with respect to pre-Old English processes like *i*-umlaut (Lass and Anderson 1975: 67, n. 1) and in its subsequent history. No such evidence supports the postulation of [ɔ:], rather than [o:] before nasals. (Such fluctuations in spelling as we find may be due to analogy — cf. note 5.)

The diphthongs involve combinations of the mid vowels, either extra- or intra-segmentally ((1a) vs. (2a)): [e] + [o̞] ⟨eo⟩ and [ɛ] + [ɔ] ⟨ea⟩, though at some point the second element of [ɛ(:)ɔ̞] is unrounded.[4] Consider Table 13.2, class II PRES and PRET₁ and class IIIa PRES and PRET₁, representing the diphthongs [e:o̞], [ɛ:ɔ̞], [eo̞] and [ɛɔ̞], respectively.

We turn now to a consideration of the principles governing the distribution of stem vowels displayed in Tables 13.1 and 13.2. Like Lass and Anderson, I shall argue that the differences in nuclear vowels are not lexical but rule-governed; but the derivations I shall propose are strongly concrete.

2.

The vowel in PRES forms in classes III–V is [e], except before nasals, where we find [i], and before Breaking clusters (as in IIIa) — i.e. in this case −[x, rC] (Lass and Anderson 1975: Chapter 3) — where we find [eo̞]. The variation is predictable from the environment. With class II PRES, the first part of the diphthong is also in articulatory terms i;a. If lexically the second element of the diphthong has the same status as [l], [r] or [n] in class III, i.e. as a separate (dependent) segment, in accordance with the representation in (1a), then again the NUCLEAR PEAK is [e]. Similarly, if we decompose the [i:] of class I PRES into two parts [i] + [i] (cf. (1b)), then we can say that in this case the nuclear peak turns up as [i] before [i], just as it does before nasals. We derive some support for this decomposition of the stem vowel in classes I–II from the fact that the second element turns up alone in PRET₂ and PP of these classes (though modified in class II PP — see below).

Given all this, the character of the nuclear vowel in PRES is entirely predictable, as formulated in (4):

(4) PRES

~ART ⇒ |i| / —— N // |~u|

|~C| ⇒ i;a

where the diphthong in *weorpan* etc. is allowed for by the application of

Breaking, which is a phonological rule not limited to these morphological circumstances. (4) specifies that in the PRES of strong verbs a vowel (|~C| — see below) with unspecified articulatory gesture is realised as either containing only |i| in certain circumstances and otherwise as i;a. The N in (4) is the nasal sub-gesture of the articulatory gesture (Anderson and Ewen, to appear: Chapter 6). However, the alternative (//) |~u| specification (for what is realised as [i], or, rather, part of [i:]), perhaps requires some further comment.

|~u| denotes a segment whose articulatory gesture contains a single component other than u. This specification is appropriate given that |~u| is realised either as |i|, in class I PRES and $PRET_2$ and PP (as we shall see below) or as |a| in the case of class I $PRET_1$ — as again we shall see in a moment. It is in contrast with the post-peak segment in class II, which is u: i.e. the post-peak segment in class II contains in its articulatory gesture u but not necessarily just u. This again is appropriate given that this u is realised as either |u| ($PRET_2$), u;a (PRES, PP) or a;u ($PRET_1$) — i.e. not necessarily as u alone.

The important point about such lexical specifications is that they represent a NEUTRALISATION of the segments that manifest them: the lexical specification must represent only the class which consists uniquely of the manifesting segments: |i| + |a| ≡ |~u|; |u| + u;a + a;u ≡ u. Contrastivity is thus maintained, while redundancies are extracted. This is true of all the representations I shall be proposing.

In $PRET_1$ we find for the nuclear peak either |a|, before a nasal or |~u| (cf. class IIIc, IVb and I), or a;i [ε] (classes II, IIIb, IVa) or its broken equivalent (IIIa). We can thus formulate the realisation rule as in (5):

(5) $PRET_1$

~ART ⇒ |a| / —— N // |~u|

|~C|

⇒ a;i

In $PRET_2$ and PP of classes I–II we find apparently no realisation of the lexical nuclear peak as such; simply a reflex of the |~u| or u that follows it (see further section 3). This confirms the appropriateness of the |~C| in (4): this segment turns up either as a vowel or as the empty segment; but it never comes to be specified as a consonant. Either |~C| comes to be specified as |V| (a vowel) or it is removed by the EMPTY SEGMENT CONVENTION (ESC), which eliminates segments which emerge from the word phonology with only a negative specification in the categorial gesture. We should therefore add to the rules for PRES and $PRET_1$ that in (6):

(6) PRES/PRET$_1$

   $|\text{-}C| \Rightarrow |V|$

whereby the unspecified nuclear peak is specified positively as a vowel in all PRES and PRET$_1$ forms.

Application of (4) and (5) gives the representations in (7) for the PRES and PRET$_1$ of classes I–II:

(7)

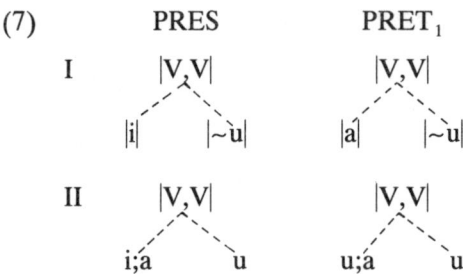

	PRES	PRET$_1$
I	|V,V|	|V,V|
	|i| |~u|	|a| |~u|
II	|V,V|	|V,V|
	i;a u	u;a u

The diphthongs in class II are subject to the general condition on Old English diphthongs that the second element agree in height with the first: i.e. Lass and Anderson's DIPHTHONG HEIGHT HARMONY (DHH). And DHH also gives |i| |i| for PRES and |a| |a| for PRET$_1$ of class I. I assume that |i| |i| and |a| |a| are interpreted by general convention as monophthongal. This ensures the representations given in Table 13.2 for PRES and PRET$_1$ of classes I–II.

PRES and PRET$_1$ of the other classes in Table 13.1 require no further comment.

3.

The nuclear peak of PRET$_2$ and PP of classes III–V is realised in a variety of ways: [ɛ:] (PRET$_2$ classes IVa, V), [o:] (PRET$_2$ class IVb), [u] (PRET$_2$ class III, PP class IVb), [o] (PP classes IIIa/b, IV), [e] (PP class V). The most that these various realisations have in common is that they do not contain a component other than u by itself: thus ~|~u|. Accordingly, we can formulate the rule in (8) for PRET$_2$ and PP:

(8) PRET$_2$/PP

$$\begin{array}{c} |\text{-}C| \\ \text{~ART} \end{array} \Rightarrow \begin{array}{c} |V| \\ \text{~}|\text{-}u| \end{array} \quad / \text{—} \; C$$

Given that the environment requires a following consonant (a segment whose categorial gesture contains C), the nuclear peak in classes I–II receives no further specification, in that it is followed in these instances by a segment whose categorial gesture contains only V (i.e. a vowel). No further rules apply to the nuclear peak in these classes in $PRET_2$ and PP forms and it is thus eliminated eventually, in terms of the empty segment convention, and its place taken as syllable peak by the following segment.

In classes III–V the nuclear peak of $PRET_2$ forms is mid and long if it is followed by only one segment: contrast classes IV–V with class III. So:

(9) $PRET_2$

$$|V| \quad \Rightarrow \quad |V,V| \quad / \, C \mathrel{\relbar\joinrel\relbar} C \}$$
$$\sim|\sim u| \quad\quad\quad \sim a, a$$

$$\Rightarrow \quad |u|$$

where } indicates the stem boundary and ~a,a is a mid vowel (a combination of a and either i or u). The inclusion of the preceding C in the environment excludes both vowel segments in the stems of classes I–II from the first part of (9). However, the vowel that follows the nuclear peak in class II, u, can undergo the second part, since it meets the $\sim|\sim u|$ requirement and also the rule is not environmentally restricted; and it therefore comes, correctly, to be specified as $|u|$ (cf. Tables 13.1 and 13.2). Before a nasal, the long mid vowel in classes IV–V $PRET_2$ is back and apparently high-mid; otherwise front and low-mid:[5]

(10) $PRET_2$

$$\sim a, a \quad \Rightarrow \quad u;a \quad / \mathrel{\relbar\joinrel\relbar} N$$

$$\Rightarrow \quad a;i$$

where N again indicates a segment whose articulatory gesture contains a nasal sub-gesture.

The nuclear vowel in PP of classes III–V is realised in accordance with the environment as in (11):

(11) PP

$$\sim|\sim u| \quad \Rightarrow \quad i;a \quad / \, C \mathrel{\relbar\joinrel\relbar} C; \}$$

$$\Rightarrow \quad u;$$

i.e. as [e] before a segment with a governing C (i.e. an obstruent) — where the preceding C in the environment again excludes the vowels in classes I–II. Otherwise, a ~|~u| stem vowel in PP is realised as a segment containing a preponderant u, and specifically as in (12):

(12) PP
|
u; ⇒ |u| /——— N

⇒ u;a

(12) also specifies the post-peak vowel in class II as [o]. As in the case of PRET$_2$ the nuclear peak in classes I–II remains negatively specified and is thus discarded, in favour of the following [i] or [u/o].

Table 13.3: Lexical representations for Old English strong verb stems

Class I	...|~C|	|V|	C;V
		|∸u|	|I|
Class II	...|~C|	|V|	C;V
		u	|I|
Class IIIa	...|~C|	V;C	|C|
		|I|	|u|
b	...|~C|	C;V	C;V
		I,u	|I|
c	...|~C|	V;C	C;V
		N	|I|
Class IVa	...|~C|	V;C	
		|I|	
b	...|~C|	V;C	
		N,u	
Class V	...|~C|	|C|	
		I;u	

170

4.

Table 13.3 presents the suggested lexical representations for the rhymes in the stem syllables of the strong verbs listed in Table 13.1, the derived character of whose nucleus is given in Table 13.2. C;V specifies a voiced plosive, V;C a sonorant consonant; |l| a non-palatal non-velar (i.e. dental/alveolar) lingual; |u|, of a consonant, a labial, l,u a palatal/velar (Anderson and Ewen 1980, to appear; Anderson, to appear c). The first segment in each rhyme is unspecified as to its articulation: the rules in sections 2–3 which invoke ~ART apply to such a segment.

Table 13.4 gives some sample derivations in relation to the forms considered so far. The derivations illustrate that the rules are not extrinsically ordered; any ordering is imposed by the stage at which there is introduced the appropriate symbols for triggering the particular rules. The rules themselves simply render the lexical specifications more specific; they are not feature-changing. We have a set of partially morphologically determined (unordered) redundancy rules. Strong derivational concreteness is ensured. Such morphophonological formulations are explicitly favoured by the notation of dependency phonology, which preferentially allows for the progressive specification of neutralised segments by rules of maximal generality. Feature-changing rules are necessarily more complex (as well as involving an arbitrary selection of underlier), in that, in particular, each input specification involves a more detailed characterisation.

5.

Many of these derivations can be replicated using binary features, particularly if the dimension of vowel height is characterised by [± high, ± mid] (Wang 1968). So, we can allow for the range of articulations associated with the unspecified vowel in PP forms as in (13):

(13)

$$[\underline{\quad}]$$
$$\Downarrow$$
$$[+\text{high}] \quad \text{(cf. rule (8))}$$

$$\swarrow \quad \searrow$$

$$\begin{bmatrix} +\text{back} \\ +\text{round} \end{bmatrix} \qquad \begin{bmatrix} +\text{mid} \\ -\text{back} \\ -\text{round} \end{bmatrix} \quad \text{(cf. rule (11))}$$

$$\swarrow \quad \searrow$$

$$[+\text{mid}] \quad [-\text{mid}] \qquad\qquad \text{(cf. rule (12))}$$
$$\;\;(a) \qquad\;\; (b) \qquad\quad (c)$$

Table 13.4: Old English strong verb sample derivations

Class				Rule
Class I	PRET₁			
bād	...|~C|	|V̄|	C;V	
		|~u|	|i|	
		⇓		
		V		(6)
		⇓		
		a		(5)
		⇓		
		a		DHH
Class II	PP			
-bod-	...|~C|	|V|	C̃;V	
		u	|i|	
		⇓		
		u;		(11)
		⇓		
		u;a		(12)
	⇓			
	∅			ESC
Class IIIb	PRES			
breġd-	...|~C|	C;V	C;V	
		l,u	|i|	
		⇓		
		V		(6)
		⇓		
		i;a		(4)
Class IVb	PRET₂			
nōm-	...|~C|	Ṽ;C		
		N,u		
		⇓		
		|V|		(8)
		~|~u|		
		⇓		
		|V,V|		(9)
		~a,a		
		⇓		
		u;a		(10)
Class V	PP			
-met-	...|~C|	|C|		
		|i|		
		⇓		
		|V|		(8)
		~|~u|		
		⇓		
		i;a		(11)

Examples: (a) *-boren*, (b) *-numen*, (c) *-meten*. However, even here the first stage in (13) is less general than rule (8), in that the developments in PRET$_2$ and PP cannot be collapsed, and the parallelism between the two in classes I–III therefore remains unexpressed. Moreover, binary features do not always lend themselves in relation to these forms to a non-feature-changing format. It is unclear, for example, what indeed would be an appropriate underlier corresponding to the ~|~u| of PRET$_2$/PP of classes III–V.

Of greater significance than such individual failures, however, is simply the inappropriateness of binary features for the expression of relationships involving (underlying) neutralisation. In order to express such neutralisation we must either invoke a third value for features or introduce the additional structural property that particular features may be absent as such from the pre-phonetic specification for particular segments (as assumed in (13)). The former option is problematical (cf. again Stanley 1967). And in the case of the latter it is unclear what significance is to be attached to a statement that a certain segment lacks a certain feature (rather than being specified as plus or minus with respect to it). A notation based on unary features and dependency relations between them, on the other hand, lends itself directly to the expression of neutralisation.

This is similarly apparent from a consideration of the status of voiced fricatives in Old English (see Anderson, to appear c), where the neutralisations are not limited to particular morphological categories. The labial and velar voiced fricatives constitute the respective realisations of the neutralisations in certain positions of the corresponding voiceless fricatives and voiced plosives. Thus, whereas in stem- and word-initial position OE /b/ is in contrast with /f/, as witnessed by e.g. *bæc* 'back' vs. *fæc* 'space', in mid-word between voiced segments we find only [v] (spelled *f*) and neither of /b/ nor /v/. Given that /b/ and /f/ are represented as in (14):

(14)a. /b/ |C;V|
                |
                |u|

b.   /f/ |C:V|
                |
                |u|

(where in (b) V and C are mutually dependent and in (a) C governs V), the associated archiphoneme is appropriately represented as (15):

(15)   C;V
          |
         |u|

i.e. a segment containing at least a C governing a V, which neutralises the distinction between voiced plosive (14a) and voiceless fricative (14c). This is realised in the highly V-full environment of between voiced segments as (16):

(16) [v]   C:V ; V
            |
            u

i.e. as a voiced fricative of identical articulatory specification, which is the only segment type which could manifest the assimilation of (15) to a voiced environment. This pattern of neutralisation and realisation is not amenable to characterisation in terms (of the standard interpretation of the status) of binary features.

6.

We have omitted from our account those verbs of class V whose forms show the results of Breaking, i.e. the equivalents in class V of class IIIa, in which (in this case) Breaking is associated with the presence of a following voiceless velar fricative. Thus we find the $PRET_1$ forms in (17):

(17) *seah* 'saw', *gefeah* 'rejoiced'

with Breaking before the [x] presumably represented by ‹h›. As elsewhere in the strong verb paradigms and indeed more generally, this historical process retains synchronic surface visibility, and is thus unproblematical for our account of the morphophonology of the strong verbs.

However, in the PRES forms of such verbs this ‹h› is present only in the second and third person singular indicative and in the singular imperative, as e.g. *seoh* (Campbell 1959: 297). Elsewhere throughout the PRES paradigm the segment represented by ‹h› is apparently absent; instead we find a 'compensatory' corresponding long diphthong and no inflexional vowel:

(18) *sēon, gefēon* infinitives

The $PRET_2$/PP show a voiced obstruent (the product of historical processes including Verner's Law), represented ‹g›. (There is no medial voiced plosive/fricative contrast: cf. above and Anderson, to appear c.)

Now, historically, the PRES forms presumably involve Breaking, loss of the consonant causing Breaking, Contraction or loss of the inflexional vowel, and Compensation; i.e. the last involve the development in (19):

(19)a.

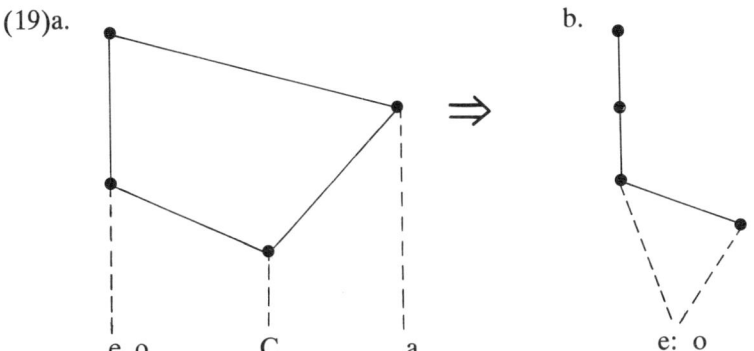

    e o   C   a   e: o

(where C is whatever consonant is lost). Loss of dependencies is compensated for by introduction of a suprasegmental dependency relation between the two elements of the diphthong, in conformity with the dependency preservation condition (Anderson, to appear a), in a rather specific manifestation. Presumably, Compensation is primarily associated with loss of the consonantal dependent of the stressed vowel, rather than of the inflexional vowel, in that Compensation has been argued to occur even if such a vowel is retained: cf. *sēoles* genitive singular of *seolh* 'seal' (Campbell 1959: section 241), and *fēolan* (below), where the consonant is lost between a sonorant consonant and a vowel rather than two vowels. That is, it is the 'weight' of the original rhyme that is preserved. See, more generally, Ingria 1980.

Similarly, the diphthong in the relevant PRES forms of the corresponding class I verbs — cf. (20):

(20) *wrēon* 'cover', PRET$_1$ *wrāh*

involves historically Breaking, of /iː/, to give /iːu/, lowered to /eːo/, followed by loss of the Breaking trigger and Contraction/loss, without (or with no non-vacuous) Compensation, given that the stem vowel is already long. In class II, on the other hand, the long diphthong is not due to Breaking (cf. *bēodan*) but is 'original':

(21) *flēon* 'flee', PRET$_1$ *flēah*

but again we have loss of the medial consonant and Contraction/loss, without Compensation.

Synchronically, throughout Old English all contracted forms lack an overt Breaking trigger. Therefore, such a derivation as is implied by the history must be suspect: it offends not just strong concreteness but also the trigger has no surface visibility. The undesirable status of such an 'abstract Breaking' derivation is mirrored in dependency notation by the complexity involved in allowing for deletion of a particular fully specified segment. The deletions we have allowed so far are an automatic consequence of the empty segment convention. But in order to trigger Breaking, the segment involved must be specified as a back continuant (cf. again Lass and Anderson 1975: Chapter 3). Let us then consider what derivation is available in the context of the concrete analysis of the strong verbs suggested in sections 3–4 above.

Suppose we represent the segment that appears as the [x] that ⟨h⟩ presumably represents in (17) as simply ~V; with ~ART. In final position this gives a velar fricative, whereas, if we presume it also to be present lexically in (18), between sonorants it is not so specified and so is discarded by the empty segment convention (cf. section 2 above), except that in $PRET_2$/PP it becomes a voiced obstruent (or a development thereof): *gefægon, wrigon, flugon.*

We need, then, first of all, the following rules:

(22) ~V;   ⇒ |C:V| / ##
       |
      ~ART

That is, the segment is a voiceless fricative word-finally and word-initially.[6] Finally it is velar:

(23) ~ART   ⇒   l,u / V; ——
       |
      C:V

whereas initially it is usually assumed to be glottal — which, following Lass and Anderson (1975: Chapter 5) and Lass (1976: Chapter 6), I take to be a fricative without an articulatory gesture. Thus, (23) is limited to post-sonorant position; initially such segments remains unspecified as to articulation. (22) and (23) are general phonological rules of Old English, applying outside the verb paradigm.

However, the $PRET_2$/PP alternant is clearly morphologically restricted:

(24) $PRET_2$/PP
       |
      ~V;   ⇒   V, C;
       |
      ~ART

The resultant specification is for a segment neutral between voiced plosive and voiceless (or voiced) fricative: its categorial gesture contains at least V and a C that governs. (On this archiphoneme, see again Anderson, to appear c.) The archiphoneme is realised in accordance with (25):

(25) V, C; ⇒ V:C ; V
      |
      u

i.e. as a voiced fricative. This is again a general phonological rule of Old English, which, as indicated in the formulation, applies also to labials (cf. the discussion of (15) above). So that the only addition to our set of rules required by the morphophonology of strong verbs is (24).

However, there remains the vowel in the contracted PRES forms. If we assume that synchronically the diphthong results from contraction of the nuclear vowel of the stem and that of the inflexion, regulated by DHH, then class V contracted forms already possess the appropriate sequence, and we need add nothing to the rules to provide for them. Breaking will not occur before ~V;. Rather, after discarding of the unspecified ~V;, the resulting sequence of vowels is simply subject to DHH, as in (26):

(26) i;a a ⇒ i;a u;a

giving /e:o/. However, classes I and II would show the sequences /i:a/ and /e:oa/, respectively, after loss of ~V;, given the present rules only. These could certainly be modified to allow for removal before the sequence ~V; |V| of the segments that were specified as |~u| and u in table 13.3.[7] Again, the sequence i;a a would result after removal of ~V;, giving, with DHH, i;a u;a, as required.

Problematical for such an account, however, are contracted verbs of class III, not so far considered here, such as (27):

(27) fēolan 'press on', PRET$_1$ fealh, PRET$_2$ fulgon

where the diphthong in PRES forms cannot result from contraction, prevented by the intervening liquid. It is usually assumed (Campbell 1959: 311) that the PRES forms show compensatory lengthening, as shown in (27).

We seem, then, after all, to need a rule creating the appropriate diphthong before contraction. To avoid an 'abstract Breaking' account we are forced to another rule with undesirable properties, but not involving deletion of a fully specified segment such as [x]. It might take the form of (28), which allows for all the contracted PRES forms we have considered:

177

(28) PRES

$$(|V|) \Rightarrow ||\underset{||\mathrm{u}||_{art}}{V}||_{cat} / |{\sim}C| \mathrm{\rule{1cm}{0.4pt}} (\ ;C\ ) {\sim} V;\ |V|$$

i.e. either a u vowel segment is inserted or, in classes I and II, the existing post-nuclear V segment (bracketed on the left of (28)) has its articulatory gesture modified to u. The optional ;C specification on the right allows for the presence of a post-nuclear sonorant (in class III — cf. (27)). Substitution of whole gestures is indicated by the double verticals notation. This account would also require absorption of the vowel of the inflexion, to leave only the appropriate sequence.

(28) and its ramifications are rather costly. In order to ensure that the representation on the right replaces the entire categorial and articulatory gestures rather than being added to them (which is the normal interpretation of a dependency rule with positive components on the left[8]), recourse has to be had to a special notational device, the double verticals of (28). Its appeal to surface visibility (or even credibility) depends on the postulation of a (negatively specified) segment whose existence is extrapolated from surface morphological regularities. Strong verb stems do not end in a vowel otherwise; strong verb stems with a long vowel in PRES do not end in a liquid.[9] Thus, *wrēon* must contain a stem-final non-vowel; and so must *fēolan*. At most such a segment can be specified in the fashion adopted here.

(28) also creates derivational neutralisation: in such instances the class of a strong verb of classes I, II and V is no longer determinate on the surface in PRES forms: the infinitive *wrēon* could belong to any of them.

Thus it is not clear that such a derivation fares any better, in terms of complexity, than one based on 'abstract Breaking', whose complexity with respect to a dependency notation resides, as we have seen, in the need to characterise removal of a particular fully specified segment (rather than there being automatic elimination by the empty segment convention).

Unsurprisingly, the classification of such verbs breaks down in the language. So, *tēon* 'accuse', historically class I, shows already in early West Saxon a class II paradigm: *teah, tugon*. And later such class-shifting is rather common (Campbell 1959: 308). A shift in the other direction (class II to class I) is illustrated by the PP of *of-tēon* 'withdraw', which appears as *-tigen* as well as *-togen*. A further complication is introduced by a verb like *þēon* 'thrive'. Historically, this is class III: so we find the PRET$_2$ form *þungon*. But the nasal is lost before a voiceless fricative, as in the ancestors of PRES and PRET$_1$ forms, with stem ending in [x]. With loss of the [x] between vowels we get contraction. The surface paradigm is thus rather irregular. And we find that the verb early acquires a (slightly more regular) class I paradigm as well, and later a class II. Thus, we find the alternative PRET₂ and PP forms in (29):

(29) PRES   PRET₂   PP

                  ⎧ þungon   -þungen
      þēon   ⎨ þigon   -þigen
                  ⎩ þugon   -þogen

Not uncommon too is the existence of alternative weak verb paradigms.

All this suggests an instability due to the failure of such derivations (as are required if we assume the operation of the usual rules for strong verbs) to maintain surface visibility. The difficulty is characterised by any account compatible with the notation of dependency phonology in terms of the costliness of the formulation required. It would appear that such verbs are reinterpreted as irregular; their paradigms are not derivable by the morphophonological rules which apply to strong verbs.

7.

Space prohibits the examination here of classes VI and VIII of the strong verbs. Lass and Anderson's analysis of these involves even greater abstractness: specifically, the postulation of a segment of a type that never surfaces as such in Old English. Again, a more concrete analysis which is equally general is available: it involves once more a stem peak which is specified as |~C| categorially, but which differs from that in classes I-V in being partially specified with respect to its articulatory gesture. And again such an analysis is preferred by the notation of dependency phonology. However, as indicated, I shall not pursue this analysis in the present context. The conclusion concerning the concrete character of the notation employed here is, I hope, sufficiently clear without taking into account the distinctive properties of classes VI and VIII.

Consider again, for example, the characterisation of the peak in the PRET₁ forms in classes I-V. The suggested strongly concrete formulation was given in (5) above. Suppose that instead we offer an analysis in which 'feature values' are changed rather than added to: the peak is given an underlying specification which may be changed by the rules of the morphophonology. Say, further, that we take the vowel of PRES as underlying (though this particular selection is unimportant in the present context — except perhaps in its arbitrariness). In this case we must substitute for (5) something like the formulation in (30):

(30) PRET_1

$$\begin{matrix} \text{i;a} \\ |V| \end{matrix} \Rightarrow |a| \;/\; \text{———}\; N \;//\; |i|$$

$$\Rightarrow \text{a;i}$$

which on the basis of any rational measure of relative complexity is more complex than (5), specifically in specifying the character of the input segment. Notice that we cannot simply specify this segment as |V|, since this characterisation is shared with the post-peak segments in classes I and II. Moreover, each strong verb peak must, on such an analysis, be represented redundantly in this way (as i;a) in the lexicon. The notation prefers a more concrete analysis. Indeed, the instability resulting from the complexity associated with non-concrete derivations is well illustrated by the contracted verbs discussed in the preceding section.

NOTES

Not even Fran Colman — and certainly not Bob Stockwell — is to blame for the inadequacies of this paper. The account of the strong verb paradigms offered by Lass and Anderson is a revision and extension of the analysis suggested in Anderson (1970).

1. We need to distinguish between segments that are 'abstract' in the sense of not fully specified and those that are 'abstract' in (also) not being realised as such. Thus, Hogg's criticism of Lass and Anderson's 'laryngeal' is just, but only on the latter grounds.

2. 'Weak' verbs do not manifest ablaut variation: their paradigms are differentiated by affixation and modification due (historically) to i-umlaut.

3. For discussions of dependency phonology, see e.g. Anderson and Jones 1974, 1977; Anderson 1980; Ewen 1980; Lass 1984: Chapter 11; Anderson and Ewen 1980, to appear.

4. On early spellings such as ‹æo› (for later ‹ea›) see, e.g. Campbell (1959: sections 135, 276, 278). Colman (forthcoming) suggests that ‹ie› when it represents a diphthong is also associated with a round second element: [iy]. The date of unrounding of these various second elements is uncertain.

5. There is considerable fluctuation in spelling, between ‹o› and ‹a›, in the stem of PRET_2 forms of class IVb: *nāmon* as well as *nōmon*. As indicated, this is usually taken to reflect intra-paradigmatic levelling rather than the existence of a distinct low-mid back vowel found only before nasals — parallel to the short [ɔ]. None of the evidence giving support for the suggestion of [ɔ] pertains in the case of a putative [ɔː].

6. The formulation in (23) acknowledges that in early West Saxon [x] and [ɣ] are in contrast finally. For late West Saxon the representation on the right can be simplified to C:V (i.e. without verticals), given that only voiceless velars occur

finally. Indeed, for this period (23) and (25) can be collapsed. See Anderson (to appear c).

7. In this case the categorial gesture for $|\sim u|$ and u should be modified to $|\sim C|$: cf. the nuclear peak, which may also be absent (in classes I and II $PRET_2$ and PP).

8. As in all the other rules discussed here, or, for example, in the vowel shift rule proposed in Anderson (1980).

9. Even if ‹feolan› is interpreted as not showing compensatory lengthening, it remains anomalous for West Saxon in showing a short [eo] diphthong not before a Breaking cluster. However, [e] breaks before [l] only if [x] follows (or [s] precedes) (Lass and Anderson 1975: Chapter 3). And we are thus back with 'abstract Breaking'!

REFERENCES

Anderson, John M. 1970. '"Ablaut" in the Synchronic Phonology of the Old English Strong Verb', *Indogermanische Forschungen* 75: 166-97.
—— 1980. 'On the Internal Structure of Phonological Segments: Evidence from English and its History', *Folia Linguistica Historica* 1: 165-91.
—— To appear a. 'Structural Analogy and Dependency Phonology', ALH.
—— To appear b. 'Suprasegmental dependencies', *Indiana University Linguistics Club*.
—— To appear c. 'The status of voiced fricatives in Old English', *FLH* 6.
—— and Colin J. Ewen (eds.). 1980. *Studies in Dependency Phonology. Ludwigsburg Studies in Language and Linguistics* 4. Ludwigsburg: Reinhard Strauch.
—— To appear. *Principles of Dependency Phonology*. Cambridge: Cambridge University Press.
—— and Charles Jones. 1974. 'Three Theses Concerning Phonological Representations', *Journal of Linguistics* 10: 1-26.
—— 1977. *Phonological Structure and the History of English*. Amsterdam: North-Holland.
Campbell, A. 1959. *Old English Grammar*. London: Oxford University Press.
Colman, Fran. 1983. 'Old English /ɑ/ ≠ /æ/ or [ɑ] ~ [æ]', *FLH* 4: 265-85.
—— Forthcoming. 'OE *ie*: Quid est?', *Lingua* 67: 1-23.
Dresher, B.E. 1978. Review of Lass and Anderson 1975. *Language* 54: 432-46.
Ewen, Colin J. 1980. 'Aspects of Phonological Structure with Particular Reference to English and Dutch'. University of Edinburgh dissertation.
Hogg, R.M. 1976. Review of Lass and Anderson 1975. *York Papers in Linguistics* 6.
—— 1982. 'Was There Ever an /ɔ/ -Phoneme in Old English?', *Neuphilologische Mitteilungen* 3: 225-30.
Hooper, Joan B. 1976. *An Introduction to Natural Generative Phonology*. New York: Academic Press.
Ingria, Robert. 1980. 'Compensatory Lengthening as a Metrical Phenomenon', *Linguistic Inquiry* 11: 465-95.
Kiparsky, Paul. 1973a. 'How Abstract is Phonology?', in O. Fujimura (ed.), *Three Dimensions of Linguistic Theory*. Tokyo: TEC, 5-56.
—— 1973b. 'Elsewhere in Phonology', in S. Anderson and P. Kiparsky (eds.), *A Festschrift for Morris Halle*. New York: Holt, Rinehart and Winston, 93-106.
Kuhn, Sherman M. 1961. 'The Syllabic Phonemes of Old English', *Language* 37: 522-38.
Lass, Roger. 1976. *English Phonology and Phonological Theory: Synchronic and Diachronic Studies*. Cambridge: Cambridge University Press.

—— 1984. *Phonology: An Introduction to Basic Concepts.* Cambridge: Cambridge University Press.
—— and John M. Anderson. 1975. *Old English Phonology.* Cambridge: Cambridge University Press.
Stanley, Richard. 1967. 'Redundancy Rules in Phonology', *Language* 43: 393–436.
Vennemann, Theo. 1972. 'Phonological Uniqueness in Natural Generative Grammar', *Glossa* 6: 105–16.
Wang, William S.-Y. 1968. 'Vowel Features, Paired Variables and the English Vowel Shift', *Language* 44: 695–708.

14

The late Old English Type *leinten* 'Lent'

KLAUS DIETZ

The diphthongization of ME *e* > *ei* before a palatal nasal in words such as *leinten* < OE *lenȝten, lencten* has long been regarded as a minor sound change in the history of English because of its relatively limited functional significance. It has been variously treated in the standard handbooks and grammars since it was briefly noted for the first time by Morsbach (1896: section 107, n. 3). The fullest treatment is still that of Jordan (1925, 2nd edn 1934: section 103), who believed that the change *e* > *ei* before the palatal groups *nct, ngd* and *ngþ* — and sporadically before *nš* — in texts written in the South and Midlands from about 1200 until well into the fifteenth century was so common as to argue for a vowel shift. Accordingly, Berndt (1960: 65) regarded spellings of the *leinten* type in the same areas as evidence of a dialectal change *e* > *ei* before the consonant groups '*ndž, ntš, nš, nþ* und *nt*' due to the palatal quality of the nasal. On the other hand, Wright and Wright (1928: sections 263, 287, 295) more or less follow the view of Kluge (1901: 998) in proposing that the spelling ‹ein› indicated a palatal nasal rather than a diphthong. In the second part of his historical grammar, which appeared posthumously, Luick (1940: section 689) favoured a similar interpretation of such spellings, whereas in the first part (1921: section 404) the possibility of interpreting the spelling ‹ein› as [ein] or [eɲ] is left open. Brunner (1938, 6th edn 1967: section 13D, 3) cautiously believed that diphthongization might have occurred.

A comparison of the various attempts to explain the *leinten* type by the acknowledged authorities on Middle English phonology reveals not only basic theoretical differences but even lack of consensus concerning the phonotactic conditions, treated recently by Lass (1976: 181) in a highly complicated rule. It is obvious that a reconsideration of the whole question, in particular of the chronology and dialectal distribution, is long overdue. In addition, Schlemilch's evidence (1914: 9) of diphthongized forms in late Old English texts of the twelfth century has been ignored by later scholarship. In fact, the earliest examples go back to even earlier than 1100.[1]

The earliest forms are found in the glosses to Aldhelm in MS. Brussels,

Bibl. Royale 1650, a text which dates from the first half of the eleventh century (ed. Goossens 1974; cp. Ker 1957: No. 8). There are six examples: *acweinte* 4008, *adreintum* 895, *aseintum* 893, *beseinte* 2979, *ʒemeind* 3746, and *leintentime* 3725 (but *acwyncte* 4270, *ʒeʒlencdan* 622, *-dum* 232 and *tostencte* 2542). All the examples are in the same hand, whose linguistic profile, in so far as it differs from the characteristic *Schriftsprache* of the southern English scriptoria, exhibits both south-eastern characteristics and early Middle English features which exclude the possibility of having their origin in the scribe's exemplar. The glosses found in MS. Bodl. Digby 146 (ed. Napier 1900: No. 1; cp. Ker 1957: No. 320), a mid-eleventh-century copy of the Brussels MS. made at Abingdon (Berks.), contain the following examples: *acweinte* 4125, *adreintum* 832, *aseintum* 829 (but *besente* 3078, *lententima* 3837 and *tostente* 2621 beside *acwencte* 4391, *ʒeʒlencdan* 539, *-dum* 128). The lesser number of ‹ein›-spellings in MS. Digby is a result of the copyist's attempts to conform to the late West Saxon *Schriftsprache*. Accordingly, the non-West Saxon (south-eastern) element is less well represented than in the exemplar (Napier 1900: xxviii ff[2]). However, the remaining interlinear glosses to the prose version of Aldhelm's *De laude virginitatis*, in particular those found in another manuscript of the Abingdon group, MS. Royal 6 B. VII (c. 1075; Ker 1957: No. 255), contain no ‹ein›-spellings. It is unclear whether the form *leʒnten* 244 in the handbook for a confessor in MS. Corpus Christi Coll. Cambridge 201, a mid-eleventh-century manuscript (ed. Fowler 1965; cp. Ker 1957: No. 49), should be included here, since it may represent a scribal error (transposition of *nʒ*).

The next example is found in the interlinear version of the *Salisbury Psalter* (ed. Sisam and Sisam 1959; cp. Ker 1957: No. 379), dating from about 1100 and probably written in a south-western scriptorium:[3] *dreintes* 35.9, besides which there are over two dozen undiphthongized forms, for example: *besencte* 68.3; *drenctest* 59.5; *lenʒte* 73.17; *strenʒþ(e)* 30.4, 47.14; *strenð(e)* 42.2, 67.12; *swencton* 12.5, *ʒeswente* 33.19; *tosten(c)ð* 32.10, 77.38. Somewhat later, in Corpus Christi Coll. Cambridge MS. 303 (Ker 1957: No. 57), a compilation associated with Rochester and dated about 1125, there are at least six further examples. The *Life of St Giles* (ed. Picard 1980) has *ʒeʒlæinde* 17, with *i* added over the line,[4] and *ʒeswæint* 230, 746 beside *ʒeswæn(c)ʒte* 59, 681. The *Life of St Nicholas* (ed. Ahern 1975) has *ʒeswæinte* 241[5] and *ʒesweinte* 288 beside *swæʒnten* 739, and the so-called *Excommunicatio VII* (ed. Liebermann 1903–16: 438 ff) has *acwæint* 23; both homilies, attributed to the second scribe, are without parallel textual transmission and contain a number of Kenticisms (Ahern 1975: 22; Picard 1980: 33). The mid-twelfth-century Old English interlinear glosses in the *Eadwine Psalter*, a Canterbury book (ed. Harsley 1889; Liles 1967; cp. Ker 1957: No. 91), have *leinten* 73.17 added on erasure by one of the correctors, as well as *streinʒþo* 32.16 and *tosteincte*

Hy. 10.51. However, spellings in ‹enc› and ‹enȝ› are usual in this manuscript, and such is also the case with the compilation in MS. Cotton Vesp. D. XIV (Ker 1957: No. 209),[6] a text probably associated with Rochester or Canterbury, whose linguistic forms suggest East Saxon provenance. *The Weather Prophecies* (ed. Warner 1917: No. XXVI) contain, beside *læn(c)ten* 66.15, 22, four occurrences of *læinten* 66.17, 19, 21, 24. The anonymous homily *Concerning St Neot*, also without parallel textual transmission, has *ȝlæinȝde* 130.15, *ȝeteiȝnde* 131.14, but *tostæncte* 131.36 (ed. Warner 1917: No. XLII). Finally, there are a number of examples in the sermons contained in MS. Bodley 343, a manuscript from the second half of the twelfth century and perhaps of south-west Midland provenance (Ker 1957: No. 310). The section edited by Belfour (1909) has *imeind* 110.20 beside *besencte* 46.13 and *þencð* 110.19; Skeat's collation (1881–1900) of Ælfric's *Homily for St Martin's Day* has *iswæinte* 31.1370,[7] beside *ȝeȝlenȝde* 31.1494.

Thus, spellings of the *leinten* type appear in seven manuscripts written between about 1025 and 1175. The surprisingly high number of forms — twenty-seven certain examples — suggests that we are not dealing here simply with scribal errors, particularly as a number of occurrences of the same form are repeated in, for example, the short text of the *Weather Prophecies* in MS. Cotton Vesp. D. XIV. All the above manuscripts belong to the transition period of the southern *Schriftsprache*, yet show at the same time graphemic, phonological, and morphological forms which typify the development of early Middle English. This is true of the Brussels Aldhelm glosses (Goossens 1974: 137 ff) and the copy of it contained in MS. Digby 146 (Napier 1900: xxvii ff), as well as of the *Salisbury Psalter* (Sisam and Sisam 1959: 28 ff). Three of the four twelfth-century manuscripts, CCCC 303, Cotton Vesp. D. XIV and Bodley 343, are for the most part compilations of Ælfric's Homilies. Apart, however, from the sermon for St Martin's Day in MS. Bodley 343, which MED rightly regards as Middle English, manuscripts of the Ælfric-canon offer no examples, since the eleventh Bodley Homily is not Ælfrician (cp. Pope 1967–8: I, 16). With one exception the examples are limited to anonymous pieces without parallel textual transmission. It is obvious that the copyists had only contemporary or near contemporary exemplars available. Indeed, it is difficult to understand why the *leinten* type, according to Glaeser's (1916) accurate study, is totally lacking in the thirty-four Ælfrician homilies in MS. Cotton Vesp. D. XIV. An examination of the variant readings of MS. CCCC 303 in the editions of Skeat (1881–1900), Assmann (1889), Pope (1967–8), and Godden (1979) leads to similar conclusions.

Five of the seven manuscripts containing ‹ein›-spellings either are the products of Kentish scriptoria or demonstrate characteristic south-eastern forms. Only the *Salisbury Psalter* can be regarded as West Saxon on linguistic, palaeographical, and codicological grounds (cp. Sisam and Sisam

1959: 28). The main hand in MS. Bodley 343 has predominantly southwestern forms (cp. Pope 1967-8: I, 17 ff; Godden 1979: xl), but the assignment of this text to this part of the country rests mainly on Napier's analysis of the *History of the Holy Roodtree* (1894: xlvii ff). The regional spread of the graph ‹ein› corresponds with that of the analogical preterite of the type *sente*, first attested about 1100 (Dietz 1981a: 83 ff). This agreement is by no means fortuitous: both occurrences, besides being morphologically related, have in common a voiceless dental following a voiced consonant as, for instance, in verbs of the type *cwenčan – cweinte – ȝecweint* (albeit a regular phonological development in the latter group). Such, however, is only later the case in verbs of the type *menȝan – meinde* with final voiced root consonant, and thus the role of the *leinten* type as a model for the development of weak preterites of the *sente* type should not be exaggerated.

Examples of the spelling ‹ein› before 1200 may be divided as follows: (a) the nouns *lenȝten* sb., adj. < WGmc. **langitīn-* and *strenȝþ(u)* 'strength' < Gmc. **strangiþō; (b)* preterites and past participles of Class I weak verbs *(a-)cwencan* 'to quench', *(a-)drencan* 'to submerge', *(ȝe-)-ȝlenȝzan* 'to decorate', *menȝan* 'to mix', *(a-, be-)sencan* 'to sink, submerge', *(to-)stencan* 'to scatter', *(ȝe-)swencan* 'to trouble' and *(ȝe-)-tenȝan* 'to hasten' < Gmc. **-angjan* or **-ankjan*, pret. **-angida/ *-ankida*. The underlying structure common to all examples is of the kind $\check{a}$ + n [ŋ] + velar (g, k) + i + dental $(d, t, þ)$. It is also attested in OE *(ȝe)enȝþu* 'distress' and *lenȝþu* 'length' and the verbs *blencan* 'to deceive', *(be)clencan* 'to hold fast', *clenȝan* 'to adhere', *denȝan* 'to beat', *(ȝe)enȝan* 'to vex',[8] *ȝenȝan* 'to go', *(ȝe)hlencan* 'to twist', *lenȝan* 'to lengthen', *lenȝan* 'to belong', *(a)rencan* 'to exalt', *scencan* 'to pour out', *screncan* 'to cause to stumble', *screncan* 'to cause to shrink', *senȝan* 'to singe', *sprenȝan* 'to scatter', *strenȝan* 'to strengthen', *swenȝan* 'to shatter', *twenȝan* 'to pinch', *wlencan* 'to enrich', and *wrencan* 'to twist'; in addition, 2nd and 3rd person sg. pres. ind. of *brenȝan* 'to bring' and *þencan* 'to think'. There are altogether some thirty lexical items if compounds, derivations such as *brenȝnes* or *lenctenlic*, and prefixed verbs are excluded. The lexical frequency of the *lencten* type with the development of *ei* turns out to be rather limited, and the majority of the examples of the development constitutes only the inflected forms of verbs which have undergone syncope. The paucity of potential examples is a consequence of the complex phonemic sequence of OE $\check{e}$ < *$\check{a}_i$ and a following triple consonant cluster comprising nasal + velar + dental.

Now, syncope of *-i-* in medial syllables took place on the one hand after *i*-Umlaut and thus after the primary palatalization of root-final velar stops [ŋk/g] > [ɲc/ɟ], in which the preceding homorganic nasal automatically took part, on the other hand, however, in the prehistoric period. Accordingly, assibilation of palatal stops, which did not occur until the historical period, could not have taken place in preconsonantal position. The consonant groups resulting from this process, which has been insufficiently, if not incorrectly, dealt with in more recent handbooks and in the latest studies (van der Rhee 1978, Cercignani 1983), are as follows: *nct* [ɲct] and *nʒd* [ɲɟd] (cp. Bülbring 1902: sections 497, 500) and *nʒt* [ɲɟt], *nʒþ* [ɲɟθ]. In the case of the last two groups assimilation to the following voiceless dental produces the groups *nċt* (*lencten*) and *nċþ* (*strencþ*); however, the historical spelling with ‹ʒ› is often retained, just as it is in the case of the devoicing of final *-ʒ* > *-h* (Campbell 1959: sections 480, 482). No matter how one interprets a form like *leinten* phonologically, the existence of spellings of this type powerfully refutes the views of Campbell (1959: sections 431, 435) and Sievers and Brunner (1965: section 206.2, n. 2) that such palatalized velars reverted to velar stops again when a consonant followed.

The further development of the resulting triconsonantal groups *nʒd*, *nċt* and *nċþ* in Old English is completed in two ways, both of which result in the disappearance of the medial palatal. First, loss of the medial palatal in the group, particularly in heterosyllabic position, leads by simplification to *nt, nþ,* and *nd*; cp. Merc. *lenten*, WS *strenþ*, Kt. *ʒemende*. Nevertheless, these changes are often disguised by etymological spellings or by restoration — in the spelling at least — of the original triple group under the analogical influence of related forms (Luick 1921–40: section 677; Campbell 1959: sections 476 f, 751). Yet forms like *leinten* demonstrate that such spellings involve more than simply adherence to orthographic convention: the adjectives *lanʒ* (*lenʒra*) and *stranʒ* (*strenʒra*) effect preservation and levelling in the derived nouns *lenʒð(u)* and *strenʒð(u)*, and the same is true of the morphophonological alternation (not reflected in spelling) in verbs of the kind /[g ~ ɟ]/ ≈ /ǧ/ and /[k ~ c]/ ≈ /č/. *Lencten*, however, alone of all such forms, stands etymologically isolated, and while it might be possible that the spelling influenced the pronunciation, such an interpretation is hardly convincing. Those rare occurrences of spellings of the type ‹nt, nþ~nð, nd›,[9] particularly in earlier texts suggest rather that the triple groups *nċt, nċþ* and *nʒd* were still widely current around 1000.

A complex process of assimilation results in late Old English forms of the *leinten* type and offers the second way in which these triple groups could develop. Assimilation of the palatal to the following dental leads to an intermediate stage with fricative articulation: [ɲċt > ɲçt > ɲjt], or [ɲɟd > ɲjd]. The resulting [j] merges with the preceding palatal nasal, in whose articulation it is already implicit. Assimilation of the palatalized nasal to the dental now immediately following results in the development of a glide which combines with the preceding vowel to give rise to a diphthong: [ɲt > int, ɲd > ind]. Such a process is seen in the Gallo-Roman development of Latin *nct* > *ñçt* > Prim. OF *ñt* > OF *int* (for example, OF *saint* < *sanctum*, *feint* < *finctum*; cp. Fouché 1966: 815 ff, 838 ff, 841; Pálfy 1966, 1975). This disengaging in the simultaneous articulation of the palatal nasal corresponds, moreover, to the treatment of ñ in French loan-words in Middle English. An alternative development [ɲct] > [ɲt] (> [int]) with loss of the palatal as the medial element in a triple group is much less likely, since the glide which arises demands that ñ be fully palatal, an unlikely development without the intermediate stage [ɲċt].

The proposal that the *leinten* type had undergone some sort of palatal diphthongization was rejected by Luick in ignorance of its actual spread in Middle English and by Wright without any discussion. However, their analysis is of little value for the Old English examples. Although ‹i› is commonly used alongside ‹e› in Old English as a diacritic to indicate palatalized and assibilated consonants, in late Old English ‹i› stands exclusively before the back vowels represented by the graphs ‹u› and ‹o› (*ecium, dryʒʒium, secʒium*; Campbell 1959: section 45; Sievers and Brunner 1965: sections 206.7c, 216.1) and in addition serves to distinguish orthographically phonemes which are otherwise undifferentiated. To suppose that ‹i› has merely a diacritic function in words of the *leinten* type is not supported by any of the spellings in the seven manuscripts in which the examples are found.[10] Furthermore, it necessitates acceptance of the highly dubious opposition ‹n› /n/ ≠ ‹in› /ɲ/ in pairs such as 1st sg. pres., pret. *hente*: *dreinte* or pret. *(a)tende*: *teinde*. If such were the case, this opposition would have had to exist until well into the fifteenth century. On the other hand, assumption of a diphthong *ei* involves no addition to the phonological system of late Old English or even early Middle English, as Old English already possessed *i*-diphthongs. They first arise out of the combination of the front vowels $\bar{e}$ and $\bar{æ}$ with tautosyllabic ʒ/j/ which has been vocalized. Later, with the fusion of heterosyllabic ʒ/j/, they are phonemicized in the course of the eleventh–twelfth centuries. The *i*-diphthongs are augmented by the addition of /oi/, which is already to be found in native words at the time of the Norman Conquest (cp. Dietz 1981b, 1981c). Examples from the early twelfth century, such as *ʒeswœinte* in MS. CCCC 303 must therefore be treated in a similar fashion to *Sœintes* 695 (< OF *saint*) in the *Life of St Nicholas* in the same manuscript. The same is true for *læinten* or *ʒeteiʒnde* in MS. Cotton Vesp. D. XIV in view of frequently attested *Sœinte* ~ *Seinte* (ed. Warner 1917: 24.4, 129.3, 130.3, 134.1), which must now be numbered among the very few French loan-words encountered before 1150.[11]

The development of vowels before a following nasal in the prehistoric period determines that OE $\breve{e}$ is the only vowel which can be involved in the late Old English diphthongization before a palatal nasal. Only $\breve{a}$, $\breve{i}$ and $\breve{u}$ can stand before a preconsonantal nasal in late Prim. Germanic. *I*-Umlaut, which also sets up the conditions for the rise of *nċ/nʒ*, produces OE $\breve{e}$ and $\breve{y}$; the latter becomes $\breve{e}$ in Kentish, while in West Saxon it falls together before palatals with original $\breve{i}$ (cp. WS *þincþ* 'seems'; *ʒeþinʒþo*, OHG *thungida*[12]). No diphthong can arise from *i*. Besides $\breve{e} <$ *$\breve{a}n_i$ there remains only its East Saxon equivalent ǣ: this ǣ may be present in *leinten* and other instances with ‹æi› in MSS. CCCC 303 and Cotton Vesp. D. XIV. In both manuscripts ‹æ› is by far the commonest spelling for *i*-mutated *ă before a nasal (cp. Ahern 1975: 27, Picard 1980: 19 ff; Glaeser 1916: 19), but no certainty is possible without a more thorough examination of the early Middle English material.

Just as the number of vowels before a preconsonantal nasal in Old English is restricted by the development in the prehistoric period, so are those consonants which may follow *nȝ* and *nc*. Therefore, only consonants which stand in suffixes and inflexions with an original *i*-element need be considered. According to the rules governing syllabic and morphemic structure in late West Saxon, only dental and alveolar plosives with the features [+ant, +cor] may follow the clusters /ng/ and /nk/ (cp. Pilch 1970: 68 ff). From examples which are attested, suffixes with *st* and *þ* are affected in the first instance (cp. Awedyk 1975: 65 ff), but so, too, are combinations with *t* and *d* in late West Saxon (Sievers and Brunner 1965: section 406, n. 2), since analogy with preterite and inflected forms with syncope (for example, pl. *adrencte, ȝeȝlenȝde*) is responsible for forms like *adrenct* and *ȝeȝlenȝd*. Such instances argue for palatal stops, not affricates as suggested by Pilch (1970: 70). The same conditions apply in medial clusters, for which, however, only *nȝd* and *nc + t,þ* are attested; compare the list in Awedyk (1975: 70 ff), who failed to notice examples of the clusters *-nȝd-* and *-ncþ-*. Whether medial combinations with *-st-* could have existed depends upon the interpretation of the West Saxon superlatives *lenȝsta* (<*langist-*) and *strenȝsta* (< *strangist-*). They are alleged to appear so late in the sources that syncope could have taken place only after assibilation (cp. Campbell 1959: section 352; Sievers and Brunner 1965: sections 161, 311). Alternatively, such instances may be examples of older forms, such as is the case with *hiehsta* (< *χauχist-*) and *niehsta* (< *nǣχist-*) in which *-i-* was syncopated in the prehistoric period (cp. Luick 1921–40: section 306, n. 2). The fact that syncopated *strenȝsta* is attested much earlier than has been previously thought, occurring three times in Orosius (ed. Bately 1980: 3.17, 72.13, 75.1), supports the latter suggestion. Furthermore, *lenȝsta < lenȝesta* and *strenȝsta < strenȝesta* might have been reformed as *lenȝsta and strenȝsta* by analogy with their comparatives *lenȝra* and *strenȝra*. Consequently the clusters *nȝ, nċ + d, (s)t, þ* must be taken into consideration in both medial and final position. The structure underlying the *leinten* type is as follows:

(1) $\begin{bmatrix} -\text{cons} \\ -\text{high} \end{bmatrix} \begin{bmatrix} +\text{cons} \\ +\text{nasal} \end{bmatrix} \begin{bmatrix} +\text{cons} \\ -\text{ant} \\ -\text{cor} \\ \alpha\text{voice} \end{bmatrix} \begin{bmatrix} +\text{obs} \\ +\text{ant} \\ +\text{cor} \\ \alpha\text{voice} \\ \langle+\text{strid}\rangle \end{bmatrix}$ ‹+cons›

In medial position, obstruents and also the sonorants *r*, *l*, and *n* may follow the groups *nȝ* and *nc*: *lenȝra, enȝlisc, brenȝnes, tostencnes*; compare Awedyk (1975: 71), whose list must now be extended to include *-ncn-* and *-nȝr-*. The spelling ⟨ein⟩ for ⟨enȝ ~ enc⟩ before liquids is, however, unattested in either Old English or Middle English. It is attested only once before a nasal, in *æfterȝeinnysse* 3501 in the Brussels glosses on Aldhelm, compared with *æfterȝencȝnysse* 2613 and *æfterȝencnyssum* 912, for Latin *posteritas*, and all by the same scribe who wrote the other examples for ⟨ein⟩. There may be several reasons why the diphthongization *enȝ/enć* > *ein* has apparently not taken place before *r*, *l* and is not productive before *n*. In the case of liquids, the nature of their articulation makes palatalization unlikely (on this, cp. Lass and Anderson 1975: 83 ff; Lass 1977, 1983). Possible combinations with a nasal comprise either deverbative abstracts (*menȝnes, swencnes*) which in late West Saxon are formed from past participles (*menȝednes, swencednes, tostencednes*; cp. Vleeskruyer 1953: 129 ff) rather than from verbal stems, or derivations from adjectives with root-final assibilation (*ȝlenȝnes*).

A comparison of the Old English occurrences with the treatment of the Middle English evidence in the handbooks reveals full agreement with Wright and Wright (1928) and substantial agreement with Jordan (1934), who believed that the process affected not only the clusters *nct*, *ngd*, and *ngþ*, but should be extended to include *nš*. Yet the sole example he cites for *nš* does not belong here: the final consonant cluster in ME *Freinsh* < OE *frencisc*, in which syncope is unattested before early Middle English, is in fact *nćʃ*. This consonant group is similar in structure to the other three clusters associated with the diphthongization *e* > *ei*; the structural formula (1) is accordingly extended to include *nćʃ* in Middle English.

Berndt's (1960: 65) treatment of the genesis of the *leinten* type is very different, but demonstrably wrong in its theoretical argument. Like Jordan he proposes a development *enʃ* > *einʃ* for ME *Freinsh*, yet argues at the same time for an identical path of change for OE *lenȝþ(u)* and *lencten*, namely ME *lenth* > *leinth, lenten* > *leinten*. Furthermore, he includes here assibilated forms such as *sengde* > *seinde* and *drenchte* > *dreinte*. The consequence of Berndt's analysis is that the *leinten* type is divided into two groups which are associated by the resulting diphthong, because he has failed to notice the role played by the palatal stop. His view that OE *lencten* develops to ME *leinten* by a process *-ŋkt-* > *-ŋt-* > *nt* > *-int-* is questionable on phonetic grounds. Moreover, it implies that diphthongization should have taken place in, for example, ME *henten* < OE *hentan*. Even more unlikely is Berndt's suggestion of an '*Einschub eines i ... vor den Konsonantenfolgen* ndž, ntš'; remarkably *i* is lacking in the present forms of verbs such as *sengen* and *drenchen*, yet appears in the preterite, which never contained an affricate at any stage of its history.

The findings of Lass (1976: 181) are no more enlightening. He interprets Jordan's material as evidence for *i*-epenthesis 'before ... a dental nasal + palatal cluster and a velar nasal + velar cluster'; the first combination must refer to the sequence *n* + *č, ǧ* and thus depends upon his earlier assibilation rule (Lass and Anderson 1975: 146 ff), which is in this respect inadequate, since it produces affricates in preconsonantal position. Such a shortcoming not only demands a restatement of the assibilation rule, it also makes necessary the extension and reordering of the complete set of rules, as the assibilation rule precedes the *i*-Umlaut rule in Lass and Anderson. Examples such as *lencten* require in addition a syncope rule which is operative after *i*-Umlaut but before assibilation. Finally, there is no evidence whatsoever for Lass's proposal that the velar groups [ŋg, ŋk] caused an *i*-diphthong to arise in Middle English.[13]

Lass's rule for the *leinten* type must be restated as follows:

$$(2) \quad \emptyset \longrightarrow \begin{bmatrix} -\text{cons} \\ +\text{high} \\ -\text{back} \end{bmatrix} \bigg/ \begin{bmatrix} -\text{cons} \\ -\text{high} \end{bmatrix} \longrightarrow \begin{bmatrix} +\text{nasal} \\ +\text{high} \\ -\text{back} \end{bmatrix} \quad [+\text{obs}]$$

The rules for palatalization of the nasal and loss of the following palatal stop must be ordered before rule (2):

$$(3) \quad [+\text{nasal}] \longrightarrow \begin{bmatrix} +\text{high} \\ -\text{back} \end{bmatrix} \bigg/ \longrightarrow \begin{bmatrix} +\text{cons} \\ +\text{high} \\ -\text{back} \end{bmatrix} \begin{bmatrix} +\text{obs} \\ +\text{ant} \\ +\text{cor} \end{bmatrix}$$

$$(4) \quad [+\text{cons}] \longrightarrow \emptyset \bigg/ \begin{bmatrix} +\text{nasal} \\ +\text{high} \\ -\text{back} \end{bmatrix} \longrightarrow [+\text{obs}]$$

Up to now the diphthongization of /e/ > /ei/ in the *leinten* type has been considered a Middle English sound change first attested in 1200. Its existence is variously doubted or even dismissed, whereas the development evidently took place two hundred years earlier. It is attested from the first half of the eleventh century and cannot be regarded as a purely orthographic phenomenon; ⟨ei⟩-spellings are attested in eleventh- and twelfth-century Old English manuscripts which were mostly written in the southeast or whose linguistic forms indicate an East Saxon/Kentish origin. Viewed in the light of linguistic history, the kind of palatal diphthongization represented in the *leinten* type is a late continuation of the Prim. Old English palatalization of original velar stops. Its functional significance in Middle English is obvious, especially in the preterite forms of Class I weak verbs with root-final *nʒ/nc*. The dialectal distribution of such forms can only be determined by a study of the Middle English evidence, which is to appear at a later date. This forthcoming analysis of the *leinten* type in

Middle English should help to dispel any final doubts about the existence of a phonological change which had its basis in Old English.

NOTES

For reasons of space it has proved impossible to include a discussion of the Middle English material. This evidence will be considered at a later date. I am grateful to David Lewis (FU Berlin) for drawing up the English version of this paper.

1. The material presented here is based on an examination of the Microfiche Concordance to Old English (1980), as well as on a number of texts not included in the Concordance.
2. Napier's view, also shared by Ker (1957: 382), of Kenticisms in the text must be modified in the light of Goossens's (1974: 26, 136) interpretation.
3. While Sisam and Sisam (1959: 12, 28) regards Shaftesbury as the place of origin for the manuscript, Stroud (1979) regards Wilton as more likely.
4. The Microfiche Concordance records the form as ʒeʒlænde, but Ahern (1975) reads ʒeʒlæinde 14.
5. The Microfiche Concordance, whose editors were not aware of Ahern's edition, has instead ʒeswæncte. My examination of a microfilm of MS. CCCC 303 confirms Ahern's reading of both ʒeswæincte and ʒeʒlæinde. The transcripts of the homilies LS 9 (Giles) and LS 29 (Nicholas) prepared for the Concordance are clearly unreliable.
6. For this manuscript, compare Godden (1979: xl ff), Schmetterer (1981: 5 ff) and the literature cited there.
7. The Microfiche Concordance does not record this form.
8. The verb ʒeenʒan, as well as ʒeenʒþu, is not recorded by Hall and Meritt (1960).
9. For the syncopated forms of the 2nd and 3rd sg. pres., compare the material in Hedberg (1945: 138 ff, 147).
10. Compare the editions of Goossens (1974: 57 ff) and Sisam and Sisam (1959: 21 ff); on the *Eadwine Psalter*, compare Hein (1903); on MS. Cotton Vesp. D. XIV, compare Glaeser (1916) and Straub (1908, 1921).
11. The Microfiche Concordance also records *Seintes* in the *Peterborough Chronicle*, s.a. 1127, but this refers to the name of the administrative centre of the Saintonge.
12. Other examples in Old English for *-*ungi*/*-*unki* + dental are apparently lacking.
13. The supposed parallels in the English of the southern United States (Lass 1976: 183) depend upon a different set of conditions.

REFERENCES

Ahern, D.E. (ed.) 1975. *An Edition of Two Old English Saints' Lives: The Life of St Giles and The Life of St Nicholas*. University of Arizona dissertation.

Assmann, B. (ed.) 1889. *Angelsächsische Homilien und Heiligenleben*. (Bibl. der ags. Prosa, 3.) Repr. 1964. Darmstadt: Wissenschaftliche Buchgesellschaft.

Awedyk, W. 1975. *The Syllable Theory and Old English Phonology*. Wrocław: Polska Akademia Nauk.

Bately, J. (ed.) 1980. *The Old English Orosius*. (EETS, SS, 6.) London: Oxford University Press.
Belfour, A.O. (ed.) 1909. *Twelfth-Century Homilies in MS. Bodley 343*. (EETS, OS, 137.) Repr. 1962. London: Oxford University Press.
Berndt, R. 1960. *Einführung in das Studium des Mittelenglischen*. Halle: Niemeyer.
Brunner, K. 1938. *Abriß de mittelenglischen Grammatik*. 6. Aufl. 1967. Tübingen: Niemeyer.
Bülbring, K.D. 1902. *Altenglisches Elementarbuch*. I: Lautlehre. Heidelberg: Winter.
Campbell, A. 1959. *Old English Grammar*. Repr. 1974. Oxford: Clarendon.
Cercignani, F. 1983. 'The Development of */k/ and */sk/ in Old English'. *Journal of English and Germanic Philology* 82: 313–23.
Dietz, K. 1981a. 'Die englischen Präterita des Typus *went*', in P. Erlebach, W.G. Müller, and K. Reuter (eds.) *Geschichtlichkeit und Neuanfang im sprachlichen Kunstwerk: Studien zur Englischen Philologie zu Ehren von Fritz W. Schulze*. Tübingen: Narr, 71–89.
—— 1981b. 'Mittelenglisch *oi* in heimischen Ortsnamen und Personennamen: Der Typus *Croydon*', *Beiträge zur Namenforschung*, NF 16: 269–340.
—— 1981c. 'Mittelenglisch *oi* in heimischen Ortsnamen und Personennamen. II. Das Namenelement *Boi(e)* und die Etymologie von *boy*', *Beiträge zur Namenforschung*, NF 16: 361–405.
Fouché, P. 1966. *Phonétique historique du français*. Vol. 3, 2nd edn. Paris: Klincksieck.
Fowler, R. (ed.) 1965. 'A Late Old English Handbook for the Use of a Confessor', *Anglia* 83: 1–34.
Glaeser, K. 1916. *Lautlehre der Ælfricschen Homilien in der Handschrift Cotton Vespasianus D. XIV.* Leipzig (1913) dissertation. Weida.
Godden, M. (ed.) 1979. *Ælfric's Catholic Homilies. The Second Series*. (EETS, SS, 5.) London: Oxford University Press.
Goossens, L. (ed.) 1974. *The Old English Glosses of MS. Brussels, Royal Library, 1650*. Brussels: Koninklijke Academie voor Wetenschappen, Letteren en Schone Kunsten.
Hall, J.C. Clark and H.D. Meritt. 1960. *A Concise Anglo-Saxon Dictionary*. 4th edn. Cambridge: Cambridge University Press.
Harsley, F. (ed.) 1889. *Eadwine's Canterbury Psalter*. (EETS, OS, 92.) London: Trübner.
Hedberg, J. 1945. *The Syncope of the Old English Present Endings*. (Lund Studies in English, 12.) Lund: Gleerup.
Hein, B. 1903. *Die Sprache der altenglischen Glosse zu Eadwine's Canterbury salter*. Würzburg dissertation.
Jordan, R. 1925. *Handbuch der mittelenglischen Grammatik. I: Lautlehre*. 2nd edn. 1934, 3rd edn. 1968. Heidelberg: Winter.
Ker, N.R. 1957. *Catalogue of Manuscripts Containing Anglo-Saxon*. Oxford: Clarendon.
Kluge, F. 1901. 'Geschichte der englischen Sprache', in H. Paul (ed.). *Grundriss der germanischen Philologie*. Vol. 1, 2nd edn. Strassburg: Trübner, 926–1151.
Lass, R. 1976. *English Phonology and Phonological Theory*. Cambridge: Cambridge University Press.
—— 1977. 'On the Phonetic Specification of Old English /r/', *Studia Anglica Posnaniensia* 9: 3–16.
—— 1983. 'Velar /r/ and the History of English', in M. Davenport, E. Hansen and H.F. Nielsen (eds.), *Current Topics in English Historical Linguistics*. Odense: Odense University Press, 67–94.

—— and J.M. Anderson. 1975. *Old English Phonology*. Cambridge: Cambridge University Press.
Liebermann, F. (ed.) 1903–16. *Die Gesetze der Angelsachsen*. 3 vols. Halle: Niemeyer.
Liles, B.L. (ed.) 1967. *The Canterbury Psalter*. Stanford dissertation.
Luick, K. 1921–40. *Historische Grammatik der englischen Sprache*. Repr. 1964. Stuttgart: Tauchnitz.
Morsbach, L. 1896. *Mittelenglische Grammatik*. Halle: Niemeyer.
Napier, A.S. (ed.) 1894. *History of the Holy Rood-tree*. (EETS, OS, 103.) London: Trübner.
—— (ed.) 1900. *Old English Glosses*. Oxford: Clarendon.
Pálfy, M. 1966. 'Traitement -/n/kt- > -i/n/t-', *Revue des Langues Romanes* 77: 131–4.
—— 1975. 'Conditions du traitement -(n)kt- > -i(n)t- en ancien français', *Revue Roumaine de Linguistique* 20: 37–41.
Picard, B. (ed.) 1980. *Das altenglische Aegidiusleben in MS CCCC 303*. Freiburg dissertation.
Pilch, H. 1970. *Altenglische Grammatik*. München: Hueber.
Pope, J.C. (ed.) 1967–8. *Homilies of Ælfric. A Supplementary Collection*. 2 vols. (EETS, 259, 260). London: Oxford University Press.
van der Rhee, F. 1978. 'Palatalisierung, Mouillierung und Assibilierung von urgerm. /k/ im Altenglischen und Altfriesischen', *Us Wurk* 26: 33–44.
Schlemilch, W. 1914. *Beiträge zur Sprache und Orthographie spätaltengl. Sprachdenkmäler der Übergangszeit (1000–1150)*. (Studien zur englischen Philologie, 34.) Halle: Niemeyer.
Schmetterer, V. (ed.) 1981. *Drei altenglische religiöse Texte aus der Handschrift Cotton Vespasianus D XIV*. Wien dissertation.
Skeat, W.W. (ed.) 1881–1900. *Ælfric's Lives of Saints*. 2 vols. (EETS, OS, 76, 82, 94, 114.) London: Trübner.
Sievers, E. and K. Brunner. 1965. *Altenglische Grammatik*. 3rd edn. Tübingen: Niemeyer.
Sisam, C. and K. Sisam (eds.) 1959. *The Salisbury Psalter*. (EETS, 242.) London: Oxford University Press.
Straub, F. 1908. *Lautlehre der jungen Nicodemus-Version in Vespasian D. XIV*. Würzburg dissertation.
—— 1921. *Lautlehre der altenglischen Übersetzung des Pseudo-Alcuinischen Liber de virtutibus et vitiis in Vespasianus D. XIV*. (Schulprogramm Wunsiedel 1920/21.) Wunsiedel.
Stroud, D.I. 1979. 'The Provenance of the Salisbury Psalter', *The Library*, 6th ser. 1: 225–35.
Vleeskruyer, R. (ed.) 1953. *The Life of St Chad. An Old English Homily*. Amsterdam: North Holland.
Warner, R.D.-N. (ed.) 1917. *Early English Homilies from the Twelfth Century MS. Vesp. D. XIV*. (EETS, OS, 152.) London: Oxford University Press.
Wright, J. and E.M. Wright. 1928. *An Elementary Middle English Grammar*. 2nd edn. Oxford: Clarendon.

15

Prothetic Alif and Canonical Form in Egyptian

CARLETON T. HODGE

It has long been known that Semitic, at least in its historically classical forms, does not allow any initial clusters (Moscati *et al.* 1964: 59–60, 64). Should the root and pattern produce CCV-, this must be resolved into CVCV- or ʔVCCV-. This was well known in the nineteenth century (e.g. Nöldeke 1880: 35 *re* Syriac) and was applied to Egyptian by Renouf in 1887. In discussing several Egyptian forms, he identified an initial reed-leaf (Gardiner 1957: Sign List, M17) as 'prosthetic vowel', noting that it 'is most commonly prefixed to words beginning with two consonants (as in the Semitic and other languages)' (Renouf 1903: 2.224 and n. 2).

Sethe, observing this phenomenon in the Egyptian verb, wrote his dissertation on it (1892). In some cases the verb had an initial reed-leaf (M17), in some cases not. For example, *wn* 'open' could be *ʔwn* in the imperative (1892: 8). Further, such a form frequently had an initial vowel in Coptic: *aouōn* 'open!' (1892: 26). Sethe concluded that this reed-leaf represented a prothetic glottal stop (plus unwritten vowel), such as occurs in Semitic before a two-consonant cluster. In Egyptian it was characteristic of certain forms of the verb, which he presented in detail in his *Verbum* (1899–1902).

Sethe's view won wide acceptance. Erman felt that his statement could hardly be doubted by any scholar (1900: 319), and the principle found a place in both his Egyptian grammar (e.g. 1911: 72) and his Late Egyptian grammar (1933: Index). Gardiner accepted Sethe's interpretation and strongly supported it when he came to write the section on vocalization in his grammar (1927: 209 [= 1957: 209]). Lefebvre agreed (1955: 120–1).

In 1923 Sethe made use of his thesis about prothetic alif in a general treatment of Egyptian vocalization. On comparing the results with Semitic he concluded that the forms with prothetic alif reflected the patterns of historical Egyptian but that the prehistoric period had a vowel between the consonants (1923: 202):

Historical   ʔ ˘ C C ´ -   *entṓret   'goddess'

195

Prehistoric   CVC-   *natarata

Our concern here is with the first pattern, though the second has had considerable influence.

More recently there has been either outright rejection or only partial acceptance of Sethe's thesis. Thacker has the most serious critique (1954: 55–67). Restricting his discussion to the morphology of the verb, he concludes that the reed-leaf was an effort to write a medial root consonant (63). There are, he says, practically no prothetic reed-leafs elsewhere (57). Edel, in the first volume of his Old Egyptian grammar, published a year after Thacker, states that the prothetic alif in the verb is not related to syllable structure (1955: 202–3). Fecht (1960) treated Sethe's prehistoric pattern (CVC- for ʔVCC-) as the historical one. For the prehistoric period he reconstructs a completely open syllable pattern: CVCVCV (1960: 189). (Sethe's allows CVCCVC, etc.) In his opinion, prothetic alif does not always occur before two consonants, citing as evidence the preposition *m* 'in', which has prothetic alif before pronouns. He reconstructs *(j ˀ)ma-*. Vergote (e.g. 1965) and Osing (1976) have both followed Fecht in reconstructing CVC- rather than ʔVCC-, though Vergote often has ʔVCC- derived from CVC-. Meltzer 'does not think it has been demonstrated conclusively that initial consonant clusters were absent from pre-Coptic Egyptian' (1978: 143).

In view of these more recent doubts and reinterpretations, the situation calls for additional study. It is proposed, in this and related articles, to test Sethe's hypothesis. Can we, combining his assumptions regarding prothetic alif and Edgerton's formulation of the relationship between Egyptian syllable structure and Coptic vowel quantity (1947), make consistent and probable reconstructions of the older Egyptian syllable structure and stress patterns? In the process we shall discover whether following the hypothesis to its logical conclusions will shed any new light on our reading of the hieroglyphs.

The hypothesis states that when a root plus vowel pattern results in an initial consonant cluster (as in CCVC), a glottal stop (plus vowel) is prefixed. A corollary is that the occurrence of a prothetic glottal stop presumes that a two consonant cluster follows. We therefore look upon any form as suspect if it sometimes occurs with a glottal stop and sometimes without. (Hereinafter reed-leaf will be transcribed as ʔ, it being a glottal stop (see Hodge 1977 and references).)

We first examine a noun which has not hitherto entered the prothetic alif discussion. This is ʔḥ 'bull', ʔḥt 'cow', Co. SBA *ehe*, F *ahē* (Crum 1939: 64a). Coptic *ehe* has been taken to be from ʔḥt (e.g. Černý 1976: 41). This assumes that the stress fell on the ending: *ʔ ˘ ḥ ´ t. If ʔ is part of the root, we would expect the pattern *ʔ ´ ḥ ˘ t (compare Eg. *snt* 'sister', Co. *sōne*), which would give *ēhe. Neither of these would yield the F form, which assumes a stressed open syllable: *ʔ ˘ ḥ ´ C ˘ C. The position of the stress here shows that the first syllable was unstressed. We therefore ask whether it is possible that ʔ- is here prothetic and that we have a cluster following: *ʔ ˘ ḥ C ´ C or *ʔ ˘ C ḥ ´ C. If so, what evidence is there for the consonant next to ḥ? The *Wörterbuch* gives ḥww 'Bez. für (kämpfende) Stiere' and ḥwjw 'allgemeine Bez. für Rinder' (Erman and Grapow 1957: 3.45); Faulkner has ḥww 'class (?) of bulls, ... cattle in general' (1962: 165). Here is evidence for -ḥw- after the ʔ- of ʔḥ and ʔḥt.

There remains the problem of the third root consonant. The -w of ḥww is probably the plural ending, reflected in the Coptic plural forms, such as S *ehow, ehēw.* The last should come from a pattern such as *ʔ ˘ ḥ w ´ C ˘ C. There is a Middle Egyptian spelling ḥwyw (where y is double reed-leaf), which would give us *ʔ ˘ ḥ w ´ y as the singular form back of Co. *ehe.* It is possible that -y- is secondary and the root is really *ḥwʔ or some other unknown. At this point we cannot go back to the y.

Turning to Semitic, we find a root reconstructed by Fronzaroli as *ḥayiy-, a West Semitic form for 'alive' (1964: 263). Dolgopolsky gives the root as *ḥwy or *ḥyw (1973: 156). In Arabic *ḥayyun* means 'a living creature' and has a plural ʔaḥyaaʔun. Deleting the ending -un, the latter has the pattern ʔ ˘ C C ´ C which we have reconstructed for Egyptian. As the stressed syllable is closed without the ending, we should have a short vowel in Coptic, and so we do: *ehe,* i.e. /ʔehé/. (The root occurs not only in Egyptian and Semitic but also in Cushitic and Indo-European.)

We now consider the case of the Egyptian independent pronouns. The forms which interest us include the later ones for second and third persons singular. The first plural does not appear before the New Kingdom. Table 15.1 gives the spelling of the attested forms, a transcription based on Edel (changing j to ʔ), a transliteration of the Coptic spelling and a phonemic interpretation of the latter. Forms not dated MEg or LEg are attested in Old Egyptian. (See Edel 1955: 79, Gardiner 1957: 53, Černý 1941: 106-7, Černý and Groll 1978: 11.)

Gardiner gives ʔnwn as a variant for 1pl. This is based on Černý (1941), who gives the spelling as ʔnwnn. Gardiner's ʔnwn is probably right as an interpretive transcription, considering the Coptic.

Of the second and third person forms, prothetic alif is written in variants of the third person plural. Edel has generalized this to all second and third persons, as the transcription shows. The Coptic, where n̄ is to be read /ʔən-/, supports him in this. We have, then, the pattern ʔ ˘ C C ´ C(-) for these forms.

Turning to the first person singular we note that the spelling nwk, on the basis of the alternate spelling ʔnk and Coptic *anok,* has been taken as ʔnk (cf. Gardiner 1957: 530, W24 and 531, W25 [nw-pot with legs, read ʔn] and Edel 1955: 20-1). However, if we read the nw-pot (W24) as nw, we find a striking parallelism between the first person spellings and those of

Table 15.1: Egypto-Coptic independent pronouns

		Spelling	Transcription	Coptic	Transcription
1sg.		nwk	ʔnk	anok	ʔanók
		ʔnk			
		nwkʔ			
		ʔnwk			
2sg. m.	MEg	ntk	ʔntk	ñtok	ʔɔntók
f.	MEg	ntč	ʔntč	ñto	ʔɔntó
3sg. m.		ntf	ʔntf	ñtof	ʔɔntóf
f.	MEg	nts	ʔnts	ñtos	ʔɔntós
2du.	MEg	ntčn	ʔntčnʔ		
3du.		ntsn	ʔntsnʔ		
1pl.	LEg	ʔnn	ʔnn	anon	ʔanón
		ʔnwnn			
2pl.	MEg	ntčn	ʔntčn	ñtōtñ	ʔɔntó:tɔn
3pl.		ntsn	ʔntsn		
		ntʔsn			
		ʔntsn			
		ʔntʔsn			

the second and third persons:

alif-less	plus alif
nwk	ʔnwk
ntk	ʔntk
ntsn etc.	ʔntsn etc.

If we add the first person plural, we have a form with prothetic alif regularly written but with optional -w-:

w-less	plus w
ʔnn	ʔnwn

The forms plus -alif and plus -w fit into the ʔ ˘ C C ´ C pattern used in the other persons. We therefore consider *ʔnwk* and *ʔnwn* to be the correct transcriptions for 'I' and 'we'. They clearly have prothetic alif as do all the others. The -w- of *ʔnwk* and *ʔnwn* is to be identified with the dependent pronoun *wʔ* 'me'. The difference in Coptic vocalization (/ʔa-/ vs. /ʔə-/) may be attributed to the difference between ʔ ˘ Cw- and ʔ ˘ Ct-. The -w- is lost and the preceding vowel made a full one. It should be noted that the possibility of reading *ʔnwk* was previously considered — and rejected (e.g. Erman 1912: 962 n.1).

Prothetic alif also occurs with certain prepositions, as has long been recognized (see, e.g., Edel 1955: 61). Consider Table 15.2.

Table 15.2: Egypto-Coptic prepositions with ʔ-

	Egyptian Without ʔ-	Egyptian With ʔ-	Spelling	Coptic Transcription	Meaning
1.	m r	ʔ m r			'like'
2.	ḥ r		hi- N	hi-	'on'
		ʔ ḥ r P	hioo- P	(ʔə)hyóːʔə-	
3.		m N	ñ N	ʔən-	'in'
			/ m̄ N	ʔəm-	
		ʔ m P	m̄mo- P	ʔəʔmó-	
4.	n N/P	ʔ n N/P	ñ- N	ʔən-	'to, for'
			/ m̄- N	ʔəm-	
			na- P	ná-	
5.	r N/P	ʔ r N/P	e- N	ʔe-	'to, toward'
			ero- P	ʔeró-	

Note: N = noun. P = suffix pronoun.
1. Edel 1964: 391–2. 2. Gardiner 1957: 127 n. 11, 209 n. 6. 3. Edel 1964: 388–9, 1955: 61; Steindorff 1951: 89–90; Till 1961: 110. For m̄ = /əʔ/, Hodge 1981. 4. Edel 1964: 387–8; Steindorff 1951: 89; Till 1961: 110–11. 5. Edel 1955: 61, 1964: 390–1; Steindorff 1951: 89; Till 1961: 110.

Edel considers the spelling *ʔmr* to be a graphic metathesis of *mrʔ* (a composite writing of *mʔ* from *mr*) (1964: 391). He specifically denies the existence of an 'old form' *ʔmr* (with reference to Firchow 1953: 108 n.1). Considered in the light of the prothetic alif overall, this is unjustified. His examples of apparent metathesis listed in 1955: 41 should be re-examined.

Both *mr* and *ḥr* have two consonants each, and the forms *ʔmr-* and *ʔḥr-* fit the pattern we have been discussing: *ʔVCCV-*. (Only *ʔḥrk* 'on you (sg. m.)' is attested (Gardiner 1957: 127 n. 11, 209 n. 6). It is logical to assume that we are dealing with the same pattern when it comes to the other three prepositions (3–5) and that we have *ʔmC-*, *ʔnC-* and *ʔrC-*. This is confirmed by the Coptic in the case of *m*, where /ʔəʔmó-/ could easily result from the metathesis of /*ʔəmʔo-/. (The metathesis of *-Cʔ-* to *-ʔC-* is very common.) We therefore tentatively reconstruct **mʔ* as the phonetic value of the preposition in the older language. The Late Egyptian spellings of *m* as *mʔm-*P, *nʔm-*P are apparently efforts to represent /ʔəʔm-/ (Erman 1933: 292-3, Černý and Groll 1978: 92). The same use of *m-* to represent /ʔə-/ (before a nasal) is found in the late Egyptian spellings of the independent pronouns, e.g. *mntf* for *ʔ˘ntˊf*, Co. /ʔəntóf/ above (Erman 1933: 45; cf. Černý and Groll 1978: 4–5, where this convention is not understood). Fecht notes the occasional use of *mʔ* for the preposition *m* in Late Egyptian names (1960: 40 n.129). This is another, also late, evidence for *mʔ* as the root.

One expects a similar explanation for *n* ~ *ʔn*, but there is less evidence. Coptic does show /ʔən-/ before nouns (/ʔəm-/ before labials), but here the forms have fallen together with those of *m*. Unlike *m* but like *r*, the form with ʔ- occurs before both nouns and pronouns. As of now, we have no evidence for the early value of C in *ʔ˘ n C-.

Analogy suggests that we are dealing with the same pattern in the case of *r* (5). It has long been recognized that the word for 'mouth', written with *r* (D21), has two consonants (e.g. Gardiner 1957: 429). *Faut de mieux*, the second of these is taken to be ʔ: *rʔ*, Co. *ro* (where the short vowel in Coptic shows that the syllable was closed in older Egyptian). If we assume that the preposition is the same morpheme as 'mouth', we understand the presence of the prothetic alif: *rʔ-f* 'to him' is CCVC, so must be ʔ˘ rʔ´ f, which is reflected in Coptic /ʔeróf/. The prothetic alif occurs before both noun and pronoun, the difference being presumably ʔ˘ rʔ˘ -N and ʔ˘ rʔ´ -P. The difference of stress affects the outcome, resulting in Coptic /ʔe/-N and /ʔeró/-P. It is probable that the latter involves metathesis, as *rC* generally becomes *ʔC*. We therefore assume ʔ˘ rʔ´ -, ʔ˘ ʔrʔ´ -, ʔ˘ rʔ´ - (= /ʔeró-/). Before nouns we have ʔ˘ rʔ-, ʔ˘ ʔ-, ʔ- (= /ʔe-/).

We conclude that the prepositions *m*, *n*, and *r* were all bi-consonantal: *mC*, *nC*, and *rC*, but that there is insufficient evidence to determine what consonant(s) C represents. We tentatively read *mʔ* and *rʔ*.

Well over a hundred other Egyptian examples have been examined, where prothetic alif is either attested or must be deduced. The ones cited above are sufficient to show that the problem of potential initial clusters (i.e., the existence of patterns such as CCVC) was resolved from the earliest observable periods by using a prothetic glottal stop plus vowel, ʔV-CCVC. The alternative, breaking the cluster by adding a vowel, C-V-CVC, may also be found (e.g. in Coptic), but it is rare. The dominant pattern is ʔV-CCVC. Sethe's hypothesis is in this respect completely upheld. Contrary to Sethe, there is no reason to doubt that this was also the prehistoric pattern — pre-Egyptian certainly and probably into the reconstructable past.

NOTE

It is a pleasure to submit this article in honor of a former colleague and long-time friend, Robert P. Stockwell. It was first presented at the 195th meeting of the American Oriental Society (joint session with the North American Conference on Afroasiatic Linguistics) Ann Arbor, April, 1985. It is part of a larger study of the phenomenon in Egyptian and related languages (including Indo-European).

REFERENCES

Černý, Jaroslav. 1941. '*INN* in Late Egyptian', *Journal of Egyptian Archaeology* 27: 106–12.

—— 1976. *Coptic Etymological Dictionary*. Cambridge: Cambridge University Press.
—— and Sarah Israelit Groll. 1978. *A Late Egyptian Grammar* (Studia Pohl, Series Maior, 4). Rome: Biblical Institute Press.
Crum, W.E. 1939. *A Coptic Dictionary*. Oxford: Clarendon Press.
Dolgopolsky, Aharon B. 1973. *Sravniteljno-istoričeskaja Fonetika Kušitskix Jazykov*. Moscow: Nauka.
Edel, Elmar. 1955, 1964. *Altägyptische Grammatik* I, II (Analecta Orientalia, 34, 39). Rome: Pontifical Biblical Institute.
Edgerton, William F. 1947. 'Stress, Vowel Quantity, and Syllable Division in Egyptian', *Journal of Near Eastern Studies* 6: 1–17.
Erman, Adolf. 1900. 'Die Flexion des aegyptischen Verbums', *Sitzungsberichte der Preussischen Akademie der Wissenschaft* 317–53.
—— 1911. *Ägyptische Grammatik*, 3rd edn (Porta Linguarum Orientalium, 15). Berlin: Reuther and Reichard.
—— 1912. 'Zur ägyptischen Wortforschung. II. III.' *Sitzungsberichte der Preussischen Akademie der Wissenschaft* 904–63.
—— 1933. *Neuaegyptische Grammatik*, 2nd edn. Leipzig: Wilhelm Engelmann.
—— and Hermann Grapow. 1957 [1926–39]. *Wörterbuch der aegyptischen Sprache*. 7 vols. Berlin: Akademie-Verlag.
Faulkner, Raymond O. 1962. *A Concise Dictionary of Middle Egyptian*. Oxford: Oxford University Press.
Fecht, Gerhard. 1960 *Wortakzent und Silbenstruktur* (Ägyptologische Forschungen, 21). Glückstadt: J.J. Augustin.
Firchow, Otto. 1953. *Grundzüge der Stilistik in den altägyptischen Pyramidentexten* (Deutsche Akademie der Wissenschaften zu Berlin, Institut für Orientforschung, 21). Berlin: Akademie-Verlag.
Fronzaroli, Pelio. 1964. 'Studi sul Lessico Comune Semitico. II. Anatomia e Fisiologia', Atti della Accademia nazionale dei Lincei. Rendiconti della Classe di scienze morali, storiche e filologiche. Roma, Series VIII, 19: 243–80.
Gardiner, Alan H. 1927, 1957. *Egyptian Grammar*, 1st edn./3rd edn. London: Oxford University Press.
Hodge, Carleton, T. 1977. Review of John B. Callender, *Middle Egyptian Language* 53: 930–40.
—— 1981. 'Coptic Double Consonants,' in Yoël L. Arbeitman and Allan R. Bomhard (eds.), *Bono Homini Donum: Essays ... in Memory of J. Alexander Kerns* (Amsterdam Studies in the Theory and History of Linguistic Science, 4). Amsterdam: John Benjamins, 659–64.
Lefebvre, Gustave. 1955. *Grammaire de l'égyptien classique*, 2nd edn. (Bibliothèque d'Étude, 12). Cairo: Institut Français d'Archéologie Orientale.
Meltzer, Edmund S. 1978. Review of Jürgen Osing, *Die Nominalbildung des Ägyptischen*. *Journal of the American Research Center in Egypt* 15: 142–4.
Moscati, Sabatino (ed.). 1964. *An Introduction to the Comparative Grammar of the Semitic Languages* (Porta Linguarum Orientalium). Wiesbaden: Otto Harrassowitz.
Nöldeke, Theodor. 1880. *Kurzgefasste Syrische Grammatik*. Leipzig: T.O. Weigel.
Osing. Jürgen. 1976. *Die Nominalbildung des Ägyptischen*. 2 vols. Mainz: Philipp von Zabern.
Renouf, Le Page. 1903. *The Life-Work of Sir Peter Le Page Renouf*, Vol. 2, ed. by Édouard Naville and W. Harry Rylands. Paris: Ernest Leroux.
Sethe, Kurt. 1892. *De Aleph Prosthetico in Lingua Aegyptiaca Verbi Formis Praeposito*. (Dissertatio) Berlin: Gustavus Schade (Otto Francke).
—— 1899–1902. *Das aegyptische Verbum*. 3 vols. Leipzig: J.C. Hinrichs.

—— 1923. 'Die Vokalisation des Ägyptischen', *Zeitschrift der Deutschen morgenländischen Gesellschaft, Neue Folge* 2: 145–207.
Steindorff, Georg. 1951. *Lehrbuch der koptischen Grammatik*. Chicago: University of Chicago Press.
Thacker, T.W. 1954. *The Relationship of the Semitic and Egyptian Verbal Systems*. Oxford: Clarendon Press.
Till, Walter C. 1961 *Koptische Grammatik*, 2nd edn (Lehrbücher für das Studium der orientalischen Sprachen, 1). Leipzig: VEB Verlag Enzyklopädie.
Vergote, Josef. 1965. *De Verhouding van het Egyptisch tot de Semietische Talen* (Mededelingen van de Koninklijke Vlaamse Akademie voor Wetenschappen, Letteren en Schone Kunsten van België 27.4). Brussels: Paleis der Academiën.

16

Proto-Burmese as a Test of Reconstruction

ROBERT B. JONES

Historical linguists are generally agreed that there is necessarily a gap between reconstructed proto-languages and the linguistic reality they indicate must have existed at some past time. The question then arises of whether it might be possible to assess the nature and extent of the gap, a question that can surely only be approached through the study of test cases in which rigorously controlled reconstructions can be assessed against historical documentation. Few such tests have, however, been undertaken, with the notable exception of R.A. Hall's exacting work in Proto-Romance. It is to provide another, and rather more restricted, test that the present study of Burmese is undertaken, limited to major aspects of the phonological systems involved in order to focus on systemic change and omitting minor aspects which are less revealing and lexical citations which would be required in a complete study.

Historical documentation for Burmese begins in the early twelfth century, the earliest dated inscription being c. AD 1113. Through approximately half of the thirteenth century, a period generally referred to as pre-standard Old Burmese, the inscriptions show considerable variation in spelling, no doubt reflecting use of a newly adapted writing system in part, but also a period of phonetic change in which there was considerable uncertainty or experimentation in devising accurate spellings. The resulting variation provides the data from which it is possible to reconstruct an earlier more stable state in the phonology which is here called Pre-Old Burmese but is also reflected in large part in one unique inscription dated c. AD 1165 in which an original and quite consistent spelling system is used. In addition we have also the evidence of modern Written Burmese which arrived at its present form in about the sixteenth to seventeenth centuries but even so was no doubt archaic by that time. The writing system is an adaptation from devanagari script(s) by way of Mon script which had been in use for several centuries and continued in use along with Burmese through the twelfth century.

Modern varieties of Burmese are not greatly differentiated, but sufficiently so to provide excellent data, not excessively complex, for the reconstruction of a Proto-Burmese. The language includes three modern major dialect areas: the central plains regions of modern standard Burmese, both spoken and written; the western region encompassing the state of Arakan; the eastern region which extends from the vicinity of Taunggyi southward to Tavoy. Within each region there is of course variation, both geographic and social, but for purposes of this reconstruction one representative from each region has been chosen which shows maximum differentiation from the other regions. These are Myohaung representing the western region, Rangoon representing the central region, Tavoy representing the eastern. In considering consonantal correspondences, however, it has been necessary at one point to include the evidence of an additional representative from the eastern region, Intha (near Taunggyi), to complete the relevant sets of correspondence.

Table 16.1 provides the basis for assessing Proto-Burmese, which involves primarily its comparison with another level of reconstruction, Pre-Old Burmese, but including also the evidence of Old Burmese variants and that of modern Written Burmese.

Table 16.1, in three sections, is a complete statement of vowels, finals, and pitch registers. For all varieties of modern Burmese and the reconstructed Proto-Burmese a final /-n/ represents nasalization of the preceding vowel. A final /-ʔ/ represents a full stop in low pitch register but glottal constriction in the high register. Vowels which are both nasalized and constricted occur only in the high pitch register. Plain constricted vowels are in general included in the open vowel correspondences, but Tavoy is exceptional. There, although constricted /i, a, u/ correspond like their open counterparts, others shift to low register with full stop final. Furthermore, *ìʔ and *ùʔ shift to high register with constriction. The relevant sets have therefore been included and set off in the table by heavy lines.

The vocalic system reconstructed for Proto-Burmese is little different from those of the modern varieties. Given the close similarity between the modern varieties it could hardly have been otherwise. Pre-Old Burmese, however, shows a quite different system, and Old Burmese appears clearly now as transitional. The spelling variants document the emerging shifts among the vowels and some of the finals with resulting expansion of the earlier three-vowel system to a new seven-vowel system. A symbol for /e/ was already in use in OB, in competition with /iy/, but it was largely restricted to use in certain grammatical affixes. The corresponding back vowel was beginning to develop but the very considerable variation that occurred is clear evidence that it had not yet become distinctive, indeed the low back vowel appears nearer to having distinctive status (and the developing open syllable symbol continues in standard Burmese to have the alternate pronunciation /au/ in closed syllables), although a new

Table 16.1: Correspondences of vocalic nuclei and pitch registers

Plain and nasalized vowels

M	R	T	*PB	WB[1]	*PreOB	OB variants[1]
en[2]	i	i	i	i	i	i, iy
i						
en[2]	e[3]	e	e	e	iy	iy, eiy, e
we	we	we	we	we	uy	uy, wuy, wiy, uiy, wɔy
e	ɛ	ɛ	ɛ	ay ~ ɛ	ay	ay, ɛ[4]
a	a	a	a	a	a	a
u	u	u	u	u	u	u, ɔ, ɔu
o	o	o	o	iu[5]	iw	iw, iu, iuw, uw, aw, ei, eiw
ɔ	ɔ	ɔ	ɔ	ɔ[6]	aw	aw, au, ɔw, ɔ, u
en	en	i	in	in	in	in
				im	im	im
				im̊[7]	im̊	im̊, im̊m, im
ɔn	in	in[8]	ɛn	aŋ	aŋ	aŋ, eŋ
	an	an	an	an	an	an, en, am̊n
ɛn				am	am	am, em
	un[9]	un[9]		am̊	am̊	am̊, am
aun	aun		ɔn	ɔŋ	uŋ	uŋ, ɔŋ
on	on	u	un	un	un	un
				um	um	um
		au	aun	um̊	um̊	um̊, um̊m, ium
ain	ain	ai	ain	iuŋ	iŋ	iŋ, iuŋ, uŋ, eiŋ

Pitch register

ˊ	ˊ	ˊ	ˊ	--˳	--h	h, ˳, ∅[10]
ˊʔ	ˊʔ	ˊʔ ˋʔ	ˊʔ	--˳	--ʔ	ʔ, ˳, ∅
ˋ	ˋ	ˋ	ˋ	∅	∅	
ˋʔ	ˋʔ	ˊʔ ˋʔ	ˋʔ	(final oral stops p, t, c/s, k)		

Laryngealized vowels

M	R	T	*PB	WB	*PreOB	OB variants
áiʔ	íʔ	íʔ[8]	èʔ	as	ac	ac, ec, ic, et, yat
ɔ́ʔ	έʔ		έʔ	ak	ak	ak, ik, ek, ec
έʔ	áʔ	áʔ	áʔ	ap, at	ap, at	ap, at
	ùʔ[9]	ùʔ[9]				
òʔ	òʔ	áuʔ	òʔ	up	up	up
áiʔ	áiʔ	áiʔ	áiʔ	iuk	ik	ik, iuk
áuʔ	áuʔ	ɔ́ʔ	ɔ́ʔ	ɔk	uk	uk, ɔk
èʔ	èʔ	íʔ	íʔ	ip, it,	ip, it	ip, it
òʔ	òʔ	úʔ	ùʔ	ut	ut	ut
énʔ[2]	éʔ	èʔ	éʔ	e₀	iyʔ	
íʔ						
éʔ	έʔ	έʔ	έʔ	ɛ₀	ayʔ	
óʔ	óʔ	òʔ	óʔ	iu₀	iwʔ	(as above)
ɔ́ʔ	ɔ́ʔ	ɔ́ʔ	ɔ́ʔ	ɔ₀	awʔ	
áunʔ	áunʔ		ɔ́nʔ	ɔŋ₀	uŋʔ	
ɔ́nʔ	ínʔ	áʔ	έnʔ	aŋ₀	aŋʔ	
		íʔ[8]				

Notes

1. In WB and OB two symbols are used to represent each of the vowels /i, u, a/, the two being usually referred to as 'long' and 'short' (the 'short' *a* is inherent and represented by the lack of any other vowel symbol). In fact the distinction is only graphic and basically the 'long' symbols are used in open syllables, the 'short' in closed syllables, and variation in OB perhaps represents a developing allophonic difference. In WB rules for their use are unambiguous. Variants listed for OB should be understood to include both possibilities.

2. In M *i and *e merge as /en/ after nasal initials.

3. In R *wi > /we/.

4. A symbol for /ɛ/ does not appear in the inscriptions until the end of the twelfth century.

5. The vertical digraph which this transcription represents is usually written *ui*. The present transcription is better justified both historically and graphically.

6. The phonological symbol is used here for the discontinuous digraph *e-a* which is usually transcribed as *o*, a transcription which would be ambiguous in the present analysis.

7. This transcription represents the superscript *anusvāra* of Sanskrit.

8. In T *ɛC > /iC/ after palatals.

9. In both R and T *CwaC > /CuC/, *waC > /wuC/.

10. No attempt is made here to represent the various reduced forms of final /h/ and /ʔ/ which occur on the way toward their final standardized forms. The final form of OB final /h/ has the appearance of Sanskrit *visarga* with which it is often understandably, but mistakenly, identified.

symbol for the corresponding low front vowel does not appear until near the end of the twelfth century. It would seem then that the four new vowels appeared in somewhat asymmetrical sequence, /e, ɔ, o, ɛ/, though we cannot know their phonetic features at that time and the supposed asymmetry may well be fictitious. It can reasonably be inferred, however, that the vowels /i, u/ had lower and probably more central allophones in closed syllables. In terms of spelling they still do in modern Burmese — lower before nasal finals, central with upward glides before stop finals. Except for the final palatal and labial semivowels, neither Old Burmese spelling nor that of later times provides evidence for the weakening of final consonants and we cannot know just when that was accomplished. The occasional appearance of the double final nasals ṁm and ṁn may be a possible exception, perhaps an indication that nasal distinctions were merging into nasalization.

The most striking shift results from the loss of final /-h/ with the concomitant development of a distinctive high pitch register. This change was probably in process for some time before the twelfth century. The full form of final /-h/ occurs with regularity only in two of the early inscriptions. Elsewhere it is represented by a variety of reduced forms, and often by nothing. The present written form was regularized at a considerably later date.

The full form of final /-ʔ/ continued in use during the twelfth century, then it too began to appear in various reduced forms over several centuries before the present form became standard. In this case, however, the phonetic features represented are never fully lost and it continues to represent glottal constriction of the preceding vowel, which in addition acquires the new distinctive high pitch, allophonically higher than that of unconstricted vowels, judging from modern Burmese.

Syllables which did not terminate in final /-h/ or /-ʔ/ remained at low pitch. The present syllabic structure was completed at that as yet unspecifiable time when the final stops had all merged into a new full glottal stop, at which time the affected syllables also acquired a higher allophone of the low pitch register. It is reasonable to assume that these pitch features were redundantly present as long as the relevant finals were intact and that the process of development into fully contrastive features of the phonology covered a longish period of time, perhaps as long as two hundred years, and surely by the time the laryngeal finals begin to appear in reduced graphic form. And the sequence is clear: final /-h/ disappears and high pitch develops first, followed by weakening of the glottal final to constriction, and finally the development of a new final glottal stop at some later time.

A final palatal nasal also occurs in writing but has not been included here. The modern varieties of Burmese present no clear evidence for reconstructing such a nasal since the pronunciation of forms with this spelling varies between /i, e, ɛ/ (occasionally /in/) and are therefore included for the most part in the correspondence sets for each of those vowels. We can only assume that in OB it probably did represent a palatal nasal which was lost very early but with varying effects on the preceding vowel. The corresponding palatal stop /-c/, however, developed quite regularly as indicated in Table 16.1.

The reduction of final consonants must have taken place in some sequence but neither the time nor the sequence can be determined in general. In Tavoy, however, a sequence for certain of the final stops is quite clear. Final labial and alveolar stops after high vowels, excepting /up/, merged with final /-ʔ/ before any weakening of that final had taken place, and before the lowering of the preceding vowel that occurred elsewhere. Thereafter such syllables developed quite regularly, shifting to high pitch register as the glottal final weakened to constriction. Only after this process was completed could the remaining oral stops have merged into a new glottal final, providing a new allophone of the structural glottal final already present in the high register. Here we have clear evidence that Tavoy was the first to split off from the main group, possibly, but not necessarily, after the development of pitch registers, but certainly before any of the changes reflected in the other dialect areas. Further support of this position is found in the final consonant clusters involving glottal stops which in Tavoy develop like the remaining oral stops, but elsewhere develop like simple glottal finals.

None of the above discussion can be derived from the reconstructed Proto-Burmese and virtually all statements that could be made concerning development from the proto-type into the modern varieties would in fact be wrong. Again Tavoy would be a striking example, for statements concerning register shifts cannot be motivated, only listed. It is possible that a reconstructed west–central stage, which has not been included, might be considerably more realistic, but it is not clear that western and central Burmese did in fact share a common period after Tavoy split away. In Myohaung it seems clear that the earlier /iy/ merged with /i/, whereas a reconstruction would indicate that it developed first into /e/ which then merged with /i/, the previous /e/ then being replaced by a new one derived from *ε. Further, such shifts as *εn > /ɔn/, *an > /εn/ raise doubts which do not arise in relation to the shifts indicated from Pre-Old Burmese, /aŋ/ > /ɔn, /an, am/ > /εn/, and similarly with the corresponding sets with stop finals. Such cases provide also a more specific kind of evidence for independent development in western and central Burmese in that velar finals induced backer vowels in Myohaung but fronter vowels in Rangoon, and variants in Old Burmese give evidence only for the fronting effect. Thus in spite of the close similarity between Myohaung and Rangoon it was probably not the case that they still constituted a common group in the twelfth century, whereas comparative reconstruction would indicate that such a grouping continued to exist for a considerable time after that period. It appears then that the language represented by Old Burmese inscriptions was the direct ancestor of central Burmese but not of western and eastern Burmese. Pre-Old Burmese, however, does appear to represent the ancestor of all three areas, with the proviso that it probably included also the two spirants *s and *sh required by comparative evidence as noted below.

Simple initial consonants show little variation, provide no useful evidence for subgrouping, and reconstructions are fully confirmed by the historical documentation. For this reason only a small group of key correspondence sets are included for the simple consonants as the first section of Table 16.2. It is here that the important evidence from the Intha variety of eastern Burmese has been included, for it is only at this point that contrasts must be reconstructed which are not represented in inscriptional Burmese, namely *s and *sh, which had already merged to /s/ prior to the twelfth century. The contrast was, however, restored at some time which cannot be accurately determined but may well have occurred during the twelfth century. We cannot be certain of the phonetic values of the Old Burmese symbols transcribed as /ch, c/, but we can be reasonably sure that they no longer represented palatal stops by the time palatal affricates had developed from palatalized velar stops, a process already in evidence in the variations that occur in Old Burmese.

Initial consonant clusters are the principle defining features of the dialect areas and the reconstruction of them is fully confirmed by the historical evidence which includes as well spelling variations indicating that the medial elements were already beginning to merge toward the palatal. Even

Table 16.2: Correspondences of selected consonants and clusters

Simple consonants

M	R	T	I	*PB	WB	OB
sh	sh	sh	sh	ch = sh	sh =	ch
θ	θ	θ		s	θ =	s
s	s	s	s	c =	s =	c
r	y	y	y	r	r	r, ry
y				y	y	y

Consonant clusters

M	R	T	*PB	WB	*PreOB	PB variants
Py	Py	Py	Py	Py	Py	Py, Pl, Ply
Pr			Pr	Pr	Pr	Pr, Pry, Pl
		Pl	Pl		Pl	Pl
Kr	Ty	Ty	Kr	Kr	Kr	Kr, Kry
		Kl	Kl		Kl	Kl, Kly
Ty		K	K	Ky	K/–i	K/–i, e
		(ty)	Ky		Ky	Ky
hr	hy	hy	hr	hr	hr	hr, rh, rhy
h ~ hy			h(y)		h/–i	h, hy
(K)rw	(T)yw	(K)w	(K)rw	(K)rw	(K)rw	(K)rw

Note: In the above table the equals sign indicates a change in phonetic value of the written symbol. Capital letters indicate classes of initial consonants: P, labials; T, alveolars; K, velars. In Tavoy OB *ky* > /ty/ but *khy* > /hy/.

as the epigraphers were evidently uncertain of an appropriate spelling for the newly emerging vowels so were they at times uncertain of a medial consonant. Such variants as *-ly-* for *-l-* and *-ry-* for *-r-* are reminiscent of the current situation in standard Thai where /r/ has generally merged with /l/ in the spoken language but is still distinguished in the written language, with the result that one often hears pronunciation which combines features of both sounds.

The development of clusters in Tavoy again distinguish it from the other dialect areas. Palatalization of velars before the high front vowel did not take place in Tavoy which still reflects the Old Burmese situation. The old palatalized aspirated velar stop /khy/ lost the stop onset before the merger of medial /-r-/ with medial /-y-/. After that merger the new /khy/ was then fronted to /thy/ as in the other dialect areas. (The old /ky/ was not affected by the first shift and old /kr/ merged with it, after which the velar was fronted to /ty/.) In general, clusters with medial /-w-/ are unremarkable and have not been included here as such, but in Tavoy the cluster /rw/, both initially and medially, is an exception in that the /r/ was dropped before the remaining occurrences merged with /y/. In as much as the inscriptions indicate that medial /-r-/ was already beginning to shift toward the palatal the development in Tavoy again indicates separation before the twelfth century. These developments in consonant clusters are evidenced in our reconstruction although the chronology can of course only be relative there.

On the assumption that the Pre-Old Burmese that has been reconstructed may date from at least a hundred years earlier than the first inscriptions, say approximately AD 1000, the Proto-Burmese we have reconstructed appears to span a period of possibly four hundred years. Except for the spirant *sh the reconstructed consonantal system is confirmed for the twelfth century and can probably be considered valid for the previous century as well, possibly earlier, so it can be said to agree with Pre-Old Burmese. It is reasonably certain, however, that pitch register was not fully developed until at least the thirteenth century, some two hundred years later, during which time the new expanded vowel system also emerged. It was also during this period, or shortly after, that the simplification of consonant clusters was probably completed, although since in central Burmese medial /-r-/ continues to be written we cannot know just when the merger with /-y-/ was completed. For the same reason we cannot know when the reduction of finals was completed. From the Tavoy evidence we do know, however, that the reduction in that branch of Burmese had probably begun by the twelfth century.

English accounts from the late seventeenth and eighteenth centuries are often difficult to interpret but it is clear that the reduction of finals was complete by the middle of the seventeenth century, and that the palatalized velars were still in use in western and central Burmese. By the end of the eighteenth century they had been fronted to alveolar affricates in central Burmese but remained velar in western Burmese until the early nineteenth century. It also appears that in western Burmese there was still at the end of the seventeenth century variation between /θ/ and the older /s/, indicating that this shift had not yet been completed and implying that the shift of /ch, c/ to /sh, s/ had not yet taken place.

It will now be apparent that Written Burmese of today represents Old Burmese only in part. Simple consonants, both initial and final, are generally accurate with the exception that the final palatal and labial semivowels are missing. The vowels represent a somewhat later period, probably the late thirteenth or early fourteenth century, and pitch register probably about the same time. Consonant clusters, however, represent an unknown period in which medial /-l-/ had already merged with either medial /-y-/ or medial /-r-/, depending on the initial, with the result that these remaining medials are ambiguous. Spelling reforms have of course taken place at various times, and it is perhaps such reforms that account for occasional mis-spelling of finals, some of which can be deduced from Tavoyan forms as well as Old Burmese.

For Proto-Romance, Hall (1976) is able to date his reconstruction within the first century BC and to estimate ninety-five percent accuracy for the phonology. This is considerably better than has been possible for the Burmese case with a time span only about half as long. Two reconstructions have been undertaken from modern Indic languages by Southworth and Pattanayak. They differ somewhat in method, results, and partly in source data, and neither includes detailed comparison with Sanskrit. A survey of their results seems to indicate a fair degree of accuracy for consonants, less so for clusters and vowels. By combining the two studies and avoiding certain self-made pitfalls this estimate might be considerably improved.

It is perhaps not surprising that reconstruction of consonants appears to provide a higher degree of accuracy than do reconstructed vowels. In present-day languages simple consonants are much less subject to variation than vowels. Even so we are still without reasonable criteria for assessing the accuracy of reconstructions in the absence of historical documentation. If such criteria can be developed they will surely depend on many more test cases.

REFERENCES

Ba Shin, Bohmu. 1962. *Lokahteikpan, Early Burmese Culture in a Pagán Temple.* Rangoon: Burma Historical Commission.

Government of Burma. 1919–. *Epigraphia Birmanica.* Archaeological Survey of Burma. Rangoon.

Hall, Robert A., Jr. 1950. The Reconstruction of Proto-Romance, *Language* 26: 6–27.

—— 1974–6. *Comparative Romance Grammar.* (Vol. 1, *External History of the Romance Languages*, 1974. Vol. 2, *Proto-Romance Phonology*, 1976.) New York: American Elsevier.

Jones, Robert B. 1972. 'Sketch of Burmese Dialects', in E. Smith (ed.), *Studies in Honor of George L. Trager.* The Hague: Mouton.

—— 1976 'Prolegomena to a Phonology of Old Burmese', in C.D. Cowan and O.W. Wolters (eds.), *Southeast Asian History and Historiography: Essays Presented to D.G.E. Hall*, Ithaca, NY: Cornell University Press.

Luce, Gordon, H. 1969–70. *Old Burma – Early Pagán.* (3 vols.) Locust Valley, NY: J.J. Augustin. (Also unpublished manuscript of volume IV.)

Nishi, Yoneo. 1976. 'Medials in Burmese', in Mantaro J. Hashimoto (ed.), *Genetic Relationships, Diffusion and Typological Similarities of East and Southeast Asian Languages.* Tokyo: Japan Society for the Promotion of Science.

Pattanayak, D.P. 1966. *A Controlled Historical Recontruction of Oriya, Assamese, Bengali, Hindi.* The Hague: Mouton.

Pe Maung Tin and Gordon H. Luce. 1933–56. *Inscriptions of Burma.* Vol. I, 1933. Vol. II, III, 1939. Vol. IV, V, 1956: Oxford University Press.

—— 1960. 'Pagán, Dhammayangyi Pillar', *Bulletin of the Burma Historical Commission*: Vol. I, Pt. II.

Southworth, Franklin C. 1958. *A Test of the Comparative Method (A Historically Controlled Reconstruction Based on Four Modern Indic Languages).* Yale University dissertation. (University Microfilms, Inc., 66–5415.)

17

Redefining the Scope of Phonology

PETER LADEFOGED

ABSTRACT

The functions of speech and language interact in a way that has a considerable effect on our view of phonology. If we are mainly concerned with the way language functions to convey objective information we will pay particular attention to the phonological oppositions that distinguish meaningful units such as words and phrases. But if we are more concerned with the sociolinguistics and attitudinal information conveyed by the sounds, we will have to pay attention to phonetic details that are not used for indicating phonological oppositions. The implications of these differences are discussed, and it is suggested that a viable phonology that is concerned only with strictly linguistic patterning will be somewhat different from the current view of phonology.

Speech has many functions; and not all of them are part of language. Similarly language has many functions; and not all of them are part of speech. One of the major functions of language that is not part of speech is to act as a mirror for the world. Language provides us with symbols for our experiences, and thus gives us ways of grouping these experiences into categories, and ways of qualifying and relating one experience to another. As a result we are able to form concepts and manipulate ideas. Some kinds of thinking may be possible without language, but we could never develop scientific theories without words. Our language acts as a model of the world as we know it, much as a map serves as a model for a piece of the terrain, enabling us to plan journeys. This function of language has little or no effect on our views of phonology — though it does, obviously, have a considerable effect on how we view semantics.

Of much greater importance for our view of phonology is the fact that one of the functions of both speech and language is the conveying of objective information (or misinformation). In order to convey this information, meaningful units have to be distinguished from one another. Of course, when we consider language as a model of our world, the symbols used for categorizing and relating our experiences have to be distinguished from one another as well. But when language is functioning in this way it does not matter how the distinctions are achieved. Language acts as our mirror of the nature of things, irrespective of whether the words are written, spoken, or simply mental images. We do not need to speak the words of our thoughts.

In order to convey objective information in spoken form, languages typically contrast between 20 and 35 segmental phonemes (Maddieson 1984), supplemented by a few suprasegmental devices. This is a comparatively small number out of the total set of possibilities available. On the basis of listening tests I have previously estimated (Ladefoged 1967) that it is possible to distinguish about 50 vowels in the plane of the primary cardinal vowels, i.e. in which front vowels are unrounded and back vowels are rounded, with the degree of rounding being predicted from the height. Adding the possibility of front rounded vowels and back unrounded vowels, together with so-called under-rounded and over-rounded vowels (such as the Assamese low back vowel which has the close lip rounding normally associated with a vowel such as [u]) would almost double this number. With the addition of nasalized vowels (which, even with training and experience, are not as distinct as oral vowels), rhotacized (*r*-colored) vowels, and other possible secondary articulations, the total number of distinguishable voiced monophthongs (to add further constraints) is undoubtedly well above 100. This is all without considering various types of diphthongs that are traditionally considered as single segments with on-glides or off-glides. We must also note possible variations in phonation type. Many languages distinguish sets of laxly voiced vowels from regularly voiced vowels (e.g. Jingpho and other languages of Southeast Asia). Others (such as Mpi) contrast laryngealized and non-laryngealized vowels. In calculating the total number of vowels we should consider each vowel as potentially occurring on three different phonation types; it is not at all difficult to distinguish at least this number of different voice qualities.

When we consider all these possibilities it seems that Shaw (1920) may have considerably underestimated the number of distinguishable vowels. In the play *Pygmalion* (and in the *My Fair Lady* version, Lerner and Loewe 1956) Colonel Pickering expresses admiration for the expert phonetician, Henry Higgins, who is able to distinguish 130 different vowels, as opposed to Pickering's 24. Shaw probably based his estimate of the number of vowels on his reading of Sweet (1890), the acknowledged prototype for Higgins, who provided 72 distinct symbols for vowels without considering diphthongs, differences in phonation types, and other aspects of vowel quality for which he provided diacritics. I would estimate that an expert phonetician could distinguish more than 250 vowels of all types. And what an expert phonetician can distinguish, anyone who has been brought up speaking a languge that uses one of these distinctions can do just as well.

The number of distinct consonants is also considerable, even if we limit ourselves fairly strictly to what must be called single segments (i.e. disregarding all affricates, prenasalized stops, etc., although many of them function as single phonological segments). The IPA (1979) chart has 81 symbols for consonants, without taking account of oppositions such as that between dental and alveolar stops (which contrast in many Australasian languages), voiceless nasals (as in Burmese), or differences between aspirated and unaspirated obstruents (Sindhi has 25 stop consonants, only 10 of which appear as distinct symbols on the IPA chart). We must also consider all the secondary articulations, such as labialization, palatalization, velarization, and pharyngealization, which would far more than double the number of possibilities. And again we have to note differences in phonation type, as well as airstream mechanisms of the kind that form clicks, ejectives, and implosives. A very conservative estimate would place the total number of consonantal segments as being up in the hundreds, making the total number of possibly contrasting segments as high as 600–800. A comparable number occurs in Maddieson's (1984) survey of the phonological segments that occur in 317 languages carefully selected so as to exemplify the range of the world's languages. He found that when he considered each phonological segment to be represented by its principal allophone he had to recognize about 650 phonetically distinct segments, without considering variations in length.

There are many reasons why languages do not use such a large number of segmental oppositions. Perhaps the most important is that they are not necessary; languages can have a sufficiently large stock of morphemes while using only a small number of segmental oppositions. The phonological devices used by languages do not require the wealth of phonetic possibilities.

Many of the subtle distinctions that can be made among sounds are used by some of the other functions of speech. Whenever we talk, we convey not only information about the topic under discussion, but also information about the sociolinguistic group to which we belong. Some of this information is conveyed in the same way as distinctions among words, using differences among phonemes. Thus Gershwin and Gershwin (1937) describe a case of different individuals with the same set of possible phonemic contrasts, using them in different words, as in 'You say [iðər] but I say [aiðər].' (It should be noted that Gershwin and Gershwin's phonetic observations are not always reliable. They correctly observe that some people pronounce the word *tomato* as [tə'meɪtoʊ], whereas others say [tə'mɑtoʊ]. But they further claim to have observed the word *potato* pronounced as [pə'tɑtoʊ]. This seems very unlikely.) A great deal of sociolinguistic information is conveyed in more subtle ways. It is rigidly codified, although not in terms of discrete oppositions of the kind used in phonemic oppositions. It is difficult to say exactly what degree of diphthongization in the vowel in *mate* marks a person as belonging to a particular social class in London (or Australia, or anywhere else that uses this distinguishing characteristic). But anyone familiar with the regional accents in question can easily place a speaker by pronunciations of this kind.

Because this information is codified in speech in an arbitrary way, we may want to regard it as part of language. But there is no reason to expect the sociolinguistic information to be conveyed by the same aspects of speech sounds as those that are used for distinguishing the linguistic oppositions discussed above. Evidence has been accumulating recently that demonstrates quite conclusively that languages and dialects are differentiated from one another in ways that are not used to distinguish oppositions within any single language. For example Ladefoged and Bhaskararao (1983) have demonstrated differences in the retroflex stops in Hindi and those in Telugu that depend on features of speech that are not used to distinguish oppositions within any single language. Similar points with respect to differences among fricatives have been made by Ladefoged and Wu (1984). Cross-linguistic differences in phonation types that characterize different languages have been described by Lindau (1982). These and many other papers suggest that the sociolinguistic functions of speech **cannot** be described entirely in terms of the same features as those that are used for describing phonological oppositions. There is no way in which small but reliable differences in retroflexion, or fricative noise, or phonation type can be expressed in terms of phonological feature classifications. Nevertheless, this is what standard feature theories attempt to do, becoming continually more complicated as a result. Thus Jakobson and Halle (1956) can express more phonetic detail than Jakobson, Fant and Halle (1952); Chomsky and Halle (1968) add still more features; and Halle and Stevens (1971) add complexities so as to be able to describe phonetic differences between languages. All this is done in order to be able to describe how the speech of one group of people differs systematically from that of another group of people. But there is no theoretical or empirical reason to expect speech systems to use the same devices for phonological and sociolinguistic purposes.

I do not mean to imply that speech systems never use the same devices for linguistic and sociolinguistic purposes. Quite obviously the ways in which vowels are distinguished within a language often involve the same mechanisms as those used for distinguishing the vowels of one accent from another. Thus the feature Vowel Height (or High) may be used phonologically for classifying vowels or, by means of its scalar values, for phonetic descriptions. But many differences between languages are not of this kind. There is no phonological feature system that allows for the degree of phonetic detail necessary for characterizing the differences between the fricatives in English, Pekingese, Tamil, and Polish (Ladefoged and Wu 1984). Attempting to specify phonetic detail in phonation types and stop consonants led Halle and Stevens (1971) into proposing a feature system that is reasonable for characterizing phonetic differences but is unacceptable for phonological classification (Anderson 1978). The Halle–Stevens proposal replaces the feature Voice by a set of four features, Stiff, Slack, Spread, and Constricted, so that they can characterize the phonetic difference between, for example, English [p] as in 'spy' and the Korean so-called lax [p]; but the cost is that they no longer have the more phonologically useful opposition voiced–voiceless.

There are also other aspects of speech that cannot be expressed in terms of any of the traditional sets of phonological features. Another function of speech is to convey the attitude of the speaker to the topic under discussion, to the person addressed, and, indeed, to the world in general. It is not at all clear how much of this is codified. Some parts of the speaker's attitude to the topic under discussion are normally considered as conveyed by systematically different intonations. Thus we speak of statement versus question intonation in different languages, and emphatic and non-emphatic statements and questions. But what about sarcastic or simpering intonations? Are they part of language?

Similarly, it is not clear how we should consider emotional effects. There seems to be something in common to expressions of anger, astonishment, sorrow, doubt, and love, for example, in many different languages. But they are probably not the same in all languages. An angry Frenchman does not sound like an angry German. But is the anger part the same, and are the differences due to the regular linguistic differences between the two languages? And how do we separate out the universal tendencies from those that are plainly learned, cultural, aspects of behavior? Many Englishmen consider it normal to speak in a phlegmatic way with a narrow intonation range that Americans consider as indicative of boredom. The Navaho tend (by American English standards) to speak very softly. As Nihalani (1983) has pointed out, Indian English typically sounds rude or aggressive to speakers of British or American English. All these are learned aspects of the culture. But do we want to consider them part of language?

Yet another aspect of speech, which probably nobody would call a function of language, is that it signals the identity of the speaker. When I walk into a house and call out 'Hi, it's me' this is all the information I am conveying. I am not really making a declarative statement. Everyone recognizes that the personal information is not part of language. But it is sometimes not clear what should be regarded as personal information and what is codified sociolinguistic information. We each speak in the way that we do partly because our particular vocal organs have certain characteristics, but also because we choose to use, within limits, our own personal style of speech. Often what might seem to be a personal characteristic of a particular speaker is in fact something that he or she has chosen to copy, which is shared by a small sociolinguistic group. Where does the family unit end, and the local group begin?

Summing up so far, the basic question is how much of all these different kinds of information conveyed by speech do we want to consider as part of language? We can get some help on this problem by considering the differences between spoken and written language. Is it appropriate to speak of a language being **reduced** to writing — this implying that some part of spoken language is not present in the written form? Or would it be better to say that (virtually) all that is **language** can be expressed in speech or in writing — and all the sociolinguistic, emotional, and personal, information that is left out is not part of what we want to define as language?

Writing conveys some but not much sociolinguistic information. It is impossible to tell from these printed pages whether this paper has been written by an Englishman or an American, or indeed, by a speaker of one or many other forms of English. You could gain some sociolinguistic information if I were to use certain marked phrases or lexical items such as talking about a full stop as opposed to a period. When the written language does convey sociolinguistic information it does so by means of precisely those phonological devices that are used to convey information about the topic under discussion. We do not need anything beyond a feature system that is capable of identifying linguistic oppositions to handle sociolinguistic information of this sort.

Writing also conveys certain aspects of intonation. From the syntax, morphology, word order and punctuation (period, comma, query, quotes, parentheses, italics and space marks) we can determine something (but far from everything), about the intonation that a given sentence could have. As Bolinger (1977) has pointed out, the semantics also often circumscribes the possible intonations, but again only to a limited extent. When speakers of Irish, Welsh, American, or Scottish English read a printed page such as this one there will be differences in their intonation patterns that cannot be ascribed to anything written down. But are these differences part of their language, or do they convey only sociolinguistic information about the speakers?

It is worth considering what kind of phonological theory we would need if we limited ourselves to accounting for the linguistic information that is conveyed by a written language with a good orthography (i.e. a written language such as Finnish or Swahili in which there are few letter-to-sound ambiguities such as written English 'read' which can be [rid] or [rɛd]; and no sociolinguistic variations, such as British English *colour* and American English *color*). It is difficult to define the linguistic information conveyed by such a written language in positive terms, but we could say that it is all the encoded aspects of speech except those that convey information about the speaker's identity, attitude, emotions or sociolinguistic background, in so far as these are not conveyed by syntactic word order or lexical devices. This last proviso is especially necessary if we are to include (as most linguists would) some but not all patterns of intonation within phonology.

The role of intonation is undoubtedly the most problematic part of this proposal for phonology. The formulation suggested above is designed to include differences in intonation such as those between statements of the form *That is a cat.* and questions such as *Is that a cat?* But it would relegate to a difference in attitude some things that can be expressed in writing such as the incredulous question *That is a cat?*. In other words, it would consider as **linguistic** only those intonation patterns that had syntactic or lexical correlates.

Past work on intonation is the only extensive body of phonological work that is not in fact confined to a spoken equivalent of the written language. Thirty years ago, linguists used to argue whether four pitch levels and a number of junctures were sufficient to capture all the meaningful contrasts in English (see, for example, Trager and Smith 1951, Stockwell 1960). Similar discussions are still in progress using a different set of phonetic devices. But in all these discussions of intonation the notion of a meaningful contrast is not the same as it is in discussions of other aspects of phonology. It includes aspects of the emotional functions of speech that are conveying the speaker's attitude. Phonology is not usually considered to include comparable aspects of segments, such as lengthening to indicate superlatives [ɪt wəz bɪ::g], [hi wəz gr:eɪt]. (A possible exception is Prince 1980, which has a brief discussion of the realization of emphasis in Finnish.) It would seem appropriate to constrain studies of intonation to those aspects of speech that convey simply linguistic information.

If we limit phonology in this way the relation between phonological and phonetic units becomes much more straightforward. The phonologist is no longer under an obligation to describe the phonetic details that characterize the sounds of one language as opposed to another. Consequently there is no need for a complex feature system. As it is so obvious that languages differ in ways that are not used to differentiate phonological oppositions we should clearly give up trying to devise a feature system that can characterize differences between languages. Features should simply be distinctive.

In fact, this view of phonology is fairly similar to the early Jakobsonian view. Thus Jakobson, Fant and Halle (1952) and Jakobson and Halle (1956) were plainly striving to minimize the number of distinctive features needed to account for phonemic oppositions in the languages of the world. They were willing, for example, to subsume under the one feature, Tense/Lax, four consonantal features listed by Trubetzkoy — 'the tension feature, the intensity or pressure feature, the aspiration feature and the preaspiration feature' (Jakobson and Halle 1956: 28), on the grounds that no language uses these phonetic possibilities independently. Their emphasis was on what was distinctive within a language. This is very different from the theory propounded by Chomsky and Halle (1968), who do not use the term **distinctive** features, but instead emphasize that features reflect general phonetic capabilities.

The only problem with a phonology of the kind that concerns itself simply with the patterns of linguistic distinctions is that it is largely untestable. If I say that a certain opposition in a given language is describable in terms of the feature Fortis/Lenis, and you prefer the feature Voiced/Voiceless, there is no way of deciding which of us is right. In fact, there is no way of deciding whether any one set of distinctive features is preferable to any other. All one can do is appeal to traditional scientific criteria, such as the parsimony, the observational adequacy and the explanatory elegance of a description. As Murdoch (1981: 6) somewhat obscurely comments, 'Linguistic idealism [is] a dance of bloodless categories.'

The view that phonology should not consider sociolinguistic information is, as I have noted, not that theoretically held by most phonologists. For example, Schane (1973), in his statement of how phonetics is part of phonology, says that 'Linguistically significant differences are those which characterize native control of a language' (p. 5). It is also different from the view that I have myself expressed elsewhere: 'When giving a precise account of what makes a particular language sound the way it does, it is necessary to describe the phonetic properties of individual segments' (Ladefoged 1980: 499). But it is an option, and one that represents the practice (but not the stated purpose) of probably the majority of phonologists. Its particular advantage is that it does not require phonologists to think very deeply about phonetics, or about the realization of phonological features. It would make the difference between one dialect and another, or one language and another, a part of sociology, describable (probably in traditional phonetic terms) in the same way as any other indexical behavior, such as the dress, appearance, or patterns of belief that characterize a particular group. Such things are part of culture; and as even Stalin (1950) knew: 'Linguistics is not to be confused with culture.' It would also regard phonetic differences conveying emotion, or those aspects of the speaker's attitude that cannot be expressed by syntactic or lexical devices, as part of the subject matter of psychology. In this view, phonologists are left with their own special field: describing and explaining in terms of general linguistic principles the patterns of speech that can convey what we have defined as objective linguistic information. If phonologists are not prepared to consider the phonetic realization of phonological units in detail, this is all phonology could be.

Finally, I might mention another speech gesture that is not used distinctively in any language: the possibility of speaking with tongue in cheek; and I will admit to something of the written equivalent (pen in word processor?) in this paper. I think that the arguments I have proposed for an alternative view of phonology are plausible. But accepting them goes against all my previous endeavours, and I am not yet prepared to regard phonetic detail as not part of phonology.

REFERENCES

Anderson, S.R. 1978. 'Tone Features', in V. Fromkin (ed.), *Tone: A Linguistic Survey*. New York: Academic Press, 133–76.
Bolinger, D. 1977. 'Another Glance at Main Clause Phenomena', *Language* 53: 511–20.
Chomsky, N., and M. Halle. 1968. *The Sound Pattern of English*. New York: Harper and Row.
Gershwin, George, and Ira Gershwin. 1937. 'Let's Call the Whole Thing Off'. New York: Gershwin Publishing Corporation, G-20-4.
Halle, M., and K. Stevens. 1971. 'A Note on Laryngeal Features', *MIT Research Laboratory of Electronics Quarterly Progress Report* 101: 198–213.
IPA. 1979. *The Principles of the International Phonetic Association*. London: University College.
Jakobson, R., C.G.M. Fant, and M. Halle. 1952. *Preliminaries to Speech Analysis*. MIT Acoustics Laboratories Technical Report, 13.
―― and M. Halle. 1956. *Fundamentals of Language*. The Hague: Mouton.
Ladefoged, P. 1967. *Three Areas of Experimental Phonetics*. London: Oxford University Press.
―― 1980. 'What are Linguistic Sounds Made of?', *Language* 56: 485–502.
―― and P. Bhaskararao. 1983. 'Non-quantal Aspects of Consonant Production: A Study of Retroflex Consonants', *Journal of Phonetics* 11: 291–302.
―― and Z.-J. Wu. 1984. 'Places of Articulation: an Investigation of Pekingese Fricatives and Affricatives', *Journal of Phonetics* 12: 267–78.
Lerner, A.J., and J. Loewe. 1956. *My Fair Lady*. New York: Coward-McCann.
Lindau, Mona. 1982. 'Phonetic Differences in Glottalic Consonants', *UCLA Working Papers in Phonetics* 54: 66–77.
Maddieson, I. 1984. *Patterns of Sounds*. Cambridge: Cambridge University Press.
Murdoch, I. 1981. *Nuns and Soldiers*. Harmondsworth: Penguin.
Nihalani, P. 1983. 'Voice Quality and its Implications', *Abstracts of the Tenth International Congress of Phonetic Sciences*, 743. Dordrecht: Foris.
Prince, A. 1980. 'A Metrical Theory for Estonian Quantity', *Linguistic Inquiry* 3: 511–62.
Schane, S. 1973. *Generative Phonology*. Englewood Cliffs, NJ: Prentice-Hall.
Shaw, G.B. 1920. *Pygmalion: A Romance in Five Acts*. London: Constable.
Stalin, Josef V. 1950. 'Marxism and Problems of Linguistics', *Pravda*, 20 June 1950. Moscow.
Stockwell, Robert P. 1960. 'The Place of Intonation in a Generative Grammar of English', *Language* 36: 360–7.
Sweet, H. 1890. *A Primer of Phonetics*. Oxford: Clarendon Press.
Trager, G., and H.L. Smith. 1951. *An Outline of English Structure*. Norman, Oklahoma.

18

The 'Akzentumsprung' of Old English ēo

ROGER LASS

1. THE PROBLEM

Every student of the history of English knows that if things had gone as they should in the transition from Old to Middle English, *choose* and *lose* (OE *cēosan, lēosan*) would be **cheese, *leese.* As of course they often were in Middle English. The same is true of a number of other forms. That is, the normal Middle English reflex of isolative OE *ēo*[1] (unshortened, etc.) is /e:/, which gives NE /i:/ via the Great Vowel Shift. Forms like *choose*, etc. with NE /u:/ presuppose ME /o:/ shifted to /u:/; therefore something happened to some OE *ēo* words that led to ME /o:/ rather than expected /e:/.

The interfering process is traditionally called *Akzentumsprung*, translated as 'accent-shift' or 'stress-shift'. I argue in this paper that there was in fact no such process (at least not in these or similar terms), but that the aberrant developments of *ēo* (and *ēa*) are simply phonetically different versions of the processes that led to the normal developments, and require no extra descriptive or conceptual machinery. And further, that they fall in quite naturally with the differential developments of the 'short' *eo* as well: EML *herte*, WML *horte* < OE *heorte* are no different in principle from standard NE *freeze* (*frēosan*) and *choose, lose*.

The classic description of the process, as usual, is Luick's (1964: section 265):

> Außer den ... normalen Entwicklungen der altenglischen Diphthonge trat noch eine besondere ein: der Akzent rückte von ihrem ersten Teil auf den zweiten und das so unsilbisch gewordene *i, e, œ* schwand ... Die Bedingungen, unter welchen er eintrat, sind noch nicht genau erkannt. Soweit es sich um *betont bleibende* Silben handelt, ist nur deutlich, daß vorausgehendes *s* oder Palatal, folgendes *w* ... ferner wohl auch Stellung im Anlaut ihn begünstigen. (Emphasis in original.)

This seems to sum up the situation, including its uncertainties, very nicely. But there is a question that Luick does not raise, and which nobody appears to have answered: if the sequence of developments is supposed to have been, e.g. cḗosan > ceósan > chǭsen (cf. Jespersen 1961: section 3.602), why was it that **length** apparently got shifted as well as 'stress' or syllabicity?[2]

That is, within the framework presupposed by Luick and most of the earlier scholars, the Old English 'long diphthongs' had long first elements; but there is nothing in that framework to make us expect length to be a concomitant of accent or syllabicity in general. One might just as easily, especially considering Luick's claim that the first elements of the diphthongs were lost, expect a sequence like cḗosan > ceósan > chŏsen (loss of accent being more naturally correlated with shortness than presence of accent with length). This, however, would not work, since open syllable lengthening would then give ME *chǭsen, NE *chose. (The Modern English preterite chose, incidentally, must be the result of Akzentumsprung of ēa, since cēas should give *chease: ēa > ME /ɛ:/ > NE /i:/.)[3]

2. THE DATA

There are a large number of OE ēo forms that show NE /u:/, but not all are to be treated under the *Akzentumsprung* heading. The main group we can get rid of are those involving a following /w/; these are not the same thing, though they have some illustrative significance. This group includes *you, rue, chew, true, brew, blew, threw* (OE ēow, hrēowan, cēowan, trēow, brēowan, blēow, þrēow), and *strew, ewe* (OE streowan, eowu).[4] In these, the NE /u:/ is expectable, since their Middle English nuclei derive from 'vocalization' of /w/ and loss of the second element of the original diphthong. Or, to put it more accurately, from monophthongization of the original diphthongs, vocalization of /w/, and neutralization of length before the new /u/ < /w/ (cf. Lass and Anderson 1975: 194–200). The result of the older sequences ēow, eow, is apparently /eu/, later /iu/, which, except after coronal stops in some dialects, would give NE /u:/. (Though the /iu/ stage, either as /iu/ or /ju:/, is attested in all environments in ENE: cf. Dobson 1968: section 179–89.)

The *ēaw* case is similar, though there are a number of etymological problems. Here we have items like *show, shrew* (OE scēawian, scrēawa); the expected development is /əu/, and the /u:/ in *shrew* seems aberrant (but cf. the older /iu/ in *show* as evidenced by the spelling *shew*, and contrariwise the traditional pronunciation of *Shrewsbury* < Scrēawesbyrig as /ʃrəuzbrɪ/).

Another group of forms that can be eliminated, perhaps untraditionally, are those showing *eo* spellings from 'palatal diphthongization': e.g. *yoke*, *yolk, short, youth* (OE *geoc, geoloca, sceort, geoguþ*). For scholars who believe that palatal diphthongization was a sound change rather than an orthographic device for indicating that *g* or *c* are to be pronounced as palatals before back vowel graphs, there is a convenient point of departure for treating the whole problem. Thus Jespersen (1961: section 3.601) says of instances like *sceort, geoc* that these are really /o/, 'modified after a front element', like the *ēo* in *scēoh*, which is 'only a long *ō* preceded by a front glide on account of *sc*', as also in *scēoc*. Thus the developments here are normal: /ʃo:x/ > /ʃu:/, /ʃo:k/ > /ʃɔk/ (the latter with prevelar shortening as in *book, look*). In the *Akzentumsprung* cases like *cēosan*, then, we can invoke a similar explanation:

> But in some words the first element of an OE diphthong, though not originally due to a preceding palatal, was treated in the same manner, the first element being absorbed into the palatal consonant, and the stress, as it were, shifted onto the second element.

Thus Jespersen's strategy is to take the palatal cases as primary, and have the non-palatal instances (e.g. *lose*), as well, presumably, as the palatal instances where the palatal is not 'causal' (*cēosan*) treated as due to a kind of 'phonetic analogy'.

This approach first of all fails to account for the length of the reflexes. If the first element of the diphthong is 'absorbed' into the palatal, why should the resulting vowel be long? This is certainly not a reasonable environment for compensatory lengthening, which in English at least seems to occur after deletion of a **post**vocalic element (cf. Ingvaeonic nasal loss before fricatives with compensatory lengthening in cases of the *five, goose, tooth* type).

In addition, it has a kind of conceptual oddity: how do we motivate this rather strange development, which in one case (the palatals) is supposedly phonetic, and in the others apparently analogical on the lexical level, without the usual morphological–paradigmatic conditions obtaining in analogical adjustments? We have to account here not only for *lose*, but for many non-surviving Middle English doublets in /o:/ for OE *ēo* forms, like *yǭde* < *ēode, rǭrd* < *rēord*, etc. (the palatal in *yǭde* is not original, and would not have been there at the time of the change; for these forms and discussion, see Jordan 1968: section 34, Anm. 2).

But the most serious problem is that there seems to be no very good evidence that 'palatal diphthongization' was in fact a phonetic or phonological phenomenon; it seems most likely to have been purely graphic (cf. the original argument in Stockwell and Barritt 1951, and the reassessment in Lass and Anderson 1975: Appendix III). If the 'modification' of vowels following initial palatals is purely graphic, then all the *ēo* forms come under the same rubric: something in general has happened to some OE *ēo* causing them to develop as ME /o:/ instead of /e:/. And the environment — unlike the case with following /w/ — is not phonetic.

In addition, this account and similar ones fail to group along with the 'shifted' ēo another set of developments of the same nucleus: the differential split into /ø:/ in the WML and parts of the South, and /e:/ elsewhere, and the parallel development of short eo into /ø/ and /e/ (cf. Jordan 1968: sections 66-9, 73, 84-5). It seems on the face of it that an analysis that can group these together in a natural way is preferable to one that can't; and I will offer one in section 4 below.

3. THE NATURE OF THE OLD ENGLISH DIPHTHONGS

But first we need a clarification — or at least a firm position — with respect to just what I assume is being represented by ēo and eo. The problem of the 'long' and 'short' diphthongs in Old English is a venerable one, and has been an issue in the Anglistic community now, in one way or another, for over forty years (Daunt 1939 picked up by Stockwell and Barritt 1951, Hockett 1959; the orthodox assailants of the revisionists like Kuhn and Quirk 1953, Kuhn 1961, through the revival of a semi-orthodox position but with special generative trappings in Lass and Anderson 1975; the revival of the Stockwell–Barritt position in Keyser and O'Neill 1983; the revival of the traditional position in Lass 1984a).

There is no need to go into the debate in detail here; I will simply sketch out its parameters, and reintroduce the position I have already argued for (Lass 1984a). The problem — which is fundamental for our topic here — is just what kind of systemic entities the Old English digraphs *ea, eo* represented. The traditional view (maintained in all the standard handbooks, e.g. Mossé 1945, Brunner 1965, Wright and Wright 1925, Campbell 1959) is that the Old English vowel system was dichotomized by a length opposition, and that each length category (short, long) contained two kinds of nuclei (monophthongal, diphthongal). The revisionist view (Stockwell and Barritt, Hockett, Daunt in different ways) allows the dichotomy, but has diphthongs only in the long (or 'complex') set, and monophthongs only in the short set. So in this view any digraph which represents either a Germanic diphthong (*bēam, cēosan*) or the breaking of a Germanic long monophthong (*nēah, fēol*) represents a diphthong; any digraph representing breaking or velar umlaut of a Germanic short vowel (*seah, heorte, bealu, heofon*) represents a short monophthong. (One issue that exercised many participants in the debate — whether the short digraphs represent independent phonemes or allophones of short vowels — will not concern us here.)

Two main issues raised in the long controversy are germane to this discussion. First, is it possible for a language to have a contrast of long and short diphthongs? And second, if, as is now reasonably well accepted, 'length' is a matter primarily of moric structure (long and diphthongal /VV/ vs. short /V/), what can a 'short diphthong' (or for that matter a 'long' one) possibly be? (Leaving aside the typologically and genetically unlikely possibility of Estonian-type *Überlänge*, which would also be ruled out by the patterning of the 'long' diphthongs not as an independent class, but like the long vowels.) The first is less of a problem now than it was: there are clear instances both of languages with phonemic length contrasts in diphthongs (Welsh, Afrikaans, some varieties of English: Lass 1981, 1984a) and of languages with phonetic length distinctions (Scots: Lass 1974; Icelandic, and most varieties of English). We can probably now take 'universalist' arguments against the possibility of two diphthong types as not tenable.

The serious problem however is conceptual: if both monophthong vs. diphthong and short vs. long are defined in terms of nuclear constituency, how do you get short diphthongs? I proposed a solution to this in Lass 1984a, which I will outline briefly here (see that paper for full argumentation, and Lass 1984b for further discussion). My suggestion was that phonological and phonetic moric structure be separated, in such a way that one tier of a multi-tiered representation of syllable structure be taken as specifying phonological moric structure or quantity (a prosodic level), and another, lower-level tier as specifying phonetic nuclear constituency. Thus syllable peaks are two-tiered structures, with non-unique mappings possible between tiers, as I will show below. The overall model of the syllable looks like this (with a CVC structure as the example):

(1)

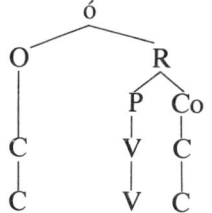

1 Syllabic Tier
2 Rhyme Tier
3 Rhyme-constituent Tier
4 Moric (Prosodic) Tier
5 Segmental Tier

In such a model, we can allow the branching of a peak (or of a coda) to be non-identical at tiers 4 and 5; a not unnatural suggestion of tier-autonomy in a multi-tiered structure, now familiar from autosegmental phonology.

Thus, given the possibility of differential branching, we can define the four nucleus types posited in the traditional account of Old English vowel phonology in this way:

THE 'AKZENTUMSPRUNG' OF OLD ENGLISH ĒO

(2)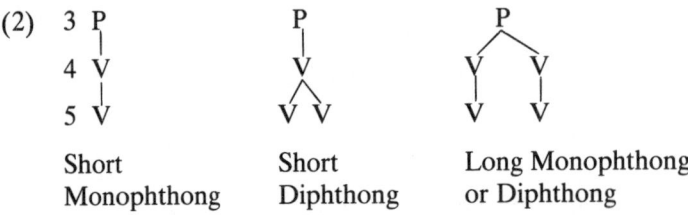

    Short   Short   Long Monophthong
    Monophthong   Diphthong   or Diphthong

That is, a 'short' diphthong is monomoric at tier 4, like a short vowel; and a long vowel or 'long' (= normal) diphthong is bimoric at 4. The distinctions at 5 are not relevant to phonological quantity. This enables us not only to give a reasonable characterization of languages with four nuclear types, but also of languages with no length or syllable-weight oppositions, but still having monophthongs and diphthongs (e.g. Yiddish). In this classification, the inventory of peak types for English and German, Afrikaans and Old English, and Yiddish would be:

(3)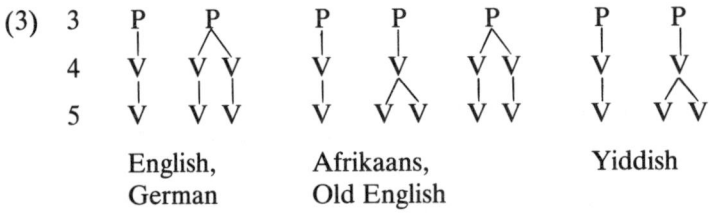

    English,   Afrikaans,   Yiddish
    German   Old English

The difficulty of course is giving a **segmental** representation of these distinctions: the usual convention, e.g. [eo] vs. [e:o] or [eo:] places the length on a particular element of the diphthong. Whereas what we're interested in is the difference in overall quantity, which is often not (see below) reflected in a way appropriate to this sort of transcription. But regardless of phonetics, we want to indicate that quantity here is not strictly a segmental property, but a structural one; and that a 'long diphthong' is not longer than a long monophthong, as implied by the above notations.

So I shall use here, where necessary, a segmental notation that signals the differences diacritically: if long vowels and 'long' diphthongs are [VV], then 'short' diphthongs, the 'odd' or 'marked' category, are [V̆V]. Such a notation is to be interpreted as referring to tier 4, i.e. [˘] indicates non-branching at that level. Thus a transcription [VV] is shorthand for a bracketing [p[vV]v[vV]v]p, and [V̆V] represents a bracketing [p[vVV]v]p.

For the rest of the argument I will assume in the traditional manner that Old English had a four-way opposition of nuclear types segmentally (tier 5) and a two-way opposition prosodically (tier 4):

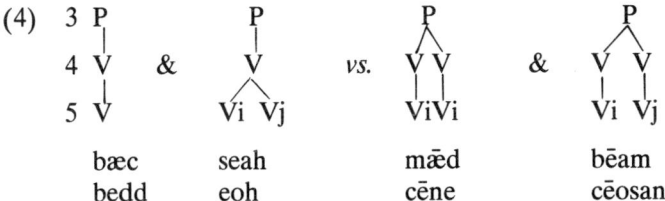

Phonetically, then *ēo* is [eo] and *eo* is [ĕŏ]; i.e., they are segmentally identical, but prosodically and phonetically (almost certainly durationally) different. The difference might have been of either of two types: (a) with the duration spread relatively evenly over both morae, or (b) with one or the other mora (most probably the first) longer in the long diphthong. That is, it might have been either the type shown in the Icelandic pair *læs/læst* 'literate' (common vs. neuter), in the system adopted here [laes] vs. [laĕst]; or that in Afrikaans *baie* 'very'/*baaie* 'bays', [bɐiə] vs. [bɑ·iə]. In the first type, the time occupied by each mora of the long diphthong equals (roughly) that occupied by a short vowel; while the duration of each mora of the short diphthong is roughly that of half a short vowel (cf. Árnason 1977: 371–2). In the second, the first mora of the long diphthong is (say) about half again as long as a short vowel, and the second mora quite short, while the short diphthong behaves as in the first case. Schematically:

(5)

Long Vowel	Vi	Vi		Vi	Vi
Long Diphthong	Vi	Vj		Vi	Vj
Short Vowel	Vi			Vi	
Short Diphthong	Vi Vj			Vi Vj	
	Icelandic			Afrikaans	

I suspect that the Icelandic 'equal' type is more likely to be a good model for the Old English situation. As we will see in the following section, the second morae of the diphthongs, both short and long, play as important a part in their histories as the first morae, suggesting that we ought not to downgrade them to 'offglide' status.

4. *AKZENTUMSPRUNG* UNVEILED; OR, THE EMPEROR SEEN IN HIS PROPER GARMENT

We now have a notation and conceptual framework sufficient (a) to characterize the process itself, and (b) to deal with the question of why length should be retained while accent and/or syllabicity shift (cf. section 1). As I suggested cryptically in note 2 above, both (a) and (b) are pseudoproblems.

The three dimensions potentially involved — accent, syllabicity, length — do not in themselves play a distinctive role. Or better, the first two are irrelevant and the third redundant.

The first two are in fact probably one. That is, if 'accent' or 'stress' in the usual sense denotes a (relational) property defining prominence in a string of syllables, then 'syllabicity' denotes a similar property defining the prominence of one mora of a bimoric nucleus. Or they denote the same property at two different levels; e.g., within a relational framework like that proposed in the more reductive versions of metrical phonology (Kiparsky 1979, Giegerich 1983), 'accent' and 'syllabicity' are two exponents of the category 'prominence' at different hierarchical levels, i.e., they are S-dominated.[5]

Now syllabicity of diphthongal morae — even if easily notated in (say) a metrical or dependency framework (e.g. Ewen 1980) — is not unproblematical. For one thing, it is often, within a given language, either impossible to perceive consistently, variable, or both. To revert for a moment to personal experience, I find that the Afrikaans diphthongs /ëə öə/ in *geel* 'yellow', *hoog* 'high' appear variably as what I would transcribe as [ë̯ə ö̯ə] and [ëə̯ öə̯] (the element marked [̯] being, among other things, shorter than the other). Given speakers will produce, say, [ɦöə̯χ] and [ɦöə̯χ] in the same discourse under similar prominence conditions, and they do not appear to notice — or to value either positively or negatively — such variation in themselves or others.

In addition, syllabicity of diphthongal morae is never as such, as far as I know, distinctive; at least in Germanic (as far as I want to go in my ignorance) I cannot conceive a phonemic distinction of the type /ai̯/ vs. /a̯i/. Even if a language does have both rising and falling diphthongs, their moric composition is different: e.g. Icelandic [i̯ɛ] vs. [ɛi̯]. We can probably take the distribution of syllabicity in this context anyhow as a low-level matter.

And in fact, from a perceptual point of view, as at least partly conditioned by purely segmental factors. For example, *ceteris paribus* the opener of two non-central morae will sound 'more prominent' (due to greater inherent length and/or sonority), the more peripheral mora will sound more prominent than the more central, etc. These are (at best) 'perceptual tendencies', but they suggest why syllabicity within complex nuclei is probably not to be taken as having much — if any — systemic import.

If we can dismiss intranuclear prominence as an operative factor, this leaves us only with length. And I suggest that this is, for our purposes, redundant. *Akzentumsprung*, I argue, is a purely segmental (tier 5) process, unaffected by and not affecting prosodic structure (tier 4). The only role that tier 4 plays is its usual one as the locus for original length, which is maintained unchanged.

Our process (which needs a new name, since *Akzent* is now out of con-

THE 'AKZENTUMSPRUNG' OF OLD ENGLISH ĔO

sideration, as *Umsprung* will be shortly) is simply one among many affecting the Old English diphthongs, and is perhaps best seen in a historical perspective. It seems fairly clear (cf. Lass and Anderson 1975: Ch. 3) that the Old English diphthongs were of a 'height-harmonic' type, i.e. both morae at the same height, as opposed to the earlier (and later) [ai au] diphthongs of Proto-Germanic and Middle English. The *ĕa* nuclei were segmentally [æɑ], the *ĕo* [eo], and the *ĭe* either [iu] or [iy].[6]

Now the height-harmonic diphthongs arise from earlier non-harmonic sequences: e.g. [æɑ] < *[au] (*bēam*), [eo] < *[eu] (*lēoht*), etc. Thus early Old English shows, as one of its modes of vocalic behaviour, internal assimilation in complex peaks. This process-type occurs again at the end of the Old English period, in the treatment of the 'long' diphthongs. As a kind of prelude (by hindsight) to the typological shift from height-harmonic to closing [-i, -u] diphthongs in Middle English, the originals assimilated their second morae to their first, and merged with the long monophthongs corresponding to their first morae (cf. Lass and Anderson 1975: 194–200). Thus:

(6)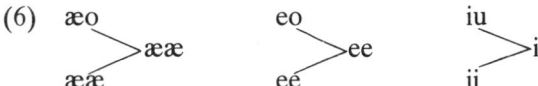

This sounds like a roundabout way of saying 'they monophthongized'; and indeed I have deliberately avoided this term, as it covers a number of different processes. Monophthongization in the case of (6) (diphthong to long vowel) is simply a case of internal harmonization (here for backness, not height); but monophthongization of the short diphthongs is something different. Here we have:

(7)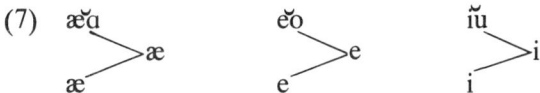

This is — granted — 'monophthongization', but a rather different kind, by deletion of a half-mora rather than assimilation of one full mora to another. Using the notational system developed earlier, we can represent the monophthongizations of *ēo* and *eo* as follows:

(8)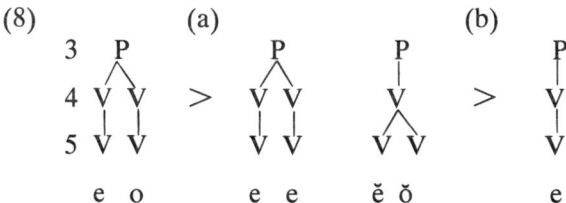

229

(Where [V̆] represents a (durational) half-mora.) These two process-types are sufficient to account both for the 'normal (*ēo* > /e:/) and 'aberrant' (*ēo* > /o:/) developments, as well as the differentiated reflexes of *ĕo* in the WML and elsewhere.

To begin with *freeze* vs. *choose*. If (8a) represents the development leading to ME /e:/ in *freeze*, that leading to /o:/ in *choose* would be:

(9)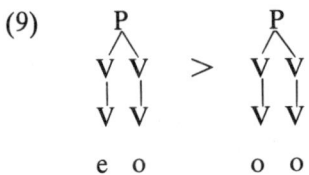

That is, instead of progressive assimilation of backness and roundness, we have regressive assimilation of the same properties: the '*Akzentumsprung*' is simply the mirror-image of the normal evolution, with no extra apparatus needed. Nothing in fact has 'shifted' except the direction of the intra-nuclear harmonization. Hence the *Umsprung* is now gone; we have a development that is (perhaps) *umgekehrt*, but not *umgesprungen*.

The WML developments of *ĕo* can be captured in much the same way. We observe that in dialects where there is merger of *ĕo* with other segments, *ēo* merges with *ē*, and *ĕo* with *e* (cf. (8)). In the WML, where there is no merger, both *ēo* and *eo* emerge as mid front rounded vowels, respectively long and short. These latter developments are:

(10) (a)   (b)

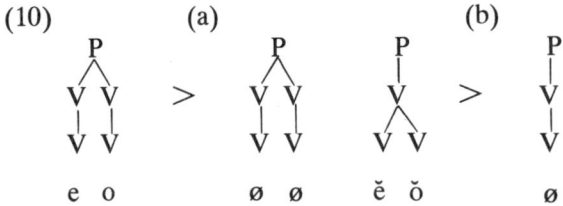

In (10a), we have progressive assimilation of backness (as in [eo] > [ee]), plus regressive assimilation of rounding; in (10b) presumably regressive assimilation of both backness and rounding, followed by deletion. Or, if we want to visualize it this way (which may be preferable), the results in (b) are the same as in (a): both morae are involved, but the result is [ø̆ø̆], i.e. two half-morae of [ø]-quality, which are of course equivalent to one full mora, i.e. short [ø].

This account, though it invokes a more complex notion of syllable structure than others, is nonetheless in the end more parsimonious than any 'special case' account. At least it is if we allow that extending a piece of machinery so that it copes naturally with a number of hitherto unrelated processes is in effect a descriptive simplification.

NOTES

I am grateful — as are all Anglicists interested in the history of the English vowel system — to Bob Stockwell, for setting up more than thirty years ago a framework for discussion which has touched all subsequent work of any quality on the topic. If it weren't for Stockwell and Barritt (1951), and later work of Stockwell's, the issues could never have been debated with clarity. And indeed, having spent the last decade and a half in periodic bouts of dialogue with Bob, both in person and by letter, on our two radically different conceptions of this field, I can attest by experience that whether I'm right or wrong (and I'm not sure yet) I would not have had the opportunity to be either without the challenge of Stockwell's work, and the certain knowledge that whatever I came up with was sure to meet a sharp and informed challenge.

It is perhaps ungracious on the surface to offer a paper that disagrees with a scholar's basic position on some issue to his *Festschrift*; the poor guy has no chance to defend himself. But I do so in a spirit of dialogue that I'm sure Bob would appreciate, and as a gesture of gratitude for an important and formative influence on my own work.

1. I am deliberately using orthographic representation here; phonetic and phonological specification will be taken up in section 3.

2. Lass and Anderson (1975: 8) consider the process to involve not 'accent' or 'stress' but syllabicity. Our analysis in terms of 'right syllabification' also misses the point. In this paper I argue that the question — obvious as it is in terms of the exposition so far — is misdirected, since length isn't involved either, in the sense of an entity that has been 'shifted'. The traditional question is also begged by Wright and Wright (1928: section 65, note) and Jespersen (1961: section 3.602), among others.

3. An analysis where 'accent' shifted but length didn't would account for a number of Modern English forms with /əu/ for OE *ēo*, e.g. *choke* < (*ā*)*cēocan*, *float* < *flēotan*, etc. That is, a short /o/ vocalism would be left, which with open syllable lengthening would give ME /ɔ:/, ENE /o:/, NE /əu/. But of course the vocalism could also come from past participles (-*floten*, etc.), treated the same way. This possibility is suggested by the frequency of analogical disturbance of strong verb paradigms by migration of vocalisms to morphosyntactically inappropriate places (in the etymological sense), e.g., short participle or pret. pl. vocalism in the preterites of Class I verbs like *bite*, the same in the present of *shit*, etc.; or the migratory consonantism going the other way with present /z/ moving into the past participle *chosen* (OE -*coren*).

4. Jordan (1968: sections 107–8) suggests that *eow* merged with *ēaw* in /ɛu/, not /eu/; but the modern evidence does not make this very firm. In any case the /eu/: /ɛu/ opposition was short-lived, and the two merged quite early on in /iu/.

5. Part of the muddle leading to such terminology as 'initial-stressed' falling vs. 'final-stressed' rising diphthongs in discussions of the history and structure of English is perhaps due to Luick's and other German scholars' unfortunate use of *Akzent* (vs. in Luick's case, syllable-level *Betonung*), and its rather unreflective adoption into English.

6. Lass and Anderson (1975: 122–9) argue for [iu]; McLaughlin (1979) suggests [iy]; and the most recent discussion (Colman, MS) suggests both values in different circumstances for those *ie* that represent diphthongs and not either V + diacritic or a disyllabic sequence.

REFERENCES

Árnason, K. 1977. *Quantity in Icelandic: A Historical and Comparative Study*. University of Edinburgh dissertation.
Brunner, K. 1965. *Altenglische Grammatik, nach der angelsächsischen Grammatik von Eduard Sievers*. 3rd edn. Tübingen: Niemeyer.
Campbell, A. 1959. *Old English Grammar*. Oxford: Oxford University Press.
Colman, F. MS. 'Old English *ie*: Quid est?'. University of Edinburgh, Department of English Language.
Daunt, M. 1939. 'Old English Sound Changes Considered in Relation to Scribal Tradition and Practice', *Transactions of the Philological Society*: 108–37.
Dobson, E.J. 1968. *English Pronunciation 1500–1700*. 2 vols. Oxford: Oxford University Press.
Ewen, C.J. 1980. *Aspects of Phonological Structure*. University of Edinburgh dissertation.
Giegerich, H. 1983. *Studies in Metrical Phonology: German and English*. University of Edinburgh dissertation.
Hockett, C.F. 1959. 'The Stressed Syllabics of Old English', *Language* 35: 575–97.
Jespersen, O. 1961. *A Modern English Grammar on Historical Principles*. Part I: *Sounds and Spellings*. Reprint. London: Allen and Unwin.
Jordan, R. 1968. *Handbuch der mittelenglischen Grammatik*. 3rd edn. Heidelberg: Winter.
Keyser, S.J., and W. O'Neill. 1983. 'Exceptions to High Vowel Diphthongization in the Vespasian Psalter and their Explanation', in M. Davenport, E. Hansen, H.F. Nielsen (eds.), *Current Topics in English Historical Linguistics*. Odense: Odense University Press, 137–64.
Kiparsky, P. 1979. 'Metrical Structure Assignment is Cyclic', *Linguistic Inquiry* 10: 421–42.
Kuhn, S.M. 1961. 'The Syllabic Phonemes of Old English', *Language* 37: 522–38.
—— and R. Quirk. 1953. 'Some Recent Interpretations of Old English Digraph Spellings', *Language* 29: 372–89.
Lass, R. 1974. 'Linguistic Orthogenesis? Scots Vowel Quantity and the English Length Conspiracy', in J.M. Anderson and C. Jones (eds.), *Historical Linguistics*, vol. I. Amsterdam: North-Holland, 311–52.
—— 1981. 'Undigested History and Synchronic "Structure"', in D. Goyvaerts (ed.), *Phonology in the 1980s*. Ghent: E. Story-Scientia, 525–44.
—— 1984a. 'Quantity, Resolution, and Syllable Geometry', *Folia Linguistica Historica* 4: 151–80.
—— 1984b. 'Vowel System Universals and Typology: Prologue to Theory', *Phonology Yearbook* 1.
—— and J.M. Anderson. 1975. *Old English Phonology*. Cambridge: Cambridge University Press.
Luick, K. 1964. *Historische Grammatik der englischen Sprache*. 2 vols., Reprint. Oxford: Blackwell.
McLaughlin, J.C. 1979. 'The *i*-Umlaut of the Old English West Saxon Diphthongs', *Journal of Linguistics* 15: 289–94.
Mossé, F. 1945. *Manuel de l'anglais du moyen âge*. I, *Viel-anglais*. Paris: Aubier.
Stockwell, R.P., and C.W. Barritt. 1951. 'Some Old English Graphemic–Phonemic Correspondences: *æ, ea, e*', *Studies in Linguistics*, Occasional Papers, 4.
Wright, J., and E.M. Wright. 1925. *Old English Grammar*. Oxford: Oxford University Press.
—— 1928. *An Elementary Middle English Grammar*. Oxford: Oxford University Press.

19

From Latin to Romance: The Vowel Systems

CARLOS P. OTERO

There are a number of unmistakable systematic differences between Latin and the Neo-Latin or Romance languages. A major one is the position of the verb within the verb phrase: Latin was a V-final language, whereas the Romance languages are not. This syntactic difference is perhaps not unrelated to an obvious morphological difference: Latin had both a 'rich' verb morphology and a 'rich' noun morphology, whereas no Romance language has a rich morphological case system, and at least one (French) does not have a rich verb morphology either, its ancestral morphological endings having been eroded over the centuries by general phonetic processes. One particularly striking phonological difference is the sharp contrast in vowel pattern between Latin and the earliest Romance. In fact, one of the most debated questions in Romance historical linguistics, and still a controversial one, is the nature of the evolution of the Latin vowel system into the three distinct Neo-Latin prototypes, which for some specialists is the outstanding sound change undergone by the Latin system.[1] It is this problem that I would like to address here. In particular, I would like to reexamine it from a new perspective and try to offer a more satisfactory account than the one I gave a decade ago.[2]

This paper is organized as follows: section 1 provides some of the relevant Latin background. Section 2 lays out, in relatively theory-neutral terms, our central topic, the 'quantity to quality' issue. Section 3 focuses on what are taken to be crucial aspects of the available evidence. The heart of the paper is section 4, which contains the descriptive proposal. Its main claims are the following: the three Proto-Romance vowel systems are derived from classical Latin by a rule of Lengthening (not Delengthening, as is wisely assumed) and, in the case of two of them, a rule of Laxing (applying to stressed mid vowels in Western Romance, and only to front stressed mid vowels in the asymmetric system exemplified by Rumanian). No other rules are needed. It is also claimed that the operation and effects of the stress rule did not change as a result of the loss of phonemic length. An Appendix on the effects of stress and syllabification is provided as a supplement to section 1.

1. THE LATIN BACKGROUND

As is well known, Latin was a language with an ordinary five-vowel pattern /i e a o u/, inherited from late Indo-European, plus a phonemic distinction of 'length', which also went back to Indo-European. This distinction was crucial in more than one way. To begin with, it gave rise to such minimal pairs as the following:[3]

(1) a. mala 'bad (FEM.)'   ma:la 'apples'
       malus 'bad (MASC.)'   ma:lus 'mast of ship'
       levis 'light (not heavy)'   le:vi:s 'smooth'
       os 'bone'   o:s 'mouth'
       solum 'sole; soil'   so:lum 'alone'
       populus 'people'   po:pulus 'poplar-tree'
       cecidi (cado, PERFECT)   ceci:di (caedo, PERFECT)
    b. Roma (NOMINATIVE)
       Roma: (ABLATIVE)
       legit '(s)he reads'   legimus 'we read' (PRESENT)
       le:git '(s)he reads'   le:gimus 'we read' (PERFECT)

As these and similar examples show, vowel length was used not only to mark lexical oppositions (1a), but also to mark other grammatical contrasts (1b), as in some present-day languages, among them some Bantu languages (Ladefoged 1971: 82).

The distinction between long and nonlong vowels was also crucial for the operation of the well known (classical) Latin Stress Rule and for Latin versification. As is often the case with stress systems, the Latin rule was sensitive to syllable 'weight' (see Zirin 1970: Ch. 5; cf. Pulgram 1975). In traditional terms, the essential principle of the rule may be expressed as follows:[4]

(2) (i) Assign accent to the antepenult unless (ii) obtains;
     (ii) Assign accent to the penult if it is a 'heavyweight' or if there is no antepenult.

A standard formalization of (2) in segmental terms is (3):

(3) $V \rightarrow [+\text{stress}] / \underline{} C_o (V^*C)VC_o \# \#$ $V^* = \text{nonlong } V$

Although the facts of Latin follow from this simple rule, an account of this nature is far from satisfactory, as shown in Hayes (1980). Hayes demonstrates that a metrical theory of stress is far superior to a segmental one, in particular to the theory proposed in Chomsky and Halle (1968). As a necessary first step, we must posit an internal structure for syllables (cf.

McCarthy 1979a,b). It is now widely assumed that syllables are universally divided into an ONSET, consisting of the segments preceding the syllabic peak, and a RIME, consisting of everything else. A crucial observation is that the existence of a rime node offers a simple way of characterizing a syllable as 'light' or 'heavy'. A 'light' syllable is one of the form C_oV, in contrast with a 'heavy' one, which in Latin is of the form C_oV: or C_oVC, a curious disjunction. The fact that in a syllable of the form C_oVC there is a slot after V suggests that C_oV: is to be represented as C_oVV at some level. If long vowels correspond to two V slots, then instead of the curious disjunction of (3) we have a distinction between branching and nonbranching rimes, as shown in (4), with typical Latin examples as illustration (cf. Allen 1973: 50ff):

(4)

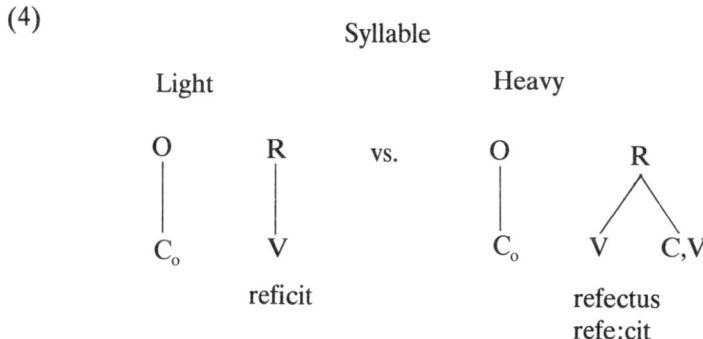

The criterion of branching appears to be especially appropriate to stress rules, which, it has been argued, apply to what is sometimes called the RIME PROJECTION, a special representation consisting solely of the rimes of the phonological string.[5]

Hayes provides an analysis of Latin stress within the framework of his metrical theory. His analysis also derives the facts of Latin stress, but it does so in a far more satisfactory way than rule (3). It is not possible to go into details here (see Hayes 1980, 1982 for extended discussion). However, it must be emphasized that a distinction between nonbranching and branching rimes, which subsumes that between light and nonlight syllables, is central to our topic. Also central to our topic are the implications of the informal statement given in (2), which are to be related to Hayes's principle of maximality of foot construction, and in particular to the idea that feet must always have the maximum size compatible with the appropriate (in our case, Latin) foot template.

A fact of crucial significance for the question under study is that we have every reason to assume that the syllable stressed immediately after the loss of phonemic length is regularly the syllable stressed by the classical Stress Rule (i.e., the position of stress remains the same). In fact, 'the accent has continued generally in the same place from our earliest documents to the present day' (Sturtevant 1940: 187) in most Neo-Latin dialects (French again being a special case, in a way — see Pope 1952: Ch. 5). Only in two small classes of words do we find that the syllable stressed in late Latin or early Romance is not the one that was stressed in the period of classical literature, and both changes are an automatic consequence of a difference in syllabification (see Appendix).

2. THE PROBLEM: 'QUANTITY TO QUALITY'

Virtually everyone who has studied this topic agrees that an important difference between Latin and Romance is that the contrast in phonemic length typical of classical Latin is not found in the earliest Romance phonology. There is also general agreement that from the very beginning we have three different vowel patterns, which are found today side by side in Southern Italy.[6] These three prototypes are generally assumed to have the following inventories:[7]

    I.   /i, e, a, o, u/
    II. /i, e, E, a, o, u/
    III. /i, e, E, a, O, o, u/

2.1. The three basic prototypes

The simplest prototype is exemplified by Proto-Sardinian.[8] Since it had the standard five-vowel pattern, for ease of identification I will refer to it as S5. It is widely assumed (explicitly or implicitly) that S5 can be derived from the system with phonemic length by a delengthening rule that yields the following correspondences with classical Latin vowels:

(5)   Sardinian prototype (reconstruction of common view)

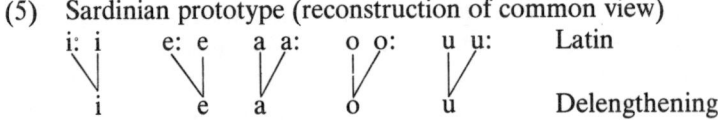

A proposal of this nature can be interpreted synchronically or diachronically. Under the first interpretation, we are dealing with a low-level phonetic rule, and our basic problem is left unresolved; under the second interpretation, a prediction is made that is immediately falsified by the documentary record. Since there is no reason to assume that the lexical restructuring that would result would lead to any modification of the Stress Rule itself (that is, the fact that the reflexes of words such as *mendi:cu-*, *me:su:ra:re, me:su:ra* and so on no longer have phonemically long vowels tells the children nothing about the Stress Rule — see n. 4), we would expect that all and only those words with a long vowel in the penult would exhibit a change in accentuation: stress would no longer be assigned to the penult, but rather to the antepenult. This is clearly not the case. In our detective story this is therefore the dog that did not bark.

The prototype that differs the most from S5 had two additional vowels, i.e. a total of seven, although these two vowels never appear in unstressed positions. I will refer to it as S7. It is best exemplified by Proto-Galegan, and it corresponds very closely to the system of present-day Galegan.[9] This is perhaps the most characteristic, and certainly the most pervasive, Romance system — the one reconstructed not only for other Western Romance dialects such as Spanish, Catalan, French, and so on, but also for Proto-Italian. The Latin-Galegan correspondences are as follows (E,O stand for lower mid vowels found only in a stressed position):

(6) Galegan prototype (reconstruction of common view)
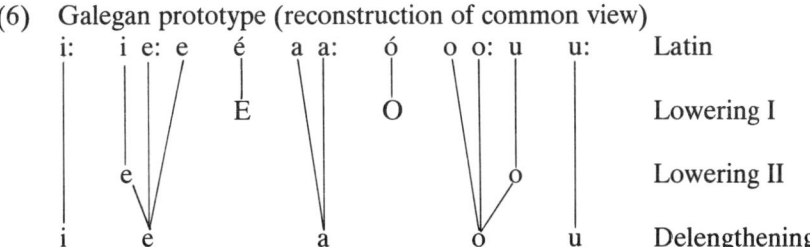

Between the 'extremes' schematized in the displays of (5)–(6), there is a sort of 'half-way house' (Elcock 1960: 46): the system reconstructed for, e.g., Proto-Rumanian.[10] In this prototype the front vowels have evolved as in S7, the back vowels as in S5. It therefore has six different vowels under stress, but only five in unstressed positions, as schematically shown in (7). I will refer to it as S6.

(7) Rumanian prototype (reconstruction of common view)
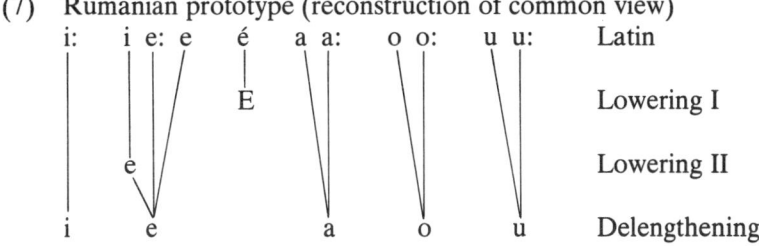

This prototype, together with the data from diphthongization which we will examine directly, offers, to my mind, the most revealing evidence, as I hope that the discussion that follows will show.

3. THE EVIDENCE

3.1. Diphthongization

As implied above, the Galegan vowels have not changed very much to this day, so we find Latin-Galegan-Italian correspondences such as the following:

(8) Latin   Galegan   Italian
     mele-   mEl   miele
     novu-   nOvo   nuovo

This minimal but representative sample of the three languages is enough, in my view, to illustrate the main steps in the evolution, which within Italian constitutes a single line of descent. The contrasting dialectal forms provide us with a fairly transparent picture, the Galegan vowels mirroring an earlier stage in the development. It therefore seems reasonable to hypothesize that between the stage essentially exemplified by Galegan and the stage exemplified by Italian (and for E, also by Spanish or French), there was an intermediate stage that may be represented as *mEEle, nOOvo*, as suggested a decade ago.[11] It was also suggested at that time that a sequence consisting of a vowel preceded by a homorganic glide is to be expected in the case of a sequence of two adjacent lax lower mid vowels that undergo diphthongization. We could represent this fact by analyzing the nucleus that evolves into a rising diphthong in (8) as typically occupying two positions in the segmental sequence. Phonetic lengthening is typically associated with stressed vowels in many languages, and the extralengthening at issue, which subsequently results in diphthongization, may be plausibly attributed to the extraordinary intensity of stress in Latin and early Romance (see Appendix). Once the two positions of the segmental sequence are filled (a highly marked structure under the Obligatory Contour Principle — see Hayes 1984), the tendency of the two identical lax lower mid vowels to diphthongize could then be viewed as a direct consequence of two things: (1) The fact that they are associated with two positions in the CV skeleton; (2) their deviation from their intended configurations at the very beginning of the articulation, a deviation that presumably makes diphthongization more likely than with tense long vowels. Thus, we can regard corresponding tense and lax long mid vowels 'as sharing to a great extent an articulatory target, and as differing primarily in that the tense vowel is more likely to reach and maintain that target than the lax vowel' (Anderson 1984: 95). In contrast, with tense long nuclei the closing tends to occur at the end of the articulation, giving rise to a sequence consisting of a vowel followed by a homorganic glide (a falling diphthong), as

FROM LATIN TO ROMANCE

in English or in the subsequent history of French (e.g. Old French *mei*, *flour*, now *moi*, *fleur*, from Latin *me:*, *flo:re*), which again differs on this point from the rest of Romance.[12]

3.2. Laxing

Next we ask what the difference is between, e.g., *mEEle*, *nOOvo*, and their immediate ancestral forms. It seems reasonable to assume that the nucleus of identical vowels derives historically from a long vowel.[13] This is likely to come as a surprise for those inclined to think of a lax vowel as being necessarily nonlong or less long than a tense one. Since the stressed vowels of the class of words exemplified by *mele-*, *novo-*, and so on, was not long in classical Latin, a lengthening of lax mid vowels under stress must be posited to explain the fact that they diphthongize (cf. Hyman 1977: 48). There is reason to assume that this lengthening process did not distinguish between mid and nonmid vowels, but rather applied to every stressed vowel. It is this process that brings about the loss of phonemic length, as we will see directly.

Evidence in favor of positing both length and laxness comes from the fact that the reflexes of the new (lax) long mid vowels in Western Romance did not merge with the reflexes of the stressed long mid vowels of classical Latin. It is then reasonable to infer that the new Western long vowels differed from the old tense long vowels in at least one property. A very natural assumption is that this property was inherited from their original difference in phonetic laxness and/or in phonetic height. If so, a way to account for the absence of merger is to say that the two contrasting long mid vowels differed phonemically in laxness and/or in height. From what was said before about the systematic difference between the (regularly tense) source of falling diphthongs and the (regularly lax) source of rising diphthongs, we must conclude that a difference in phonological laxness is necessary. It is precisely the reflexes of the originally (lax) nonlong vowels (not the continuously long ones) that diphthongize in Western Romance, and the resulting diphthongs are rising ones (in contrast with the falling diphthongs that emerge later in French, which are the reflexes of tense long vowels, as are the falling diphthongs of Germanic, including sixteenth-century English).[14] The only remaining question is whether phonological laxness is sufficient.[15]

Some non-Romance evidence that is directly observable today may be of help at this point. It is generally recognized that for many speakers English /æ/, a tense low vowel, is raised before nasals, the resulting segment having approximately the height of /E/, not /e/; however, like /e/, it is phonetically tense. Phoneticians often point out that the two 'mid front' vowels of English, the lax vowel of *met* and the tense vowel of *mate*,

239

differ in tongue height. In view of the contrast between tense /e/ and the raised reflex of /æ/, Kahn (1976: 126) added that 'even among [+tense] vowels there appear to be two heights distinguished within the "mid" range'. In any case, it seems reasonable to see the tense long mid vowel of early Romance as the analogue of English tense /e/ and the new Romance lax long vowel as not unlike the raised reflex of /æ/.

Is it possible to construct an argument in favor of a height distinction between mid vowels for early Romance? It does not appear to be the case. If the analysis presented so far is essentially correct, in Proto-Western Romance there is only one front mid vowel that is tense, namely /e/, and only one front mid vowel that is lax, namely /E/. The two vowels can therefore be distinguished as tense and lax counterparts of the same height. It is true that they can also be distinguished as higher and lower mid vowels, but the height distinction does not account for the rising Romance diphthongization. Since, at least as a first approximation, we need the phonological feature [tense] or an equivalent feature, by Occam's razor we retain this feature and leave out the (dispensable) height distinction.[16] We therefore conclude that the new Romance long vowels differed from the old long vowels both in laxness and in height, and that at least the difference in laxness came to be a phonological one. A more interesting proposal would be to show that in this case laxness is simply the phonetic interpretation of the fact that a 'lax' long vowel of the class under consideration is linked to a VV sequence, while the typical 'tense' long vowel (in particular, a long vowel resulting from 'compensatory lengthening' of the usual kind) must be a VC unit in the CV skeleton (cf. n. 17). That topic, however, is beyond the scope of this paper.

An important clue to the chronology of the laxing process, in particular the one that laxes short *e*, is provided by the evolution of the Latin diphthong *æ*, most of whose reflexes merge in Romance with those of short *e*. A few, however, do not, or do so only in Italian. Thus, from Latin *faenum, saepe*, we get Italian *fieno, siepe*, but Spanish *heno*, and French *foin, soif* (like *moi, toi* from *me:, te:*). The spelling *ae* began to replace *ai* (the spelling of our earliest documents) about 200 BC, and became usual before 100 BC. According to Sturtevant (1940: 124, 126), 'the orthography *ae* must reflect merely a more open pronunciation of the second member of the diphthong: the earlier *ai* stood for a diphthong ending in a close *i*, as in It. *mai*, while the later *ae* denoted a diphthong ending in a more open sound approaching a close *e*, somewhat as in Eng. *my* or German *mein*'. Two Latin authors (Lucilius and Varro) refer to a 'rural' pronunciation of *praetor* as *pretor*, and there appears to be epigraphic evidence that other Italic dialects had monophthongized inherited /ai/ to /e:/. 'Apparently this type of monophthongization spread at an early date over nearly all Central Italy west of the Appennines, except for the region of the lower Tiber' (Sturtevant 1940: 125–6), and it has been suggested that the few words that show the same result as inherited long *e* in most Romance languages might have been introduced into standard Latin by country people.

However, it is a fact that in most cases *ae* merged with short *e* (e.g., *aequus* 'equal' came to be pronounced like *equus* 'horse'). It is then highly plausible that *ae* evolved only into [E:], that is, a monophthong that was both long and lax — a segment perhaps differing only slightly from the nucleus of English *man* in the pronunciation of some speakers, as we have just seen. Presumably, this [E:] could merge with the reflexes of short *e* only after this segment became long, or at least after it became phonologically [−tense]. This merger is first attested in Pompeii and in Rome. Pompeiian graffiti, which can be precisely dated (the city was destroyed by the eruption of Mt Vesuvius in AD 79), show a thorough confusion of *ae* and originally short *e*, and so do a few, roughly contemporary, plebeian inscriptions in the city of Rome. In the second century the confusion was widespread. It seems reasonable to assume that the reflexes of *ae* that did not merge with those of originally short *e* merged with the reflexes of long *e* **before** the emergence of E, certainly before the emergence of long E. Since there was no long **lax** segment to associate with the long lax reflex of *ae*, it was presumably associated with tense **long** *e*. If so, there was only one monophthongization of *ae* (*contra* Sturtevant 1940: 128), but the resulting [E:] could at first be associated only with long *e*, presumably because short *e* had not yet become [E:], or at least [E].

If these speculations are on the right track, they suffice to undermine the basis for any 'structuralist' interpretation (cf. n. 1) which assumes that the monophthongization of *ae* was more or less directly responsible, as a sort of subversive agent, for the shift from quantity to quality that brought about the fall of Rome's vowel system.

3.3. Delengthening

There is some evidence that the loss of the length distinction in unstressed vowels was not uncommon, particularly in final syllables (cf. Schane 1983). In fact, in some environments it occurred long before the loss of phonemic length. Thus, 'long vowels were regularly shortened before final *m*, *t*, *nt*..., and, except in monosyllables, before final *r* and *l*'. Also, 'long vowels were generally shortened before another vowel'. And, as we will see in the Appendix, 'there was a marked tendency in colloquial speech, as reflected in early poetry, to shorten the final syllable, especially a final long vowel, in iambic words' (Buck 1933: 95–6).

4. A NEW PROPOSAL

We are now ready to characterize the Proto-Romance vowel systems more precisely. We will begin by focusing on Proto-Rumanian because its development is the most transparent of the three, and it offers what seems to be the crucial clue to the solution. But first some general considerations are in order.

4.1. Stress and gemination

The framework assumed here is that of generative phonology enriched with the autosegmental representations introduced in recent work (cf. Clements and Keyser 1983, Halle and Clements 1983, Steriade 1982, Hayes 1984). However, for the purposes of this paper only a small part of this framework is relevant, namely, the part that has to do with the representation of length and gemination (cf. McCarthy 1979a, 1981b; Leben 1980; Stemberger 1984; Harris 1984). Essentially we need to be able to contrast, on the one hand, nonlong and long vowels and, on the other, long vowels (monosegmental or bisegmental) and sequences of two adjacent heterosyllabic nonconsonants. To accomplish this it is necessary to distinguish at least two tiers in the representation (see McCarthy 1981b): the generally assumed tier of segments, which will be referred to as the segmental tier, and a more abstract tier formed of C or V slots, which will be referred to as the CV tier or CV skeleton (cf. (4) above). To allow for representations that make a four-way distinction we need to assume (1) that nonlong vowels occupy a single segmental position in the segmental tier, while long vowels may occupy one (unmarked case — see Hayes 1984) or two (marked case); and (2) that both long vowels and tautosyllabic or heterosyllabic sequences of two vowels are linked to two slots in the CV skeleton (except that a long vowel or a tautosyllabic pair of vowels is associated with only one rime, while adjacent heterosyllabic vowels are associated each with a different rime. If we further assume that in the appropriate autosegmental representation a lax long vowel is associated with a VV skeleton, while a tense long vowel is associated with a VC skeleton (see section 3.2), we have the following contrasting representations (x = an arbitrary vowel):[17]

(9) a. Nonlong b. Lax Long c. Geminate d. Heterosyllabic vowels

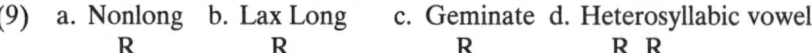
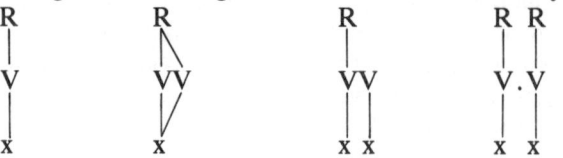

Long vowels (b) are then monosegmental (like nonlong vowels) and binonconsonantal (like vowel clusters), while geminates (c) and heterosyllabic sequences (d) are both bisegmental and binonconsonantal; the difference

between the latter two is that they are associated with one and two rimes, respectively. A linear model cannot differentiate between (9b) and (9c), or between (9c) and (9d). An example of (9d) is Spanish *prove.er, prove.en* ('to provide', 'they provide'). Examples of the other three cases are the partial underlying representations given in (10):

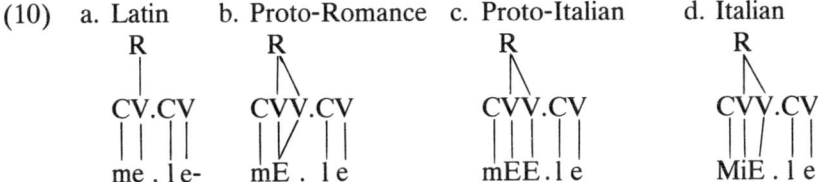

The changes from (10a) to (10b) and from (10b) to (10c) are both presumably due to the intensity of the Latin/Romance stress, as suggested above. Thus, the diphthongizing vowels are represented underlyingly, first (10b) as a single segment linked to two V positions dominated by a single rime (an unmarked structure), later (10c) by two identical segments analogously linked to two V positions and a single rime (a marked structure), and finally (10d) by the same structure with a glide in place of the first of the two identical segments (diphthongization). This final step may be formulated as a rule that states that if a rime associated with a VV skeleton contains two lax vocalic segments, the first must be high.[18] It is reasonable to attribute these changes to the dynamics of a particularly intensive stress: Since 'the tendency towards lengthening is the most obvious feature observed as a physiological correlate to stress' (Fant 1957: 43), it is natural for a strongly stressed vowel to become phonetically long, and for a strongly stressed long vowel to become extralong: extralength encourages diphthongization. Our main topic, however, is not diphthongization (cf. Romeo 1968, Spore 1972), but rather the changes that paved the way for diphthongization.

4.2. The emergence of the Rumanian prototype

The claim that must now be made explicit is that the S6 prototype underwent two diachronic processes: laxing and lengthening. To derive the appropriate phonetic reflexes from the underlying representations postulated for the pre-Romance vowel system, the following two low-level rules must be added to the grammar of the adult speakers (the first, a quality rule, is expressed on the segmental tier: the second, a quantity rule, on the CV tier):[19]

FROM LATIN TO ROMANCE

(11) (i) Laxing
   a. Informally:
   e* --------► E*   *=stressed
   b. Formally:

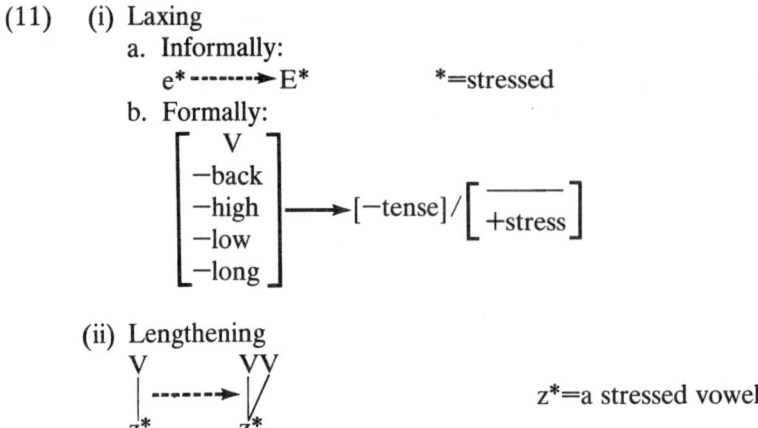

   (ii) Lengthening

   V   VV
   |------►|/   z*=a stressed vowel
   z*   z*

After diphthongization, we get *fir, negru, stele, miele, nou, nod, lut, luna*, from Latin *fi:lu-, nigru-, stellae, mele-, novu-, no:du-, lutu-, lu:na-* (see Meyer-Lübke, ss.vv-; Lausberg 1963).

It is usually assumed that at least one additional rule is needed to lower nonlong *i* to *e*. One of my basic claims is that this rule is not necessary. To understand this, all we need to do is to place the diachronic changes in the perspective of language acquisition. As we all know or should know by now, 'when children learn their mother tongue, they are exposed not to its grammar directly but rather to the output of this grammar as it is actualized in the utterances of the parents, and it is on the basis of these utterances that children construct the grammar of the language' (Chomsky and Halle 1968: 251). It is a fact known from the beginning of the century that the highest point of the tongue arch in the lax short vowel [I] is sometimes lower than in the tense vowel [e] (see Ladefoged *et al.* 1972, and Halle 1983 referring to Wood 1982; cf. Lindau 1978: 543-4). For the Latin speakers with a phonemic length distinction, (lax) short *i* and (tense) long *i* belonged together, regardless of their phonetic implementation (as they usually do for speakers of languages with phonemic length contrasts), because certain phonological rules of their mental grammar grouped them together (cf. Halle 1983).[20] But the grammar constructed by their children was quite different in this respect from the grammar of the adults. Once length became a concomitant of stress (see (11ii)), the reference to a branching rime was still crucial for the operation of the stress rule (2); there was, however, no place for phonemic length, or for any phonological rule that referred to phonemic length, in the grammar of the child. Not having internalized this part of the mental phonology of their parents, all the children had to guide them was the phonetic facts they directly observed in the output of the adults, so the auditory quality of the vowel became the only relevant cue in the primary data.

Consider now the distribution of the available acoustic space for each of the front vowels in a system such as that of S6, exemplified in the earliest Rumanian. Even though 'at this stage in our study of language, we have a somewhat better grasp of the issues in the articulatory domain than in that of speech perception and processing' (Halle 1983: 96), since the position in the available acoustic space of a particular vowel in a particular language depends, among other factors, on the number of vowels in the system (see Lindau and Ladefoged 1984), it is reasonable to assume that the new long vowel E took over some of the space formerly appropriated by old long *e*, which as a result came plausibly to be pronounced as a sort of higher mid vowel.[21] It is therefore highly likely that nonlong *i* was articulated at a point that was closer to long *e* than to long *i*. Since in a situation like this lax vowels are acoustically quite similar to tense vowels one step down, it is reasonable to assume that for the child lax (short) *i* sounded more like tense *e* than like the reflex of inherited tense (long) *i*, and as a result lax *i* and tense *e* merged as an automatic consequence of general phonetic properties, a fact that need not be expressed in the phonological part of the child's grammar. On the other hand, there was no O in S6, so the articulation of nonlong *u* was plausibly closer to long *u* than to *o*. It is often the case that 'when a language does not have to distinguish between two possibilities, it produces a sound that is between the two' (Ladefoged 1982: 209). It is then reasonable to assume that the Rumanian child identified nonlong *u* with long *u*.

4.3. The emergence of the Galegan prototype

In contrast, Western Romance developed both E and O, so that in the process of internalizing the representation of the earliest Italian or Western Romance vowels the child was confronted with a situation that was parallel to the one she/he faced with respect to the front vowels. In other words, once Laxing was effected, the symmetry or asymmetry of the vowel system was an automatic consequence of the articulatory properties of the vowels as they appeared in the output of the adults. Again, the fact that in the asymmetric system nonlong *u* merges with the reflex of Latin long *u*, while in the symmetric seven-vowel system it merges with the reflex of Latin long *o*, is not something to be expressed in the phonological part of the grammar at all; rather, it is an automatic consequence of general phonetic properties. This is then a clear case in which a phonetic fact finds no place in the phonology internalized by the children.[22]

We therefore assume that the immediate ancestor of Western Romance added two low-level rules to its grammar. The first one is a more general form of (11i) in which /e*,o*/ and /E*,O*/ are substituted for /e*/ and

/E*/, respectively, in (a), and [−back] is eliminated from (b).²³ The second is identical to (11ii). After diphthongization, we get Italian *filo, pelo, catena, miele, nuovo, nodo, loto, luna,* from Latin *fi:lu-, pilu-, cate:na-, mele-, novu-, no:du-, lutu-, lu:na-.*

4.4. The emergence of the Sardinian prototype

What of S5? In this case we have no evidence from the early processes of diphthongization, which occurred only in S6/S7. This does not mean that there is no evidence of what transpired, however. To begin with, the three systems emerged side by side in Southern Italy, and chances are that they developed concurrently. The two decisive processes might have appeared almost simultaneously (in diachronic terms), since Laxing did not have enough time to generalize in S6, and S5 completely escaped its effects. S5 does not differ from the other two prototypes with respect to these two crucial facts:

1. phonemic length is lost;
2. this loss has no known systematic consequences for the position of the stress; in particular, the words with an originally long vowel in the penult position continued to be stressed on the same syllable (see section 1).

Given these two facts, plus the fact that there is no reason to assume that the (Neo-) Latin Stress Rule did not survive the loss of phonemic length (cf. section 2.1), it is highly plausible that in all three systems the penultimate syllables that had originally had long vowels continued to have branching rimes after phonemic length distinctions had disappeared from the evolving grammar. To account for this we need only posit that the Lengthening Rule (11ii) was also part of S5. Where S5 differs from S6/S7 is in that the Laxing Rule (11i) is not part of its history at all. Everything else is the same, contrary to what is generally assumed.²⁴ (We have *filu, pilu, kadena, mele, nou, nodu, lutu, luna,* from Latin *fi:lu-, pilu-, cate:na-, mele-, novu-, no:du-, lutu-, lu:na-.*) A consequence of this analysis is that, in a technical sense, the vowel system of Proto-Sardinian was essentially identical to that of classical Latin: it continued to have five nonlong vowels and five 'long' ones (i.e. five vowels associated with two positions in the CV skeleton). What was entirely different was the new distribution of the five pairs of vowels: no nonlong vowel was stressed, and no 'long' vowel was unstressed. This being the case, there was no longer a possibility of contrasts such as those in (1). Distinctive phonemic length had become a thing of the past.²⁵

APPENDIX

Latin stress and syllabification

In a standard periodization of the history of Latin (Duff 1960: Ch. 3), the period of the earliest Latin (usually treated as pre-literary) begins about 500 BC, and is mainly represented by inscriptions and by legal and ritual remains. The first phase of the literary period begins a quarter of a millennium later, starting with the early Epic (in particular, Ennius, 239–169 BC) and the early Comedy (Plautus, c. 254–184, and Terence, c. 195–159). Literary Latin attains its 'Golden Age' at the end of the Republic and the beginning of the Empire, including the immediately pre-Augustan as well as Augustan oratory and poetry, which reach their greatest height at the hands of Cicero (106–43 BC) and Virgil (70–19 BC), respectively. The third phase or 'Silver Age' begins roughly with the Christian Era, including the writers of the early Empire, among them Petronius, in whose work we find some of the available testimony on the contemporary vernacular or 'Vulgar Latin'. The fourth and final phase ('Late Latin'), represented mainly by Christian writers, begins towards the end of the second century AD.

As Sturtevant (1940: 176) writes, 'the history of Latin is characterized by a considerable amount of loss of short vowels', and 'such loss of vowels is known to occur in the unaccented syllables in languages that have a strong stress accent, and it is not known to occur under any other circumstances'.

From weakening to syncope

There is general agreement that in prehistoric times Latin had a 'stress accent', and that primary stress was invariably assigned to the initial syllable of the word. Here is a small sample of relevant data (* stands for unattested):

(12) (i) Weakening
　　　a. Open syllables
　　　　　difficilis ($<$ *dis-facilis)　　debere ($<$ *de-habere)
　　　　　occido ($<$ *ob-cado)　　　　inci:do ($<$ *in-caedo)
　　　　　afficio ($<$ *ad-facio)　　　　conclu:do
　　　　　　　　　　　　　　　　　　　　($<$ *con-claudo)
　　　　　colligo ($<$ *con-lego)　　　exigo ($<$ *ex-ago)
　　　b. Closed syllable
　　　　　incestus ($<$ *in-castus)　　accentus ($<$ *ad-cantus)
　　　　　ineptus ($<$ *in-aptus)　　　inermis ($<$ *in-armis)

         biennis (< *bi-annus)   condemno
                                      (< *con-damno)
         confectus (< *con-factos)   affectus (< *ad-factos)
  (ii) Early syncope
         aetas (< *aevitas)   iu:nior (< *iuvenior)
         novitas (< *novotas)   pergo (< perrego)
         no:nus (< *novenos)   nuntio (< *noventio:)
  (iii) Both weakening and early syncope
         undecim 'eleven' (< unodecem < *oino-decem)
         quindecim 'fifteen' (< quinquedecem)
         auceps (< *avicaps)
         princeps 'prince' (< *primo-caps)
         officina (< *opifacina — cf. opifex)

Notice that the diachronic relation between the two members of each of these pairs shows that every one of the words outside the parentheses was stressed on the first syllable at an earlier time: most of the words exhibited would not have been assigned stress on the initial syllable by rule (3).

This initial stress is therefore in sharp contrast with the system of classical Latin, which is essentially found already in the works of Plautus, although with some interesting exceptions.[26] It has been argued, however, that the nature of the Latin accent has not changed since prehistoric times.[27] The following quotation is illustrative:

> In languages with a stress accent, like English, an unaccented short vowel is often suppressed. So in NE *chapter* from *chapiter*, *captain* from *capitain*, colloquial and poetic *ev'ry* beside more formal *every*, *gen'ral* beside *general*, and countless others. Such syncope of short vowels is unknown in ancient Greek with its pitch accent [NB-C.O.], but is very common in Latin (Buck 1933: 98–9; cf. Palmer 1961: 211–14, Allen 1978: Ch. 5).

There is persuasive and abundant evidence in support of the idea that the Latin accent was quite strong at every period of its history. To begin with, the interrelated phenomena of vowel weakening and syncope just illustrated were widespread and continuously found in all periods of Latin (and early Romance). It is well known that the weakening and loss of vowels in unaccented syllables correlates with a strong stress accent in many languages (cf., for example, English *had* with Gothic *habaida*). The following are examples from a much later period, when the (classical) Stress Rule (3) was already part of Latin phonology (cf. Väänänen 1982: II.A.4):

(13) tabla/tabula   fabla/fabula
      valde:/valide: caldus/calidus
      donna/domina   balneum/balineum
      calfacere/calefacere maldicere/maledicere
      oclus/oculus   articlus/articulus
      infra/inferus   raucus/ravis

Another type of evidence found in the classical and post-classical period is the loss of syllabicity of a front vowel when followed by a back vowel, resulting in rime mergers such as the following (the symbol '.' stands for syllable boundary):

(14) bal.ne.o   > bal.ni.o > bal.n̯i̯o
      mo.ne.o: > mo.ni.o   > mo.n̯i̯o
      ca:.se.o   > ca:.si.o > ca:.si̯o
      a.le.a   > a.li.a   > a.li̯a
      va.le.at   > va.li.a   > va.li̯a

Thus, weakening and syncope, commonly found as a concomitant of a strong stress accent, appear to have occurred in all periods of the history of the language.

Also suggestive is the phenomenon of so-called 'iambic shortening' (*brevis brevians*), which delengthens a vowel if it is preceded by a nonlong one (e.g. *modo, cito, ego, mihi, bene, male, duo*, from *modo:, cito:, ego:*, etc., whereas *ambo:, longe:*, etc., with a heavy penult, are not affected). In colloquial speech the tendency to delengthen the final syllable was even more common, to judge from imperatives such as *ama, puta*, found in Plautus and his contemporary Terence. In fact, in these authors the reduction in the force of articulation is apparent even in final syllables ending in a diphthong or in a cluster of consonants (see Allen 1978: 82). Also, in words of four syllables or more, there was a secondary stress (e.g. *aedifica:vit, tempesta:tem*). The evidence comes from versification (it counted as a metrical stress) and from consonantal gemination in Italian immediately following the secondary stress (e.g. *scellerato* from *scelera:tum*).

From syncope to resyllabification

It is now widely recognized that in some cases a process of syncope (vowel deletion) is associated with resyllabification, as in

(15) ta.bu.la- > tab.la
      o.ku.lu-   > ok.lV
      e.re.mu-   > er.mV

249

There is evidence that the new syllabification just illustrated persisted for an extensive period of time.[28] Thus, under certain conditions, the consonant segment that was resyllabified in, e.g., *ok.lV*, underwent a process of assimilation in voice to the following sonorant. This suggests that the syllable division is as indicated, since the assimilation rule requires that the cluster undergoing it be heterosyllabic; more precisely, that the two consonants not belong to the same onset.[29] This type of resyllabification seems to be at the root of the difference in stress position within a word between Latin and early Romance referred to in section 1. It is found in two small classes of words. One is a set of the form XKLV## (where K = obstruent and L = liquid), the two clearest examples being those given in (16a) together with their Galegan reflexes; the other class includes words of the form XKV*VLV (where V* = front vowel, stressed before the change, i.e. in the forms of the left-hand column), of which those in (16b) are representative examples:[30]

(16) a. Latin stage   Later stage of (Neo-) Latin
          in.te.gru-   >   in.teg.ru-   (Gg. enteiro)
          ca.the.dra   >   ca.ted.ra   (Gg. cadeira)
      b.
          len.te.o.lus   >   len.tio.lo   (cf. Italian lenzuolo)
          a.vi.o.lus   >   a.vio.lo   (cf. Spanish abuelo)
          ca.pre.o.lus   >   ca.prio.lo   (cf. French chevreuil)

Given this syllabification, both classes of words exemplified in (16) have a branching penult, which is automatically assigned stress by rule (2).

NOTES

It is a real pleasure to be able to offer this study to Robert P. Stockwell, to whom I owe perhaps the most inspiring and determinative experience in my life. A fleeting mention I once overheard, shortly after becoming a member of the UCLA faculty, led me to sit in on one of his graduate classes in generative grammar in the early 60s, and subsequently in several others (including an unforgettable preview of *Aspects of the Theory of Syntax* months before it was published). Although I had already completed doctoral studies in Madrid and in Berkeley, never had I come close to a teaching experience remotely comparable in caliber or intensity. The sheer wonder of the revolutionary new ideas (which, as we know, appear infrequently), the conviction and convincingness with which they were being presented, the overflowing contagious enthusiasm, the generosity with which a seemingly inexhaustible supply of copies of yet-to-be-published papers was being made available simply for the asking — all of that was new, impressive, and fascinating to me. Even more importantly, my long quest for definite signposts towards that twentieth-century reality I, somewhat hazily, envisioned, was at last satisfied; in fact, the proliferating effects still continue. I shudder to think what my life might have been had I not had such an experience. My initially profound debt to the man that made it possible increases with the passage of time.

Thanks are due to Mona Lindau, who most willingly and promptly provided me with several papers, answered a seemingly unending series of questions, and later sent, from afar and without delay, comments on a preliminary draft of this study that led me to carefully reconsider section 3.2, and then to rewrite it anew (I hope the present version is more cogent and persuasive than the earlier one). Bruce Hayes was no less helpful and supportive, providing comments and suggestions at successive points. I am also indebted to James W. Harris for comments on a preliminary draft, to Judith Strozer for comments at various stages, and to Paula Kempchinsky and Susan Plann for a careful reading of the prefinal version.

1. Väänänen 1982: para. 42. For a critique of outstanding 'structuralist' treatments, see Spence 1965 (his proposal is in turn criticized in Klausenburger 1975). The first account within the framework of generative phonology is found in Walker (1971). A quite different account, within a new framework, is given in Schane (1983), which I found very helpful, even though the view presented below differs substantially from Schane's — a consequence, in part, of a somewhat different interpretation of some crucial evidence. (I am indebted to Sanford Schane for a typed copy of the paper and for identifying for me one of his references.)

2. In the first two sections (pp. 13–67) of Otero (1976), actually written in September 1973; an English version of the first section was presented at the First Convocation in Romance Linguistics at the University of California (Berkeley) in the Fall of 1974.

3. The symbol ':' after a vowel is used to indicate that the vowel is long; all other vowels in (1) are nonlong.

4. This statement is intended to bring out the special character of surface penultimate stress in Latin (in contrast with, say, that of Polish, Swahili, or Piro — cf. Hyman 1977: 62; Halle and Clements 1983), a crucial point with nontrivial consequences. In contrast with a syllable of the form CV (the unmarked type of syllable, which is of course 'light'), a syllable of the form CVC or CV: is something special (many languages do not have nonlight syllables). A word of more than two syllables becomes proparoxytonic if the penult loses its heaviness (see Otero 1985).

5. But see now Everett and Everett (1984). See Clements and Keyser (1983), p. 14 n., and Otero 1985 n. 31.

6. See Lausberg (1939); see also Lausberg (1963), Rohlfs (1966). Also found in this region are two other systems (exemplified by Sicilian and one variety of Calabrian), both with a five-vowel pattern, but with a vowel distribution different from that of the Sardinian prototype. There are different views on the reconstruction of their development, but everyone agrees that the two are derivative (cf. Mazzola 1976, Otero 1976: 22–8). Perhaps it should be added here that Strabo (66 BC–AD 21) expressly testifies that by his day the Lucanians had become Romans, that is, they spoke Latin. The Latinization process had begun long before, however. As is well known, the epic poet Quintus Ennius (239–169 BC), who was about five years younger than Plautus, was a Lucanian whose birth at Rudiae, 'an old Calabrian town in touch with Hellenism, made him a "semi-Graecus", to use the phrase of Suetonius' (Duff 1960: 100, 16).

7. The first system, a very simple one, is of course extremely common. The third one, which is not uncommon, is found in many language families (see Otero 1976 and references given there; cf. now Ruhlen 1976, Maddieson 1984). From the perspective of this paper, perhaps the most intriguing seven-vowel system is that of Hill Nubian. It seems to derive historically from a system that was similar or identical to the five-vowel system of Central (or Mahas) Nile Nubian (or Nobíin Nubian), which apparently is identical to that of Latin except that in addition to phonemic length it has two tones, high and low (see Tucker and Bryan 1966: 313–28, Bell 1971).

8. Prior to Lausberg's pioneering research, it was generally thought that this development was limited to Sardinia, but it is also found in an area extending along both sides of the frontier between Lucania (now Basilicata) and Calabria, and reaching the Gulf of Taranto. Now there are also some reasons to suspect that this is an independent phenomenon, rather than the result of immigration from Sardinia (cf. Mazzola 1976: 127ff). The matter is of some interest for us, as we will see in section 4.4 (cf. n. 10).

9. Renaissance Portuguese is a slightly evolved form of Medieval Galegan, but the vocalism of modern Portuguese differs considerably from that of Galegan, and is far less close to that assumed for Western Proto-Romance.

10. It is also found in the region of Lucania (see Mazzola 1976), again a fact of some interest (cf. n. 8).

11. Otero (1976: 5.2); cf. Harris 1984. From our vantage point, the 'alternative theory' favored in Stockwell (1961) may be seen as an early anticipation of current ideas.

12. This is said to be due to the fact that 'under the Frankish influence the intensity of the ... stress was considerably increased'. There is no question that this characteristically French diphthongization (within Romance) is much later than the one in (8), almost general for Western Romance. In French, a diphthongization analogous to that of (8) occurred earlier than a general process of Syncope, while the diphthongization particular to French followed Syncope (see Pope 1952: 100, 106).

13. The idea that, under a strong stress, the originally short vowels were first lengthened, is not new:

Ce qui montre que les voyelles accentuées ont subi par rapport aux autres un allongement, c'est qu'elles ont tendu à se diphtonguer ... On observe le phénomène d'un bout du domaine à l'autre, et il résulte de là que la condition initiale, qui est une durée relativement longue des voyelles accentuées, était amorcée, sinon réalisée, des le "latin vulgaire"' (Meillet 1928: 244).

14. For a contrary view, see Fouché (1926: 212); observe that in each of his examples the tenseness of the source vowel is not beyond question.

15. We are not concerned here with the phonetic implementation of the phonological feature here labeled 'tenseness'; cf. Halle and Clements (1983: 7), Halle (1983), Lindau and Ladefoged (1984), and references cited there.

16. See Schane: 'How are we to express formally the relationship between laxness and lowered height? The standard notation of generative phonology, although it can describe the Latin changes, fails to provide any insight into the mechanism underlying them. This deficiency follows from the current conception of features as independent traits. The notation has no way of showing the interrelationships among length, tensity, and height, the essential parameters in the Vulgar Latin changes.' For some discussion as to whether the pairs of phonemes symbolized here by /e,o/ and /E,O/ are or are not structurally of the same height see, in addition to Kahn (1976), Lopez (1979: 2.1, and references cited there).

17. See Steriade (1982: Ch. 2). In this context we may note that the diphthong in, e.g., Galegan *enteiro, cadeira*, from Latin *in.teg.ru, ca.thed.ra*, is of the same form as that in Old French *mei, tei*, from Latin *me:, te:*.

18. Cf. the Height rule in Harris (1984).

19. It is reasonable to assume that there were no longer any long unstressed vowels in the adults' systems (cf. section 3.3 and Appendix). Alternatively, a rule such as (iii)

(iii) $V \rightarrow [-\text{long}]$

ordered after (11ii), might be proposed (as in, e.g., Otero 1976). It seems, however, that this rule is unnecessary. Since it is not possible to go into this question here, I will assume that after (11ii) is introduced, the children reconstructing the grammar have no reason to set up long vowels other than those generated by (11ii). See below.

20. In the acoustical vowel diagram Lehiste (1970, 31) gives for Czech, a language with a vowel system plausibly not unlike that of Latin, the average position of short *i* is much closer to the average position of /e:/ than to the average position of /i:/.

21. The term 'higher mid' is being used here in a way similar to the way it is used in Maddieson (1984: 204).

22. Cf. Stockwell and Macaulay (1972: ix). This should not be identified with the generally recognized (even by Fouché) phonetic difference between the long and nonlong realizations of a particular vowel (cf., e.g., Sturtevant 1940: 107ff, Straka 1959, Klausenburger 1975), which yields no explanation for either S6 or S5, since presumably the general phonetic difference obtained also in their ancestral forms.

23. 'Here I must agree with those scholars who maintain that the tense/lax opposition began as a gradual change, first affecting the front vowels. In this area of Eastern Romance it never reached the rounded ones' (Schane 1983: cf. Fouché 1926: 230). As repeatedly pointed out, the three systems developed side by side in Southern Italy.

24. Cf. Schane (1983): 'In Sardinian ... a five-vowel system emerged due to the coalescence of original pairs of long and short vowels. Romance scholars point out that this system evolved in a remote region of the Roman empire. This suggests that Sardinia was immune from changes that were occurring elsewhere.' See Fouché (1926: 231).

25. To account for this, Walker (1971: 144) posits these two rules:

(i) Vowel Shift:
$$\begin{bmatrix} V \\ -\text{tense} \\ \langle -\text{high} \rangle \end{bmatrix} \longrightarrow \begin{bmatrix} -\text{high} \\ \langle +\text{low} \rangle \end{bmatrix}$$

(ii) Tenseness Neutralization:
$$\begin{bmatrix} V \\ \alpha \text{ stress} \end{bmatrix} \longrightarrow [\alpha \text{ tense}]$$

If the analysis proposed in this paper is essentially correct, the angle bracket part of rule (i) is inadequate, for the reasons given in section 3.2: the other part is unnecessary (see section 4.2). Rule (ii), which in a way is quite insightful, appears to be, however, totally at odds with the facts, since it is the nontense long mid vowels that diphthongize in several Western Romance dialects, including French, while their tense counterparts diphthongize only in French (see note 12).

Schane assumes that unstressed *i:*, *u:* merged immediately with the reflexes of *e:*, *o:*. There is evidence that this is not the case. For data of a more reliable character than the data discussed by Gulsoy (1969), see Otero (1976: 79).

26. On the possible significance of some of these exceptions, see McCarthy (1979a).

27. It seems worth mentioning that some of the reasons given by those who advanced the idea that classical Latin had a pitch accent obtain also in Arabic, which does not have a pitch accent. (The relevance of Arabic in this respect was brought to my attention by Bruce Hayes.)

28. This brings to mind the double syllabification attested in Golden Age literature, sometimes within a single line of verse, as in line 663 of the second book of

Virgil's *Aeneid*, where we find both *pa.tris* and *pat.rem*.
   gnatum ante ora patris, patrem qui obtruncat ad aras
   'who butchers the son before the father's eyes, the father at the altars'
   29. See the discussion on heterosyllabicity as a possible condition on assimilation rules in Steriade (1982: III.5.6).
   30. Of the class examplified in (16b), Niedermann (1953: 15–16) has this to say: Probablement *i-o* et *i-e* sont devenus d'abord des diphtongues descendantes *io*, *ie*, puis l'élément le plus sonore, qui était le second, attirait l'accent sur lui, d'où les diphtongues ascendentes *io*, *ié*. C'est de cette façon que *io* (du latin *égo*) est devenu *yo* en espagnol.

REFERENCES

Allen, W. Sidney. 1973. *Accent and Rhythm. Prosodic Features of Latin and Greek: A Study in Theory and Reconstruction*. Cambridge: Cambridge University Press.
—— 1978. *Vox Latina: A Guide to the Pronunciation of Classical Latin*. 2nd edn. Cambridge: Cambridge University Press.
Anderson, Stephen R. 1984. 'A Metrical Interpretation of Some Traditional Claims about Quantity and Stress', in Mark Aronoff and Richard Oehrle, with Frances Kelly and Bonnie Wilker Stephens (eds.), *Language and Structure*, Cambridge, Mass.: MIT Press, 83–106.
Bell, Herman. 1971. 'The Phonology of Nobíin Nubian', *African Language Review* 9: 115–39.
Buck, Carl Darling. 1933. *Comparative Grammar of Greek and Latin*. Chicago: University of Chicago Press.
Chomsky, Noam, and M. Halle. 1968. *The Sound Pattern of English*. New York: Harper and Row.
Clements, George N. and Samuel Jay Keyser. 1983. *CV Phonology: A Generative Theory of the Syllable*. Cambridge, Mass.: MIT Press.
Duff, J. Wight. 1960. *A Literary History of Rome: from the Origins to the Close of the Golden Age*. Edited by A.M. Duff. London: Ernest Benn/New York: Barnes and Noble. (First published in 1909.)
Elcock, W.D. 1960. *The Romance Languages*. London: Faber and Faber.
Everett, Dan, and Keren Everett. 1984. 'On the Relevance of Syllable Onsets to Stress Placement', *Linguistic Inquiry* 15: 705–11.
Fant, C.G.M. 1957. *Modern Instruments and Methods for Acoustic Studies of Speech*. Report no. 8 of Speech Transmission Laboratory, Stockholm.
Fouché, Pierre. 1926. 'Questions de vocalisme latin et préroman', *Revue des Langues Romanes* 63: 195–260.
Gulsoy, J. 1969. 'The *-i* Words in the Poems of Gonzalo de Berceo', *Romance Philology* 23: 172–87.
Halle, Morris. 1983. 'On Distinctive Features and Their Articulatory Implementation', *Natural Language and Linguistic Theory* 1: 91–105.
—— and G.N. Clements. 1983. *Problem Book in Phonology*. Cambridge, Mass.: MIT Press.
Harris, James W. 1984. *Spanish Diphthongization and Stress: A Paradox Resolved*. Mimeographed, MIT.
Hayes, Bruce. 1980. *A Metrical Theory of Stress*. MIT dissertation. (Reproduced, with some revision, by the Indiana Linguistics Club, in 1981.)
—— 1982. 'Extrametricality', *Linguistic Inquiry* 13: 227–76.
—— 1984. *Inalterability in CV Phonology*. Mimeographed, UCLA.

Hyman, Larry M. 1977. 'On the Nature of Linguistic Stress', in Larry M. Hyman (ed.), *Studies in Stress and Accent*. Los Angeles: Department of Linguistics, University of Southern California, 37–82.

Kahn, Daniel. 1976. *Syllable-based Generalizations in English Phonology*. MIT dissertation. (Published by Garland, New York/London, 1980.)

Klausenburger, Jurgen. 1975. 'Latin Vocalic Quantity to Quality: a Pseudoproblem?' in Mario Saltarelli and Dieter Wanner (eds.), *Diachronic Studies in Romance Linguistics*. The Hague: Mouton, 107–17.

Ladefoged, Peter. 1971. *Preliminaries to Linguistic Phonetics*. Chicago: University of Chicago Press.

—— 1982. *A Course in Phonetics*. 2nd edn. New York: Harcourt Brace Jovanovich.

—— Joseph DeClerk, Mona Lindau, and George Papcun. 1972. 'An Auditory-motor Theory of Speech Production'. *UCLA Working Papers in Phonetics* 22: 48–94.

Lausberg, Heinrich. 1939. *Die Mundarten Suedlukaniens*. Halle: Max Niemeyer. (ZRPh 90.)

—— 1963. *Romanische Sprachwissenschaft*. Zweite, durgesehene Auflage. Berlin: Walter de Gruyter. (Spanish translation, Madrid: Gredos, 1965.)

Leben, William. 1980. 'A Metrical Analysis of Length', *Linguistic Inquiry* 11: 497–509.

Lehiste, Ilse. 1970. *Suprasegmentals*. Cambridge, Mass.: MIT Press.

Lindau, Mona. 1978. 'Vowel Features', *Language* 54: 541–63.

—— and Peter Ladefoged. 1984. 'Variability of Feature Specifications', in J. Perkell (ed.), *Invariance and Variability in Speech Processes*. (To appear.)

Lopez, Barbara Strodt. 1979. *The Sound Pattern of Brazilian Portuguese (Cariocan Dialect)*. UCLA dissertation.

McCarthy, John J. 1979a. 'On Stress and Syllabification'. *Linguistic Inquiry* 10: 443–65.

—— 1979b. *Formal Properties of Semitic Phonology and Morphology*. MIT dissertation.

—— 1981a. 'The Representation of Length in Hebrew', *Linguistic Inquiry* 12: 322–7.

—— 1981b. 'A Prosodic Theory of Nonconcatenative Morphology', *Linguistic Inquiry* 12: 373–418.

Maddieson, Ian. 1984. *Patterns of Sound. With a Chapter Contributed by Sandra Ferrari Disner*. Cambridge: Cambridge University Press.

Mazzola, Michael L. 1976. *Proto-Romance and Sicilian*. Lisse: Peter de Ridder Press.

Meillet, Antoine. 1928. *Esquisse d'une histoire de la langue latine*. Paris: Hachette. (3rd edn, 1933; 6th edn, 1952; nouvelle edn, 1966.)

Meyer-Lübke, W. 1935. *Romanisches etymologisches Wörterbuch*. Dritte Auflage. Heidelberg: Carl Winter Universitätsverlag, 1968. (Reprinting.)

Niedermann, Max. 1953. *Précis de phonetique historique du latin*. Paris: Klincksieck. (3rd edn., rev. et augm.; 4th edn., 1959.)

Otero, C.P. 1976. *Evolución y revolución en romance, II*. Barcelona: Seix-Barral.

—— 1985. 'A Unified Metrical Theory of Spanish Stress' (written for a volume of studies presented to Sol Saporta).

Palmer, L.R. 1961. *The Latin Language*. 3rd impression (with corrections). London: Faber and Faber.

Pope, M.K. 1952. *From Latin to Modern French with Special Consideration of Anglo-Norman. Phonology and Morphology*. Rev. edn. London: Butler and Tanner. (Reprinted by Manchester University Press, 1966.)

255

Pulgram, E. 1975. *Latin-Romance Phonology: Prosodics and Metrics.* Muenchen: Wilhelm Fink Verlag.
Rohlfs, Gerhard. 1966. *Grammatica storica della lingua italiana e dei suoi dialetti. Fonetica.* Torino: Giulio Einaudi.
Romeo, Luigi. 1968. *The Economy of Diphthongization in Early Romance.* The Hague: Mouton.
Ruhlen, Merrit. 1976. *A Guide to the Languages of the World.* Language Universals Project. Stanford University.
Schane, Sanford. 1983. 'Some Observations on the Evolution of the Vulgar Latin Vowels'. Paper presented at UCLA in mid July.
Spence, N.C.W. 1965. 'Quantity and Quality in the Vowel System of Vulgar Latin', *Word* 21: 1-18. Reprinted in James M. Anderson and Jo Ann Creore (eds.), *Readings in Romance Linguistics.* The Hague: Mouton, 1972.
Spore, Palle. 1972. *La diphthongaison romane.* Odense: Odense University Press.
Stemberger, Joseph Paul. 1984. 'Length as a Suprasegmental', *Language* 60: 895-913.
Steriade, Donca. 1982. *Greek Prosodies and the Nature of Syllabification.* MIT dissertation.
Stockwell, Robert P. 1961. 'The Middle English "Long Close" and "Long Open" Mid Vowels', *Texas Studies in Literature and Language* 2: 529-38.
—— and R.K.S. Macaulay (eds.) 1972. *Linguistic Change and Generative Theory.* Bloomington: Indiana University Press.
Straka, Georges. 1959. 'Durée et timbre vocaliques. Observations de phonétique générale, appliquées à la phonétique historique des langues romanes', *Zeitschrift für Phonetik und algemeine Sprachwissenschaft* 12: 276-300.
Sturtevant, Edgar H. 1940. *The Pronunciation of Greek and Latin.* 2nd edn. Philadelphia: Linguistic Society of America.
Tucker, A.N., and M.A. Bryan. 1966. *Linguistic Analyses: The Non-Bantu Languages of North-eastern Africa.* Oxford: Oxford University Press.
Väänänen, Veikko. 1982. *Introduzione al latino volgare.* A cura di Alberto Limentani. Traduzione di A. Grandesso Silvestri. 3a. edn. italiana. Bologna: Patron Editore. (Originally published in 1963 in French.)
Walker, Douglas Charles. 1971. *Old French Phonology and Morphology.* University of California, San Diego, dissertation.
Wood, S. 1982. *X-ray Model Studies of Vowel Articulation.* Working Paper 23, Lund University, Department of Linguistics.
Zirin, Ronald A. 1970. *The Phonological Basis of Latin Prosody.* The Hague: Mouton.

20

The Rule Dependence of Syllable Structure

THEO VENNEMANN

The goal of this paper is to point out some problems inherent in current views of syllable structure and to suggest ways in which these problems may be solved.

I would like to begin by sketching a few positions of the sort that can be or have been taken concerning the internal organization of syllables. The minimal assumption is that any syllable merely comprises a sequence of speech sounds and nothing else. The resulting structure may be called LINEAR; graphically it would appear as in (1a) or (1b).

(1) Linear structure for syllables

It does not matter for this discussion whether such sequences are believed to be generally definable as subsequences of longer sequences by language specific or universal rules (a belief which I consider mistaken) or whether they are introduced axiomatically, according to the belief that syllable structure, even at this simple level, may be contrastive. (The analogous neutrality will be maintained also in what follows.)

A more complex assumption views the syllable as a pair consisting of a sequence of speech sounds, the SYLLABLE BASE, and an index, the NUCLEUS MARKER, distinguishing a subsequence of the syllable base, the NUCLEUS, from the rest of the base. A special version of it assumes the nuclear subsequence always to contain at most one speech sound (Vennemann 1982). Further differences may arise from the answers to the question whether the nucleus may be empty, as Hockett (1955: 57) assumes, or not, which is the more traditional assumption. In any event, the resulting structures may uniformly be represented as in (2a), and since with

257

THE RULE DEPENDENCE OF SYLLABLE STRUCTURE

a given base and nucleus marker one may define ONSET and OFFSET in a straightforward way, it may also be graphically represented as in (2b), a representation which covers a variety of traditional and contemporary views. This type of structure may be called FLAT.

(2) Flat structure for syllables

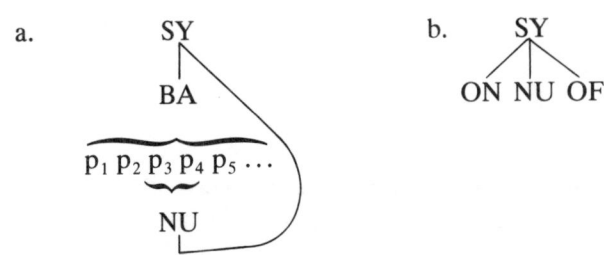

In a description with phrase structure rules, flat structure may be generated by a single rule, viz. (3a) or (3b).

(3) Flat structure rules

    a.   SY → (ON) NU (OF)

    b.   SY → $\begin{cases} \text{(ON) NU (OF)} \\ \text{ON (OF)} \end{cases}$

On the basis of flat structure it is easy to define additional concepts and to express relationships among them and the original ones, as in (4).

(4) a. RHYME   RY $=_{def}$ NU ∪ OF
    b. BODY   BO $=_{def}$ ON ∪ NU
    c. SHELL   SH $=_{def}$ ON ∪ OF
    d. Base   BA =   ON ∪ RY
    e.   =   BO ∪ OF
    f.   =   SH ∪ NU
    g.   =   ON ∪ NU ∪ OF
    h. Nucleus NU =   BA − SH
    i.   =   RY − OF
    j.   =   BO − ON

The relationships (4a–f) may be represented graphically as in (5).

(5) a. b. c.

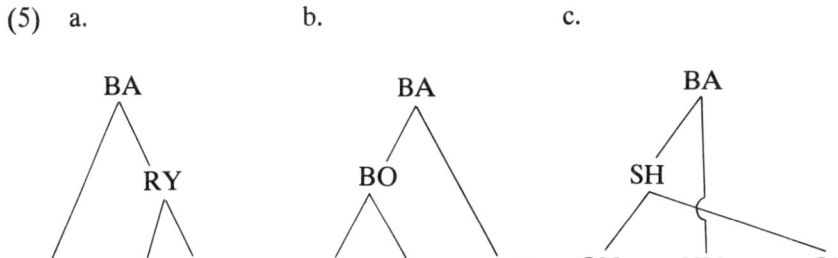

The subgraphs, read from bottom to top, here represent set-theoretical union. It is also possible, however, in the case of (5a) and (5b) to consider phrase structure analogs and thus to assume that the syllable consists not of a base and a portion marked off as nuclear but, e.g., of an onset and a rhyme, the latter in turn consisting of a nucleus and an offset, each in the order given. Viewed in this way, the syllable assumes HIERARCHICAL STRUCTURE, viz. RHYME STRUCTURE or BODY STRUCTURE depending on how the three basic constituents — onset, nucleus, and offset — are grouped in the phrase structure, cf. (6).

(6) Hierarchical structure for syllables

a. Rhyme structure   b. Body structure

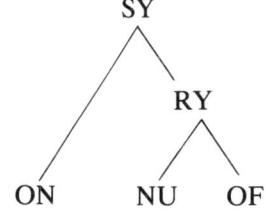
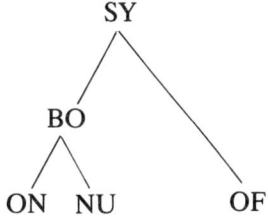

The phrase structure description of hierarchical structure, as opposed to that of flat structure, requires two phrase structure rules rather than one, cf. (7).

(7) Hierarchical structure rules

    a. Rhyme structure rules

        1. SY → (ON) RY
        2. RY → NU (OF)

b. Body structure rules

1, SY → BO (OF)
2. BO → (ON) NU

Donegan and Stampe (1978: 30) assume a structure for syllables that combines the two hierarchies 6a and 6b.

> Let us regard syllables as having two 'slopes', one (the 'rise') including everything up through the syllabic, and the other (the 'fall') including the syllabic and everything which follows it. For example, the rise and fall of [klɑ̯ɒnz] are [klɑ] and [ɑ̯ɒnz], respectively. The reason for including the syllabic in both slopes is simply that the principles governing both slopes include the syllabic.

See diagram (6c).

(6) c.
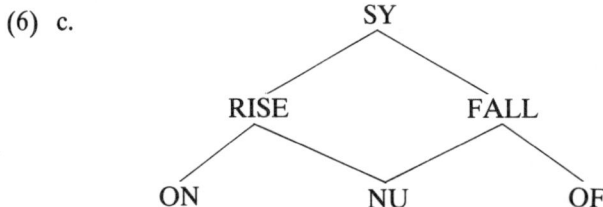

The authors warn against attributing too much importance to these divisions. 'We remark here that there is little to recommend any particular internal analysis of syllables: virtually any linear breakdown of a syllable can be found in the evidence of alliteration, rhyme, secret languages, singing Yankee Doodle, etc.' (30). This anticipates some of the discussion that follows, though the conclusions will turn out to be quite different.

Rhyme structure is extremely popular. Some representatives are Pike and Pike (1947), Kuryłowicz (1948), and, more recently, Selkirk (1982), Cairns and Feinstein (1982), Kiparsky (1979, 1981). There exist among these proposals considerable differences of detail. For example, Cairns and Feinstein introduce rhyme structure by means of rules of the sort (7a), while Kiparsky can define rhyme structure on the basis of a metrical tree of weak and strong positions within the syllable, cf. (8).

(8)
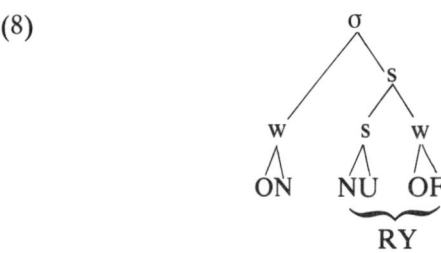

THE RULE DEPENDENCE OF SYLLABLE STRUCTURE

For example, the one syllable of the English word *flounce* receives the metrical representation (9a) (cf. Selkirk 1982: 343).

(9) a.

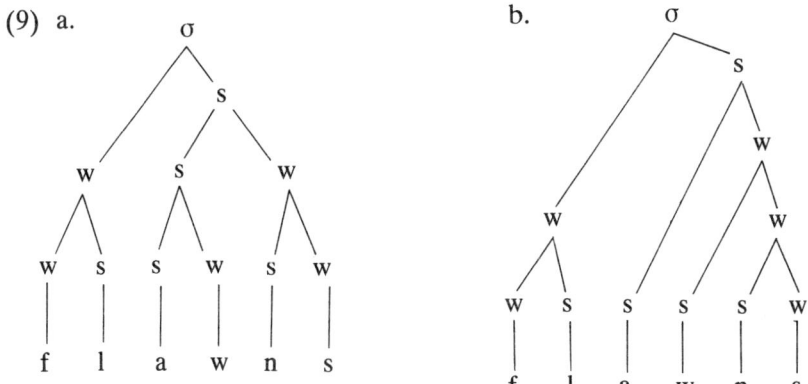

b.

In Kiparsky's own system the example would be represented differently, viz. with a more direct reflection of the 'prominence profile of the syllable' (Kiparsky 1981: 250), cf. (9b). Rhyme structure may be recognized by comparing (9) with (8). But such differences will here be ignored, as pointed out earlier, because what matters is that either approach imposes hierarchical structure of the sort (6a), viz. binary branching structure such that the nuclear segments are contained in the top right branch.

Both the flat structure views and the hierarchical structure views may be adjusted to the idea that the nucleus is itself not linear but has flat or hierarchical structure. E.g., one may consider a triphthong such as /iau/ a flat structure consisting of a PEAK and two SATELLITES, viz. an ONGLIDING SATELLITE and an OFFGLIDING SATELLITE (ONGLIDE and OFFGLIDE for short), cf. (10).

(10) Flat structure for nuclei

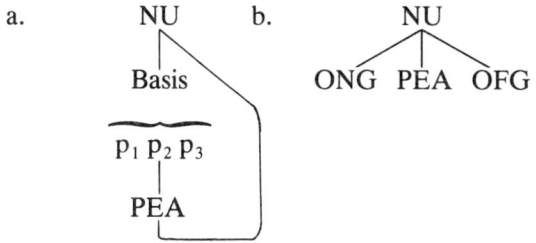

(11) Phrase structure rule for flat structure for nuclei

NU → (ONG) PEA (OFG)

THE RULE DEPENDENCE OF SYLLABLE STRUCTURE

But one may also consider such a triphthong a hierarchical structure, viz. right-branching (ASSONANCE STRUCTURE) or left-branching (HEART STRUCTURE) on the analogy of (6a) and (6b), as in (12).

(12) Hierarchical structure for nuclei

    a. Assonance structure   b. Heart structure

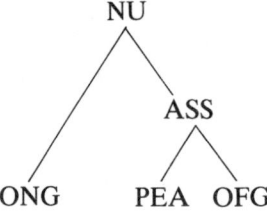 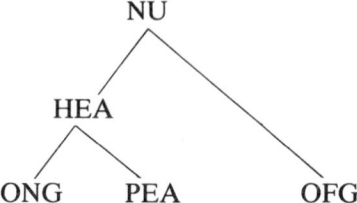

(13) Phrase structure rules for hierarchical structure for nuclei

    a. Assonance structure rules

        NU → (ONG) ASS
        ASS → PEA (OFG)

    b. Heart structure rules

        NU → HEA (OFG)
        HEA → (ONG) PEA

A version of the phrase structure approach to complex nuclei (but only expressing the flat structure view) is contained in Cairns and Feinstein (1982). The metrical approach to syllable structure easily permits complex nuclei. If triphthongs are admitted — and this can easily be avoided in any theory, e.g. by considering satellites as parts of the shell — then this approach necessarily imposes hierarchical structure, cf. (14).

(14) a.   b.

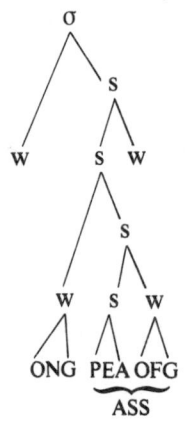 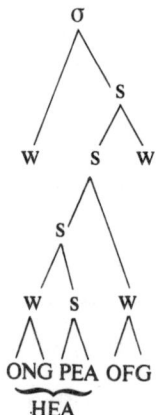

THE RULE DEPENDENCE OF SYLLABLE STRUCTURE

Since in Kiparsky (1979, 1981) only right-branching, i.e. rhyme structure, is admitted at the syllable level, I would expect that only a single kind of branching would be admitted at the nucleus level as well, and I feel that the option taken would again be right-branching, i.e. assonance structure as in (14a). Thus, a triphthong /iau/ would likely be represented as in (15).

(15)

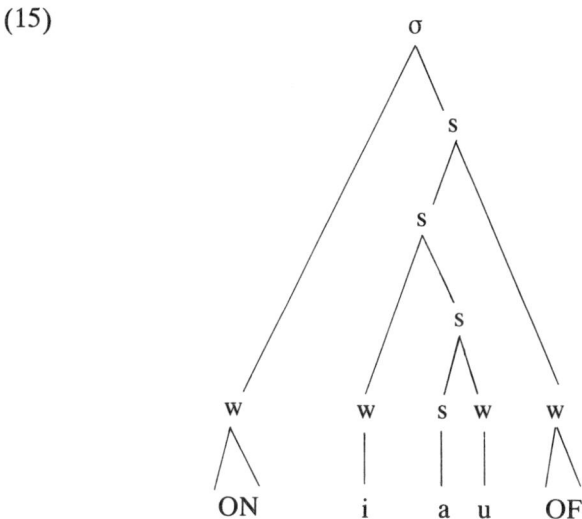

Arguments for and against the assumption of some particular internal syllable structure — usually for rhyme structure — have been presented by a great many authors. Those in favor of rhyme structure have been conveniently classified in Davis (1982). Davis distinguishes four sorts of evidence:

(16) a. 'The existence of phonotactic constraints between peak and coda' (i.e., between nucleus and offset, in the terminology used here);

b. 'Reference to the rhyme in stress assignment';

c. 'Mention of the rhyme in other language specific rules';

d. 'The existence of a durational relationship between peak and coda' (i.e. between nucleus and offset).

One may also mention the use of rimes in the poetic use of many languages; rimes may, of course, be defined in a straightforward way by reference to rhyme structure, which is indeed the very basis for this piece of terminology.

With regard to (16a), Davis correctly points out that evidence from phonotactic constraints may also be produced in favor of body structure and even in favor of shell structure. (I take the liberty of freely using my own terminology even where it differs from that of cited authors.) For example, in Mazatec, nasalized vowels may not be preceded by (clusters containing) /vylrmnñ/. This clearly is a constraint on the structure of syllable bodies rather than rhymes. And in English, syllables may not take the shape *(s)ClVl* or *CN'VN"* (*C*: any consonant; *V*: any vowel; *N'*, *N"*: any two nasals). This clearly is a constraint on the structure of syllable shells, rather than on either rhymes or bodies.

As for (16b), it is undoubtedly the case that stress rules are usually sensitive only to rhymes. For example, in English adjectives such as *anecdótal, dialéctal* vs. *díffident, lúdicrous*, heavy penults — penults heavy by the complexity of their rhymes — arrest the accent, whereas light penults let it pass to the antepenult; that body structure is immaterial here is shown by pairs such as *cataclýsmic* vs. *cýclical* with penultimate onsets of identical complexity. The equally well known stress rule for Early Latin polysyllables likewise puts the accent on the penult if it is heavy, otherwise on the antepenult.

(17) a.má.tus   mo.lés.tus   dó.mi.nus   ín.te.grum

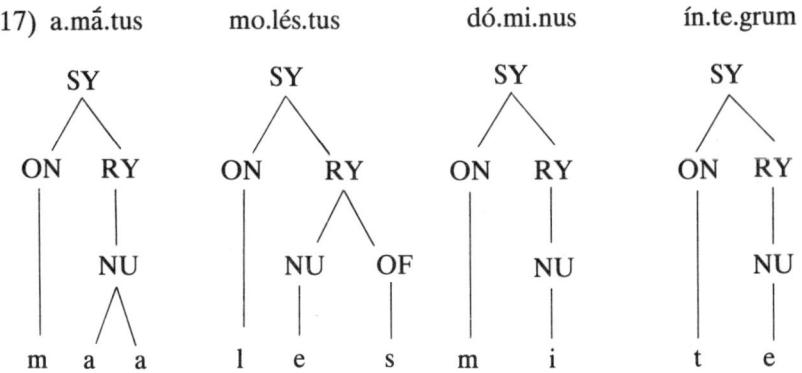

Conversely, whereas in Latin a light penult syllable cannot be stressed, in Icelandic a stressed syllable cannot be light; more precisely, a stressed open syllable must contain a long nucleus. This was not so in Old Icelandic; the regularity came about by a lengthening of nuclei in stressed open syllables, no matter whether the nucleus was monophthongal or diphthongal.[1] With some suggestive abbreviations as in (18), the regularities can be captured in neat informal rules such as (19) and (20).

(18) a. $\vec{S}$: an OPEN SYLLABLE   (a syllable with an empty OF)
         $\overset{\leftharpoonup}{S}$: a CLOSED SYLLABLE   (a syllable that is not open)

THE RULE DEPENDENCE OF SYLLABLE STRUCTURE

b. Š: a LIGHT SYLLABLE   (a syllable with a simple RY, i.e. an open syllable with a short NU)

Ŝ: a HEAVY SYLLABLE   (a syllable that is not light)

(19) Early Latin stress rule

S → Ś / ⎯⎯ (Š)S #

(20) Icelandic length rule

NU → long / in Š́

While no one will contest the relevance of such examples — and they are plentiful — Davis cites a contrary case: in Aranda (Central Australia), stress in polysyllables goes on the first syllable if its onset is not empty, otherwise on the second syllable; e.g., tárama 'to laugh', but imáŋa 'arm'. Let me introduce abbreviations on the analogy of (18a).

(21) S̗: a NAKED SYLLABLE   (a syllable with an empty ON)
S̄: a COVERED SYLLABLE   (a syllable that is not naked)

Then the Aranda stress rule may informally be presented as in (22).

(22) Aranda stress rule

S → Ś / # (S̗) ⎯⎯

Reference to naked syllables is reference to body structure in the same sense as reference to open syllables is reference to rhyme structure, as is shown by the symmetry of the graph in (23).

(23) a. an open syllable   b. a naked syllable

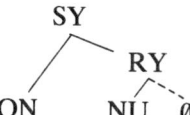   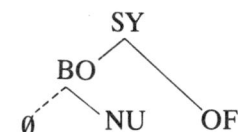

To this extent Davis has thus produced a stress rule that is sensitive to body structure. Whether there are stress rules that make reference to the body structure counterpart of light syllables rather than merely to that of open syllables I do not know.

With regard to (16c), Davis points out that, e.g., spreading rules for nasality, palatality, etc. are not always restricted to rhymes but may also

265

THE RULE DEPENDENCE OF SYLLABLE STRUCTURE

involve onsets or be restricted to bodies. Examples — especially of the palatalization and labialization of onsets before palatal or labial nuclei — are so common that none need be cited here. It seems to me that the syllable body is indeed the preferred domain of coarticulation processes.

As regards (16d) Davis points out that durational relations occur not only inside rhymes but even across syllables. Since I am not a phonetician I will leave the argument at that.

Davis concludes that in general, phonological processes cannot be constrained to any particular constituent such as the rhyme, not even to the syllable as can be seen from numerous cases of vowel harmony, dissimilation, and metathesis. We may add that such processes are often not even limited to the word as a constituent but may spill over, so to speak, resulting in rules of external sandhi.

Finally Davis cites evidence that in transposition speech errors not only rhymes and onsets play a role but also bodies and offsets, cf. (24) and (25).

(24) Rhyme structure transpositions
    a.   *wine   racks* → *Rhine   wacks*
          ON_1 ON_2 ON_2 ON_1
    b.   *our backyoad is full of tards*
                RY_2 RY_1

(25) Body structure transpositions
    a.   *pussy cat* → *cassy put*
          BO_1 BO_2 BO_2 BO_1
    b.   *pitch and stress* → *piss and stretch*
          OF_1 OF_2 OF_2 OF_1

or   c.   *stress and pitch* → *piss and stretch*
           BO_1 BO_2 BO_2 BO_1

Concerning the poetic rime evidence in favor of rhyme structure that we added earlier, we may now cite poetic assonance as an argument in favor of shell structure, in view of the fact that assonance technique refers directly to nuclei rather than to either rhymes or bodies; cf. (26).

(26) [= 6c] Shell structure

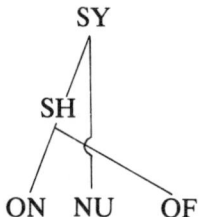

Davis's overall conclusion is that the syllable has no rhyme constituent (virtually the same argument is developed, independently, in Clements and Keyser 1983: 19–24); and he implies, even though he does not say it in these words, that it has no body constituent either; 'a flat or level structure is the only possibility' because, as he says, 'only such a structure can allow for the different possible interactions of onset, peak, and coda' (531), i.e. of onset, nucleus, and offset.

Davis's seems to me to be a very good argument against hierarchical structure — both rhyme and body structure as well as shell structure — and in favor of flat structure. But I will now produce evidence of the same sort to argue against a general version of flat structure, namely that version which allows polyphthongal nuclei.

Let us first look at decreasing (offgliding) diphthongs. Contemporary Standard German has three such diphthongs, /aɪ̯ aʊ̯ ɔʏ̯/. There are at least two sorts of evidence in favor of the view that these are entirely nuclear elements. First, each diphthong assonates only with itself, not with monophthongal /a/ or /ɔ/. Second, before a vowel of the same simplex word, the offglide remains in the first syllable rather than moving to the second syllable, as an offset speech sound would, forming either a syllable head or an interlude:

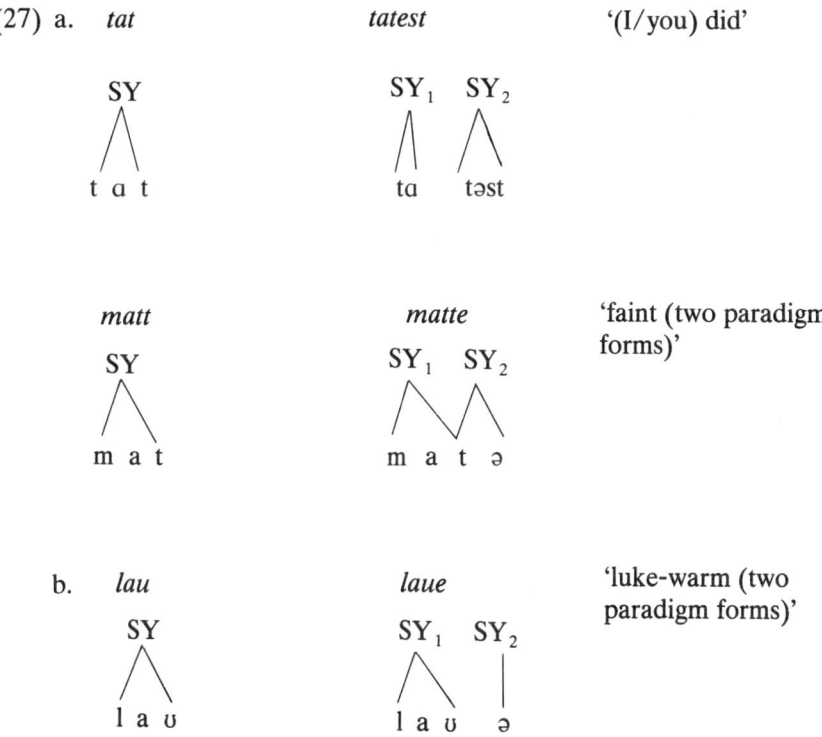

THE RULE DEPENDENCE OF SYLLABLE STRUCTURE

Thus, assuming flat structure, *matt* and *lau* differ as in (28a) and (b).

(28) a.   b.

In (28b), NU may also appear as a more complex structure, e.g. as in (10) or (12) above. However, there is also at least one kind of evidence suggesting that the offglide of these diphthongs is part of the syllable offset. After a monophthong, all consonants are permitted within the same syllable, all the way from the strongest to the weakest;[2] in particular, /r/ may occur freely after both tense and lax vowels: *Jahr* /jɑr/ 'year', *Rohr* /ror/ 'cane', *Bier* /bir/ 'beer', *Uhr* /ur/ 'clock', *Kür* /kyr/ 'free skating'; *Narr* /nar/ 'fool', *Torr* /tɔr/ '(id.)', *wirr* /vɪr/ 'confused'; *Murr* /mʊr/ (name of a tomcat), *dürr* /dʏr/ 'dry'. After diphthongs, however, only the stronger consonants — down to /l/ — are permitted whereas /r/ is not: *Beil* /baɪ̯l/ 'axe', *faul* /faʊ̯l/ 'rotten', *Geheul* /gə.hɔʏ̯l/ 'howling'; */aɪ̯r/, */aʊ̯r/, */ɔʏ̯r/ within syllables. If a sequence /aɪ̯r aʊ̯r ɔʏ̯r/ occurs within a simplex word, the /r/ has to go to the second syllable; cf. (29).

(29) /faɪ̯r/   →   /faɪ̯.r/   *Feier* 'celebration'
     /maʊ̯r/ →   /maʊ̯.r/   *Mauer* 'wall'
     /fɔʏ̯r/   →   /fɔʏ̯.r/   *Feuer* 'fire'

The offglides here seem to occupy the first slot of the offset, and while /l/ and the stronger consonants may occupy the second slot, /r/ may not: *Karl* /karl/ 'Charles', but */Vlr/ within syllables. This then is evidence in favor of offset membership for the offglides of German diphthongs.

As a second example, let us consider the English diphthong /i̯u/ (or triphthong, /i̯uʊ̯/, according to some analyses), as in *cute*, *fuse*, and, in some dialects, *dew* and *suit*. Since in the core vocabulary tautosyllabic /Ci̯V/ is restricted to /Ci̯u/ while other groups, e.g. /Cʊ̯ Cr Cl sN sP/, are never restricted in such a seemingly arbitrary way, /Ci̯/ does not appear to be an onset; thus /i̯u/ seems to be a somewhat exceptional kind of diphthongal nucleus, exceptional also in that it appears as plain /u/ after alveolars in some dialects (*dew* /di̯u/ or /du/, *suit* /si̯ut/ or /sut/). On the other hand, diphthongal /i̯u/ and monophthongal /u/ assonate and rime, e.g. *fuse* and *booze*; and this would make /i̯/ appear to be outside the nucleus, i.e., part of the onset.

We may thirdly consider diachronic evidence showing that there is no firm line of division between nuclei and margins. In Greek, offglides — for all that is known — used to be nuclear (note the position of the accent marks); and the monophthongization of αι /ai/ underscores this interpretation. But in Contemporary Greek the earlier υ-offglide of αυ, ευ /au eu/ has become a labiodental fricative: φαίνομαι /pʰaí.no.mai/ > /fé.no.me/ '(I) appear', φεύγω /pʰeú.gō/ > /fé.vγo/ '(I) flee', Ζεῦς /dᶻéùs/ > /zéfs/ 'Zeus', ταῦρος /taú.ros/ > /tá.vros/ 'bull', αὐτός /au.tós/ > /a.ftós/ 'this'. The opposite development, the weakening of postvocalic liquids, nasals, fricatives, and even stops into glides, often with subsequent monophthongization, is also well attested; e.g., Latin *alba* > French *aube* /ob/ 'dawn', Lat. *āctum* > Spanish *auto* 'decree'. Similar developments may be found with onglides, e.g. Proto-Germanic ⁺/béu.dan/ > Old Icelandic *bjúða* 'to offer'.

All of these examples argue against a general version of flat structure just as Davis's own examples argue against hierarchical structure. Admitting the validity of both sets of arguments, we have to conclude that syllables have either linear structure or a restricted version of flat structure, namely that in which the nucleus never contains more than one speech sound. Linear structure cannot, of course, be defended because the position of the nucleus may be contrastive in some languages: compare English *lantern* /læn.tr̩n/ and *apron* /ei.pr̩n/ — both /læn.tr̩n/ and /ei.pr̩n/ are possible phonological word forms; Sanskrit *urvī́* /ur.uí̯/ (= /ur.u̯í/) 'earth' and *vṛdhá-* /ur̥.dʰá-/ (= /ur̥.dʰá-/) 'friend'. Also developments such as Icelandic ⁺/beu.dan/ > ⁺/biu̯.ða/ > /bjū.ða/ *bjúða* 'to offer', Middle High German *ie* /ie̯/ (= /ie̯/) > /ie̯/ (= /i̯e/) > Contemporary German *je* /je/ 'ever' can only be understood as changes in the position of nuclearity within a syllable. Therefore, all the evidence taken together argues in favor of the restricted version of flat structure, which we may call PEAK STRUCTURE or simply NUCLEAR STRUCTURE. It is the structure of syllables assumed in Vennemann (1982).

The syllable has nuclear structure; that is a clear-cut and sober conclusion. But can we be satisfied with it? What happened to all the arguments in favor of rhymes, bodies, satellites, etc.? Were they not good arguments? In my opinion the arguments were good but the conclusions were wrong. I believe the correct conclusion to be the following, and it comes in two parts. The first is that syllables — rather than having none — actually have all the sorts of structure that have been proposed; more precisely, that they can assume any one of those structures depending on the syllable-related phenomenon under study. Regularities of accent, rime, and meter are typically sensitive only to that part of the syllable which consists of the peak and what follows; they only look at the 'rhyme projection' of a

(30) Nuclear structure

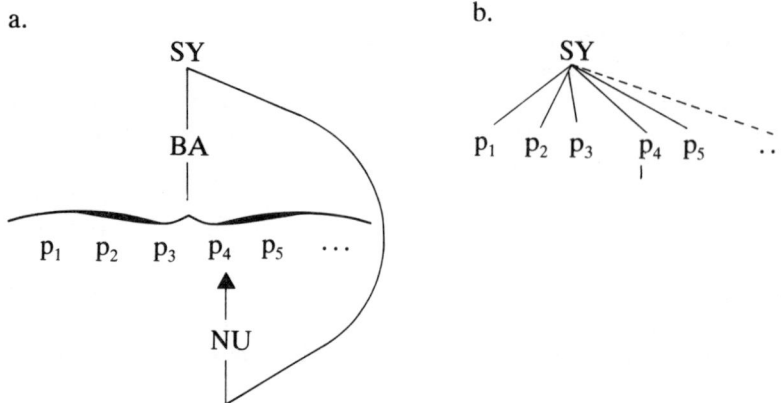

text, as it has been called (Halle and Vergnaud 1978, cited in Van der Hulst and Smith 1982a: 17). The rules we formulate to capture those regularities will thus make reference to rhyme structure: they impose rhyme structure on certain syllables. But exceptions do occur, and they are not really damaging to a theory of what such regularities are usually like. For example, stress in Aranda seems to be sensitive only to that part of the first syllable of a word which consists of the peak and what precedes it; it only looks at the 'body projection'. The rule that has been formulated for Aranda word stress imposes body structure on the first syllables of Aranda words. Conversely, phonological rules expressing regularities arising from coarticulation usually impose body structure on syllables; but there are others that impose rhyme structure. For certain phonotactic constraints the 'shell projection' is relevant, and for assonance only the 'peak-plus-satellite projection' counts.

I think it would be a methodological error to insist that, even despite all the conflicting evidence cited, the syllable must have — *an sich*, so to speak — one or the other of the structures discussed. In linguistics, this error has caused a lot of unfruitful discussion. Perhaps the best known is the controversy over whether affricates are mono- or diphonematic. The answer is, they may be either or both, depending on the regularity under study. For example, in English, the affricate /ts/ appears as diphonematic because the vast majority of instances arise morphologically from the affixation of /s/-suffixes to stems ending in /t/. In German, /ts/ may also arise in this way, e.g. in *Trott+s* /trɔts/ 'trot (gen.)', but then /ts/ is also very common within stems, e.g. *Trotz* /trɔts/ 'spite', *zwei* /tsvaɪ/ 'two', and arguments may be presented for the view that it is a single speech sound, exactly like the affricate /pf/ which only occurs within stems. An analogy of the rhyme vs. body structure ambivalence is known from syntax. Consider a simple nominative–verb–accusative sentence of English, e.g. *he loves them*. In addition to those for flat structure, arguments for both kinds of hierarchical structure may be produced, viz. PREDICATE STRUCTURE and CORE STRUCTURE; cf. (31).

(31) a. Predicate structure   b. Core structure

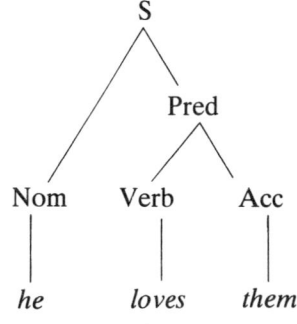
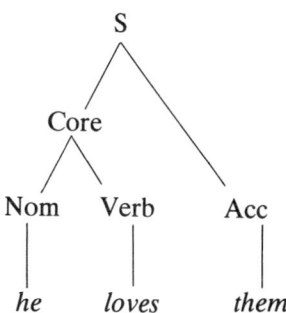

For example, rules of infinitive formation induce predicate structure (*love them*, **he love*), and the rule of number agreement induces core structure. The same kind of ambivalence is found wherever we look. Perhaps the best known example outside linguistics is the structure of light: light assumes wave structure or corpuscle structure, depending on which light-related regularities are formulated in natural laws.

Turning next from the internal structure of syllables to the syllabic organization of larger units, we find similar kinds of ambivalence. For the sake of brevity, let me mention only one problem, that of ambisyllabicity. For words such as English *hammer* /hæmɾ/, German *Hammer* /hamɾ/, three positions can be taken — and have been taken — concerning their syllabic division, cf. (32).

(32) a. Right-bonding   b. Left-bonding   c. Ambisyllabicness

S_1 S_2 S_1 S_2 S_1 S_2

ha   mɾ   ham   ɾ   h a m   ɾ

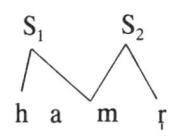

For German, the following arguments can be advanced against (32a) and (32b), besides the intuitive response that the first syllable 'feels' closed and the second, covered. In monosyllables, lax vowels occur only if the syllable is closed; assuming left-bonding structure in cases like *Hammer* allows one to formulate the general rule that lax vowels (in stressed syllables) occur only before tautosyllabic consonants (in 'checked' position) — and this argues against (32a). Again in monosyllables, voiced obstruents are not tolerated in offsets. Assuming syllabications like (32a) would allow one to formulate a general rule of final devoicing because words such as *Ebbe* 'ebb', *Kladde* 'rough copy', and *Roggen* 'rye' would be /ɛ.bə kla.də rɔ.gn̩/ and thus remain outside the domain of the rule, whereas (32b)-type syllabications would require the exceptional exemption of these cases from the rule — and that argues against (32b). One may now conclude that therefore (32c), ambisyllabicness, is the true structure of these cases, as I did in Vennemann (1982) (others have reached this conclusion on other grounds as early as the nineteenth century); for under this analysis the first syllable of, say, *Roggen, qua* /rɔġn̩/, is /rɔg/ and thus closed, so that the lax vowel rule may be formulated in full generality, while at the same time the /g/ is not in a coda, heads and codas being defined as free onsets and offsets, respectively, viz. onsets and offsets not containing ambisyllabic speech sounds, so that final devoicing of obstruents can be formulated in full generality as coda unvoicing. But then it may be argued that (32c) is not a proper constituent structure, or that it does not make sense that one and the same segment is both in a weak position, viz. an offset, and a strong position, viz. the beginning of an onset.

In this situation one may be driven to the conclusion that the very idea of syllable boundaries, i.e. the idea that sequences of speech sounds may always be divided into syllables, is untenable — exactly as earlier on in this discussion one could be driven to the conclusion that the idea of boundaries between nuclei and margins was untenable. But again I think this would be a *non sequitur*: words such as *Hammer, Roggen*, etc. — and similar words in English — assume right-bonding or left-bonding syllabication, depending on the regularities we recognize.

So far I have implicitly characterized two possible positions concerning syllable structure: one which assumes that syllable structure of the sort studied above is simply there and we have to discover it and base our rules on it, the other which says that syllable structure of the sort studied above is only induced by the rules we formulate. Adherents of the former position would naturally claim that rules are structure-dependent; adherents of the latter position would equally naturally claim that structure is rule-dependent. With labels used in Popper (1972: 103–11) and *passim*, the former position may be called ESSENTIALIST, the latter, INSTRUMENTALIST. Both positions have their obvious virtues, but one cannot really be happy with either. To be sure, adherents of one or the other version of the essentialist position for syllable structure have to live with all the evidence pointing in the opposite direction from theirs, and that is more than I for one would be willing to live with. But a staunch adherent of the instrumentalist position for syllable structure would — or should — be troubled by the question why it is that one and the same expression may take on different phonological structure depending on which of its aspects we happen to investigate — and I for one would not be willing to evade this question, even if I were in possession of a perfectly workable theory neatly relating all types of syllabic structurings to the various types of phonological rules.

In short, what is needed is a more general theory of phonological structure, one which permits the definition of all the sorts of syllabic structure considered above not as arbitrary groupings but on the basis of phonological properties that characterize the grouped constituents as intrinsically different. Such a theory would have to accommodate the insight that such groupings are in large measure language-specific but also the insight that, if looked at from their phonetic side, there is a great amount of similarity. Such a theory would certainly have to account for phenomena related to the concept of consonantal strength as well as for cross-language similarities among strength scales by reference to their universal phonetic counterpart, sonority, however defined. But such a theory should also be more flexible than one merely relying on strength relations because, as is well known, speech sounds of one and the same strength class may relate quite differently to some given speech sound. There may be some special attraction, as between /p/ and /f/ in German where /p/ is the only plosive after which /f/ may occur in simplex words; but there may also occur some special repulsion, as between /t/ and /l/ in Faroese where the sequence /tl/ is always heterosyllabic in simplex words while the sequences /pl/ and /kl/, as well as /pr kr tr/, are always tautosyllabic in the same environment. In short, such a theory would have to define a number of relations of phonological cohesion, such as would characterize groups of positioned speech sounds with respect to each other, to the nucleus, to the accent, to morphosyntactic boundaries, and perhaps to some further factors. Except for the position of nuclearity, all the syllabic aspects of expressions should fall out as consequences of the action and interaction of the cohesion relations. In order to distinguish them terminologically from syllabic phonologies which consider syllables as basic, let us call such theories NUCLEAR PHONOLOGIES.

The foundations for such a theory have, I believe, been laid in an article by Alan Bell (1979) and elaborated to some extent in Kreitmair (1984). Bell considers four cohesion relations which he calls SEGMENT BONDS (13):

1. the proximity bond
2. the segmental bond
3. the sequence bond
4. the onset bond

These are characterized as follows:

> 1. The proximity bond. All segments are bound by the proximity bond. The strength of the proximity bond decreases with greater distance between segments, increases with faster rate of articulation, and

decreases inversely with level of self-monitoring ...

2. The segmental bond. The segmental bond closely binds a sequence of articulatory gestures together into a complex segment. Affricates and diphthongal nuclei are held together by the segmental bond ...

3. The sequence bond. Simple and complex segments with closer connection than proximity or juxtaposition are connected together and form sequences within a segment string ...

4. The onset bond. Simple and complex segments may also be bonded together to form an onset sequence (Bell 1979: 13).

There are a number of points in Bell's paper that I consider insufficient or else I do not understand. For example, he says, 'It is assumed that the only segment organization specified in the lexicon is the sequence of segments. Also represented, but separate from the segment sequence, is the accentual pattern of lexical items' (13). Whereas the latter part of the statement is clear enough (assuming that 'accentual' here means the same as 'prosodic'), the former is inconsistent with the fact that the position of nuclearity may be contrastive, as pointed out earlier in this paper. Bell writes: 'The approach that I take here requires that vowels and vocalic glides be distinguished in the lexicon. This is the only vestige of the feature SYLLABIC that remains' (14). But first of all, this is not enough, because not only do /i̯u/ and /iu̯/ (i.e. /iu̯/ and /i̯u/) have to be able to be distinguished, but also /r̩l/ and /rl̩/, /l̩n/ and /ln̩/, etc. And secondly, nuclearity is inadequately represented by a feature, because the difference between, e.g., /i̯/ and /i̩/, is not on a par with, say, that between /t/ and /d/; as a matter of fact, there is no /i̯/ vs. /i̩/ but only /i/, the difference between nuclearity and marginality belonging to a different plane than the internal structure of (the phonetic correlates of) speech sounds which is the descriptive domain of features. Clearly structural information such as the positions of nuclearity has to be able to be stored lexically over and above segment sequences and prosodic properties. It is immaterial that this information is frequently — and in some languages always — predictable; the same is, after all, true for prosodies: to the extent that structural and prosodic properties are redundant this will be expressed in rules. I also believe that among the structural properties at least some cohesion properties have to be part of the phonological word form. For example, in the German words *eklig* /éklɪç/ 'disgusting' and *jeglich* /jéklɪç/ 'every', only the sequential [2]/kl/ of *eklig* is onset-bonded, [3]/kl/ of *jeglich* is not (in other words, *eklig* is /é.klɪç/ while *jeglich* is /jék.lɪç/. The reason is that the *-lich* of *jeglich* is felt to be the adjectival suffix *-lich*, even though there is no stem *jeg-* (but compare *täglich* /tǽk.lɪç/ 'daily'). This, however, cannot be expressed in a phonological rule but only in a morphosyntactic rule, and therefore the difference between onset-bonded and non-onset-bonded

/kl/ is in German of the nature of that between /χ/ and /ç/ in *Kuchen* /kú.χn̩/ 'cake' and *Kuhchen* /kú.çn̩/ 'cow (dimin.)', i.e. it is a phonological contrast, even though this contrast is here predictable on morphological grounds.

Another point in Bell's approach with which I have problems is his concept of adhesion:

> *Adhesion.* One last feature of the theory is that the organization of segments is manifested in their *adhesion*, a property which, together with other factors, governs the strength with which segments affect one another as well as their resistance to processes that would separate them. Since adhesion is recognized by its effect on the application of phonological processes, among other things, it follows that such processes are to be described in part in terms of the adhesion of the segments within the domain of the processes. This is contrasted to the prosodic interpretation of a string, which is governed by and affects the bonds of segment organization directly (14–15).

As I view cohesion relations, their job is precisely to express the attractions and repulsions obtaining among speech sounds, (a) *qua* speech sounds *per se*, i.e., when their phonetic correlates are considered, on the basis of their phonetic properties, and (b) *qua* prosodically determined structure; and these relations may be changed in realization phonology by such factors as rate of speech. In short, I do not understand the function of 'adhesion' over and above the cohesion captured by the various bonding relations.

Another point on which I disagree with Bell is his treatment of onsets in relation to vocalic and consonantal nuclei. Bell observes that, in general, syllables with consonantal nuclei have more restricted — in particular: shorter — margins than syllables with vocalic nuclei. He accounts for this by assuming the onset bond to bind consonants only to vocalic, not to consonantal nuclei. I think this is wrong. A way to account for Bell's observation in a more natural and a more general fashion will be pointed out directly.

A refinement and further development of Bell's approach is presented in Kreitmair (1984). Kreitmair assumes five types of bonding (30-1):

1. φ-bonding (segment sequence bond)
2. κ-bonding (complex segment bond)
3. σ-bonding (syllabic bond)
4. ω-bonding (onset bond)
5. ν-bonding (nucleus bond)

The sequence bond simply defines the sequence of segments. The complex segment bond binds sequences of segments into complex segments such as affricates and diphthongs. The syllabic bond binds segments into syllabic complexes; the syllabic bond may leave segments unbonded. The onset bond is responsible for the greater cohesion of segments within the body than within the rhyme. The nucleus bond binds segments into complex nuclei.

In addition to the bonding types, Kreitmair assumes various types of AFFINITIES which are in part responsible for the presence or absence of the various bonds. The following three types of affinity he considers to be the most relevant (31-2):

1. peak affinity
2. peak environment affinity
3. sequence affinities
    a. onset affinity
    b. offset affinity

Peak affinity is the affinity between syllable peaks and the other segments bonded to it by the syllabic bond (σ-bond); the stronger this affinity, the closer the segment tends to stand to the peak. Peak environment affinity is the affinity between syllable bonded segments standing before and after the peak; this affinity is responsible for the degree of compatibility of onset and offset types. Sequence affinities are the affinities between contiguous segments within onsets and within offsets.

Kreitmair points out two advantages of his approach over those which are based directly on the concept of sonority. First, the relations of affinity are defined, for any given language system, independently of considerations concerning sonority. They may then be compared to it. Congruity between the affinities on one hand and the sonority hierarchy on the other may exist but need not: language specific patterns appear equally normal to the native speaker, whether they agree with the universal sonority hierarchy or not; and the bonding approach is perfectly suited to express this. Congruity of language-specific affinities with the universal sonority hierarchy may thus be interpreted as a universal preference, as this concept is developed in Vennemann (1983). Secondly, whereas approaches based on sonority have to assume greater sonority for the syllable peak than for the neighboring segments — contrary to fact as pointed out earlier in this paper — Kreitmair's approach implies no such restriction for syllable peaks; even syllables such as /sţ^h sç^h sķ^h sţ'/, which occur in North-west American languages, are in no way excluded by the theory.

Even though a great many questions are still left open by the bonding theories as so far developed, the basic idea of explicating syllabic phenomena by means of a theory of phonological cohesion appears to me to be very promising. Even those phonologists who take a friendly view of theories incorporating some concept of segmental hierarchy, such as a universal sonority hierarchy or even a language-specific consonantal strength scale, have been disturbed by blatant violations of syllabic organization in terms of the hierarchy. One recurring complaint is the existence of appendices in so many languages, such as with initial fricative plus plosive clusters (as in English) or final plosive or fricative plus liquid clusters (as in French); clearly the very notion of appendices argues against segment organization theories, including syllabic theories, that employ no more general concepts than that of a segmental hierarchy. Another complaint is the occurrence of seemingly arbitrary exceptions to otherwise general combinatorial rules. Very many languages tolerate word-initial clusters of plosives and liquids with just one set of exceptions: sequences of dentals plus laterals. For example, sets such as (33) are quite common.

(33) pr   tr   kr   pl   *tl   kl
      br   dr   gr   bl   *dl   gl

One may, of course, point to all sorts of phonetic explanation for deviations from an orderly patterning such as some standard segment hierarchy could allow us to predict. Research leading to phonetic theories explaining such language-specific patterning, or rather the universal preferences from which the patterns result (e.g. the work of John J. Ohala and his students, most recently Kawasaki 1982), is extremely valuable in its own right. But in the context of this discussion it does not help at all because the problem is a phonological one, and evidently phonological descriptions cannot be based on phonetic explanations.

It seems to me that some sufficiently rich concept of affinity within a theory of phonological cohesion is precisely the instrument to handle such seemingly aberrant patterning. For example, it is easy to develop such a theory to the point where it can be expressed formally that in English the affinity between /s/ and the plosives is strong enough to induce word-initial onset bonding, whereas that between alveolar plosives (and /θ/) and the lateral liquid is so weak that no onset bonding is possible in word-initial position (or anywhere else, for that matter). The affinities can be defined for any two (or more) segments individually or by more or less general rules; the more general the rules, the more clearly the contours of a segmental hierarchy will emerge in the description. Segmental hierarchies are epiphenomenal in theories of phonological cohesion. That is as it should be: a new theory conceived in the general spirit of an older one proved to be insufficient will permit the definition of concepts corresponding to the primitive concepts of the older theory. The affinities may even be defined as functions of prosodic properties. For example, the peak affinity of a post-nuclear segment increases if the syllable of the peak is stressed, and it decreases if the peak segment is long. The former property makes the /t/

of *atom*, but not that of *atomic*, ambisyllabic in English. The latter property makes a sequence such as *tr* in a configuration $\acute{V}trV$ in pre-West Germanic tautosyllabic, $\acute{V}.trV$, if the vowel in the stressed syllable is long, but heterosyllabic, $\acute{V}t.rV$, if it is short; the latter appears as $\acute{V}t.trV$ in the attested West Germanic languages (cf. Murray and Vennemann 1983).

Bell's observation concerning the margins of syllables with consonantal nuclei already mentioned above can be easily and naturally accommodated by a theory of segment affinities. It is a well known fact that the ability of segments to form syllable nuclei in general matches their sonority. Looking only at the most common segment types, the order of increasing nucleability is plosives – fricatives – nasals – lateral liquids – central liquids – high vowels – mid vowels – low vowels. The order of increasing marginability is, of course, the exact opposite. The peak affinity of a segment increases with its own degree of marginability, the degree of nucleability of the peak segment, and the linear closeness of the two segments — in general, as there may be specific as well as typical exceptions. It follows from the combination of these factors that the margins of syllables will be the more restricted the less nucleable is its peak segment. For example, in one language all consonants may have sufficient peak affinity to nuclear vowels to form margins with them, but only obstruents may have sufficient peak affinity to nuclear liquids. In another language the peak affinity may be sufficient to allow the margins /n/, /k/, and /kn/ before vowels while before liquids, only /n/ and /k/, but not /kn/, remain possible: the generally lesser peak affinity to liquids would disallow the /k/ to syllable-bond at a distance.

Would developing nuclear phonology as a theory of phonological cohesion imply the abandonment of the goals and insights of syllabic phonology? Bell said in an earlier article, 'One conclusion I do not draw yet is that phonology can do without the syllable' (1976: 261). I take this to be an evaluation of the *status quo* because he also says: 'It follows that the syllable is not likely to be a unit derivable from abstract phonological properties, just as at the phonetic level it has not been possible to derive it from phonetic features' (260), and

> For the concept of the syllable to contribute to phonology, it should be promising to assume, just as we assume that speech is organized into segments, that segments are organized into syllables, both phonetically and at more abstract levels. Let us, however, guard against too narrow a view, against confusing a tool with the problem. 'Defining the syllable' and 'proving the existence of the syllable' are pseudo-problems. Segment organization is the problem. If assumption of a syllabic unit leads to explanation of regularities of segment organization, so much the better. If not, we will be awaiting a more general theory of organization, and the syllable may enter the museum's Hall of Scientific Constructs, taking its place beside ether, the noble savage, and the like (261).

It seems to me that in a properly developed theory of phonological cohesion the concept of a syllable will be definable. In this sense I can say that the syllable is epiphenomenal in a theory of phonological cohesion. Does this make the concept superfluous? I do not think so. It is normal for theories of all sorts to introduce some of their most important concepts not as basic but as defined ones. For example, one of the central concepts of the theory of natural numbers, the prime number, is normally introduced there in terms of more primitive properties, among them divisibility. The advantage of a general cohesion theory is that it gives us a chance to define the syllable in such a way that the paradoxes of syllabic theories can be avoided. For example, there is no necessity to postulate that all parts of segment strings be associated with syllables; those that do not enter the syllabic bond relation (Kreitmair's σ-bonding) would simply stay outside and be 'extrasyllabic'. And if Hyman is right in his 'claim that Gokana has no syllable structure' (1985: 27), even this could be accommodated in such a theory: the cohesion theory for this language could, e.g., be formulated in such a way that the syllabic bonding relation remains empty. Defining a grammatical concept does not, of course, imply that entities of the defined sort have to occur in every language. Assuming that the concept of an infinitive can be defined in a general syntactic theory, it does not follow that all languages have infinitives. On the contrary, only a well developed concept of a syllable (or an infinitive) allows us to make negative statements such as Hyman's. Clearly the observation that Gokana has no syllabic structure does not, if correct, offer an argument against carrying a concept of syllables in general phonological theories. As long as there are languages for which syllabic structure has been demonstrated, the exact opposite is true.

Returning now in closing to the main theme of this essay, I would like to suggest that the apparent rule-dependence of syllable structure may find its explanation in a theory of phonological cohesion. Both Bell and Kreitmair assume, over and above more general kinds of bonding, an 'onset bond' tying pre-nuclear segments to the peak; let me call it the BODY BOND because a special cohesion of segments within syllable bodies, not onsets, is really what is meant. Kreitmair has, in addition, the syllabic bond tying segments into syllable bases. It seems to me that this already suffices, together with a marking of nuclei in segment strings, to account for some aspects of the dilemma described above. For example, that rules of coarticulation typically look out for especially tightly bonded sequences is not surprising; they find them in the body-bonded body. And conversely, that accent rules and rules of poetic meter typically look out for loosely bonded elements such as syllables in larger strings, or loosely bonded segments within syllables, is equally to be expected: such rules scan the segment string for elements that are worth counting and are likely to consider segments body-bonded to the peak as merely an uninteresting annex. However, such a cohesion theory does not preclude the assumption of rules that penetrate even the most tightly bonded segment sequences, such as rules of alliteration whose specialty it is to look deep into the body and even into the onset itself.

Seen in this way, the rule-dependence of syllable structure is only an illusion. Phonological form is structured in a syllabically relevant way quite independently of individual rules, namely by the various affinities of the phonological elements operating in lexically and morphosyntactically determined domains. But it is structured in more intricate ways than simple syllabic theories have suggested. It is this more intricate structure that permits the appearance of simplistic divisions such as in body structure and rhyme structure, just as it is the intricate structure of the human organism that makes it appear as consisting sometimes of a left half and a right half, sometimes of an upper and a lower half, of a heart and all the rest to the cardiologist, of two feet and a connecting part to the shoemaker, of a neck and two protuberances to the hangman. While it is easy to define various structures for syllables, as done earlier in this essay, it is the intricate structure induced by the bonding relations (and their effect on rule application) that motivates these definitions: the division into body and coda (offset) is motivated by the body bond, that into head (onset) and rhyme by the loose connection between segments not body-bonded to each other. Appendices seem to be especially tightly bonded to their support, i.e. the stronger segment they flank, because to the Germanic rules of alliteration, prependices form a constituent with their support, whereas the weaker elements that follow are never included.[3] Thus an appendical bond would motivate a division of (stressed) syllables into an ALLITERANT and a TRUNK, cf. the two lines from *The Battle of Maldon*, vv. 136–7 in (34).[4]

(34) hē SCĒAF þā mid ðām SCYLde   þæt se SCEAFT tōBÆRST

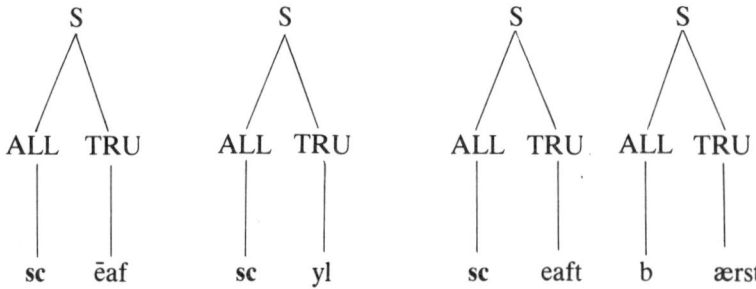

and þæt SPEre SPRENGde   þæt hit SPRANG OnGĒAN

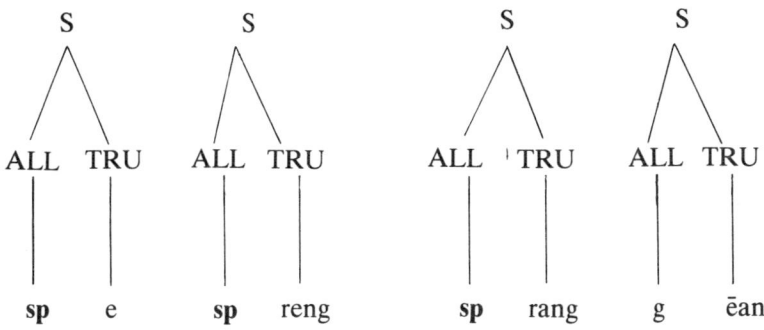

It seems to me that theories of phonological cohesion promise to be able to incorporate all our best insights into phonological structure without giving up any of the proven advantages of syllabic phonologies. Developing such theories should be a great challenge to the linguistic community.[5]

NOTES

1. Also stressed final syllables (including monosyllables) closed by a single consonant were lengthened in Icelandic (and those closed by two or more consonants were shortened). Kristján Árnason (1980: 127) leaves open the question of whether the two lengthenings are one process or two, even though he seems to slightly favor a uniform treatment both descriptively and in terms of causation (159–60, 181–5); and earlier authors have usually assumed a single unified 'quantity shift' (Árnason 1980: 121–2). I consider the two processes, open syllable lengthening and singly-closed syllable lengthening, to be independent of each other. One reason is that each of the two processes may occur without the other in other languages (cf. Árnason 1980: 122); another is that the motivations for the changes are different: open syllable lengthening (as well as closed syllable shortening of non-final syllables) results from the universal preference for stressed syllables of exactly two moras, whereas singly-closed syllable lengthening (as well as multiply-closed syllable shortening) is in my opinion part of a maneuver in Icelandic to underline the contrast of single consonants and geminates in the precarious final position, innocuous because the vowel length contrast had been transformed into one of tenseness; e.g. *risa* $^+$[rī^{s}sa] > [ri:^{s}sa] 'to rise', *ristu*$^+$[rīs þu] > [ris^{s}tʏ] 'rise!', *risum*$^+$[ri^{s}sum] > [rɪ:^{s}sʏm] '(we) rose', *risnir* $^+$[ris^{s}nir] > [rɪs^{s}nɪɾ] 'risen (masc. pl. nom. strong)'; *is* $^+$[īs] > [i:s] 'ice (nom.)', *iss* $^+$[īs] > [is:] 'ice (gen.)', *mis-* $^+$[mis] > [mɪ:s] 'mis- (prefix)', *viss* $^+$[ṷis̃] > [vɪs:] 'certain (e.g. masc. sg. nom)'; *reisa* $^+$[rei^{s}sa] > [rei:^{s}sa] 'to raise', *reisti* $^+$[reis^{s}ti] > [rĕis^{s}tɪ] '(I) raised', etc. Rule 20 below is the open syllable length rule.

2. The terms STRONGER and WEAKER refer to two arrangements of the speech sounds of a language system on a scale of CONSONANTAL STRENGTH which is, in the preferred case and quite commonly in actual fact, the inverse of the phonetic parameter of SONORITY. Vowels usually occupy the lowest portion of the strength scale, followed by the liquids, then the nasals, and finally the obstruents, with the voiceless

plosives at the top of the scale. Among the vowels, the high ones occupy the highest position on the scale, in German as in many other languages: they, and no others, may occur in syllable margins, a position most typically occupied by consonants. Among the liquids, /l/ ranks higher (is stronger) than /r/, a property which German likewise shares with many other languages. For example, /r/, much more than /l/, tends to vocalize in nuclear as well as in offset position, both in German and in English; and if /rl/, but not /lr/, may occur as an offset in both German (see below) and English, this is so precisely because /r/ is weaker (more vowel-like and thus possessing greater affinity to the nuclear position) than /l/. See Vennemann (1982: 283-96) for a detailed demonstration of the concept of phonological strength in the phonology of Standard German.

3. This is the interpretation that first comes to mind: rules of alliteration scanning onsets of stressed syllables for the segment of greatest consonantal strength plus any segments prependix-bonded to it, exactly as rules of assonance scan syllables for the syllable peak (usually the segment of least consonantal strength) plus any segments complex-segment-bonded (Kreitmair's κ-bonded) to it, viz. in the case of diphthongs. And it may be the right account. But then things may also be the other way around: rules of alliteration may look for the strongest onset segment and consider everything tightly bonded to it as an uninteresting annex, but regard any segments of the same onset not so bonded to it as a co-alliterating element. In this case the analogy would be rules of poetic rime within my above bonding-theoretical account of the relevance of rhymes to accent and poetic meter: rules of alliteration count everything up to the first strength peak of the stressed syllable and disregard the tightly bonded material that follows, whereas rules of riming count everything down from the resonance peak of the stressed syllable (to the end of the word) and disregard the tightly bonded (body-bonded) material that precedes. Which bond it is that prependices would thus be excluded from — the body bond? the syllabic bond? — depends on the details of the bonding theory. The fact that prependical /s/ is sometimes detatched from its syllable, e.g. $\#sT\ldots > \#is^sT\ldots$ as in the prothesis of the Western Romance languages, seems to point to an especially loose rather than tight cohesion within the alliterant. There is no need, however, to choose between the alternatives within the present context.

4. From a metrical point of view, the alliterating unit is the foot rather than the syllable. The two domains coincide for heavy syllables, but for light syllables foot formation requires 'resolution', the integration of the following syllable into the trunk of the alliterating foot. Thus the trunk of the first alliterating unit of the second verse is actually *e.re.*

5. A short version of this paper was presented at the Fifth International Phonology Meeting, Eisenstadt/Austria, 25-28 March 1984.

REFERENCES

Árnason, Kristján. 1980. *Quantity in Historical Phonology: Icelandic and Related Cases.* Cambridge: Cambridge University Press.
Bell, Alan. 1976. 'The Distributional Syllable', in Alphonse Juilland (ed.), *Linguistic Studies Offered to Joseph Greenberg on the Occasion of his Sixtieth Birthday.* Saratoga, California: Anma Libri, 249-62.
—— 1979. 'The Syllable as Constituent versus Organizational Unit', in Paul R. Clyne *et al.* (eds.), *The Elements: A Parassession on Linguistic Units and Levels.* Chicago: Chicago Linguistic Society, 11-20.
Cairns, Charles E., and Mark H. Feinstein. 1982. 'Markedness and the Theory of

Syllable Structure', *Linguistic Inquiry* 13: 193-226.
Clements, George N., and Samuel Jay Keyser. 1983. *CV Phonology: A Generative Theory of the Syllable*. Cambridge, Mass.: MIT Press.
Davis, Stuart. 1982. 'Rhyme, or Reason? A Look at Syllable-Internal Constituents', *Proceedings of the Annual Meeting of the Berkeley Linguistic Society* 8: 525-32.
Donegan, Patricia J., and David Stampe. 1978. 'The Syllable in Phonological and Prosodic Structure', in Alan Bell and Joan Bybee Hooper (eds.), *Syllables and Segments*. Amsterdam: North Holland, 25-34.
Halle, Morris, and Jean-Roger Vergnaud. 1978. 'Metrical Structures in Phonology', Unpublished MS. Cambridge, Mass.: MIT.
Hockett, Charles F. 1955. *A Manual of Phonology*. Baltimore: Waverly Press.
Van der Hulst, Harry, and Norval Smith. 1982a. 'An Overview of Autosegmental and Metrical Phonology', in Van der Hulst and Smith 1982b, Vol. 1, 1-45.
—— (eds.). 1982b., *The Structure of Phonological Representations*, 2 vols. Dordrecht: Foris.
Hyman, Larry M. 1985. *A Theory of Phonological Weight*. Dordrecht: Foris.
Kawasaki, Haruko. 1982. *An Acoustical Basis for Universal Constraints on Sound Sequences*. University of California, Berkeley dissertation. Ann Arbor, Mich.: University Microfilms.
Kiparsky, Paul. 1979. 'Metrical Structure Assignment is Cyclical', *Linguistic Inquiry* 10: 421-42.
—— 1981. 'Remarks on the Metrical Structure of the Syllable', in Wolfgang U. Dressler *et al.* (eds.), *Phonologica 1980: Akten der Vierten Internationalen Phonologie-Tagung, Wien, 29. Juni-2. Juli 1980* (= *Innsbrucker Beiträge zur Sprachwissenschaft*, 36), Innsbruck: Institut für Sprachwissenschaft, Universität Innsbruck, 245-56.
Kreitmair, Wolfgang. 1984. *Untersuchungen zur Silbenstruktur des Standarddeutschen*. University of Munich, Department of German Philology MA thesis.
Kuryłowicz, Jerzy. 1948. 'Contribution à la théorie de la syllabe', *Biuletyn Polskiego Towarzystwa Językoznawczego* 8: 80-114. Reprinted in Jerzy Kuryłowicz, *Esquisses linguistiques I* (= *International Library of General Linguistics*, 16.I), Munich, Wilhelm Fink, 2nd edn., 1973, 193-220.
Murray, Robert W., and Theo Vennemann. 1983. 'Sound Change and Syllable Structure [:Problems] in Germanic Phonology', *Language* 59: 514-28.
Pike, Kenneth L., and Eunice V. Pike. 1947. 'Immediate Constituents of Mazateco Syllables', *International Journal of American Linguistics* 13: 78-91.
Popper, Karl R. 1972. *Conjectures and Refutations: The Growth of Scientific Knowledge*. London: Routledge and Kegan Paul.
Selkirk, Elisabeth O. 1982. 'The Syllable', in Van der Hulst and Smith 1982b, Vol. 2, 337-83.
Vennemann, Theo. 1982. 'Zur Silbenstruktur der deutschen Standardsprache', in Theo Vennemann (ed.), *Silben, Segmente, Akzente*. Tübingen: Max Niemeyer, 261-305.
—— 1983. 'Causality in Language Change: Theories of Linguistic Preferences as a Basis for Linguistic Explanations', *Folia Linguistica Historica* 4: 5-26.

Part III

Syntactica

21

Objects (Direct and Not-So-Direct) in English and Elsewhere

STEPHEN R. ANDERSON

Despite the radical attempts of structuralists in the 1930s, 40s, and 50s to do away with her influence, the Miss Fidditch of Henry Lee Smith Jr and Martin Joos continues to assign us much of our homework. Although the concerns of grammarians in the era of generative syntax include many indisputable novelties, the great majority of tools and analytical categories in use today are inherited fairly directly from the same traditional theories of grammar in western Europe that formed Miss Fidditch's views.

This is especially obvious in the case of the problem described by Stockwell (1980) as that of determining the 'primitive alphabet' in terms of which the rules of the syntax are stated: the basic terms and relations of a theory of syntax which are to be taken as primitives in individual statements. As Stockwell notes, theories today differ as to whether they accept, as undefined elements of such a primitive alphabet, parts of speech (plus constituency relations) alone, or semantic roles, or syntactic grammatical relations — but they all seem to assign some place in a syntactic description to the last of these, the set of structural relations which we inherit from a tradition reaching back at least to the grammatical theories of early Greek philosophers.

Miss Fidditch taught us (or at least, most of us) to identify the SUBJECT, DIRECT OBJECT, and INDIRECT OBJECT in a sentence, and most of us learned the lesson well enough. It is indeed quite easy to agree on the assignment of these labels as in (1) — much easier, say, than getting agreement on the correct extension of a term like VOWEL HARMONY in phonology, or the difference between SOURCE and AGENT, GOAL and PATIENT in traditional semantics.

(1) a. *Jones* bit *his dog*.
         SBJ.   DO
   b. *Jones* threw *his dog a stick*.
         SBJ.   IO   DO

This is not to say that scholars do not differ on the status of such labels: indeed Stockwell's discussion referred to above is precisely a concise comparison of theories that derive them from information about constituent structure alone, theories that derive them from information about semantic roles, and theories that take them as primitives. But virtually everyone agrees that they have **some** place in the theory.

The present paper investigates one important notion from this tradition: the relation of direct object (and those closely related to it, particularly indirect object). The goal of such an investigation is to determine just how solid a conceptual basis underlies our assignment of direct object-hood to sentence constituents, and indeed whether this notion corresponds to a unitary category at all. In the process, we will be led into a variety of other areas of sentence structure which may turn out to have some intrinsic interest.

Discussions of the traditional grammatical relations generally start with an analysis of the status of subjects — and nearly as often end there, as far as their substance is concerned. It is assumed that if good arguments can be provided for the validity of a category of subjects, a simple 'and so on' will suffice to bring along the rest of the grammatical relations from school grammar. Such arguments for the coherence of the notion of Subject are indeed rather easy to find, in the domains of morphology, syntax and even (to a limited extent, given the general fuzziness of theories) semantics. For example, English is a language with rather impoverished inflectional morphology, but much of what it has is devoted to distinguishing subjects from non-subjects. Verbs agree in number (always, except for modals, and only) with their subjects (e.g. *Jones likes cats* vs. *Cats like Jones*), and the only formal reflection of case relations in the language is in the shape of pronouns, which distinguish a subject form from a non-subject form (e.g. *I saw her with him* vs. *He saw me with her*).

In more straightforwardly syntactic terms, subjects also occupy a distinct structural position. This is shown, for example, by the fact that it is precisely the subject that constitutes the 'missing NP' in association with infinitives: *Jones intended [∅] to arrest his neighbor*, but **Jones intended his neighbor to arrest [∅]* (cf. also *Jones intended [∅] to be arrested*, for evidence that the semantic role of the NP involved is not the determining factor). The literature on syntactic and semantic properties of subjects in a variety of languages is by now quite vast, and the well defined nature of subject-hood is not seriously in doubt. Of course, that still does not solve the problem of whether 'subject' is a primitive or a derived notion, and if the latter, what it is to be derived from — but the legitimacy of calling certain NPs (and not others) Subjects is quite generally admitted.

Whether the success of subjects furnishes a license to treat other traditional grammatical relations as equally well founded, however, remains at least logically in question. In fact, when we look at the traditional literature on the notions of direct object and indirect object, it quickly becomes clear that these are much less securely founded. In the following sections, we will survey several attempts to provide criteria for direct object-hood, and to distinguish direct objects from other complements (especially indirect objects and objects of prepositions). The issues thereby raised lead to the discovery of a number of fundamental aspects of linguistic structure, but the notion of 'direct object' itself turns out to be merely a convenient descriptive label for a cluster of properties that are related as a 'family resemblance' rather than being co-extensional. Our conclusion is that direct objects (*per se*) have much less theoretical relevance than subjects.

1. SOME BASIC PROPERTIES OF 'OBJECTS'

Plato founded the notion of 'subject' on the relation between what we are talking about and what we have to say about it, whilst Aristotle saw subjects as the particular individuals of which a universal is predicated. In both cases, the underlying intuition was that 'subject-hood' was fundamentally an aspect of the semantic structure of sentences, susceptible to a unitary definition in terms of the nature of the judgment. Following a similar line, traditional grammar attempted to define the direct object semantically as well.

Jespersen (1924, 1927) surveys a number of attempts of this sort. Considering pairs of sentences in which the same verb appears with or without an object, he notes that *He doesn't smoke* differs from *He doesn't smoke cigars* in that 'the object serves to make the meaning contained in the verb more special, or to limit its sphere of applicability' (Jespersen 1927: 230); but immediately points out that all sorts of other complements fall under this vague criterion as well (compare *He doesn't smoke in public*, etc.).

The most common attempts Jespersen finds in the literature to define objects are in terms of what we would today call 'thematic relations': definitions such as 'the person or thing to which something is done', 'the receiver of the action', 'the thing directly affected by the action', etc. But as Henry Sweet (1898) among others had already noted, such a definition cannot possibly encompass the full range of noun phrases which we would like to call objects. In the case of perception verbs, for instance, the 'person to whom something is done', who 'is directly affected', etc., is surely the subject:

(2) a. Jones saw a pink elephant in his sleep.
    b. The elephant heard Jones coming.
    c. Jones fears more dreams like that.

Consideration of a representative sample of verb types makes it clear that there is no unitary semantic role which is consistently filled by direct objects.

Another sort of problem for the attempt to define direct object-hood semantically is that it is often possible to describe the same state of affairs in more than one way, using the same verb and the same NPs, where the difference lies precisely in the choice of one or another NP to serve as direct object. In pairs like the following, there is surely no difference whatsoever in the semantic role filled by a given post-verbal NP in the (a) and the (b) sentences:

(3) a. Jones made a silk purse out of a sow's ear.
     b. Jones made a sow's ear into a silk purse.

(4) a. Our chess club furnishes arms to the Montenegrin rebels.
     b. Our chess club furnishes the Montenegrin rebels with arms.

(5) a. Jones pounded his fist on the table.
     b. Jones pounded the table with his fist.

If it is indeed possible for the same NP to fill the same role with respect to the description of the same state of affairs, using the same verb, by two different sentences, it is obvious that specific semantic roles cannot be criterial for direct objects.

If it is not its semantic role that makes a given NP a direct object, then what is it? Considering the pairs (3–5) above, it is evident that (in English, at least) 'direct objects' are the otherwise-unmarked NPs that come immediately after the verb. In other languages, criteria such as overt case-marking or (non-subject) agreement in the verb might be more important; while others such as word order might be irrelevant. Nonetheless, it is clear that direct objects are much more centrally a formal class than a substantive semantic one.

When we consider any given English verb, we might expect that we could at least predict, from a consideration of the semantic roles that are implied for the participants in the state of affairs it describes, what formal possibilities are employed for the complement phrases that represent these participants. Even this much of a match between semantic and syntactic structure does not seem to be possible, however. Different lexical items describing (at least grossly) similar situations differ considerably in the sets of complements with which they occur:

(6) a. Jones hung his walls with pictures / *hung his walls / hung pictures on his walls / hung pictures.
     b. Jones covered his walls with pictures / covered his walls / *covered pictures on his walls / *covered pictures.

c. Jones put pictures on his walls / *put pictures /
*put his walls with pictures / *put his walls.

Each of the verbs in (6) describes the fact that Jones established a relation between a set of pictures and a set of walls; each can in fact occur with both a direct object and a prepositional phrase, but they differ as to which of the two sets can be referred to by a direct object alone, or which of the two appears as direct object when the other is described in a prepositional phrase.

From such considerations (which could be multiplied without effective limit), we see that the set of complements (unmarked NPs, prepositional phrases, etc.) taken by a given verb is an idiosyncratic lexical property, together with the particular ways in which these complements are integrated into its semantic interpretation. It is necessary to describe, as a part of the lexical specification for each verb in the lexicon of the language, just what sorts of complements it can be associated with: what specific prepositions appear with such complements, and whether some complement can appear with no associated preposition whatsoever.

There are two aspects to this specification — the formal description, such as 'appears with an *on*-phrase', 'appears with a *with*-phrase', 'appears with an unmarked NP', etc.; and the interpretation to be assigned to each such formally characterized complement. Obviously there is an intimate connection between these two: *on*-phrases describe locations, but not instruments, etc. The relation is not one of complete predictability, however, and it is precisely in the area of the association between direct objects and their interpretation that the most evident ambiguity arises (cf. the variants of (6a) vs. (6b) with direct object alone, for example). The fact that syntactic and semantic structure are related in such a fashion is an aspect of the claim that syntax is 'autonomous', and the observation of this autonomy is hardly a new one. An exactly parallel point is made by Stockwell (in Hill (ed.) 1962: 27), who notes that languages can differ in the formal categories that realize complements whose semantic roles are essentially the same, and that this argues that 'one cannot hope to discover the syntactic structure of a language from a set of semantic absolutes'.

Now in fact, although it is not possible to associate the relation of direct object with a unitary semantic role, this does not mean that there are no semantic correlates of the direct object relation. One such correlate was noted some years ago (Anderson 1971), and has been investigated by a number of authors. When a given 'participant' associated with a particular verb can appear either as an unmarked NP or in a prepositional phrase, it is (often) the case that the unmarked NP is interpreted HOLISTICALLY (as affected more completely, definitively, successfully, etc. by the action), as opposed to PARTITIVELY. To see the nature of this distinction, consider the following pairs:

(7) a. Jones assembled the Linguistics Department into a volleyball team.
b. Jones assembled a volleyball team from the Linguistics Department.

(8) a. Every night I read *War and Peace* to my wife.
b. Every night I read to my wife from *War and Peace*.

(9) a. Rosie ran the New York Marathon two years ago.
b. Rosie ran in the New York Marathon two years ago.

(10) a. A disappointed diner shot Girardet last week.
b. A disappointed diner shot at Girardet last week.

Each of these pairs describes essentially the same situation, but with subtle differences. In (7a), for instance, it is at least strongly implied that the entire Linguistics Department was pressed into service, while (7b) says only that a team was assembled whose members were from the Linguistics Department. Taken at its word (8a) describes an astonishing amount of reading, since it (and not the otherwise parallel (8b)) implies that I read the entire novel each evening. The sentences in (9) relate to the famous incident a few years ago in which one runner in the New York Marathon appears to have run only a short distance (a couple of miles or so), and then slipped away to take the subway to a point near the finish, where she rejoined the course and finished well before any other woman in the race. Describing this event, one could perhaps use (9b), since she did indeed run *in* the race, but not (a), since she didn't in fact run all of the race. Finally, my concern for the health of the world's greatest chef will be much more acute if I hear (10a), which implies Girardet was in fact hit by the shot, than if I hear only (10b).

In each instance, an NP is interpreted as 'holistically' affected when the variant is used in which that NP appears as a direct object, but not when it appears as an oblique complement. Of course, not all verbs admit such a holistic interpretation of their direct object. In particular, it appears to be a phenomenon associated (in English) with the specific case of verbs which can take the same participant as either a direct (unmarked) or an oblique (prepositional phrase) complement. Verbs like *examine, discuss, convince, destroy*, etc., whose objects are always direct, do not present any contrast. Still, it seems that holistic interpretation (where it arises) is a consistent property of direct objects.

Relatively little search, however, turns up cases in which holistic interpretation appears to be a property not of direct objects, but of subjects:

(11) a. The seeds we planted grew/sprouted into opium poppies.
b. Opium poppies grew/sprouted from the seeds we planted.

(12) a. John broke out in a rash.
b. A rash broke out on John.

In (11a), it is implied that all of the seeds we planted (or at least all of those for which we have evidence) grew or sprouted into opium poppies; while (11b) only asserts that opium poppies were among the results of the germination. Similarly, (12a) asserts (if construed literally, though perhaps exaggeratedly) that John was covered with a rash, while (12b) only says that he had one somewhere. With these intransitive verbs, it is apparently the subject NP that is interpreted holistically. Of course, subjects share with direct objects the property of being otherwise unmarked (i.e., of appearing without a relation-specifying preposition); and the intransitive verbs in such sentences are exactly the ones in which any one of several semantic roles may be realized by the subject NP, with others realized in prepositional phrases. From this, we might conclude that there is a unitary generalization at work: the possibility of a holistic interpretation is a property of unmarked NPs that alternate with prepositional phrases, rather than a property of (direct) objects *per se*.

The sort of alternation between holistic and partitive interpretation which we can see in English is far from isolated in the languages of the world. Many other languages show similar pairs of sentences, differing in approximately the same way semantically, and differing formally in that the holistically interpreted object is formally 'direct' (in some language-particular sense) while the partitively interpreted one is 'oblique'. Polish, for instance, shows pairs in which the holistic object is case-marked in the accusative, while the partitive object is in a prepositional phrase.

(13) a. Kocham Anię
I-love Ann (acc.)
'I love Ann.'
b. Marysia kocha się w słynnym aktorze
Mary loves refl. prep. famous actor
'Mary is in love with a famous actor.'

(13a) and (13b) differ in a fashion similar to their English glosses: in (13b), the actor may not even know of Mary's existence, while (13a) carries much more of an implication of the object's involvement (though not necessarily reciprocation).

Many languages, in fact, make much more systematic use of such a device than the lexical idiosyncrasies of English or Polish. In Warlpiri, for example (cf. Hale 1973), objects of transitive verbs are usually marked in the absolutive case (while transitive subjects are in the ergative). Systematically, however, it is possible to indicate that an action was incompletely or unsuccessfully carried out by marking the object with the dative:

(14) a. njuntulu-lu Ø-npa-tju pantu-ṇu ṇatju
       you-ergative Aux.-2-1 spear-past me
       'You speared me.'
   b. njuntulu-lu Ø-npa-tju-la pantu-ṇu ṇatju-ku
       you-ergative Aux.-2-1-obl. spear-past me-dative
       'You speared at me; you tried to spear me.'

Some languages even have a distinct case with exactly this function. In Finnish, for example, the partitive case is used for the object when the action is incompletely carried out, the object is incompletely affected, or simply to indicate an imperfective aspect:

(15) a. Hän luki   kirja-n
       He read-past book-gen./acc.
       'He read the book.'

   b. Hän luki   kirja-a
       he read-past book-partitive
       'He was reading the book.'

In contrast (cf. (15a)), completely affected objects in perfective sentences are marked with the accusative (distinct only for pronouns; syncretic with the genitive for singular nouns, and with the nominative for plural nouns).

In the Polish and Warlpiri cases, the contrast which marks holistic vs. partitive is formally an aspect of the marking of objects of transitive verbs, and so examples parallel to (11) and (12) in which the same distinction is marked with intransitive verbs do not arise. In Finnish, however, the partitive case can appear on the subjects of intransitives, where it marks a difference of definiteness:

(16) a. Huonee-ssa leikki lapsi-a.
       room-in   play   child-partitive
       'There were children playing in the room.'

   b. Lapse-t   leikki-vät huonee-ssa.
       child-nom.pl. played-pl. room-in
       'The children were playing in the room.'

The distinction found in intransitive subjects clearly shares at least a family resemblance with that found in objects, and one would probably want to subsume them under the same generalization — as in English.

We conclude, therefore, that there is no unitary semantic characterization available for the notion of 'direct object'. Attempts to base such a definition on semantic roles founder on the general semantic diversity of objects, together with the fact that the same role may be realized with a given verb both as objects and as oblique (prepositional) complements. The one semantic characteristic which does seem to be associated with objects, on the other hand, is the possibility of holistic vs. partitive interpretation, and this exists for subjects as well as for objects. It is clearly a generalization about certain formal properties of surface NPs (in English, unmarked ones), rather than about a class of elements filling a syntactic structural position (direct objects).

2. DIRECT VS. INDIRECT OBJECTS

From the evidence of the preceding section, we conclude that the notion of direct object is a formal one, rather than being based on semantic factors: direct objects are otherwise-unmarked NPs that follow the verb. By itself, however, this definition is insufficient. A central class of problem cases is presented by the traditional indirect object construction:

(17) a. The committee offered the position to Jones.
      b. The committee offered Jones the position.

(18) a. Surreptitiously, Jones picked an edelweiss for his mother.
      b. Surreptitiously, Jones picked his mother an edelweiss.

Like the constructions discussed above with regard to the difference between holistic and partitive interpretation of objects, the indirect object construction involves an alternation between complements introduced in a prepositional phrase (the (a) sentences in (17) and (18)), and the same complements introduced as unmarked NPs (the (b) sentences). In the latter cases, of course, sentences contain two post-verbal unmarked NPs; and if this notion is to be well defined, it is necessary to resolve the issue of which of these (if either, and not both) should be considered the 'direct' object.

Consider this issue as it is addressed by Jespersen (1927: 279): 'the direct object is more essential to the verb and more closely connected with it than the indirect object', as shown by the fact that 'it is possible to isolate the direct object (*they offered a reward*), but not the indirect object ([*] *they offered the man*)'. Jespersen's claim is thus that, when a verb takes two unmarked complements (one of which alternates with a prepositional phrase with *to* or *for*), one of these (but not the other) is obligatory, and it is this object that should be called 'direct'.

With some verbs, however, neither complement can be isolated in Jespersen's sense:

(19) a. hand Jones a hot potato / hand a hot potato to Jones
          *hand a hot potato / *hand Jones

  b. promise Jones a job / promise a job to Jones
    *promise a job / *promise Jones

Such verbs would have to be interpreted as having no direct object if the criterion of isolability were taken as a necessary one — surely an unappealing conclusion.

  With other verbs, on the other hand, either of the two associated complement NPs can be isolated, as Jespersen observes (1927: 295). In this case, his criterion leads him to claim that there must in fact be two 'direct objects':

(20) a. strike him
    strike a heavy blow   strike him a heavy blow

  b. ask John
    ask a question   ask John a few questions

Maintaining logical consistency, Jespersen agrees to call both complements with verbs like those in (20) 'direct' objects, but he justifies this conclusion by appealing to the fact that neither complement has a prepositional phrase alternant with *to* (or *for*). Where one 'direct object' corresponds to a *to*-phrase, Jespersen prefers to consider it 'indirect':

(21) a. he teaches boys   he teaches the boys French
    he teaches French   he teaches French to the boys

  b. I told the teacher   I told the teacher my story
    I told my story   I told my story to the teacher

In these cases, both objects can appear alone, and thus by his initial definition Jespersen should call both of them 'direct'. Apparently, however, the existence of a *to*-phrase paraphrase marks a complement as an indirect object, and this criterion is seen as taking precedence.

  The existence of a *to*-phase paraphrase cannot be taken as an absolute requirement for indirect objects, however. Even if we agree (counterintuitively) to say that both objects with verbs like those in (20) are 'direct', other cases exist where a complement which is clearly 'indirect' by Jespersen's first criterion (optionality) has a paraphrase with a preposition other than *to* (or *for*):

(22) a. play a nasty trick / play Jones a nasty trick / *play Jones
    play a nasty trick on Jones / *play a nasty trick to Jones

  b. bear a grudge / bear Jones a grudge / *bear Jones
    bear a grudge against Jones / *bear a grudge to Jones

When we consider a full range of verbal NP complements, it is clear that the criteria of optionality and existence of *to*-phrase paraphrases cannot provide us with necessary and sufficient conditions for assigning the labels 'direct' and 'indirect' to objects. Consider, for example, the verb *bet*. This verb takes up to three complements: (a) a sum wagered; (b) the party with whom the wager is made; and (c) a proposition with respect to which the wager is made. The first of these can appear alone; the second can appear unmarked, but not alone. It would thus appear that the sum wagered is the direct object, and the person with whom the bet is placed the indirect object — but the latter has only a *with*-phrase paraphrase, and not a *to*-phrase. Further, the sum wagered is not an obligatory complement, since it can be omitted if the subject of the wager is mentioned. This latter can appear as an *on*-phrase if nominal (or a gerund), or as a bare complement if sentential:

(23) a. Smith bet $10 (with Jones) (on a horse / on Mary's being fired).
b. Smith bet Jones $10 / *bet Jones / *bet $10 to Jones.
c. Smith bet (Jones) that Mary would be fired.
d. *Smith bet a horse / Mary's being fired.

Jespersen's definitions fairly clearly do not provide us with a way of satisfactorily identifying the various complement NPs in association with many verbs. Note that there is no particular objection to saying that a single unmarked NP following a verb is its direct object: the problem arises exactly with verbs which can take more than one such complement. Here Jespersen attempts to provide us with a basis for saying that one of these is the 'real' direct object, while the other is an indirect object. The goal is to specify properties that designate one of the complements (defined by its semantic role) as direct object. As we noted initially, it does not appear possible to specify the notion of direct object in terms of a constant semantic role; Jespersen thus attempts to base his selection on formal properties (unmarked NP as direct object, and *to*-NP as indirect object). Where more than one NP meets the formal condition for being a direct object, the reference must be to other, related structures in which the same verb occurs. We have just seen, however, that the attempt to refer to optionality or the presence of a *to*-phrase in such structures does not in fact solve the problem completely.

Quirk *et al.* (1972: 349) attempt to resolve these problems by introducing an additional criterion for distinguishing between direct and indirect objects in sentences with two unmarked NPs, one not making reference to other related structures: 'An INDIRECT OBJECT, where both are present, precedes the DIRECT OBJECT, and is semantically equivalent to a prepositional phrase; a direct object may occur without an indirect object, but not vice versa ...' In fact, their definition incorporates both of Jespersen's criteria (equivalence to a prepositional phrase, though they do not specifically limit this possibility to *to*-phrases, and optionality), as well as a factor of linear order. If the notions of direct object and indirect object correspond to real and unitary aspects of grammatical structure, then, they are implicitly claiming that these factors will coincide in all cases.

We have already noted above (cf. (20)–(21)) that it is not always the case that indirect objects are optional, while direct objects are not. We can also note that some 'indirect objects' do not correspond to a prepositional phrase:

(24) a. fine miscreants $10 / *fine $10 to miscreants
 b. envy bankers their wealth / *envy their wealth to bankers
 c. spot the Bruins ten points / *spot ten points to the Bruins

In these cases, we are left with only the criterion of relative linear order to distinguish 'direct' from 'indirect' objects. This would appear to conflict, however, with the fact that for the verbs in (24), if either NP is optional it is not always the one corresponding to the first of the two complements:

(25) a. fine repeat offenders / *fine more than they can pay
 b. envy the rich / envy Jones' new job
 c. *spot Milan / *spot three goals

Furthermore, there are some complements which can appear unmarked but which alternate with prepositional forms (and thus ought to be called indirect objects), but which do not occur with another unmarked complement following them:

(26) a. write (telephone, wire, etc.) mother / write to mother
 b. signal the waiter / signal to the waiter

Is the single complement in structures such as these a direct object or an indirect object? Neither Jespersen nor Quirk *et al.* have a satisfactory way to resolve this problem.

In identifying direct objects, it is apparently a necessary (though not sufficient) condition that a post-verbal complement be unmarked by a preposition. Indirect objects (at least in the traditional acceptance of this term) are typically optional, typically have prepositional phrase paraphrases (usually with *to* or *for*), and typically come before the direct object when unmarked. We have seen above, however, that none of these characteristics can really be treated as definitional for indirect objects.

Another property of indirect objects has been noted by Stowell (1982): it is generally the case that when both direct and (unmarked) indirect objects co-occur, the indirect object can be interpreted as having some sort of (generalized) possessor relation with regard to the direct object. Sometimes, a verb that occurs with direct and indirect objects, so long as this relation can be imposed on the two, appears only with a direct object and a prepositional phrase if the apparent indirect object cannot be interpreted in this way:

(27) a. Jones sent a telegram to Canada.
 b. *Jones sent Canada a telegram.
 c. Jones sent Smith a telegram.

(28) a. Clean your room for Aunt Mary!
 b. *Clean Aunt Mary your room!
 c. Clean Aunt Mary a nice plump chicken!

The status of this condition is not clear, however, and it is surely not definitional for indirect objects. On the one hand, it cannot be a necessary condition, since there is no obvious sense of 'possession' that applies to the presumptive indirect objects of sentences like (22, 23, 24a), but not to otherwise parallel cases where indirect object constructions are not possible. And it is also not a sufficient condition, since it is well known that many verbs for which such an interpretation is possible do not allow unmarked indirect objects:

(29) a. Jones donated $10 to the Red Cross / *donated the Red Cross $10.
 b. Jones appointed a nurse for his son / *appointed his son a nurse.

Thus, while it is probably a general principle of English that the first of two unmarked post-verbal NP complements in interpreted where possible as standing in some sort of abstract possessive relation to the second, this cannot be taken as a definition of the indirect object relation.

We may note that 'indirect objects' may sometimes also be subject to holistic interpretation, as with other unmarked NPs like direct objects:

(30) a. Jones left a dog and cat hospital all of his money.
 b. Jones left all of his money to a dog and cat hospital (but the will was invalidated).

(31) a. Jones handed the butler his hat (who then dropped it).
 b. Jones handed his hat to the butler (who didn't take it).

Judgments are moderately subtle in such cases, but at least to my ear, (30a) implies that in fact the dog and cat hospital actually received the money, while (30b) in contrast is consistent with the state of affairs in which for some reason Jones' testamentary wishes were not carried out. Similarly, (31a) implies that the butler received the hat, while (31b) only implies that it was directed toward him. If this description is accurate, it would appear that the unmarked indirect objects are interpreted as more holistically implicated in the action described by the verb than the otherwise synonymous prepositional phrase paraphrases — surely a fact to be described by whatever principle is responsible for holistic interpretation.

On the basis of the considerations adduced in this section, then, we conclude that however convenient the labels 'indirect object' and 'direct object' may be (especially for the case in which two unmarked complements occur together), the traditional difference is not based on a set of significant and generally applicable criteria. Again, we come down to the fact that lexical specification for each verb must describe the exact set of complements that it can occur with, and the role to be assigned to each of them in its interpretation. There are surely many partial predictabilities in this domain, but these have the status of limited generalizations over the lexicon, rather than rules of syntactic structure. Similarly, there are undoubtedly rules of semantic interpretation that operate on the basis of syntactic structure (such as the rules of holistic interpretation and the possessive rule discussed by Stowell), but these rules are not definitional for categories in that structure. Indeed, there is no evidence that they need access to the information that would be represented in the labeling of such categories as direct and indirect object.

3. OBJECTS AND PASSIVIZATION

A particularly notable characteristic of objects, in English at least, is their susceptibility to passivization. The two notions of object-hood and passivization, indeed, are often regarded as virtually synonymous. As Jespersen (1927: 299) succinctly puts it, '[w]hat in the active is an object, is made the subject in the passive'.

(32) a. A man in uniform demanded my passport at the border.
b. My passport was demanded at the border by a man in uniform.

As the relation between (32a) and (32b) illustrates, the direct object of a transitive verb with no other unmarked NP complement appears as the subject of the corresponding passive.

With verbs taking more than one unmarked complement (i.e., those taking an 'indirect' object), as in (33a), the 'direct' object may be passivized as in (33b). It is also possible to passivize the 'indirect' object, as in (33c) — but only if this appears unmarked. The virtually synonymous sentence with a prepositional phrase does not have a variant with passivized indirect object:

(33) a. The railway gave Jones a gold watch when he retired.
 b. A gold watch was given Jones by the railway when he retired.
 c. Jones was given a gold watch by the railway when he retired.
 d. *Jones was given a gold watch to by the railway...

It seems, then, that there is a simple generalization at work: unmarked NP complements of verbs, their 'objects' in a generalized sense, can appear as the subjects of corresponding passives. Unfortunately, however, this claim is falsified in both possible directions: some unmarked post-verbal NP complements of verbs are not passivizable, and some NPs that **can** be passivized are apparently objects of prepositions.

Turning to the first of these cases, we can note with Jespersen (1927: 300) that '[n]ot every object can be made the subject of a passive sentence. Some verbs do not admit of a passive turn, although according to the analysis here preferred they take an object in the active [...].' Such verbs include the following:

(34) a. *40 tons is/are weighed by the Soviet space station.
 b. *Four is equalled by the square of two.
 c. *Too much is cost by the new edition of my book.
 d. *Jones' children are resembled by him.

The usual reaction to this observation is to claim that 'obviously' the post-verbal NPs in such sentences are not 'real' objects at all, but rather some sort of quasi-adverbial complements. This is not, however, to solve the problem, but simply to restate it. If we confine the Primitive Alphabet of syntactic description to information about word class (and phrasal type, derived from word-class information in some variant of an $\bar{X}$-theory) plus an indication of constituent structure, there is no reason to deny that the phrases following verbs like *weigh, equal, cost, resemble,* etc. really are NPs. And since the verbs in question are apparently just as much sub-categorized for their complement phrases as a verb like *beat* is for its object, there is equally no reason to deny that they occupy a position in constituent structure parallel to that occupied by 'real' objects.

Of course, if we extend the Primitive Alphabet of syntactic description to include labels for grammatical relations borne by particular constituents, we could simply deny the label 'object' to the complements of such verbs. Aside from the difficulties encountered above in deciding what status the relations direct and indirect object should have, however, are those that will be noted below with the claim that exactly objects of verbs can be passivized, Jespersen (1927: 232) notes another problem:

If I call *two pounds* and *three years* objects in "it costs two pounds" and "it will last three years", my chief reason is that it is possible to say "it will cost you two pounds" and "it will last you three years", where it is most natural to speak of an indirect and a direct object ... but then we must also call *two pounds* in "it weighs two pounds" an object; and probably also *two miles* in "he walked two miles".

In other words, the complements in question are integrated into the system of 'direct' and 'indirect' objects in the same way other direct objects are. Their failure to undergo passivization remains an idiosyncrasy which cannot be eliminated simply by saying that they are not 'real' or 'full-fledged' objects, at least in any coherent and explicit sense of that term.

The second problem noted above is that the subject of a passive may correspond to a prepositional object or some other complement rather than to a 'direct object', as in the following examples:

(35) a. Our Mr Jones is looking into your request with care.
 b. Your request is being looked into with care by our Mr Jones.
 c. Jones made use of Zorn's Lemma in proving his theorem.
 d. Zorn's Lemma was made use of by Jones in proving his theorem.
 e. Use was made of Zorn's Lemma by Jones in proving his theorem.

(35b) illustrates the possibility of passivizing what is apparently the object of a preposition in the corresponding active (35a). In (35d) we have the same sort of relation, made still more complex by the fact that the prepositional phrase in question is apparently not a complement to the verb *make* itself, but rather to its object *use* — which is independently passivizable as well, as shown by (35e).

The usual account of sentences like (35b,d) is to appeal to the fact that many verbal lexical items in English actually consist of a verb plus a preposition-like element: the 'Verb-Particle' construction. Jespersen (1927: 312ff) suggests such a line:

> What in the active is the object of a preposition connected with a verb or with a verb and its object may be made the subject of a passive construction. [From this] we see that the particle has greater cohesion with the verb than with what (in the active) is the object either of the particle alone (preposition) or of the whole phrase.

If we interpret this 'greater cohesion' as the claim that the verb plus its particle form a constituent (a verb), we can then say that the apparent prepositional objects in such cases are actually the (unmarked) direct objects of this complex verbal unit.

In fact, as a substantial literature argues (see for example Fraser 1965, Palmer 1965, Bolinger 1971, and many other works), it is possible to distinguish genuine verbal particles from prepositions accompanying other post-verbal complements. One important distinguishing property, for instance, is the fact that genuine particles, but not prepositions, may follow objects:

(36) a. Jones looked up Smith's telephone number.
 b. Jones looked Smith's telephone number up.
 c. Jones looked into Smith's request.
 d. *Jones looked Smith's request into.

Unfortunately for the attempt to appeal to the Verb–Particle construction (36a,b) as the basis for passives such as (35b,d), it is not only in these cases that passivization is possible. Both of the passives in (37) are well formed:

(37) a. Smith's telephone number was looked up by Jones.
 b. Smith's request was looked into by Jones.

Despite the possibility of passivizing either (36a) or (36c), the contrast between (36b) and (36d) suggests that *into Smith's request* in (36c) is actually a prepositional phrase, and thus a constituent, as opposed to a sequence of verbal particle plus unmarked NP like *up Smith's telephone number* in (36a). This conclusion is reinforced by other considerations as well. For instance, prepositions, but not particles, form a phrase with the object, as shown by their moving together with it in the formation of relative clauses and questions:

(38) a. The request into which Jones was looking was Smith's.
 b. Into which request do you imagine Jones is looking now?
 c. *The telephone number up which Jones was looking ...

Similarly, with reference to the construction in (35c–e), there is good reason to believe that both *of X* and *use of X* are constituents in the phrase *make use of X*:

(39) a. Zorn's Lemma, of which Jones made use in proving his theorem, is equivalent to the Axiom of Choice.
 b. Zorn's Lemma, use of which was made by Jones ...

If this is correct, however, it is difficult to see how X in this construction can be construed syntactically as the direct object of a hypothetical complex verb *make use of*, parallel to the structural position of *the number* in *look up the number*.

Another argument against the proposal that the subjects of 'prepositional passives' like (35b,d) correspond to the direct objects of Verb–Particle constructions, rather than to objects of prepositions, can be constructed from the facts of 'Heavy-NP Shift'. Essentially, NPs that are (in some sense that remains to be explicated) heavy or internally complex can appear sentence-finally, out of their normal structural position.

(40) a. The constable watched patiently the building which the suspect had been seen to enter.
b. The constable told to move along the last few of the spectators who had surrounded the vandalized statue.

There are, however, two classes of NP which are not in general subject to displacement in this way: subjects, and objects of prepositions.

(41) a. *Finally moved along the last few of the spectators who had been standing around the vandalized statue.
b. *The constable waited before all afternoon the building which the suspect had been seen to enter.

By this criterion, we can determine that *work on X* and *work in X* in sentences like those in (42) below are sequences of verb plus prepositional phrase, while *dig up* is a Verb–Particle combination taking an object structurally parallel to that of simple verbs like *cultivate*:

(42) Jones has been $\begin{Bmatrix} \text{cultivating} \\ \text{digging up} \\ \text{*working on} \\ \text{*working in} \end{Bmatrix}$ for weeks a pathetic little

garden plot in which he hopes to raise vegetable marrows.

However, the NP object following any one of these may be the subject of a corresponding passive:

(43) This garden looks like it has been recently $\begin{Bmatrix} \text{cultivated.} \\ \text{dug up.} \\ \text{worked on.} \\ \text{worked in.} \end{Bmatrix}$

From these facts, we conclude that the phenomenon of 'prepositional passives' cannot be reduced to the existence of Verb–Particle sequences. As a result, we are left with the two difficulties we originally noted for the view that exactly objects of verbs can be passivized in English. On the one hand, some apparent verbal objects cannot be passivized, while on the other, some NPs that can be passivized are evidently objects of post-verbal prepositions, not of the verbs themselves directly. In the next section, we suggest a line of inquiry that may lead to an account of these problems.

4. THE NOTION OF 'GRAMMATICAL PERSPECTIVE'

The difficulty raised in the preceding section concerns the circumstances under which a given post-verbal complement can serve as the subject of a corresponding passive sentence. It would of course be of considerable interest if it were possible to give a purely syntactic solution to this question, in the form of a set of necessary and sufficient syntactic conditions for passivization. In traditional grammar, what is commonly proposed is that direct objects can passivize; but we have already seen that the notion of direct object is not an altogether satisfactory one; and in any event, indirect objects as well as direct objects can be passivized in English. A natural refinement would be to abandon the relational characterization and say that what can be passivized is an unmarked post-verbal NP complement; but we saw in the previous section that this is both too strong and too weak, since some passive subjects correspond to objects of prepositions on the one hand, and some unmarked post-verbal NP complements cannot be passivized on the other.

In the absence of a compelling syntactic alternative, we might examine the possibility that some other area of grammatical structure is central to determining the well-formedness of passives. A point made above in section 2 may have some methodological relevance: it is often the case that the same gross semantic content can be presented in more than one grammatical form, but when this happens, there are frequently subtle semantic distinctions associated with the difference. We suggest that there are semantic properties of passive sentences which furnish a key to the problem at hand.

The relevant aspect of semantic interpretation can be described, following suggestions of Fillmore (1977), as a theory of 'Grammatical Perspective'. Fillmore observes that the semantic content of a sentence is represented from a particular (not necessarily unique) grammatical point of view. This 'perspective' is oriented by one of its purportedly referring expressions (NPs), which is taken as central to its content. Much previous work (e.g. Anderson 1977, Wasow 1980, Bresnan 1982a) has identified this central NP with a particular semantic role (the *theme*) in a theory of Thematic Relations; but there are reasons to believe that no one particular semantic role can be identified with the participant which anchors the Grammatical Perspective of a sentence. Still following Fillmore's insight, we propose to call this NP the GRAMMATICAL FIGURE (as in 'figure' vs. 'ground'). The designation of a Grammatical Figure is not the only aspect of the determination of a sentence's Grammatical Perspective. Other relevant aspects include the assignment of responsibility (Agency) to some participant in some sentences, an aspect of sentence semantics which is interestingly grammaticalized in the Salish languages (Thompson 1976); abstract 'Source–Goal' patterns for movement or change, etc.

The Grammatical Figure is a sort of 'logical topic' (not to be confused with the **discourse** topic). It is the argument of a logical relationship of predication which forms part of the interpretation of a sentence. Since Plato is no longer around to defend himself, it might in fact be possible to identify this notion with his conception of ONOMA (the thing about which something is said) as opposed to RHEMA (which says something about it). When a sentence is logically 'about' the fact that an event results in a change in the state of some object, it is that object which constitutes its central orientation or Grammatical Figure. In a sentence describing motion, it is typically the Grammatical Figure that moves; if a sentence describes an event that results in the creation of some object, this object is the Grammatical Figure. In the description of perceptions, it is usually the source of the perception rather than its experiencer which is the Grammatical Figure. In so far as a sentence ascribes some identifying property, attribute, or (possibly abstract) location to an object, it is the object so identified that is the sentence's Grammatical Figure. It will be seen that this characterization is quite similar to that usually given of the *theme* in a theory of semantic roles; but as we will note below, there are some reasons to believe the two concepts should be kept separate.

In the most usual cases, the Grammatical Figure is identifiable from the grammatical relations borne by various NPs in the sentence. Usually the Grammatical Figure in a sentence containing a 'garden-variety' transitive verb is its direct object; with an intransitive verb, it is the subject.

Since the Grammatical Perspective of a sentence is an independent aspect of its semantic interpretation, however, the association of grammatical relations with this structure is not completely mechanical. Though most structurally transitive verbs have their direct object as Grammatical Figure, for example, a few must be construed as making something else occupy this place. Verbs such as *resemble* have this property: in *Jones' children resemble him*, the natural interpretation is that in which an identifying property is ascribed to Jones' children, rather than to Jones. Thus, with such verbs, the subject is the Grammatical Figure rather than the object. With some (especially locative) verbs describing essentially symmetrical relations, either subject or object may be the Grammatical Figure.

These remarks hardly constitute an articulated 'theory' of Grammatical Perspective, but they suggest the direction in which such a theory could be constructed. For further discussion, see Fillmore (1977). On the assumption that a full theory of this sort could be developed, we can suggest the following hypothesis in relation to our original concern: the Grammatical

Figure of a passive sentence cannot be in non-subject position unless the corresponding active also has its Grammatical Figure in the same position. The latter possibility is intended to accommodate examples like (44) below:

(44) a. Jones served Smith a dead fish.
 b. Smith was served a dead fish (by Jones).
 c. Jones has put an end to Smith's intransigence.
 d. An end has been put to Smith's intransigence (by Jones).

In (44a), it may be the fish which is the Grammatical Figure, since the action of serving it results in its conveyance from Jones to Smith. This remains the case in the passive (44b), and the structural position of the Grammatical Figure is the same in both cases. In (44c), it is *Smith's intransigence* which constitutes the Grammatical Figure, since it is this which undergoes change as a result of the event described. In the corresponding passive, the Grammatical Figure remains the same, and occupies the same structural position as in the active.

The more usual case, however, is that in which the (non-subject) Grammatical Figure in the active becomes the subject in the passive:

(45) a. Jones' slovenliness incensed his mother.
 b. Jones' mother was incensed (at/by his slovenliness).

Assuming that the Grammatical Figure must either remain in place or become the subject in the passive immediately accounts for the standard class of exceptions to passivization, such as *equal, resemble, weigh, cost, lack*, etc. We can call such verbs 'pseudo-transitive', since their semantic interpretation is not normally consistent with taking their 'object' as their Grammatical Figure. In the passive, the post-verbal NP becomes the subject, and the original subject (which is the Grammatical Figure) would thus have to move to a non-subject position:

(46) a. Jones lacks confidence / *Confidence is lacked (by Jones).
 b. The cheese weighs a kilo / *A kilo is weighed by the cheese.

Interestingly, there are exceptional circumstances in which these verbs can be given such an interpretation:

(47) a. In the result of this peculiarity, it [Othello] is resembled only by Antony and Cleopatra. (Bradley, *Shakespearean Tragedy*, *apud* Jespersen 1927: 300)
 b. Jones' world record has recently been equaled by a Swiss.

In these examples, we can note that *resemble* is normally used to assert a property of its subject, but in (47a), the property under discussion is a characteristic of the post-verbal NP in the related active: that is, because of the peculiarity in question, *Othello* has the property that only *Antony and Cleopatra* resembles it. Similarly, in ordinary uses of *equal* (e.g., *Pi equals 3.1415926...*), some property of the subject (*pi*) is asserted, but in (47b) the sentence describes a change which the post-verbal NP has undergone.

While the Grammatical Perspective of a sentence can be thought of as a sort of organization imposed on its basic semantic content, it is not the case that it is uniquely determined by this content. With many verbs, the logical predication relationships that can be expressed are unambiguous, but in other cases there is more than one possible mode of interpretation. For example, (48) below can be interpreted as expressing a property either of the troops (their present location), or of the territory beyond the river (that of being occupied by our troops):

(48) Our troops have crossed the river.

On the first of these readings, it is the subject (*our troops*) that constitutes the grammatical figure, while on the second it is the object. If the generalization suggested above is correct, we would predict that a passive could only be formed on the latter reading, in which the Grammatical Figure becomes subject, and not on the former, in which the Grammatical Figure would have to be deleted (or displaced to a *by*-phrase). This is of course correct, since (49) can only be used to describe the current state of our conquest, and not to tell someone where to forward mail addressed to the troops:

(49) The river has been crossed by our troops.

Transitive verbs that do not admit of an appropriate Grammatical Perspective do not have directly corresponding passives:

(50) a. The list includes your name.
      b. *Your name is included by the list.
      c. Your name is included on the list.

Sentence (50a) describes a property of the list, not of the name, and thus does not directly passivize; while the related adjective *included* expresses a property of its subject (like other adjectives), and thus allows for sentence (50c).

In some cases, it is clear that not only the verb of the sentence but the entire state of affairs it describes can determine the range of possible Grammatical Perspectives. Thus, (51a) cannot plausibly be interpreted as expressing a property of the stadium, though (51b) **can** be interpreted as describing the *surprising result* (as an EFFECTED OBJECT or OBJECT OF RESULT, in traditional terms). Correspondingly, the latter has a passive (51c) while the former does not (51d):

(51) a. Jones arrived at the stadium.
 b. Jones arrived at a surprising result.
 c. A surprising result was arrived at by Jones.
 d. *The stadium was arrived at by Jones.

An area of grammatical structure in which an account similar to that offered here has been suggested (cf. Anderson 1977) is the phenomenon of 'Visser's Generalization', whose significance was pointed out by Bresnan (1976). This is the observation that when a verb takes a complement phrase, the passive is only possible if that complement refers to the immediately preceding NP:

(52) a. John will make Mary a docile wife.
 b. Mary will be made a docile wife by John.
 c. John will make Mary a docile husband.
 d. *Mary will be made a docile husband by John.
 e. The vision struck John blind.
 f. John was struck blind by the vision.
 g. John strikes his friends as pompous.
 h. *John's friends are struck by him as pompous.
  (cf. John's friends are struck by his pomposity)
 i. John persuaded Mary to take a taxi.
 j. Mary was persuaded (by John) to take a taxi.
 k. John promised Mary to take a taxi.
 l. *Mary was promised (by John) to take a taxi.

These facts have been discussed by a number of writers. Bresnan (1982b) treats a wide range of cases, and argues that the central principle is one which follows from the assumptions of Lexical Functional Grammar. On that theory, the relevant complements (in (52c,g,k)) are subject to the condition that the subject of the basic verb serve also as the subject of the complement: ($\uparrow$SUBJ) = ($\uparrow$XCOMP SUBJ). Accordingly, the lexical rule of Passive must transfer the control relation to an oblique phrase, which is not a well formed functional control structure. In (52a,e,i), however, the control relation in the basic verb is ($\uparrow$OBJ) = ($\uparrow$XCOMP SUBJ), and the lexical Passive rule transfers the functional control relation in a well formed way to the subject of the derived passive.

We are essentially in agreement with Bresnan's account, but would like to derive it from other aspects of grammatical structure if possible. In particular, we would like to suggest that the difference between verbs with the property that (↑SUBJ) = (↑XCOMP SUBJ) and those with (↑OBJ) = (↑XCOMP SUBJ) follows from the difference between verbs whose subjects are interpreted as Grammatical Figures and those whose objects are so interpreted. In other words, only Grammatical Figures are eligible to serve as (↑XCOMP SUBJ). The advantage of this account is that it allows us to encompass the complementation facts, the absence of passives like (50b) and (51d), and the unambiguous interpretation of (49), under the same principle. Since these latter examples do not involve complements at all, it cannot be the simple failure of functional control to transfer from subjects to obliques that is at work. We suggest that it is really the failure of 'Grammatical Figure-hood' to transfer to obliques that is responsible both for the examples with complements (52) and for those without them.

If the preceding observations are essentially correct, they furnish a basis for determining which of a verb's complements is eligible to serve as its Grammatical Figure in some cases. Assuming that certain ('verb phrase internal') complements are interpreted as predicated of the Grammatical Figure, we can suggest that the 'direct object' but not the 'indirect object' of *give* has this function, regardless of whether the latter appears with a preposition or unmarked.

(53) a. The fish came raw to the table.
 b. The Japanese will often serve tuna to you raw.
 c. *They give the tuna a special sauce raw.

With *present*, on the other hand, the status of the THEME as Grammatical Figure or not depends on whether it is the unmarked complement (the direct object) or appears in a *with*-phrase:

(54) a. I presented Jones' cat to him dead.
 b. *I presented Jones with his cat dead.

With some verbs, either subject or direct object can serve as Grammatical Figure by this test:

(55) a. The government abandoned Cleveland as a slum.
 b. Jones abandoned Cleveland as a boy.

As expected, however, only the first of these readings undergoes Passive:

(56) a. Cleveland was abandoned by the government as a slum.
 b. *Cleveland was abandoned by Jones as a boy.

Similarly, the classic set of exceptions to Passive (*cost, weigh, resemble,* etc.) only allow complements predicated of their subjects, as we would expect if this is necessarily the Grammatical Figure of sentences containing them:

(57) a. As an adult, Jones resembles his late father.
 b. *As a child, Jones' new son resembles his late father.

It may be appropriate to characterize certain grammatical constituents other than complete sentences as having a specific (internal) grammatical perspective. Noun phrases in particular, as is well known, often have interpretations parallel in many ways to those of clauses, and these interpretations might be presumed to have similar internal structure. An instance in which the grammatical perspective established by specific lexical items has consequences for the well-formedness of noun phrases is the following. Given a $[N-N]_N$ compound, one element of which is derived from a verb, the other noun must usually be interpreted as the Grammatical Figure in the interpretation of the deverbal element:

(58) a. birdsong, rainfall, babytalk, earthquake
 playboy, rattlesnake, glowworm, crybaby
 b. punchcard, pushbutton, callgirl, scarecrow
 handshake, lionhunt, birth control, haircut

The compounds in (58a) correspond to intransitive verbs, whose only argument is of course the Grammatical Figure of interpretations based on them. The examples in (58b) are based on transitive verbs. Regardless of whether the deverbal part of the compound precedes the other noun in the compound (as in the *punchcard* examples) or follows it (as in the *handshake* examples), this other noun is interpreted as an argument corresponding to the direct object of a related sentence, which would in fact be the Grammatical Figure of such a clause. Interestingly, some verbs have both transitive and intransitive uses, and both may serve as the base of a compound. The interpretation of the compound, however, depends on what the Grammatical Figure of the corresponding clause would be:

(59) a. bird call ('call of a bird' or 'thing to call birds with'), turntable vs. turncoat
 b. bee-sting, frostbite, heartbeat, sound change

The compounds in (59b) appear to be built on transitive verbs, with the other noun representing the direct object. The verbs that serve as the basis of such compounds, however, are those that also have intransitive uses (*bees sting, that dog bites, his heart beat wildly,* etc.) which can be taken to be the foundation of the compounds in question.

Crucially for our purposes, those transitive verbs whose objects are not the Grammatical Figure of their clause (as shown by their inability to passivize) are interpreted differently from the ones in (58b):

(60)   family resemblance, women's equality, food costs, engine weight

A *family resemblance* is a way in which (members of) a family resemble each other, rather than a way in which someone resembles a family. *Women's equality* is the condition of women being equal (to something) rather than that of something's being equal to women (contrast this with *women's liberation*, the act of liberating women rather than an act of women liberating someone). Similarly, *food costs* and *engine weight* refer to what food costs or engines weigh, rather than to something that costs (as much as) food or weighs (as much as) an engine.

The sort of phenomenon discussed above has been associated, in previous work, with the semantic role of THEME, defined in rather vague terms as the participant whose location is specified, which undergoes movement, etc., together with metaphorical extensions of these. We suggest, however, that it is not correct to identify all of the various ways the Grammatical Figure of a clause may be integrated into its semantic interpretation as a single role relationship. In any event, there is good reason to believe that the theme in this sense does not always constitute the Grammatical Figure:

(61)   a.   Giant pussycats inhabit the north woods.
       b.   The north woods are inhabited by giant pussycats.

Sentence (61a) presumably asserts the location of giant pussycats, and thus its subject should be its theme. The passive in (61b), however, shows that the sentence may nonetheless be interpreted as asserting a property of the north woods, in which case the Grammatical Figure is not the same as the theme. It seems preferable, therefore, to separate these two notions, reserving the notion of theme for a role in the core semantic interpretation of a sentence; and using the conception of Grammatical Perspective (including the notion of a sentence's Grammatical Figure) to refer to a distinct aspect of its meaning, perhaps related to the notion of 'predication structure' appealed to by various authors in recent work (e.g. Williams 1980, Hellan 1983).

We have no illusions that these issues have been satisfactorily resolved by the sketchy remarks above. Our aim here is rather more limited, however: starting from a discussion of the conditions on passivization, we have uncovered a set of properties associated with certain NPs in a clause. Our goal was to show that these properties are related to an aspect of semantic structure, and that they are not uniformly associated with the grammatical relation 'direct object'. As such, they cannot serve to substantiate the content or the significance of this relation.

5. CONCLUSION

In concluding, we must stress that the skepticism implicit in the above remarks about the notions of direct object and indirect object do not at all imply a corresponding disbelief in the possibility of representing formally a difference between them within (any one of a number of) current syntactic theories. The formal apparatus of phrase markers obviously can distinguish two structural positions for unmarked post-verbal complements (cf. Stowell 1982 for some possibilities). Similarly, Relational Theories can simply incorporate these two distinct terms as undefined primitives. The point of view taken here is probably closest to that of Lexical Functional Grammar, which simply allows for one or two unmarked post-verbal complements called 'OBJ' and 'OBJ2' (in addition to prepositional objects); but within this theory, it would of course be perfectly possible to distinguish direct and indirect objects in Functional (as well as Constituent) Structure if this were warranted.

Rather than maintaining that the traditional terms direct object and indirect object are unrepresentable, we have tried to show that they are unwarranted — or at least that they do not represent significant and unitary grammatical categories in syntactic structure. It is of course convenient to have these labels available for discussing the parts of particular sentences, and in a large central core of cases, we can determine their reference with little risk of ambiguity. This convenience does not by itself justify them as terms of a theory of grammar, however.

Theoretical status would only follow if it could be shown that they correspond to some non-trivial set of syntactic and/or semantic properties. As we have seen above, the 'canonical' direct object in English is (a) an unmarked NP which comes immediately after the verb; (b) an obligatory complement of the verb; (c) interpreted holistically; (d) capable of serving as the subject of a corresponding passive; and (e) interpreted as the Grammatical Figure of its sentence. Since these properties are independent of one another, however, there is no motivated set of generally applicable criteria which define 'direct objects' (and by extension, 'indirect objects') in a uniform and non-arbitrary way. A principled theory thus should not include them as part of what Stockwell (1980) calls its Primitive Alphabet — or even as important derivative terms.

REFERENCES

Anderson, Stephen R. 1971. 'On the Role of Deep Structure in Semantic Interpretation', *Foundations of Language* 7: 387–96.
—— 1977. 'Comments on the Paper by Wasow', in P. Culicover, T. Wasow and A. Akmajian (eds.), *Formal Syntax*. New York: Academic Press, 361–77.
Bolinger, Dwight. 1971. *The Phrasal Verb in English*. Cambridge, Mass: Harvard University Press.
Bresnan, Joan W. 1976. 'Toward a Realistic Model of Transformational Grammar'. Paper presented at MIT–AT&T Convocation on Communications, *New Approaches to a Realistic Model of Language*. MIT.
—— 1982a. 'The Passive in Lexical Theory', in J. Bresnan (ed.), *The Mental Representation of Grammatical Relations*. Cambridge, Mass.: MIT Press, 3–86.
—— 1982b. 'Control and Complementation', in J. Bresnan (ed.), *The Mental Representation of Grammatical Relations*. Cambridge, Mass.: MIT Press, 282–390.
Fillmore, Charles. 1977. 'The Case for Case Reopened', in P. Cole and J. Sadock (eds.), *Grammatical Relations (Syntax and Semantics*, 8). New York: Academic Press, 59–81.
Fraser, Bruce. 1965. *The Verb-Particle Construction in English*. MIT dissertation, later published in revised form by Taishukan Publishers, Tokyo.
Hale, Kenneth. 1973. 'Person Marking in Walbiri', in S. Anderson and P. Kiparsky (eds.), *A Festschrift for Morris Halle*. New York: Holt, Rinehart and Winston, 308–44.
Hellan, Lars. 1983. 'Reflexives in Norwegian and Theory of Grammar'. Unpublished manuscript, University of Trondheim.
Hill, Archibald A. (ed.) 1962. *Third Texas Conference on Problems of Linguistic Analysis in English*. Austin: The University of Texas.
Jespersen, Otto. 1924. *The Philosophy of Grammar*. (Reprinted 1965) New York: W.W. Norton.
—— 1927. *A Modern English Grammar* (Part III: *Syntax*, second volume). Copenhagen: Ejnar Munksgaard.
Palmer, Frank R. 1965. *A Linguistic Study of the English Verb*. London: Longmans.
Quirk, Randolph, S. Greenbaum, G. Leech, and J. Svartvik. 1972. *A Grammar of Contemporary English*. New York: Seminar Press.
Stockwell, Robert P. 1980. 'Summation and Assessment of Theories', in E. Moravcsik and J. Wirth (eds.), *Current Approaches to Syntax (Syntax and Semantics*, 13). New York: Academic Press, 353–81.
Stowell, Timothy. 1982. 'The Origins of Phrase Structure'. Unpublished MIT dissertation.
Sweet, Henry. 1898. *A New English Grammar*. Oxford: Oxford University Press.
Thompson, Laurence C. 1976. 'The Control System: A Major Category in the Grammar of Salishan Languages', in B. Efrat (ed.), *The Victoria Conference on Northwestern Languages*. Victoria: British Columbia Provincial Museum [proceedings published 1979], 154–76.
Wasow, Thomas. 1980. 'Major and Minor Rules in Lexical Theory', in T. Hoekstra, H. van der Hulst and M. Moortgat (eds.), *Lexical Grammar*. Dordrecht: Foris Publications, 285–312.
Williams, Edwin. 1980. 'Predication,' *Linguistic Inquiry* 11: 203–38.

22

A Note on the Definition and Description of True Anacolutha

NILS ERIK ENKVIST

1.

1.1.

In this paper I shall try to describe, not the ideal norms that people use when steering their linguistic behaviour, but one detail of what they actually do in speech (as well as writing, though here my data come from speech alone). Those who believe in distinctions between competence and performance might therefore like to classify my essay as a contribution to performance linguistics.

1.2.

Anacolutha have often been regarded as one instance of performance gone awry. They have been grouped together with hesitation and correction phenomena as instances of human frailty. But we may well ask what impromptu communication would be like if there were no mechanisms for hesitation (pause, vocalized hesitation with schwa, repetition, stretching, use of verbal fillers, and semantic softening and hesitation with hedges), correction, and melioration (addition of another correct but somehow more appropriate expression). All these devices are obviously important in helping communication partners to overcome the strains imposed upon them by on-line language processing in real time. Indeed one of the characteristics of a good, fluent speaker is his skilful handling of hesitation and correction devices, especially those that are least conspicuous. Foreign-language teachers too are beginning to pay attention to the importance of giving students some experience of hesitation devices common in the target language but unattainable through spontaneous transfer from L1.

1.3.

Thus a linguist may well study hesitation, correction, melioration, and perhaps anacolutha too, in the conviction that they are part and parcel of normal communication. Such phenomena are particularly characteristic of impromptu speech. Their investigator will be readily tempted to adopt a stance of what one might call teleological optimism. 'Tout,' said Pangloss in Chapter One of *Candide*, 'étant fait pour une fin, tout est nécessairement pour la meilleure fin. Remarquez bien que les nez ont été faits pour porter des lunettes, aussi avons-nous des lunettes.' In a similar spirit one might say that there are situations, not least in impromptu speech, where human beings cannot, and perhaps should not, follow the syntactic patterns normally expected in, say, literate writing. We need devices such as hesitation patterns, correction, melioration, and anacolutha, *pour la meilleure fin.*

2.

2.1.

The term *anacoluthon* (from Greek *an-* 'not' + *akólouthos* 'following', hence 'lacking proper sequence') has been used by linguists in senses ranging from the very broad to the very specific. In the broad sense, any structure deviating from some standard of well-formedness has been labeled as an anacoluthon. To remind the reader that I am using the term in a more specific sense I shall here opt for the collocation 'true anacoluthon'. A concrete and precise description of true anacolutha has been given by Loman and Jörgensen (1971: 54–5), as well as by Linell (1981: 176ff), with a comprehensive set of Swedish examples. The following definition and description of true anacolutha is heavily indebted to these principles, though some of Linell's more detailed observations may not apply to English-language data.

2.2.

A TRUE ANACOLUTHON is definable as a blend of two overlapping structures, as in

(1) S.2.11.1526–7[1]   I have been (for the last year) I have been doing that thing

Thus a true anacoluthon consists of two parts, each of which is syntactically correct in itself, as far as it goes (though it can be subject to hesitation, correction, and melioration). It qualifies as one type of STRUCTURE SHIFT in those instances where the INITIAL STRUCTURE, here *I have been for the last year*, remains incomplete. The FINAL STRUCTURE, here *for the last year I have been doing that thing*, can be either an incomplete structure or a complete one. We can now define the CENTRE of a true anacoluthon, here put between parentheses *(for the last year)* as the overlap string shared by both constructions, the initial and the final. The initial string is correct up to the second parenthesis) ; the final structure is correct after the first parenthesis (. Following Linell we can label the part before the (the INITIAL PERIPHERY and the part following the) the FINAL PERIPHERY of the true anacoluthon. The overlap can be illustrated by the tree diagram of Figure 22.1.

Figure 22.1

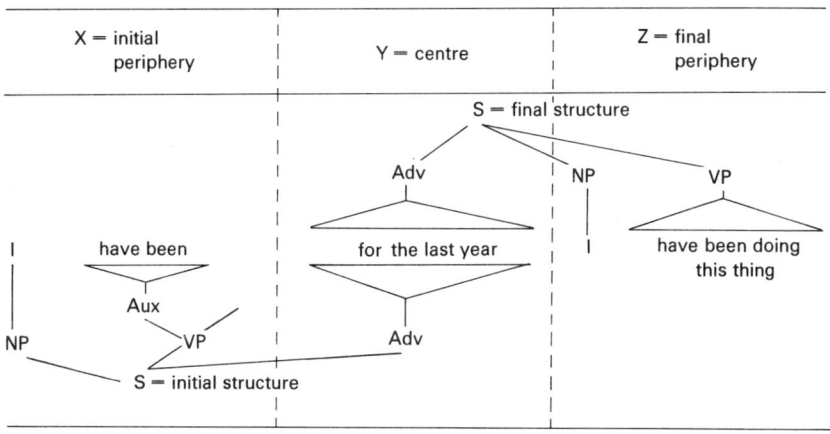

The definition can also be given as a process grammar with three rules:

(2) (i) produce an initial structure consisting of a well-formed complete or incomplete string X + Y,
 (ii) syntactically disregard X (which may nevertheless go on contributing to the total semantic and pragmatic information of the discourse, particularly if it is not repeated or paraphrased), and
 (iii) produce an element or string Z which makes Y + Z a well-formed string.

In such a context, well-formedness should be defined so as to allow phenomena characteristic of normal impromptu speech, such as hesitation, correction, and melioration, rather than in terms of stricter well-formedness criteria appropriate to other types of communication and text, such as literate writing.

2.3.

Having now defined a true anacoluthon, we can proceed to a set of further problems such as difficulties in the identification of true anacolutha, and the structure of the centre and peripheries of true anacolutha. Another problem not discussed here is the relation between true anacolutha and other types of structure shift (for instance, where do hesitation patterns and repair occur in the structure of the anacoluthon?).

3.

3.1.

True anacolutha are not always easy to identify. In corpora of authentic impromptu speech, they seem to be comparatively rare in comparison with instances of hesitation, correction, and melioration. Further, there are instances which can be analysed both as true anacolutha and as other types of structure shift. A few examples:

(3) S.2.1.670–5.   it's it's it's (now obviously with thirty thousand items) it's got to be [xh] much closer to an STC type of treatment than / to / [uh m] I was going to say Emily Skeel's / Brewer Webster bibliography

How can we tell whether the initial periphery + centre, *it's now obviously with thirty thousand items*, qualifies as a well-formed structure (allowing for the hesitation manifested as a repetition of *it's*)? Those opting for the view that (3) is a true anacoluthon would support their analysis by saying that the structure could go on, as in

(4) It's now obviously, with thirty thousand items, perfectly possible to adopt a treatment such as that of the STC. (Fabricated.)

Another kind of problem often met with occurs in

(5) S.2.8.9-12.   I mean when it came to the crunch you see it was uh / (England's trouble over the miners) / took precedence over / Ireland's problems with Sunningdale

What is missing here is a relative pronoun. Had the text been *it was England's trouble over the miners that took precedence*, it would be all right; it would not be a true anacoluthon. Dropping an obligatory relative thus results in structure shift. Finally, the analyst may wonder whether he should classify some instances as true anacolutha or left dislocations or both, as in

(6) S.2.14.23-5.   The evening class I went to / (we all agreed) / that it should start at a quarter to eight

Compare (6) with the non-dislocated (7):

(7) We all agreed that the evening class I went to was placed at a very awkward hour. (Fabricated.)

Such overlaps between categories need not embarrass us until we want to start counting incidences of different types of structure shift. Then we must have discrete categories and make up our minds how to classify our findings.

3.2.

What structures, then, occur in the centre and in the respective peripheries of true anacolutha? Presumably the peripheries and the centre consist of constituents or strings of constituents rather than of random non-constituent strings. But obviously we cannot define their structure in terms of specific constituents or constituent groupings: the elements indicated by X, Y, and Z in (2) are rather in the nature of 'essential variables', like topicalized elements definable as slots that can be filled with various syntactic contents.

3.3.

As Linell's Swedish examples and their analyses show, it is nevertheless possible to list certain categories of elements that often recur in the initial periphery and in the centre of true anacolutha. Thus the initial periphery contains elements occurring in the slot or field Scandinavian grammarians call 'fundament', that is, sentence- or clause-initial thematic or topical elements of the lighter kind (such as anaphoric pronouns) and of a nexus consisting of a high-frequency verb (*e=är, va=var, har* 'is, was, has'). Prototypically the centre is heavier and may contain a subject, an adverbial, a parenthetic insertion, or other materials more rhematic and informationally weighty than those in the initial periphery. The centre is then restructured into a new thematic element or theme–rheme complex, to which the new, final periphery consisting of a possible new nexus and a rhematic element are added. What should be emphasized here is the importance of informational categories explicable in terms such as old or given, and new information (or theme and rheme or topic and comment if such terms are used to indicate given and new information). Such informational categories are likely to be more relevant here than syntactic structures as such. Element weight is also relevant but as part of information structure: weighty elements become long and weighty because of the amount of new information they contain.

3.4.

All the same there is nothing to prevent us from classifying individual anacolutha or categories of anacolutha by syntactic structure. A few examples from a limited sample of texts from the London–Lund corpus follow. The initial periphery can, for instance, consist of

(8) (a) a (light) subject NP and finite verb
  S.2.11.1526–7   I have been (for the last year) I have been doing that thing
  S.11.3.122–33   he's getting thinner he looked (no longer) looked like Diaghilev
  S.1.7.855   it's just (the shop on the bridge) just does everything cheaper
  S.1.9.253–5   I did see (on LMS) / some carriages had gone in for this idea
 (b) a (light, anaphoric) fronted object NP
  S.6.6.665–6   for some of them (we didn't have to tell) them
 (c) a (heavier) NP with modifier
  S.2.14.23–5   the evening class I went to / (we all agreed) / that it should start at quarter to eight
 (d) a clause with a (heavy) NP complement which is then restructured as subject

S.10.10.107ff   but they're they're they're mostly the [s] the [?] (the squarer young / you know / ... the sort of university young of course /) are the usual woolly lot / you know / who won't have a bar of it

S.2.7.114–22   C: and another was — uh — I can't remember the bloke's name / something like Tom Jones / or (laughs)
a: (laughs)
C: or To ... no / no / (Tony Scott) / I'd never heard of / but they were quite that's all though

(e) an adverbial (adverb)
S.2.7.544–6   before / (we got on pretty well and shared a flat) before /

(f) a clause, the centre being a reporting clause
S.6.6.102–4   I went to England nearly every year (/ that was stipulated by my parents) / that I should go almost every year home

The number of examples is too small to allow any estimates of densities of such types of anacolutha in different types of impromptu-speech texts.

3.5.

Another approach to the syntactic description and classification of true anacolutha would start from the centre. The essential requirement is that the centre must be capable of occurring as an overlap between the initial and the final structures. There are two possibilities: either the centre has the same function in both the initial and the final structure, as in

(8a) S.2.11.1526–7   I have been (for the last year) I have been doing that thing

or the centre is restructured so that it comes to have different functions in the initial and the final structure, as in

(8c) S.2.7.114–22   (simplified) I can't remember the bloke's name — something like (Tony Scott) I'd never heard of

Here the predicative complement of the initial structure is restructured as the fronted objectival complement of the final structure.

3.6.

Such examples in which a noun phrase still retains its character of complement, despite partial restructuring, suggest that one should pay attention to the degree of syntactic and semantic similarity that obtains between the initial and the final periphery of a true anacoluthon. Thus in

(8b) S.6.6.665–6   for some of them (we didn't have to tell) them

some of them and *them* are closely related in form and referent (to the point where *some of them* might be regarded as a dislocation). But in

(8g) S.3.2.592ff   My understanding of the AUT's position / is that / [hm] they don't insist on / (people [hm] below the age of you) could be appointed / and still not offend the AUT at the bottom of the scale

Here the centre is a complement in the initial structure and is restructured into the subject of the final structure. As the nexal relation between subject and verb phrase may require little semantic prediction it is clear that the choice of semantic content for the final periphery can be relatively independent of the initial periphery. In other words, in such instances the final periphery need not recapitulate matter already expressed in the initial periphery. Again a far larger collection of examples would be necessary to show what actually happens in such instances in different types of impromptu speech.

3.7.

Linell's extensive collection of Swedish anacolutha contains examples of several other categories. They also provoke the question to what extent true anacolutha might differ between Swedish, which is thematically somewhat more flexible, and English, which is thematically somewhat more rigid. (In other terms: Swedish is somewhat less subject-dominated and somewhat more theme-dominated than English because it allows some types of topicalization disallowed in English.) At this point a contrastive study might be in order.

4.

4.1.

Another empirical question whose study needs more extensive materials has to do with the co-occurrence of hesitation, correction, and melioration with true anacolutha. Such a study would throw light on the process by which a speaker monitors his output, checking whether it conforms to his plans or not. We can model a monitor as a more or less complex device whose basic function is pattern matching (Laver 1980). Both plans and actual output go into the monitor, which decides whether the output is identical with what the speaker wanted to say (according to certain specific criteria of identity or similarity), or whether the output differs from what he desired. If it does differ, the speaker must decide (consciously or not) whether he will let the slip go uncorrected, or whether he wants to correct his utterance by activating the appropriate correction mechanism (cf. Levelt 1983).

4.2.

Anacolutha differ from those slips that activate correction and melioration patterns in that they are presumably either undetected by the speaker, or approved because he is prepared to abandon the initial periphery — that is, abandon syntactically: semantically, the initial periphery, like a noun phrase in left dislocation, may still play an important role in text comprehension.

5.

What, to indulge in a final speculation, is the function of anacolutha? They are one way in which a speaker can change his mind and shift structures, perhaps more often subconsciously or unconsciously than consciously. An anacoluthon is the smoothest of all types of structure shift. It does not overtly signal the break in syntactic patterning but bridges the discrepancy by means of the centre shared by the initial and the final structures. In this sense anacolutha hide, or embellish, the break in syntactic continuity between the initial and the final structures. Anacolutha are also economical in making use of the same centre in two structures. Many anacolutha seem to be difficult to detect; it would be interesting to know to what extent receptors are capable of spotting anacolutha as they occur in rapid impromptu dialogue. In brief: however severely we may wish to stigmatize anacolutha in literate writing, they do provide impromptu speech with a smooth means of structure shift.

NOTE

1. My materials come from the Survey of English Usage's London–Lund Corpus, some of the texts being available in Svartvik and Quirk (1980) and some

remaining unprinted. I am grateful to Randolph Quirk, Sidney Greenbaum, and Jan Svartvik for their characteristically generous permission to consult the files of the Survey and use its texts. Numbers preceding quotations refer to locations in the London-Lund corpus. I also owe thanks to my assistant Martina Björklund, who found and classified several of the examples cited here.

REFERENCES

Boardman, G.N. 1977. 'A Study of Certain Kinds of Anacolutha in a Corpus of Spoken English', in Wolf-Dietrich Bald and Robert Ilson (eds.), *Studies in English Usage* (= Forum Linguisticum 6). Frankfurt/M. and Bern: Lang, 183-228.

Laver, John. 1980. 'Monitoring Systems in the Neurolinguistic Control of Speech Production', in Victoria A. Fromkin (ed.), *Errors in Linguistic Performance.* New York: Academic Press, 287-306.

Levelt, Willem J.M. 1983. 'Monitoring and Self-Repair in Speech', *Cognition* 14: 41-104.

Linell, Per. 1981. 'Svenska anakoluter', in Sigurd Fries and Claes-Christian Elert, *Svenskans beskrivning 12* (= Acta Universitatis Umensis. Umeå Studies in the Humanities, 37). Umeå: Umeå University, 173-83.

Loman, Bengt, and Nils Jörgensen. 1971. *Manual för analys och beskrivning av makrosyntagmer* (= Lundastudier i nordisk språkvetenskap C.1). Lund: Studentlitteratur.

Svartvik, Jan, and Randolph Quirk (eds.). 1980. *A Corpus of English Conversation* (= Lund Studies in English 58). Lund: Gleerup.

23

On the Principle of 'Weight' in English

PETER ERDMANN

THE HEAVIER CLAUSE ELEMENT PRINCIPLE

The principle of 'weight' is an old one. It has been observed in both synchronic and diachronic investigations of English and other languages. In word-order studies it has played a particularly prominent rôle. In the fifties and sixties it fell into eclipse among some linguists with modern, more formal approaches to language, but it has reemerged in recent years as part of 'textual pragmatics' (see, e.g., Leech 1983: Chapter 3.3.3). In other linguistic schools, especially functional approaches like that of the Prague School, the notion has had a continuous application (see, e.g., Firbas 1964). I will begin by documenting some of its history in this century.

One of its earliest formulations is Otto Behaghel's *Gesetz der wachsenden Glieder*, presented and copiously illustrated in an article entitled 'Beziehungen zwischen Umfang und Reihenfolge von Satzgliedern' (Behaghel 1909/10: 139). Behagel's *Gesetz* is a description of the tendency to be found in many languages to put heavy clause elements after light ones, i.e. towards the end of a clause or sentence.

> Das Gesetz [der wachsenden Glieder] lautet: Von zwei Gliedern von verschiedenem Umfang steht das umfangreichere nach. (Behaghel 1930: 85)

This 'heavier element principle' (Stockwell 1977: 68) belongs to a group of word-order tendencies based on the physical appearance of constituents. In Behaghel's own words, they are word-order patterns where 'lediglich die Körperlichkeit der Wörter den Ausschlag gibt ...' (1930: 84). This group of principles interacts with a second one which is based on the content of clause elements. They are word-order patterns where 'die Anordnung in irgendwelcher Beziehung zum Inhalt der Satzglieder [steht]' (Ibid.). One of the principles of this second group concerns the positioning of given or less important, and new or more important information within the clause.

Behaghel states that the new — or more important — information tends to follow the given — or less important — information, i.e. the former is to be found with elements towards the end of the clause, the latter with clause elements at or near the beginning. In his own words:

> Ein beherrschender Satz ist der, daß im allgemeinen das Wichtigere die spätere Stellung, das weniger Wichtige die frühere Stellung erhält ... Statt der Ausdrücke 'weniger wichtig' und 'wichtiger' kann man vielfach auch einsetzen: das Alte und das Neue: dasjenige, das bereits im Bewußtsein vorhanden ist, und das, was ihm erst zugeführt werden soll. So drängen Begriffe, die bereits in einem vorausgehenden Satz Ausdruck gefunden haben, nach dem Eingang des Satzes. (Ibid.)

Behaghel surmises that this tendency to put the new information towards the end of a clause underlies historically the 'heavier clause element principle':

> ... der Begriff des Umfangreicheren wird sich weithin mit dem des Gewichtigeren decken, aber nachdem die zweckmäßige Stellung zur überlieferten geworden ist, entsteht daraus ein unbewußtes rhythmisches Gefühl, das gebietet, einem kürzeren Glied einen längeren Abklang folgen zu lassen. (Behaghel 1930: 85)

Among the six principles or tendencies of word order which Jespersen discusses in volume seven (Chapter 2.1) of his Modern English grammar, he mentions the 'principle of relative *Weight*' (Chapter 2.1.5(D)), and gives the following examples from English:

> Lighter elements can be placed near the centre, while heavier ones are relegated to more peripheral places: *take it off / take off your hat* ... Whole clauses are generally placed either at the very beginning or at the end of the sentence of which they form parts — thus really in 'extraposition' ...

> The light little word *it* is frequently placed with the verb to avoid clumsy collocations, thus as subject in *It is fortunate that he has come / it is a pleasure to see so many people here*; as object in *I take it for granted that he will come* ...

Reszkiewicz (I owe this reference to Jacek Fisiak), in a study on word-order patterns in Late Old English prose, sets up the following principle, which he calls the 'fundamental ordering formula' for two-element sequences in the post-nuclear or tail section of a clause, i.e. after the finite verb form: '... the heavier the element as a class is, the further toward the end it is placed' (1966: 51). He distinguishes this 'fundamental principle' from the 'communicative principle' developed especially by representatives of the Prague School. According to the latter principle, 'elements which are new in the communicative process are stressed and, consequently, placed later on in the sequence and elements which are known are unstressed and, consequently, ... placed earlier in the sentence ...' (61ff). The former principle does not derive from the grammatical, semantic, or communicative functions of the clause but is based on the physical volume of its elements. The fundamental principle divides a clause into 'ordering classes', i.e. 'sentence elements, or portions of these, capable of being placed separately, which are isolated and defined not relationally but in complete isolation, i.e. independently, of each other and primarily in terms of such physical characteristics as size, weight, and the complexity of the structure of each of them' (9). Although the two principles have to be kept apart, they often interact and work together, 'since normally the short and light elements express datum, what is known, and the longer and more complex they become the more new information they communicate' (62).

Quirk and his three collaborators in the *Grammar of Contemporary English*, in dealing with factors that affect the sequential organization of a clause or sentence as a message, likewise point to two tendencies they call the 'principle of end-focus' and the 'principle of end-weight'. The first refers to the tendency to place new information in the 'neutral position of focus ..., that is (generally speaking) chief prominence on the last open-class item or proper noun in the clause ...' (1972: Chapter 14.3), as illustrated in their sample sentence *Dylan Thomas was born in SWANsea*. The second principle directs attention to the 'tendency to reserve the final position for the more complex parts of a clause or sentence' (Chapter 14.8). The weight of clause elements is determined in the following way: 'The "weight" of an element can be defined in terms of length (e.g. number of syllables) or in terms of grammatical complexity (number of modifiers, etc)' (Leech and Svartvik 1975: section 423).

The authors quoted above agree that the weight of clause or sentence elements is one of the principles influencing the organization of syntactic structures as messages. This principle of weight interacts with, but is independent of, the grammatical (e.g. subject, object, complement, adjunct), semantic (e.g. participant rôles like agent, patient, instrument, location) and communicative (e.g. theme/rheme, given/new information) structure of the clause or sentence.

LIGHT AND HEAVY CLAUSE ELEMENTS

According to the principle of weight, clause elements are counted as **light** or **heavy**. The two syntactic phenomena looked at in this article, i.e.

extraposition and clefting, concern the weight of verbal and nominal groups. In this area, both co- and subordination are involved; the number of joined elements and the type of modification used are important. Counting a nominal group as heavy means either that two or more nominal groups, which are coordinated or which stand in apposition to one another, show up as the clause elements to be clefted, or that the head noun of a nominal group is **post**modified by a phrase or clause. It is striking that nominal postmodification plays a decisive rôle in establishing a nominal group as heavy. My corpus material allows no conclusions as to whether some types of nominal premodification are important for counting a nominal group as heavy. Nominal groups which do not have the grammatical build-up just mentioned are counted as light. Let me illustrate some of the structures in question.

1. Juxtaposition of nominal groups
   (a) by coordination
       governors and managers; doctors, artists, lawyers; their love of flying, their spirit of adventure or their curiosity
   (b) by apposition
       tennis, his favourite sport; entertainment (movies, TV, plays); her usual attire — baggy dungarees, a mantailored shirt and sturdy oxfords

2. Postmodification of head noun
   (a) by a relative clause
       a relationship that is cold but not violently hostile; the image he had seen; the thorough way in which the quality and refinement have been improved
   (b) by a *that*-clause
       the consideration that it would diminish our security; the fact that he cared; the hope he would conduct himself in an orderly fashion
   (c) by a prepositional phrase
       an urgent look at our secondary education; the need for a certain humility; the balancing of knowledge against blind instinct
   (d) by a participial clause
       overall laws governing the development of a society; theorems concerned with civil disobedience; a belief shared by many people
   (e) by an infinitival clause
       the will to follow through; the chance to earn a living; his obdurate refusal to yield the floor to any of his opponents

Counting the weight of verbal groups in our instance means, as will become apparent in the following section, looking at the length or structural complexity of the superordinate predicate adjective. When this is not coordinated with other predicate adjectives or when it is not postmodified by a phrase or clause, the verbal group is counted as light. Verbal groups whose adjectival core shows these characteristics are counted as heavy. Let me give some examples of heavy verbal groups met with in the corpus for extraposed sentences.

1. Juxtaposition of predicate adjectives
    (a) by coordination
        it is exciting and surprising that ...;
        it was odd, almost frivolous, that ...;
        it is not just meaningless but dangerous to ...

2. Postmodification of predicate adjectives
    (a) by a clause
        it is as appropriate as it is significant that ...; *it was less self-evident than he thought that* ...
    (b) by a prepositional phrase
        it is clear from the sheer volume that ...;
        it was obvious to anyone who bothered that ...; *it is far from my intention to* ...
    (c) by an adverbial phrase
        it is astonishing in this day and age that ...; *it is important, however, on general grounds of policy, that* ...; *it is advantageous, therefore, on the input side to* ...

EXTRAPOSED AND NON-EXTRAPOSED CLAUSES

The first construction I will take up is extraposition, which has repeatedly been said to interact with the principle of weight. Take for example the characterization given by Jespersen quoted above or Stockwell's statement in his *Foundations of Syntactic Theory* (68): 'The "heavier element" principle is the basis for an important set of transformational rules called **extraposition** rules ...' The type of extraposition to be looked at is illustrated by the following two sentence pairs.

1. (a) It is important that their time should not be wasted.
   (b) That their time should not be wasted is important.
2. (a) It is sweet to sip in the proper place.
   (b) To sip in the proper place is sweet.

That is, I will restrict my analysis to (non-)extraposed sentences having a *that*- or *to*-clause as their subject and an adjective as their predicate in the superordinate clause. The reasons for choosing this type of extraposition are twofold: first, it allows both extraposition and non-extraposition, and, second, it is the structure most representative of (non-)extraposed sentences, both grammatically and lexically speaking. The statistics given are derived from analysis of a corpus of written Standard British English comprising 15 novels, 15 book-length (popular) scientific writings, 15 editions of the *Daily Telegraph* (daily newspaper), and 15 editions of the *Spectator* (weekly newspaper).

The overall numbers for both extraposed and non-extraposed sentences exemplified under (1) and (2) above clearly show that extraposition is the favoured construction. The corpus contains 452 examples of structures with a *that*-clause as sentential subject, like (1a) and (1b). Of this total, 416 cases extrapose the subject *that*-clause by introducing the pro-form *it* as in (1a), while 36 cases keep it in subject position as illustrated by (1b); i.e. 92.04 per cent of the examples attested in the corpus extrapose their *that*-clause subject, while only 7.96 per cent do not.

These differing rates of occurrence are a reflection of the distribution of light and heavy clause elements in the sentence. Clausal *that*- and infinitival *to*-subjects count as heavy elements; they consist of several elements, whether of the full range of clause elements as in the case of *that*-subjects or of an infinitive and complements or adjuncts as in the case of the attested *to*-subjects. The predicate in the superordinate clause, however, tends to be light; i.e. it consists of only an adjective, which is at times premodified by an adverb. Cases where it is postmodified by a prepositional phrase or an adjunct are rare. The figures gained from the corpus are as follows: of the 416 examples showing extraposition, 365 have no postmodification of the superordinate adjective while 51 do; i.e. 87.74 per cent display the sequence 'light predicate – heavy subject', and 12.26 per cent the distribution 'heavy predicate – heavy subject'. Of the 36 examples showing non-extraposition, 20 have no postmodification of the superordinate adjective while 16 do; i.e. 55.56 per cent follow the weight pattern 'heavy – light', and 44.46 per cent the positioning 'heavy – heavy'.

Table 23.1: Extraposed and non-extraposed *that*-clauses

total		*it* + adj. + *that*-clause				*that*-clause + adj.			
number	%	number		%		number		%	
452	100	416		92.04		36		7.96	
		adj. light		adj. heavy		adj. light		adj. heavy	
		number	%	number	%	number	%	number	%
		365	87.74	51	12.26	20	55.56	16	44.46

The figures are similar for (non-)extraposed infinitival *to*-subjects. The corpus contains 649 examples of structures like (2a) and (2b). Of this total, 617 cases extrapose their clausal *to*-subject by introducing the pro-form *it* as in (2a), while 32 examples keep it in subject position, as illustrated by (2b); i.e. 95.07 per cent of the examples attested in the corpus extrapose their infinitival subject, while only 4.93 per cent do not. Comparing the weight of the superordinate adjective with that of the *to*-clause, corresponding results obtain. Of the 617 examples showing extraposition, 549 have no postmodification of the superordinate adjective while 68 do; i.e. 88.98 per cent display the sequence 'light predicate – heavy subject', and 11.02 per cent the distribution 'heavy predicate – heavy subject'. Of the 32 examples showing non-extraposition, 22 have no postmodification of the superordinate adjective while ten do; i.e. 68.75 per cent follow the weight pattern 'heavy – light', and 31.25 per cent the positioning 'heavy – heavy'.

Table 23.2: Extraposed and non-extraposed *to*-clauses

total		*it* + adj. + *to*-clause				*to*-clause + adj.			
number	%	number		%		number		%	
		617		95.07		32		4.93	
		adj. light		adj. heavy		adj. light		adj. heavy	
649	100	number	%	number	%	number	%	number	%
		549	88.98	68	11.02	22	68.75	10	31.25

To conclude, the distribution of extraposed and non-extraposed sentences in English displays a tendency that could be called the 'principle of balanced weight'. If the superordinate predicate adjective is light, the heavy clausal subject tends to be extraposed; if the adjective is heavy, the tendency not to extrapose the heavy clausal subject is less clear-cut. What is striking is that the ratio of light to heavy superordinate adjectives in non-extraposed structures is less favourable for light predicates than it is in extraposed sentences. Taking the two types illustrated above together, the following picture emerges: in non-extraposed sentences, light superordinate predicates are favoured over heavy ones by approximately six to four; in extraposed sentences, the ratio is roughly nine to one. Let me give some corpus examples for the tendencies described:

(a) (non-)extraposed *that*-clauses

It is evident that one reform calls for another ...
(*Daily Telegraph*, 13 March 1975, 16:7)

It is true that every word the teacher utters counts.
(Britton, *Language and Learning*: 188)

... it has long been known to physiologists that the succeeding portions of a meal are arranged in corresponding layers in the stomach.
(Cleave, *The Saccharine Disease*: 143)

That we have living architects in our day is certain; but that they will be given their opportunity is not sure at all.
(Sitwell, *British Architects*: 270)

That I was in love with Kitty and that this was a love letter was clear to me well before one o'clock.
(Murdoch, *A Word Child*: 223)

(b) (non-)extraposed *to*-infinitives

It is dangerous to trust the word even of a scrupulous diarist ...
(*Spectator*, 25 January 1975, 93: 3)

It was rather pleasant to give instructions after receiving so many.
(Hartley, *The Go-Between*: 173)

It was good of Mr Weekley to give you those driving lessons.
(Sillitoe, *A Start in Life*: 63)

To be alone, to think alone, to read quietly is difficult.
(Hoggart, *The Uses of Literacy*: 36)

To be fat was to be prosperous. To be big was to be at an advantage. To be as huge as Maud was worthy of the wife of God.
(Pownall, *The Raining Tree War*: 17)

As mentioned in the introductory section, the notion of weight interacts with other word-order principles. There are clear-cut textual differences between the use or non-use of (non-)extraposed sentences, which I cannot go into here. The tendencies observed for (non-)extraposed structures with adjectives as their superordinate predicates are as pronounced with other predicators. Take for example (non-)extraposed sentences with finite passive verb forms as their superordinate predicates. I will restrict myself to illustrating (non-)extraposed sentences with *that*-clause subjects, which are far more numerous in the corpus than infinitival subjects. There are 311 cases in the corpus. Again, the extraposed group (277 examples) is more numerous than the non-extraposed class (34 examples); i.e. 89.07 per cent extrapose the clausal subject while 10.93 per cent do not. The interesting point to note is the occurrence of *by*-phrases with the finite passive verb forms in the superordinate clause. According to the principle of balanced weight mentioned above, these sentences should show a strong tendency to leave out their *by*-phrase with extraposed sentences, since this would make the superordinate predicate heavy; *by*-phrases should be favoured in non-extraposed sentences. The figures confirm this tendency. Of the 277 examples of extraposed sentences, 268 have no *by*-phrase while nine do; i.e. 96.75 per cent comply with the principle of balanced weight, 3.25 per cent do not. Of the 34 examples of non-extraposed sentences, 23 have a *by*-phrase while 11 do not; i.e. 67.65 per cent go along with the tendency, 32.35 per cent run counter to it. Typical corpus examples of the distribution to be observed are the following.

It is hoped that forming a Parliamentary committee will allow emotions to cool.
(*Daily Telegraph*, 18 March 1975, 5: 2)

That Krushchev's concern that his large eastern ally [= China] might entangle the Soviet Union in war with the United States ... was evidenced also by Soviet criticism of Peking during the first round of the Sino-Indian border dispute in 1959.
(Buchan, *The End of the Postwar Era*: 22)

IT- AND *WHAT-*CLEFTS

The second area to be looked into is that of grammatical prominence. I will compare *it-* with *wh-*clefts in regard to the notion of weight. There has been a great deal of work done on the focusing constructions of English (see, e.g., Akmajian 1979, Higgins 1979), and there have been perceptive studies of some of the discourse functions of both *it-* and *wh-*clefts (see, e.g., Jones 1977: Chapter 6; Prince 1978). The principle of weight, however, has not played a rôle so far. In what follows, I take sentences like (3a) and (3b) to be *it-*clefts, structures like (4a) and (4b) to be *wh-*clefts (cp. Prince 1978:883, fn. 1).

3. (a) It was fear that made him draw the revolver.
   (b) It is the look in his eyes I'm worried about.
4. (a) What is even more alarming is the high rate of teenagers involved in fatal crashes in which alcohol is a factor.
   (b) What no one understood was Mike's answer to the question of how to cope with inflation.

In some cases, clefts like those mentioned under (3) and (4) can be ambiguous. Working with actual data normally rules out such problems, because the context disambiguates the structures in question. To compare *it-* and *wh-*clefts in regard to the notion of weight, it was necessary to concentrate on focused nominal groups in subject and object position which denote non-persons, because they are the only clausal groups which offer a choice of highlighting a constituent in an *it-* or *wh-*cleft. Nominal groups denoting persons are not focused in *wh-*clefts in my corpus, which is the same as that used for extraposition. Sentences like *Who Nixon chose was Agnew* (Akmajian 1979: 18) are ruled out by the five speakers of British English I asked. The few examples I have collected since are all from writings by American authors, so there may be a difference involved between these two national standards of English. There are likewise no examples in my corpus of *wh-*clefts for adverbial groups like the following, frequently found in generative publications: *When John arrived was at 5 o'clock, Why Fillmore sent Perry was to exploit the Japanese, How he did that was by using a decoder* (the sentences are taken from Akmajian 1979: 18). The only adverbial group found in my corpus, with six examples, is the locative; the number is too small to be of any significance in a comparison of *it-* and *wh-*clefts. Finally, focusing of non-finite verb forms can only occur with *wh-*clefts. So again a statistical comparison with *it-*clefts is ruled out, and we are left with nominal groups in subject or object position which denote non-persons, as stated above.

This structural option is a grammatical prerequisite for observing distinctions between the two focusing constructions in regard to the principle of weight. In the introductory section, I remarked that a nominal group (in *it-* or *wh-*clefts) is considered heavy when it consists of two or more simple or complex nouns which are coordinated or which stand in apposition to one another, or when a head noun is postmodified by a further phrase or clause. Nominal groups which do not show this structural build-up are counted as light. Applying the principle of weight to the two focusing constructions brings out a marked difference, which can be summarized as follows: nominal groups in *it-*clefts tend to be light, whereas nominal groups in *what-*clefts are preferentially heavy. The distribution of the attested examples is displayed in Table 23.3.

Table 23.3: *It-* and *what-*clefting of nominal groups

cleft		nominal group (not denoting persons)								
		subject					object			
		total	light	%	heavy	%	total	light	%	heavy	%
	it-	85	46	54.12	39	45.88	60	30	50	30	50
	what-	154	17	11.04	137	88.96	97	21	21.65	76	78.35

It- and *what-*clefting of nominal groups is more frequent in subject than in object position. The tendency of *it-*clefts to focus light clause elements mentioned above is slight; maybe it is better to speak of an even distribution between light and heavy nominal groups being *it*-clefted. *What*-clefts on the other hand strongly favour the focusing of heavy constituents; taking the figures for subjects and objects together, *what*-clefting of light nominal groups occurs in 15.14 per cent of the attested cases, whereas *what*-clefting of heavy nominal groups occurs in 84.86 per cent. The following examples are typical of the distribution just mentioned.

(a) *it*-clefting

It is the colleges which are the outstanding characteristics of Oxford and Cambridge.
(Burgess, *A Guide to English Schools*: 186)

I can't help thinking that it may well be his incompetence and laziness that were the cause of this accident.
(Wilson, *Old Men at the Zoo*: 37)

It's only tragedy which people bother to imagine or invent.
(Greene, *The Honorary Consul*: 16)

It is, of course, unemployment and its attendant consequences that politicians fear most.
(*Spectator*, 15 February 1975, 74: 13)

(b) *what*-clefting

What was needed was a political breakthrough.
(*Daily Telegraph*, 21 March 1975, 32: 4)

What was to Henry's credit was his whole state of mind, which encompassed the welfare of Ireland, as something quite separate from that of England, and at the same time perfectly desirable.
(Fraser, *Cromwell*: 579)

What is important for us is the contingent relation of this circumstance of continuous warfare to the character of a modern European state as an association of human beings and to that of the office of its government.
(Oakeshott, *On Human Conduct*: 272)

What he wanted to know was Pamela's whereabouts.
(Powell, *Books Do Furnish a Room*: 80)

What he misses, of course, is the rapidly emerging fact that Mrs Thatcher is a politician of star quality.
(*Spectator*, 29 March 1975, 366: 1)

What we want is the chance to earn a living, as we know we can.
(*Daily Telegraph*, 25 March 1975, 2: 7)

This tendency of having heavy subjects or objects in *what*-clefts is emphasized by the distribution of nominal clauses in the two focusing constructions under consideration. Because nominal clauses are heavy, one would expect *what*-clefts to favour marking their grammatical prominence. The statistics bear out this expectation. Table 23.4 gives their distribution as found in the corpus.

Figure 23.4: *It-* and *what*-clefting of nominal clauses

cleft		nominal clause			
		subject (total: 121)	%	object (total: 105)	%
	it-	9	7.44	0	0
	what-	112	92.56	105	100

To give some examples:

It was seeing Mary Hawkins that softened Jimmy.
(McIlvanny, *Docherty*: 158)

To discover what Aquinas thought about magic one has to look at quite different parts of his work; and what emerges then is that for him magic means almost exclusively ritual or ceremonial magic.
(Cohn, *Europe's Inner Demons*: 175)

What had to be decided was whether the problems were sufficiently great to require a legislative remedy ...
(*Daily Telegraph*, 25 March 1975, 10: 6)

What I can't see is why I'm here.
(Amis, *I Want it Now*: 126)

I cannot **want** 'happiness': what I want is to idle in Avignon or to hear Caruso sing.
(Oakeshott, *On Human Conduct*: 53)

THE PRINCIPLE OF 'WEIGHT' AND SYNTACTIC PROCESSING

Ordering clause and sentence elements according to the principle of weight has been linked to perceptual restrictions guiding our way of processing syntactic structures. There have been several attempts to account for this correlation, of which I will mention three. In the late fifties, Yngve (1960, 1961) developed the 'depth hypothesis' for English, which says that, because of constraints on the span of immediate memory, English tolerates only a certain number of left-branching structures. In several articles, Bever (1970, 1971) has proposed a series of universal perceptual restrictions that he sees reflected in language structure. His 'Principle G' covers the principle of weight, which is paraphrased in the following way: 'in ordering phrases we save the hardest for the last' (1971: 76). Edwards (1980), in a study on the influence of syntactic complexity on the comprehension of sentences, argues that the difficulty of understanding a sentence is a function of the clarity of its syntax, which can for example be impaired by constructions not following the principle of weight. All the studies alluded to characterize the principle of weight as a device which facilitates the processing of syntactic structures.

Of the proposals mentioned, I find Yngve's 'depth hypothesis' the most appealing. What is intriguing about it is the dominant tendency this hypothesis ascribes to right-branching structures (Yngve calls them 'progressive') in English, as for example compared with German. Relying on psychologists' measurement of the span of immediate memory, which is said to comprise seven items, Yngve hypothesizes 'that the grammar of English is so constructed that excessively deep constructions are actively prevented, and alternatively constructions of lesser depth are provided' (1961: 136). A sentence containing two *that*-clauses before its main verb, for example, is ungrammatical, because it exceeds the mentioned memory restriction: **That that it is true is obvious isn't clear.*

English syntax has developed a right-branching construction — extraposition — to remedy the situation — *It isn't clear that it is obvious that it is true.* The extraposition construction, which our material showed to be preferred to non-extraposed, i.e. left-branching, structures (Yngve calls them 're-gressive') in more than ninety per cent of the examples attested in the corpus, thus can be interpreted as a device to reduce depth in the subject-position of the sentence. Edwards, who builds on Yngve's hypothesis, relates its findings to his own proposal that the avoidance of top-heavy clausal subjects improves the perceptual task facing the reader in the comprehension of a sentence, which is 'to identify the subject and main verb and relate the two successfully. This crucial cognitive process is impaired, if the main verb is delayed too long in the sentence' (Edwards 1980: 32), as is the case in non-extraposed constructions.

This compound theory of taking the avoidance of heavy subjects and its proposed concomitant cognitive interpretation (impairment of the comprehensibility or memorability of a construction) as a guide to make sense perceptually of the principle of weight has been applied, so far, to non-focused structures only. There have been no comparable psycholinguistic studies on questions of weight in *it*- and *wh*-clefts. And I will not venture into this area.

NOTE

This work was supported in part by a grant from the Volkswagenstiftung.

REFERENCES

Akmajian, A. 1979. *Aspects of the Grammar of Focus in English*. (Outstanding Dissertations in Linguistics.) New York: Garland.
Behaghel, O. 1909/10. 'Beziehungen zwischen Umfang und Reihenfolge von Satzgliedern', *Indogermanische Forschungen* 25: 110–42.
―― 1930. 'Von deutscher Wortstellung', *Zeitschrift für Deutschkunde*, Jahrgang 44 der Zeitschrift für den deutschen Unterricht, 81–9.
Bever, T.G. 1970. 'The Cognitive Basis for Linguistic Structures', in J.R. Hayes (ed.) *Cognition and the Development of Language*. New York: Wiley and Sons, 279–362.
―― 1971. 'The Influence of Speech Performance on Linguistic Structure', in T.G. Bever, J.J. Katz, and D.T. Langendoen (eds.), *An Integrated Theory of Linguistic Ability*. Hassocks: Harvester, 65–88.
Edwards, N. 1980. 'Difficulty' in Text as a Function of Syntactic Complexity: A Study of Syntactic Complexity Within and Between Sentences. Unpublished Master of Philosophy thesis, Open University, Walton Hall, Milton Keynes.
Firbas, J. 1964. 'From Comparative Word-order Studies', *Brno Studies in English* 4: 111–26.
Higgins, F.R. 1979. *The Pseudo-cleft Construction in English*. (Outstanding Dissertations in Linguistics, 17.) New York: Garland.
Jesperson, O. 1949. *A Modern English Grammar on Historical Principles*. Part VII. 1974. London: Allen and Unwin.
Jones, L.K. 1977. *Theme in English Expository Discourse*. (Edward Sapir Monograph Series in Language, Culture, and Cognition, 2.) Lake Bluff, Ill.: Jupiter Press.
Leech, G.N. 1983. *Principles of Pragmatics*. (Longman Linguistics Library, 30.) London: Longman.
―― and J. Svartvik. 1975. *A Communicative Grammar of English*. London: Longman.
Prince, E.F. 1978. 'A Comparison of *wh*-clefts and *it*-clefts', *Language* 54: 883–907.
Quirk, R., S. Greenbaum, G.N. Leech, and J. Svartvik. 1972. *A Grammar of Contemporary English*. London: Longman.
Reszkiewicz, A. 1966. *Ordering of Elements in Late Old English Prose in Terms of their Size and Structural Complexity*. (Komitet Neofilologiczny Polskiej

Akademii Nauk.) Wrocław: Zakład Narodowy Imienia Ossolińskich Wydawnictwo Polskiej Akademii Nauk.

Stockwell, Robert P. 1977. *Foundations of Syntactic Theory.* (Foundations of Modern Linguistics Series.) Englewood Cliffs, NJ: Prentice-Hall.

Yngve, V.H. 1960. 'A Model and an Hypothesis for Language Structure', *Proceedings of The American Philosophical Society*, Vol. 104, No. 5, 444–66.

—— 1961. 'The Depth Hypothesis', in R. Jakobson (ed.), *Structure of Language and its Mathematical Aspects* (*Proceedings of Symposia in Applied Mathematics*, Vol. XII). Providence, RI: American Mathematical Society, 131–8.

24

Tale of Two Passives:
Internal Reconstruction in Ute

TALMY GIVÓN

1. INTRODUCTION[1]

This is an attempt to reconstruct the history of two grammatical morphemes in Ute on the basis of purely internal evidence. The first of the two is the suffix -*ta*, synchronically marking the IMPERSONAL-PASSIVE construction (see Givón 1980, 1981). Clustering with it is the root -*ra*, which synchronically forms the base for the verb 'be'. The second morpheme is the suffix -*ka*, synchronically the ANTERIOR/PERFECT marker (see Givón 1980, Ch. 4 or Givón 1984, Ch. 8). Related to it is the suffix/ formative -*ga*, used synchronically as either the verb 'have', the simultaneous-participial marker, or (in various combinations) in several tense–aspect markers. In the course of surveying the internal evidence concerning the synchronic distribution of these markers, I will try to show how it is possible to reconstruct an older use of -*ka* as a passive suffix. I will argue that the putative older passive with -*ka* must have been typologically different from the current impersonal-passive with -*ta*. I will try to assess the interplay between these two passives in the light of some parallel cross-linguistic evidence.

The exclusive use of internal evidence in historical reconstruction is of course risky. It is, nonetheless, in many ways superior to the strict application of traditional comparative reconstruction and a much more rewarding exercise. In applying the internal method, one must rely heavily on one's concepts of universality and naturalness, however implicit those may be. Ultimately, however, any suggestions made in this paper must tally with comparative evidence from other Numic languages.

2. PHONOLOGICAL PRELIMINARIES

There are good grounds in Ute phonology, both synchronic and diachronic, for interpreting the voicing variation of -*ta*/-*ra* and -*ka*/-*ga* as arising from an earlier allophonic variation in Ute. In this section I will sketch the arguments for this briefly, but for more detail see Givón (1980, Ch. 1). Currently, only the voiceless variants of stops (p, t, k) can appear in word-initial position in Ute, but not the voiced counterparts (v, r, g, respectively). Compounding — and thus placing the initial consonant in a word-medial position — normally brings about voicing. Thus consider[2]

(1) a. tuá-ci 'child' → núu-ruá-ci 'Ute-child'
    b. píą-pi 'female' → kavá-víą-pi 'mare' (lit. 'horse-female')
    c. káni 'house' → núu-gáni 'tipi' (lit. 'indian-house')

Synchronically one finds minimal pairs with voiceless stops and voiced variants in word-medial positions, as in

(2) a. 'ipí-ci 'red body paint' vs. 'iví-ci 'stick'
    b. 'áapa-ci 'boy' vs. 'áava-ci 'broadbeans' (from Sp. *hábas*)
    c. paná-qa-rų 'money' vs. sá-ĝa-rų 'white'
    d. sakų́-paĝáy- 'limping' vs. pagų́ 'fish'
    e. sá-x̂a-ka-tų-mų 'white' (AN, PL) vs. sá-ĝa-rų-mų 'white' (AN, SG)
    f. tųká-ti 'cause to eat' vs. tamári 'Spring'

Because of extensive word-final devoicing of vowels, erstwhile medial voicing contrast may become phonetically word-final, as in

(3) a. sá-ĝa-rų 'white' vs. tųká-qa-tų 'he who ate'
    b. sináâ-vi 'wolf' vs. pía-pi 'female'
    c. puwá-vų 'medicine power' vs. kwicá-pų 'feces'

The semantic–pragmatic plausibility of assuming that the *-ta / -ra* and *-ka / -ga* morpheme pairs are historically related is thus further reinforced by a plausible phonological connection.

3. THE IMPERSONAL-PASSIVE AND THE *-ta/-ra* CONNECTION

3.1. The Ute impersonal-passive

The Ute impersonal-passive has been described in detail elsewhere (Givón 1980, Ch. 6; Givón 1981), and thus will be covered here only briefly. Typologically there are two extreme types of passives, well exemplified by those of English and Ute. They may be contrasted as follows (for further discussion see Givón 1981):

(4) THE PROMOTIONAL PASSIVE (English)   THE AGENT-DELETION PASSIVE (Ute)

a. Object of active promoted to NOMINATIVE/SUBJECT in the passive

object of active retains its old case-marking in the passive

b. subject of active can appear in the passive, but must be marked by some OBLIQUE case

subject of active cannot appear in the passive clause

c. range of case-roles that can become subject/topic of passive is severely limited

fewer restrictions — if any — on case-roles that can become subject/topic of passive

d. passive clause tends to be semantically STATIVE

passive clause tends to be semantically ACTIVE

One may thus say that in the agent-deleting passive type, the new topic of the passive clause is assigned 'by default' rather than by formal structural 'promotion' to full subjecthood. Consider first the following examples:

(5) a. Active: ta'wá-ci sivą́ątu-ci paxá-xa
       man-SUBJ goat-OBJ kill-ANT
       'The man killed the goat.'

   b. Passive: sivą́ątu-ci paxá-ta-xa
       goat-OBJ kill-PASS-ANT
       'Someone killed the goat.'
       'The goat was killed (by some unspecified person).'

In the passive clause (5b) the agent cannot be mentioned, although it must be singular/dual. Indeed, the unspecified agent retains control of plural agreement on the verb in Ute, as can be seen by contrasting (5) with (6):

(6) a. Active: táata'wa-ci-u sivą́ątu-ci paxá-xa-qa
       men-PL   goat-OBJ kill-PL-ANT
       'The men killed the goat.'

   b. Passive: sivą́ątu-ci paxá-xa-ta-xa
       goat-OBJ kill-PL-pass.-ANT
       'Some persons killed the goat.'
       'The goat was killed (by some unspecified persons).'

Clitic/pronominal subject or object agreement on the verb is optional in Ute, and is controlled by complicated discourse-structure considerations of topicality and thematicity. In the active, the clitic pronoun on the verb may agree with either subject/agent or object.

(7) a. Agent agreement:
   táata'wá-ci-u sivą́ątu-ci pax̂á-x̂a-qa-amų
   men-PL   goat-OBJ kill-PL-ASP-they
   'The men killed the goat.'

   b. Object agreement:
   táata'wá-ci-u sivą́ątu-ci pax̂á-x̂a-qa-'u
   men-PL   goat-OBJ kill-PL-ANT-him
   'The men killed the goat.'

In the passive, however, only the object — or new topic — can control clitic agreement, but never the unspecified agent. Thus compare

(8) a. Agent agreement:
   *sivą́ątu-ci pax̂á-x̂a-ta-x̂a-amų
   goat-OBJ kill-PL-PASS-ANT-him

   b. Object/topic agreement:
   sivą́ątu-ci pax̂á-x̂a-ta-x̂a-'u
   goat-OBJ kill-PL-PASS-ANT-him
   'The goat was killed (by some persons).'

The permissiveness of what can become the topic of the passive clause (or what sentence types can be passivized; cf. (4c) above) is illustrated in (9):

(9) a. DO as topic of passive:
   tųkúa-vi tųká-ta-x̂a
   meat-OBJ eat-PASS-ANT
   'The meat was eaten.'/'Someone ate the meat.'

   b. IO as topic of passive:
   kaní-naag̑a tųká-ta-x̂a
   house-in   eat-PASS-ANT
   'Someone ate in the house.'

   c. Manner adverb as topic of passive:
   tų́ų-tųká-ta-x̂a
   well-eat-PASS-ANT
   'Someone ate well.'

   d. Verb complement as topic of passive:
   tųká-vaaci 'ásti-ta-x̂a
   eat-COMP want-PASS-ANT
   'Someone wanted to eat.'

   e. No element to serve as topic of passive:
   *tųká-ta-x̂a
   eat-PASS-ANT

343

The unacceptability of (9e) is essentially a pragmatic restriction, rendering the passive infelicitous if no argument exists to be its 'default' topic. Such an argument may be an anaphoric pronoun, in which case a comparable passive sentence is acceptable, as in[3]

(10)   tųká-ta-x̂a-ux
        eat-PASS-ANT-it
        'It was eaten.'/'Someone ate it.'

3.2. The use of -*ta* in action nominals

The suffix -*ta* is used with verb stems — without any finite trimmings of tense–aspect, plural agreement, or pronominal clitics — to mark action nominal(ization)s. Such derived nominals are, in essence, VPs excluding only the subject/agent, a restriction that is of course reminiscent of the passive, and may be used in reconstructing the history of the Ute passive. In such nominals, which are not full sentences, no argument on top of the verb is required:

(11) a. tųká-ta   tų́ų̨'-a-tų
        eat-NOM good-NOM
        'Eating is good.'

    b. sivą́ątu-ci pax̂á-ta ka-'áy-wa-tų
        goat-OBJ kill-NOM NEG-good-NEG-NOM
        'Killing the goat is bad.'

    c. sivą́ątu-ci pax̂á-vaacı̨́ásti-ta ka-'áy-wa-tų
        goat-OBJ kill-COMP want-NOM NEG-good-NEG-NOM
        'Wanting to kill the goat is bad.'

3.3. The root -*ra* and the verb 'be'

Synchronically, the most common verb 'be' in Ute is derived from the suffixal base -*ra*. This 'defective verb' is usually augmented with a deictic prefix, most commonly the remote-invisible *'u-*.

(12) a. 'ína   sarí-ci   'urá- 'ay
        this-SUBJ dog-PRED be-IMM
        'This is a dog.'

    b. 'ína   sarí-ci   tų́ų'a-tų   'urá-'ay
        this-SUBJ dog-SUBJ good-NOM be-IMM
        'This dog is good.'

Another erstwhile deictic prefix, *'a-*, is still used in a number of frozen contexts, as in the following question:

(13) 'íca̱-'ará 'íni   'ará-'a̱y
      this-be WH-PRED be-IMM
      'This thing there, what kind (of a thing) is it?'

In another partially frozen use, *'u-* alternates with the distant-visible deictic suffix *ma-*:

(14) a. 'u-rá-tu̱-ni
         that-be-NOM-SUBJ
         'like that one (there-invisible)'
     b. ma-rá-tu̱-ni
         that-be-NOM-SUBJ
         'like that/this one (there-visible)'

In addition to all these frozen or semi-frozen uses of *-ra* as 'be', one also finds in oral Ute texts various attestations of it without the most common augment *'u-*. The following are some examples from our text collection:[4]

(15) a. '... "áavu̱ púupa ma-rá-vàni" máy-pu̱gá ...'
         now   manner that-be-FUT say-REM
         '... "now you'll be just like this," he said ...'
         (H. Richards, 1 September 1976, 'How Bobcat and Coyote Got Their Shapes')
     b. ... 'aĝá-ra̱-pu̱gá-vaci̱ ...
         WH-be-REM-BKGR
         '... whichever way it was ...'
         (Ibid.)
     c. ... ma-rá-vaci̱-'urá ...
         that-be-BKGR-be
         '... it was like that ...'
         (Ibid., 'The Footrace')
     d. ... ka-tu̱vú̱ci-toĝó-ma̱kú-tu̱ ma-rá-wa-tu̱-mu̱   'urá-vaci̱ ...
         NEG-very-long-NOM-OBJ that-be-NEG-NOM-AN be-BKGR
         '... he wasn't very tall, not like this (gesture) ...'
         (Ibid.)

In some of these contexts, one finds both *-ra* and *-ta* alternating in virtually identical grammatical environments:

345

(16) a. ... sináa̠-vi-ra-x̂a-tu̧-mu̧ ...
         wolf-OBJ-be-ANT-NOM-AN
         '... he was (like) a wolf ...'
         (J. Cloud, 'Ute Creation Story')

   b. ... "'iní-'a-ta-vaa-pu̧-u-na̠-'urá?" máy-pu̧gá-ni ...
         WH-OBJ-be-HYPOTH-REL-be   say-REM-think
         '..."I wonder what it would have been?" he thought ...'

   c. ... mo̧vó̧t'o̧-a-'u pa'á-to̠ĝó-tu̧ mo̧vó̧t'o̧-ta-pu̧gá ...
         nose-GEN his long-OBJ   nose-be-REM
         '... and his nose became a very long nose ...'

   d. ... 'u̧vú̧s pa'á-to̠ĝó-tu̧ kwasí-ta-pu̧gá ...
         end long-OBJ   tail-be-REM
         '... and lo, (his) tail became very long ...'
         (H. Richards, 1973, 'How Bobcat and Coyote Got Their Shapes')

3.4. From 'be' through action nominal to passive

The naturalness of deriving a passive marker from a copular verb 'be', as in English, is fairly well attested cross-linguistically. Langacker and Munro (1975) have noted this tendency in both Uto-Aztecan and elsewhere, albeit within the context of a synchronic argument. However, there are a number of reasons why the *-ta* impersonal-passive of Ute, unlike the current passive of English, is not likely to have arisen directly from the verb 'be' *-ra/-ta*.

(i) Such a development would have left the topic-of-passive (and erstwhile object of the active) as grammatical subject of 'be' — and thus of the derived passive verb, as in English. But the Ute *-ta* passive is, as we have seen, non-promotional.

(ii) The English-type passive tends to be semantically stative, in a way reflecting the stative nature of a 'be' plus adjective construction. But as we have noted before, the *-ta* passive in Ute is semantically active.

A more attractive alternative is to assume that the verb 'be' *-ra* first gave rise to the action-nominalization suffix *-ta*, and the latter then gave risei to the passive construction with *-ta*. The following reasons make this alternative attractive:

(i) Phonologically, the passive and action-nominal markers are both *-ta*, while 'be' is *-ra*. The split between nominalization and the passive thus presumably is a later split, following the split between the two erstwhile allophones *-ra* and *-ta*.

(ii) The action nominal and the passive share the agent-deletion restriction. Deriving the passive from the action nominal would give a natural diachronic motivation to this restriction, as well as to the case-marking preservation of the non-agent arguments in passive clauses.
(iii) This derivation would presumably explain the non-stative nature of the Ute passive, something that direct derivation from 'be' would not predict.
(iv) Egerod (1975) has suggested that the Philippine voicing system, i.e. what used to be called the various 'focus' constructions, arose historically from nominalizations. Presumably, then, such a derivation of passive from nominalization is plausible on general grounds.[5]

There is, in addition, another fact about Ute discourse style which has some bearing on preferring the derivation of the passive via nominalization. It is an extremely common usage in Ute discourse to nominalize the main verb of a clause and subordinate it under the verb 'be', which is then grammatically the main verb. Consider the following examples, all taken from the same expository text:

(17) a. ... kác-'urá mámų naná-ma wų́ųka-x̂a-wa-tų-mų
NEG-be   they together   work-PL-NEG-NOM-PL/PRED
'urá-'ąy ...
be-IMM
'... and they don't work together ...'

b. ... ka-naná-maní-kya-wa-tų-mų   'urá-'ąy ...
NEG-together-do-PL-NEG-NOM-PL/PRED be-IMM
'... (we) don't work together ...'

c. ... 'umų́s-'urú pǫ'ǫ́-miyą́-rų-mų   'urá-'ąy ...
they-that   write-go/PL-NOM-PL/PRED be-IMM
'... since they do go to school (nowadays) ...'

d. ... 'úu-pa-ni-ax̂ 'urá-tų   'urá-'ąy ...
that-way-like-it be-NOM/PRED be-IMM
'... that's the way it (really) is ...'
(R. Cloud, 13 April 1977, Speech to Ute Language Committee)

4. THE ANTERIOR-PERFECT -ka AND THE RECONSTRUCTION OF AN EARLIER PASSIVE

4.1. The anterior-perfect

The anterior-perfect marker -*ka* (with predictable allophones -*x̂a*, -*kya*, -*kwa*, -*x̂wa*, -*qa*) covers two major functions in the Ute tense-aspect system synchronically.⁶ First, it is used as the 'anterior', 'out-of-sequence' aspect in narrative, as in

(18) a. ... 'uwás-'urá kaní-naaĝa-tux yu̱gá-y,
           he-be   house-in-to   enter-IMM
           '... So he then enters the house,

   b. mamá-ci   'uwáy   pu̱níkya;
      woman-OBJ the-OBJ see (-IMM)
      and he sees the woman;

   c. 'uwá-vaa-tu̱ nu̱ká-qa-y;
      her-LOC-DIR hear-ANT-IMM
      he **has heard** about her before;

   d. x.'urá máy-(y)
      then   say-(IMM)
      so then he says ...'

Clauses (18a, b, d) above relate events in the natural sequence in which they occurred. Clause (18c), on the other hand, reports an event which occurred prior to (18b) and, for that matter, prior to (18a). This use of the Ute anterior is akin to the English perfect or pluperfect.

The other major use of the Ute marker -*ka* is a predictable and widely attested extension of the perfect-anterior (see Givón 1982 for discussion). Discourse initially or in disconnected short exchanges in conversation, the -*ka* marker is used to establish 'past tense'. This is particularly true of the informal register, where the remote past marker -*pu̱gá* is inappropriate (cf. (18) above), but rather the 'immediate' aspect is used as a narrative-past marker. Under such conditions, if the 'immediate' were used at the onset, it may be confused with 'present-progressive', its other major function. As illustration of this usage consider:

(19) a. Speaker A: sivá̱a̱tu-ci 'uwáy   'áa   pax̱á-qa-'u?
                   goat-OBJ the-OBJ who kill-ANT-him
        'The goat, who **killed** it?'

   b. Speaker B: 'áapa-ci   'u   'iní-**kya**-ax̂
                 boy-SUBJ the-SUBJ do-ANT-it
        'The boy **did** it.'

4.2. The defective verb -*ga* 'have'

The defective verb formative -*ga* 'have' in Ute must incorporate, as prefix, the possessed noun (or nominal element). It takes major tense–aspect markers like a verb, but its stem pluralization is problematic, requiring first-syllable reduplication of the possessed noun. Most characteristically, it tends to appear in a nominalized, non-finite form with the subject nominal suffix -tu̱. Possessive expressions thus occupy in Ute an intermediate status, between syntax and the lexicon. Consider the following examples:

(20) a. puwá-ĝa-tu̱   (i) 'he has medicine-power' (sentential)
       power-have-NOM   (ii) 'he who has medicine-power' (relative)
                                          (iii) 'medicine-man' (noun)

      b. piwá-ĝa-tu̱   (i) 'he has a wife' (sentential)
         spouse-have-NOM   (ii) 'he who has a wife' (relative)
                                          (iii) 'a married person' (noun)

      c. kaní-gya-tu̱   (i) 'she has a home' (sentential)
         house-have-NOM   (ii) 'she who has a home' (relative)
                                          (iii) 'a home-owner' (noun)

All the possessive expressions in (20) above denote **inalienable** possession. To mark alienable possession, -ga is augmented by 'uni-aa-. Contrast (20c) above with (21) below:

(21) 'avá'na̱-tu̱ ka-ĝáni   'uní-aa-ĝa-tu̱
      many-OBJ RED-house-OBJ POSS-have-NOM
      (i) 'He owns many houses.'
      (ii) 'a person who owns many houses'

Existential expressions in Ute are constructed with the possession verb -ga augmented by the suffixal element -aa-. The location is thus, historically, the 'possessor' of what is in it. As an example consider

(22) 'i-vá̱a̱-tu̱   'avá'na̱-tu̱ kaní-aa-ĝa-tu̱
      here-LOC-NOM many-OBJ house-POSS-have-NOM
      (i) 'This place here has many houses.'
      (ii) 'There are many houses here.'

A morphological peculiarity of -ga 'have' is the suppletive negative -'a 'lack':

(23) a. kaní-gya̱-tu̱
         house-have-NOM
         'home-owner'

      b. ka-kaní-'a̱-tu̱
         NEG-house-have/NEG-NOM
         'homeless'

4.3. The use of *-ga* as tense–aspect marker

A fairly transparent development from *-ga* 'have' is the 'remote' tense–aspect market *-pųgá*. The first element, *-pų*, is a nominal suffix. The construction was thus originally a nominalized complement verb under the main verb 'have'. The suppletive negative of *-pųgá*, *-pų(')á*, is transparently related to the suppletive negative of 'have'.

(24) a. 'apáĝa-pųgá
  speak-REM
  'He spoke.'

  b. ka-'apáĝa-pųá
   NEG-speak-REM/NEG
   'He didn't speak.'

The augmented form *-a(a)ĝa*, derived from *-ga* 'have', is also used as the 'closure' aspectual in narrative (see details in Givón 1980, Ch. 4), as in

(25) ... 'úvway-ax̂-'urá 'ųvų́s 'urá-pųgá, qox̂óy-kya-pųáy-aĝay-amų ...
  then-it-be   end be-REM   slaughter-ANT-REM-have-them
  '... so that was the end then, he had slaughtered them all ...'

4.4. The use of *-ga* as participial-adverb marker

This is again a fairly transparent extension of 'have', to mark the verb in participial adverbs most commonly denoting progressive-simultaneous action. Thus consider

(26) a. káa-ĝa wų́ų ka-pųgá
  sing-PART work-REM
  '(she) worked singing.'

  b. káa-x̂a-ĝa-x̂a wų́ų ka-x̂a-pųgá
   sing-PL-PART-PL work-PL-REM
   '(they) worked singing.'

  c. ka-káa-'way-sapa̱ wų́ų ka-pųgá
   NEG-sing-NEG-MOD work-REM
   '(she) worked without singing'

  d. ka-káa-x̂a-'way-sapa̱ wų́ų ka-x̂a-pųgá
   NEG-sing-PL-NEG-MOD work-PL-REM
   '(they) worked without singing.'

4.5. The reconstruction of an earlier -*ka*-marked passive

In the preceding sub-sections we saw the various synchronic uses of the perfect-anterior -*ka* and the defective verb 'have' -*ga* with its various offshoots. In this section we will survey the evidence suggesting that at some earlier time Ute must have had a passive construction, of the PROMOTIONAL type, marked with -*ka*.

4.5.1. Frozen object nominalizations with -ka

The synchronic pattern of subject relativization and nominalization in Ute involves the nominalizing suffix -*tų*, which is typically used with animate subjects.[7]

(27) a. Finite: 'uwás-'urá pǫ'ǫ́-mi
           he-be   write-HAB
           'He habitually writes.'
   b. Nominalized: 'uwás-'urá pǫ'ǫ́-mi-tų 'urá-'ạy
           he-be   write-HAB-NOM be-IMM
           'He is a writer.'
   c. Relativized: ta'wá-ci̱   'u   pǫ'ǫ́-mi-tų ...
           man-SUBJ the-SUBJ write-HAB NOM
           'The man who writes habitually ...'

In contrast, the nominal suffix -*pų* is found with many frozen, non-productive COGNATE-OBJECT nominalizations:

(28) a. kwicá-   'defecate'   →   kwicá-pų   'feces'
   b. si'í-   'urinate'   →   si'í-pų   'urine'
   c. 'uú-   'fart'   →   'uú-pų   'a fart'
   d. nhká-   'dance'   →   'nhká-pų   'a dance'
   e. 'ųá-   'cultivate' →   'ųá-pų   'a field'

This cognate-object nominalization pattern is closely related to another non-productive pattern using -*pų*, that of ABSTRACT ACTION/QUALITY nominalization:

(29) a. naĝámi- 'be sick' → naĝámi-pų 'sickness'
   b. sųrí'aa- 'be afraid' → sųrí'aa-pų 'fear'
   c. wavųá- 'have sore throat' → wavųá-vų 'sore throat'
   d. ------- puwá-vų 'medicine power'
   e. ------- tagú-pų 'Sundance power'
   f. ------- 'ųnų́-pų 'madness'

A semi-productive nominalization pattern for objects of more transitive verbs uses a combination of the suffix -*ka* with the nominalizer -*pu̧*, as in

(30) a. cikávi'ná- 'cut' → cikávi'na-qa-pu̧ 'broken piece'
 b. wunu̧'a- 'notch' → wunu̧'a-qa-pu̧ 'a notched piece'
 c. kukwá- 'gather wood' → kukwá-qa-pu̧ 'gathered firewood'
 d. cu̧kú̧r'a- 'splinter' → cu̧kú̧r'a-qa-pu̧ 'splintered piece'

One may argue that the -*ka* suffix (here as allomorph -*qa*-) used above is still a 'perfective/resultative' marker, and that while -*pu̧* is a fairly prototypical inanimate object nominal suffix, it is not necessarily a **subject** suffix in usages such as (30). However, the most productive object nominalization pattern in Ute requires the -*ka*- suffix as well as the subject nominalizer -*tu̧*:

(31) a. po̧'ó̧- 'write' → po̧'ó̧-qwa-tu̧ 'book', 'letter', 'text'
 b. tu̧sú- 'grind' → tu̧sú-kwa-tu̧ 'flour'
 c. cox̂ó- 'grind' → tu̧kúa-vi cox̂ó-qwa-tu̧ 'ground meat'
 d. cíira- 'fry' → tu̧kúa-vi víira-qa-tu̧ 'fried meat'
 e. tavási-ti- 'dry' → tu̧kúa-vi tavási-ti-kya̧-tu̧ 'dried meat'
   dry-caus.
 f. 'iní- 'make' → taví-iní-kya̧-tu̧ 'sun-made', 'sunshine'
 g. kwiy'á- 'fence around' → kwiy'á-qa-tu̧ 'fence'
 h. wht ó̧pina- 'bundle' → wht ó̧pina-qa-tu̧ 'medicine bundle'

For the use of the subject nominalizing suffix -*tu̧* to be explicable, one must assume that the suffix -*ka* marked a **de-transitivized** construction whose grammatical subject was the object of the corresponding transitive verb. In the next section I will show that passive-looking usages of -*ka* can still be found in texts produced by Ute elders. The frozen evidence of the nominalization pattern in (31) is thus reinforced by semi-synchronic evidence culled from the speech of the oldest surviving generation of speakers.

4.5.2. *Residual use of the* -ka *passive in texts*

In this section I will cite a number of examples, all from texts obtained from Ute-speaking elders during the 1970s, showing the use of the suffix -*ka* as marking a passive-like construction. In many cases the examples are not unambiguous, and alternative less-than-passive interpretations of their structure may be constructed. Functionally, however, they all fall within the range of the passive's three functional domains (topicalization of non-agent, agent suppression, detransitivization; see Givón 1981).

What complicates clear-cut determination in Ute is, of course, the fact that -*ka* is synchronically the perfect-anterior marker, as well as a homonym of the stem-plural suffix -*ka*. This creates, in principle, the following — cross-linguistically rather plausible — three-way ambiguity, paraphrased in

(32) a. Passive: Joe was killed.
  b. Anaphoric-perfect: (He) has killed Joe.
  c. Impersonal-plural: They killed Joe.

In at least some of the examples cited below, interpretations (32b, c) are ruled out by the context. However, the passive may functionally cover the range of 'agents predicted anaphorically' (Givón 1979, Ch. 2), and thus a structure such as (32b) may serve as an equivalent to passivization. Similarly, the use of plural impersonals to code the impersonal-passive function is widely attested cross-linguistically (Givón 1981). For all these reasons, the force of the Ute text examples remains, at least to some extent, tentative.

Let us consider first the following example:

(33) a. ... 'iná-kwa-pu̱ núu-ci̱   'aví-pu̱gá, pu̱-pú̧i-pu̱gá;
      there-go-NOM person-SUBJ lie-REM   RED-sleep-REM
      '... and there was a person lying there, fast asleep;

  b. 'uwás-'urá 'u-vwáa-tugwá-pu̱gá, pu̱ní'ni-pu̱gáy-'u;
     he-be   there-LOC-go-REM   look-at-REM-him
     so he went over there and looked at him;

  c. 'úniguni to̧cá̧y'a̱   to̧'ma-x̂a-qa-pu̱gá ...
     lo   prairie-dog-SUBJ roast-PL-ANT/PASS-REM
     and lo — the prairie-dogs had been roasted ...'
     (H. Richards, 1973, 'How Bobcat and Coyote Got Their Shapes')

There are several features of example (33) which make it impossible to interpret the second -*ka* suffix in (33c) as anything except a passive marker:

1. The topic of clause (33c), 'prairie-dog(s)', is marked as a **subject**. This automatically rules out interpretations (32b, c).
2. The plural suffix in (33c) could only correspond, according to the story's context, to the prairie-dogs, but not to the other likely protagonist (the one who was seen asleep in clauses (33a, b), who is definitely a **singular**.
3. As we have seen from the nominalization examples in (31) above, if the -*ka* suffix indeed marked an older passive construction in Ute, that construction must have been of the 'promotional' type. And this is precisely what one finds in (33c), with the topic-of-passive marked as subject and controlling verb-plural agreement.

Let us consider the next example:

(34) a. ... 'iví-ci̱   'urá-pу̱gá 'icá-ta-ni,
           stick-SUBJ be-REM   this-be-like
    '... they were (like) sticks, like this,

   b. cuwáxi̱-kya-pу̱gá,   kу̱ná-vу̱-naag̑a-amу̱-'urá ...
      stuff-ANT/PASS-REM bag-OBJ-in-they/them-be
      stuffed into the bag ...'
      (J. Cloud, 16 June 1983, 'Ute Creation Story')

An impersonal-plural (i.e. 32c) interpretation of (34b) is ruled out by the story's context. However, an anaphoric-perfect (i.e. 32b) interpretation is quite natural, whereby one of the two **singular** main protagonists is the understood subject of 'stuffed', with the -*ka* suffix thus functioning as anterior-perfect.

The next two examples involve the use of the verb *wacу̧-* 'put'. In its minimal form, it is a bi-transitive verb. However, with the suffix -*ka* it has just about become lexicalized as the intransitive 'be there', used for inanimates only.[8] One thus finds -*ka* here as a frozen detransitivization marker, as in this constructed example:

(35) pǫ́'ó-qwa-tу̱ tу̱ká'na-pу̱ 'u-vwán wacу̧́-ka
     book-SUBJ table-OBJ there-on put-ANT/PASS
     'The book is on the table.'

The two examples from text are

(36) ... 'urú pu̱-púcucugwa-vaa-ku̱,
         that RED-know-FUT-SUBJ
     pǫ'ǫ́-qway-kwa̱-ax̑-'urú wacу̧́-ka-y ...
     write-PL-SUBJ-it-that put-ANT/PASS-IMM
     '... so that they may know it, if it is put into writing ...'
     (R. Cloud, 13 April 1977, Ute Language Committee Meeting)

(37) ... 'u-vwáa-tux 'i-vą́g̑a-ax̑-'urú wacу̧́-ka-y ...
         there-LOC-to here-LOC-it-that put-ANT/PASS-IMM
     '... it was (put) right there ...'
     (H. Richards, 1 September 1976, 'Sináwavi̱, Buffalo and Crane')

The subject of the two potentially-passive clauses in (36) is an inanimate, the Ute language. The allomorph of -*ka* following the stem 'write; could not be a perfect-anterior, for semantic reasons, nor could it be a plural agreeing with 'language'. Thus it must be an anaphoric/impersonal-plural marker (cf. (32c)). The -*ka* marking the verb 'put' in (36) could not be an anterior-perfect for similar semantic reasons, though it could equally well be either a passive-detransitivizer morpheme or an impersonal-plural one. In (37), however, -*ka* could easily be interpreted as a detransitivizer-passive, although an anaphoric perfect-anterior interpretation (cf. (32b)) cannot be ruled out.

The next pair of examples are of interest because, being taken from the same story told by the same speaker, they related virtually the same event in a parallel fashion, once with the -*ka* anterior-or-passive marker, the other with the passive marker -*ta*. While the first of those could be interpreted as an impersonal-plural (cf. (32c)), the parallelism makes it reasonably clear that the speaker intended both as passives.

(38) ... pyní-ti-pyáy-aĝay-'u ... mǫ'ǫ́-av   'urú,
      see-CAUS-REM-have-him   hand-OWN that-OBJ
      '... and he showed him his hand,
      py-m-'urú   tapáx̂a-qa-pyá-na-av-'urú ...
      REL-LOC-that nail-ANT/PASS/PL-REM-REL-OWN-that
      { 'where he had been nailed (to the cross) ...'
      { 'where they had nailed him (to the cross) ...'

(39) ... 'awáta-py-'u py-paa-ty   tǫná-ta-pyá-na-av ...
      rib-OBJ-his REL-LOC-DIR stab-PASS-REM-REL-OWN
      '... his ribs, where he had been stabbed ...'
      (M. Cloud, 16 December 1976, 'Story of Sundance')

Let us consider the final example, in which two -*ka*-markers appear in succession on the same verb in clause (40d):

(40) a. ... manúx-taa-s-'urú nỹ' 'ymýy-rugwá-vaani,
        all-OBJ-CONJ-that   I   you-give-FUT
        '... and I will also give you everything,

    b. 'urú   py-aa-my   'uní-vąąni,
        that-OBJ REL-OBJ-you do-FUT
        those (things) that you'll use,

    c. 'iní-wyný-vaa-na,
        do-stand-FUT-REL
        when you stand (in the Sundance),

    d. 'iní-kya-x̂aa-vaa-na ...
        do-PL-ANT/PASS-FUT-REL
        (the things) that will be worn (by y'all) ...'
        (Ibid.)

The first -*ka* in the sequence in (40d) cannot be the anterior, since neither the passive nor the plural could follow in Ute verb morphotactics. If it were the passive, then the sceond -*ka* could only be the anterior (the plural again being excluded on morphotactic grounds). However, an anterior interpretation of the second -*ka* is incompatible with the future tense -*vaa*. Therefore, the first -*ka* in the sequence in (40d) could only be the plural marker. Next, we have already noted that the second could not be the anterior, which is semantically incompatible with the future. The only remaining interpretation of the second -*ka* in (40d) is therefore that of the passive. And indeed, substituting -*ta* for it would have been quite natural, so that one suspects that the speaker can use either, more or less interchangeably.[9]

4.5.3. *Reconstructing a relationship of anterior, passive, and have*

It is well known that both synchronically and diachronically 'have', 'perfect', and 'passive' are members of closely-related semantic and pragmatic functional domains. This relationship is well documented in many unrelated language families (see, for example, Anderson 1982). If Ute indeed had an earlier passive construction marked with -*ka*, one displaying the characteristics of the 'promotional' type of passive, then one could suggest three plausible scenarios for the interrelationship between 'have' -*ga* and the -*ka* of the perfect and passive.

SCENARIO I: The marker -*ka* was originally the passive marker, and both the perfect and 'have' -*ga* developed from it.
SCENARIO II: The marker -*ka* was originally the perfect marker, and both the passive and 'have' -*ga* developed from it.
SCENARIO III: The marker -*ga*, originally 'have', is the source of both the passive and perfect -*ka* as either related or independent developments.

I think scenarios I and II can both be ruled out on general grounds, namely that grammatical morphology tends to evolve out of lexical stems, rather than vice versa (Givón 1971, *inter alia*). In addition, a specific phonological reason also militates against scenarios I and II for Ute. The *k/g* variation in Ute was almost certainly a predictable allophonic variation, with [g] being the natural variant in intervocalic environments. For a suffix, then, -*ga* is most likely to have been the **older** form, and -*ka* the more recent development, one which presumably exploited an erstwhile allophonic split growing into a phonemic one.

The fact that perfect and passive share the -*ka* form may be taken as weak evidence that the split between them is a secondary one, post-dating the original split of one of them from 'have' -*ga*. Our scenario III may now be further elaborated to accommodate such further detail. The most likely elaboration must take account of the naturalness of interpreting an anaphoric-perfect-impersonal construction as an 'impersonal passive', by downgrading the referentiality of the agent. This is an extremely subtle reinterpretation, since in many languages the passive construction with its agent-suppression function may be used in either ANAPHORICALLY-PREDICTABLE or GENERICALLY-PREDICTABLE environments. Thus consider the following two examples from English text, cited from Givón (1979, Ch. 2):

(41) a. Passive in an anaphoric-agent context:
'... since **he** didn't want to throw up, he forced himself to eat lightly. Anubis resented **being fed** small portions ...'
b. Passive in a generic-agent context:
'... When the ship **was** first **equipped** with the drive, The Golden Goose **had been revved up** to top speed ...'

In (41a), Anubis, a dog belonging to the character 'he', was clearly fed by its owner, whose identity is recoverable from the immediately preceding anaphoric context. On the other hand, the agent of the two passives in (41b) must be some generically assumed 'mechanics' or 'operators'.

One may thus suggest a two-step reinterpretation leading from an impersonal — perhaps plural-subject — perfect to an agentless passive:

(42) a. Anaphoric-perfect: They had roasted it [with 'they' actually referring]
b. Generic-perfect: They had roasted it [with 'they' not referring]
c. Agentless passive: It had been roasted.

It is thus the subtle shift from anaphoric to impersonal — (42a) to (42b) — which creates the potential for later restructuring as a passive construction. And in Ute, specifically, either the perfect -*ka* or the plural agreement -*ka* could have contributed to the rise of a passive -*ka*.[10]

There is one reason why scenario III, as amplified above, may not be our ultimate best choice: such a scenario would predict a non-promotional passive, with the topic-of-passive marked as **object**. But it was shown above that if -*ka* was a passive marker in Ute, that earlier passive construction must have been a **promotional** passive. I see two ways of resolving this difficulty. First, one may suggest that a restructuring in the case-marking system occurred, via which an earlier non-promotional passive with an object-marked topic became a promotional passive, with the topic acquiring the case-marking of subject. The feasibility of such a development is discussed by both Kennan (1975) and Givón (1976).

Alternatively, one may wish to suggest that scenario III be modified as follows:

1. Both the passive and perfect developed independently from 'have' -*ga*.

357

2. Both then underwent, separately, a change from -*ga* to -*ka*.

In order to make such a scenario feasible, one must posit a change from -*ga*, the main verb of a complex construction, to -*ga*/-*ka*, the grammatical verb-suffix coding the passive. Unlike the main verb 'be' which is used very widely cross-linguistically as a passive marker, 'have' is less common in such a capacity. However, we have already seen that Ute 'have' also shades into 'be' in existential expressions. Further, there are still, synchronically, expressions marked by -*ga* but functioning as 'be' or 'become'. As examples consider

(43) a. núu-ci̱ 'person'
    b. 'uwás-'urá núu-ci-**gya**-pu̱gá
       he-be   person-**be/have**-REM
       'He was (like) a person.'

Expressions such as (43b) are very common in Ute traditional stories, where animals are described as having been, in the olden days, 'like people'. In sum, then, such a modificiation of scenario III is feasible on both general and Ute-specific grounds. As to a choice between the two versions of scenario III, one suspects it will have to await the availability of more facts, either Ute-internal or comparative Numic.

5. TALE OF TWO PASSIVES

So far I have attempted to justify separately the development of the current Ute passive marked by -*ta* from 'be' -*ra* and the development of an earlier Ute passive marked by -*ka* from 'have' or 'be' -*ga*, perhaps via the perfect-anterior -*ka*. There remains now the question of why Ute changed from a promotional passive with -*ka* to a non-promotional passive with -*ra*. Such a question can only be answered tentatively, citing the many precedents of unrelated languages which have undergone wholly or partially similar developments. Various agent-suppressing impersonal constructions are available in most languages and quite often replace, eventually, older 'promotional' passive constructions. This is happening now in colloquial French, is virtually complete in non-literary Spanish, and has been recently documented in Dutch (Kirsner 1976) and in Kimbundu (Givón 1976). The feasibility of subject-topic coding properties acquired gradually by the non-agent topic of the passive has been discussed in detail by Keenan (1975), where it was observed that the last subject-coding property to be acquired is most commonly the nominative case-marking, i.e. full 'promotion'. Further, Ute also exhibits the typical pattern of the older passive receding into LEXICAL DERIVATION. In the diachronic replacement of one construction by another within the same — or roughly similar — functional domain, a conflation of potentially independent — and thus not mutually predictable — conditions must occur. These may be summarized as follows:

1. Functional and/or structural similarity: Another construction must exist in the language in close functional — and/or structural[11] — **proximity** to the 'receding' structure, for ANALOGICAL REINTERPRETATION to occur.
2. Loss of code-efficiency: The older construction must have developed considerable MORPHOPHONEMIC VARIABILITY for purely phonological reasons; or, and perhaps in conjunction, it must have undergone a number of functional splits and thus increased HOMOPHONY. Either one of these decreases the code-efficiency of a construction and increases the likelihood of its replacement by another.
3. Functional density along the two domains: The 'receding' construction must be moving into an area of LOW CODE DENSITY, i.e. where a few coding points cover a large functional domain. Such a condition may be likened to 'functional vacuum'. On the other hand, the 'invading' construction must be moving from an area of HIGH CODE DENSITY, where several constructions code a relatively small — or over-coded — functional domain. Such a condition may be likened to 'functional pressure'.

We have already suggested that many of these independent factors did exist in Ute. The ultimate way in which they may have conspired to come together is, of course, a matter of conjecture.

NOTES

1. I am indebted to Ron Langacker and Wick Miller, as well as to a number of participants in the Friends of Uto-Aztecan Conference, UCSD, June 1984, for many helpful suggestions on an earlier draft of this paper.
2. We use underscore in our Ute orthography to mark silent/devoiced vowels. The circumflex accent [ˆ] over a velar consonant is used to indicate an allophonically predictable change to uvular position. The cedilla under [ʉ̧] marks it as a high back unrounded, phonemically distinct vowel; with [ǫ] it marks the allophonically predictable mid front rounded vowel; with [ą] it marks the allophonically — or historically — predictable fronted [æ] variant of [a].
3. In other languages with similarly 'permissive' impersonal passives, such as Dutch (Kirsner 1976) or Latin (Keenan 1975), passivization without a surviving topic/argument is acceptable. Perhaps it is also acceptable in Ute, under some discourse-pragmatic conditions yet to be discovered. One may perhaps contend that the use of -*ta* in Ute action nominalizations is an instance of such a condition, though I would prefer not to argue in that direction.
4. The texts are recorded Ute traditional stories and legends, collected and transcribed since 1973 by the Ute Language Program of the Southern Ute Tribe. The examples below are from the oldest layer of surviving speakers.
5. The Philippine 'passive' has more recently been shown to have undergone a

further shift toward an **ergative** construction. See discussion in Payne (1982), Givón (1981) or Cooreman *et al.* (1984), *inter alia.*
  6. For further detail see Givón (1980, Ch. 4; 1984, Ch. 8).
  7. This condition is not absolute. An offshoot of *-tụ, -rụ,* is used with many adjectives even with inanimate subjects. The restriction here is rather probabilistic/pragmatic, based on the normal assumption that in human discourse the most frequent topics — thus subjects — tend to be human.
  8. For animates 'being there' *'uni-'ni-* a reflex of the verb 'do', is used.
  9. Since the topic of the passive clause is only anaphorically alluded to in clause (40d), one cannot judge whether it was 'promoted' or not.
  10. Wick Miller, in personal communication, has suggested to me that in fact the intimate relationship between 'perfect', 'passive', and 'plural-impersonal' may explain the homophony in Ute of the plural and perfect, both *-ka.* This is a rather attractive suggestion, and may ultimately shed further light on our various reconstructions. At the moment I am not in a position to pursue it further.
  11. We tend to think of the exploitation of similarity for analogical change in grammar as involving primarily functional similarity/proximity. For reasons of general iconicity considerations in grammar, however, one should not rule out some role, however secondary, for structural similarity in influencing analogical change (for a general discussion of iconicity in grammar, see Haiman (ed.) 1984).

REFERENCES

Anderson, L. 1982. 'The "Perfect" as a Universal and as a Language-particular Category', in P. Hopper (ed.), *Tense and Aspect* (TSL Vol. 1). Amsterdam: J. Benjamins.
Cooreman, A., B. Fox, and T. Givón. 1984. 'The Discourse Definition of Ergativity', *Studies in Language* 8.1.
Egerod, S. 1975. 'Typology of Chinese Sentence Structure'. Paper read at the 8th Annual Conference on Sino-Tibetan Languages and Linguistics, University of California, Berkeley. MS.
Givón, T. 1971. 'Historical Syntax and Synchronic Morphology: An Archaeologist's Field Trip'. CLS no. 7. University of Chicago: Chicago Linguistics Society.
—— 1976. 'Topic, Pronoun and Grammatical Agreement', in Li 1976: 149–88.
—— 1979. *On Understanding Grammar.* New York: Academic Press.
—— 1980. *Ute Reference Grammar.* Ignacio, CO: Ute Press.
—— 1981. 'Typology and Functional Domains', *Studies in Language* 5.2.
—— 1982. 'Tense–aspect–modality: The Creole Prototype and Beyond', in P. Hopper (ed.), *Tense and Aspect* (TSL Vol. 1). Amsterdam: J. Benjamins.
—— 1984. *Syntax: A Functional–Typological Introduction.* Amsterdam: J. Benjamins.
Haiman, J. (ed.). 1984. *Iconicity in Syntax* (TSL Vol. 6). Amsterdam: J. Benjamins.
Keenan, E. 1975. 'Some Universals of Passive in Relational Grammar', *CLS* 11: 340–52.
Kirsner, R. 1976. 'On the Subjectless "Pseudo-passive" in Standard Dutch and the Semantics of Background Agent', in Li 1976: 385–415.
Langacker, R., and P. Munro. 1975. 'Passives and their Meaning', *Language* 51: 789–830.
Li, C. (ed.) 1976. *Subject and Topic.* New York: Academic Press.
Payne, T. 1982. 'Role and Reference Related Subject Properties and Ergativity in Yup'ik Eskimo and Tagalog', *Studies in Language* 6.1.

This chapter is © Talmy Givón, 1988.

25

The Unity of English/German Contrasts: Inferring a Typological Parameter

JOHN A. HAWKINS

I think contrastive studies are important and useful and that we need more of them; I think that ... the most hopeful basis for insightful contrastive analysis is entirely theoretical; ... and ... that the notion that the primary audience for such studies is a pedagogically oriented one is mistaken in part (R.P. Stockwell 1968: 25).

1. INTRODUCTION

A comparison of the grammars of Modern English and Modern German presents the theoretical linguist with a tantalizing challenge. These two genetically related languages, so similar at the time of the earliest historical records, now exhibit considerable contrasts in their grammars. And one is led to ask: why is the balance between similarity and contrast the way it is, i.e. why do the areas of contrast involve the structures they do rather than the shared structures? And why do those structures that contrast actually contrast the way they do, rather than in other conceivable ways? This paper addresses these two questions and relates the conclusions to issues of current concern in both general linguistic theory and language typology.

The hypothesis to be pursued is that the contrasting structures are in some way related, despite first appearances, and that this relatedness explains the divergences. Thus, it is assumed that there are general principles, awaiting discovery, which unite the contrasting rules in question and which explain why they, rather than others, have undergone historical change in one or the other language and why they have changed the way they have.

In order to support this point I shall discuss some generalizations underlying a large range of English/German contrasts involving inflectional morphology, word order, basic grammatical relations, clause-external movement rules, deletions, and rules of semantic interpretation. I shall suggest that these generalizations are, in turn, instances of a much broader principle of variation involving the relationship between form and meaning. Roughly, where the morphological and syntactic rules of English and German contrast, those of English introduce a greater distortion of semantic representation than those of German, in ways that can be specified quite precisely given standard assumptions about the exact nature of the surface forms and semantic representations in question.

The contrasts between English and German can therefore contribute to an important goal of recent linguistic theory, which is to discover the 'regularities in the ways languages may differ from one another' (Keenan 1978: 90). By imposing principled limits on this variation, the theory will define the notion 'possible human language'. Contrasts provide us with a ready-made pool of variation data, with suggestive consequences for the nature of the principles that explain why grammars have the sets of co-occurring rules and properties that they do, rather than the imaginable but non-co-occurring rules and properties. Just how generalizable the typological principles underlying English/German variation will turn out to be must await similar research in other language families. Clearly, there will be numerous differences from the Germanic case, and the precise logic of the proposed correlations between variant properties will need to take account of these. In the meantime, evidence will be presented of an intriguing regularity underlying large numbers of contrasts between English and German.

2. GRAMMATICAL MORPHOLOGY

German has richer inflectional morphology than English. In general, all the grammatical distinctions that are drawn in English inflectional morphology are drawn in German as well, though not vice versa.

For example, both English and German express a singular/plural distinction on their nouns (E. *book/books*; G. *Buch/Bücher*); verbs express a past/present tense distinction (E. *say/said*; G. *sage/sagte*); and third person singular pronouns distinguish masculine/feminine/neuter forms (E. *he/she/it*; G. *er/sie/es*). But numerous grammatical distinctions drawn in German inflectional morphology are not drawn in English. German has inflectional morphemes distinguishing four cases within the noun phrase, nominative/accusative/genitive/dative (cf. *der Mann/den Mann/des Mannes/dem Mann(e)* respectively). English has collapsed its nominative, accusative, and dative forms into a common *the man*, though it still retains a separate genitive *the man's*. The definite article *the* is invariable (as are English adjectives). German still has an indicative/subjunctive distinction on its verb, whereas English employs (almost exclusively) a single form for both (cf. G. *gab/gäbe*; E. *gave*). The German verb also carries person and number markings, whereas the bare stem in English is used for all persons and numbers except for the third person singular, and for both imperative and non-imperative forms.

What we are witnessing in Modern English is the product of considerable syncretism in inflectional morphology compared to Old English. The morphology of Old English was very similar to that of German today. And whereas German has preserved much of its inflectional system intact, English has reduced it. Since both languages originally had a common West Germanic inflectional system, and since change in English has been in a consistent direction, towards syncretism, we now have a precise relationship between the morphologies of the two languages. For each individual area of inflectional morphology (e.g. indicative versus subjunctive marking), the grammatical distinctions drawn in English are a subset, proper or otherwise, of those drawn in German.

Sapir (1921: 168) refers to the loss of inflectional morphology in English as 'the drift towards the invariable word'. He also makes a profound observation about the semantic consequences of this process:

> This striving for a simple, unnuanced correspondence between idea and word, as invariable as may be, is very strong in English. It accounts for a number of tendencies which at first sight seem unconnected. Certain well-established forms, like the ... plural -s of *books*, have resisted the drift to invariable words, possibly because they symbolize certain stronger form cravings that we do not yet fully understand ... As soon as the derivation runs danger of being felt as a mere nuancing of, a finicky play on, the primary concept it tends to be absorbed ..., to disappear as such ... [An] instance of the sacrifice of highly useful forms to this impatience of nuancing is the group *whence, whither, hence, hither, thence, thither*. They could not persist in live usage because they impinged too solidly upon the circles of meaning represented by the words *where, here* and *there*. In saying *whither* we feel too keenly that we repeat all of *where*. That we add to *where* an important nuance of direction irritates rather than satisfies. We prefer to merge the static and the directive (*Where do you live?* like *Where are you going?*) ... Now, ... we do not object to nuances as such, we object to having the nuances formally earmarked for us (Sapir 1921: 169-70).

In more modern parlance, invariable words, and the absorption of semantic nuances, result in greater ambiguity (or vagueness) for the morphemes in question.[1] That is, the range of meanings covered by English grammatical form classes is larger than it was, and larger than in German. Distinct forms for the directional/static opposition have merged into ambiguous (or vague) undifferentiated forms: *where/whither* has been replaced by *where* alone. This same directional/static opposition lives on in German in *hinter den Tisch* (acc.: directional) and *hinter dem Tisch* (dat.:

static), both of which correspond to the invariable *behind the table* in English. The definite article in English now does service for, and is semantically neutral to, all genders, cases, and numbers, whereas German has six definite article forms (*der/den/des/dem/die/das*) dividing up the same grammatical and semantic terrain to which English is neutral. Indicative and subjunctive have merged in English by and large, with the indicative carrying both sets of meanings. And the English verb stem (e.g. *say*) is now compatible with all person, number, and imperative distinctions that are kept apart in German (cf. *sage/sagst/sagen/sagt/sag*).

The drift towards the invariable word has consequences for the relationship between semantics and pragmatics. Semantic distinctions which are no longer expressed formally in Modern English may be recovered pragmatically in language use, by exploiting linguistic context plus real world knowledge. The ambiguity of *where* is disambiguated by the semantics of *live* (stative) versus *go* (active) in *Where do you live?* versus *Where are you going?*. Similarly, the presence and nature of the subject of a verb and its syntactic position makes clear the non-imperative or imperative force of a verb. Linguistic context typically resolves the irrealis/realis or reported/non-reported speech status of clauses, which was hitherto explicitly signalled by subjunctive/indicative marking, etc. Alternatively, English must express these distinctions in other ways, by paraphrase, longer and more expressive linguistic forms, etc. But the important point is that German speakers are forced to make certain semantic distinctions which can regularly be left unspecified in English.

Summarizing, what Sapir appears to be drawing attention to is a general realignment in the assignment of meanings to linguistic forms. Languages can vary in the extent to which numerous semantic distinctions are explicitly drawn in surface morphology. Not to draw these distinctions in surface does not render them inexpressible and does not make the language in any sense impoverished — it simply means that their expression is carried by fewer linguistic forms, each with broader semantic coverage (i.e. more ambiguity and vagueness). And the precise interpretation that is explicitly marked in the one language will typically be pragmatically derived in the other.

3. WORD ORDER FREEDOM

It is often observed that word order in German is freer than in English. The greater freedom of the relevant movement rules in German does **not** extend to rules crossing clause boundaries (cf. sections 4 and 5), and hence we need to restrict our claim to clause-internal movements only. The relative freedom of German word order comes about in two ways: German has movement rules effecting word order rearrangements which are without parallel in English; and where there are similar movement processes they apply more productively in German than in English, i.e. in more environments.

It is plausible to argue that the case system of German is responsible for this contrast. Across languages the existence of rich surface case marking typically correlates with extensive word order freedom. The reason most commonly advanced for this is that fixed word order at the sentence level in a language like English is used to encode grammatical relations such as subject, direct object, and indirect object, which are morphologically encoded in a case-marked language. And word order permutations are possible in a case-marked language because grammatical relations are recoverable morphologically. This insight has been expressed as the 'principle of covariation of functional equivalents' by Keenan (1978: 120–1). His principle predicts that the loss of the case system in the history of English should be accompanied by a relative freezing of the permitted word order permutations, and this is, of course, what happened.

But the relative rigidity of word order in Modern English has an interesting consequence for the relationship between form and meaning. Languages whose morphology makes possible the kinds of word order permutations that exist in German can use these options for pragmatic purposes, marking old versus new information, topic, focus, etc. These pragmatic rules have been extensively illustrated for languages such as Czech (cf. Firbas 1966, 1971) and Russian (cf. Comrie 1979), cf. also Thompson (1978) for a discussion of 'pragmatic word order languages'. Now, assuming that such pragmatic differences exist, it follows that the fixed word orders of English are correspondingly more ambiguous (or vague) with respect to these pragmatic functions. That is, many pragmatic distinctions which receive their own syntactic encoding in German and Russian etc., do not receive distinct encoding in English, and one and the same syntactic form of English ranges over pragmatic differences in meaning which can be disambiguated in these languages.

In fact, the word order permutation possibilities of German are not as free as those of Russian or Czech, and so German occupies a position intermediate between these languages and English (cf. Sgall 1982). The precise function of the different word order options is less transparent as a result, and there is more disagreement in the German linguistic literature on this question than one finds in the Slavic literature. One of the major determinants does seem to be old versus new information, however (cf. Kirkwood 1969, 1970, 1978 and Lenerz 1977), though a number of other subtle pragmatic functions appear to play a role as well (cf. Hawkins 1986).

4. BASIC GRAMMATICAL RELATIONS AND THEIR SEMANTIC DIVERSITY

There is greater semantic diversity to the basic grammatical relations in English than in German (cf. Hawkins 1981). Consider first direct objects. The class of direct objects in English has expanded relative to German. German verbs which are two-place predicates most often take an accusative-marked NP as their second, non-subject argument. But there are numerous verbs which take a dative:

(1) a. Ich liebe ihn. Die Frau sieht meinen Vater.
      [+Acc.]   [+Acc.]
      'I love him.'   'The woman sees my father.'
    b. Er half ihm.   Die Frau antwortete meinem Vater.
      [+Dat.]   [+Dat.]
      'He helped him.' 'The woman answered my father.'

The syntactic rules of German are sensitive to this case-marking distinction (cf. Hawkins 1986). For example, only an accusative-marked NP can be converted to a nominative-marked subject by Passive:

(2) a. Er wird geliebt.   'He is loved.'
    b. *Er wurde geholfen.   'He was helped.'

Such considerations suggest that accusative NPs only should be equated with direct objecthood in German. As a result, the class of English direct objects properly includes that of German, since it comprises both the accusative-marked NPs of German and (regularly) the dative-marked NPs as well. The number of direct objects has expanded in the history of English to subsume NPs that were formerly not accusative-marked.

There is an important semantic consequence of this morphological and syntactic contrast. Numerous grammarians of German have tried to come up with a semantic generalization distinguishing dative-taking verbs from others. Curme (1977: 494) talks of the dative 'indicating the direction of an activity towards a goal', and classifies dative-taking verbs into several subtypes, e.g. those signifying 'a. Inclination or aversion, a pleasing or displeasing, a serving or resisting; b. Benefit or injury'; etc. Plank (1980, 1981) talks of accusative objects being diametrically opposed to subjects with regard to control over and influence on an event, with dative (or indirect) objects being less opposed and more like subjects.

Now, however we characterize these facts, one thing is clear. Semantic distinctions are operative here, and German is systematically excluding certain semantic roles from being mapped onto the (accusative) direct object relation with the predicates in question. By contrast, English regularly collapses the semantic roles of both accusative- and dative-taking verbs into a grammatical entity, direct object, and into a common surface form. And hence there is correspondingly greater semantic diversity to the direct object relation in English than in German. English surface structures frequently make no distinction between semantic roles which receive distinctive encoding in German.

The same holds true for subjects. Subjects can regularly be semantic agents in both languages. But English and German contrast over the extent to which non-agentive semantic roles can be mapped onto the subject relation. Rohdenburg (1974) has made a systematic investigation of the subject-forming possibilities of both languages using a huge corpus of literature in translation, as well as numerous native speakers. He argues that the subject-forming possibilities of German are in general a proper subset of those in English. Wherever German has grammatical subjects expressing non-agentive semantic roles, so does English, but not vice versa. Many cases of subject formation are judged ungrammatical by German native speakers for sentence types in which they are judged grammatical in English. And on other occasions German native speakers are uncertain, where English native speakers are quite certain, about the grammaticalness of subjects. The semantic roles assigned in the following examples are based on the theory of Fillmore (1968, 1971):

(3) a. *The king* visited his people.
    b. *Der König* besuchte sein Volk.
    (Su. = agent)

(4) a. *The garden* swarmed with bees.
    b. *Der Garten* wimmelte von Bienen.
    (Su. = locative: *in the garden*...)

(5) a. *This hotel* forbids dogs.
    b. **Dieses Hotel* verbietet Hunde.
    (Su. = locative: *in this hotel*...)

(6) a. *My guitar* broke a string.
    b. **Meine Gitarre* (zer)riß eine Saite.
    (Su. = locative: *on my guitar*...)

(7) a. *A penny* once bought 2 to 3 pins.
    b. **Ein Pfennig* kaufte früher 2 bis 3 Stecknadeln.
    (Su. = instrumental: *with a penny*...)

(8) a. *This advertizement* will sell us a lot.
    b. **Diese Anzeige* verkauft uns viel.
    (Su. = instrumental: *with this ad*...)

(9) a. *The latest edition of the book* has added a chapter.
    (Su. = ?; *to the latest edition*...)

b. *Die letzte Ausgabe des Buches hat ein Kapitel hinzugefügt.

(10) a. *I* like the book. (Su. = experiencer)
b. *Mir* gefällt das Buch. (*mir* = dative non-subject)
c. *Ich* habe das Buch gern (*ich* = nominative subject)

(11) a. *Tomorrow* will be rather cold in most places.
b. **Morgen* verspricht meistenorts ziemlich kalt zu sein. (Su. = time specification)

(12) a. *John* wounded his leg in the war.
b. ?*Johann* hat sich im Krieg das Bein verwundet. (Su. = dative)

Even where subject formation is fully grammatical in the two languages, Rohdenburg's corpus shows that non-agentive roles are converted to subjects significantly less frequently than they are in English, and that English subjects correspond regularly to prepositional phrases or to dative-marked NPs in German, e.g. *mit einem Pfennig kaufte man früher 2 bis 3 Stecknadeln* 'with a penny one once bought 2 to 3 pins' for (7), *in diesem Hotel sind Hunde verboten* 'in this hotel dogs are forbidden' for (5). Both in terms of grammaticality and in terms of frequency, therefore, the subject-forming possibilities of non-agentive arguments in English are greater than those of German.

I would argue that the loss of the case system is ultimately responsible for the greater semantic diversity of basic grammatical relations in English. The different surface cases of German are available to distinguish a variety of semantic roles for arguments. This then naturally results in less semantic diversity for the basic grammatical relations, subject and object, since the oblique roles, experiencer, instrument, etc., have their own characteristic (though still relatively ambiguous) morphology arranged within a closed system of morphological oppositions, one member from which must always be chosen. And this deprives the subject (nominative) and object (accusative) classes of these oblique members, making subject and object less semantically diverse.

When the comparable case system of English is lost, we get an identity in surface form between hitherto non-identical NPs. In Middle English, direct objects collapse the semantic roles of many accusative, genitive, and dative NPs of Old English, and subjects collapse the semantic roles of earlier nominative, accusative, and dative NPs. The set of English subjects has also increased beyond the set predicted by case syncretism alone, for which Kirkwood (1978) offers a plausible speculation. His argument rests on two simple and indisputable facts: Modern English has more fixed SVO word orders than it used to; and yet there are certain very general pragmatic principles of word order rearrangement (e.g. old before new information) which seem to be present to some extent at least in all languages, and whose productivity is correspondingly reduced as fixed SVO word order gradually asserts itself. The result is a form of conflict: the syntactic rules force fixed word order; pragmatic principles favour word order rearrangements in accordance with the information structure of a whole discourse. The conflict is naturally resolved by permitting more types of NPs to actually be subjects, and hence to occupy immediately preverbal position. Many NPs representing old information can now occupy subject position which could not do so hitherto. And the result is a semantically more diverse class of subjects compared with the more conservative German, whose word order is correspondingly freer.

One consequence of this semantic diversity contrast is that transitive and intransitive surface structures in English

(13)   a.   SU-V-DO
       b.   SU-V

can be mapped onto a considerable diversity of semantic propositions. For example, (13a) can be realized as *I love him, he helped him, I like the book, this hotel forbids dogs, my guitar broke a string, a penny bought 2 to 3 pins, John wounded his leg*, etc., i.e. a variety of predicate types selecting argument types with different semantic roles. In any mapping, therefore, between surface structure and a semantic representation which specifies these semantic roles, the surface structure SU-V-DO is going to be potentially ambiguous between a variety of interpretations, and there is nothing in the surface structure itself to indicate the appropriate interpretation. The sentence interpreter has to rely on knowledge of the semantics of predicate and arguments in order to assign the appropriate interpretation. By contrast, the German translations regularly force a disambiguation, either on the basis of case marking alone (*mir gefällt das Buch/ich sehe das Buch* versus *I like/see the book*), or by a structural rearrangement of the whole sentence in which the subject in English shows up as an oblique NP (*an meiner Gitarre riß eine Saite* versus *my guitar broke a string*, i.e. OBL-V-SU versus SU-V-DO). Hence, the German surface structures exhibit less ambiguity than English. There is greater differentiation between distinct predicate types in surface, and less collapsing of diverse semantic structures onto one and the same surface structure.

5. RAISING STRUCTURES

English has a productive rule of Subject-to-Subject (S–S) Raising, operating as illustrated in (14), and triggered by a reasonably large class of higher predicates, some sixty or more according to Postal (1974: 292):

(14)　John seems (△ to be ill)　　*cf.* It seems (that John is ill)

(15)　a.　John seems to be ill.
　　　b.　The noise seems to get on his nerves.
　　　c.　John happens to be ill.
　　　d.　The noise happens to get on his nerves.
　　　e.　John continued to be ill.
　　　f.　The noise continued to get on his nerves.
　　　g.　John ceased to be ill.
　　　h.　The noise ceased to get on his nerves.

But German, according to König (1971), presents apparent S–S Raising in surface structure only for *scheinen* 'seem' and for a handful of other triggers which are exactly properly included in the corresponding English class:

(15′)　a.　Johann scheint krank zu sein.
　　　　b.　Der Lärm scheint ihn aufzuregen.
　　　　c.　*Johann geschieht krank zu sein.
　　　　d.　*Der Lärm geschieht ihn aufzuregen.
　　　　e.　*Johann fuhr fort krank zu sein.
　　　　f.　*Der Lärm fuhr fort ihn aufzuregen.
　　　　g.　?Johann hörte auf krank zu sein.
　　　　h.　?Der Lärm hörte auf ihn aufzuregen.

Even for *scheinen* Ebert (1975) has argued that (15′a) involves clause-union rather than raising, since the 'raised' constituent need not be a subject:[2]

(16)　a.　Ihm　　scheint geholfen zu werden.
　　　　　　'to-him seems　to be helped'
　　　　b.　An dem Wagen scheint noch gearbeitet zu werden.
　　　　　　'on the　car　　seems still　to be worked'

Postal (1974) has also argued, convincingly to my mind, for a rule of Subject-to-Object (S–O) Raising, operating as illustrated in (17), and triggered again by a reasonably large class of some sixty verbs:

(17) I believe John (△ to be ill)   cf. I believe (that John is ill)

(18) a. I believe John to be ill.
      b. I believe the farmer to have killed the cow.
      c. I understand him to be stupid.

German has no translation equivalents here, and any attempt to construct them results in violent ungrammaticality:

(18′) a. *Ich glaube Johann krank zu sein.
      b. *Ich glaube den Bauer die Kuh geschlachtet zu haben.
      c. *Ich verstehe ihn dumm zu sein.

Attempts to find evidence for German S–O Raising in *lassen* constructions and with verbs of perception have met with negative results (cf. Reis 1973, Harbert 1977). One might argue that structures like *er glaubte sich betrogen* 'he believed himself deceived' provide evidence for S–O Raising in German. If they do, they represent an extremely limited phenomenon. *Er glaubte sich betrogen zu sein* 'he believed himself deceived to be' is ungrammatical, and hence the semantically appropriate or underlying verb *sein* must be deleted. Yet structures like *er glaubte sich betrogen* are only possible when *sein* is the semantically appropriate and deleted verb of the lower clause.

What is significant, therefore, about both S–O and S–S Raising in German is that the few predicates which appear to provide at least some support for it are, in translation, exactly a proper subset of the English raising triggers.

Tough Movement (or Object-to-Subject Raising), whose operation is illustrated in (19), is quite productive in English, but limited in German.

(19) Linguistics is { easy / tough } (to study △)

      cf. (To study Linguistics) is { easy / tough }

English Tough Movement is more productive than German Tough Movement with respect to the number of triggering verbs, the class of NPs which undergo it, and the unboundedness versus boundedness of the rule (cf. further Hawkins 1986: Ch. 5):

(20) a. He is easy to convince.
      b. Linguistics is boring to study.

c. The boy is easy to help/to work with.
d. This book is easy for me to force Harry to read.

(20') a. Er ist leicht zu überzeugen.
b. *Die Linguistik ist langweilig zu studieren. (fewer triggers)
c. *Der Junge ist leicht zu helfen/mit zu arbeiten. (raise DO only)
d. *Dieses Buch ist leicht für mich Heinrich zu lesen zu zwingen. (bounded)

The net result is a precise proper inclusion relation between Tough Movement structures in the two languages: wherever German can tough-move, so can English, but not vice versa (cf. further Hawkins 1986: fn. 32).

The three raising rules of English involve a change in grammatical relations whereby a subject or non-subject in one clause assumes the subject or object relation in the higher clause. *The noise* is a derived subject in *the noise ceased/seemed to get on his nerves*; *the farmer* is a derived object in *I believe/assume the farmer to have killed the cow*; and *Linguistics* is a derived subject in *Linguistics is boring to study*. But the semantic interpretations of these surface sentences involve, in effect, undoing the grammatical relation-changing rule, by interpreting the derived subjects and objects as arguments of the lower, embedded, clause out of which they have been raised, and not as arguments of the predicates within the clause that most immediately contains them. *The noise* in the S–S Raising structure did not itself necessarily *cease* (and there is no sense in which *the noise* can *seem*!), but the noise did get on his nerves and this whole event then ceased (cf. *the noise ceased to get on his nerves when he bought ear plugs — even though the noise itself continued louder than ever*). Similarly, in the S–O Raising structure it is not being claimed that I believe the farmer in any way (and one certainly cannot *assume the farmer*!) but rather that the farmer killed the cow, and this whole proposition then stands in the belief relation to me. And in the Tough structure it is not necessarily claimed that Linguistics is boring — only that studying it is.

This situation contrasts with Equi-type structures, in which the surface (matrix) subject or object **is** interpreted as an argument of its immediate clause and also of the embedded clause:

(21) a. John wants to be ill.
b. I persuaded John to visit the doctor.
c. John is eager to please.

In (21a) John does want something, and so is an argument of *want*, and his desires do not necessarily extend to anyone else being ill apart from himself, and hence he is also an argument of *be ill*. In (21b) John is the individual who is being persuaded, and hence he is an argument of *persuade*, and it is his rather than anyone else's visit to the doctor which the matrix subject *I* is trying to bring about through persuasion, and so John is also an argument of *visit*, and similarly for (21c). German and English are, in general, equally rich in Equi structures, but German is clearly resistant to raising.

The derived subjects and objects formed by raising therefore exhibit a rather extreme form of departure from their corresponding semantic representations, for these raised arguments are interpreted as belonging in an altogether different clause from the one in which they are physically situated in surface structure. The Equi constructions are semantically more normal in that even though they involve 'spreading' the argument of a surface NP over two predicates (by binding a variable in the lower clause), the argument of the higher NP still contracts a semantic relation with the immediate predicate of the clause that it is in in surface structure (i.e., John does want something in (21a), etc.). There is no 'skipping over' surface predicates in semantic interpretation. Thus, the arguments of an immediate predicate in English surface structures are to a greater extent than in German not arguments of this predicate in semantic representation.

I believe that the causes of the greater productivity of raising in English are twofold. First, these structures extend the semantic diversity of subject and object even further than in the examples of the last section, by requiring the raised argument to be interpreted as belonging in an altogether different clause from the one in which it is physically situated in surface. But since the semantic diversity of subject and object has been considerably expanded in English quite independently, it is predictable that it should be English rather than German which has the productive raisings. Second, the greater productivity of raising rules must surely be connected with the fact that all clause-external movements are more productive in English than in German (cf. below).

A consequence of this productivity of raising rules in English is that English now has regular syntactic ambiguities with Equi structures:

(22) a. NP–V–to–VP   S–S Raising   John ceased to be ill.
                                     Equi   John wanted to be ill.
      b. NP–V–NP–to–VP   S–O Raising   I believe John to be ill.
                                     Equi   I persuaded John to be ill.
      c. NP–be–Adj–to–VP   S–S Raising   John is certain to please.
                                     Tough   John is easy to please.
                                     Equi   John is eager to please.

This is reminiscent of the greater ambiguity of SU–V–DO and SU–V structures in English (i.e. NP–V–NP and NP–V), which also involved greater semantic diversity for basic grammatical relations. By contrast, the structures corresponding to (22) in German are almost always assigned Equi interpretations only, since raising of all kinds is either non-existent or extremely limited. Once again, there is that much less structural ambiguity in German, and that much more of a one-to-one mapping between surface form and semantic representation.

6. EXTRACTIONS

Unbounded movement rules such as Relative Clause Formation, Cleft, Question Formation, etc. (i.e. Chomsky's 1977 WH-Movement) apply in more environments in English than in German. In fact, it is argued in Hawkins (1986) that the contrastive situation is as precise as in the raising examples: wherever German can extract, so can English, but not vice versa. In this context, we will merely illustrate the direction of contrast with one or two examples.

Extractions out of finite (i.e. tensed) object complement clauses are possible in English, but typically impossible in German. (23a), which derives from (23b), is perfectly grammatical in English. Its counterpart in German, (23'a), is ungrammatical.

(23) a. The man who you believe that you saw is my friend.
 b. The man $_{S1}$ (who you believe $_{S2}$ (that you saw Δ)) is my friend.

(23') a. *Der Mann, den du glaubst, daß du gesehen hast, ist mein Freund.
 b. der Mann $_{S1}$ (den du glaubst $_{S2}$ (daß du Δ gesehen hast)) ist mein Freund.

The effect of WH-Movement is similar to that of Raising and Tough Movement in an important respect: even though this rule does not create derived grammatical relations, it can still move an NP (the WH-element) into a clause in which it cannot be interpreted as an argument of that clause. *Who* is semantically an argument of *saw* in S_2, and is in no sense a semantic argument of *believe* in S_1. Thus, the WH-argument contracts no semantic relation with the predicate of the clause which most immediately contains it in surface structure, and the language interpreter must, in effect, skip over *believe* and assign WH to the lower predicate *saw*. In a similar way, *the noise* must skip over *ceased* and *seems* and be assigned to the lower predicate in raising structures such as *the noise ceased/seems to get on his nerves*, etc.

The descriptive regularity which unites both bounded and unbounded clause-external movements is one of 'argument trespassing'. In all these contrasting structures, the moved NP is situated in a surface clause in which it contracts no semantic relation with its immediate predicate (and in which it did not originate in more remote structures). We will say that an NP 'contracts no semantic relation with' its immediate predicate, if and only if 'the argument to which the NP corresponds in semantic representation is not an argument of' this immediate predicate. And an 'immediate predicate' can be defined as 'that predicate separated from the NP constituent in question by fewer branches than any other predicate in the surface structure tree'. We can now define the contrastive Argument Trespassing Generalization as follows:

(24) ARGUMENT TRESPASSING GENERALIZATION
The set of German surface structures in which an NP c(onstituent)-commands an immediate predicate with which it contracts no semantic relation is properly included in the corresponding English set.

Another precise contrast between English and German which I shall argue is very much related to these extraction contrasts involves Pied Piping rules (cf. Ross 1967). This time it is German that is more productive: wherever English can pied pipe, so can German, but not vice versa. For example, German has a rule of VP Pied Piping, which creates structures like (25):

(25) a. der Mann, *den zu töten* ich öfters versucht habe, ...
'the man *whom to kill* I often tried have'
b. der Mann $_{VP}$ (den zu töten) ich △ öfters versucht habe

English has no such rule:

(25') *the man to kill whom I have tried ...

In terms of the Argument Trespassing Generalization, it is no accident that it should be German rather than English which has the rule of VP Pied Piping. For this rule enables moved NPs to keep as their immediate predicate that predicate of which they are an argument. And we have seen that it is consistently German which is reluctant to move its NPs into positions in which they contract no semantic relation with their immediate predicates.

The ultimate cause of the greater tolerance for argument trespassing in English may be, once again, the loss of the case system. NPs in German are that much more resistant to leaving their dominating phrasal categories PP, VP, NP, etc., i.e. the categories that contain the head categories, P and V, etc., which assign case to their governed NPs. The effect of pied piping is to keep WH-NPs within their dominating VPs (and PPs and NPs). WH-Movement extracts WH-NPs from these categories, and Raising also moves NPs out of their respective dominating categories. Hawkins (1986) argues that the absence of a rich morphological case system in English facilitates the extraction of surface NPs out of their immediately dominating categories, and more generally that the number of morphological case distinctions drawn in a language correlates negatively with the possibility of removing NPs from the c-command domains that assign case. A similar position has been argued for in Lightfoot (1981). I will not summarize the details here.

This negative correlation can be extended to cover NP deletions as well, which are also more restricted in German compared to English. For example, differently case-marked NPs typically cannot undergo conjunction reduction where in English they can, and the deletion of case-marked NPs is frequently blocked in environments such as PPs from which extraction is blocked as well (cf. Hawkins 1986: Ch. 7).

Notice now the semantic consequences of raising, extraction and pied piping rules. In previous sections we have seen that major English/German contrasts all conspire to create greater ambiguity in surface forms in English. The extraction and pied piping contrasts, on the other hand, do not appear to be packing a greater number of semantic or pragmatic types into a limited set of common surface forms in English, thereby making these more ambiguous or vague. But they do have another interesting effect from the point of view of the mapping between surface form and meaning. If we think (following Keenan 1973, 1978) in terms of the 'conservation of logical structure' in these surface structures, we can say that the effect of argument trespassing is precisely not one of conserving logical structure in surface, but rather of destroying it by rearranging arguments and predicates. English frequently permits arguments in surface structure in positions where they do not belong semantically, while German allows less rearrangement, and rearrangement over smaller syntactic domains.

The freer deletions of English are also relevant here. If a deletion process removes an argument of logical structure from surface, the relevant clause will be lacking an argument which belongs logically in it, and which will be assigned to it in the process of semantic interpretation. But both removal of an argument from a position in which it does belong logically, and insertion of an argument (by Raising etc.) into a position in which it does not belong logically, would seem to be two complementary ways in which a surface structure can deviate from its corresponding logical structure, and thereby fail to conserve it.

7. THE UNITY OF ENGLISH/GERMAN CONTRASTS: INFERRING A TYPOLOGICAL PARAMETER

The contrastive typology of English and German can be summarized as follows:

(26) German   English
      More grammatical morphology   Less grammatical morphology
      More word order freedom   Less word order freedom
      Less semantic diversity of GRs   More semantic diversity of GRs
      Less raising   More raising
      Less extraction   More extraction
      More pied piping   Less pied piping
      Less deletion (of NPs)   More deletion (of NPs)

I would argue that the distribution of the 'more' and 'less' values in (26) admits of a unifying generalization, which can be summarized as follows:

(27) THE UNITY OF ENGLISH/GERMAN CONTRASTS
      Where the grammars of English and German contrast, the surface forms (morphological and syntactic) of German are in closer correspondence with their associated meanings, in the following ways:

   a. AMBIGUITY (AND/OR VAGUENESS)
      There is greater ambiguity (and/or vagueness) of surface forms in English, i.e. greater collapsing of semantic distinctions and of different semantic types onto common surface forms. The result is more of a one-to-one mapping between form and meaning in German, with distinct forms carrying distinct meanings to a greater extent:
         cf. ambiguity (and/or vagueness) in English grammatical morphology;
             pragmatic ambiguity (/vagueness) in fixed word order;
             ambiguities in semantically diverse SVO and SV sequences;
             ambiguities in Raising and Equi structures.

   b. DESTRUCTION OF SEMANTIC CLAUSE STRUCTURE
      There is less correspondence between surface clause structure and semantic clause structure in English:
      (i) The arguments of an immediate predicate (V or Adj) in English surface structures are to a greater extent than in German not arguments of this predicate in semantic representation, but must be matched with a predicate lower in the sentence. That is, English frequently permits arguments in surface structure in positions where they do not belong semantically. German allows less rearrangement of arguments and their predicates, and rearrangement over smaller syntactic domains.

377

cf. more raising in English;
more WH-extraction;
less pied piping.
(ii) Conversely, there is greater removal in English surface structures of arguments which are present in semantic representation, i.e. greater deletion of arguments from surface structures in which they do belong semantically. cf. more deletions (of NP) in English.

German is therefore giving us a 'tighter fit' between surface form and semantic representation. Even though linguists may differ over what they consider a semantic representation to look like, they are all agreed on the following essentials: semantic representations cannot be ambiguous; arguments must stand 'together with' the predicates with which they are associated semantically; and material that is semantically understood, even though deleted or absent from surface structure, must be present in semantic representation. Now it is precisely these essentials that we are concentrating on in our comparative study. German has less surface ambiguity, less rearrangement of arguments and predicates, and less deletion of arguments than English.

This comparative typology for which English and German provide evidence raises more general questions of explanation. Why should languages differ over the tightness of fit between form and meaning? What are the respective advantages and disadvantages of preserving essential features of semantic structure in surface structure? Hawkins (1986: Ch. 8) provides some speculative answers to these questions. But before too much mental energy goes into this kind of speculation, we need to check the generality of our descriptive regularity for English and German. Does variation within and across other language families admit of a similar unifying generalization across major areas of the grammar? Clearly, the specific contrasts will differ from case to case. But is there still a common directionality to the contrasts, regardless of differences in detail? And what is the precise nature of the universal correlations between variant properties in this area (e.g., if a language has no morphological case system, then ...; or if a language allows preposition stranding, then ...)? These are questions that require further research. In the meantime, the contrasts of English and German point to an intriguing regularity, suggesting that variation throughout a whole grammar may be constrained by rather abstract typological principles involving the degree of correspondence between surface form and semantic representation.

NOTES

1. I shall generally use the cover term 'ambiguity' for both ambiguity and vagueness, as these are discussed in, e.g., Kempson (1977: Ch. 8). Within a purely semantic context it is crucial to keep ambiguity and vagueness clearly distinct (or at least to try to!). But within the present context, the primary focus is on how large a semantic range is covered by given morphemes, and the precise semantic status of any distinctions within this semantic range is of only secondary importance. Hence the choice of the single (and more standard) cover term 'ambiguity'.

2. In König's (1971: 68-73) analysis, *scheinen* is an optional raising trigger. König also proposes that *beginnen* 'to begin', *anfangen* 'to begin', and the epistemic modals are obligatory (S-S) Raising triggers in German. These constitute a proper subset of the class of obligatory triggers which Postal (1974) proposes for English, namely *begin*, epistemic modals, *continue, cease, prove, tend, be apt, be liable*, etc. Hence, all the proposed triggers for German (including *scheinen*) constitute a proper subset of the proposed English S-S Raising triggers. If *scheinen* is not a raising trigger (cf. Ebert 1975), the proper subset relation will still hold between the remaining (obligatory) raising triggers of German, and the obligatory and optional raising structures of English. If the obligatory raising analysis is not accepted for either language (in an approach which base-generates all these structures and assigns different semantic interpretations only), English will still have optional raising triggers without parallel in German. If even the optional raising analysis is not accepted, English will still have syntactic structures corresponding to the outputs of the would-be optional and obligatory rules in the raising analysis, which are without parallel in German. The advantage of the Argument Trespassing Generalization to be given in section 6 is that it succeeds in capturing a significant contrastive generalization in this area, while remaining neutral between such competing synactic analyses. It is defined on the relevant surface structures (the constituency of which is in most cases not in serious doubt, though cf. Hawkins 1986: Ch. 5) and their associated semantic representations, irrespective of the (increasingly undecidable) best analysis of the syntactic rules involved.

REFERENCES

Chomsky, N. 1977. 'On WH-Movement', in P. Culicover, T. Wasow and A. Akmajian (eds.), *Formal Syntax*, New York: Academic Press.

Comrie, B. 1979. 'Russian', in T. Shopen (ed.), *Languages and their Status*, Cambridge, Mass.: Winthrop Publishers.

Curme, G.O. 1977. *A Grammar of the German Language*. 2nd Edition. New York: Ungar.

Ebert, R.P. 1975. 'Subject Raising, the Clause Squish, and German *scheinen*-constructions'. *Papers from the Eleventh Regional Meeting of the Chicago Linguistic Society*, University of Chicago.

Fillmore, C.J. 1968. 'The Case for Case', in E. Bach and R.T. Harms (eds.), *Universals of Linguistic Theory*, New York: Holt, Rinehart and Winston.

——— 1971. 'Some Problems for Case Grammar', *Working Papers in Linguistics* (Ohio State) 10: 245-65.

Firbas, J. 1966. 'Non-thematic Subjects in Contemporary English', *Travaux linguistiques de Prague* 2: 239-56.

——— 1971. 'On the Concept of Communicative Dynamism in the Theory of

Functional Sentence Perspective', *Sbornik Praci Filosoficke Fakulty Brnenske University* A-19: 135–44.

Harbert, W. 1977. 'Clause Union and German Accusative Plus Infinitive Constructions', in P. Cole and J.M. Sadock (eds.), *Grammatical Relations (Syntax and Semantics,* 8), New York: Academic Press.

Hawkins, J.A. 1981. 'The Semantic Diversity of Basic Grammatical Relations in English and German', *Linguistische Berichte* 75: 1–25.

—— 1986. *A Comparative Typology of English and German: Unifying the Contrasts.* London: Croom Helm and Austin: University of Texas Press.

Keenan, E.L. 1973. 'Logical Expressive Power and Syntactic Variation in Natural Languages', in E.L. Keenan (ed.), *Formal Semantics of Natural Language,* Cambridge: Cambridge University Press.

—— 1978. 'Language Variation and the Logical Structure of Universal Grammar', in H. Seiler (ed.), *Language Universals,* Tübingen: Gunter Narr Verlag.

Kempson, R.M. 1977. *Semantic Theory.* Cambridge: Cambridge University Press.

Kirkwood, H.W. 1969. 'Aspects of Word Order and its Communicative Function in English and German', *Journal of Linguistics* 5: 85–107.

—— 1970. 'Some Systemic Means of "Functional Sentence Perspective" in English and German', *IRAL* 8: 103–14.

—— 1978. 'Options and Constraints in the Surface Ordering of Noun Phrases in English and German', *Journal of Pragmatics* 2: 225–45.

König, E. 1971. *Adjectival Constructions in English and German: A Contrastive Analysis.* Heidelberg: Julius Groos.

Lenerz, J. 1977. *Zur Abfolge nominaler Satzglieder im Deutschen.* Tübingen: Gunter Narr.

Lightfoot, D.W. 1981. 'The History of Noun Phrase Movement', in C.L. Baker and J.J. McCarthy (eds.), *The Logical Problem of Language Acquisition,* Cambridge, Mass.: MIT Press.

Plank, F. 1980. 'Verbs and Objects in Semantic Agreement: Minor Differences between Languages that Might Suggest a Major One'. MS, Technische Universität Hannover.

—— 1981. 'Object Cases in Old English: What do They Encode? A Contribution to a General Theory of Case and Grammatical Relations'. MS, Technische Universität Hannover.

Postal, P. 1974. *On Raising.* Cambridge, Mass.: MIT Press.

Reis, M. 1973. 'Is There a Rule of Subject-to-Object Raising in German?'. *Papers from the Ninth Regional Meeting of the Chicago Linguistic Society,* University of Chicago.

Rohdenburg, G. 1974. *Sekundäre Subjektivierungen im Englischen und Deutschen: Vergleichende Untersuchungen zur Verb- und Adjektivsyntax.* PAKS Arbeitsbericht 8, Bielefeld: Cornelsen-Velhagen und Klasing.

Ross, J.R. 1967. 'Constraints on Variables in Syntax'. MIT dissertation.

Sapir, E. 1921. *Language: An Introduction to the Study of Speech.* New York: Harcourt Brace.

Sgall, P. 1982. 'Wortfolge und Fokus im Deutschen', in W. Abraham (ed.), *Satzglieder im Deutschen,* Tübingen: Gunter Narr Verlag.

Stockwell, R.P. 1968. 'Contrastive Analysis and Lapsed Time', in J.E. Alatis (ed.), *Contrastive Linguistics and its Pedagogical Implications* (19th Round Table Meeting). Washington: Georgetown University Press.

Thompson, S.A. 1978. 'Modern English from a Typological Point of View: Some Implications of the Function of Word Order', *Linguistische Berichte* 54: 19–35.

26

The Group Genitive and Type 24 Languages

FRED W. HOUSEHOLDER

What Jespersen (1933: 140) calls the group genitive of English sometimes surprises native speakers of other European languages.[1] Bloomfield's (1933: 178) example is fairly typical: *The man I saw yesterday's* [sc. *hat*], though in literary contexts you're more likely to see ones like: (Jespersen's examples) *The King of Denmark's castle* or *The son of Pharaoh's daughter was the daughter of Pharaoh's son*. Neither Bloomfield nor Jespersen gives a clear statement of the rule; Jespersen says 'The *s* is appended to a group of words if it forms a sense unit,' and (141) 'is felt as belonging nearly as much to the word following it as to the preceding one.' Bloomfield says 'the [-z] is in construction with the entire preceding phrase, so that the two are united into a single long word'. From neither of these accounts could a stranger appreciate the fact that this is not some free, semantically or stylistically controlled phenomenon, but an almost or quite exceptionless syntactical rule:

> RULE 1: In a construction of the form $_{NP}$[possessor NP + possessed Nom.]$_{NP}$, **if the 's [-z] morpheme is used at all**, it must follow the last word of the possessor NP and immediately precede the first word of the possessed Nom. (i.e. N̄, NP lacking any determiner — whose place is filled by the possessor NP), no matter what those words are.

When Jespersen says 'forms a sense unit', judging by some of his examples, he seems to be thinking of short idioms like *heir-apparent, commander-in-chief, somebody else*. But there is no such restriction in ordinary use, which is better represented by *The man I saw yesterday*. We can easily say (though we rarely write) *The man I'm talking about's hat* or *The man I came in with's hat* or *The man I saw's hat*, though some combinations, partly because of possible ambiguity (as suggested by Jespersen) and partly because of what he calls the 'peculiar difficulties' related to the personal pronouns, are avoided. I doubt if you're likely to say [*The man who came with Jane*]*'s hat* (it's sure to be wrongly bracketed) or **One of us's hat* or even, though Jespersen finds some such examples, *One of our hat(s)* to mean 'The hat of one of us'. Yet *one of them's hat* sounds possible. And Bloomfield's 'single long word' stems from a clear prejudice against suffixes (phonologically word-parts) being construed with phrases syntactically.

In English, since both relative clauses and attributive prepositional phrases normally follow the head noun, the *'s* [-z] element can be affixed to any word which may be last in either of those. (We are not forgetting conjoinings — *Adam and Eve's children* — or appositives — *Smith the bookseller's office* — because in these cases the last word is always a noun, perhaps even the head noun, for some analyses, so that no difficulty arises.) An English prepositional phrase virtually always ends with a noun (exceptions mainly involve *with* — *The man with the plaid coat on's brother*). Much the same possibilities as for prepositions exist with participial modifiers: *The man wearing the red coat's brother is my friend* or *[The candidate defeated last year]'s running mate is a woman*. All of these can easily be regarded as reduced relative clauses.

I have taught syntax courses for many years, and since about 1954 or so I have frequently used problems taken from the SIL workbook (the latest edition I own bears the names Merrifield, Naish, Rensch and Story, and is dated 1974). One of my favorite problems in that book has long been the Cashinahua problem (no. 164 in the 1974 edition). For readers unfamiliar with the problem, it consists of 85 sentences with semi-literal English translations, carefully designed to reveal a number of interesting structural facts about the language.[2] Among them are: (1) nominal direct (and indirect) objects (O) and intransitive subjects (S) are unmarked, transitive subjects (A) are marked — i.e., it is or has been or is about to become at least a split ergative language (this, incidentally, is the fact most often missed by my students); (2) it is basically an SOV language; (3) the noun phrase has possessor (unmarked) before possessed (also unmarked), but adjective after head (and intensifier 'very' after adjective); (4) the case endings (besides ergative only an instrumental occurs in the problem) are suffixed to the last word in the NP, whatever it is — and, in this set of examples, it may be an attributive adjective or the intensifying adverb as well as the head noun. (A few sentences are translated with a present participle following and modifying the head noun, but those NPs are always subjects of intransitive verbs, and hence unmarked.)[3] This fourth feature provides, of course, the connection you have been expecting with English group genitives. Last year one of my students (Alicja M. Gorecka-Polewczak) challenged me to find other languages exhibiting this feature.

A hasty leaf-through of recent issues of *IJAL* soon turned up what seem to be two parallel examples, Wappo and Diegueño, in Li, Thompson and Sawyer (1977) and Gorbet (1979), respectively.

What are some of the salient features of Wappo? (1) Direct or indirect object is unmarked, S and A are equally marked with a suffix (*-i*). So

Wappo is not now ergative. (2) The word order is SOV. (3) Possessor (marked if alienable) precedes possessed, adjectives follow the noun, but I cannot discover either here or from Radin (1929) where words for 'very' (Radin lists *enya*) are placed. (4) The case-ending is last (Li, Thompson and Sawyer 1977: 92: 'The SM [subject marker] must be the last word in the phrase.') except when quantifiers are present. So also in conjoinings (93) 'only the second noun shows the SM'. If the NP is a headless relative clause (97), the dative case marker -*thu* follows the verb. All Radin says (1929: 137) is 'An adjective always agrees with its noun in case', which **allows** the case marker to occur last, but **also** on the head noun. Radin appears to have been relatively uninterested in syntactic facts.[4]

For Diegueño, besides Gorbet 1979 we may also use Gorbet 1976, where (1) we read (15) that 'the grammatical subject of a verb, whether transitive or intransitive' takes the subject case marker (-č); but (1979: 252) 'the object case [direct or indirect] is unmarked; (2) 'Diegueño is a fairly strict SOV language' (7); (3) possessor (unmarked 'object case') precedes possessed (1976: 17); (4) case affixes occur on the last word of the noun phrase, whatever it is (1976: 13; 1979: 252), and it may be an adjective, verb or noun. The expression for 'very' is said to be a verb (1976: 122), and so probably may be followed by a case-ending, though I could find no examples in Gorbet (1976) or (1979), nor in Langdon (1970).

From a hint in the Li, Thompson and Sawyer (1977) article I inferred that Mojave might be similar (and it is also closely related to Diegueño), and a quick glance at Munro (1976) shows that that is indeed the case. For point 1, see pp. 18–19; point 2, 24 and 139; point 3, 17–18, 22; point 4, 22 and 45 — I can't find the information on 'very'.[5]

All three are clear-cut type 24 languages, in the Greenberg-Hawkins scheme (Greenberg 1966, Hawkins 1979), i.e. SOV, postposition,[6] Gen. + N, N + Adj., and this type offers the best chance of finding languages with an NP-last rule, though, as we shall see, 16, 17 and 21 are also possible. (In type 23 case will automatically be NP-last, but the head N will always be right before it. Gorbet (1976) does find parallels in Japanese, which is a type 23 language, but has relative clauses in which the head is internal.) So I have tried hard to discover the relevant facts about the type 24 languages listed in Hawkins (mostly following Greenberg), and with a little success. Greenberg (1966: 95, Universal 40), reports that Basque has an NP-last rule for case suffixes (see also Tovar 1957: 69, and Wilbur 1979: 59), and Dixon (1980: 443) mentions Kuuku-Ya?u as having a similar rule, though most Australian languages have either agreement (i.e. case-ending last **as well as** on head — see Dixon 1980: 293 for an instance from Warrgamay in which this case-ending is added on top of the genitive case-ending of a following possessor) or, like Ngiyambaa (Donaldson 1980), have a rule of case-ending once, either on head or on adjective (which may either precede or follow, i.e. four possibilities). Haas (1940: 62, 130) gives a similar rule for Tunica, and Parfionovich (1982: 73) gives one for Classical Tibetan (*-sa*), both type 24 languages. The Cushitic languages Oromo and (probably) Dasenech are also type 24 languages with a case-last rule (and zero inflection for Objects), according to Gragg (1976) and Sasse (1976). Athapascan Hare (Rice 1977), is probably another such language. From type 16 (which is SVO instead of SOV), Hoijer's Tonkawa (1931: 25) offers a similar rule for the accusative suffix *-ʔa˙lak*, which has rather more phonological substance than most of the other examples we have observed. Of these five languages (Basque, Kuuku-Yaʔu, Classical Tibetan, Tunica and Tonkawa), the first three are ergative in some degree, with zero marking for S and O, but not the two American Indian languages, and all (in accordance with the definitions of types 16 and 24) have adjectives after nouns, though I can verify 'very' after adjective only for Tonkawa and Basque.

English, however, is not type 16 or type 24, but probably either 10 or 11, which include mainly IE languages (though I also examined Efik and Maya — in vain), in which case endings are pretty thoroughly fused.

The uneasiness shown by Jespersen and Bloomfield appears also in Cromack (on Cashinahua, 1968: 88) who calls all these case morphemes (and some modal morphemes) enclitics, rather than suffixes — and compares English *The King of England's (hat)*. Gorbet (1976: 45) compares English *The man that I talked to's mother* and *The friend that I remember's face*, but successfully avoids the word 'suffix' and 'enclitic', speaking always of 'cases' and 'case-marking', except on p. 13 where the term 'suffixes' appears. Gorbet (1979) has no such qualms, using the word 'suffix' from p. 251 on. Li, Thompson and Sawyer (1977) also have no qualms, referring to 'suffixes' by that name from p. 90 on, though on p. 92 they say 'The SM must be the last word in the phrase'; this may be a slip for 'be suffixed to the last [etc.]'.

Why should anyone have qualms? There seem to be two partially related factors, both having to do with the notion of wordhood. (1) Most linguists accept the definitional restriction that all syntactically relevant parts of a sentence must be either groups of words, words, or parts of words. And (2) they also feel that, to be a word, a 'formative' must have a certain phonological freedom and (3) that phonological boundaries (e.g. word-ends) must coincide with syntactic ones — i.e. that a phrase cannot end in the middle of a word. These three principles sometimes lead to contradictory judgments.

Let us examine the qualms involved. Consider the examples of group genitive cited above: is *yesterday's* in the Bloomfield example; or *Denmark's* in Jespersen's; or *about's*, *with's* or *saw's*; or *them's* in mine; or *England's* in Cromack's; or *to's* or *remember's* in Gorbet's a word? As wholes, *about's* and *them's* and *saw's* don't seem to be words because they are not interpretable by themselves, but constituents or constitutes, violating principle 3. But, by itself, *'s* violates principle 2. However, on reflection, we cannot maintain this principle in its strongest form. There are in English a good handful of words with equally short forms as variants: *is, are, has, have, had, will, would* and sometimes *did, an, in, it* reduce to a single consonant (*z, r, s, v, d, l, n, t*) or less (as in [jə] for *did you*). It's true that they all have emphatic stressed variants, whereas possessive *'s* does not. The case may well be stronger in our American Indian languages. In Mojave, all three case-endings consist of a single consonant (*-č, -lʸ, -m*), and Munro says (1976: 4) that 'the basic root of the word consists minimally of a vowel'. In Diegueño, four of the five alleged suffixes consist of a single consonant (*-č, -lʸ, -m, -k* — the fifth is *-i*), and a rule of lenition (Gorbet 1976: 3–5) shows that at least *-č* and *-k* cannot be words. (See also Langdon 1970: 50.) In Wappo, only one potential suffix is a bare consonant (*-h*), but here again the minimal word (Radin 1929: 18) must contain a vowel. The other Wappo cases are either *-CV* or *-CV?*, except for the subject case-ending *-i*. Finally, the Cashinahua agent (A) case as given in problem 164 is even shorter: nasalization of the last vowel, which may even be only the penultimate segment (as in the word *des* 'nephew'). Cromack, however, gives the case marker ('enclitic') as *-n*, presumably an underlying form, and offers variant forms with more substance (1968: 341): *-nen, -nin, -pan, -wan*, which are possible words. All the other cases except one (*-a*, a locative ending) are at least *CV*.

The two possible ways of easing our qualms (if we have any) are either Bloomfield's (and implicitly Jespersen's) way — *'s* is a suffix, it's in IC relation to the whole preceding NP, but that NP has been magically converted into a single word (therefore, presumably, NP + *'s* is also a single word); or Cromack's way — *'s* is an enclitic **word**, not a suffix at all, but a postposition.[7] This second solution is possible for English (in spite of the nonexistence of a stressed variant and of other postpositions), for Cashinahua, and perhaps for Wappo, though it seems difficult for Mojave and Diegueño. But it does seem hard to justify the first solution for any language; the postulated 'word' has few word-like qualities other than phonological ones. Admittedly some linguists deny that the verb inflections in IE and other similar languages are in IC relation to the rest of the verb, but at least those inflections are always added to the verb, not to whatever happens to turn up in the right spot.

Our final question might be the one implied in our title; why is it mainly type 24 languages (if this is true) that have a rule like Rule 1 above? The preconditions, or some of them, are easy to state: (1) the language must have at least two cases; (2) it must be predominantly suffixing; (3) it must allow some subordinate clauses with V last or NPs with Adj. or other qualifier last. No one of these three conditions enters into the definition of the 24 types. But it is fairly easy to see that condition 3 more or less eliminates VSO languages (and any VOS which may exist) — types 1–8, though some type 1 languages might be possible. Most of 9–11 are Indo-European languages, and I could find none in them or in the other languages I checked of types 9 and 10 (other than English). Nor could I find any in types 12–15. In 16 we find Tonkawa, which we mentioned above, and in 17 Persian (the definite object suffix *-ra*, as described in Lambton 1963: 9), nothing in 18–20, probably Teda (as described in C. and M. Le Coeur 1956: 36–43) in 21; and types 17 and 21 look as if they may have other examples. No languages are listed for 22, and we have already discussed the problem with 23, where other languages besides Japanese may have a relative clause type with incorporated antecedent, but most surely don't. It looks as if the main typological features are numbers 1 and 2, case suffixing, and these can be related to ergativity as follows:

Ergative languages are necessarily either marked on the verb (as in Sierra Popoluca) where the NPs are uninflected, or by case affixes.

The largest number of case-marking languages in the Greenberg–Hawkins sample is found in types 9, 23, and 24. This explanation does not account for the other similarities between Wappo and Diegueño (and Mojave), for which areal influence seems a possible reason.

It would be nice to have a new typological classification which included the features [± case system] and [± suffixing] or [± prefixing], and even [± ergative].

NOTES

1. This paper has benefited from the criticism of my colleague Linda Schwartz.
2. The best way to check these inferences is to look at the whole problem, since it is easily available but too long to reproduce here. I will quote sentences 30 and 64 to illustrate some of the points, using tilde instead of cedilla for nasalization.

(30) isu ɨwopa haidã pia ũĩnũ.
 spider-monkey big very+nas. (A) arrow will-see
 'A very big spider monkey will see the arrows.'

(64) habũ dẽs pia haidawɨ isu cakašũ.
 he-nas. (A) nephew-nas. (A) arrow many-Instr. spider-monkey shot
 'His nephew shot spider monkeys with many arrows.'

Note that the 3rd person singular pronoun possessor takes the agent marker. Other pronouns have the same form for all subjects (S and A) and possessors, but a different form for objects. *haidã* is variously 'much', 'many', and 'very'.

3. All this information can also be gathered, though much less easily, from Cromack (1968), although Cromack never uses the term ergative, and the SOV order is only with difficulty extracted from Figure 14 on p. 83. A focusing rule is

also easily inferred from the problem, and hard to get out of Cromack.
4. There are no NPs in the examples or the one short text which provide evidence on this point.
5. The structural similarity of these three languages (grouping Mojave with Diegueño) suggested possible kinship, and the first items I checked were surprisingly similar — the short person markers (one syllable or less) for first and second persons (singular).

	Cashinahua	Wappo	Diegueño–Mojave
'I, me, my'	ʔį	ʔi	ʔ-
'you, your'	mį	mi	m-

That looks very close. But nothing else confirms it. (Cromack actually gives a Swadesh list.) Wappo is said to be a Yukian language, Diegueño and Mojave are Yuman, while Cashinahua is Panoan.
6. 'Suffixing' is not used as a criterion in this scheme, and, as remarked above, 'suffixes' like these are often considered postpositions.
7. This is also the solution adopted for English by Zwicky (1977).

REFERENCES

Bender, M.L. (ed.) 1976. *The Non-Semitic Languages of Ethiopia*. Lansing: Michigan State University.
Bloomfield, L. 1933. *Language*. New York: Holt, Rinehart and Winston.
Cromack, R.E. 1968. *Language Systems and Discourse Structure in Cashinawa*. Hartford Seminary Foundation dissertation. Hartford Studies in Linguistics (typescript).
Dixon, R.M.W. 1980. *The Languages of Australia*. New York: Cambridge University Press.
Donaldson, Tamsin. 1980. *Ngiyambaa* (Cambridge Studies in Linguistics, 24). New York: Cambridge University Press.
Gorbet, L.P. 1976. *A Grammar of Diegueño Nominals*. New York: Garland.
—— 1979. 'The Case Marking of Diegueño Complement Clauses', *IJAL* 45: 251–66.
Gragg, G. 1976. 'Oromo of Wellegga,' in Bender (ed.), 1976: 166–95.
Greenberg, J.H. 1966. 'Some Universals of Grammar with Particular Reference to the Order of Meaningful Elements,' in J.H. Greenberg (ed.), *Universals of Language* (2nd edn). Cambridge, Mass.: MIT Press, 73–113.
Haas, Mary R. 1940. *Tunica* (Handbook of American Indian Languages, vol. 4, no. 40, part 4a). New York: J.J. Augustin.
Hawkins, J.A. 1979. 'Implicational Universals as Predictors of Word Order Change', *Language* 55: 618–48.
Hoijer, H. 1931. *Tonkawa, an Indian Language of Texas* (Handbook of American Indian Languages, vol. 3). Reprinted by the University of Chicago Libraries.
Jespersen, Otto. 1933. *Essentials of English Grammar*. London: Allen and Unwin.
Lambton, A.K.S. 1963. *Persian Grammar*. New York: Cambridge University Press.
Langdon, M. 1970. *A Grammar of Diegueño* (University of California Publications in Linguistics, 66). Berkeley: University of California Press.
Le Coeur, C. and M. Le Coeur. 1956. *Grammaire et textes Teda-Daza*. Dakar: Ifan.

Li, C.N., S.A. Thompson, and J.O. Sawyer. 1977. 'Subject and Word Order in Wappo', *IJAL* 43: 85–100.

Merrifield, W.P., C.M. Naish, C.R. Rensch, and G. Story. 1974. *Laboratory Manual for Morphology and Syntax*. Santa Ana, California: Summer Institute of Linguistics.

Munro, P. 1976. *Mojave Syntax*. New York: Garland.

Parfionovich, Y.M. 1982. *The Written Tibetan Language*. Moscow: Nauka.

Radin, P. 1929. *A Grammar of the Wappo Language* (University of California Publications in American Archaeology and Ethnology, 27) Berkeley: University of California Press.

Rice, Keren. 1977. *A Preliminary Grammar of Fort Good Hope Slave (Hare)*. Ottawa: Department of Indian and Northern Affairs.

Sasse, Hans-Jürgen, 1976. 'Dasenech', in Bender (ed.), 1976: 196–221.

Tovar, A. 1957. *The Basque Language*. Philadelphia: University of Pennsylvania Press.

Wilbur, T.H. 1979. *Prolegomena to a Grammar of Basque*. Amsterdam: Benjamins.

Zwicky, A.M. 1977. *On Clitics*. Indiana University Linguistics Club. Also in W.V. Dressler and D.E. Pfeiffer (eds.), *Phonologica 1976*, Innsbruck, 29–39.

27

Transitivity: Intransitivization vs. Causativization: Some Typological Considerations Concerning Verbs of Action

YOSHIHIKO IKEGAMI

1.

This paper discusses two contrasting semantic behaviors observable with verbs of action — a tendency to be intransitivized and a tendency to be causativized — and suggests that the dominance of one tendency over the other can be correlated with certain typological features of the language in question.

2.

A verb of action is typically a linguistic means of representing an action performed by a human agent. Such an action will normally involve two components — one referring to how the human agent behaves and the other referring to what effect is produced. Since, normally, the human agent is presumed to act with a certain goal in mind, the second feature can also be characterized as referring to the attainment of the intended result or the achievement of the goal. For brevity's sake, I will be referring to the two components as 'action component' and 'achievement component', respectively.

3.

Although both components are presumably involved in the action seen as an extralinguistic event, a verb of action, which represents it linguistically, may or may not involve the component of achievement as part of its meaning. Thus there are (1) verbs of action which imply the achievement of the goal intended by the action and (2) verbs of action which do not necessarily imply the achievement of the goal intended by the action. (There is a third possibility, i.e. verbs of action which regularly do not imply the achievement of the goal intended by the action. We will leave aside this possibility for the moment.)

The two types of verbs can be illustrated by the English verbs *kill* and *invite*. The goal of 'killing' a person is to bring about the consequence that the person dies. This consequence is implied by the verb *kill*. Thus sentence (1) would be semantically anomalous:

(1) *John killed Bill, but Bill didn't die.

The goal of 'inviting' a person is to bring about the consequence that the person in question comes. This consequence does not have to be implied by the verb *invite*. Thus sentence (2) is not anomalous:

(2) John invited Bill, but Bill didn't come.

We will call verbs which behave like *kill* 'achievement' verbs and verbs like *invite* 'non-achievement' verbs.[1]

4.

An interesting fact in this connection is that an action verb in one language does not necessarily behave in the same way as its semantically corresponding counterpart in another language. Theoretically, there are four foreseeable cases of correspondence:

	Language$_1$	Language$_2$
(i)	'achievement'	'achievement'
(ii)	'non-achievement'	'non-achievement'
(iii)	'achievement'	'non-achievement'
(iv)	'non-achievement'	'achievement'

What interests us is those cases in which the corresponding verbs behave differently, namely (iii) and (iv).

If we compare English and Japanese verbs of action with maximal semantic correspondence between them, there emerges a very interesting contrast. We have, quite expectedly, cases (i) and (ii), where there is no difference in the behavior of the corresponding English and Japanese verbs. Thus the Japanese verbs *korosu* and *shotaisuru*, which maximally correspond in meaning to the English verbs *kill* and *invite*, behave in the same way as the latter in terms of the implication of 'achievement'/'non-achievement'. Sentences (3) and (4) correspond to (1) and (2) given above:

(3) John wa   Bill o   koroshita kedo, Bill wa   shinanakatta.
       TOPIC   OBJECT killed   though TOPIC didn't die

(4) John wa   Bill o   shotaishita kedo, Bill wa   konakatta.
       TOPIC   OBJECT invited   though TOPIC didn't come

There are numerous pairs of English and Japanese verbs which behave in this way.

There are, on the other hand, also quite a few pairs of English and Japanese verbs which do not behave identically with regard to the implication of 'achievement', and what is remarkable in this respect is that whenever there is a discrepancy in behavior between the English and Japanese verbs of maximally corresponding meanings, it is invariably the English verbs which imply 'achievement' and their Japanese counterparts which do not necessarily imply 'achievement'. In other words, we find examples for case (iii) but not for (iv). Some examples for case (iii) are given below:

(5) a. *I boiled the water, but it didn't boil.
    b. Wakashita kedo, wakanakatta.
       boiled   though didn't boil

(6) a. *I burned it, but it didn't burn.
    b. Moyashita kedo, moenakatta.
       burned   though didn't burn

(7) a. *I counted how many there were, but it was impossible to count.
    b. Ikutsu   aru ka   kazoeta kedo, kazoerarenakatta.
       how many are QUESTION counted though couldn't count

(8) a. *The child divided ten by three, but it was impossible.
    b. Kodomo wa   ju o   san de watta   kedo,
       child   TOPIC ten OBJECT three by divided though
       warenakkata.
       couldn't divide

(9) a. *I dropped a bomb on the target, but it didn't hit it.
    b. Mokuhyo ni   bakudan o   otoshita kedo, ataranakatta.
       target   GOAL bomb   OBJECT dropped though didn't hit.

(10) a. *I helped Mary solve the problem, but she couldn't solve it.
     b. Mary ga   mondai o   toku no   o
        SUBJECT problem OBJECT solve NOMINALIZER OBJECT
        tetsudatta kedo, Mary wa   tokenakatta.
        helped   though TOPIC couldn't solve

391

(11) a. *I measured the height of the mountain, but didn't succeed.
 b. Yama no takasa o hakatta kedo,
  mountain POSSESSIVE height OBJECT measured though
  damedatta.
  didn't succeed

(12) a. *I mixed oil and water, but they didn't mix.
 b. Abura to mizu o mazeta kedo, majiranakatta.
  oil and water OBJECT mixed though didn't mix.

(13) a. *I persuaded John to go, but he wouldn't go.
 b. John o yuku yoni settokushita kedo, ikoto shinakatta.
  OBJECT go to persuaded though will go didn't do

(14) a. *I thawed the frozen food outdoors, but it didn't thaw.
 b. Reito shokuhin o sotode tokashita kedo,
  frozen food OBJECT outdoors thawed though
  tokenakatta.
  didn't thaw

(15) a. *I woke Mary, but she was fast asleep.
 b. Mary o okoshita kedo, gussuri nemutteita.
  OBJECT woke though fast asleep was

Other verbs which behave more or less in the same way include *cheat – damasu, classify – bunruisuru, dry – kawakasu, float – ukaberu, inflate – fukurakasu, peel – muku, scoop – sukuu, stand* ('to put in an upright position') *– tateru*, etc. In all these examples, the English verbs imply the achievement of the goal intended by the action, while their Japanese counterparts do not have to imply that the intended goal is achieved. I have so far been unable to find a pair of English and Japanese verbs which behave the other way around, i.e. a pair which represents case (iv).

5.

It is tantalizingly desirable to know how widely languages whose verbs of action behave like those of Japanese are distributed over the world. It would then be possible to determine whether any other features commonly found in those languages might perhaps be correlated with the particular feature we are now concerned with. In the absence of such information, I can only proceed with building a hypothesis on the basis of my linguistic intuition as a native speaker of Japanese. I will attempt to identify those other features of the language which seem to have a high probability of being responsible for the way in which the Japanese verbs of action so characteristically behave.

5.1.

The first point to be considered concerns the nature and status of the grammatical object. The grammatical object of a transitive verb of action represents the goal to which the action is directed. A goal-directed action is achieved when it reaches its goal, and a very natural inference is that the goal is affected when it is reached by the action. Hence a grammatical object added to the verb of action will certainly help support the implication of 'achievement'. Since a transitive verb is by definition a verb accompanied by a grammatical object, it should imply, insofar as the verb refers to a goal-directed action, the achievement of the goal as well as the action directed to the same goal.

With the intransitive verb, things are otherwise. Since an intransitive verb is, by definition, not accompanied by a grammatical object (which would refer to the goal of the action), the semantic focus is naturally on the action. An action represented by an intransitive verb can also be directed to a certain goal to be possibly affected by the action, but the goal is then not represented as the grammatical object but as a prepositional phrase. In English, the typical preposition will be *to* in such cases, e.g. *Mary sang to the baby*. The semantic focus, however, is still on the action, and there is no implication that the baby was affected in a particular way. In fact, with certain verbs that can be used either transitively or intransitively, there is a systematic contrast between their transitive uses with an implication of achievement and their intransitive uses without an implication of achievement. Thus compare *shoot a person – shoot at a person, strike a person – strike at a person, bite a person – bite at a person, seize something – seize at something, snatch something – snatch at something, catch something – catch at something*. Other verbs behaving in the same way include *hit, kick, lash, slap, smash, punch; clutch, grab, grasp,* and *grip*.

Now a syntactic characteristic of Japanese is that the grammatical object can freely be suppressed in the discourse as actually used in context, insofar as it can be inferred from the context. (Thus the Japanese sentences in (5)–(15) above represent the English pronominal objects by zero-forms, taking this fact into consideration.) From the preceding discussion, it will be clear that the quite common suppression of the object may have a certain effect on the meaning of the transitive verb. In Japanese, transitive verbs are frequently used without the grammatical object — in other words, used as if they were intransitive verbs; hence it is quite foreseeable that the Japanese transitive verbs tend to become semantically intransitivized — which, in the case of transitive verbs of goal-directed action, means that the semantic focus shifts from the 'achievement' component to the 'action' component. This can account for the non-obligatoriness of the implication of achievement with the Japanese verbs of action.

In fact, the acceptability of the Japanese sentences does seem to become lower when the verb is accompanied by the object. A particularly interesting case in point is the verb *wakasu* 'to boil'. This verb is usually used with an 'object of result', i.e. the word *yu* 'warm water'. It can also be used, quite logically, with the word *mizu* 'water'. There is a decrease in acceptability as we go from (16) (=(5): with object suppressed) though (17) (with an affected object) to (18) (with an object of result):

(16) Wakashita kedo, wakanakatta.
      boiled   though didn't boil

(17) Mizu o   wakashita kedo, wakanakatta.
      water OBJECT boiled   though didn't boil

(18) (?)Yu   o   wakashita kedo, wakanakatta.
      warm water OBJECT   boiled   though didn't boil

The fact that the acceptability is lowest with the example with an object of result shows that the specification of the grammatical object has the effect of shifting the semantic focus from the 'action' component to the 'achievement' component.

5.2.

The second point to be noted is the nature and status of the grammatical subject. With verbs of action, the grammatical subject represents an agent, typically a human being acting on his own will and power. If the grammatical object of a verb of action represents the goal to which the action is directed, its grammatical subject then represents the source from which the action is directed.

It may safely be assumed that as the source of action intensifies its agentivity (i.e. its role of acting on the goal to which the action is directed), the goal becomes increasingly more markedly affected and that this increase in affectedness will be marked by a change in the status of the object from simply the 'patient', which only suffers the action, to the 'causee', which undergoes a certain change as a consequence of being affected. A good illustration is the causativization of transitive verbs:

(19) a. Mary rocked her baby (in the cradle).
      b. Mary rocked her baby to sleep.

(20) a. Mary washed her clothes.
    b. Mary washed her clothes clean.

The same causativization process may start with an intransitive verb and jump over the stage of the (non-causative) transitive use:

(21) a. Mary sang to her baby.
    b. Mary sang her baby to sleep.

(22) a. Mary danced with her friend.
    b. Mary danced her friend weary.

Modern English is known to have a strong tendency toward causativization (which, in other words, means the intensification of the notion of agentivity; cf. Ikegami 1984).

Now just as with the grammatical object, Japanese can also quite freely suppress the grammatical subject when it can be inferred from the context. Many of the illustrative sentences (5)–(15) in section 4 are given without their subject (particularly, one referring to the speaker). This common suppression of the subject will also have an effect on the meaning of the verbs referring to a goal-directed action. It will certainly work to weaken the notion of agentivity (which is to be implied by the subject) and thus help to obliterate the 'achievement' sense of the goal-directed action verbs — a tendency which is quite opposite to the tendency toward causativization. Thus the non-obligatoriness of the subject in Japanese seems to conspire with the common suppression of the object to shift the semantic focus of the action verbs onto the 'action' rather than the 'achievement' component.

5.3.

There is one more point about the subject of the goal-directed action verbs that must be considered — the selection restriction. The kind of noun that can stand as subject of a goal-directed action verb in Japanese must as a rule be a 'human' noun. This is in clear contrast with the situation in a language like English, where an inanimate and even an abstract noun can with comparative ease stand for the agent. Of the following three sentences, frequently cited in the discussion of case grammar, only (23) would be fully acceptable in Japanese; (24) would sound odd and (25) would be taken as clearly involving the personification of the wind:

(23) John opened the door.

(24) The key opened the door.

(25) The wind opened the door.

English, for that matter, will also allow an abstract subject to cooccur with such verbs: *The magic word opened the door, This trick will open the door*; both of these would sound odd in Japanese, if not artificially rhetorical.

It is not very difficult to see that the use of non-human nouns has an effect on the meaning of the goal-directed action verbs. If the subject is a human noun, one can always more or less visualize the action performed by the human agent. (Thus, even in the case of the verb *open*, usually treated as a 'causative' verb, one can still draw a mental picture of a human agent touching, turning, and then pushing the door-knob.) If, on the other hand, the subject is an inanimate noun (and still more so, if the subject is an abstract noun), it will then in principle be impossible (unless indirectly via 'personification') to visualize the performed action. This obliterates the 'action' component of the goal-directed action verbs and shifts the semantic focus onto the 'achievement' component. In other words, the use of inanimate and, especially, abstract nouns as subjects of action verbs will change the status of the verbs from non-causative to causative.

In fact, this is what is involved when the different degrees of acceptability of pairs of sentences like the following are discussed:[2]

(26) a. John taught Mary how to behave.
     b. The experience taught Mary how to behave.

(27) a. John taught Mary how to behave.
     b. *The experience taught to Mary how to behave.

The indirect object construction is said to imply mastering what is taught, whereas this is not the case with the construction with a prepositional phrase. In our terms, the former construction is associated with the 'achievement' sense and the latter with the 'action' sense. Since an abstract noun like *experience* cannot be associated with the action of 'teaching', it is not quite compatible with the construction which predominantly implies 'action' rather than 'achievement'.

5.4.

There seems to be one further linguistic feature, which at first sight looks quite unrelated, but which in fact is very relevant to the characteristic behavior of the Japanese verbs of goal-directed action we are considering. This feature is the lack of grammatical means (corresponding to English articles) for specifying 'definite' vs. 'indefinite' contrast with Japanese nouns. How this feature bears on the semantic tendency of the goal-directed action verbs toward a 'non-achievement' sense (and consequently, toward an 'action' sense) is conveniently illustrated by the semantic contrast observable with English sentences like the following:

(28) a. *John dried the dishes for Mary, but he didn't dry all the dishes.
b. John dried dishes for Mary, but he didn't dry all the dishes.

(29) a. *John cleared the snow from the path, but there was still some left.
b. John cleared snow from the path, but there was still some left.

(30) a. *I picked up the fallen beads on the floor, but there were so many of them scattered over the floor that I couldn't pick them all up.
b. I picked up fallen beads on the floor, but there were so many of them scattered over the floor that I couldn't pick them all up.

There may be ambiguous cases like *John poured the milk into the pot*, where the definite article for *milk* may simply refer to the 'given-ness' of milk, but the function of the definite article to assign 'definiteness' and the consequent effect of this on the meaning of goal-directed action verbs should be clear enough. By being assigned 'definiteness', the goal of the action is presented as an entity having a definite contour — something 'discrete'. When such is the case, it is not difficult to conceive of the goal of an action as holistically (and not just partially) affected, since the entire extension of the goal is defined. When, however, such is not the case, the choice between 'holistic' and 'partitive' interpretation must remain open.

The absence of obligatory marking of 'definiteness' in Japanese has the effect of obliterating the extensional contour of the goal of an action. Coupled with this, there is also the lack of obligatory marking for the 'singular' vs. 'plural' contrast on nouns in Japanese. These factors combine to represent the goal of an action not as a clearly discrete entity, but rather as a mass or a continuum, where, because of the indefinite extensional contour, the contrast between 'holistic' and 'partitive' tends to be neutralized. It is clear that the 'achievement' sense is difficult to establish where a holistic and a partitive interpretation are neutralized.

6.

Before concluding, I would like to refer to a few other points which are relevant to the topic I have been discussing.

6.1.

The first point is the behavior of Japanese verbs of motion, which seems to parallel closely the behavior of the Japanese verbs of action so far discussed. That there is a parallelism between the structure of an action and that of a motion will be clear enough.[3] The action starts from a certain source and reaches a certain goal; similarly, the motion starts from a certain source and reaches a certain goal. It will then be no surprise if the verbs of (goal-directed) motion behave in the same characteristic way as the verbs of (goal-directed) action. In fact, this is exactly what is observed with Japanese verbs of motion.

One peculiar characteristic of Japanese verbs referring to locomotion by a human agent is that, in contrast to their English counterparts, they are not generally directly combined with a phrase indicating the goal to which they are supposedly directed. Thus in contrast to the English sentences (31a) and (32a) below, which are quite acceptable, the corresponding Japanese sentences (31b) and (32b) will sound odd:

(31) a. John ran to the station.
      b. (?)John wa   eki   e hashitta.
              TOPIC station to ran

(32) a. John swam to the shore.
      b. (?)John wa   kishi e oyoida.
              TOPIC shore to swam

There are two ways in which the acceptability of the Japanese sentences can be improved:

(31) b′. John wa   eki   e hashitte itta/kita.
              TOPIC station to running went/came
      b″. John wa   eki   made hashitta.
              TOPIC station till   ran

(32) b′. John wa   kishi e oyoide   itta/kita.
              TOPIC shore to swimming went/came

      b″. John wa   kishi made oyoida.
              TOPIC shore till   swam

The (b′) sentences are roughly equivalent to the English sentences, *John went/came running to the station* and *John went/came swimming to the shore.* The (b″) sentences say literally, 'John ran till the station' and 'John swam till the shore' (meaning, of course, that John ran till he reached the station and John swam till he reached the shore).

The behavior of the Japanese verbs of motion can be accounted for if we assume that their semantic focus is on the 'motion' component rather than on the 'achievement (of the goal)' component. The (b) sentences above are odd because the verbs *hashiru* and *oyogu* lack the notion of 'directedness' (which their English counterparts, *run* and *swim*, seem to have). The (b') sentences, on the other hand, are acceptable, because the verbs, *iku* and *kuru*, supply the lacking notion of 'directedness'. The (b") sentences are acceptable because the prepositional phrase no longer refers to the goal to which the locomotion is directed but to the time at which the locomotion, continued so far, terminates.

All this seems to suggest that Japanese verbs of motion are not really verbs of motion in the same sense as their English counterparts. Two notable exceptions are, as we have seen above, *iku* 'go' and *kuru* 'come'. But the use of these two verbs is not restricted to a human agent. And as far as verbs referring to a human agent's locomotion are concerned, the semantic focus seems to be on the process of change in locus rather than the attainment of a certain goal. Taking into consideration what we have already observed with the verbs of action, we can say that the Japanese verbs, both of action and of motion, are 'process-oriented', whereas their English counterparts are 'goal-oriented'.

6.2.

The second point concerns verbs of action of the third type mentioned in section 3 and left for later discussion — namely, verbs of action which always imply non-achievement of the goal to which the action is directed. (The first type is of those verbs (i.e. *kill*) which always imply achievement of the goal, and the second type is of those verbs (e.g. *invite*) which do not necessarily imply achievement of the goal.)

Our immediate impression is that such verbs do not seem to be numerous, although the same notion can be represented periphrastically by using the verb *fail* (e.g. *fail to kill*) or the adverbial phrase *in vain* (e.g. *invite in vain*). What happens is that in most of those cases where we would expect the sense 'to act but fail to achieve the intended goal', we would in fact find the sense 'to act and achieve a different or wrong goal'. The latter sense is apparent in most verbs of action with the prefix *dis-* or *mis-* (e.g. *displace* and *misplace*).

This replacement of 'fail to achieve the goal' by 'achieve a different or wrong goal' is not at all peculiar; it is, on the contrary, a process whose analogues are not difficult to find in language. If we represent 'fail to achieve the goal' as NOT (GO TO X), the latter implies either BE FROM X or GO TO X̄. What generally happens semantically with verbs with the prefixes *dis-* or *mis-* is that, of the two possible implications, it is the latter choice (i.e. the choice involving TO rather than FROM) that is selected. This is, in fact, one instance of the general predominance of the notion of 'goal' over that of 'source' in language, of which abundant evidence is adduced with discussion in Ikegami (1982).

6.3.

The third point concerns the performance of the speaker when confronted with an apparently contradictory sentence involving the use of a verb of action. In section 3, I referred to the Japanese verb *korosu* as counterpart of the English verb *kill* and assumed that the Japanese verb behaves in the same way as the English verb insofar as the implication of achievement of the intended goal is concerned. There seemed to be absolutely no room for doubting this assumption — at least to my own intuition and probably to that of many others.

But an informant test conducted by a member of the National Language Institute in Tokyo produced a rather unexpected result. The test was given to several groups of junior-high-school and college students, and the responses given to the Japanese equivalent of the English sentence *John killed Bill, but Bill didn't die* (cf. sentence (1) in section 3) showed that approximately one out of ten found the sentence acceptable. This proportion was very much higher than I had ever imagined — in fact, I had expected to find a nearly one hundred percent agreement on the unacceptability of the sentence. This led me to give a similar test to a group of college students, and I took the opportunity to ask those who responded affirmatively on the acceptability of the sentence why they did so. One reply — a typical one — went something like the following: 'On TV, you often see a drama in which one person believed he had successfully murdered someone. Actually, however, the latter was not dead; he came out again fully alive, to the immense surprise of the murderer.' To me, the sentence would still sound odd enough even referring to circumstances like these. But what happens here is that, to some speakers at least, 'X thought X had killed Y' can be an approximate equivalent of 'X killed Y'. Such an equivalence would be possible only under the condition that the 'achievement' component of the meaning of the verb is irrelevant (i.e. on the assumption that the verb is, in fact, of the same semantic type as *invite*). I strongly doubt that speakers of English would ever think of interpreting the verb *kill* in the same way. The fact, however, that the verb referring to killing can be interpreted, at least by some Japanese speakers, as not involving the achievement of the goal intended, again seems to reflect the general tendency of the Japanese verbs of goal-directed action to place their semantic focus on the 'action' rather than the 'achievement' component.

7.

In this paper I have shown that verbs of action do not necessarily behave semantically in the same way between languages and have suggested that the characteristic behavior of Japanese verbs of action may very likely be correlated with certain syntactic features of Japanese. Whether or not the suggested correlation is in fact the valid one will have to be checked against data from other languages which we hope that future typological research will afford. The current typological investigations across different languages are focused predominantly on readily and 'objectively' identifiable linguistic features only and are consequently yet unable to pass judgment on the hypothesis offered in this paper.

NOTES

1. Because of the difference of framework, the 'achievement' verb here is not the same as that used by Vendler (1967). The problem of 'implication' was once discussed by Karttunen (1971), but he concentrated on those verbs whose semantic implications are expressly specified linguistically (e.g. by an infinitive following the verb in question). For a discussion of the whole problem from a wider perspective, see Ikegami (1981).
2. Cf. Green (1974).
3. Cf. Anderson (1971).

REFERENCES

Anderson, John M. 1971. *The Grammar of Case: Towards a Localistic Theory*. Cambridge: Cambridge University Press.
Green, Georgia. 1974. *Semantics and Syntactic Regularities*. Bloomington: Indiana University Press.
Ikegami, Yoshihiko. 1981. '"Activity" – "Accomplishment"–"Achievement": A Language That Can't Say *I burned it, but it didn't burn* and One That Can'. Paper No. 87, Series A, Linguistic Agency, University of Trier.
—— 1982. 'Source vs. Goal — A Case of Linguistic Dissymmetry', in Robert St. Clair and Walburga von Raffler-Engel (eds.), *Language and Cognitive Styles*. Lisse: Swets and Zeitlinger.
—— 1984. 'How Universal is a Localist Hypothesis? A Linguistic Contribution to the Study of "Semantic Styles" of Language', in Robin Fawcett, M.A.K. Halliday, Sydney Lamb, and Adam Makkai (eds.), *The Semiotics of Culture and Language*, Vol. 1. London: Frances Pinter, 49–79.
Karttunen, Lauri. 1971. 'Implicative Verbs', *Language* 47: 340–58.
Vendler, Zeno. 1967. *Linguistics and Philosophy*. Ithaca: Cornell University Press.

28

Minor Movement Rules

FREDERICK J. NEWMEYER

This paper explores the properties of grammatical processes known as 'minor movement rules' or simply as 'minor movements'.[1] This class of rules is characterized by the movement of a nonmaximal projection, i.e. of a nonphrasal node. Typical examples are Particle Movement in English (1), Leftward Quantifier Movement in French (2), and Verb Fronting in German (3):[2]

(1) John looked [$_P$up] the answer

(2) elle les a [$_Q$tous] lus

(3) ich [$_V$habe] das Buch gelesen

Specifically, the paper will address two questions pertaining to minor movements. First, given current government binding assumptions, in which component do they apply? I take it as *a priori* desirable that they all apply either in the syntax or all apply in PF. Second, can all minor movements be subsumed under Move-Alpha? Chomsky (1980) specifically excludes movements of nonphrasal nodes from Move-Alpha, as does much subsequent work. However, other work in the GB framework has assumed the contrary. The question is not an empty one, of course; if Alpha can be nonphrasal, then there must exist a set of independent principles that interact with Move-Alpha to predict the full distribution of nonphrasal nodes.

Only one work, to my knowledge, has raised these questions, namely Fiengo (1980). Fiengo concludes that minor movements all apply in PF and that they can be subsumed under Move-Alpha. However, he presents no arguments whatsoever for the former conclusion, and only the sketchiest ones for the latter. My conclusions will be the opposite of Fiengo's. I will argue that, where relevant evidence exists, such rules can be shown to apply in the syntax (i.e. in the mapping between DS and SS). Furthermore, there is little evidence at all that Alpha can be nonphrasal. I will further argue that my conclusions have important implications for both framework-internal and framework-external debate. As far as the former is concerned, they allow the PF component to be constrained in a highly desirable way, namely, by the reduction, if not the total elimination, of syntactic operations that may apply there. As far as the latter is concerned, they lead to a convergence of certain central theoretical claims of the Government Binding Theory with those more 'surface-based', particularly Generalized Phrase Structure Grammar (GPSG).

The following five considerations are relevant to the determination of the position of minor movements in the grammar.

1. WHETHER THEY FEED MOVE-ALPHA OR ARE FED BY MOVE-ALPHA. If a minor movement can be shown to feed Move-Alpha, then obviously it cannot apply in PF. If a minor movement can be shown to be fed by Move-Alpha, then it might well apply in PF, but only necessarily so if it applies on a deeper cycle than the Move-Alpha that feeds it.

2. HOW THEY BEHAVE WITH RESPECT TO CONDITIONS THAT APPLY AT S-STRUCTURE. For example, if the binding conditions are sensitive to the output of minor movements, then they must apply in the syntax. On the other hand, if minor movements destroy configurations relevant to binding, then they must apply in PF. The same point can be made with respect to Case assignment, which I will assume, along with Chomsky (1981), takes place at S-Structure.[3] If a minor movement creates an input relevant to case assignment, then it must apply in the syntax.

3. HOW THEY BEHAVE WITH RESPECT TO PROPERTIES OF LOGICAL FORM. If the operation of a minor movement affects the logical form of the sentence in any way, then it cannot (given the simplest assumptions) apply in PF. Likewise, if a minor movement is relevant to the ECP in any way (whether the ECP is stated at S-Structure or at LF), then it cannot apply in PF.

4. HOW THEY BEHAVE WITH RESPECT TO PF PRINCIPLES. Jaeggli (1980) and Chomsky (1981) have suggested that the only empty category 'visible' to rules applying in the PF component is case-marked trace. If this is correct and if visibility is somehow relevant to the operation of a particular minor movement, then that minor movement must apply in PF.

5. WHETHER THEY FEED, OR ARE FED BY, STYLISTIC RULES. It has been argued that there exists a class of 'stylistic rules', including Extraposition of PP, Heavy NP Shift, and Stylistic *There*-Insertion, that apply in PF. If this is correct, and it can be shown that a minor movement follows such a rule, then that minor movement must also apply in PF. On the other hand, if a

minor movement can be shown to precede a stylistic rule, then we have perhaps weak evidence that that minor movement applies in the syntax. I will argue below, however, that we must call into question the claim that stylistic rules **do** apply in PF.

Let us now examine some of the best studied minor movements in English, French, and German. We will see that, where evidence bearing on the question exists, it points to that movement applying in the syntax.

First, consider the English rule of Subject-Aux-Inversion, illustrated in (4).

(4) has Mary left

Several properties of this rule indicate that it applies in the syntax. First, it acts as input to LF. To state an obvious truth, declaratives and questions do not mean the same thing. **If** this difference of meaning is encoded at LF **and** meaning is interpreted off S-Structure, then it follows that Subject-Aux-Inversion must apply in the syntax. More concretely, this rule affects the interpretation of quantifier–negative scope, another argument that it must apply in the syntax. Note (5a–b), related by this rule.

(5) a. many people haven't left
 b. haven't many people left

Also, as noted in Chomsky (1971), Subject-Aux-Inversion can even affect the interpretation of lexical meaning, as the following pairs show:

(6) a. I shall go downtown
 b. shall I go downtown

Subject-Aux-Inversion may also apply before a stylistic rule, suggesting (weakly) its syntactic nature. Rochemont (1978) distinguishes between two types of *There*-Insertion: syntactic and stylistic. Notice that each type interacts differently with Subject-Aux-Inversion:

(7) a. was there a fire in the store? (**syntactic**)
 b. *does there stand in the plaza a statue of Juarez? (**stylistic**)

These facts can be explained if the application of Subject-Aux-Inversion follows syntactic *There*-Insertion, but precedes its stylistic counterpart, a state of affairs consistent, at least, with the rule in question being syntactic.

A more complex argument for the syntactic nature of Subject-Aux-Inversion is based on Safir (1982). Safir attempts to explain the matrix/subordinate asymmetry of many rules without recourse to stipulating a root vs. structure preserving distinction. The core of his proposal is the 'Head Uniqueness Principle' (HUP) stated as follows:

(8) S' must have a unique governed head (assuming INFL to be the head of S').

In main clauses (where there is a *Wh*-phrase in COMP), Inversion must apply, so INFL can be governed by the adjacent *Wh*-phrase. An uninverted INFL would remain ungoverned, violating the HUP. However, in embedded clauses, the reverse holds true. If inversion were to apply, both INFL and its trace would be governed (the former by COMP, the latter by percolation), violating the HUP. An uninverted INFL would be governed only once, by percolation.

Safir argues that the HUP applies at S-Structure. Very briefly, he considers it the 'natural assumption' since other government relations are defined there. And secondly, he provides arguments that since PRO appears to be visible for purposes of inflection-government (though invisible to the rules of PF), the HUP must apply at S-Structure.

If Safir's arguments are correct, then Subject-Aux-Inversion must apply prior to the HUP and thus be syntactic.[4]

Let us now turn to the English minor movement rule of Particle Movement. I will assume, along with Emonds (1976), that the rule moves an intransitive preposition leftward, as in (9):

(9) a. John [$_V$looked] [$_{NP}$the answer] [$_{PP}$[$_P$up]]
    b. John [$_V$looked] up [$_{NP}$the answer]

Note that this movement is inapplicable to **transitive** prepositions:

(10) a. *I threw [$_P$in] the ball [$_{PP}$[$_P$e] the basket]
     b. *John dumped [$_P$out] the garbage [$_{PP}$[$_P$e] the window]

In fact, it is in general impossible to extract a head from a complement in English, as has been noted independently in Wilkins (1979), Newmeyer (1980), Fiengo (1980), and Wexler and Culicover (1980). While there are a number of ways of achieving this result in GB, an obvious one is to utilize a principle argued for in Stowell (1983), namely that a lexical head must govern its complements. If we make the natural assumption that this principle applies at S-Structure, then we can explain the ungrammaticality of (10) beside grammatical (9). But such an assumption demands that Particle Movement be syntactic.[5]

The next rule to be examined is English Participle Movement. I will assume that prenominal progressive participles arise through movement, as illustrated in (11).

(11)   the baby [$_{VP}$[$_V$crying]] > the [$_{VP}$[$_V$crying]] baby e

Note that this movement is impossible if the participle has an object:

(12)   a.   *the [$_V$eating] man [$_{VP}$[$_V$e] meat]
       b.   *the [$_V$slicing] butcher [$_{VP}$[$_V$e] the salami with a knife]

Again, given the principle that a lexical head must govern its complements, we can explain the ungrammaticality of (12) if Participle Movement is syntactic.

A third English minor movement that fails to apply if the moved element has a complement is discussed in Fiengo (1980). Fiengo noted that intransitive verbs can be fronted over their subjects in sentences headed by prepositional phrases, while transitive ones cannot:

(13)   a.   in the hallway stood a coatrack
       b.   *in the hallway stood John a coatrack

Again, these facts follow if the minor movement in question applies in the syntax.

Now consider the minor movement rule of Quantifier Float in English, which I will assume applies as in (14).

(14)   all the men have left > the men all have left > the men have all left

There are at least two reasons to consider this rule syntactic. First, as noted in Fiengo (1980), it affects the scope of quantifiers and negation:

(15)   a.   all the men haven't left
       b.   the men haven't all left

Second, it appears to feed the rule of Topicalization which, since Chomsky (1977), has been subsumed under Move-Alpha. Note that in order to derive the following sentences, the quantifier must have floated off the subject (in GB terms, a *Wh* place-holder) prior to movement:

(16)   a.   the guests, I think ____ all left hours ago
       b.   the guests, I don't think ____ all like anybody

Turning to German and Dutch, there is an argument based on Safir's HUP for regarding the rule of Verb Movement, which places the tensed verb in second position in main clauses, as applying in the syntax. In main clauses, the verb must front in order to be governed by the subject which has been moved into COMP. But were the verb to be moved in an embedded clause, both it and its trace would be governed, thereby violating the HUP.

Again, assuming that the HUP applies at S-Structure, this analysis supports the idea that Verb Movement applies in the syntax.

One way that Dutch differs from German is that in the former language the inflected verb is leftmost in the line of verbs in the subordinate clause. Many linguists assume a minor movement rule of Verb Raising, which extracts the infinitive and raises it to the right:

(17) dat Richard [$_{VP}$[$_S$PRO het boek te lezen] belooft
 that Richard the book to read promises
 >
(18) dat Richard [$_{VP}$[$_S$PRO het book [$_V$e]$_j$] belooft te lezen$_j$

The only GB analysis of this construction of which I am aware, Reuland (1981), requires that the rule of Verb Raising be in the syntax. The basic core of Reuland's argument is that infinitives in Dutch are verbs, but are nominal 'enough' to be able to be assigned case by a tensed V. But since they are defective and **cannot** be assigned case, they must move outside the VP. Since their movement is prior to case assignment, it must be syntactic.

A minor movement rule in French worth examining is Leftward Quantifier Movement or 'L-*Tous*'. This rule, originally formulated, I believe, in Kayne (1975), moves a bare quantifier to the left over a verb:

(19) elle les a lus tous > elle les a tous lus

I can extract no argument from Kayne (1975) for the rule being syntactic (or for its applying in PF, for that matter). However, in later work, Kayne (1981) suggests a possible extension of this rule. Apparently the quantifiers *tout* and *rien* can be moved out of **tensed** clauses, though the resultant sentences are admittedly of low acceptability:

(20) ?Je veux tout que tu leur enlèves.
 'I want you to take everything away from them.'

But apparently this movement is possible only if the quantifier is moved from object position; extraction of the quantifier from subject position leads to clear unacceptability:

(21) *Je veux tout que ____ leur soit enlevé.
 'I want everything to be taken away from them.'

This subject/object asymmetry is a classic ECP situation. If the movement of *tout* and *rien* can be collapsed with L-*tous*, then this rule must be in the syntax, so it can apply before the operation of the ECP.

We have now examined seven well known minor movement rules and have found that all must apply in the syntax, rather than in PF. The only problematic minor movement known to me is the familiar rule of Affix-Hopping in English. Given certain central theoretical assumptions in Chomsky (1981), it is crucial that this rule **not** apply in the syntax. In order for INFL to govern the subject at S-Structure, it cannot 'hop' until PF:

(22)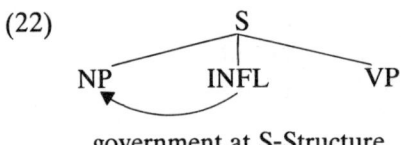

government at S-Structure

It is important to stress, however, that Affix-Hopping is different from the other minor movements we have examined in one fundamental way: it is a **morphological** rule. Perhaps, as suggested in Anderson (1982), rules of inflectional morphology **do** apply in PF. In any event, Affix-Hopping is distinct enough from the other rules examined so as not to pose a grave threat to the hypothesis that minor movements are all syntactic.[6]

This brings us to the question of whether Move-Alpha can be expanded to include minor movements, or whether each one must be stated individually. Obviously, the former alternative is *a priori* more desirable; our goal is always to reduce the need for *ad hoc* stipulation in the theory. Yet, unfortunately, it seems very unlikely that Move-Alpha can be extended in such a way. Certainly most of the best-motivated constraints and principles proposed to date have little to say about minor movements. The binding theory, the A-over-A Principle, theta theory, control theory, and so on are silent on the operation of minor movements. The structure preserving constraint is clearly inapplicable to the regulation of minor movements, since it is such rules that most typically **violate** the constraint. Indeed, there is a close relationship between nonphrasal movements and local structure-destroying movements. But, nevertheless, we cannot go so far as to claim that all minor movements are local, since we are faced with the obvious counterexample of German and Dutch Verb Fronting.

The number of logically possible minor movements that do not occur is enormous. For example, no rule occurs that inverts a prenominal adjective over an article (23a), a determiner over a preceding preposition (23b), or a head noun over an article (23c):

(23) a. ↑the red book
 b. the refusal ↑of the offer
 c. ↑a tendency to be rude

No doubt some universal (or parameterized) principles could be found to block the movements sketched in (23). The deviance of *red the book* might result from some universal ordering between DET and A. Perhaps the case filter could be extended to block *the refusal the of offer*. And perhaps *tendency a to be rude* is ruled out by a prohibition against the movement of a head within its phrase, along the lines suggested by Schwartz (1972). Nevertheless, there is no reason to think that all illegitimate minor movements can be blocked by some independently motivated constraint. While, clearly, sharp constraints do exist on their operation, there are not enough, it appears, to allow them to be subsumed under Move-Alpha. We must conclude — tentatively and reluctantly — that learning a language involves learning a finite number of minor movement rules.[7]

There is a broader implication of the syntactic nature of minor movements that is worth calling attention to. Since the principal rival models of syntactic description are GB and GPSG, one might ask what the areas are of their fundamental incompatibility. Many assume that this incompatibility lies in the fact that the former theory allows both transformations and empty elements. But this assumption is incorrect. In GB, if S-Structures were to be generated directly (without D-Structures and Move-Alpha) the theory's essential core would remain unchanged. And furthermore, GPSG allows empty elements. Even an analysis containing empty subjects occurring with infinitival complements is not incompatible with GPSG. But there is one fundamental difference between GPSG and GB, as they now stand: in GPSG, there is one level (surface structure) at which the class of grammatical sentences can be characterized; in GB, on the other hand, rules applying at many different levels combine in the characterization of the class of grammatical sentences.

One feature of the development of GB in the past few years, however, is the steady diminution of the types of syntactic operations performed in PF. The role of filters has grown steadily less, as has that of deletion rules. Likewise, it is becoming more and more clear that there is no distinct set of 'stylistic rules' confinable to PF. Consider three rules which in the past had been considered stylistic PF rules: 'Stylistic' *There*-Insertion, Heavy NP Shift, and PP Extraposition. The first of the three cannot be in PF, since it feeds Move-Alpha. As noted originally in Aissen (1975), *there* is subject to Raising:

(24)   there seems to hang on the wall a Mexican serape

Interestingly Chomsky (1981) cites *There*-Insertion with the verb *arrive* as a standard example of **syntactic** *There*-Insertion.

Given current assumptions, Heavy NP Shift cannot be in PF either, since it licences parasitic gaps (see Engdahl 1983):

(25) John offended t by not recognizing e immediately, his favorite uncle from Cleveland

And finally, PP Extraposition must be syntactic, since it creates configurations relevant for anaphor-antecedent binding (see Guéron 1980):

(26) a. a picture of **Mary** was sent to **her**
     b. *a picture was sent to **her** of **Mary**

Since the above rules are the three best studied which had been purported to be stylistic rules applying in PF, it seems safe to conclude that there are **no** such rules.

But if minor movements can be excluded from PF as well, what is left to apply there of a syntactic nature? Nothing at all. We therefore may hypothesize that all syntactic processes in human language apply in the mapping between D-Structure and S-Structure; that PF is syntax-free. Furthermore, rules of the LF component typically filter out impossible readings of otherwise grammatical sentences; they do not in themselves distinguish the set of grammatical sentences from the set of ungrammatical ones. Thus we are faced with a highly interesting convergence between the claims of GB and those of GPSG: there exists one level (S-Structure) at which the class of grammatical sentences can be characterized.

I do not thereby wish to underemphasize the great differences that still exist between the two models, not the least of which is that GB wishes to ascribe principles of phrase structure to those of independently functioning systems, while the goal of GPSG is to derive linguistic universals from principles of phrase structure. Nevertheless, it seems clear to me that the result of eliminating all syntactic operations in PF is a major step toward a reconciliation between the competing frameworks.

NOTES

1. This paper was presented at the GLOW Colloquium in York, England on 29 March 1983, and in earlier versions at UCLA, UC-San Diego, and at the University of Southern California. I would like to thank Professor Robert Stockwell for his part in arranging for me a Visiting Professorship at UCLA, where the paper was written.
2. This sense of 'minor movement' is not to be confused with the sense of the term as it was first used in Emonds (1970), where it refers to a rule which moves an element only over an adjacent node. But not all minor movements, as the term is used here, meet the adjacency criterion (e.g. German Verb Fronting). Emonds now (see Emonds 1976) calls his original minor movements 'local transformations'.
3. Since assigned case is relevant to both LF and PF, assignment cannot take place later than S-Structure. I will also make the simplifying assumption that the case filter applies at S-Structure, though such an assumption is not crucial to my arguments.

4. While Safir's arguments are very neat given his assumptions, some of the assumptions strike me as rather *ad hoc*. For example, he must allow an abstract 'Q' in COMP to be a governor, to account for inversion in yes/no questions. And he must assume that in simple declaratives, INFL carries the illocutionary force and hence needs no external governor.

5. In many other languages, such as German, Dutch, Spanish (see Torrego 1984), and Kru (see Koopman 1982), there is no comparable restriction on extracting heads from complements. In such languages, apparently, Stowell's principle applies at D-Structure, or it is reformulated to specify (at S-Structure) that a lexical head **or its trace** must govern its complements.

It would be nice to be able to derive Stowell's principle directly from the projection principle. Case (ii) of the projection principle states, essentially, that subcategorization relations must be preserved at every syntactic level. If a head is moved away from its complement, after movement it has ceased, in the strictest sense, to subcategorize for its complements.

6. If Stowell's (1983) idea that subjects are governed from COMP is correct, then there would be no need at all for Affix-Hopping to apply in PF.

7. The alternative treatment of minor movements — base generation — is not appealing at all. It is their (typically) non-structure-preserving nature that makes them the best candidates for transformational analysis. A transformational derivation is a formal way of expressing the fact that they result in non-optimal phrase structure configurations.

REFERENCES

Aissen, Judith. 1975. 'Presentational There-Insertion: A Cyclic Root Transformation'. *Papers from the Eleventh Regional Meeting of the Chicago Linguistic Society*, 1–14.

Anderson, Stephen. 1982. 'Where's Morphology?', *Linguistic Inquiry* 13: 571–612.

Chomsky, Noam. 1971. 'Deep Structure, Surface Structure, and Semantic Interpretation', in Steinberg and Jakobovits (eds.), 1971: 183–216, and Chomsky 1972: 62–119.

—— 1972. *Studies on Semantics in Generative Grammar*. The Hague: Mouton.

—— 1977. 'On *wh*-Movement', in Culicover, Wasow, and Akmajian (eds.), 1977: 71–132.

—— 1980. 'On Binding', *Linguistic Inquiry* 11: 1–46.

—— 1981. *Lectures on Government and Binding*. Dordrecht: Foris.

Culicover, Peter, Thomas Wasow, and Adrian Akmajian (eds.). 1977. *Formal Syntax*. New York: Academic Press.

Emonds, Joseph. 1970. *Root and Structure-Preserving Transformations*. Bloomington: Indiana University Linguistics Club.

—— 1976. *A Transformational Approach to English Syntax*. New York: Academic Press.

Engdahl, Elisabeth. 1983. 'Parasitic Gaps', *Language and Philosophy* 6: 5–34.

Fiengo, Robert. 1980. *Surface Structure*. Cambridge, Mass.: Harvard University Press.

Guéron, Jacqueline. 1980. 'On the Syntax and Semantics of PP Extraposition', *Linguistic Inquiry* 11: 637–78.

Heny, Frank (ed.). 1981. *Binding and Filtering*. Cambridge, Mass.: MIT Press.

Jaeggli, Oswaldo. 1980. 'Remarks on *to* Contraction', *Linguistic Inquiry* 11: 239–46.

Kayne, Richard. 1975. *French Syntax.* Cambridge, Mass.: MIT Press.
—— 1981. 'Binding, Clitics, Quantifiers, and Control'. In Heny (ed.). 1981: 191–212.
Koopman, Hilda. 1982. 'Verb Movement'. Paper presented to Generative Linguists of the Old World meeting, 26 March, Paris.
Newmeyer, Frederick J. 1980. 'The Flanked Trace Filter'. Unpublished manuscript, University of Washington.
Reuland, Eric. 1981. 'On Extraposition of Complement Clauses', in *Proceedings of the Eleventh Annual Meeting of the Northeastern Linguistic Society,* 296–318.
Rochemont, Michael. 1978. *A Theory of Stylistic Rules in English.* Amherst: Graduate Student Linguistic Association, University of Massachusetts.
Safir, Ken. 1982. 'Inflection Government and Inversion', *Linguistic Review* 1: 417–67.
Schwartz, Arthur. 1972. 'Constraints on Movement Transformations', *Journal of Linguistics* 8: 35–86.
Steinberg, Danny, and Leon Jakobovits (eds.). 1971. *Semantics: An Interdisciplinary Reader.* Cambridge: Cambridge University Press.
Stowell, Timothy. 1983. 'Directional Government'. Unpublished paper presented to West Coast Conference on Formal Linguitics meeting, University of Southern California.
Torrego, Esther. 1984. 'On Inversion in Spanish and Some of its Effects', *Linguistic Inquiry* 15: 103–30.
Wexler, Kenneth, and Peter Culicover. 1980. *Former Principles of Language Acquisition.* Cambridge, Mass.: MIT Press.
Wilkins, Wendy. 1979. *The Variable Interpretation Convention.* Bloomington: Indiana University Linguistics Club.

29

On the Basicness of Certain Types of Passives: Some Evidence from Child Acquisition

SUZANNE ROMAINE

The passive is a syntactic construction which displays features associated with so-called complex syntax, and is acquired relatively late. Evidence for 'delayed acquisition' comes from languages such as English (cf. Horgan 1978, Bever 1970, Turner and Rommetveit 1967, 1968, Strohmer and Nelson 1974) and French (cf. Sinclair and Ferreiro 1970). The 'errors' made by children cross-linguistically are similar, thus indicating that there are some common syntactic, semantic, and pragmatic difficulties inherent in passives, e.g. understanding that the grammatical subject is not necessarily the agent. In English there is a tendency for nouns which function as agents to occur in sentence-initial position. By and large, this principle works as an interpretive strategy, except where surface word order does not correspond to the underlying semantic relations.

Most of the evidence on children's acquisition of passives comes from psycholinguistic tasks of comprehension and imitation. There has been little attempt to study children's spontaneous production of passives, partly due to their general infrequent occurrence even in adult discourse (cf. for example, Givón 1979; and also Rickford 1975 on the general problem of eliciting syntactic constructions). In this paper I will discuss children's spontaneous production of passives within the context of a face-to-face 'sociolinguistic interview', which was designed to elicit speech on a variety of topics (cf. Wolfson 1976 for a discussion of the constraints and norms governing this interaction). The children were all born and raised in Edinburgh, and of working class background. A total of 24 children were studied, four males and females in each of three age groups, six-, eight-, and ten-year-olds.

Before examining the data I will make some brief remarks about the notion of passivization in relation to some of the findings of studies of children's acquisition of passives.

ON THE BASICNESS OF CERTAIN TYPES OF PASSIVES

1. SOME REMARKS ON PASSIVIZATION

The types of constructions which grammarians call passives have figured prominently in hotly debated issues in syntactic theory. There is no general agreement on how best to treat this class of constructions. Chomsky (1981: 120-1) has observed that the category called 'passive' may not constitute a natural class, either within or across languages.

The most general definition that can be offered would be to describe the passive as a syntactic means for encoding the same semantic role in a different way. If we compare (1) and (2), we can see how they might be thought of as alternatives for expressing the same proposition.

(1) Mary hit John. (active)

(2) John was hit by Mary. (passive)

More specifically, we can say that passivization is a syntactic process which allows the direct object of an active verb to appear as the subject. The original subject is deleted or demoted to an agentive phrase, e.g. *by Mary*, and the object *John* advanced to subject position. This movement and reordering of noun phrases within the sentence does not, however, entail a change in semantic roles. In the formation of the passive English makes use of the auxiliary BE (or GET, as in *John got hit by Mary*), and a prepositional phrase (usually with *by* at its head) is used to mark the agent. In English word order and grammatical relations correlate very closely: passivization destroys the correspondence between semantic roles and grammatical relations in that subjects are generally agents and patients do not usually appear in subject (i.e. sentence-initial) position. It is partially due to this factor that passives pose comprehension problems for children. Although they can produce well formed passives spontaneously at age two, their full productive and receptive skills do not match those of adults until as late as thirteen years. Baldie (1976: 338), for example, reports that by age eight all children can comprehend and imitate passives, but the rate of production is 80 per cent.

The examples given in (1) and (2) are generally referred to as FULL or AGENTED PASSIVES, since they contain at least two NPs, one of which is expressed by an agentive phrase. Since the role of agent correlating with subjecthood tends to be thought of as a more basic semantic role than that of patient (cf. Comrie 1981), syntacticians have generally favored treating the active as the more basic structure.

Another factor which has been cited in favor of taking the passive as the more complex structure is the verb form, which in English, at any rate, bears the marks of passive verb morphology (cf. also Matthews 1981: 106-7; Huddleston 1984). In early models of transformational generative grammar the full passive was regarded as related to its active equivalent by means of the so-called passive transformation (cf. Chomsky 1957, 1965). Some analyses postulated the existence of a further optional rule which allowed the deletion of the agentive phrase to produce what has been called the TRUNCATED or AGENTLESS PASSIVE, as in (3) and (4).

(3) Mary was hit.

(4) The plate got broken.

In these sentences the logical subject is not expressed.

As Horgan (1978: 68) points out, this derivational history is suspect when seen from the perspective of child language acquisition. Truncated passives are frequently used by children, whereas full passives are rare. For those who believe that the order of acquisition is dictated either fully or partly by grammatical complexity (cf. Brown and Hanlon 1970, Slobin 1980), and that the latter in turn corresponds to derivational depth (cf. Yngve 1972), it is hard to explain why children should acquire the seemingly more complex construction first. Let us look now at some of the comparative data from studies of children's acquisition of passives.

2. SOME COMPARATIVE DATA ON CHILDREN'S ACQUISITION OF PASSIVES

Horgan presents longitudinal data from children aged two to 13, which shows the separate route of development of agentless and agented passives. The use of the full passive begins at age two, but is very infrequent; approximately ten per cent of the children in her sample use it. There is a slight drop at age six in the percentage of children using it, but thereafter a steady increase until age eleven, at which point the construction is used by about 30 per cent of the children. By comparison, the use of the agentless passive is more frequent at earlier and later stages. At age two, nearly 60 per cent of the children use it, and by age thirteen 100 per cent do. Similarly, Baldie (1976) reports that the agentless passive is both produced and comprehended earlier than either the reversible or non-reversible types illustrated in (5) and (6).

(5) The girl was hit by the boy. (reversible)

(6) The plate was broken by the girl. (non-reversible)

In sentences like (6) the hearer does not need to pay attention to syntactic or other linguistic cues such as the morphology of the verb in order to assign the correct semantic role to the NPs *the plate* and *the girl*. 'Common-sense knowledge' tells us that only the plate could be the recipient of the action, even though from its syntactic position, the 'normal' tendency would be to assign it the role of agent. Passives of this type are non-reversible since the nature of the NPs does not allow the roles of agent and patient to be exchanged. Sentence (5), on the other hand, illustrates a reversible passive, where either *the girl* or *the boy* could be agent or patient. The only way to be sure is to pay attention to the order of constituents, the morphology of the verb, and the agent phrase beginning with *by*. Horgan (1978: 72–3) found that when children began using passives, some used only reversible and others non-reversible ones initially. The non-reversible ones, however, were of the instrumental type (e.g. *the plate was broken with a hammer*) rather than of the agentive type. The agentive non-reversible type (e.g. *the plate was broken by the girl*) did not appear until age nine, and until age eleven no child in Horgan's study produced both reversible and non-reversible passives. Baldie (1976) studied production, comprehension, and imitation of various types of passive constructions by children between the ages of three and seven. He found that all the age groups showed a higher rate of comprehension for non-reversible than reversible passives (with the exception of the six-year-olds, who comprehended both equally well). There was, however, asymmetry in the production results; non-reversible passives were less often produced than reversible ones.

We can compare Horgan's results with the passives produced by the Edinburgh schoolchildren. There is a total of 144 passives. Table 29.1 shows the rate of production of agented and agentless passives for each age group. There is a progressive increase in the number of passives produced as children grow older, with the greatest difference occurring between the six- and eight-year-olds. Most of these passives are agentless, 90 per cent (N = 130), and most of them are produced by the ten-year-olds, although the relative proportion of agentless to agented passives remains about the same throughout all the age groups. Horgan (1978) managed to elicit 81 agented passives from the five- to 13-year-old groups and 32 from the two- to four-year-olds. Although the rate of occurrence is higher than that of the Edinburgh children, this probably reflects the nature of the task. Otherwise, Horgan's findings and mine are similar: the younger the child, the less the tendency there is to produce agented passives.

Table 29.1: Agented and agentless passives produced by Edinburgh schoolchildren

	Age 10		Age 8		Age 6		Total	
	N	%	N	%	N	%	N	%
Agented	8	11	4	8	2	10	14	10
Agentless	63	89	49	92	18	90	130	90
Total	71	49	53	37	20	14	144	100

Three of the examples which I have included under the heading of agented passives are cases in which the agent is not expressed in a prepositional phrase headed by *by*.

(7) I got battered *off* my big brother. (eight-year-old girl)

(8) I never got hurt, just my arm that got hurt *on* the chair. (eight-year-old boy)

(9) Josie got hit *with* a cricket bat. (ten-year-old girl)

It is arguable whether the second of these is really an agentive phrase. In the first of the examples the agent is animate, and in the second and third, inanimate. All of the other agented passives involved the use of *by*; of these 13 per cent (N = 8) were animate and 27 per cent (N = 3) inanimate.

Table 29.2 shows the agented and agentless passives produced by the children in relation to the animacy of the logical objects (i.e. patients) and subjects (i.e. agents). As far as the agentless passives are concerned, we can see that most of the logical objects are also animate, viz. 87 per cent (N = 130). All the logical objects in agented passives are animate (N = 14). Thus, the results confirm a close relation between animacy and agentivity as well as animacy and patienthood. These findings are not in agreement with Horgan's observation that agentless passives produced by younger children tend to have inanimate logical objects. Thus, one major difference between the agented and agentless passive with respect to animacy of object is not supported by my data.

This discrepancy could of course reflect the nature of the context in which her and my data were elicited. She asked children to describe pictures which presented a wide range of situations with both animate and

Table 29.2: Animacy of logical objects and subjects in agented and agentless passives

	Age 10		Age 8		Age 6		Total	
	+agent	−agent	+agent	−agent	+agent	−agent		
Animate object	8	53	4	45	2	15	14	113
Animate subject	8	53	2	—	2	—	9	—
Sub-total	13	53	6	45	4	15	23	113
Inanimate object	0	10	0	4	0	3	0	17
Inanimate subject	3	—	2	—	0	—	5	—
Sub-total	3	10	2	4	0	3	5	17
Total	8	63	4	49	2	18	14	130

inanimate potential agents. It could be the case that since most agents tend to be animate, the children selected only those agents which were inanimate in the pictures for special attention. In other words, her data may reflect the tendency of speakers to encode deliberately what they think the hearer is unlikely to assume. This would follow from a more general discourse principle which endows agents with higher presuppositionality than patients (cf., e.g., Givón 1979), and the tendency for agents to be animate and human. By contrast, my data were more spontaneous but less controlled, since the children had a wider range of topics to draw on when answering my questions in the interview. It is well known that topic acts as a constraint on both productivity and style. I also did not try to elicit information regarding inanimate topics.

Another possible reason for the difference in our results may be due to age. The youngest children in Horgan's sample were two to four years of age. She did not study the development of the agentless passive through to adulthood; however, it could be the case that there is a shift with increasing age to favor animate logical subjects. She found a shift from inanimate logical subjects to animate ones in full passives, which was age-related. The youngest children used 75 per cent inanimate logical subjects in agented passives, while children aged five to 13 had only 39.5 per cent. This is quite closely paralleled by the Edinburgh data, where 36 per cent of the agented passives had inanimate logical subjects. Two of the inanimate logical subjects have appeared in examples (8) and (9) above. The other three are (10)–(12).

(10) The horse got scraped by a bad wire. (ten-year-old girl)

(11) He's been knocked by a car. (ten-year-old girl)

(12) He's getting banged by the pram. (eight-year-old girl)

Given the way in which Horgan and I obtained our data, neither of us is able to separate the effects of animacy from those of agenthood vs. patienthood. Experiments done by Angiolillo and Goldin-Meadow (1982), however, have controlled for the fact that agents tend to be animate and patients inanimate, in order to see whether children could separate the notion of animacy from that of agentivity.

They asked children between the ages of two and three to describe actions involving animate and inanimate entities, which played both agent and patient roles. They found that eight out of nine children differentially placed agents and patients in their utterances. Patients, whether animate or inanimate, were placed postverbally, while agents, animate or inanimate, seldom occupied this position. Thus, the children were using word order systematically to mark agents differentially from patients, independently of animacy. Angliolillo and Goldin-Meadow (1982: 641) claim that their findings constitute evidence for the psychological reality of semantic categories like agent and patient in young children's language.

As far as the choice of verbs made in agentless and agented passives is concerned, it does not appear to be the case that a wider variety of verbs is used with agented than agentless passives, although this is what Horgan found in her data. This factor is, however, difficult to assess since the agentless passives far outnumber the agented ones. Of the fourteen verb forms which appeared in the agented passives in my data, only four do not appear in agentless passives: *got scraped, got called up, got splattered, has been stopped*. There appears to be nothing unusual about the semantics of these verbs. All of the other verbs (ten) appear in both types of passives; two of these, *got beat* and *got caught*, are very frequently used. Horgan suggests that in her data the difference in the verb types found with each of the passive constructions reflects a semantic opposition between stative and dynamic. I do not think this interpretation is correct for my data. Another factor, which Horgan does not take into account in her discussion, may be responsible. That is the difference between passives formed with GET or BE as the auxiliary. The two types are illustrated with examples from the Edinburgh data:

(13) BE passive: Everybody was captured. (ten-year-old boy)

(14) GET passive: I got knocked down. (eight-year-old boy)

(15) BE/GET passive: The leader wasn't pleased at all of them getting shot because he wasn't shot. (ten-year-old boy)

Most of the passives produced by the Edinburgh children were GET passives, as can be seen in Table 29.3, which shows the occurrence of both types in each age group. Overall, BE passives are produced with a frequency of 22 per cent (N = 31). We can see that the youngest group uses almost exclusively GET passives; this is also true for the eight-year-olds. Only in the oldest group do the BE passives amount to a sizable proportion of the passives, viz. 35 per cent (N = 25). This finding is in agreement with a number of studies of both children and adults. Turner and Rommetveit (1968), for example, say not only that BE passives are infrequent in everyday language, but also that children probably do not acquire them until they are at school.

Table 29.3: GET and BE passives

	Age 10	Age 8	Age 6	Total
GET	46	48	19	113
BE	25	5	1	31
Total	71	53	20	144

3. DISCUSSION

Two conclusions emerge from the literature on child acquisition of passives: firstly, agentless passives are more frequent than agented passives; secondly, GET passives are more basic than BE passives. Furthermore, if frequency and order of emergence in child acquisition are to be given any credibility in arguments about basicness, then we have here a good case for saying that the agentless passive with GET is the most basic type.

The argument in favor of the basicness of the agentless construction can be strengthened by looking at cross-linguistic evidence. Agentless passives seem to be more frequent, and not all languages have agented passives. Many more have agentless ones. In fact, Keenan (1975) predicts that the existence of an agented passive in a language implies the presence of an agentless one. Moreover, Lyons (1968) maintains that the function of passivization in languages of the world is to make the agentless construction possible. In other words, it allows the deletion of an agent, whereas the subject of an active sentence cannot ordinarily be deleted.

A few more points can be added with regard to the relation between children's output and the input they receive. Brown (1973) claims that one reason why children produce so few agented passives is that they hear so few from adults as input. He found that in a sample of 713 utterances used by three sets of parents to their children no agented passives appeared. Harwood (1959) reports that in a sample of 12,000 utterances of five-year-olds there were no full passives. Slobin's (1968) observation that agentless passives account for all occurrences of passives is well in line with Svartvik's (1966), Jespersen's (1924), and Stein's (1979) estimates of its frequency among adults, viz. that 75–80 per cent of passives are agentless. In his study of texts Givón (1979: 51) found that the frequency of actives and passives varied according to genre. Passives occurred most frequently in non-fiction texts, but even there they amounted to only 18 per cent. The average for all the texts was eight per cent. A number of sociolinguists have commented on the difficulty of obtaining instances of agented passives in spontaneous speech (e.g. van den Broeck 1977, Weiner and Labov 1983).

With regard to the argument that GET passives appear to be more basic than BE passives, one could add a few more points. Both GET and BE can occur with verbal and adjectival passives, but GET passives are almost always dynamic. There are also informal stylistic connotations to GET: it tends to be avoided in formal contexts (cf. the discussion in Svartvik 1966). This may explain another reason why children acquire GET passives earlier; namely, because they acquire language largely through informal interaction in the first instance. It may also be the case that the notion 'dynamic' is more salient. There is more ambiguity in BE passives since they are more likely to have both stative and dynamic interpretations. Compare sentences (16) and (17), where *break* supports the distinction between adjectival and verbal passive.

(16) The cup was broken.
 i. NP verb adjective (adjectival/stative)
 ii. NP Aux past participle (verbal/dynamic)

(17) The cup got broken. (dynamic)

Under one interpretation of (16), (i), *broken* functions as an adjective to refer to the state of the cup, i.e. its brokenness. In (ii) the interpretation is dynamic and verbal; *broken* is analysed as the past participle of the verb *break* and therefore part of the verb. Most adjectival passives are obligatorily agentless. A sentence like (18) can only be verbal (unless the phrase *by John* is construed as a locative complement).

(18) The cup was broken by John.

Perhaps one reason why children have less difficulty in comprehending agentless passives is that these can be interpreted as basic sentence types (compare *The house was pretty*) and the problem of the assignment of a semantic role to an agent does not arise. The agented passive, however, is structurally (though not semantically) related to a basic sentence type, e.g. *John was standing by Mary*, when *by Mary* is a locative complement rather than an adjectival complement to the verb. Indeed, it is partly due to the structural similarities between these two types of constructions on the one hand, and to the less direct relationship between adjectival and verbal passives, and their active counterparts on the other, that the notion of a generalized passive transformation has come into dispute in more recent versions of generative grammar.

Simplistic interpretations of claims about the psychological reality of grammars have tended to assume isomorphism between children's and linguists' grammars. It is important to remember, however, that data from developing grammars can provide insights into claims made for the basicness of certain structures and for the nature of certain relationships among structures, but these do not in any sense determine the form of grammars. The evidence from comprehension and production indicates considerable divergence between these two modes of processing, and thus may be consistent with a number of possible grammars. From the data presented here it would appear to be the case that the syntactic relationship between the agented and agentless passive may not be as close as some grammarians have argued. The infrequentness of passives (by comparison to actives) — particularly the full agented BE passive — is due partly to the existence of other available syntactic options which put a non-agentive NP into topic/subject position, e.g. topicalization and semantic focus, and partly due to the fact that passives tend to presuppose animate agents. If most agents are predictable from discourse, then it is in unusual or pragmatically marked circumstances that agents will be specified. Thus, the basic choice appears to be between the active and the agentless passive.

REFERENCES

Angiolillo, C.J., and S. Goldin-Meadow. 1981. 'Experimental Evidence for Agent-Patient Categories in Child Language', *Journal of Child Language* 9: 627–43.
Baldie, B. 1976. 'The Acquisition of the Passive Voice', *Journal of Child Language* 3: 331–48.
Bever, T.G. 1970. 'The Cognitive Basis for Linguistic Structures', in Hayes (ed.), 1970.
Brown, R. 1973. *A First Language: The Early Stages.* Cambridge, Mass.: Harvard University Press.
—— and C. Hanlon. 1970. 'Derivational Complexity and Order of Acquisition', in Hayes (ed.), 1970.
Chomsky, N. 1957. *Syntactic Structures.* The Hague: Mouton.
—— 1965. *Aspects of the Theory of Syntax.* Cambridge, Mass.: MIT Press.
—— 1981. *Lectures on Government and Binding.* Dordrecht: Foris.
Comrie, B. 1981. *Language Universals and Linguistic Typology.* Oxford: Blackwell.
Givón, T. 1979. *On Understanding Grammar.* New York: Academic Press.
Harwood, F. 1959. 'Quantitative Study of the Speech of Australian Children', *Language and Speech* 2: 236–70.
Hayes, J.R. (ed.). 1970. *Cognition and the Development of Language.* New York: Wiley.
Horgan, D. 1978. 'The Development of the Full Passive', *Journal of Child Language* 5: 65–80.
Huddleston, R. 1984. *Introduction to the Grammar of English.* Cambridge: Cambridge University Press.
Jespersen, O. 1924. *The Philosophy of Grammar.* London: Allen and Unwin.
Keenan, E.L. 1975. 'Some Universals of Passive in Relational Grammar'. *Papers from the Eleventh Regional Meeting of the Chicago Linguistic Society.* Chicago, Illinois.
Lyons, J. 1968. *Introduction to Theoretical Linguistics.* Cambridge: Cambridge University Press.
Matthews, P. 1981. *Syntax.* Cambridge: Cambridge University Press.
Rickford, J. 1975. 'Carrying the New Wave into Syntax: The Case of Black English BIN', in R. Fasold and R. Shuy (eds.), *Analyzing Variation in Language.*

Washington, DC: Georgetown University Press, 162-84.
Sinclair, H., and E. Ferreiro. 1970. 'Production et répétition des phrases au mode passif', *Archives de Psychologie* 40: 1-2.
Slobin, D. 1968. 'Recall of Full and Truncated Passives in Connected Discourse', *Journal of Verbal Learning and Behavior* 7: 876-81.
—— 1980. 'The Repeated Path Between Transparency and Opacity in Language', in U. Bellugi and M. Studdert-Kennedy (eds.), *Signed and Spoken Language: Biological Constraints on Linguistic Form.* Berlin: Chemie, 229-43.
Stein, G. 1979. *Studies in the Function of the Passive* (Tübinger Beiträge zur Linguistik, 97). Tübingen: Gunther Narr.
Strohmer, H., and K. Nelson. 1974. 'The Young Child's Development of Sentence Comprehension: Influence of Events Probability, Non-Verbal Context, Syntactic Form and Strategies', *Child Development* 45: 567-76.
Svartvik, J. 1966. *On Voice in the English Verb.* The Hague: Mouton.
Turner, E., and R. Rommetveit. 1967. 'Experimental Manipulation of the Production of Active and Passive Voice in Children', *Language and Speech* 10: 169-80.
—— 1968. 'Focus of Attention in Recall of Active and Passive Sentences as a Function of Subject or Object Focus', *Journal of Verbal Learning and Verbal Behavior* 7: 246-50.
van den Broeck, J. 1977. 'Class Differences in Syntactic Complexity in the Flemish Town of Maaseik', *Language in Society* 6: 149-83.
Weiner, E.J., and W. Labov. 1983. 'Constraints on the Agentless Passive', *Journal of Linguistics* 19: 29-59.
Wolfson, N. 1976. 'Speech Events and Natural Speech: Some Implications for Sociolinguistic Methodology', *Language in Society* 5: 189-211.
Yngve, V. 1972. 'The Depth Hypothesis', in F. Householder (ed.), *Syntactic Theory I: Structuralist.* Harmondsworth: Penguin, 115-24.

30

Non-Restrictive Relative Clauses

JAMES PETER THORNE

The chapter on relative clauses in Jackendoff (1977) makes an important contribution to our understanding of the syntactic structure of both restrictive and non-restrictive (appositive) relative clauses. The modifications required to fit the analyses he proposes into the theory set out in Chomsky (1981) are for the most part obvious and comparatively straightforward. However, further consideration of the logical form of non-restrictive relative clauses raises certain questions about the position that Jackendoff assigns to these clauses in deep structure. According to Jackendoff restrictive relative clauses are N^2 complements and non-restrictive relative clauses are X^3 complements (where X is a cover symbol for the major categories N, V, A and P).[1] I believe that a re-examination of the evidence makes it appear more likely that non-restrictive relative clauses are S (in Jackendoff's theory V^3) complements.

The rule Jackendoff gives for mapping into logical form in the case of non-restrictive relative clauses is

$$\begin{bmatrix} X \\ +wh \end{bmatrix}^3 \text{ is anaphoric to } Y^3, \text{ in the configuration}$$

$$[Y^3 \text{---} Y^2 \, [_{\bar{S}} \, [_{Comp} \text{---} X^3 \text{---}] \, _S]]$$

The rule he gives in the case of restrictive relative clauses is

$$\begin{bmatrix} X \\ +wh \end{bmatrix}^3 \text{ is bound to Art}^3, \text{ in the configuration}$$

$$\text{Art}^3 \, [_{N^2} \text{---} [_{\bar{S}} \, [_{Comp} \text{---} X^3 \text{---}] \, _S] \text{---}]$$

It is clear that Jackendoff assumes that these are mappings from deep structure, and that it is the relative pronoun that is interpreted as a pronoun in the case of the non-restrictive relative clause and as a variable in the case of the restrictive relative clause. Following Chomsky (1981) I shall assume that mappings to logical form are from surface structure and that it is not the relative pronoun but the trace that is left after it has been moved that is interpreted in the first case as a pronoun and in the second case as a variable.

The theoretical issues involved here are, of course, extremely important but they should not be allowed to obscure the significance of Jackendoff's insight. The thesis that non-restrictive relative clauses contain a pronoun and restrictive relative clauses a variable explains several of the most striking differences between them. First, it explains why restrictive relative clauses attach only to NPs. If these clauses contain a variable which must be bound by a quantifier lying outside the clause, then, because it is only NPs that contain a node Art, and because it is only this node that contains elements that can be interpreted as quantifiers, it follows that it is only to NPs that relative clauses can (indeed must) be attached. Second, it explains why it is only to certain kinds of NPs that restrictive relative clauses can be attached: not NPs consisting only of proper nouns or NPs containing a possessive NP or pronoun.

(1) a. *Xavier that speaks fluent Greek wasn't invited.
    b. *Xavier's father that is a tax expert disagrees.
    c. *His father Bill always argues with was there.

None of these sentences is well-formed, because in no case does the subject NP contain a node that can be interpreted as a quantifier at the level of logical form.

Third, it explains why (unlike restrictive relative clauses) non-restrictive relative clauses can be attached not only to NPs but to APs, PPs and Sentences.

(2) a. Xavier spoke to the girl, who was standing by the door.
    b. Xavier spoke to the girl that was standing by the door.
    c. She is beautiful, which is something you will never be.
    d. *She is beautiful that is something you will never be.
    e. His brother works in London, which is where he would like to work.
    f. *His brother works in London that is where he would like to work.
    g. Harry was late, which bothered Sam.
    h. *Harry was late that bothered Sam.

It is also why they can be attached to NPs without an Art node,

(3) a. Xavier, who speaks fluent Greek, wasn't invited.
    b. Xavier's father, who is a tax expert, disagrees.
    c. His father, who Bill always argues with, was there.

but not to NPs in which the Art node contains a quantifier such as *every* or *no*.

(4) a. *Every hotel, which he tried, was full.
    b. Every hotel he tried was full.
    c. *No student, who takes this course, ever fails.
    d. No student that takes this course ever fails.

If a non-restrictive relative clause contains a pronoun which must have an antecedent outside the clause, it follows that, if it is to be well-formed, a sentence containing a non-restrictive relative clause must contain an NP capable of acting as an antecedent. As the following examples show, APs, PPs and Sentences can be antecedents.

(5) a. She is beautiful, and $\begin{Bmatrix} \text{that} \\ \text{it} \end{Bmatrix}$ is something you will never be.

    b. His brother works in London, and $\begin{Bmatrix} \text{that} \\ \text{it} \end{Bmatrix}$ is where he would like to work.

    c. Harry was late, and $\begin{Bmatrix} \text{that} \\ \text{it} \end{Bmatrix}$ bothered Sam.

And so can NPs containing only proper nouns or possessive NPs.

(6) a. Xavier wasn't invited, and he speaks fluent Greek.
    b. Xavier's father disagrees, and he is a tax expert.
    c. His father was there, and Bill always argues with him.

But NPs containing quantifiers such as *every* and *no* cannot.

(7) a. *Every hotel was full, and he tried it.
    b. *No student ever fails, and she takes this course.

   The deep structure that Jackendoff proposes for restrictive relative clauses is shown in Figure 30.1.
   The deep structure he proposes for non-restrictive relative clauses when they are attached to NPs is shown in Figure 30.2.
   The only purely syntactic argument that Jackendoff gives for making restrictive relative clauses N^2 complements and non-restrictive relative clauses N^3 complements is based on the fact that in a sentence containing

Figure 30.1

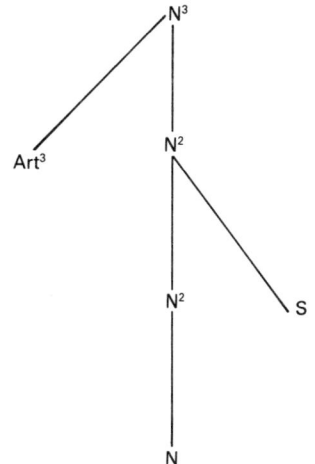

Figure 30.2

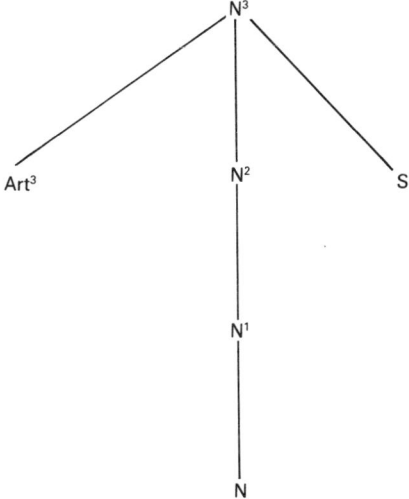

both a restrictive and a non-restrictive relative clause the former must precede the latter.

(8) a. Xavier went off with the girl I introduced him to, who was very beautiful.
    b. *Xavier went off with the girl, who was very beautiful, I introduced him to.

A grammar in which restrictive relative clauses are N^2 complements and non-restrictive relative clauses N^3 complements predicts this result. As Jackendoff puts it, it is guaranteed by 'the geometry of the sentence'.

All the other arguments Jackendoff gives for making restrictive relative clauses N^2 complements and non-restrictive relative clauses N^3 complements derive from a generalization which he claims can be made about the semantic function of complements. Jackendoff claims that all complements attaching at the same level have the same semantic function. Thus all complements attached, say, to X^3 have the same kind of semantic function irrespective of whether X is taken as N, V, A or P.

Considering how much weight Jackendoff places on this generalization, it is surprising how little space he devotes to establishing it. The fullest discussion of the semantic functions of complements attaching at X^2 and X^3 is to be found in his discussion of those attaching at V^2 and V^3 (which in his theory replaces S). Examples of V^2 complements include adverbials of manner, means, instrument, and purpose. Of these Jackendoff says that 'Semantically, they map predicates into predicates of the same number of arguments and they contribute to the main assertion of the sentence' (1977: 61). Examples of V^3 complements include sentential adverbs, parentheticals (such as the expression *I believe* in the sentence *Your house, I believe, is very old*) and various types of clauses including concessive clauses. Of these Jackendoff says that they 'add no conditions to the assertion of the sentence, but rather add some sort of auxiliary assertion (one of whose arguments is usually the main assertion)' (61–2).

Jackendoff does not state the semantic function of restrictive relative clauses but presumably he would say they map properties into arguments. How far one is justified in describing this as the same kind of function as mapping predicates into predicates I am not sure. On the other hand, it is certainly the case that in a sentence containing a main clause and either a restrictive relative clause or a non-restrictive relative clause the restrictive relative clause adds truth conditions to the proposition contained in the main clause and the non-restrictive relative clause does not. If there is a semantic criterion for classing restrictive relative clauses as X^2 complements and non-restrictive relative clauses as X^3 complements, then that is what it comes down to. But notice that, even if this does provide a criterion for establishing the level at which these complements attach, it does not provide a criterion for establishing the category to which they attach. In particular, while it may show that non-restrictive clauses attach at a different level from restrictive relative clauses, it does not show that they can attach to Ns.

In fact, as I have already said, I believe that there are good grounds for saying that non-restrictive relative clauses never form part of a noun phrase (or a prepositional phrase or an adjectival phrase) and that they are always S complements. That is to say, I take the deep structure of sentences (3a–c) to be as shown in Figure 30.3.

I must immediately make it clear that I am not attempting to revive the thesis originally put forward by Ross (1967), and subsequently argued for by Thompson (1971), that non-restrictive relative clauses are really conjoined clauses. That is, that the deep structure of sentences (3a–c) is really that shown in Figure 30.4 and that transformations delete *and*, substitute a relative pronoun for the deleted conjunction, and move the newly constructed relative clause to a position next to the subject noun phrase in the first clause. The evidence provided by the following sentences (all taken from Jackendoff) is sufficient to demolish such a claim.

Figure 30.3

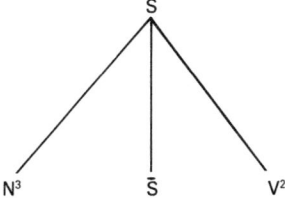

Figure 30.4

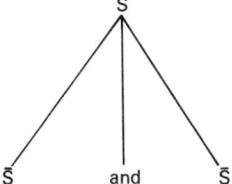

(8) a. Go to Cincinnati, which is on the Ohio River.
  b. Are we landing in Washington, which is on the Potomac?
  c. *Go to Cincinnati, and it is on the Ohio River.
  d. *Cincinnati is on the Ohio River, and go there.
  e. *Are we landing in Washington, and is it on the Potomac?
  f. *Washington is on the Potomac, and are we landing there?

Instead, like traditional grammarians, I want to distinguish between apposition and co-ordination, and I believe that this distinction is properly reflected in the difference between Figures 30.3 and 30.4.

My main reason for rejecting Jackendoff's analysis is that I do not see how one can reconcile the claim that non-restrictive clauses form part of a major constituent of the sentence with the claim that 'they add no condition to the assertion of the sentence but rather add some sort of auxiliary assertion'. If this second claim is true then it surely must be the case that at the level of logical form a non-restrictive relative clause makes up one proposition and the constituent that acts as the antecedent to the pronoun it contains is part of another. Therefore, for both these claims to be true it must mean that in sentences (3a–c) the non-restrictive relative clause is attached to the subject noun phrase in the main clause at the levels of deep and surface structure but separated from it at the level of logical form. On the other hand, if non-restrictive relative clauses are S complements then they do not form part of any other constituent within the sentence. Thus the constituent structures of all three levels are isomorphic and the mapping from surface structure to logical form are optimally simple.

This analysis opens the way to a simple but important generalization. Subordinate clauses (that is, clauses which form part of a major constituent), for example, restrictive relative clauses, form part of the same proposition as the head of the constituent to which they are attached. Independent clauses (that is, clauses which are S complements), for example non-restrictive relative clauses, form independent propositions. Consider sentences like

(9) Xavier failed the test, although he is the smartest in the class.

Clearly, in this sentence the proposition contained in the concessive clause is separate from the proposition contained in the main clause and, therefore, can be used to make a separate assertion. Equally clearly, concessive clauses are S complements — independent clauses.

We can now see why, despite the obvious difficulties involved, linguists like Ross and Thompson were encouraged on the evidence of sentences like

(10) Xavier failed the test, and he is the smartest in the class.

to suggest that non-restrictive relative clauses derive from deep structures containing co-ordinate clauses. As I have already pointed out, it is important to distinguish between appositive clauses and co-ordinate clauses, but logically co-ordinate clauses are like appositive clauses, and not like subordinate clauses. And this is because (or, depending on which way you look at it, why) they are S complements.

According to Jackendoff, all X^3 complements show four characteristics which distinguish them from X^2 or X^1 complements: each of these characteristics being a consequence of X^3 complements not forming part of the main assertion of the sentence. He claims that they cannot contain foci, that they cannot be clefted or negated, and that they are set off by what he calls 'comma intonation'. As far as the evidence from focusing and clefting is concerned, it neither supports nor weakens the thesis that non-restrictive relative clauses are S complements. The evidence from intonation and negation strongly supports it.

Jackendoff points out that, as with sentential adverbs and parentheticals, elements in non-restrictive relative clauses cannot be focused.

(11) a. *John opened the letter, **of course**.
 b. *He opened the letter, **I believe**.
 c. *I didn't see the man, who brought the **strawberries**.

Compare

(12) a. John opened the letter **willingly**.
 b. He opened the letter with a **paper-knife**.
 c. I didn't see the man that brought the **strawberries**.

Other examples are clauses with *although* and *unless*. Like sentential adverbs and parentheticals these are also S complements. In fact, if non-restrictive relative clauses are N complements then (as far as I can discover) they are the only example of a complement which cannot contain foci which is not an S complement. If, on the other hand, non-restrictive relative clauses are S complements then they are no longer exceptional, and Jackendoff's generalization about X^3 complements is replaced by a generalization about S complements.[2]

There are two points to be made about clefting. The first is that it is unreliable as a criterion for distinguishing between second- and third-level complements. Jackendoff's claim that second-level complements can be clefted but third-level complements cannot is weakened by the fact that, although there are good reasons for thinking that both manner adverbial and instrumental phrases are second-level complements, whereas a sentence like

(13) It was with a hammer that Arnold hit the nail.

is well-formed, sentences like

(14) ??It was softly that Arnold hit the nail.

seem very dubious. The second point is that in any case it is of no help in determining at which level either restrictive or non-restrictive relative clauses are attached because neither can be clefted.

(15) a. *It was who I liked that the girl left.
 b. *It was, who I liked, that the girl left.

431

Like sentential adverbs, parentheticals, and concessive clauses, non-restrictive clauses are marked by 'comma intonation'. If they are all S complements then it is possible to see these breaks in the intonation pattern as having a function: they signal that the constituent 'bracketed', as it were, at the phonological level is separate from all the other constituents of the sentence at the syntactic levels.

Jackendoff says that X^3 complements are 'not affected by sentence negation' (1977: 62). Unfortunately, it is not easy to be sure what he means by this. The source of the difficulty is that on several occasions when he is talking about X^3 complements he says that they cannot be 'negated and focussed', giving as examples sentences like

(16) a. *He didn't find it, **of course**.
 b. *I haven't met his friend, who is a **vet**.

But the fact that these sentences are not well formed is sufficiently explained by the fact that sentential adverbs and non-restrictive relative clauses cannot be focused. There is certainly nothing wrong with the sentences

(17) a. He found it, of course.
 b. I haven't met his friend, who is a vet.

Counter-examples like

(18) *I didn't buy a dog, which had a large tail.

are simply a consequence of the fact that an indefinite noun phrase cannot act as an antecedent when it occurs within the scope of a negative. Compare, for example,

(19) a. *I didn't buy a dog, and it had a large tail.
 b. *I didn't buy a dog, although it had a long tail.

Sentences like (18) are, therefore, further evidence for the thesis that non-restrictive relative clauses contain a pronoun.

All this is not to say that there are not important points to be made about the behaviour of sentential adverbs and about the behaviour of non-restrictive relative clauses when they occur in negative sentences. But they are different points; in the case of sentential adverbs, it is that at the level of logical form they always have wider scope than a negative in the same clause: in the case of non-restrictive relative clauses, it is that anything within them remains outside the scope of a negative in another clause. Witness

(20) a. He would not talk to individuals who had any interest in the case.
  b. *He would not talk to individuals, who had any interest in the case.

The trouble with Jackendoff's generalization is that it explains both too much and too little. It explains too much because it covers both sentential adverbs and non-restrictive relative clauses. But there is no reason to suppose that there could be a generalization about negation that would cover both of these. Like negatives, sentential adverbs are operators. Non-restrictive relative clauses are clauses which may contain operators. It explains too little for two reasons. The first is that the contents of a non-restrictive relative clause fall outside the scope not just of negatives in another clause but also of quantifiers in another clause. A sentence like

(21) Everyone there had a wife who loved him.

has an interpretation in which *him* is taken as a variable, as well as an interpretation in which it is taken as a pronoun. This is because the restrictive relative clause is a subordinate clause and so, at logical form, part of the same proposition as the main clause, enabling the variable that *him* maps into at logical form to come within the scope of *every*, just as the variable that the trace maps into comes within the scope of *a*, an existential quantifier at logical form. On the other hand a sentence like

(22) Everyone there had a wife, who loved him.

has, because the non-restrictive clause contains a separate proposition from that contained in the main clause, only one interpretation, that in which *him* is a token as a pronoun at logical form. Even this interpretation is only possible if the existential quantifier is taken as having wider scope than the universal quantifier in the proposition contained in the main clause, because only then can the noun phrase *a wife* act as an antecedent for the pronoun that the trace maps into at logical form.

The second reason why Jackendoff's generalization says too little is that it ignores the fact that the constituents of any clause that is an S complement are outside the scope of logical operators in another clause — because they form separate propositions.

(23) a. *Everyone there had left his wife, although she loved him.
  b. *No one there had brought his wife, although she loved him.

The fact that in a sentence containing both a restrictive and a non-restrictive relative clause the restrictive must precede the non-restrictive, which Jackendoff sees as a consequence of making non-restrictive relative clauses N^3 complements, is also a consequence of making them S complements: since in that case it is impossible for them to occur inside a major constituent. However, there is one fact about ordering that at first sight might appear to favour Jackendoff's analysis. Making non-restrictive relative clauses N, P, and A complements, as well as S complements, provides an immediate explanation of why it is they always come next to the constituent that acts as an antecedent to the pronoun they contain. On the other hand, if non-restrictive clauses are always S complements, it might be expected that (like concessive clauses, for example) they could occur anywhere in the sentence. There are two points to be made here. First, there are good reasons for thinking that all matters concerning the order in which constituents can occur are properly explained not by rules but by constraints on rules. Second, there are particular reasons for not thinking that the distribution of non-restrictive relative clauses is to be accounted for by rules that stipulate the places at which they can be attached at deep structure. The fact that they contain a pronoun makes it far more likely that the explanation is to be found in a condition on the relation between this pronoun and its antecedent. Certain similarities between the pronoun in a non-restrictive relative clause and the pronoun *that* and (in one of its uses) *it* were pointed out above, illustrated by sentences (5a–c). A comparison of sentences (24a–c) with (5a–c)

(24) a. *$\left\{ \begin{matrix} \text{That} \\ \text{It} \end{matrix} \right\}$ is something you will never be, and she is beautiful.

b. *$\left\{ \begin{matrix} \text{That} \\ \text{It} \end{matrix} \right\}$ is where he would like to work, and his brother works in London.

c. *Which bothered Sam, Harry was late.

and a comparison of sentence (25a) with sentence (25b).

(25) a. *She was standing by the door, and Xavier spoke to the girl.

(where *the girl* is taken as the antecedent of *she*).

(25) b. *Who was standing by the door, Xavier spoke to the girl.

strongly suggests that the positions in which non-restrictive relative clauses can occur is determined by a condition which states that the pronoun in them must be bound by an antecedent which is in another clause and precedes it.

Taking non-restrictive relative clauses as S complements has the further advantage of explaining something which Jackendoff's analysis fails to explain. There is a rule which moves restrictive relative clauses, as in

(26) There is a painting going to be auctioned next week which was done using this technique.

Since the movement leaves a trace it is subject to subjacency, so that a sentence like

(27) *There is a painting by every painter going to be auctioned next week who ever used this technique.

is not well-formed. This is well known, but, as far as I am aware, it has not been pointed out that non-restrictive clauses are not subject to this constraint. For example

(28) There is a painting by Delacroix going to be auctioned next week, who was the first painter ever to use this technique.

If, like restrictive relative clauses, non-restrictive relative clauses can be N complements, then the only conclusion that can be drawn is that the movement of non-restrictive relative clauses constitutes an exception to subjacency. Obviously this is a very unsatisfactory conclusion to have to draw. But if non-restrictive relative clauses are always S complements the problem disappears. Since S complements can occur at any point within the sentence (outside a constituent) there is no need to explain the position the non-restrictive relative clause occupies in sentence (28) as the result of a movement rule, so that the question of whether or not subjacency is violated simply does not arise.

It might seem that this solution is only achieved at the cost of raising another problem. For, if non-restrictive relative clauses are not N complements, how are we to explain the fact that relative pronouns cannot be extracted from them?

(29) *Who the girl I liked left.

is not well-formed, and yet to reach the complement of the main clause the relative pronoun has only to cross one S node. Here too the explanation lies in the difference between subordinate and independent clauses. As examples like

(30) *What did Harry hesitate although Bill offered.

show, independent clauses are absolute barriers to movement.

435

NOTES

1. For the sake of argument I accept Jackendoff's premise that all major categories have three levels, though I am not convinced that this is so.
2. The fact that non-restrictive relative clauses cannot contain foci also explains why they cannot be stacked. For discussion see Jackendoff (1977: 184–90).

REFERENCES

Chomsky, N. 1981. *Lectures on Government and Binding.* Dordrecht: Foris Publications.
Jackendoff, R. 1977. *X̄ Syntax: A Study of Phrase Structure.* Cambridge, Mass.: MIT Press.
Ross, J.R. 1967. *Constraints on Variables in Syntax.* Diss. MIT, Cambridge, Mass.
Thompson, S.A. 1971. 'The Deep Structure of Relative Clauses', in C. Fillmore and D.T. Langendoen (eds.), *Studies in Linguistic Semantics,* New York: Holt, Rinehart and Winston, 76–96.

31

On the Subject of Bare Imperatives in English

ARNOLD M. ZWICKY

SUMMARY

In transformational grammar there is a tradition for deriving superficially subjectless imperatives in English from structures containing a subject NP *you*, via a rule deleting this pronoun. There are a number of difficulties with this analysis (detailed in section 1). In part in response to these difficulties, though in larger measure as a consequence of shifts toward restricted theories of syntax, one feature of the traditional analysis (the *You*-Deletion rule) has been generally abandoned. Another feature, a second-person (hereafter, 2P) pronoun subject in (some or all) imperative sentences, remains, at least as an option; rather than the specific lexical item *you*, however, the pronoun in question is a phonologically empty abstract element.

What evidence is there for this analytical construct? Section 2 surveys the relevant arguments, which depend on properties of two classes of phenomena: anaphoric elements with syntactic conditions on their distributions, and syntactic processes creating derived subjects. Every relevant datum appears to support the positing of a 2P pronoun subject.

However, section 3 observes that there are substantial arguments that the phenomena providing so much evidence in favor of *you*-subjects are to be described not by syntactic rules, but by rules in other components of grammar — the lexicon and semantics, in particular. It then seems that there are no syntactic arguments whatsoever for this analysis, possibly that there cannot be any. No known facts about English distinguish between a syntactic analysis positing 2P pronoun subjects that can be phonologically empty and one positing structures lacking subjects, with 2P-subject interpretations supplied by interpretive principles. As matters stand, the choice is not an empirical one, but instead follows from theoretical assumptions.

1. UNDERSTOOD *YOU* AND ITS TRIALS

The traditional wisdom on English grammar has it that sentences like (1) and (2) — which I will refer to as BARE IMPERATIVES, because they lack visible subjects — have an 'understood *you*' as their subject.

(1) Get that drunken kangaroo out of here!

(2) Open up the window and let the bad air out!

Just what is meant by 'understood' in this context is not at all clear; the traditional grammarians who used the locution were not, after all, aiming to provide a precise and complete description of the language, and the terminology was adequate for their purposes, conveying at least that if one must supply a grammatical subject for bare imperatives, then that subject will be one referring to the addressee.

In classical transformational grammar the traditional wisdom is embodied in an analysis that posits *you* in the remote structure of sentences like (1) and (2). As a result, all major sentences have subjects in base structure. This is usually seen as a benefit of the analysis, since the treatment of the category S is uniform in this analysis.

Bare imperatives are then derived by the application of a syntactic rule deleting *you*-subjects in imperatives. *You*-Deletion can be assumed to be optional, so that if it is not applied (3) and (4) are generated instead of (1) and (2).

(3) You get that drunken kangaroo out of here!

(4) You open up the window and let the bad air out!

The rule will not affect third-person subjects in imperatives, as in (5) and (6).

(5) Somebody get that drunken kangaroo out of here!

(6) Everybody open up their windows and let the bad air out!

Three sorts of objection have been raised against this line of analysis.

First, it may be objected that analyses that posit material in a remote structure for a sentence that does not actually contain that material are inherently suspect, or at least require an extended defense. This is the starting point of such criticisms of the standard analysis as Downes (1977) and Schmerling (1977).

Second, it may be objected that the standard analysis incorrectly gives imperatives the same sort of remote structures as declaratives. This is the line taken by Goodman (1973) in his attack on early transformational treatments of bare imperatives:

> My feeling for English is that it is highly unlikely that 'Watch out!' has a 'You' to be understood as the subject of the verb, as traditional grammars have asserted, and ... Chomsky is trying to construct the 'simplest grammar' [here, a grammar with only one type of base S — AMZ]. It is less artificial to take the absence of the subject at face value and say that imperatives never were sentences talking about the world, but were direct actions (21).
>
> My claim is that Chomsky's derivation is too simple and misses the actual use and depoverishes it: the essence of imperatives is direct action, not declaration about (125).

Since Goodman never provided anything like a precise description of the sort that would satisfy linguists, his criticism was ignored. Moreover, it is met to some degree by analyses that provide different underlying structures for imperatives and declaratives, as all analyses since that of Katz and Postal (1964) have done, either via an underlying mood marker like IMP (which might be a formative or a feature of some node) in imperatives, or via different hypersentential structures in imperatives and declaratives.

A third line of objection builds on the fact that imperative sentences differ from declaratives and interrogatives both in their internal syntax and in their external privileges of occurrence. As a result, any analysis that treats the three sentence types as all having remote structures in which some indicator # of sentence type combines with a sentential constituent S will require some rather complex mechanisms (a) to solve INTERNAL PROBLEMS, that is, to provide for different expansions of S depending upon which # it is combined with, and (b) to solve EXTERNAL PROBLEMS, that is, to ensure that S can occur with different constituents depending upon which # it is combined with. I remarked above that the assumption of *you* as remote subject for sentences like (1) and (2) may be defended in part on the grounds that the category S will no longer require a different expansion for imperatives from the expansion for the other sentence types. This small saving in descriptive complexity must be weighed against the cost of the mechanisms for (a) and (b), insofar as these are required in the standard analysis of imperatives.

Evidence supporting this line of objection has been offered by a number of writers, including Schmerling, who proposes an alternative to the standard analysis; and the UCLA grammarians (Stockwell, Schachter, and Partee 1973: Ch. 10), who provide what is undoubtedly the most extensive formalization of the standard analysis. I will first list some of the ways in which imperatives differ from declaratives and interrogatives (using declaratives as the basis for comparison) with respect to their internal syntax. These internal problems include, beyond the optional nonappearance of a subject in imperatives, those characterized and exemplified in List 1.

LIST 1. INTERNAL DIFFERENCES BETWEEN IMPERATIVES AND DECLARATIVES

1. The absence of tense/person marks in imperatives:

   Imp.: (You)   be/*are/*were   quiet!
   Decl.: You   *be/are/were   quiet.

2. The absence of modals in imperatives:

   Imp.: *Will/*Must/*Be about to   respond!
   Decl.: You   will/must/are about to   respond.

3. The absence of perfective *have* in imperatives:

   Imp.: *Have eaten/Eat/Finish eating   dinner by 8!
   Decl.: You   have eaten/ate/finished eating   dinner by 8.

4. The possibility of *do, do not,* and *don't* in combination with an imperative verb — including the verb *be*, with which *do, do not,* and *don't* may not occur in declaratives and interrogatives:

   Imp.: Do/Do not/Don't   be unintelligible!
   Decl.: *You   do/do not/don't   be unintelligible.

5. The **im**possibility of *do* in imperatives when the subject is expressed rather than understood:

   Imp.: *You do/*Do you   move slowly.
   Decl.: You do move slowly.

6. The failure of negation to be located after *be* in imperatives, though negation appears after inflected forms of *be* in the other sentence types:

   Imp.: Do not be/Don't be   sluggish!
         *Be not/*Ben't   sluggish!
   Decl.: *You not/*Youn't   are sluggish.
          You   are not/aren't   sluggish.

7. The ability of *don't* to precede *you* in imperatives but not in declaratives:

   Imp.: Don't you/?You don't   touch me!
   Decl.: *Don't you/You don't   touch me.

8. A failure of parallelism between *do not* and *don't*, with only the latter occurring with subject *you* in imperatives:

   Imp.: *Do not/Don't   you touch me!
   Decl.: You   do not/don't   touch me.

9. A restricted set of expressed subjects in imperatives as opposed to the other types:

   Imp.: (two of) you, everybody (from Skokie),
         the boy with the huge penguin,
         *Herbert Hawkins, *many people, *she,
         *a boy with a huge penguin
   Decl.: permits all of the above

10. The occurrence of sentence-initial *please* in imperatives, but not in the other types:

    Imp.: Please help me!
    Decl.: *Please you will help me.

(I exclude from this list differences that can reasonably be explained as following straightforwardly from the meaning or function of imperative sentences — for instance, the absence of epistemic adverbs like *probably* or *maybe* in imperatives, the absence of past time expressions like *yesterday* in them, and the nonoccurrence of imperative VPs like *contain monosodium glutamate* or *comprise a trio*, which describe states not under human control.)

There are many possible analytic responses to facts like those in List 1. With respect to items 1 and 2, for instance, it has often been suggested that the imperative rule deletes tense/person markers and some specified modal, so that the absence of these surface elements is predicted. The UCLA grammarians opt for an analysis in which imperatives are treated as parallel to such 'bare subjunctives' as those in (7)–(9),

(7)   I insist that you be more careful with that ham.

(8)   They will ask that Simon be allowed to continue his administrative duties.

(9) Myra requested that she be given the southern half of Honshu.

with the result that the indicator # is analyzed as a constituent of the auxiliary in remote structure. I do not intend to survey the literature responding to such facts as those in List 1. It suffices for me to say that these internal problems present serious challenges to the standard analysis of imperatives.

An external problem, having to do with the syntactic environments in which imperatives occur, arises from the fact (stressed by Schmerling) that English has nothing that amounts to an embedded imperative construction, though both declaratives and interrogatives occur embedded, as in (10) and (11).

(10) I am sure that there are artichokes in this soufflé.

(11) I wonder how often these little green bits will turn up.

Thus, the imperative is in an important way not parallel to the other major sentence types of English. It is a 'root' construction, in the sense of Emonds 1976. Moreover, the special character of the imperative in this respect is not a peculiarity of English, but rather represents a very widespread pattern, as noted by Sadock and Zwicky (1985).

I have supplied a considerable list of detailed objections to the traditional assumption that every English bare imperative has a *you*-subject (at some level of analysis), which is deleted by rule. There are actually three interlocked assumptions in the traditional analysis, and these must now be prised apart. First, there is the choice of an analysis with a subject NP for bare imperatives, over an analysis in which some Ss lack subjects; in the latter sort of analysis, an interpretive principle must supply a 2P-subject interpretation for these truly subjectless Ss. Second, given that bare imperatives are to have subjects, there is the choice of an actual English word, *you*, as that subject, over the positing of a 2P, but phonologically empty, pronoun. Third, there is the choice of this analysis for all instances of bare imperatives.

It is the second assumption that requires *You*-Deletion and so leads to the internal and external problems just listed. Assuming **either** an absent subject **or** an empty 2P subject (or sometimes one and sometimes the other) will permit facts like those in List 1 to be described, by brute force if necessary. Moreover, the move towards more restricted theories of syntax would speak against any solution requiring a transformational deletion rule; the transformational aspect of the traditional analysis for bare imperatives is now unappealing within a wide range of theoretical frameworks (including at least GB, LFG, and GPSG), while absent-category (AC) and empty-category (EC) analyses are both available in these frameworks.

2. EVIDENCE FOR A SECOND-PERSON SUBJECT

I now survey the evidence favoring the EC alternative over its AC competitor. The textbook arguments against absent subjects in bare imperatives rely on two phenomena: ordinary reflexive objects and tagged imperatives. The first of these turns out to be only the tip of an evidential iceberg. The second is seriously flawed, and I will pass over it quickly (section 2.1) before taking up anaphoric processes subject to syntactic constraints (section 2.2), which is the class of phenomena to which ordinary reflexive objects belong, and, then, syntactic processes deriving subjects (section 2.3), whose importance in the context of imperatives Schmerling (1977) seems to have been the first to stress. Section 2.4 briefly evaluates the evidence in the two sections preceding it.

2.1. Tagged imperatives

A standard argument for a 2P subject in bare imperatives involves the appearance of 2P, and only 2P, pronouns in tags to imperatives:[1]

(12) Give me a hand with this penguin,
won't you/would you/will you/could you/why don't you?

(13) Give me a hand with this penguin,
*won't he/*would I/*should she/*when did they?

This argument carries through only if the analysis of tagged imperatives is to be referred to the analysis of tagged declaratives, where there is an echo relationship between the (expressed) subject of the declarative and the pronoun in the tag:

(14) You aren't happy, are you/*is he/*am I?

(15) He would be happy, wouldn't *you/he/*I?

But there is no reason to think that the two types of tags have anything in common syntactically (or even semantically). In fact, Sadock (1974: 105–7) has suggested that tagged imperatives like (12) are 'fractured whimperatives', directly related to interrogatives that request:

(16) Won't you/Would you/Will you/Could you/Why don't you hand me that penguin?

Although this argument fails to go through it is useful, since it illustrates

443

what a relevant case would be like. What would be probative is a syntactic association, requiring identity of person features, between the subject position in a construction and some other NP in the construction. If bare imperatives act 'as if' they had 2P subjects for the purpose of this association, we have reason to say that, syntactically, bare infinitives have 2P subjects (even though these are inaudible); otherwise, a generalization about person identity would be split into two unrelated (but virtually identical) generalizations, one about the construction when it has a subject (mentioning identity of grammatical person), the other about the construction when it lacks a subject (prescribing 2P).

2.2. Anaphora with syntactic conditions

The crucial phrase in the preceding paragraph is *syntactic association*. If the requirement is merely that two NPs be coreferential, we learn nothing about the syntax of the construction they occur in. But a requirement that **NPs standing in a certain syntactic relationship to one another** be coreferential could be a powerful tool. Just such a requirement is claimed in the other textbook argument for a 2P subject in bare imperatives, the argument from ordinary reflexive objects, as in (17).

(17)   Make   yourself/*himself   Prince Regent!
       Make   yourselves/*ourselves a drink!
       Shave yourself/*myself   before dinner, please!

What is important here is that normal reflexive objects in English are subject to the 'clause-mate' condition, the requirement that a reflexive object NP must have an antecedent earlier in its clause:

(18)   He made   *yourself/himself   Prince Regent.
       He thought you had made   yourself/*himself   a drink.

In bare imperatives, it appears that this requirement is not satisfied, but that instead an (unrelated) requirement holds requiring 2P reflexives.

I now enumerate some further cases of this sort, involving anaphoric elements with a syntactic condition (at least putatively) associated with them. For the sake of brevity, I merely name the phenomena and give crucial examples involving bare imperatives, leaving to the reader the exercise of discerning the syntactic condition that might be at play. I make no claim that phenomena discussed under different names must be analyzed separately; but I have tried not to make any startling conflations of phenomena under a single heading.

2.2.1. Overt anaphors

The examples in (17) have reflexive NPs filling open slots as objects of verbs. Similar conditions hold for all the overt anaphors in the following list:

LIST 2. OVERT ANAPHORA TO SUBJECT NPs

1. 'Picture reflexives', which appear in prepositional complements to certain nouns:

    Draw a picture of   yourself/*himself!
    Write another article about   yourself/*ourselves!

2. 'Reflexives of independence', which fill adverbial slots:

    Do it   yourself/*myself!
    Get there by   yourselves/*herself!

3. 'Absolute reflexives', which are (semantically intransitive) idioms containing an obligatorily reflexive NP:

    Behave   yourself/*himself!
    Absent   yourselves/*ourselves   as soon as possible!
    Make   yourself/*herself   scarce!

4. Ordinary *own*-possessives:

    Make   your/*our   own drinks!

5. '*Own*-possessives of independence':

    Do it on   your/*her   own!

6. 'Absolute possessives', parallel to absolute reflexives:

    Do   your/*their   best!
    Give   your/*my   all, boys!

2.2.2. Zero anaphors

Another set of relevant phenomena is exemplified by verb complements without surface subjects; a condition requires coreference between the empty subject in the complement and the subject of the verb. The paradigm example is the Equi-NP construction with verbs like *try*:

(19) He keeps trying to express himself in Norwegian.

Bare imperatives, as in (20a), have 2P subjects, as can be seen in (20b):

(20) a. Try to be more thoughtful.
      b. Try to express yourself in Gwamba-Mamba.

Zero anaphors in general support the positing of a 2P subject, a fact that would follow if there was only one zero anaphor, PRO, whose coindexing with other NPs was achieved by one rule. This proposal has been widely adopted, and under it all the phenomena in this section would be interpreted merely as further instances of a single phenomenon, already illustrated in (20). It is not clear to me that a single zero anaphor and a single coindexing rule will suffice for the full range of cases, so that I will break the data into subsets. With the understanding, then, that there might be only a single argument in all of these data, I present further instances of zero anaphors giving evidence about the subjects of bare imperatives. These appear in two lists, one for zero anaphors in verb complements, another for zero anaphors in adverbial subordination.

LIST 3. ZERO ANAPHORS IN VERB COMPLEMENTS

1. Infinitival *wh*-complements:

    Figure out how to open the door!
    Ask him how to express yourself better.

2. Infinitival 'hidden question' complements:

    Figure out a way to open the box!
    Ask her the time to absent yourself.

3. Some gerundive complements:

    Work at being more thoughtful.
    Give some thought to behaving yourself better!

LIST 4. ZERO ANAPHORS IN ADVERBIAL SUBORDINATION

1. Marked-infinitive constructions:

Open that door (in order) to give yourself a treat.
Watch him (so as) to find out how to express yourself clearly in a topic-prominent language.

2. Unmarked-infinitive constructions:

Give me a hand rather than just sit there.
Stay and fight rather than absent yourselves!

3. Finite-verb constructions (in B's contribution to the second exchange below):

A: Herman sang. B: He danced instead of sang.
A: I think I'll sing. B: Dance instead of sing!

4. Subjectless complements related to copular constructions; these can include (at least) past participles, present participles, predicate adjectives, and prepositional phrases:

Give Gorgo the book when addressed.
Look intelligent when expressing yourself to them!
Give them your attention instead of making yourself such a pest.
Speak up (even) though unhappy.
Answer the door even if in pajamas.

2.3. Derived subjects

The remaining source of evidence about the subjects of bare imperatives, at least in terms of classical TG and related frameworks, comes from syntactic processes creating derived subjects. Schmerling (1977) cites three such processes that derive human subjects, which are then (in the traditional analysis) available for the rule of *You*-Deletion.

What is important about these processes is that the NPs that are turned into subjects must be available in the structures to which the processes apply, a fact that argues against the AC analysis for the subjects of bare imperatives and in favor of the EC analysis. The crucial examples include the following, involving Raising to Subject in (21), *Tough* Movement in (22), and Passive in (23):[2]

(21) Do (not) stop writing when the bell rings.
   Just happen to be here when I arrive.
   Appear to be going through the files when the boss comes in.
   Look as if you're having fun when the inspectors arrive.

(22) Do (not) be easy for us to spot.
Be tough to deal with when these people bargain with you.

(23) Do (not) be examined by a doctor.
Be as pleased by these offers for your flying pig as you can be.

2.4. Evaluation

The evidence in the two preceding sections is much more impressive than might appear at first glance. It is not merely that there are n arguments for an empty 2P pronoun subject in bare imperatives; that would be worth little if the n arguments were based on samples selected from a large population of potentially relevant data, within which lurked unexamined data that might well constitute counterevidence. The cogency of the evidence above arises from the fact that it covers all the data I know of that might be relevant. Every anaphoric process with a syntactic condition on it supports the same conclusion about the subjects of bare imperatives. Every syntactic process creating (human) derived subjects says the same thing.

I stress this fact because not all the arguments alluded to above are equally compelling. It might turn out, for instance, that some of the zero anaphors in List 4 obey a condition requiring coreference between the empty subject in the adverbial subordinate clause and **some** NP in the main clause, not necessarily the subject; if so, these anaphors would tell us little about what the main-clause subjects were like in particular examples. It might be discovered that some of the conditions were not even syntactic in character. However, the possibility that some of the arguments I have given will turn out to be beside the point does not affect the general conclusion, which is that every piece of evidence I know of which has a conceivable bearing on the matter indicates that bare imperatives have empty 2P pronouns as subjects, rather than lacking subjects entirely.[3]

3. CONCLUSIONS

I do not claim to have presented an analysis (syntactic, semantic, or pragmatic) of the English imperative. The full range of syntactic facts is considerable — see Bolinger (1967), who emphasizes the connection between imperative verb forms and bare infinitives, for some indication of this range — and the semantic and pragmatic description of imperatives presents many knotty problems (see, e.g., Schmerling 1982 and Huntley 1984). I have merely demonstrated that insofar as English syntax has anything to say on the question of how to analyze the subjects of bare imperatives, it appears to speak with one voice: these subjects are 2P, and they are present (though phonologically empty) in syntactic structure.

But now consider what current theories of grammar have to say about the phenomena in sections 2.2 and 2.3. Considerable evidence has been amassed, first of all, that anaphoric linkages are not to be described by rules of syntax; instead, principles of interpretation (subject, to be sure, to conditions referring to syntactic structure) are responsible for indicating when such linkages are possible, necessary, or prohibited. The phenomena in section 2 are no longer viewed as syntactic at all, in the sense that syntactic rules are responsible for describing the distribution of particular pronouns and zero anaphors. For the most part — I am about to discuss the possible exceptions — pronouns and zero anaphors are freely distributed NPs. It follows that the evidence of section 2.2 is not syntactic.

The possible exceptions in the previous paragraph are the phenomena of section 2.2.1, of which ordinary reflexive objects and absolute reflexives can serve as representatives, and Equi-NP constructions. Absolute reflexive constructions are quite clearly lexical items; no syntactic rule distributes the reflexive pronouns in *make oneself scarce, make a nuisance of oneself,* and the like. Ordinary reflexive objects and Equi-NP constructions make a natural class with the phenomena of section 2.3: Reflexivization, Equi-NP Deletion, Raising to Subject, *Tough* Movement, and Passive are five of the standard **cyclic** transformations of English — the remaining standards being *There*-Insertion, Raising to Object, and Dative Movement, plus of course *You*-Deletion, or Imperative.

Two facts about the standard cyclic rules are important here. First, they are mutually motivating, via what Bach (1974: 171–2) calls 'arguments from other rules'; positing Dative Movement motivates Passive, which in turn motivates Raising to Subject, and so on — which means, of course (by contraposition) that rejecting Raising to Subject means rejecting Passive, and then in turn Dative Movement, and so on. Second, they have been widely abandoned as syntactic rules, in favor of lexical and/or semantic-interpretive treatments. See Brame (1978a, b) and Bresnan (1978, 1982) for discussion of both points, Brame emphasizing the bounded character of the cyclic rules, Bresnan their susceptibility to lexical exceptions.

It follows that in many widely held syntactic frameworks there is no **syntactic** support for the EC position. But neither is there any **syntactic** evidence against it. All the available evidence concerns the lexicon, semantics, or pragmatics, and it is consistent with either a thoroughgoing EC approach or a thoroughgoing AC approach, the choice between these being determined by theoretical assumptions rather than empirical facts.

NOTES

Earlier versions of this paper were presented at University College London, Sussex University, and Lancaster University in 1977, and portions of another version were distributed at the Ohio State University in 1979. A Fulbright research fellowship in Theoretical Psychology at Sussex enabled me to begin work on imperatives, and a visiting appointment at the Center for the Study of Language and Information, Stanford University, enabled me to consolidate some of my earlier thoughts on the matter.

1. I assume that sentences like *Give me a pink wrench, will he!* are to be treated as exclamations with interrogative form, not as imperatives.

2. In each case, the first example is Schmerling's.

3. The arguments apply equally to imperatives with the marker *do* and to those without it, undercutting a suggestion of Schmerling's (1977) that the former be analyzed as subjectless, the latter as having a subject. Moreover, the arguments as a set speak very strongly against the proposal of Downes (1977), who considers only the argument from ordinary reflexive objects and then proposes to posit a subject pronoun only where it is actually needed to trigger reflexivization.

REFERENCES

Bach, Emmon. 1974. *Syntactic Theory*. New York: Holt, Rinehart and Winston.
Bolinger, Dwight. 1967. 'The Imperative in English', in *To Honor Roman Jakobson: Essays on the Occasion of his Seventieth Birthday*. The Hague: Mouton, 335–62. Revised version: 'Is the Imperative an Infinitive?' in *Meaning and Form*. London: Longman, 1977, 152–82.
Brame, Michael K. 1978a. *Base Generated Syntax*. Seattle: Noit Amrofer.
—— 1978b. 'The Base Hypothesis and the Spelling Prohibition', *Linguistic Analysis* 4: 1–30.
Bresnan, Joan W. 1978. 'A Realistic Transformational Grammar', in Morris Halle, Joan Bresnan, and George Miller (eds.), *Linguistic Theory and Psychological Reality*. Cambridge, Mass.: MIT Press, 1–59.
—— (ed.). 1982. *The Mental Representation of Grammatical Relations*. Cambridge, Mass.: MIT Press.
Downes, William. 1977. 'The Imperative and Pragmatics', *Journal of Linguistics* 13: 77–97.
Emonds, Joseph E. 1976. *A Transformational Approach to English Syntax: Root, Structure-Preserving, and Local Transformations*. New York: Academic Press.
Goodman, Paul. 1973. *Speaking and Language: In Defence of Poetry*. London: Wildwood House.
Huntley, Martin. 1984. 'The Semantics of English Imperatives', *Linguistics and Philosophy* 7: 103–33.
Katz, Jerrold J., and Paul M. Postal. 1964. *An Integrated Theory of Linguistic Descriptions*. Cambridge, Mass.: MIT Press.
Sadock, Jerrold M. 1974. *Toward a Linguistic Theory of Speech Acts*. New York: Academic Press.
—— and Arnold M. Zwicky. 1985. 'Speech Act Distinctions in Syntax', in Timothy Shopen (ed.), *Language Typology and Syntactic Description*. Cambridge: Cambridge University Press, Vol. I, 155–96.
Schmerling, Susan F. MS. 1977. 'The Syntax of English Imperatives'.
—— 1982. 'How Imperatives Are Special, and How They Aren't', in Robinson Schneider, Kevin Tuite, and Robert Chametzky (eds.), *Papers from the Parasession on Nondeclaratives*. Chicago: Chicago Linguistic Society, 202–18.
Stockwell, Robert P., Paul Schachter, and Barbara H. Partee. 1973. *The Major Syntactic Structures of English*. New York: Holt, Rinehart and Winston.

Addresses of Authors and Editors

John M. Anderson, Ph.D., Department of English Language, University of Edinburgh, David Hume Tower, George Square, Edinburgh EH8 9JX, Scotland

Stephen R. Anderson, Ph.D., Professor, Department of Linguistics, University of California, Los Angeles, CA 90024, USA

Dr Renate Bartsch, Professor, Centrale Interfaculteit, Universiteit van Amsterdam, Grimburgwal 10, gebouw 13, 1012 GA Amsterdam, The Netherlands

William Bright, Ph.D., Professor, Department of Linguistics, University of Colorado, Boulder, CO 80309, USA

William H. Brown, Jr, Ph.D., Professor, Department of English, University of Southern California, Los Angeles, CA 90089, USA

Dr Klaus Dietz, Professor, Institut für Englische Philologie, Freie Universität Berlin, Gosslerstr. 2-4, 1000 Berlin 33, West Germany

Caroline Duncan-Rose, Ph.D., Professor Emeritus of English and Linguistics, California State University, Dominguez Hills;
home address: 3044 Greenfield Avenue, Los Angeles, CA 90034, USA

Nils Erik Enkvist, Ph.D., Professor, Research Institute of the Åbo Akademi Foundation, Kaskisgatan 2 C 14, SF-20700 Åbo/70, Finland

Dr Peter Erdmann, Professor, Fachrichtung Anglistik, Universität des Saarlandes, 66 Saarbrücken 11, West Germany

Victoria A. Fromkin, Ph.D., Professor, Department of Linguistics; Dean of the Graduate Division; and Vice Chancellor — Graduate Programs, University of California, Los Angeles, CA 90024, USA

Talmy Givón, Ph.D., Professor, Linguistics Department, University of Oregon, Eugene, OR 97403, USA

John A. Hawkins, Ph.D., Professor, Department of Linguistics, University of Southern California, Los Angeles, CA 90089-1693, USA

ADDRESSES OF AUTHORS AND EDITORS

Archibald A. Hill, Ph.D., Professor Emeritus of English and Linguistics, University of Texas, Austin; 3403 Mt. Bonnell Drive, Austin, TX 78731, USA

Carleton T. Hodge, Ph.D., Professor Emeritus of Linguistics and Anthropology, Indiana University, Lindley Hall 401, Bloomington, IN 47405, USA

Fred W. Householder, Ph.D., Research Professor of Linguistics and Classics, Indiana University, Lindley Hall 401, Bloomington, IN 47405, USA

Yoshihiko Ikegami, Ph.D., Professor, College of General Education, The University of Tokyo, Komaba, Meguro-Ku, Tokyo 153, Japan

Robert B. Jones, Ph.D., Professor, Department of Modern Languages and Linguistics, Morrill Hall, Cornell University, Ithaca, NY 14853, USA

Michael B. Kac, Ph.D., Professor, Department of Linguistics, University of Minnesota, Minneapolis, MN 55455, USA

Sherman M. Kuhn, Ph.D., Professor Emeritus, 225 Buena Vista, Ann Arbor, MI 48103, USA

Peter Ladefoged, Ph.D., Professor, Department of Linguistics, University of California, Los Angeles, CA 90024, USA

Roger Lass, Ph.D., Professor, Department of General Linguistics, University of Cape Town, Rondebosch 7700, South Africa

David Lightfoot, Ph.D., Professor, Linguistics Program, Division of Arts and Humanities, University of Maryland, College Park, MD 20742, USA

Ronald K. S. Macaulay, Ph.D., Vice President for Academic Affairs and Professor of Linguistics, Pitzer College, Claremont, CA 91711, USA

Frederick J. Newmeyer, Ph.D., Professor, Department of Linguistics, GN-40, University of Washington, Seattle, WA 98195, USA

Robert Ochsner, Ph.D., Professor, Department of English, University of Maryland, Baltimore County, Catonsville, MD 21228, USA

ADDRESSES OF AUTHORS AND EDITORS

Carlos P. Otero, Ph.D., Professor of Romance Linguistics, Department of Spanish and Portuguese, University of California, Los Angeles, CA 90024, USA

Suzanne Romaine, Ph.D., Professor, Merton College, Oxford OX1 4JD, England

Paul Schachter, Ph.D., Professor, Department of Linguistics, University of California, Los Angeles, CA 90024, USA

John Victor Singler, Ph.D., Assistant Professor, Department of Linguistics, New York University, 10 Washington Place, Room 601, New York, NY 10003, USA

James Peter Thorne, Ph.D., (1933–1988) See Preface.

Elizabeth Closs Traugott, Ph.D., Professor, Department of Linguistics, Stanford University, Stanford, CA 94305, USA

Theo Vennemann, Ph.D., Professor, Institut für Deutsche Philologie, Universität München, Schellingstr. 3RG, 8000 München 40, West Germany

Dr Wolfgang Viereck, Professor, Lehrstuhl für Englische Sprachwissenschaft und Mediävistik, Universität Bamberg, An der Universität 9, 8600 Bamberg, West Germany

Arnold M. Zwicky, Ph.D., Professor, Department of Linguistics, The Ohio State University, 63 W. Beaumont Rd., Columbus, OH 43214, USA